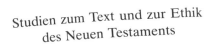

Studien zum Text und zur Ethik
des Neuen Testaments

Studien zum Text und zur Ethik des Neuen Testaments

Festschrift zum 80. Geburtstag
von Heinrich Greeven

herausgegeben von
Wolfgang Schrage

Walter de Gruyter · Berlin · New York
1986

Beiheft zur Zeitschrift für die neutestamentliche Wissenschaft
und die Kunde der älteren Kirche

Herausgegeben von Erich Gräßer

47

Gedruckt auf säurefreiem Papier
(alterungsbeständig – ph 7, neutral)

CIP-Kurztitelaufnahme der Deutschen Bibliothek

Studien zum Text und zur Ethik des Neuen Testaments
: Festschr. zum 80. Geburtstag von Heinrich Greeven / hrsg. von Wolfgang Schrage. – Berlin ; New York : de Gruyter, 1986.
(Beiheft zur Zeitschrift für die neutestamentliche Wissenschaft und die Kunde der älteren Kirche ; 47)
ISBN 3-11-010464-4

NE: Greeven, Heinrich: Festschrift; Schrage, Wolfgang [Hrsg]; Zeitschrift für die neutestamentliche Wissenschaft und die Kunde der älteren Kirche / Beiheft

Satz und Druck: Arthur Collignon GmbH, Berlin 30
Bindearbeiten: Lüderitz & Bauer, Berlin 61

Sehr verehrter, lieber Herr Greeven!

Zu Ihrem 80. Geburtstag, den Sie am 4. Oktober dieses Jahres feiern werden, grüßen Sie alle Mitarbeiter dieses Bandes und sagen Ihnen – gewiß stellvertretend auch für viele andere – herzlichen Dank für alles, was sie an menschlicher und wissenschaftlicher Bereicherung durch Sie erfahren haben. Es ist dies eine längst fällige Dankespflicht, und wir hoffen, daß Sie diese verdiente Ehrung freuen wird.

Sie haben in den vielen Jahrzehnten Ihrer Lehrtätigkeit in Heidelberg, Bethel, Kiel und Bochum keine „Schule" gegründet, und nur einige der an dieser Festschrift Beteiligten können sich Ihre persönlichen Schüler nennen. Aber alle haben Sie als anregenden und liebenswürdigen Lehrer oder Kollegen erlebt, auf dessen klugen Rat und verständnisvolle Kritik sie bei ihrer eigenen Arbeit am Neuen Testament immer gern gehört haben. Dabei haben Sie uns in Sonderheit gelehrt, sorgfältig auch auf das scheinbar Geringfügige zu achten und mit philologischer Exaktheit und methodischer Sorgfalt dem Text und seinem Sinn nachzugehen.

Wir wissen, daß diese Aufsätze die Resonanz nur auf jenen Teil Ihrer vielfältigen Lebensarbeit darstellen, der der Forschung und Lehre gewidmet war, doch kann Ihre Tätigkeit als Rektor in Kiel und Bochum, als Vorsitzender des Fakultätentages und als Präsident der Studiorum Novi Testamenti Societas hier ebensowenig die gebührende Anerkennung finden wie Ihre langjährige Mitarbeit in kirchlichen Kommissionen und ökumenischen Arbeitskreisen.

Diese Festschrift ist thematisch auf zwei Gebiete konzentriert, denen Sie vor allem Interesse und Intensität zugewandt haben. Die anderen Sachbereiche Ihrer wissenschaftlichen Arbeit sollen nicht vergessen werden, weder Ihre Dissertation bei Kurt Deißner noch Ihre dem Erbe von Martin Dibelius verpflichteten Neubearbeitungen verschiedener Kommentare, noch Ihre zahlreichen Beiträge zum Theologischen Wörterbuch. Aber seit Ihrer Habilitation in Greifswald haben Sie mit Vorrang Probleme der urchristlichen Sozialethik aufgegriffen, speziell das Thema der Ehe, und Ihr eigentlicher Forschungsschwerpunkt ist dann der Urtext der Evangelien geworden, an dessen neue Rekonstruktion Sie Jahr um Jahr intensive und geduldige Arbeit gewandt haben, die dann in der Neuedition der Synopse ihre Krönung gefunden hat. Wir hoffen, daß es Ihnen gelingen möge, Ihre Untersuchungen zur synoptischen Textkritik zuende zu führen, und Ihnen dabei weiterhin Gesundheit und Schaffenskraft erhalten bleiben. Vor allem aber wünschen wir Ihnen auch weiterhin Gottes Segen und Geleit.

Diese Festgabe wäre nicht zustande gekommen ohne großzügige Druckkostenzuschüsse von seiten der Evangelischen Kirche von Westfalen, der Christian-Albrechts-Universität in Kiel und der Gesellschaft der Freunde der Ruhr-Universität Bochum. Dank gebührt auch meinem Bonner Kollegen Erich Gräßer für die Aufnahme dieser Festschrift in die Reihe der BZNW sowie Andrea Bencsik, Rudolf Linßen, Jürgen Köllges, Daniela Rückert und Dirk Vanhauer für ihre Mithilfe beim Redigieren und Korrekturlesen.

Im Namen der Mitarbeiter grüßt Sie in herzlicher Verbundenheit

Ihr Wolfgang Schrage

Inhaltsverzeichnis

Der Text des Johannesevangeliums im 2. Jahrhundert

von Kurt Aland

(Einsteinstraße 12, 4400 Münster)

Mit P^{52} ist das Johannesevangelium die in der handschriftlichen Überlieferung am frühesten bezeugte neutestamentliche Schrift. Er wird im allgemeinen Konsens in die Zeit um 125 n. Chr. angesetzt. Als Theodore C. Skeat 1983 in Band 50 der Oxyrhynchus Papyri (S. 3–8) als Nr. 3523 den P^{90} veröffentlichte, erhielt P^{52} eine zeitgenössische Parallele. Zwar hat Skeat die in der vorangehenden Korrespondenz als möglich erscheinende unmittelbare zeitliche Nähe zu P^{52} durch die allgemein gehaltene Datierung "Second century" herabgemindert (zur Begründung im einzelnen durch den Vergleich mit P. Egerton 2, P. Ox. 656 und dem von T. W. Mackay BASP 10,57–64 edierten Homer-Papyrus vgl. S. 3). Aber dennoch ergab sich durch P^{90} die Möglichkeit einer Betrachtung unter dem angegebenen Titel, denn P^{52} mit Joh 18,31–33 und 18,37–38 und P^{90} mit Joh 18,36–19,7 gehörten in den gleichen Textbereich. Zu beiden kam dann noch P^{66} hinzu, der Kapitel 18 und 19 des Johannesevangeliums bis auf kleine Lücken vollständig enthält. Zwar wird er allgemein »um 200« datiert, aber selbst in diesem Fall reicht er mit seiner Vorlage ins 2. Jahrhundert hinein, ganz abgesehen davon, daß Herbert Hunger an seiner Ansetzung von P^{66} als »nicht ... später als Mitte des 2. Jahrhunderts« (Geschichte der Textüberlieferung I, 82) unverändert festhält (persönliche Mitteilung).

Diese dreifache Bezeugung eines neutestamentlichen Textes aus dem 2. Jahrhundert ist einzigartig, wie die frühe Überlieferung des Johannesevangeliums überhaupt einzigartig ist: P^{66} hat im Johannesteil von P^{75} eine Entsprechung von mehr als der Hälfte des Textes und in P^{45} wenigstens für Teile von Kap. 10 und 11. Aber beide Papyri gehören nach allgemeiner Überzeugung ins 3. Jahrhundert, so daß sie für den Versuch einer Feststellung des Textes im 2. Jahrhundert nicht in Betracht kommen. Auch alle anderen, relativ zahlreichen, frühen Papyri fallen aus, weil ebenfalls ins 3. Jahrhundert gehörig: P^{5} mit Versen aus Joh 1; 16; 20, P^{22} mit Versen aus Joh 15; 16, P^{28} mit Versen aus Joh 6 und P^{80} mit Joh 3,34.

Das ist ganz exzeptionell: P^{46} mit den Paulusbriefen, ebenfalls »um 200« datiert, hat als Entsprechung (mit der gleichen Datierung) nur P^{32} mit Versen aus Tit 1; 2 neben sich, aus dem 3. Jahrhundert stammen P^{27} mit Versen aus Röm 8; 9, P^{40} mit Versen aus Röm 1–4; 6; 9, P^{15} mit Versen aus 1. Kor 7; 8, P^{49} mit Versen aus Eph 4; 5, P^{65} mit Versen aus 1.

Thess 1; 2 und P^{12} mit Hebr 1,1. Damit hört es schon fast auf. Denn aus der Zeit »um 200« haben wir nur noch P^{32} mit Tit 1,11–15; 2,3–8 und P^{64+67} mit Matth 3,9.15; 5,20–22, 25–28; 26,7–8, 10,14–15, 22–23, 31–33. P^{32} ist ganz ohne Parallele in den frühen Textzeugen. Bei P^{64+67} finden sich Parallelen in P^{45} lediglich für die Verse aus Matth 26, ebenso wie bei P^{53} und P^{37}. Das ist alles, was hier aufzuführen wäre.

Selbst wenn man das dritte Jahrhundert als Basis wählte, würde man (außer beim Joh. Evang.) keine drei einander parallelen Textzeugen aufbringen: im Lukasevangelium tritt zwar zu P^{45} noch P^{75} hinzu, aber für die sonst noch in Betracht kommenden P^{4} und P^{69} fällt jeweils der eine oder der andere von beiden aus. Und so ist es überall sonst auch. So sind wir selbst im 3. Jahrhundert auf das Johannesevangelium angewiesen, wenn wir ein Urteil über die frühe Textgestalt des Neuen Testaments gewinnen wollen, um vom 2. Jahrhundert zu schweigen.

Zur nachfolgenden Präsentation des Materials ist zu sagen, daß die Wiedergabe auf Grund neuer Kollationen der im Institut für neutestamentliche Textforschung vorhandenen Fotos erfolgt. Dabei ist darauf verzichtet worden, die Papyri in der ursprünglichen Zeilenlänge wiederzugeben, weil das den Abdruck nicht nur erheblich verlängert, sondern auch den Textvergleich sehr erschwert hätte, auf den es doch entscheidend ankommt. In Z. 61 ist ein Eingriff in den Text der Erstausgabe erfolgt, weil hier die Einfügung des Versschlusses von 19,5 durch den Korrektor von P^{66} am (wahrscheinlich unteren) Rand der Seite berücksichtigt werden mußte. Zwar ist der Text selbst nicht mehr erhalten, aber zwischen ιματι]ọν und ọτε ist ein deutliches Einfügungszeichen zu sehen. Es ist vom Herausgeber auch der zweiten vermehrten (und korrigierten) Ausgabe übersehen worden (Bibl. Bodmeriana 1962, S. [134]), so daß er im Apparat και λεγει αυτοις ιδου ο ανθρωπος als vom Papyrus ausgelassen bezeichnet, während das nur für die erste Hand gilt. Darin ist ihm mancher gefolgt, der kritische Apparat zum Nestle[26] verzeichnet für die Auslassung korrekt: P^{66*}. Natürlich können wir nicht absolut sicher sein, was der Korrektor eingefügt hat (deshalb in eckigen Klammern und – wie alle Zusätze des Korrektors – oberhalb der Zeile in Petit wiedergegeben), aber alle Wahrscheinlichkeit spricht dafür, daß es sich dabei um den – mindestens auf griechischer Seite – überwältigend bezeugten wiedergegebenen Wortlaut handelte.

Um den Vergleich des Textes der drei Papyri miteinander zu erleichtern, sind ihre Abweichungen voneinander jeweils unterstrichen (wobei bei P^{66} erste Hand und »Korrektor« als Einheit genommen sind. Denn mindestens in unserem Abschnitt handelt es sich ausschließlich um Zusätze zur Berichtigung von Auslassungen des Schreibers, nicht um Textkorrekturen im eigentlichen Sinn). Um ein Urteil über ihren Text zu ermöglichen, sind die Abweichungen aller drei vom Nestle[26] (und Greek New Testament 3[illegible]) kursiv gedruckt. Auf den ersten Blick zeigt sich, daß sie bei P^{52}

P52

31 οι Ϊου
δαι[ο]ι̣ ημε[ιν ουκ εξεστιν αποκτει]
32 [ναι] ουδενα ¹ ϊνα ο λ[ογος του ι̅υ̅]
[πληρωθη ον ει]πεν σημαινω[ν]
[ποιω θανατω ημελλεν απο]
33 θνησκειν ¹ ισ[ηλθεν ουν παλιν]
[εις το πραιτω]ριον ο Π[ιλατος και]
[εφωνησεν τον ι̅ν̅] και ειπ[εν]
[αυτω συ ει ο βασιλευς των]
[Ιουδ]αιω[ν]

P90

[κοσμου ην η βασ]ιλε̣ια η εμ̣[η οι υ]
[πηρεται οι εμοι ηγ]ω̣νιζοντο α̣[ν ινα μη]
[παραδοθω]τ̣οις Ιου̣[δα]ιοις̣ [νυν]

P66

31 [¹ει]πεν ου¯
αυτο[ις ο Π]ε̣ι̣λατ̣[ος λαβετ]ε̣ *ο̣υν* αυ
[τον υμεις και κατα τον] νομον
[υμων κρινατε ᵀ ειπον αυτ]ω οι Ϊ[ου]
[δαιοι ημιν ουκ εξε]σ[τι]ν̣ αποκ̣[τει]
32 [ναι ουδενα ¹ ι]ν̣α̣ ο̣ λ̣ογος του ι̅υ̣̅
[πληρωθη ον ε]ι̣πεν σημαινω[ν]
[ποιω θανατω] η̣[με]λλεν απο
33 [θνησκειν ¹ ει]σηλθ[εν ου]ν̣ παλι̣ν̣
[εις το πραιτ]ω̣ριον ο Π̣[ειλα]τος· κ[αι]
[εφωνησεν]τ̣ον̣ ι̅ν̅ κ̣[αι ει]πεν
[αυτω συ ει ο βασιλευς των]
[Ιουδαιων]
[σ]υ̣
34 ¹ *απεκρινα̣[τ]ο* ι̅ς̅ απ̣ο σεαυ̣[του]τουτο
λε[γεις η αλ]λοι *ε[ι]πεν* σο[ι πε]ρι εμου
35 ¹ απεκρ̣[ιθη ο Πει]λατος *μη γαρ* ε᾽
γω Ϊου[δαιος ειμι]το εθνος το σον
και οι α[ρχιερεις π]αρεδωκαν σε᾽
36 εμοι [τι εποιησα]ς᾽ ¹απε[κρι]θη ι̅ς̅᾽
η βασ̣ι̣[λεια η εμη ουκ εστιν εκ του]
[κ]οσμο̣[υ τουτου ει εκ *τουτου του*]
[κ]ο̣σμου ην̣ η [βασιλεια η εμη οι υ]
[π]η̣ρεται οι ε[μοι ηγωνιζοντο αν ινα μη]
παραδοθω τοι[ς Ιουδαιοις νυν]

Z. 4 ᵀ N: + αυτον

P52	P90	P66
	[δε η βασιλεια η]εμη ουκ̣[ε]σ̣τιν̣[εν]	δε η βασιλι̣[α η εμη ουκ εστιν εν]
	[τευθεν ¦ ειπεν]ο̣υν αυτω[ο Π]ε[ιλα]	37 τευθε[ν ¦ ειπεν ουν αυτω ο Πειλα]
	[τος ουκουν βασι]λευς *συ ει α*	τος ο̣[υκο]υν βασι[λευς ει συ α]
	π̣[εκριθη ο ις ______ συ λεγεις]	πεκ[ριθη] ^T ις *κ[α]ι ειπ̣[εν* συ λεγεις]
[το]υ̣	οτι βασ̣ι̣λ̣ε̣υ̣ς̣ [ειμι εγω εις του]	[οτι βασιλε]υς ειμ̣[ι εγω εις του]
το γ[ε]γ̣εννη̣μαι [και ^T ε]	το γεγ̣ε̣ν̣ν̣η̣μα[ι και εις τουτο ε]	[το γεγεννημαι και εις τουτο ε]
[ληλυθα εις τον κο]σμον ϊνα μαρτυ	[ληλυ]θ̣α εις τ̣[ον κοσμον ϊνα μαρτυ]	[λ]ηλυθα̣ εις τ[ον] κ̣οσ̣μον [ινα μαρτυ]
[ρησω τη αληθεια πας ο ων] εκ της	[ρη]σω̣ τ̣η̣ α̣λ̣[ηθεια πας ο ων εκ της]	ρησω [τη] αληθεια̣· πας ο ω̣ν εκ της̣
αληθε[ιας ακουει μου της φωνης]	αλ̣[η]θε̣ι̣α̣[ς ακουει μου της φωνης]	αληθι̣[ας] ακουει μου της φωνης
λεγει αυτω [ο Πιλατος τι εστιν]	λ̣ε̣γ̣ει αυ̣τ̣ω̣ ο Π̣[ειλατος τι εστιν]	38 ¦λεγει *ουν* αυτω ^T Πειλατος τι εστι
[αληθεια κ]αι τουτο̣ [ειπων παλιν]	αληθεια και τ[ουτο ειπων παλιν]	αληθι[α] και τουτο ειπων πα[λιν]
[εξηλθεν προς] τους Ιο̣[υδαιους]	εξηλθεν προς τ[ους Ιουδαιους]	εξηλθ[εν π]ρος του[ς] Ϊουδαιους’
[και λεγει αυτοις εγω ουδ]εμι[αν ευ]	[κ]α̣ι λεγει αυτοις [εγω ουδεμιαν ευ]	[και λεγει αυτο]ι̣ς εγω ουδεμιαν *ευ*
Z. 30 ^T N: + εις τουτο	[ρ]ισκω εν̣ αυτ̣[ω αιτιαν ¦ εστιν]	39 *[ρισκω]αι̣[τι]α̣ν εν αυτω’* ¦εστι̣[ν]
	[δε] συνηθ[ε]ια ϋμ[ειν ινα ενα απο]	[δε συνηθεια υμιν ιν]α ε̣να α[πο]
	[λυ]σω ϋμειν [εν τω πασχα βουλε]	[λυσω υμιν εν τω] πασχα· β[ουλε]
	σθε ουν *ϊνα̣* [απολυσω υμειν τον] βασιλε	[σθε ουν απολυ]σω ϋμϊν το[ν β]ασιλ[ε]
	α τ̣[ων Ιουδαιων ¦ εκραυγ]ασα̣ν̣ ο̣υ̣ν	40 [α των Ιου]δαιων ¦ εκ̣[ραυγασαν ουν]
		λεγοντες
	π̣[αλιν λεγοντες μη] το̣υ̣[το]ν̣ α[λλα]	[παλιν *παν]τ̣ε̣ς* μη τουτο[ν α]λλα̣
		ο
	[τον Βαραββαν ην]δε ο Βαραββ̣[ας]	[τον Βαραβ]βαν· ην δε Β[αραββας]
	[ληστης ¦ τοτε ουν] *λαβων ο Πειλ[ατος]*	19,1 [λησ]τ̣ης ¦ τ̣[οτε ουν *ο Πειλατος*]
	[τον ιν και εμαστιγω]	*ελαβεν* τ[ον ιν και εμ]αστ[ιγω]
		Z. 28 ^T N: + ο Z. 34 ^T N: + ο

[σεν ¹ και οι στ]ρατιωται π̣[λεξαν]
[τες στεφαν]ο̣ν εξ α̣κανθω̣[ν]
[επεθηκαν αυτ]ο̣υ̣ τη [κε]φαλη
και̣ [ιματιον πορφυρ]ου̣[ν] περιε
βα[λον αυτον ¹ και ηρ]χ[ο]ντο
προς αυ̣[τον και ελεγον] χα̣ιρε
ο βασιλευ[ς των Ιουδαιων]κ̣αι ε̣
δ̣[ι]δ̣οσαν αυ[τω ραπισματα] ᵀ

[ε]ξ[ηλ]θεν παλιν [ο Πειλατος]
[και λεγει] αυτοις ιδε [αγω υμειν αυ]
[τον εξω ινα γ]ν̣ω̣[τε οτι *αιτιαν*]
[ε]ν̣ α̣υ̣[τω] ουχ ευρισ[κω ¹ εξηλθεν]
[ο]υν ο̣ ι̅ς̅ εξω φο[ρων τον ακαν]θι
νον στεφανον [και το πορφυρ]ουν

ιματιον κ[αι λεγει αυτοις ι]δου ο̣ αν

θρωπο[ς ¹ οτε ουν ειδον α]υτον̣
οι̣ αρχιερε̣[ις και οι υπηρεται] ε̣

κραζαν λ[εγοντες σταυρωσον ᵀ *α]υ[τον]* λεγε[ι
αυτοις]
[ο Πειλατος λαβ]ετε *υμεις [αυτον* σταυρωσα]τε
ε̣γω̣ γα̣ρ̣ [ουχ ευρισκω εν αυτ]ω̣ αιτ̣ια̣ν
¹[απεκριθησαν ᵀ οι Ιουδ]αιοι ημ̣ε̣ι̣ς
[νομον εχομεν κα]ι̣ κατα τον [νομον]

Z. 54 ᵀ N: + και
Z. 64 ᵀ N: + σταυρωσον   Z. 67 ᵀ N: + αυτω

2 [σεν ¹ και ο]ι̣ στρατιω̣[τ]αι πλεξαν᾽
τ̣ε̣ς εξ*[α]κανθω̣ν σ̣τε[φ]ανον*
επεθηκαν αυτου τη κε̣[φ]αλη·
και ϊματιον πορφυρο[υ]ν̣ περιε
3 βαλον αυτον᾽ ¹ και η[ρ]χοντο᾽
προς αυτον και ελεγο[ν] χαιρε
βασιλευ των Ϊουδα̣[ιων] και ε
4 [δ]ιδοσαν αυτω ραπι̣[σματα ¹ και]
ουν
[εξ]ηλθεν παλιν εξω̣ [ο Π]ειλα̣[τος]
[κα]ι̣ λεγει αυ[τοις ιδε αγω υμειν αυ]
το[ν ε]ξω ϊνα γνω[τε οτι *αιτιαν*]
5 *εν̣[αυτ]ω̣ ουχ ευρισκω̣* ¹ [εξηλθεν]
ου[ν ο ι̅ς̅ εξω] *εχων* τ̣[ον ακανθι]
[νον σ]τεφανον και̣ [το πορφυρουν]
[και λεγει αυτοις ιδου ο αν]
[ιματι]ο̣ν ¹
[θρωπος]
6 ¹οτε ουν ε[ιδον αυτον]
οι αρ̣[χιερεις και οι] ϋπηρετα̣[ι ε]
σ̣Ρ̣ον
κ[ραυγασαν ᵀ σΡο]ν̣ λεγει α̣[υτοις]
ο Πειλατος λαβεται ϋ*[μεις αυτο]ν* σ̣Ρα̣τ̣ε̣
εγω γαρ ουχ ευρ̣[ισ]κ̣[ω εν αυτω αιτιαν]
7 ¹απεκρι̣θη̣σαν ᵀ ο̣[ι Ι]ουδα̣ι̣[οι ημεις]
[νο]μον εχομεν· και κατα το[ν ν]ομ̣[ον]
οφιλει αποθανειν οτι υ̅ν̅ θυ̣̅[εα]υτον̣
[ε]ποιησεν·

Z. 64 ᵀ N: + λεγοντες
Z. 67 ᵀ N: + αυτω

und P^{90} im Vergleich mit P^{66} minimal sind. Nun ist bekannt, daß P^{66} nach der Definition des sog. »frühen Textes« (fester, normaler, freier Text, zu denen man noch die Radikalform des freien Textes, den »paraphrasierenden Text«, hinzurechnen kann, wenn man an seine spätere Ausformung im sog. D-Text denkt) in den Bereich des »freien Textes« gehört, der sich vom ursprünglichen Wortlaut nicht selten entfernt. Zur Dokumentation dessen sei nachstehend eine Liste aller Abweichungen von P^{66} in Joh 18,31–19,7 vom Nestle^{26} gegeben, und zwar unter Hinzufügung der wichtigsten Bezeugung. Bereits bei der Betrachtung dieser Zusammenstellung wird deutlich, daß P^{66} bei seinen Abweichungen in der Regel sekundär ist, was aufs Kräftigste durch das Faktum unterstrichen wird, daß P^{52} (soweit vorhanden) und P^{90} im allgemeinen gegen P^{66} stehen.

18,31 λαβετε] add ουν P^{66}
18,31 κρινατε αυτον] om αυτον P^{66vid} ℵ*W 087^{vid} f^{1} 28.565.892^{s}al
18.34 απεκριθη] απεκρινατο P^{66} ΑΝΘΨ087 f^{1}33.565.700.1241 al
18,34 συ] om $P^{66*.60}$ ℵ*
18,34 ειπον] – πεν P^{66} M pc
18,35 μητι] μη γαρ P^{66}
18,36 του κοσμου τουτου^{2}] 3 1 2 P^{66}
18,37 ο Ιησους] om ο $P^{66vid.60}$ LWΓΔΨ 0109.0250.28.33.565.1241 pm
18,37 Ιησους] add και ειπεν P^{66vid}
18,38 λεγει] add ουν P^{66}
18,38 ο Πιλατος] om ο P^{66} 28*
18,38 ευρισκω εν αυτω αιτιαν] 1 4 2 3 P^{66}
18,40 παλιν] add παντες P^{66vid} Α Θ 054.0250 𝔐
18,40 λεγοντες] om P^{66*}
18,40 ο Βαραββας] om ο P^{66*}
19,1 ελαβεν ο Πιλατος] 2 3 1 P^{66} Ψ 054
19,2 στεφανον εξ ακανθων] 2 3 1 P^{66}
19,3 ο βασιλευς] βασιλευ P^{66} ℵ
19,4 και εξηλθεν] εξηλθεν ουν P^{66c} WΘΨ 054.0250 f^{13} 𝔐
19,4 ουδεμιαν αιτιαν ευρισκω εν αυτω] αιτ. εν αυτω ουχ ευρ. $P^{66.90}$ (ℵ*) W
19,5 φορων] εχων P^{66} 1.565 pc
19,5 και λεγει αυτοις ιδου ο ανθρωπος] om P^{66*}
19,6 λεγοντες] om P^{66vid} ℵ 054
19,6 σταυρωσον σταυρ.] σταυρ. P^{66*} 054^{c}.1010 pc
19,6 αυτον υμεις και] 2 1 $P^{66vid.90vid}$
19,7 απεκριθησαν αυτω] om αυτω $P^{66.90vid}$ ℵ W f^{1}565

Um der Vollständigkeit des Berichtes willen sei eine gleiche Übersicht für P^{52} und P^{90} hinzugefügt. Bei P^{52} handelt es sich um eine einzige Abweichung vom Nestle^{26}, die nicht ins Gewicht fällt:

18,37 εις τουτο^{2}] om P^{52vid}

Bei P^{90} sind es deren 9, z. T. als Singulärabweichungen:

18,37 ει συ] 2 1 P^{90}
18,39 βουλεσθε ουν] add ινα P^{90} ℵ W 054.700.2193 pc
19,1 ελαβεν ο Πιλατος] λαβων ο Π. P^{90} ℵ W (⸀ L 33 pc)
19,4 και εξηλθεν] om και P^{90} ℵ f^1 565 al
19,4 εξω ο Πιλατος] 2 3 P^{90vid}28 al
19,4 ουδεμιαν αιτιαν ευρισκω εν αυτω] αιτ. εν αυτω ουχ ευρ. $P^{90.66}$(ℵ*) W
19,6 εκραυγασαν] εκραζαν P^{90} (ℵ*—ξαν)
19,6 σταυρωσον σταυρωσον] σταυρωσον αυτον P^{90vid}054
19,6 αυτον υμεις και] 2 1 $P^{90vid.66vid}$
19,7 απεκριθησαν αυτω] om αυτω $P^{90vid.66}$ℵ W $f^1$565

Wenn die Materialdarbietung S. 3–5 eine Vergleichung mit dem sog. »Standard-Text« von Nestle ^{26} – Greek New Testament 3^a einschließt, so deshalb, weil dieser Text nun einmal der heute verbreitetste ist. Es gibt neben ihm aber noch drei andere moderne Texte, die vom »Standard-Text« nicht selten abweichen: zunächst die Synopse des Jubilars selbst (Albert Huck, Synopse der drei ersten Evangelien mit Beigabe der johanneischen Parallelstellen, 13. Auflage, völlig neu bearbeitet von Heinrich Greeven, 1981), die von John Bernard Orchard (A Synopsis of the Four Gospels in Greek Arranged according to the Two-Gospels Hypothesis, 1983) sowie den sog. »Majority Text« (The Greek New Testament according to the Majority Text, edited by Zane C. Hodges, Arthur L. Farsted, 1982). Um der objektiven Berichterstattung und der Bildung eines unabhängigen Urteils willen seien die Textabweichungen der drei Ausgaben vom „Standard-Text" nachstehend verzeichnet (MT = Majority Text):

18,31 κρινατε αυτον] om αυτον Greeven P^{66vid}ℵ*W 087^{vid} $f^1$28.565.892^sal c
18,31 ειπον] add ουν MT, Orch., Greeven, P^{60} ℵ LWΨ 054.0109.0250 f^{13} 𝔐 lat
18,33 παλιν εις το πραιτωριον] 2 3 4 1 MT P^{60vid} ℵ AC^2Θ(NΨ) 087 f^1 𝔐
18,34 απεκριθη Ιησους] απεκριθη αυτω ο Ιησους MT ℵ $C^3$$f^{13}$ 𝔐 c sy^p sa^{ms} bo^{ms}
απεκρινατο ο Ιησους Greeven (P^{66})AC*D^sNWΘΨ(054). 087.33.565.700.1241 al
18,34 απο σεαυτου] αφ εαυ- MT, Orch., Greeven AC^2D^sW 054.087$f^{1.13}$ 𝔐
18,34 ειπον σοι] 2 1 MT, Greeven, P^{60} ℵ AC^3 (N) ΘΨ 054.087.0109 $f^{1.13}$ 𝔐
18,36 βασιλεια η εμη^2] 3 1 Greeven ℵ D^s NΘ 0250 pc
18,36 οι εμοι ηγωνιζοντο [αν] ινα] 4 1 2 3 5 MT, Orch., AD^s Θ 054.0250 𝔐

18,37 ο Ιησους] om ο MT $P^{60.66vid}$ LWΓΔΨ 0109.0250.28.33.565.1241 pm

18,37 ειμι] add εγω MT AΘ 0109.0250 𝔐 lat

18,38 ευρισκω εν αυτω αιτιαν] 4 1 2 3 MT, Greeven ℵ AWΘΨ $054^{(*)}$ $f^{1.13}$ 𝔐 q

18,39 απολυσω υμιν] 2 1 MT AΘ 054(*) f^{13} 𝔐

18,39 απολυσω υμιν^{2}] 2 1 MT EGHΓΔ 𝔐

18,40 παλιν] add παντες MT,Greeven P^{66vid} A(´ D^{s})Θ 054.0250 𝔐 vg sy^{h}

19,3 και ηρχοντο προς αυτον] om MT $AD^{s}Ψ$ 054 f^{1} 𝔐 f q sy^{p}

19,3 εδιδοσαν] εδιδουν MT AD^{s} 054 f^{1} 𝔐

19,4 και εξηλθεν] om και Greeven P^{90} ℵ D^{s} Γ f^{1}565 al lat sy^{h}
εξηλθεν ουν MT P^{66c} W Θ Ψ 054.0250 f^{13} 𝔐 vg^{cl}

19,4 ουδεμιαν αιτιαν ευρισκω εν αυτω] 4 5 1 2 3 MT, Greeven D^{s} Θ 𝔐 vg sy^{h}

19,5 ιδου] ιδε MT AD^{s} 𝔐

19,6 σταυρωσον σταυρωσον] add αυτον MT (P^{90}) ℵ A D^{s} Θ 054.0250 f^{13} 𝔐 it vg^{cl} sy

19,7 απεκριθησαν αυτω] om αυτω Greeven $P^{66.90}$ℵ W f^{1} 565 pc it ac^{2} pbo bo^{ms}; Or

19,7 νομον] add ημων MT P^{60vid} A Θ 054 $f^{1.13}$ 𝔐 q sy co

19,7 υιον θεου εαυτον] 3 2 1 MT ΓΔ (28).700.892^{s}.1010 al

Leider war es drucktechnisch nicht möglich, auch diese Abweichungen bei der Materialübersicht S. 3–5 zu verzeichnen, denn diese geht bereits an die Grenze des der Setzerei Möglichen. Aber ein Vergleich mit dem Text der drei Papyri, auf den es ankommt, (und der Weg über die Verzeichnung der Bezeugung der Abweichungen von P^{66} vom »Standard-Text«) ermöglichten doch eine Beurteilung der verschiedenen Textformen, ebenso wie die der vorstehenden Übersicht zugefügte Verzeichnung der Bezeugung der Varianten in den wichtigsten Handschriften (𝔐 = Mehrheitstext). In eine Diskussion im einzelnen kann hier nicht eingetreten werden, schon mit Rücksicht auf den vorgeschriebenen Umfang dieses Beitrages, der die Grenzen bereits in der vorliegenden Form überschreitet.

Aufs Äußerste bedauerlich ist, daß der Codex Bezae Cantabrigiensis für unseren Textabschnitt nicht erhalten ist, Joh 13,14–20,13 liegt nur im (beklagenswert wenig untersuchten) Supplement aus sehr viel späterer Zeit vor, das als Ersatz verständlicherweise nicht herangezogen werden kann. So ist in unserem Zusammenhang ein konkreter Nachweis der Unrichtigkeit der Behauptung von Westcott/Hort nicht möglich, daß der D-Text den eigentlichen Text des 2. Jahrhunderts darstelle. Zwar ist das ohnehin sicher, denn nirgendwo finden wir in der frühen griechischen Überlieferung die großen Zufügungen und Auslassungen bzw. Umstellungen bezeugt, die D im Gegensatz zu dieser Überlieferung bietet (zu den Einzelheiten vgl. für das Matthäus- und das Lukasevangelium K. Aland in der Festschrift Roca-Puig und für die Apostelgeschichte B. Aland in den Ephemerides Theologicae Lovanienses). Aber es wäre doch schön gewesen, das auch an dem für das 2. Jahrhundert einzigartig bezeugten Textabschnitt Joh 18,31–19,7 handgreiflich beweisen zu können. Jedoch auch sonst erwarten einen Enttäuschungen. Wer, wie ich, von Perlers Ausgabe der Pascha-Homilie des Melito in den Sources Chrétiennes 123, 1966 herkommt, glaubt hier eine verhältnismäßig umfangreiche Bezeugung unseres Textabschnitts zu finden (Perlers Register nennt Joh 18, 31, 33, 37; 19, 1, 2, 6f. als bei Melito bezeugt, z. T. in umfangreichen Abschnitten). Aber eine Nachprüfung im einzelnen erweist das als Schemen, die Ausgabe von Hall, Oxford 1979 nennt (zu Recht) keine von diesen Stellen in ihrem Register.

Nun ist es mit Evangelienzitaten bei den griechischen Vätern des 2. Jahrhunderts ohnehin eine schwierige Sache. Sie beginnen – und enden – bei Irenäus und Clemens, denn was – und wie – Justin zitiert, ist eine sehr disputable Angelegenheit und alle anderen erhaltenen Schriften des 2. Jahrhunderts fallen völlig aus. Aber unser Abschnitt wird bei Irenäus (ich fuße hier auf den im Institut für neutestamentliche Textforschung gesammelten Unterlagen) nicht zitiert, genau so wenig wie bei Clemens. Erst nach Überschreiten der Jahrhundertschwelle finden sich Zitate aus Joh 18,31–19,7. Origenes bringt eine ganze Reihe davon (wobei 18,36 sogar mehrfach zitiert wird): im Johanneskommentar XXVIII, 25 (232), GCS 10,422 aus Joh 18,31 und 35, in XXVIII, 25 (233), GCS 10,422 aus Joh 18,40, in XXVIII, 25 (234), GCS 10,422 aus Joh 19,7. Sie bieten sämtlich einen Text wie Nestle, lediglich in 18,35 steht τὸ σὸν ἔθνος als Singulärlesart und in 19,7 wird αὐτῷ mit P^{66} ℵ W f^1 565 pc it ac^2 pbo bo^{ms} ausgelassen. In 18,40 schließlich wird hinter μὴ τοῦτον zur Verdeutlichung ἀπολύσῃς eingefügt, aber das ist offensichtlich Zutat des Origenes und folglich ohne handschriftliche Bezeugung. Im selben Werk wird in I 21 (129), GCS 10,26 Joh 18,33 und 36 mit demselben Text zitiert, den auch Nestle bietet. Das gilt im Grunde auch für das Zitat von Joh 18,36 in der 14. Homilie zu Jeremia 15,17, GCS 6,123, nur daß das ἦν hier (mit W) vor ἐκ τοῦ κόσμου gestellt wird. Auch bei der Matthäuserklärung Tom. XIII,9, GCS 40,203 entspricht 18,36 ganz dem Text im Nestle mit der Ausnahme, daß auch hier das ἦν vor ἐκ κόσμου τούτου steht, und daß außerdem das ἄν (mit A D^s Θ 054.0250 𝔐) aus der sonstigen Stellung bei Origenes nach ἠγωνίζοντο hinter ὑπηρέται versetzt wird. In Contra Celsum I 61, GCS 2,112 wird 18,36 zunächst (mit Umstellung des ἦν wic in den beiden zuvor genannten Stellen) ganz wie im Nestle geboten. Nur der Schluß des Zitats läuft anders, und zwar anscheinend als Singulärlesart: νυνὶ δὲ οὐκ ἔστιν ἐκ τοῦ κόσμου τούτου ἡ βασιλεία ἡ ἐμή (wobei es offensichtlich der Argumentationszusammenhang und der Skopos der ganzen Passage ist, der Origenes zu dieser verdeutlichenden Änderung geführt hat). Im dritten Buch des Kommentars zum Hohenlied, GCS 33,215 wird der Schluß von 19,1 (beiläufig und unergiebig) zitiert, in den Homilien zu Numeri XIV, 4, GCS 30,127 wie im Kommentar zum Römerbrief VI, 12 (PG 14,1096) je einmal 19,7: untereinander und mit Nestle identisch, soweit der lateinische Text das festzustellen erlaubt.

Nun gehört Origenes mit seinen Schriften eindeutig ins 3. Jahrhundert, wenn auch in dessen Anfang. Es ist auch die Frage, ob die für Kirchenväterzitate zuständigen Mitarbeiter alle in Betracht kommenden Stellen in seinen Schriften gefunden haben (obwohl das nach dem Vorliegen von Band 3 der Biblia Patristica eigentlich angenommen werden kann). Aber trotzdem kann man sich nach dem Befund in den Papyri wie bei Origenes doch eigentlich des Eindrucks nicht erwehren, als ob das internationale Herausgeberkomitee, das den »Standard-Text« verantwortet, in Joh 18,31–19,7 den Text des 2. Jahrhunderts mindestens im wesentlichen getroffen hätte. Denn natürlich steht auch Origenes in engster Verbindung zu dieser Textepoche. Selbstverständlich liegt der Einwand nahe, daß der behandelte Textausschnitt für ein solches Urteil zu kurz ist. Aber er stellt, wie eingangs dargelegt, die optimale Möglichkeit zur Untersuchung des neutestamentlichen Textes im 2. Jahrhundert dar. Vielleicht können parallele Untersuchungen für den Text des 3. Jahrhunderts angestellt werden, sie anzuregen, war eine der Absichten dieses Aufsatzes. Zwar ist die Zahl der zum Vergleich zur Verfügung stehenden Papyri geringer, aber dafür laufen etwa im Lukasevangelium P^{45} und P^{75} mehrere Kapitel lang einander parallel. Zu den griechischen Kirchenvätern kommen dann auch die lateinischen hinzu, die in unserem Fall keine Ausbeute lieferten. Denn Tertullian bringt lediglich in De idololatria 20,1 CCL 2, 1121 ein »ecce homo«, das bestenfalls als Anspielung auf Joh 19,5 aufgefaßt werden kann. Erst bei Cyprian begegnet in Ad Quirinum II, 29, CCL 3,70 ein zusammenhängendes Zitat aus Joh 18,36–37 (übrigens ganz parallel zum »Standardtext«).

Jesus and Mary (John 20 16f.) in the Second Epistle on Virginity Ascribed to Clement

by T. Baarda

(Troskerlaan 27, 1185 BV Amstelveen, Holland)

I.

1. The Example of Jesus in Ps-Clem. de Virg. 15[1]

(1) "And, not to make our discourse[2] too long, what shall we say about our Lord Jesus Christ? He, our Lord, constantly remained with his twelve apostles, when He came to the world[3]. And not only this – but when He was sending them out[4], He sent them two and two together[5], men with men, and women were not sent with them. And neither on the road[6] nor in the house[7] did they stay with women or with virgins, and thus they pleased God in everything.

(2) Also, when He, our Lord Jesus Christ, was talking with the Samaritan (woman) at the well by himself[8], his disciples came and found Him talking with her, and they were astonished that Jesus was standing and talking with a woman[9]. Look, is this not a rule which is not (to be) broken, and a standard, an example for all generations of men?

(3) And it was not only this, but also when our Lord arose from the dead[10] and Mary came to the sepulchre[11], she ran and fell down at the feet

---

[1] For the text, cf. J. J. Wettstein, *Duae Epistolae S. Clementis Romani etc.*, Leiden 1752, 25(a): 31–40, 26(b): 1–23; J. Th. Beelen, *S. P. N. Clementis Romani Epistulae binae de Virginitate Syriace*, Louvain 1856, 108:1–16, 110:1.

[2] Wettstein: *mltn*, Beelen: *mlt'* – both of them render "sermonem *nostrum*".

[3] Cf. John 1,9. For a similar phrase, cf. Aphrahat, *Dem.* I:7(8), T. Baarda, *The Gospel Quotations of Aphrahat the Persian Sage*, vol. I, Amsterdam 1975, 63. Beelen, *o.c.*, 108 n. 1, 209 n. 1, wrongly suggests the meaning "when he came *in publicum*".

[4] Mt 10,5, Mk 6,7, Lk 9,5, 10,1.

[5] Mk 6,7, Lk 10,1.

[6] Mt 10,10, Mk 6,8, Lk 9,3, 10,4.

[7] Mt 10,12, Mk 6,10, Lk 9,4, 10,5.

[8] John 4,6ff.

[9] John 4,27.

[10] Cf. Mk 16,9; T. Baarda, *o.c.*, 254; The Resurrection Narrative in Tatian's Diatessaron according to three Syrian Patristic Witnesses, in: T. Baarda, *Early Transmission of Words of Jesus*, Amsterdam 1983, 103–115, esp. 111.

[11] John 20,1–11.

of our Lord and worshipped Him and desired to seize Him[12]. But He said to her, 'Touch me not, for I have not yet ascended to my Father'[13]. Is it not, therefore, (something) to marvel at our Lord, that He did not allow Mary, the blessed woman, to touch his feet?

(4) But you dwell with them (scil. the women), and you are served[14] by women and virgins, and you sleep where they sleep, and women are washing your feet for you[15] and anointing you . . .[16]".

2. The Epistles on Virginity ascribed to Clement

(1) The fragment given here in translation is taken from what is called the second letter on virginity, ascribed to 'the blessed Clement, the disciple of the apostle Peter'[17]. This letter, together with the first letter on virginity, is preserved only in a Syriac codex of the New Testament dating from the fifteenth century (ca A.D. 1469/1470)[18]. There is, however, a fragment of the first letter in a sixth century Syriac manuscript containing a florilegium of patristic testimonies, being a translation of a work of Timotheus of Alexandria (dating from 457 A.D.)[19]. It is clear that the Syriac text of these pseudepigrapha was existent in Syriac-speaking regions in a rather early period, most probably as a translation from the Greek. The testimonies of Epiphanius[20] and Jerome[21] concerning these letters suggest that they were known in the East during the fourth century. Their contents, partly dealing with the problem of the so-called *virgines subintroductae,* seem to imply that the pseudo-Clementine letters originated in the third or early fourth century[22].

(2) The author deals with various problems within the monastic life, especially with the behaviour of masculine and female 'virgins' in relation

---

12 John 20,16.

13 John 20,17.

14 Cf. Lk 8,3.

15 Cf. John 13,9; T. Baarda, *Quotations,* 184f.

16 Cf. John 12,3 parr.

17 Beelen, *o.c., 2:1f.*

18 The date is "anno 1781 Graecorum (i.e. 1469)" according to Wettstein (p. VI), "anno 1470 aerae Christianae" according to Beelen (p. XIII, n. 2).

19 B. M. 12. 156; cf. H. Duensing, Die dem Klemens von Rom zugeschriebenen Briefe über die Jungfraulichkeit, *ZKG* 63 (1950/51), 166–188, 167; Fr. Diekamp, *Patres Apostolici,* Tübingen ²1913, iv.

20 Beelen, *o.c.,* xxii sqq.; Diekamp, *o.c.,* i–ii; Duensing, *o.c.,* 166.

21 Beelen, *o.c.,* xxxviii sqq.; Diekamp, *o.c.,* ii; Duensing, *o.c.,* 166.

22 O. Bardenhewer, *Geschichte der altkirchlichen Literatur,* II, Freiburg i. Br. 1914, 303 (first half of the 3rd cent.); Diekamp, *o.c.,* vii; Duensing, *o.c.,* 168 ("Man darf die Briefe vielleicht noch dem 3. Jahrhundert zuweisen").

to each other[23]. The author urges his readers – both men and women – to walk worthy of the kingdom of heaven[24]. The conduct of several celibatarians gives him a cause for concern: "But we speak thus in consequence of the evil rumours and reports concerning shameless men who, under the pretext of the fear of God, have their dwelling with maidens, and so expose themselves to danger, and walk with them along the road and in solitary places alone ... Others, too, eat and drink with them at entertainments ... in loose behaviour and much uncleanness ..."[25]. This theme of the first letter is elaborated in the second one, where the author advises his virgin brothers, when they have come in a place where women are present, to say, "we holy men do not eat and drink with women, nor are we waited on by women or maidens, nor do women wash our feet for us, nor do women anoint us, nor do women prepare our bed for us, nor do we sleep where women sleep, so that we may be without reproach in everything ..."[26].

(3) In order to support this advice and to strengthen his exhortation to walk worthy of the kingdom of God, the author presents his readers with a long list of examples taken from the Old and New Testament, such as the story of Joseph and Potiphar's wife, the fall of the hero Samson, the sin of David in his relation to Bathsheba, the story of Amnon and Tamar, the ruin of Solomon under the influence of foreign women, the history of Susanna, the fact that Moses and 'the sons of Israel' sang apart from Miryam and the women after the crossing of the sea[27]. Then he continues with the examples from the life of Jesus as given in the text of ch. 15 which is found in the fragment given above in translation.

II.

3. The Gospel quotations in the Epistles on Virginity

(1) Although the Syriac text is most probably a translation from a Greek original, it is clear that the translator did not merely render the references to the Gospel text from its Greek exemplar. He rather, in more than one case, substituted the Syriac Gospel text, with which he was acquainted, for the original wording of the references in the Greek epistles, as we hope to demonstrate in this contribution. For most scholars the decisive argument for a Greek original is that there are several Greek parallels to the text of the Syriac letters to be found in the so-called 'Pandect of the

---

[23] Cf. Bardenhewer, *o.c.*, 300; Duensing, *o.c.*, 167f.; cf. F. Martinez, *L'ascétisme chrétien pendant les trois premiers siècles de l'Église,* Paris 1913, 171–186, 172f.

[24] Epist. I: 2, Beelen, *o.c., 4:7.*

[25] Epist. I: 10, Beelen, *o.c.*, 42: 8f., 44: 1–5; transl. B. P. Pratten, in: A. Roberts–J. Donaldson (Ed.), *The Ante-Nicene Library* VIII (repr.) Grand Rapids 1974, 53–66, 58.

holy Writ' of the Palestinian monk Antiochus of Mar Saba[28]. Since this work is compiled in the Greek language, it seems obvious that this author worked upon a Greek text of the pseudo-Clementine epistles. Therefore, it is appropriate to use the Greek text of Antiochus for a comparison of the quotations in the Syriac text. Since our aim is mainly to examine the author's reference to John 20,16f., of which no Greek parallel is found with Antiochus, it is not possible to discuss all of the quotations and allusions with Gospel material in this paper. We will select only a few examples to illustrate the procedure of the translator.

(2) *Epist. de Virg.* I:12.3: "this generation will not go out save by fasting and by prayer, continuous every time"[29]. Apart from the last words that remind us of Luke 18,1, the phrase is taken either from Mt 17,20 v.l. or Mk 9,29. The author's quotation closely agrees with Sy^s(Sy^c hiat.) in Mark (Sy^p has here 'cannot go out') and with Sy^p in Matthew (Sy^s and Sy^c omit the text)[30]. The striking agreement is the order *fasting – prayer*. The text of Antiochus, τοῦτο γὰρ τὸ γένος, φησίν, ἐν προσευχῇ ἐκτενεῖ καὶ πίστει μετὰ νηστείας ἐξέρχεται[31], which has the air of a paraphrase, agrees with the order *prayer – fasting* of the Greek Gospel texts[32].

(3) *Epist. de Virg.* I:12.4 presents us with the text of Mt 10,8[33]:

"Our Lord said:	ἐρρέθη γὰρ ὑπὸ τοῦ κυρίου·
'Cast out (the) demons'	Δαιμόνια ἐκβάλλετε,
– with many other healings –	μετὰ καὶ τῶν ἄλλων ἰάσεων,
and: 'without pay you received,	δωρεὰν ἐλάβετε,
without pay give!'."	δωρεὰν δότε.

At this point the Greek text closely agrees with the Syriac wording. The latter used the same word for 'demons' as is found in Sy^s(Sy^c hiat.) namely *s'd'*, whereas Sy^p uses the synonym *dyw'*. Remarkably enough, the Syriac quotation differs from both Sy^s and Sy^p in using the synonym verb *šql* for *nśb* ('you received')[34].

---

[26] Epist. II: 3, Beelen, *o.c.*, 78: 7–10; tr. Prattern, *o.c.*, 62.

[27] Epist. II: 7–14; Beelen, *o.c.*, 92–106.

[28] P. G. 89: 1421–1850; cf. B. Altaner, *Patrologie*, Freiburg i. Br. [5]1958, 482. A collection of the Greek fragments is presented by Diekamp, *o.c.*, 1–49 (cf. iii).

[29] Beelen, *o.c.*, 58: 5f.

[30] I have compared A. S. Lewis, *The Old Syriac Gospels or Evangelion Da-Mepharreshe*, London 1910; Ph. E. Pusey–G. H. Gwilliam, *Tetraevangelium Sanctum iuxta simplicem Syrorum versionem*, Oxford 1901.

[31] Diekamp, *o.c.*, 23: 10–13.

[32] Cf. K. Aland a.o. (Ed.), *Nestle–Aland, Novum Testamentum Graece*, Stuttgart [26]1979, 119 app.; 48 app.

[33] Beelen, *o.c.*, 62:3f.; Diekamp, *o.c.*, 23:20–23.

[34] The verbs are synonyms, cf. e.g. Epist. I: 5.4 (Beelen 24: 1), "Take your cross" (*nśb*) and

(4) *Epist. de Virg.* II:6.1 presents us with the text of Mt 10,16 in the form of an exhortation instead of an imperative, "Let us be wise like the serpents and innocent like the doves"[35]. Antiochus's text is slightly different as it paraphrases the saying: ... κτήσασθαι τὴν φρόνησιν τοῦ ὄφεως καὶ τὸ ἀκέραιον τῆς περιστερᾶς[36]. The Syriac wording closely follows that of the Syriac Gospel text, including the reading *ḥakkîmīn* ('wise') of Sy^p instead of *ʿarīmīn* ('wily') in Sy^s[37].

(5) There is no doubt that in these cases the translator, in his rendering of the Gospel quotations, followed the Syriac Gospel tradition with which he was acquainted. This tradition agrees partly with Sy^p, partly with Sy^s. Unfortunately, it is not possible in any of these three cases to reconstruct the Diatessaron text, since it would be of interest to know whether the translator was acquainted with this early Syriac form of the Gospel. There is, however, one quotation from John (4,27) in *Epist. de Virg.* II: 15.2 (that is, in the fragment which we gave in translation in § 1) which we can compare with the Diatessaron text. Unfortunately, there is no Greek parallel in the work of Antiochus of that passage.

4. The example of Jesus in John 4,27[38]

(1) In order to give further support to his admonition the author refers to the episode of Jesus' encounter with the Samaritan woman at the well. The main point of his argument consists in a quotation from John 4,27, but in order to give a setting for that quotation he had to add a few other elements from the context. The following phrases are to be noticed:

(a) *when he was speaking*. The author obviously quotes these words from verse 27, where Sy^p reads, 'when he (was) speaking' which is an interpretative paraphrase of ἐπὶ τούτῳ. Sy^p agrees with, or is followed by, T^A (*w-bynmʾ hw ytklm*, 'and while he spoke')[39]. This reading has an echo in several other eastern witnesses. Sy^s presents the phrase in the plural form, 'when they (were) speaking'. The Persian harmony apparently preserves the Pešiṭtā reading when it renders 'and in the word he was still'[40]. Likewise the Persian Gospel text reads 'still in the word he was'[41]. The

II: 5.5 (Beelen 86: 6), 'who in truth is carrying his cross' (*šql*), cf. Mk 8,34, Mt 16,24, Lk 9,23 (*šql*).

35 Beelen, *o.c.*, 88: 2f.

36 Diekamp, *o.c.*, 38: 3.5.

37 Cf. Gen 3,1 in the Targum Onkelos and in the Pešīṭtā (*ʿarīm*), contra Targum Ps.-Jonathan (*ḥakkīm*).

38 Epist. II: 15.2, Beelen, *o.c.*, 108: 6–10.

39 A.-S. Marmardji, *Diatessaron de Tatien, Texte arabe*, Beyrouth 1935, 204.

40 G. Messina, *Diatessaron Persiano*, Rome 1951, 160 (II: 42: *w-dar suḥan bud hanuz*).

41 B. Walton, *Biblia Sacra Polyglotta* V, London 1657, 416 (*hanuz dar suḥan bud*).

Armenian[42] and Georgian[43] Gospels replace the verb by a noun 'and in that word' (cf. also Old Latin r^1 'in hoc ser(mone)'[44]).

(b) *with that Samaritan (woman),* a necessary complement to the preceding words in order to clarify to his readers which episode was in his mind, cf. John 4,7.9 etc.

(c) *at the well.* Again a complement to the quotation. The word 'well' is found in John 4,11f. both in the Syriac Gospels, Sy^s and Sy^p, and in the Diatessaron text of Ephraem[45].

(d) *by himself,* or: *alone,* another complement to the text necessary for the course of the argument: to be alone *(mnh w-lh)* with a woman can be dangerous and asks for reproach. The same idea is expressed in Ephraem's commentary on the Diatessaron, though with a different wording *(blḥwdyh)*[46].

(e) *came his disciples.* This is again an element of verse 27. The text agrees with Sy^s, Sy^p, T^A and the Greek text.

(f) *and they found Him while He was talking with her.* This is again an addition of the author (or translator) apparently arising from the desire to underline the strangeness of the situation. There is, at least, no indication that these words were part of any text or version of John 4,27. However, there is a faint parallel in the Persian versions, for they read "and they were amazed *that they saw Him* that He spoke" etc. (Persian Harmony: "and they were amazed *when they saw* that" etc.)[47]. Was there a text of this kind which was used in our text? Since it is a characteristic reading of the Persian texts alone (for idiomatic reasons?), it is hardly probable.

(g) *and they were astonished.* This is the reading of the Syriac versions – $Sy^{s.p}$: *w-mtdmryn hww* – but Ephraem's Diatessaron text seems to have been different: *tmhw*[48].

(h) *that with the* (or: *a*) *woman . . .* in agreement with the Syriac texts ($Sy^{s.p}$, T^E, cf. T^A) and the Greek text.

(i) *was standing.* This peculiar addition to the text of verse 27 is not an invention of the author or translator, even though it is not found in the

---

42 J. Zohrab, *Astowacašownč matean hin ew nor katakaranκç,* IV, Venice 1805, 290 (*ew yayn ban*).

43 R. P. Blake, M. Brière, *The Old Georgian Version of the Gospel of John,* Paris 1950, 486 (*da (a)mas sitquasa*).

44 A. Jülicher, W. Matzkow, K. Aland, *Itala, Das Neue Testament in altlateinischer Überlieferung,* IV, Berlin 1963, 33.

45 T^E 12: 17; L. Leloir, *Saint Éphrem, Commentaire de l'Évangile concordant, Texte Syriaque,* Dublin 1963, 90: 13.

46 T^E 12: 16 (Leloir, *o.c.,* 88: 23). The same expression in Epist. I: 10 (Beelen, *o.c.,* 44: 2) in the passage quoted above (ad n. 25).

47 Walton, *o.c.,* 416; Messina, *o.c.,* 416; Messina, *o.c.,* 160.

48 T^E 12: 16, Leloir, *o.c.,* 88: 24.

Greek text or in the Syriac Vulgate. For the same reading is attested in the Old Syriac (Sy^{s}) and in Ephraem's Diatessaron, scil. "(was) standing" *(qā'ēm)*[49].

(j) *and speaking.* This is again the reading of Sy^{s} and T^{F}, whereas Sy^{p} has only '(was) speaking' due to the absence of the preceding word.

(k) *Jesus.* This may have been an addition of the translator or the author, since it is not found in any other text. However, it is surprising that he does not use a phrase as 'our Lord' or 'our Lord Jesus Christ' which he usually writes elsewhere in the epistles. Therefore, one cannot exclude the possibility that it belongs to the quotation and may have been part of the text which the translator was acquainted with or found in the Greek exemplar[50].

(2) The reference to John 4,27 would not have attracted our attention so much, if it had not contained the peculiar readings mentioned under (a) and (i). They clearly betray that the translator did not merely follow his Greek exemplar but rather a Syriac form of the Gospel which he knew by heart. It is difficult to conclude from this fragmentary reference which form of the Syriac Gospel he knew. If Sy^{p} had preserved the Diatessaron reading in (a) – cf. T^{A} – it might well be that the early Syriac harmony – cf. reading (i) – had lent him the wording of the quotation. However, it could as well have been a form of the early Syriac Separate Gospel of John which presented him with this wording.

(3) What may surprise us in the author's argument is that he wished to make a reference to Jesus' behaviour with women as an example for his readers. However, the thrust of his argument is that they should avoid speaking with a woman alone. But Jesus spoke with the Samaritan alone. Therefore, it is actually the astonishment of the disciples that provides him with the example. At this point, the author could have learned from Ephraem's exegesis: this father observes that Jesus "was not afraid of a reproach to speak with a woman alone", "in order to teach me that he who *is standing* in the truth will not be disturbed"[51]. It is exactly the addition of *qā'ēm* – cf. reading (i) – which solves the problem for Ephraem. However, it seems that the author of the epistle did not trust his readers that much, but wished to convey to them that one should avoid the company of women altogether.

(4) What may puzzle us, is why the reading "(was) standing" was introduced into the text of Sy^{s} and T^{E}. It is hard to believe that it was meant to show that Jesus – who in John 4,6 is said to be sitting at the spring – stood up as an act of respect for a woman. It rather seems to have

---

49 T^{E} 12: 16, Leloir, *o.c.*, 88: 24.

50 In comparison with the Greek text of Antiochus the Syriac text of the Epistles tends to use such designations as "our Lord Jesus Christ" etc.

51 T^{E} 12: 16, Leloir, *o.c.*, 88: 23f.

been an insertion with an ascetic touch. One does not sit with women (cf. Sirach 9,9, 'Sit not with a married woman ...'), so if one meets with a woman and talks with her, one should rather stand up. If we think of Tatian as the author of the Diatessaron, it might well have been one of the ascetic additions of this 'encratite' scholar[52]. In that case it might have been part of the early Syriac Diatessaron, which in its turn may have influenced the Old Syriac Gospel tradition (Sy^s). It is interesting to see that the translator of our letter was acquainted with that tradition, but did not see its ascetical meaning and did not exploit it the way Ephraem did.

III.

5. The example of Jesus in John 20,16f.

(1) The second Johannine example[53] is taken from the narrative of Jesus' meeting with Mary near the sepulchre at the day of the Resurrection. It is interesting that this Mary is not qualified as 'Magdalene' but as *the blessed woman,* "... he did not allow Mary, the blessed woman, to touch his feet'[54]. This epithet is specifically used for Mary, the mother of Jesus, in Syriac tradition. Could it be possible that our author used this designation because he himself was convinced that the meeting was one between Jesus and his mother? There was a tradition of this kind in Greek and Syriac traditions[55]. It is also quite evident that this was the conviction of Ephraem expressed both in his commentary on the Diatessaron[56] and in his other writings[57]. It is my view that his conviction was prompted by the way in which the story of John 20 was retold in the Diatessaron[58].

---

52 See for the ascetism in the Diatessaron e.g. D. Plooÿ, *A Further Study of the Liège Diatessaron,* Leiden 1925, 78f.; idem, Eine enkratitische Glosse im Diatessaron, *ZNW* 22 (1923), 1–16.

53 Epist. II: 15.3, Beelen, *o.c.,* 108: 10–15.

54 Ibid., Beelen, *o.c.,* 108: 14f.

55 Cf. T. Baarda, *Quotations,* 254–257, notes (485ff.), but especially R. Murray, Mary, the second Eve in the early Syriac Fathers, *ECR* 3 (1971), 372–384; idem, *Symbols of Church and Kingdom,* Cambridge 1975, 146–148; idem, Note on the Confusion of our Lady & Mary Magdalen in St. Ephrem, not in print but underlying the communication in L. Leloir, *Saint Éphrem, Commentaire de l'Évangile concordant, Version Arménienne,* Latin translation, Louvain 1954, 75 n. 3.

56 Cf. $T^{E\text{-arm}}$ 2: 17; Leloir, *o.c.,* 24: 4–10; $T^{E\text{-syr}}$ 21: 27; Leloir, *o.c.,* 228: 8–10.

57 Cf. a.o. Ephraem, *De Crucifixione,* 4: 17; *De Azymis,* 6: 6f.; *De Resurrectione,* 4: 13, E. Beck, *Des heiligen Ephraem des Syrers Paschahymnen.* Louvain 1964, 13, 59, 74; cf. *Hymn. de Fide* 81: 4, E. Beck, *Des heiligen Ephraem des Syrers Hymnen de Fide,* Louvain 1955, 249.

58 W. L. Petersen, *The Diatessaron and Ephraem Syrus as Sources of Romanos the Melodist,* Diss. Utrecht 1984, 159f. disagrees with this opinion: he thinks that it is "very

Because we have no solid evidence that the author, or should we say the translator, of the epistle actually meant to say that it was Mary, the mother of Jesus, we cannot press this point here. Meanwhile, apart from this element, the passage in which the author makes mention of Jesus' encounter with Mary is noteworthy because of several other striking features that are not found in the canonical text of John 20.

(2) The passage presents us with the following narrative[59]:

(a) She ran	
(b) and she fell down	
(c) at the feet of our Lord	
(d) and worshipped Him	
(e) and desired to seize Him.	
(f) But He said to her:	λέγει αὐτῇ Ἰησοῦς·
(g) "Touch me not,	μή μου ἅπτου,
(h) for I have not yet ascended	οὔπω γὰρ ἀναβέβηκα
(i) to my Father".	εἰς τὸν πατέρα [μου].

Unfortunately, there is no Greek parallel to the Syriac text in the Pandect of Antiochus. If we compare it with the Greek text of John 20,16f., there is only support for the author's reading in the last four lines (see above). Are the other textual elements merely the invention of the author? This seems to have been the opinion of the editor of the Syriac text, J. Th. Beelen, for he writes, "Quod Maria ad pedes Jesu provoluta ipsum manu apprehendere voluit, in Evangeliis non legitur. Sed colligitur ex eo quod Johannes narrat, Jesum ad Mariam dixisse *'noli me tangere'*"[60]. Of course, one cannot exclude the possibility that some of the textual elements could have originated as a logical inference of the author himself. However, there is ample reason to believe that he was rather indebted to existing Greek traditions (in the case that the author is responsible for these elements) or Syriac traditions (in case that the translator added one or more elements to the text of the Greek exemplar). This is, at least, what the present study seeks to demonstrate.

---

doubtful whether this is a Tatianic reading", and labels it as "a hallmark of Ephraem, not Tatian!". However, in my view, the fact that Ephraem refers to it not only in his hymns, but also in his Diatessaron commentary suggests that the text of the latter work prompted his exegesis. The great difficulties which are offered by the various narratives of the Resurrection in the Gospels suggested to the harmonist Tatian a solution in which a distinction was made between the appearances to Mary Magdalen and his mother Mary, cf. esp. Baarda, *Quotations,* 254–257.

[59] Beelen, *o.c.,* 108: 11f.

[60] Beelen, *o.c.,* 109 n. 4; for a similar reasoning see the text of Chrysostom (text ad n. 97) and Alcuin (text ad n. 118).

6. The agreements with the Greek text of John 20,17

(1) Before we examine the possible background of the additions to the canonical text, it may be useful to compare the last four lines of the Syriac text with the Greek text of John 20,17.

(a) *But He said to her.* This text differs from the Greek text and all other texts in omitting the explicit subject 'Jesus'. This does not mean much, since after twice mentioning "(our) Lord" it seems redundant to maintain the name here. Another difference is that our author adds the adversative particle "but" (*hw dyn,* i.e. 'ipse autem'), but this seems only a natural sequence in the retelling of the episode in the epistle. One may, however, notice the fact that Sy^s also differs from other texts in using *hyd-yn,* 'then, at that time', which presents a formal similarity (*–dyn*) in text, but this may be mere coincidence.

(b) *Touch me not.* This text – *l' ttqrbyn ly* – is in agreement with the wording in Sy^p and T^E[61]. From the way in which Ephraem introduces the phrase it is quite clear that this was the text of his Syriac Diatessaron exemplar[62]. The use of the *Ethpael* in these texts differs from the use of the *Peal* form *l' tqrbyn ly* in Sy^s and Sy^{pal}[63]. In his own comments Ephraem also uses the *Peal* form a few times[64], either because he wanted to vary or because he knew this other form from the early Syriac tradition. The verb *qrb* is used in Syriac tradition except from Sy^h. Since the verb *qrb* has an ambivalence, meaning both 'to approach' and 'to touch', Sy^h introduced the verb *gšf* which avoids that ambivalence, since its meaning 'to touch, to seize' corresponds with the ἅψασθαι of the Greek text[65].

(c) *for I have not yet ascended.* This is in agreement with Sy^p and the Greek text. Sy^s omits the particle γάϱ. Ephraem's commentary presupposes a text like that of Sy^p, for it has two forms,

1. "For I have not ascended" (ch. 21:27)[66].
2. "I have not yet ascended" (ch. 21:27.28)[67],

which presuppose the reading, "For I have not yet ascended", the omissions of 'yet' and 'for' being due to the nature of Ephraem's comments.

---

[61] T^E 21: 26.27; Leloir, *o.c.,* 226: 9, 228: 14.16.

[62] T^E 21: 26 ("this is what he said"), 27 ("through this which (quoth) . . ."), 27 ("quoth"), cf. 27 (Leloir, *o.c.,* 228: 18f.).

[63] Lewis, *Gospels,* 264; A. S. Lewis, M. D. Gibson, *The Palestinian Syriac Lectionary,* London 1899, 222.

[64] T^E 21: 26 (Leloir, *o.c.,* 228: 3), 28 (228: 8.9.11.21).

[65] J. White, *Sacrorum Evangeliorum Versio Syriaca Philoxeniana,* I, Oxford 1778, 551.

[66] Leloir, *o.c.,* 228: 16.

[67] Leloir, *o.c.,* 228: 22, 230: 3.

(d) *(un)to my Father,* in agreement with Sy^s, Sy^p, T^{E68} and most Greek manuscripts[69].

IV.

7. The adoration of Mary as a traditional motive

(1) The part of the passage which has no equivalent in the Greek text of John – lines (a)–(e) – speaks about the way Mary behaved when she met and recognized Jesus, before He asked her not to touch Him. Are these elements to be ascribed to the inventive mind of the author of the epistle as an inference from the words 'noli me tangere'? These words seem to imply that she was at the point of touching Him, or rather, that she had touched Him. It is, however, surprising that similar phrases are found in other retellings of this episode. This may be mere coincidence, but the reader may judge for himself whether this is so or not. In order to inform him which parallels I have in mind I shall deal with them in two different paragraphs, the first one containing a comparison of the lines b–c–d dealing with Mary's adoration; the second one presenting a comparison of lines a–e, that is Mary's attempt to seize Jesus.

8. "and she fell down at the feet of our Lord and worshipped Him"[70].

(1) Apart from the words 'of our Lord' which may have been the author's substitution for (or, in the case of the Syriac text, an addition to) 'his', it is clear that the phrases b–c–d are closely related with the text of Mt 28,9, where Jesus meets with the two women including Mary Magdalene:

Greek	αἱ δὲ προσελθοῦσαι	1	*hnyn dyn qrb*	Syriac (Sy^p)
	ἐκράτησαν	2	*'ḥd*	
	αὐτοῦ τοὺς πόδας	3	*rglw(h)y*	
	καὶ προσεκύνησαν αὐτῷ	4	*w-sgdyn lh*	

The text in our epistle agrees in the third element *rglw(h)y* and in the fourth one *w-sgdt lh.* The agreement with Mt 28,9 is even closer, when we look at the paraphrases of this text in some of the western harmonies or versifications of the Life of Jesus. First of all, the *Heliand* attracts our attention, for its text (lines 5951f.),

---

68 Leloir, *o.c.,* 228: 9.17, 228: 2, 230: 3.

69 K. Aland a.o., *o.c.,* 316 app. The reading of Sy^{pal}(*'abbā'*) is ambivalent; cf. M. Black, *An Aramaic Approach to the Gospels and Acts,* Oxford ²1954, 198, 218); cf. T^E 21: 28, Leloir, *o.c.,* 230: 7.

70 Beelen, *o.c.,* 108: 11f.

"... endi sia te is kneohon hnigun/
fellun im tô fuoton ..."[71],

partly agrees with our Syriac text in this regard. Even more so the *Pepysian Harmony* (§ 104), "*And hij fellen adoun to his feete and honoureden hym,* and heilseden hym, and kisseden his feete ..."[72]. A similar text occurs in the Dutch-German harmony tradition, cf. e.g. the Stuttgart manuscript (§ 288), "*Doe vielen si hem te voeten ende anebeidene* ende hildene metten voeten"[73]. The same is true for the so-called *Saelden Hort* (lines 9910–12), "*Si hettent im die fúesse / zů den si* minneclichen *hin / do vielen nider, an betten in*"[74]. We may also compare the so-called *Vita Rhytmica* (lines 6192f.), "*Que* cuncte viso domino *prosternunt se* gaudentes / *adorant suos* osculando *pedes complectentes*"[75]. One cannot deny the great similarity in expressing the behaviour of the women towards Jesus in these texts, nor their agreement with the phrases in our Syriac text. All this may be mere coincidence, but one may consider the possibility that there was some strong Latin textual tradition which contained the motive of the adoration of the women including the phrase 'prociderunt ad pedes eius'. If this were true, one cannot exclude the possibility that such a textual addi-

---

71 O. Behaghel–W. Mitzka, *Heliand und Genesis,* Tübingen 71958, 206 (§ 71), cf. also R. van den Broek, Jacob van Maerlant en het Nederlandse Diatessaron, *NThT* 28 (1974), 141–164, 161.

72 M. Goates, *The Pepysian Gospel Harmony,* London 1922, 104: 6–8, cf. Van den Broek, *o.c.,* 162. The "kissing" is also mentioned in the *Rymbybel* (J. David, *Rymbybel van Jacob van Maerlant,* II, Brussel 1859, 678) lines 26845f., "Ende si *custen* sine voete/ ende anebeeddene harde saen". A. H. A. Bakker (D. Plooij a.o., *The Liège Diatessaron* II, Amsterdam–London (1938–)1970, 763 app.) and Van den Broek, *o.c.,* 161, refer to the Persian Harmony IV: 53 (Messina, *o.c.,* 364) where the text reads, "both worshipped before Him *and kissed his feet*". Although the agreement is striking, one has to be cautious with attributing this reading to Tatian (Van den Broek's observation, "Het is niet onmogelijk, dat dit reeds op Tatianus teruggaat" is rather cautious, indeed). It is difficult to say, whether the Persian text developed this idea of kissing on the basis of a source. The Armenian text "and they approached, seized his feet *and kissed-the-earth* for Him" used the words *erkir-pagin* which is an idiomatic equivalent to προσκυνεῖν. The reading of the Pepysian harmony occurs in other western lifes of Jesus, cf. Ludolph of Saxony's *Vita Jesu Christi,* ch. 73 (A. C. Bolard, L.-M. Rigollot, J. Carnandet, ed., Paris–Rome 1865, 710a) "illae autem (...) accesserunt et tenuerunt *ac deosculatae sunt pedes eius* (...) et (...) adoraverunt"; cf. Hrabanus Maurus (Van den Broek, *o.c.,* 162f.): "... *osculatae sunt Domini vestigia*". The *Vita Rhythmica* (see text ad n. 75) also reads "*osculando*".

73 J. Bergsma, *De Levens van Jezus in het Middelnederlandsch,* Leiden 1895–1898, 264: 4f. Similar texts in C. C. de Bruin, *Diatessaron Leodiense,* Leiden 1970, 272: 34f.; *Diatessaron Haarense,* Leiden 1970, 118: 6f.; *Diatessaron Cantabrigiense,* Leiden 1970, 59: 1f.; Chr. Gerhardt, *Diatessaron Theodiscum,* Leiden 1970, 264: 3f.

74 H. Adrian, *Der Saelden Hort,* Berlin 1927, 183.

75 A. Vögtlin, *Vita Beate Virginis Marie et Salvatoris Rhythmica,* Tübingen 1888, 209

tion came from Greek or Syriac tradition. Unfortunately, there is not a trace of it in the early Syriac tradition due to the fact that both Sy^s and Sy^c are wanting here. Ephraem's commentary does not mention Mt 28,9, so that we are not able to reconstruct the Diatessaron text. However, that a similar tradition was present in the eastern area, is clear from the Georgian manuscripts Op-Tb-Sin[76] which read the text "but they approached *and fell down at his feet* and worshipped Him" (Ms. Ad.: "... and seized his feet ...")[77].

(3) What we wanted to demonstrate is that there is a relation between the phrases in the quotation from John 20,16 is our epistle concerning Mary's adoration *and* the text of the meeting of the two women in Mt 28,9, especially when we take into account some western and eastern witnesses to the latter text. This influence of Mt 28,9 on John 20,16 is an early phenomenon, for in the Latin version of Irenaeus' *Adversus Haereses* (V. 31.1) we read, "et Mariae, quae se prima vidit *et adoravit,* dicebat: 'Noli me tangere, nondum enim ascendi ad Patrem ...'"[78]. Did Irenaeus (or the Latin translator) know John 20,16 with the addition καὶ προσεκύνησεν αὐτῷ?

(4) Now, it is quite interesting to observe that some of the other western texts, especially in mediaeval versifications and harmonies of the Life of Jesus, have traces of this adoration in their retelling of the meeting of Jesus and Mary in John 20,16. We give here the pertinent texts including the element of recognition (another addition in many texts[79]) and that of Mary's attempt at seizing Jesus, anticipating the *second* addition which we shall comment upon later[80].

The first mediaeval versified harmony is the *Heliand* (lines 5928–32): "... Thuo gruotta sia thie hêlago drohtin / bi namen neriendero best / siu geng im thuo nâhor sniumo, / that uuîf mid uuillion guodan, / *antkenda* iro uualdand selƀan, / miðan siu is thuru thia minnia ni uuissa: / *uuelda ina* mid iro mundon *grîpan,* / thiu fêhmia an thena folko drohtin / ..."[81]. A similar text is found in *Otfrid's Gospel* (Lib. I: vii, lines 55f.): "Bi námen er sa nánta, / joh sí nan sar *irkánta / zi fúazon si sar ílta* ...[82].

---

[76] J. Molitor, *Synopsis Latina Evangeliorum Ibericorum antiquissimorum,* Louvain 1965, 284 (app. col. a).

[77] J. Molitor, *o.c.,* 283, col. a.

[78] W. W. Harvey, *Sancti Irenaei Libri Quinque adversus Haereses* II, Cambridge 1857, 412: 5–7.

[79] See for this variant the studies of G. Quispel, *Gnostic Studies,* Istanbul 1975, 70–97, esp. 86; 159–168, esp. 166; J. J. van Weringh, *Heliand und Diatessaron,* Assen 1965, 130f.; W. L. Petersen, *Romanos,* 119f.

[80] See below §§ 9f.

[81] Behaghel–Mitzka, *o.c.,* 205.

[82] O. Erdmann–R. Wolff, *Otfrids Evangelienbuch,* Tübingen [4]1962, 228; cf. 229f. (lines 33 and 42).

These Old German texts express the elements of recognition and of the attempt at seizing Jesus, which we also find mentioned in the early Dutch versification in the *Rymbybel* of Maerlant (lines 26810–13): "So seide Jhesus: 'Maria'. / *Doe kennet soene* in dat woort /ende seide: 'Meester', / *ende tart voort / Soe wildene tasten an sine voete* / ..."[83]. There are, however, other mediaeval texts which contain also the notion of adoration. The *Saelden Hort* (lines 9873–77) describes the encounter with these words, "do sprach Jesus: Maria! / und *er wart bekannt* alda / si sprach: O gůter maister min! / *und lie sich zů den fúessen sin, / die si wolt um vangen han*"[84]. This resembles what Petrus Comestor writes in his *Historia Scholastica* (ch. 188), "Dicit ei Jesus: Maria!, et statim *cognovit eum,* et ait: Rabboni ..., *et procidens voluit tangere pedes eius,* ut consueverat ..."[85]. A similar touch is found in the *Vita Rhythmica* (lines 6172–75): "Quam Jesus vocans nomine dixit: O Maria! / Mox quod esset dominus ex hac voce pia / *Novit* atque propius statim accedebat, / *se prosternens suos pedes tangere volebat*"[86]. Finally, we may refer to the *Vita Jesu* of Ludolph of Saxony (ch. 72), who wrote in his paraphrastic and interpretative comments, "Illa vero conversa ... *eum* in voce ... *recognovit* ... Dicit ei: Rabboni .... *Et currens ac procidens* Maria *ad pedes Jesu,* vestigia eius *adorando,* statim *voluit* ... *amplecti* vestigia eius *quem recognovit,* ac *pedes tangere* et osculari, ut consueverat"[87]. This last mentioned Latin text, again, agrees with the *Pepysian Harmony* (§ 103) in the features of recognition and adoration, where it reads, "And Jesus cleped hire 'Marie'. And þ an *sche knew hym* by his voice, and turned hire, and *fel adoun to his feete* and seide, 'Ha! Swete Sir, ...'"[88]. There must have been a strong Latin tradition both in the Latin harmonies and in the commentaries which gave rise to these additions in the retelling of the episode.

(5) One cannot, in my view, wholly exclude the possibility that the addition of the words 'and fell down at his feet' both in the eastern and western texts mentioned here were independent embellishments of the text, but it is more likely that there was a common origin of the addition. It would be necessary to follow the long commentary tradition on John 20,16 – which is however beyond the scope of this contribution – to establish a possible origin in the Latin textual tradition. It may have been an

---

[83] David, *o.c.*, 676. N.B. "ende tart voort" suggests a Latin reading "procedens" instead of "procidens".

[84] Adrian, *o.c.*, 182.

[85] Petrus Comestor, *Historia Scholastica,* P. L. 198, Paris 1855, 1053–1722, ch. 188 (1638 D). For "ut consueverat" cf. Ludolph of Saxony (ad n. 87) and also Euthymius Zigabenus (ad n. 99) who adds after "for she rushed to touch his feet": ὡς εἰώθει.

[86] Vögtlin, *o.c.*, 209.

[87] Bolard a.o., 708 b. – cf. Alcuin (ad n. 118).

[88] M. Goates, *o.c.*, 103: 35–37.

early Latin harmony tradition which has influenced the mediaeval commentary tradition. The same is true for the second addition which we found in our Syriac text and which, as we may conclude from the examples given above, has parallels in other eastern and western textual witnesses.

9. "And she ran ... and desired to seize Him"[89]

(1) The reading in its usual form is found in what is called the *Cae-* addition that we found in several of the western textual witnesses mentioned in § 8.4. Moreover a similar text is found in some Greek manuscripts and a few eastern and western versions of the Gospel (see below § 10).

(2) Our Syriac text, however, differs from most of these witnesses which usually present the phrase καὶ προσέδραμεν ἅψασθαι αὐτοῦ or a translation of it, in that it has *w-bʿyʾ hwt d-tlbkywhy,* "and wished (or: desired) to seize (lit. that she should seize) him". One might explain this phrase as a paraphrase of the usual form of the addition, but one has to consider the fact that a similar phrase καὶ κρατῆσαι ἠβουλήθη, is found in the first hymn of the Resurrection (Kont. 40:1) of Romanos the Melodist[90]. It has been convincingly demonstrated that the hymns of Romanos largely depend on Syriac traditions[91]. Could this poet have borrowed from the same tradition as did the author (or perhaps the translator) of the epistle on Virginity? In order to make an attempt at answering this question an examination of the usual Greek and versional addition may be helpful.

V.

10. Καὶ προσέδραμεν ἅψασθαι αὐτοῦ

(1) The reading in its usual form is found in what is called the *Caesarean* recension as appears from its occurrence in Θ *13–346–1689*[r92]. The fact that a 6th or 7th century corrector of Codex Sinaiticus (א)[93], who is supposed to have worked at Caesarea, wished to introduce these words into its text, seems to corroborate the assumption that the reading existed

[89] Beelen, *o.c.,* 108:11f.

[90] Petersen, *o.c.,* 121.

[91] Petersen, *o.c.,* 169ff. (Epilogue) and passim.

[92] The textual observations are based upon the data in the more recent critical editions (Tischendorf, Von Soden, Nestle, Merk, Aland); cf. B. M. Metzger, *A Textual Commentary on the Greek New Testament,* Stuttgart 1971, 255. I checked also W. H. Ferrar–T. K. Abbott, *A Collation of four Important Manuscripts of the Gospels,* Dublin 1877, 384; G. Beerman–C. R. Gregory, *Die Koridethi-Evangelien,* Leipzig 1913, 491 (= 246^{r}).

[93] The corrector is designated as $א^{ca}$ (Tischendorf: 'sed $א^{cb}$ rursus delet'), $א^{3}$ (Nestle), $א^{1}$ (Aland) or $א^{a}$ (Greek NT).

in Palestine manuscripts. Apart from these witnesses there are other cursives such as *1093 1195* 1230 2145* (all of them of the *Koine* type of text?) which have the addition. The origin of the *Caesarean* recension is usually sought in Egypt. As a matter of fact, the uncial codex Athous Laurensis (Ψ), which is one of the late Alexandrian witnesses, contains the same reading and consequently suggests that the addition was once present in Egyptian manuscripts. But what is more important is that it is also found in Ms. *1820* (15th cent.), since this codex contains the commentary of Cyril of Alexandria: this author presents us with the addition in the lemma (καὶ προσέδραμεν κτλ.) and with a reference to it in his comments (προσέθει)[94]. It is, however, not found in the vernacular Egyptian versions, as has been suggested by Schnackenburg[95].

(2) It is quite understandable that recent commentators discard this reading as being testified by "some lesser witnesses" (Brown) and, therefore, "textkritisch sekundär" (Schnackenburg). It is described as an interpretative gloss (Bernard, Metzger), an "interpolation by some scribe" (Westcott), which has "to prepare the reader for the following statement" (Metzger, cf. Barrett, Bultman, Brown). The words μή μου ἅπτου in verse 17 (pres. impt. with μή) imply that some action is in progress, or at least an attempt is made to perform an action (Barrett). The gist of the addition seems to be that Mary made an attempt at touching Jesus (Zahn, Bultmann, Schneider)[96].

(3) But if the words of Jesus in verse 17 actually intended to say that Mary seized Him or tried to seize Him, why then was it necessary to add such a phrase? It has been suggested that there was another factor which prompted the addition, that is, the parallel text in Mt 28,9 (cf. e.g. Bernard, Brown, Schnackenburg): Mary Magdalene and the other Mary seized the feet of Jesus. This gesture was transplanted to John's version of the meeting of Mary Magdalene and Jesus. The addition means to say that Mary seized, or was at the point of doing so, the *feet* (Bernard, Barrett), the *hand* (Zahn) or the *knees* (Lagrange, Zahn) of Jesus. If the words of the gloss (although the phrase is "selbständig formuliert") are prompted by Mt 28,9, the interpolator may have thought of the *feet* of Jesus.

(4) The other possibility is that the words were an independent and logical inference from μή μου ἅπτου, which as a commentator's comment crept into the text. As an illustration Chrysostom's homily on this text[97]

---

94 I used the edition of *S. Cyrillus Alexandrinus Archiepiscopus, In Joannem Evangelium* in Migne, P. G. 74, Paris 1857, esp. col. 692.

95 R. Schnackenburg, *Das Johannesevangelium,* III, Freiburg–Basel–Wien 1975, 375, n. 51.

96 The gist of μή + imptv. present. is rather that she already touched Him, cf. N. Turner(–J. H. Moulton), *A Grammar of New Testament Greek,* Edinburgh (1963) 1980, 75f. ("do not continue to ...": "stop touching me!").

97 S. Joannes Chrysostomus, *Homiliae in Joannem,* Migne, P. G. 59, Paris 1862, 469 (Hom. 86).

may be adduced: "For when He called her, 'Maria', then she *recognized* (ἐπέγνω) Him. Therefore, the recognition is not by sight, but by voice. But if it is asked, how is it so obvious that the angels were astonished (ἐξεπλάγησαν) [this is what Chrysostom concluded from the fact that they did not speak any more to Mary], so that this was the reason why the woman turned around? And if it is asked at the same verse, why is it so obvious that she touched Him (ἥψατο αὐτοῦ) and fell down (προσέπεσεν)? Now, just as the latter fact is clear from the saying 'Touch me not', just as clear is the first fact from the saying 'she turned around'". This exposition clearly shows how an interpreter of the usual text in verse 16 could create a more elaborate story in which mention is made of recognition[98], of touching[99], of falling down etc. which were absent from his text. It is not necessary that Chrysostom made these inferences himself, since he could have found them already in some commentary known to him.

(5) If we assume that the addition was prompted either by logical inference or by harmonization with Mt 28,9, it is quite obvious that the same form of the addition in the various manuscripts is not the result of the inventive mind of each scribe, but it is highly probable that the copyists of the manuscripts found it already in their exemplars. Who was the inaugurator of the addition? This is a question of mere guesses. Since its origin seems to lie in Alexandria, one might venture the suggestion that it may have been part of a comment made by Origen as a logical inference, which then was included in the text by some Alexandrian copyist. Or if the Matthaean text was of influence here, it could have been caused by the chimaeric Synopsis of Ammonius of Alexandria.

11. The versional evidence

(1) The addition is also found in the eastern versions: the Palestinian Syriac lectionary[100], the Harclean recension[101], the Georgian version (Mss. Op-Tb-Sin)[102], and – in a somewhat different wording – in the Si-

---

[98] A similar comment in Theophylactus, *Commentarius in Joannem* (P. G. 124, Paris 1864), 293: καὶ οὕτως ἐπιγνοῦσαν· Ῥαβουνι, εἰπεῖν. Cf. Euthymius Zigabenus, *Commentarius in Joannem* (P. G. 129, Paris 1864), 1481: καὶ αὐτίκα τοῦτον ἐπιγνῶσα, ἐβόησεν· ... Διδάσκαλε. It is apparently a constant item in the commentary tradition. Quispel's observation (*Gnostic Studies*, 86) after mentioning the element of recognition in the Heliand, the Pepysian and Liège harmonies and in Sy^s, "Dieser Zusatz liegt nicht sehr nahe" deserves modification. The recognition motive is present also in almost every recent commentary on this text. This does not mean that I disagree with him in assuming that it was a textual element in the Diatessaron.

[99] Theophylactus, *ibid.*: καὶ βούλεσθαι μὲν προσελθεῖν αὐτῷ; Euthymius, *ibid.* : ὥρμησε γὰρ ἅψασθαι τῶν ποδῶν.

[100] Lewis–Gibson, *o.c.*, 222. [101] White, *o.c.*, 551.

[102] J. Molitor, Das Adysh-Tetraevangelium, *OrChr* 46 (1962), 11; Blake–Brière, *o.c.*, 591.

naitic Syriac Gospel[103]. The origin of these testimonies is a puzzling question. There are several possibilities:

a) all of them are independent translations from various Greek exemplars. There is probably a relation between the Georgian version and the Caesarean text, and the same is said of the Palestinian Syriac. The text of Sy^{h} (it is part of the text, not of the marginal notes) may have been influenced by some *Koine* manuscript with this singular reading. Even Sy^{s} may have originated in some Greek manuscript of Alexandrian or Caesarean origin. In this case, one cannot speak of a Syriac tradition: all occurrences are independently caused by Greek models.

b) another possibility is that there was an Old Syriac reading of this kind. Sy^{h} could have preserved here an indigenous Syriac text, which originally contained a phrase like *w-rhṭt* (= Sy$^{s.pal.h}$) *d-tqrwb* (= Sy$^{s.pal}$) *bh* (= Sy$^{pal.h}$, or: *lh* = Sy^{s}), which in Sy^{h} has been assimilated to its interpretation of vs. 17 (cf. § 6.1b) by substituting the verb *qrb* by *gšf*. In this case, Sy^{h} and Sy^{pal} may be witnesses for an Old Syriac text whose origin could have been either a Caesarean manuscript or the Syriac Diatessaron. This latter source, however, has been identified by Th. Zahn[104] as an explanation for the deviating text of Sy^{s}: *w-rhṭt lppyn lwth d-tqrwb lh*. The words underlined agree with those in Sy^{pal} (cf. Sy^{h}) to a great extent, but the remaining words are peculiar to Sy^{s}: the first element *lppyn* = *l'ppyn* 'to the face', that is, 'forward' is apparently an attempt to render the Greek prefix πρός- in προσέδραμεν, 'ran up'[105]; the second element *lwth* 'towards, unto Him' is probably another attempt at rendering the gist of the Greek verb. The wording *lh* leaves open the possibility of two interpretations: Mary ran up towards Jesus *in order to approach Him*[106] or *in order to touch Him*[107]. It seems obvious that we cannot speak of one Syriac tradition. If the text of Sy^{s} originates in the Diatessaron (Zahn), the other Syriac versions must have come from another Old Syriac source. Or, if these latter versions ultimately go back to the Diatessaron, then Sy^{s} must have rooted in some Old Syriac text or must have been an independent translation.

c) these extreme solutions are presented here, in order to avoid an approach which ascribes the origin of all these testimonies to the Diates-

---

103 Lewis, *o.c.*, 264.

104 Th. Zahn, *Das Evangelium des Johannes*, Leipzig–Erlangen $^{5.6}$1921, 676, n. 47.

105 The verb *rhṭ* is equivalent to τρέχω, cf. John 20,2; Lk 15,20 etc. The rendering of *lppyn* is varying: "ante eum" (Lagrange), "en avant" (Lagrange), "forward" (Burkitt), "entgegen" (Merx), "facing him" (Jennings); no rendering in Lewis' translation.

106 So e.g. Lagrange, *Critique textuelle*, Paris 1935, 167, n. 3; 214; A. Merx, *Die vier kanonischen Evangelien nach ihrem ältesten bekannten Text, Uebersetzung*, Berlin 1897, 225 marg.

107 A. Merx, *o.c.*, 225 (text); A. S. Lewis, *A Translation of the Four Gospels from the Syriac of the Sinaitic Palimpsest*, London 1896, 107.

saron of Tatian, as so often is done. The situation may be more complicated than usually is assumed. My impression is that the Georgian text ultimately goes back to a Greek model. The fact that this version presents the verb '(she) ran' with the prefix *mi-* suggests that it was an independent attempt at accurately translating the prefix προσ- of the Greek verb. There is no relation with Sy^{s}, since it has no equivalent to *lwth* 'unto Him'. The fact that Sy^{pal} uses the reading *bh* for αὐτοῦ could suggest that the author was aware of the fact that the Greek verb meant 'to touch'; this may be an indication that he was also rendering a Greek text. But here again, just as in the case of Sy^{h}, the possibility of a Syriac tradition cannot be excluded.

(2) The addition is also found in western areas, for it is present in some Vulgate manuscripts of the so-called Irish or Celtic family[108]:

gat (8th cent.): et occurrit ut tangeret eum
D (808 A.D.): et occurrit ut tangueret eum
E (8th cent.): et cucurrit ut tangeret eum

It is often suggested that the Book of Armagh (*D*) has affinities with the Ferrar group of cursives which belong to the Caesarean family of texts. Therefore, since *gat–D–E* have close affinities, one might assume that this addition to the Vulgate text was introduced under the influence of some Greek manuscript of this type. However, since (as we shall see) the same addition is found in several witnesses of the western Diatessaron tradition, one has to take into account the possibility that an early Latin harmony was the source for this Irish interpolation.

VI.

12. The western Diatessaron traditions

(1) The harmony of the codex Casselanus was introduced into the Diatessaron research by C. W. M. Grein[109], who referred to its reading 'et occurrit ut tangeret eum' as a convincing proof that the text of the *Heliand* was not based upon the harmony text of the Codex Fuldensis, but on some

---

108 J. Wordsworth–H. J. White, *Novum Testamentum D. N. Jesu Christi Latine secundum editionem s. Hieronymi,* Oxford 1989–1898, 640 app.; J. H. Bernard, *The Gospel according to St. John,* II, Edinburgh 1928, 667 mentions: Cant., Stowe, Rawl. G. 167. Cf. J. M. Heer, *Evangelium Gatianum,* Freiburg 1910, 179; E. S. Buchanan, *The Four Gospels from the Latin Text of the Irish Codex Harleianus in an English Version,* London 1914, 49.

109 C. W. M. Grein, *Die Quellen des Heliand,* Cassel 1869, 49, 61, 113, 129, 257. Van Weringh, *o.c.,* 129f.

other Latin harmony which agreed with the Kassel text at this point[110]. It turned out that this reading was present in several other Latin harmonies examined by H. J. Vogels, scil. München 7946, München 23346, Reims A. 46, Leipzig 192 and 193, and Berlin 1707[111]. Since these harmonies are of a later date (9th, 13th and 14th century) than the Vulgate codices mentioned above, one may theoretically ask whether these Latin harmonies were influenced by this Vulgate variant reading. However, the *Heliand* proves that there was an early Latin harmony which in its turn could have influenced the Irish texts.

(2) Besides the occurrence of the interpolation in Latin harmonies there seems ample evidence that there was a similar text in the Latin *Vorlage* of the Middle Dutch and German harmonies:

$T^{N(S)}$: Doe liep si te hemwaerd ende woudene roeren[112].
$T^{N(Hr)}$: Doe liep si te hem waert ende wouden roeren[113].
$T^{N(C)}$: Doe liep si tot hem waert ende wouden roren[114].
$T^{G(MV)}$: Do lief si zv ime vnd wolt in rüren (V: tasten)[115].

The first problem is whether these manuscripts represent the original Dutch text. For the famous Liège manuscript and the manuscripts Z–N–W–U of the Middle German text do not include this interpolation. Did these latter texts suppress the text in question? This depends on the question of the genealogy of the Dutch texts. If $T^{N(L)}$ is, as is usually assumed, the crown witness of the Dutch harmony, the addition in the other manuscripts is a later interpolation. However, since $T^{N(L)}$ is a copy of an older exemplar and not completely identical with the original Dutch Diatessaron, for whose reconstruction also the other manuscripts are of much importance, I do not want to exclude the possibility that at this point the other manuscripts may have preserved the text of the common ancestor and its Latin predecessor[116].

---

110 Grein, *o.c.*, 61, "aus einer Handschrift derselben, welche dem Codex Cassellanus näher stand, als den Texten, welche Schmeller (= Sang.) und Ranke (= Fuld.) herausgegeben haben"; cf. 113; Von Weringh, *o.c.*, 130 concludes that it was present in the Latin Diatessaron behind the Heliand: "$T^{lat(hel)}$: et occurrit ut tangeret eum".

111 H. J. Vogels, *Beiträge zur Geschichte des Diatessaron im Abendland*, Münster i. W. 1919, 138.

112 J. Bergsma, *o.c.*, 264.

113 De Bruin, *o.c.*, 119: 2f.

114 De Bruin, *o.c.*, 59: 33.

115 Gerhardt, *o.c.*, 167: 15. The verb "tasten" also in the Rymbybel of Maerlant, see below.

116 D. Plooij, *A Further Study of the Liège Diatessaron*, Leiden 1925, 39, who knew only the Stuttgart variant, writes, "How such a reading could disappear from all Diatessaron texts except S is one of the riddles of textual criticism"; he apparently believed that the Stuttgart manuscript had preserved the original reading of the Latin Diatessaron or even of the original Diatessaron.

The second problem is which form of text did this Latin predecessor contain. At first sight it seems highly probable that this was the usual text *et occurrebat ut tangeret eum.* The addition of 'unto Him' in the Dutch harmony is apparently an attempt at rendering the prefix *ob-* in *occurrebat* (cf. the similar procedure in Sy^s). However, is the reading 'ende woudene roeren' an attempt at rendering the Latin *ut tangeret eum*? Or does it render a different Latin text such as *et voluit (volebat) tangere eum*? I would not have made this suggestion, if there were not a strong tradition in other Latin and German texts (see § 7.4), e.g. "si wolt um vangen" (*Heliand* 5932), "uuelda ina . . . gripan" (*Saelden Hort* 9877), "soe wildene tasten" (*Rymbybel* 26813), "voluit tangere" *(Petrus Comestor),* "tangere volebat" (*Vita Rhythmica* 6175), "voluit tangere" (*Ludolph of Saxony*)[117].

(3) The Dutch Diatessaron tradition does not make solutions easy. If the train of thought that we have developed here would be right, one has to reckon with the fact that there were two different Latin Diatessaron readings, namely

et occurrebat ut tangeret eum
et occurrebat et voluit (volebat) tangere eum,

of which the first occurs in a few Latin manuscripts and the latter only in part of the vernacular tradition. Those who would be inclined to suggest that the interpolation was absent from the original Dutch Diatessaron and only crept into the Dutch text at a later stage of the textual development avoid this difficulty. They might assume that it came into the later texts due to the influence of a commentary such as that of Petrus Comestor. They could refer to the comment of Alcuin, "Iam vero ab evangelista non subditur, quid mulier fecerit, sed ex quo innuitur, quod audivit, cui dicitur 'Noli me tangere . . .'. In his namque verbis ostenditur, quod Maria *amplecti voluit* vestigia eius quem *recognovit*"[118]. Here again, just as in Chrysostom's commentary, we meet with logical inferences from the Gospel text, including the notions of recognition and of the desire to seize Jesus. However, just as in the case of Chrysostom, such a comment may have been the result of a longer commentary tradition and does not exclude the possibility that the Dutch texts were witnesses of a different Latin harmony tradition. Those who would make firmer decisions at this point take the risk of overspeculating the textual data. What would be necessary is an overall survey and examination of all the eastern and western commentaries and glosses on John 20,16f. in order to draw conclu-

---

[117] For the addition of the auxiliary verb *voluit/volebat* cf. R. van den Broek, Enkele opmerkingen over de Latijnse archetypus van het middelnederlandse Diatessaron, *De Nieuwe Taalgids* 70 (1977), 434–458, esp. 441 ff. This phenomenon requires a more thorough investigation.

[118] Quoted by Grein, *o.c.,* 113.

sions on the basis of a more thorough understanding of the history of tradition with respect to this text. Such an examination is beyond the scope of this contribution. Meanwhile one can only register the fact that the western Diatessaron tradition at certain stages of its development has the interpolation in some form[119]. It is at this point that the Syriac text of the epistle on Virginity draws our attention.

13. Once again: the text of the Syriac Epistle

(1) The result of the preceding investigation is that two alternative readings suggest themselves as possible readings of the Latin Diatessaron, the first one with the wording *ut tangeret eum,* the second one with the phrase *et voluit (volebat) tangere eum.* It is the latter reading which presents us with an exact parallel of the wording in the Syriac translation of the Epistle on Virginity (*w-bʿyʾ d-tlbkywhy*), which as we have seen was also present in one of the hymns of Romanos (καὶ κρατῆσαι ἠβουλήθη). The question may now be posed whether these readings have preserved the Syriac Diatessaron wording.

(2) This question may be positively answered, if we may adduce the testimony of a passage in Ephraem's commentary as an indication for such a reading. I have in mind the passage of his comment on 'the wedding of Cana' in ch. 5:5[120], which unfortunately is found only in the Armenian version. We have already observed that Ephraem identified the Mary of John 20 as the mother of Jesus. Therefore, one cannot be surprised that Ephraem combines John 2,3f. and John 20,16f. It is quite interesting to see that he begins his comments with the observation that Mary, Jesus' mother, *did ran* (Arm. *antʿaçaw*)[121], a feature which is not found in John 2,3f., but which occurs in John 20,2 ($Sy^{s.p}$) and John 20,16 (Sy^{s}): *rhṭt,* cf. Epist. de Virg. II: 15.3. Now, according to Ephraem, Jesus did not comply with Mary's desire both in John 2,3f. and 20,16f., '. . . the same way, after his victory on the Sheol, when his mother saw Him, she wished (or, desired) to embrace Him (*ggowel zna*) as a mother . . .', '. . . He prevented her again that she approached Him'[122]. These last words (*zi mi mercesçi i na*) are repeated in $T^{E\text{-arm}}$ 21:27. 'Why did He, therefore, prevent Mary

---

[119] It is interesting to find a parallel of the first form in Tertullian, *Adversus Praxean,* 25: 2 (Aem. Kroymann–Ern. Evans, *Q. S. Fl. Tertulliani Opera* II, Turnhout 1954, 1195f. (= 25,18ff.), ". . .cum iam Patrem se/posset ostendere tam fideli feminae, ex dilectione, non ex/curiositate nec ex incredulitate Thomae *tangere eum adgres/sae*: 'Ne, inquit, contigeris me, nondum ascendi ad Patrem/meum . . .'".

[120] L. Leloir, *Saint Éphrem, Commentaire de l'Évangile concordant, Version arménienne* (*Texte*), Louvain 1953, 61: 6–19.

[121] Ibid., 61: 1.

[122] Ibid., 61: 12–14; 17–18.

that she approached Him?'[123], which reflect the refusal of Jesus in John 20,17 'Do not approach (*qrb*) me!'.

(3) The verb used in the Armenian (*kamim,* 'volo, desidero') presupposes a Syriac text with the wording *bʿyʾ* 'she wished (desired)' in John 20,16, an element found in the Syriac text of our Epistle. The question is whether the Armenian verb (*ggowel*) which we have rendered with 'to embrace' (Leloir: *mulcere, caresser*[124]) could have been a rendering of the Syriac verb *lbk,* which is used in the Syriac Epistle on Virginity. If this were the case, it would have been possible that the translator, in rendering the Greek *Vorlage* which may have contained the usual text καὶ προσέδραμεν ἅψασθαι αὐτοῦ followed, just as in other cases mentioned above, the textual tradition of the Diatessaron, either directly from the Diatessaron itself or from an Old Syriac text influenced by the Syriac harmony. In that case, the translator of the Epistle becomes an important witness to the Diatessaron text.

(4) If these observations are correct, we are able to venture a hypothesis concerning the course of textual tradition in John 20,16:

(a) The Greek text καὶ προσέδραμεν ἅψασθαι αὐτοῦ was originally inserted into Greek texts as an interpolation in the second or early third century, in Alexandria (Ammonius? Origen?). It has influenced the Caesarean text, and through it also the Koine text and the Irish text of the Vulgate. The latter text may have influenced some of the Latin harmonies.

(b) Independently, or under the influence of this Greek text, the Syriac Diatessaron introduced another phrase, namely *and ran up and wished to seize Him,* which was used by the author of the Syriac version of our Epistle on Virginity and by Romanos. This eastern reading then was introduced into the early Latin translation of the Diatessaron, which in its turn has influenced the wording of the Heliand, Saelden Hort, the Dutch harmonies, Maerlant's Rymbybel and many Latin commentaries on the passage of John 20,16f.

(5) This hypothesis explains both the spread of the interpolation *and* its different wording in western areas. It remains a hypothesis, and therefore, as may be observed in the preceding pages, can only be launched with some hesitation *and* with cautiousness[125]. The interpretation of tex-

---

[123] Ibid., 331: 1f.; cf. Leloir, *o.c.* (Syr.), 228: 18f.

[124] J. Miskgian, *Manuale Lexicon Armeno-Latinum,* Rome 1807 (repr. Louvain 1966), 56 mentions the meanings "ulnis amplector, recreo, nutrio, foveo". Is the reading of the Armenian text (= Ms. A, Ms. B reads *glgowel* – I cannot trace its meaning) the original reading? The verb *grkem,* "amplector" (ibid. 64) would suggest itself.

[125] An example of an over-enthousiastic and therefore uncareful approach is found in D. Plooij, *A further Study,* 39, which mentions the reading of the Middle-Dutch Stuttgart manuscript and compares it with the Greek, Latin and Syriac witnesses, and concludes, "a range of authorities which by itself would suggest a Tatianic origin", without any ex-

tual facta, especially in the field of Diatessaron research, is a task that asks for such cautiousness. This is what has been emphasized so often in the sessions of the Seminar on Textual Criticism at the annual meetings of the Studiorum Novi Testamenti Societas, devoted to the problems of the early Syriac harmony. I cherish the hope that these pages, with which I wanted to honour my colleague, meet with the demands which he always made for himself in textual studies.

planation of the differences in wording or the complications in the textual history of the interpolation; to a certain degree this is also true for the treatment by Van Weringh and Quispel. This criticism does not imply that these authors did not have a good intuition when they brought up the Tatianic problem in their examination of the text, as can be seen from the present contribution.

Johanneische Theologie und Ethik im Licht der »letzten Stunde«

von Horst Balz

(Am Herrenbusch 46, 5810 Witten 3)

Ob der 1 Joh als echter Brief gelten kann, ist umstritten[1]. Einerseits wendet sich der Verfasser eindeutig als Schreiber an einen vielschichtigen (1 Joh 2,12–14) Kreis von Lesern[2]. Als »Kinderchen«[3], »Kindlein«[4] und »Geliebte«[5] spricht er sie an. Zum anderen hat er aber auf die formalen Elemente eines griechischen und urchristlichen Briefes verzichtet. Für ihn sind die Paulusbriefe nicht – wie mehrfach sonst in den pseudepigraphischen Briefen des Neuen Testaments – zum Vorbild geworden. Er wird sie kaum gekannt haben. Dennoch schreibt er nicht minder verbindlich und mit einer persönlichen Autorität, die ihm seitens seiner »Kindlein«

---

[1] R. Bultmann, Art. Johannesbriefe, in: RGG III, ^{3}1959, 836: »ein ›Manifest‹ oder ein Mahnschreiben«; R. Schnackenburg, Die Johannesbriefe, HThK XIII/3, ^{7}1984, 2: »Letzthin ... für uns ein Rätsel«; Ph. Vielhauer, Geschichte der urchristlichen Literatur, 1975 (durchges. Nachdr. 1978), 462: Traktat oder an die ganze Christenheit gerichtetes Manifest; K. Wengst, Der erste, zweite und dritte Johannesbrief, ÖTK 16, 1978, 27: Der briefliche Rahmen einschließlich der Verfasserangabe fehlt, »weil der Briefschreiber den Eindruck erwecken will, mit dem Verfasser des Evangeliums identisch zu sein.«; H.-M. Schenke/K. M. Fischer, Einleitung in die Schriften des NT, II 1979, 219: »Er ist kein Brief ... Es kann nur eine Bestimmung vom Inhalt her gegeben werden. Danach ist 1 Joh die Entfaltung der Tradition der Augenzeugen für die Situation der Scheidung von der Irrlehre mit dem Anspruch auf Allgemeingültigkeit.« Am ehesten: »Manifest«; H. Balz, Die Johannesbriefe, in: Die »Katholischen« Briefe, NTD 10, ^{2}1980, 161: »ein predigtartiger Aufruf«; R. E. Brown, Ringen um die Gemeinde. Der Weg der Kirche nach den Johanneischen Schriften (engl.: The Community of the Beloved Disciple, 1979), 1982, 73: »eher eine Abhandlung als ein persönliches Schreiben«.

[2] γράφομεν ἡμεῖς 1 Joh 1,4; γράφω ὑμῖν 2,1.7.8.12.13 (2 mal); ἔγραψα ὑμῖν 2,14 (3 mal). 21.26; 5,13.

[3] τεκνίον begegnet im NT nur im Vok. Plur., und zwar neben Joh 13,33 nur (7 mal) im 1 Joh: 2,1.12.28; 3,7.18; 4,4; 5,21. Anders dagegen τέκνα (τοῦ) θεοῦ 3,1f.10; 5,2 von den (recht glaubenden und lebenden) Gotteskindern, im Gegensatz zu den τέκνα τοῦ διαβόλου 3,10. In 2 Joh 1.4.13 und 3 Joh 4 meint τὰ τέκνα wiederum konkret die Gemeindeglieder.

[4] παιδία 2,14 (neben πατέρες und νεανίσκοι wie zuvor τεκνία in 2,12f.); 2,18; es fehlt in den beiden kleinen Johannesbriefen.

[5] ἀγαπητοί 2,7; 3,2.21; 4,1.7.11; Sing. noch 3 Joh 1f.5.11.

wohl auch fraglos eingeräumt wird. Mag sein Brief daher inhaltlich eschatologische Belehrung (ἵνα εἰδῆτε ... 5,13) und formal ein Rundschreiben an einen Kreis von johanneischen Gemeinden gewesen sein – Grüße, Austausch von Segenswünschen und organisatorische Mitteilungen scheinen dem Verfasser dabei wenig bedeutet zu haben[6]. Wichtigeres hat er anzusagen, daß es nämlich an der Zeit ist, letztgültige Klarheit über sich selbst und andere zu gewinnen: »Kindlein, es ist letzte Stunde, und wie ihr gehört habt, daß ein Antichrist kommt, so sind nun viele Antichriste erstanden, woran wir erkennen, daß es letzte Stunde ist« (2,18). Überraschend ist der Antichrist »jetzt schon in der Welt« (4,3).

I

So schreibt einer, der sich zu den Augen- und Ohrenzeugen des Lebenswortes rechnet, ja dieses mit Händen betastet haben will (1,1f.). Das bedeutet, daß er sich ganz von dem Logos geprägt weiß, der das Leben gebracht hat (Joh 1,4.14 mit 1 Joh 1,2f.). Als ein Sprecher der johanneischen Tradition und besonders des johanneischen Evangeliums tritt er seinen Gemeinden gegenüber[7]. Wenn er von Anfang an betont, daß der Logos irdisch geschaut und begriffen werden konnte, so dürfte er gleich zu Beginn seines Schreibens solche im Blick haben, die meinen, auf diese irdische Wirklichkeit des Lebenswortes mit all ihren Konsequenzen für ihr eigenes Leben verzichten zu können[8]. Da sie wohl ursprünglich dem jo-

---

[6] Ph. Vielhauer, a.a.O. (Anm. 1), 462, vermißt den »Korrespondenzcharakter«.

[7] F. Overbeck, Das Johannesevangelium, 1911, dachte an ein »begleitendes Erläuterungsschreiben« zum 4. Evangelium (474); s. dazu aber R. Schnackenburg, a.a.O. (Anm. 1), 34–39. Die Erklärung von K. Wengst (s. o. Anm. 1) müßte präzisiert werden. Die Leser des 1 Joh sind ja johanneische Christen, denen die Umstände der Entstehung und Verbreitung des Johannesevangeliums (Evangelist, Lieblingsjünger, Bearbeiter bzw. »Anwalt« des Evangeliums, vgl. Joh 21,24f.) nicht ganz fremd gewesen sein können. Eher schon könnte man vermuten, daß der 1 Joh (in einer im einzelnen noch zu klärenden Weise) mit der Redaktion des Evangeliums zusammenzusehen sei, was vor allem durch das Motiv der glaubwürdigen Bezeugung der irdischen Wirklichkeit des Logos nahegelegt würde, vgl. 1 Joh 1,1–3 mit Joh 19,35; 21,24; ähnlich schon M. Dibelius, Geschichte der urchristlichen Literatur, II 1926, 63; s. auch J. A. T. Robinson, The Destination and Purpose of the Johannine Epistles, NTS 7, 1960/61, 56–65, bes. 58; J. Becker, Die Abschiedsreden Jesu im Johannesevangelium, ZNW 61, 1970, 215–246, bes. 233–236; G. Klein, »Das wahre Licht scheint schon«, ZThK 68, 1971, 303f. mit Anm. 180 (Lit.), der diese Vermutung allerdings skeptisch aufnimmt; G. Richter, Studien zum Johannesevangelium, BU 13, 1977, 357–381; W. Langbrandtner, Weltferner Gott oder Gott der Liebe, BBE 6, 1977, 373–404.

[8] Daß der 1 Joh das 4. Evangelium vom Prolog bis zum ursprünglichen Schluß anklingen läßt (vgl. 1 Joh 1,1–3 und 5,13), könnte man damit zu erklären versuchen, daß der Verfasser das Evanglium seinen Lesern zunächst einmal nahebringen wolle (s. o. Anm. 7).

hanneischen Kreis um den Verfasser angehört haben (1 Joh 2,19; s.u.) und nun als Lehrer zu seinen Gemeinden kommen (2,26f.; 4,1), ist für den Schreiber die Stunde der letzten Prüfung und Bewährung dieser Gemeinden angebrochen. In dieser Stunde gilt es, an der lange schon erkannten Wahrheit festzuhalten und sich von aller Lüge zu trennen (2,21)[9]. Die »Kinderchen« und »Geliebten« sollen wissen, daß sie durch ihren Glauben das ewige Leben wirklich schon haben (5,13) und daher keiner neuen Belehrung mehr bedürfen (2,27). Bleiben sie in dem, was das χρῖσμα sie gelehrt hat, und damit in Christus, dann werden sie auch mit erhobenem Haupt und ohne jede Furcht ihrem Herrn entgegensehen, wenn er sich in seiner Parusie offenbart (2,27.28).

»Letzte Stunde« könnte ein Vorwegträumen des Endgültigen, einen Tagtraum vor dem Ende der Nacht bedeuten. Es könnte sich aber auch auf eine letzte Stunde nach vorangegangenen vorletzten und drittletzten Stunden beziehen, also das Ende eines Zeitverlaufs markieren. Beides scheint hier nicht der Fall zu sein. Mit der eigenständigen Bildung ἐσχάτη ὥρα[10] spitzt der Schreiber vielmehr eine seinen Lesern aus der johanneischen Sprache wohlvertraute Wendung in unerhörter Weise zu: Nicht um die im Evangelium angekündigte Stunde geht es, in welcher die Toten die Stimme des Menschensohns hören werden (Joh 5,25.28), sondern um eine Stunde letzter Entscheidungen und Scheidungen, die lediglich noch die Parusie Christi als des Richters und Retters vor sich hat. Wohl ist mit dieser Stunde *auch* das Ende der irdischen Geschichte der angesprochenen Gemeinden angesagt, aber ihr eigentliches Gewicht erhält sie durch das Auftreten der Antichriste und Verführer, die die Gemeinden stören und zerstören könnten, also als Stunde der letzten Krise. Das Eschaton selbst wird umfassendes Licht und vollkommene Wahrheit sein, die Glaubenden werden dem Vater gleich sein und ihn sehen, wie er ist (1 Joh 3,2). Zuvor haben aber Lüge (2,22), Verführung (2,26) und der Geist der Christusleugnung (4,3) ein letztes Mal ihre Stunde. Der Kosmos greift mit Haß (3,13) nach denen, die aus dem Tod schon zum Leben hinübergeschritten sind (3,14; vgl. Joh 5,24). Obwohl sie ihren Bedrohern in keiner Weise

---

Mehr Wahrscheinlichkeit hat aber die Annahme für sich, daß er seine Gemeinden in einer schismatischen Situation mit Nachdruck bei der von ihm vertretenen wahren Botschaft ihres Evangeliums bewahren will, vgl. 2,7.21.24.26f. und grundsätzlich H. Conzelmann, »Was von Anfang war«, in: Neutestamentliche Studien für R. Bultmann, BZNW 21, 1954, 194–201, bes. 198f. (= ders., Theologie als Schriftauslegung, 1974, 211f.).

[9] Für K. Weiß, Orthodoxie und Heterodoxie im 1 Joh, ZNW 58, 1967, 247–255, steht hinter dem 1 Joh ein »Autor, der sich in das noch unentschiedene Gewoge von Rechtgläubigkeit und Irrglaube mitten hineinstellt und mit beweglicher und wechselnder Kampfführung die Position des rechten Glaubens zu gewinnen und den Irrglauben als solchen zu enthüllen und ins Unrecht zu setzen am Werke ist.« (255)

[10] Singulär im NT und in der LXX; s. zum einzelnen G. Klein, a.a.O. (Anm. 7), 295–304, bes. 303.

ausgeliefert sind, weil sie ja den weltüberlegenen Herrn in sich haben (1 Joh 4,4) und ihn glauben (5,5), sollen sie wissen, daß auch ihre Bewährung, genauer: ihr »Bleiben im Herrn« (2,28) bis hin zur Parusie auf dem Spiel steht. Erst wenn sie vollends erfahren und verstehen, daß jede Kommunikation zwischen ihnen und dem Kosmos heilsnotwendig zerbrochen ist (4,5f.), haben sie im Glauben als Gotteskinder auch wirklich den Kosmos überwunden (5,4). »Letzte Stunde« heißt also: Die Mächte des Kosmos erkennen, selbst wenn sie sich verstellen und verkleiden, und sie festmachen in Verhaltensweisen und letztlich in bestimmten Menschen, die von ihnen beherrscht werden, um sich dann endgültig zu trennen von allem Vorletzten und nur noch vom Letzten her zu leben, das zugleich von allem Anfang an gültig ist (1,1–4; 2,24f.). Nur wer sich hier bewährt, wird in Ewigkeit bleiben (2,17).

Diese eschatologische Mahnung gilt einer Kirche, deren Gemeinden Lebensgemeinschaft untereinander haben und dadurch auch Anteil haben an dem Vater und dem Sohn (1,3). Kompromisse und Verständigungsversuche als Lebensregeln der vorletzten Zeit können nicht mehr tragen, da die Gemeinden endgültig, – für das Ende gültig –, von Gott gefordert sind. Mit denjenigen, die der Gemeinschaft mit dem Vater und dem Sohn nicht entsprechen, gibt es keine Kooperation und bald darauf auch keine Kommunikation mehr (2 Joh 10f.). In der Stunde vor dem Ende bricht die johanneische Theologie also heilsnotwendig in Alternativen auseinander.

Alternative zum Denken und Leben des Kosmos ist die johanneische Theologie und damit auch das Leben der johanneischen Gemeinden von Anfang an gewesen. In der Situation des 1 Joh ist aber eine Theologie gefordert, welche diese Alternative unüberhörbar neu aktualisiert; welche die Wahrheit nur sagen kann, indem zugleich die Lüge gebrandmarkt wird und die Menschen der Lüge verworfen werden (1 Joh 2,21f.; 4,6b); welche vom Licht nur reden kann, indem zugleich alles Wandeln in der Finsternis enttarnt wird (1,7f.; 2,9–11); ja welche die Gemeinschaft mit dem Vater und dem Sohn (1,3) nur bewähren kann, indem zugleich aus dieser Gemeinschaft ausgeschlossen wird, wer ihr nicht wirklich zugehört. »Sie sind von uns ausgegangen, aber sie waren (in Wirklichkeit) nicht aus uns; wären sie nämlich aus uns gewesen, wären sie mit uns zusammengeblieben; an ihnen sollte jedoch offenbar werden, daß nicht alle (, die bei uns sind,) aus uns sind« (2,19). Wenn im 1 Joh also die johanneische Alternative zwischen Wahrheit und Lüge, zwischen Gemeinde und Kosmos nunmehr als innerjohanneische Alternative zwischen wahrer und falscher Botschaft neu ausgesagt werden muß, dann ist für den Schreiber in der Tat die Spannung zwischen Gott und dem Kosmos auf ihrem endzeitlichen Höhepunkt angekommen.

Damit ist aber der Konflikt, dem sich der Verfasser des 1 Joh ausgesetzt sieht, noch nicht vollständig erfaßt. Es ist ja offensichtlich geworden, daß hier johanneische Christen, welche die Gemeinschaft mit dem Vater und dem Sohn für sich beanspruchen dürfen, solche Christen radikal von sich weisen sollen, die ebenfalls aus der johanneischen Tradition kamen (ἐξ ἡμῶν ἐξῆλθαν 2,19), nun aber in den Kosmos ausgezogen sind (4,1) und die Glaubenden durch ihre Lehre in Verwirrung führen (2,26f.). Bei der Frage nach der Herkunft der Dissidenten darf das auffallende Gegenüber von ἐξ bzw. μεθ' ἡμῶν in 2,19 (insgesamt 5 mal) und ὑμεῖς in v. 20 nicht übersehen werden[11]. Im Abschnitt über das Wirken der Antichriste 2,19–27 vermeidet der Verfasser nämlich das ihn mit den Lesern zusammenschließende »Wir«, das zuvor die antithetischen Sätze in 1,6–2,5 bestimmt hatte[12]. Er steht also an seinem Ort, der damit zugleich der Herkunftsort der Verwirrer ist, den Orten der Gemeinden gegenüber. Die Antichriste und Falschpropheten scheinen vor allem deshalb so gefährlich zu sein, weil sie sich über eine verführerische Botschaft hinaus auch noch mit einer Autorität schmücken konnten, die der Schreiber allein für sich und seine Botschaft reklamiert. Vermutlich hat er sich in die Defensive gedrängt gesehen angesichts einer neuen »johanneischen« Botschaft, die er zunächst nicht verhindern konnte und vor der er nun auf jeden Fall die johanneischen Gemeinden zu bewahren hat. Die Ausgezogenen mögen dagegen ihn selbst als Verfälscher der johanneischen Botschaft kritisiert haben. Eine Spaltung ist jedenfalls bereits vollzogen worden, und die Dissidenten werden ihren Auszug in die Welt nachdrücklich mit eigenen theologischen Argumenten begründet haben. Aus Sorge um seine Gemeinden schreibt dann der Verfasser seinen Brief und ruft in ihm die letzte Stunde als die Stunde des Antichrists aus.

Für eine Beurteilung der Entwicklung der johanneischen Theologie ist es daher von höchster Bedeutung, den Charakter und die Gründe dieser Auseinandersetzung wenigstens in Umrissen aus dem 1 Joh zu er-

---

[11] Das betonte ὑμεῖς fällt in Weiterführung von 2,20 noch auf in v. 24 und 27. In gleicher Weise ist der parallele Zusammenhang in 4,4–6a zu beurteilen, wo mit ὑμεῖς v. 4 zunächst die angesprochenen Gemeinden, mit αὐτοί in v. 5 dann die Falschpropheten und mit ἡμεῖς in v. 6a schließlich der Kreis der Lebenszeugen um den Schreiber selbst gemeint sind. Nur so kann v. 6a als Weiterführung von v. 4f. und nicht als – im Zusammenhang störende – Verdoppelung der Aussage von v. 4 verstanden werden. Ähnlich K. Wengst, a.a.O. (Anm. 1), 175.

[12] Allein in 2,25 könnte ἡμῖν wieder als gemeinsames »Wir« des Schreibers und der Leser interpretiert werden und somit dem Befund widersprechen. Hier gilt es allerdings zu erkennen, daß v. 25 inhaltlich und weithin auch im Wortlaut (καὶ αὕτη ἐστὶν ἡ [ἐπ]αγγελία) die Aussage von 1,5 wieder aufnimmt, welche die gesamte Auseinandersetzung eröffnet hat. 2,25 bildet also mit 1,5 zusammen eine rahmende Klammer um den ersten Teil des 1 Joh (1,5–2,27), auf welche rückblickend und zusammenfassend nur noch die deutlich abgehobenen (ταῦτα ἔγραψα...) v. 26f. folgen. Wie in 1,5 geht es dann auch in 2,25 um das »Wir« der Lebenszeugen von 1,1–4, die den angeschriebenen Gemeinden gegenüberstehen.

schließen. Die pauschalen Auskünfte, hier stünden Orthodoxie gegen Häresie oder johanneischer Inkarnationsglaube gegen johanneische Gnosis, könnten u. U. ja zunächst mehr verdecken als erhellen.

II

Da der 1 Joh in einer schismatischen Situation die johanneischen Gemeinden warnen und bewahren will, muß im Grund der gesamte Duktus des Briefs zur Klärung dieser Situation herangezogen werden, also sowohl die eher lehrhaften Sätze (besonders die antithetischen Aussagen) als auch die mehr homiletischen und paränetischen Partien. Von besonderem Gewicht ist jedoch der erste Hauptteil des Briefes, der in der Ansage der »letzten Stunde« des Antichrists und der Antichriste in 2,18–25 sein Ziel findet.

Das Ende dieses ersten Teils kann m. E. nicht schon in 2,17 gegeben sein[13], sondern erst mit dem deutlichen Abschluß[14] in 2,26f. Nach dieser grundsätzlichen Klärung der Fronten findet der Verfasser zu stärker paränetisch bestimmten Aussagen (2,28–3,24), die die gewonnenen Alternativen im Blick auf das rechte Handeln und vor allem das johanneische Liebesgebot entfalten[15]. In 4,1 ff. wird die anfängliche Auseinandersetzung wieder aufgenommen, nun jedoch in der Weise, daß nach der Mahnung, »in ihm zu bleiben« (2,28), in einem neuen Schritt von den Gottesgaben die Rede ist, an denen die Glaubenden erkennen, daß Gott auch »in ihnen bleibt« (3,24). Es geht um den wahren Geist und um die Liebe, die beide von Gott ausgehen (4,1–6; 4,7–5,4). Wie der erste Briefteil durch das Stichwort μένειν (2,24.27) zum zweiten Teil hinführt, so bildet am Schluß des zweiten Teils das neue Stichwort πιστεύειν die Brücke zum dritten Teil, der dann deutlich die Leser auf ihren (rechten) Glauben hin anspricht (4,1.16; 5,1.4[16].5.10.13).

Obwohl die Auseinandersetzung ihren Schwerpunkt im ersten Teil des Briefes hat, läßt dieser die Kontroverse nicht sofort deutlich erkennen. Vielmehr will der Schreiber allem Anschein nach die Leser zunächst davon überzeugen, daß Entscheidungen und Scheidungen überhaupt geboten sind. Damit wird es zusammenhängen, daß auch seine Ansage der eschatologischen Krise erst am Ende des ersten Briefteils ihren Platz findet. Er will seine Gemeinden nicht unvorbereitet mit einer neuen, end-

---

[13] So z. B. R. Schnackenburg, K. Wengst u. a.

[14] R. Bultmann, Die Johannesbriefe, KEK XIV, ^{2}1969, 40.

[15] In 2,28 werden deutlich Konsequenzen für das Leben der Gemeinde gezogen (καὶ νῦν, τεκνία...). V. 29 spricht dann neu vom »Tun der Gerechtigkeit«, was in 3,3 mit dem Motiv der Heiligung aufgenommen wird, den Abschnitt 3,4–10 bestimmt (vgl. besonders v. 4.7f. 10b) und schließlich zu den Aussagen über das Gebot Jesu nach Joh 13,34 führt (1 Joh 3,11–24).

[16] Nur hier begegnet das Subst. πίστις im 1 Joh.

zeitlichen Deutung ihrer Situation konfrontieren, wirft er doch auch den Dissidenten vor, daß sie neue und damit falsche Lehre bringen (2,20f.24f.26f.). Vielmehr wirbt er aus der bestehenden und nunmehr erst gefährdeten Gemeinschaft mit den Lesern heraus (1,3) zunächst um ihr Verständnis für seinen Bruch mit den Ausgezogenen; vollkommene Freude will er letztlich an seinen »Kinderchen« finden (1,4). Er ist weniger Lehrer oder Wahrer des rechten Bekenntnisses, sondern eher Prediger und »Vater« seiner Gemeinden, der seine Leser nicht umsonst durch die familiäre Anrede liebevoll an seine bisher unbestrittene Autorität erinnert.

Damit dürften die richtigen Voraussetzungen für das Verständnis des Abschnitts 1,5–2,11 geschaffen sein. Die Struktur dieses Textes wird schnell deutlich, wenn man sieht, daß der Verfasser zunächst in 1,5 seine eigene johanneische Botschaft (ἀγγελία) in einer knapp gefaßten These formuliert: »Gott ist Licht, und Finsternis ist in ihm keine.« Diese Botschaft hat er (inmitten der johanneischen Lebenszeugen) von Christus, dem Lebenswort, gehört; sie ist es auch, die er den johanneischen Gemeinden (wie stets schon) weitergibt.

Anschließend folgen Sätze, die überwiegend antithetische Aussagenpaare bilden und inhaltlich eine fiktive Auseinandersetzung über die Konsequenzen dieser Botschaft wiedergeben. Sie setzen mit dem aus der These vorgegebenen Gegenüber von Finsternis und Licht ein (1,6f.) und enden im Stil einer Ringkomposition auch wieder mit diesem Gegenüber (2,9–11). Sie gehören also als Einheit zusammen. Formal sind sie besonders dadurch gekennzeichnet, daß zunächst zwei antithetische Aussagenpaare jeweils mit ἐάν + 1. Pers. Plur. gebildet werden (1,6f.8f.). Die dritte Aussage entspricht inhaltlich dem antithetischen Muster, hat ἐάν + 1. Pers. Plur. jedoch nur im ersten Glied (1,10–2,2). Die vierte und fünfte Antithese sind jeweils mit einer eigenen Einleitung versehen: »(Und) daran erkennen wir, daß wir ihn erkannt haben, wenn wir (nämlich) seine Gebote halten/daran erkennen wir, daß wir in ihm sind« (2,3.5c). Im vierten Aussagenpaar folgt dabei auf einen Partizipialsatz ein Relativsatz (2,4f.), und im fünften Aussagenpaar steht einem ähnlich wie in 2,4 formulierten Partizipialsatz (2,6) eine diesen zu einer antithetischen Einheit ergänzende Aussage über das »neue Gebot« gegenüber (2,7f.). Mit der letzten partizipial formulierten Antithese (2,9f.) kehrt die Entfaltung der Botschaft von 1,5 wieder zum Gegensatz von Licht und Finsternis zurück; zugleich sind erstmals der Bruderhaß und die Bruderliebe einander gegenübergestellt, wodurch die bisherige antithetische Erschließung der Ausgangsthese ihrem eigentlichen Ziel entgegengeführt wird: Die Liebe zu den Brüdern bzw. das Versagen gegenüber dem Liebesgebot Jesu werden den Brief im folgenden entscheidend bestimmen. Deshalb unterstreicht der Verfasser eigens noch einmal das grundlegende Fehlverhalten derer, die meinen oder behaupten, im Licht zu sein, und es dennoch nicht sind: Sie hassen den Bruder, sind und wandeln damit in der Finsternis und wissen nicht, wohin sie gehen, denn die Finsternis hat ihre Augen blind gemacht (2,11).

Soll also erkannt werden, was Licht und Finsternis als Alternativen wirklich bedeuten, so muß am Ende vom Gebot der Bruderliebe die Rede sein. Die Ausgangsthese, genauer: die Botschaft des Verfassers hat nicht den Charakter einer Information über längst Bekanntes, sondern ist selbst schon als Konsequenz aus dem überlieferten Wissen der johanneischen Theologie formuliert, eine Konsequenz, die erst jetzt angesichts des Auseinanderbrechens des johanneischen Zeugenkreises wirklich ausgesprochen werden kann: Wer den Bruder haßt und damit in der Finsternis ist, der ist notwendig nicht in Gott, denn »Gott ist Licht, und Finsternis ist in ihm keine«.

Daß diese Botschaft des Schreibers letztlich auf Trennung und Ausschließung zielt, wird besonders deutlich dadurch, daß die angeschlossenen sechs antithetischen Entfaltungen dieser Botschaft sämtlich zunächst ein negatives Verhalten markieren, das jeweils mit bloßen Behauptungen der Diskussionsgegner zusammenhängt. Die Antithesen werden entweder durch ἐὰν εἲπῶμεν (1,6.8.10) oder durch ὁ λέγων (2,4.6.9) eröffnet. Durchweg steht einem nur behaupteten Tun oder Sein ein wirkliches, positives Tun oder Sein gegenüber: im Licht wandeln 1,7; die Sünden bekennen 1,9; als (gelegentliche, vgl. 5,16f.) Sünder auf die durch Jesus Christus, den Parakleten, geschaffene Sühnung trauen 2,1f.; das Wort und Gebot Christi halten 2,5; das »alte« Gebot bewahren in dem neuen Wissen darum, daß die Finsternis vergeht und das wahre Licht schon scheint 2,7f.; den Bruder lieben und damit im Licht bleiben 2,10. Die zur Licht- und Finsternisthese komprimierte Grundbotschaft des Schreibers scheidet ein lediglich behauptetes von einem wahren Sein, hilft Verhaltensweisen erkennen, in welchen Tun und Selbstverständnis nicht übereinstimmen. Sie ist damit alles andere als lediglich ein erbauliches Predigtthema.

Nur von seiner Funktion und Intention her läßt sich also der Grundsatz von 1,5 beurteilen. Wie Gott als das Licht jede Finsternis ausschließt, so schließt rechte Gotteserkenntnis ein der Finsternis zugewandtes Leben aus. »Christen« können zwar überzeugt sein, daß ihr eigenes, erleuchtetes Dasein Gott entspricht und dennoch falsch leben, so daß sie zutiefst auch kein Wissen um Gott haben.

Dennoch dürften die Antithesen von 1,5ff. nicht jeweils die »rechtgläubige« Haltung einer »häretischen« Position gegenüberstellen, so daß die negativ qualifizierten »Behauptungen« schlicht Zitate aus der gegnerischen Lehre wären. Ein solches Vorgehen entspräche nicht dem Anliegen des Verfassers und wohl auch nicht der für ihn selbst diffizilen Situation, traten doch die Dissidenten in der Welt als johanneische Verkündiger auf. Daher ist eher anzunehmen, daß die sechs Entfaltungen der Grundthese von 1,5 den Lesern grundsätzlich vor Augen führen sollen, wie man sich über die eigene Zugehörigkeit zum Licht täuschen oder täuschen lassen kann. Das wird besonders daran deutlich, daß der Verfasser sich in 2,1f. und 2,7f. zweimal gleichsam unterbricht, um die Gemeinden direkt anzureden, als Gefestigte und doch zugleich Betroffene. Dabei weiß der Schreiber natürlich, von wem er in Wirklichkeit spricht. Die Leser werden aber Schritt für Schritt aus eigener Erkenntnis heraus zu der Einsicht geführt, daß selbst eine Botschaft, die sich der johanneischen Sprache bedient und sich auf die johanneische Tradition beruft, nicht unbedingt von Gott und seinem Licht handeln muß. Aus diesem Grund wird der Schreiber das ihn mit den Lesern zusammenschließende »Wir« besonders in 1,6ff. verwendet haben. Anhand der Antithesenreihe sollen die Leser auch im Blick auf sich selbst zu einem vertieften Verständnis der johanneischen Botschaft kommen, so daß sie in der endzeitlichen Krise nicht mehr durch Verführer um ihre Gabe des Lebens gebracht werden können.

Für den Schreiber steht dabei fest, daß seine Leser nicht nur behaupten, im Licht zu sein. Deshalb versichert er ihnen sogleich im Anschluß an die antithetische Entfaltung seiner Grundbotschaft in sechsfacher Wiederholung, daß er alles Voranstehende nicht etwa geschrieben habe, um sie damit zu treffen, 2,12–14[17]. Danach erst kommt er in 2,15–17 zu einer Ermahnung, die die Gemeinden aufruft, die Alternative zum Kosmos durchzuhalten, um so für die Ewigkeit Gottes bewahrt zu bleiben (v. 17). Sollten die Leser an diesem Punkt des Briefes verstanden haben, daß der in 2,15–17 geschilderte feindliche Kosmos ihnen auch in der Gestalt von falschen Auslegern der johanneischen Botschaft entgegentreten kann, dann hätten sie das Anliegen des Verfassers verstanden und wären somit vorbereitet für seine Ansage der »letzten Stunde« des Antichrists und der Antichriste selbst.

Von daher ist die Terminologie von 1,5 noch einmal näher zu beleuchten. Oft schon ist gesehen worden, daß dieser so johanneisch wirkende Satz eigentlich eine johanneische Neuerung darstellt[18]. Gott als Licht

---

[17] In 2,12–14 sollte das sechsfache ὅτι besser mit »daß« statt mit »weil« übersetzt werden. Der Verfasser schreibt an die Leser nicht, weil sie es sozusagen wert sind, sondern er schreibt ihnen, »daß« sie die Vergebung der Sünden haben, den Uranfänglichen erkannt haben usw., daß also die voranstehende kritische Analyse keineswegs auf sie selbst zielt, sondern ihnen lediglich ein kritisches Instrument zur Beurteilung der neuen, verführerischen »Lehre« an die Hand gibt. Entsprechendes gilt dann auch für 2,21. Es liegt dem Schreiber nicht daran, eine bereits gefestigte Gemeinde (Perfektformen) um Unterstützung in seinem Kampf anzugehen (kausales Verständnis), sondern er versichert den Gemeinden, die nach seiner Ansicht gerade in eine endzeitliche Auseinandersetzung hineingezogen werden, daß er auf ihrer Seite steht und im Grunde auf ihre Überlegenheit über den Kosmos und damit auch über die Verführer vertraut.

[18] Zwar stehen sich hier wie im Johannesevangelium Licht und Finsternis antithetisch gegenüber, aber im Evangelium sendet Gott mit dem Logos das Leben als das Licht der

hat mit Finsternis grundsätzlich nichts gemein, so wie umfassendes helles Licht alles Finstere verdrängt und nicht einmal mehr dem Schatten Raum gewährt. Weder will der Verfasser damit Gott definieren noch will er nur sagen, »was Gott für den Menschen bedeutet«[19], noch geht es ihm schließlich um die Antithese von Licht und Finsternis allein. Die zunächst tautologisch wirkenden Licht- und Finsternisaussagen von 1,5 haben dann nebeneinander einen Sinn, wenn das beide verbindende καί konsekutiv oder explikativ verstanden wird und somit den Blick der Leser auf jenen Bereich lenkt, der aus Gott per se ausgegrenzt ist, nämlich den der Finsternis. Um dieser Ausgrenzung willen wird der Verfasser seine endzeitliche Botschaft überhaupt in einem solchen Satz über Licht und Finsternis konzentriert haben und ihn wie ein Warnsignal an deutlich exponierter Stelle in sein Schreiben eingebracht haben.

Daher wäre wenig damit geholfen, dieser These Parallelen aus Qumran (z.B. 1 QS 3,20f.), aus dem hellenistischen Judentum (z.B. Test. Levi 19,1) oder der mandäischen Gnosis (z.B. Ginza R I 3, Lidzbarski 6,26ff.) an die Seite zu stellen. Die Aussage zielt weder auf den endzeitlichen Kampf zwischen Licht- und Finsternismächten noch auf die Entscheidung zwischen dem Gesetz Gottes und den Werken Beliars, noch schließlich auf den in sich reinen Lichtgott. Schon die Fortführung von v. 5 in v. 6 zeigt ja, daß sich das Interesse des Schreibers zunächst mehr auf die Finsternis richtet als auf das Licht. Das gleiche läßt sich bei der Rückkehr zum Thema von Licht und Finsternis in der letzten der sechs Antithesen von 2,9f. erkennen, denn auch hier liegt alles daran, daß solche, die die Brüder hassen, notgedrungen »noch« (ἕως ἄρτι v. 9) in der Finsternis sind, weil sie nichts von dem in sich haben, was im Lichtbereich gilt, nämlich vom Gebot der Bruderliebe. Vollends wird dies unterstrichen durch die vernichtende Schlußaussage über den Hassenden in 2,11: Weil er in der Finsternis ist, ist er ohne jede Orientierung; seine Augen vermögen nichts zu sehen, und aus dem Licht ist er ausgeschlossen.

Diese Fortführung der Ausgangsthese zeigt an, worum es dem Verfasser eigentlich geht: nicht um Gott an sich, sondern um die notwendigen Implikationen alles Redens von Gott und jeder Gottesbeziehung. Gott kann da nicht im Spiel sein, wo im aktuellen Lebensvollzug die Finsternis auch nur irgendeinen Platz eingeräumt bekommt; wer Gott auf diese Wei-

---

Menschen in den Kosmos (Joh 1,4), so daß das Licht in der Finsternis leuchtet und schließlich Jesus, der Offenbarer, selbst als das von Gott ausgehende Licht erscheint. Nicht Jerusalem, sondern nur die Nachfolger erfahren ihn aber als das Licht des Lebens (Joh 8,12ff.; vgl. weiter 1,7–9; 3,19–21; 9,5; 12,35f.46). Daß Gott selbst Licht sei, ist terminologisch und sachlich eine neue Aussage gegenüber dem Evangelium. Noch deutlicher wird dies in 1 Joh 1,7, wonach Gott selbst »im Licht ist«, φῶς also den Lichtbereich meint. S. weiter G. Klein, a.a.O. (Anm. 7), 284–291.

[19] So R. Bultmann, a.a.O. (Anm. 14), 21.

se mit der Finsternis verbindet, hat mit Gott selbst nichts zu tun. Um den wahren Gott geht es allein da, wo alle Rede von Gott und alles Bekenntnis zu Gott gedeckt ist durch einen entsprechenden Wandel im Licht. Nur hier ist der Gott im Spiel, der sich in Christus geoffenbart hat und dadurch ein Leben im Licht, nämlich im Heilsbereich der Sündenvergebung durch das Blut Jesu eröffnet hat (1,7). Während die Leser in 1,5 vordergründig hören könnten: »Gott ist Licht und hat mit der Finsternis (des Kosmos) nichts gemein«, sollen sie in Wirklichkeit lernen, daß am Licht Gottes, das alle Finsternis ausschließt, nur die Anteil haben, die auch in diesem Licht leben, und d. h. ekklesiologisch gesprochen: in der Gemeinde Jesu Christi als dem Bereich dieses Lichts, dem Ort der Sündenvergebung und des ewigen Lebens. Schon zu Beginn des 1 Joh bereitet die Botschaft des Schreibers die Trennung von den Abtrünnigen vor und gilt somit der Bewahrung des Lichtbereichs selbst, nämlich der Gemeinschaft mit dem Vater und dem Sohn (1,3) und untereinander (1,3.7).

Dieses Ergebnis würde grundsätzlich auch dann nicht in Frage gestellt, wenn der Verfasser in 1,5 nicht einen eigenen kritischen Satz formuliert, sondern eine Formel gebraucht hätte, die ihn wenigstens noch im Grundsätzlichen mit seinen Gegnern verbindet und die als Parole der Abtrünnigen u. U. schon bis zu den Gemeinden durchgedrungen sein konnte. Die Gegner hätten dann von Gott als dem Licht ohne alle Finsternis im Sinne eines spekulativen oder metaphysischen Dualismus gesprochen und – bereits auf dem Weg zur Gnosis – in der Erkenntnis des Lichtes Gottes sowie in der Erleuchtung ihres eigenen Selbst das höchste Ziel gesehen[20]. In diesem Sinn könnten in der Tat die Aussagen von 1,8 und 2,3f.5cf. interpretiert werden. Der Verfasser hätte sich diesen Satz aber zu eigen gemacht, um seinerseits ganz andere Folgerungen daraus zu ziehen und gerade unter Berufung auf Gott als Licht ohne jede Finsternis das Heil

---

[20] Die Beziehungen zwischen der gegnerischen Theologie und der Gnosis sind immer wieder hervorgehoben worden, vgl. nur R. Schnackenburg, a.a.O. (Anm. 1), 16: »Die bekämpfte religiös-sittliche Abweichung vom Christentum ist *gnostisch* (Sperrung im Original) orientiert. Das bedarf nach der ganzen Terminologie und Anschauungswelt keines näheren Beweises.« Ähnlich R. Bultmann, a.a.O. (Anm. 1), 837: »Gnostiker ..., die zwischen Jesus und Christus unterscheiden«. Nähere Begründungen sowie eine differenziertere Zuordnung finden sich besonders bei K. Wengst, Häresie und Orthodoxie im Spiegel des ersten Johannesbriefes, 1976, passim. Nach ihm stehen die Gegner »in einer Entwicklung ..., die folgerichtig zu Kerinth hinführte« (34); vgl. dazu auch R. E. Brown, a.a.O. (Anm. 1), 80ff. 144. Vorsichtiger spricht K. Weiß, Die »Gnosis« im Hintergrund und im Spiegel der Johannesbriefe, in: Gnosis und NT, hg. v. K.-W. Tröger, 1973, 341–356, bes. 353ff., zwar von Zügen, »die diese Häresie der Gnosis verdächtig machen« (353), betont dann aber eher die Unterschiede und Widersprüche zu den späteren gnostischen Systemen. Die Heimat der Gegner sei eher im hellenistischen Bereich zu suchen (356). Gegen gnostischen Einfluß wendet sich in neuerer Zeit z. B. J. M. Lieu, »Authority to become Children of God.« A Study of I John, NT 23, 1981, 210–228.

exklusiv an die Gemeinschaft, die Sündenvergebung und das Gebot zu binden. Diese Sicht hätte allerdings erhebliche Konsequenzen, wenn es nämlich darum geht, das theologische Profil der Gegner und besonders ihre Christologie zu erheben. Daß sie Jesus als den Christus und so mit dem Sohn auch den Vater geleugnet haben (2,22f.), könnte zusammen mit 4,2f. und 5,5–10 als Beleg dafür herangezogen werden, daß sie eine in irgendeiner Weise doketische[21] oder allgemein gnostische Christologie entwickelt hätten. Die Auseinandersetzung des 1 Joh hätte dann zumindest einen Schwerpunkt in diesem christologischen Streit.

Es ist allerdings kaum denkbar, daß der Verfasser das autoritative »Wir« der Lebenszeugen (1,1–4.5) für eine solche Botschaft in Anspruch genommen hätte, die zumindest auch die Basis für schwerwiegende Mißverständnisse und Verfehlungen sein konnte. Die Formulierung von 1,5a spricht also deutlich gegen eine solche Annahme. Daher kann auch die These von 1,5 nicht als Indiz dafür gewertet werden, daß die Gegner in erster Linie eine neue christologische Lehre gebracht hätten. Die gegenüber dem Evangelium neue Redeweise vom Licht geht vielmehr auf den Verfasser selbst zurück. Ist er dann aber mit seiner These auch theologisch über das Evangelium hinausgegangen?

Nach dem Johannesevangelium hat sich Gott, der Vater, aus Liebe zum Kosmos in Jesus als dem menschgewordenen Sohn dem Kosmos zugewandt, so daß die Taten Jesu die Herrlichkeit Gottes selbst offenbarten und der Gesandte dadurch als Sohn verherrlicht wurde (Joh 11,4; vgl. 1,14; 8,54; 17,5.22–24 u. ö.), als Licht des Lebens für die Menschen (Joh 1,4; 8,12; vgl. 1,9; 3,19–21; 9,5; 12,35f. u. ö.). So kennt die johanneische Gemeinde Gott allein als den, den der Sohn gebracht hat. Der in die Welt gesandte Sohn ist der Mittler des Vaters, und der Vater ist es wiederum, der sich im Sohn Unverständnis, Ablehnung und schließlich Verwerfung durch den Kosmos gefallen läßt. Daher erhalten allein die Hörer und Nachfolger das Licht des Lebens. Den sich Verweigernden wird die Rettung der Glaubenden zum Gericht, den Glaubenden aber ist das vom Sohn in den Kosmos gebrachte Leben das Licht selbst. Finsternis ist insofern nicht in ihm, als Gott sich zwar im Sohn auf die Finsternis der Welt eingelassen hat, nicht aber in sie eingegangen ist oder sich mit ihr vermischt hätte. Das Licht steht vielmehr als Gabe und Angebot der Finsternis gegenüber. Wo dieses Angebot angenommen wird, vertreibt das Licht die Finsternis, begegnet der Kosmos in einzelnen Glaubenden und schließlich in der Jüngergemeinde selbst dem Licht, das in der Gemeinde

---

[21] Kritisch dazu u. a. K. Weiß, a.a.O. (Anm. 20), 343; R. E. Brown, a.a.O. (Anm. 1), 85–87. K. Wengst, a.a.O. (Anm. 20), 24–38, möchte die Christologie der Gegner nicht als doketisch bezeichnen, weil sie nicht bestritten hätten, »daß Jesus wirklicher Mensch war« (37).

seinen Ort gefunden hat. In diesem Sinn ist der Ansatz des Johannesevangeliums im 1 Joh konsequent fortgeschrieben worden[22].

Ist die Gemeinde wirklich durch die Sendung des Lichts in den Kosmos und durch das von den Glaubenden ergriffene Leben der einzige Ort des Lichts im Kosmos, dann ist auch der Lebensvollzug der Glaubenden ganz auf das reale Zusammenleben in der Gemeinde angewiesen. In diesem Sinn kann dann auch gesagt werden, daß Gott im Licht ist (1 Joh 1,7), ja daß er das Licht selbst ist und Finsternis in ihm keine ist (1,5). Nur wer in der Gemeinschaft der Glaubenden von der Liebe Gottes zum Kosmos und von der Vergebung durch das Blut des Sohnes lebt und sich auf diese Weise an das alte und bleibend neue Gebot der gegenseitigen Liebe hält, hat das Licht und damit Gott selbst bei sich. In solchen Menschen ist »wahrhaft die Liebe Gottes vollendet« (2,5). Nur unter diesen Voraussetzungen läßt sich schließlich sagen, daß »die Finsternis bereits vergeht, und das wahre Licht schon scheint« (2,8). Wer aber diese Gemeinschaft preisgibt, fällt dem Kosmos anheim, dem er dann auch je schon zugehört hat (αὐτοὶ ἐκ τοῦ κόσμου εἰσίν 4,5). Solchen bleiben ihre Sünden, sie bleiben selbst in der Finsternis und im Tod.

III

Auf der bisher gewonnenen Grundlage kann nun das Bild des Verfassers von seinen Gegnern in seinen Grundzügen vervollständigt werden, wenn dabei auch manches skizzenhaft bleiben muß. Zunächst ist klar geworden: Die Gegner stammen aus dem johanneischen Kreis, haben sich aber von ihm getrennt und sind in den Kosmos ausgezogen (2,19; 4,1), wo sie anscheinend in einer Weise Gehör finden, die für den Verfasser beängstigend ist (4,5). Sie lehren in den johanneischen Gemeinden, aber ihre Lehre stammt nach dem Urteil des Verfassers nicht aus dem Geist Gottes, sondern aus dem des Antichrists (4,3); aus ihnen spricht nicht der Geist der Wahrheit, sondern der der endzeitlichen Verführung (2,26; 4,6). Daran, daß sie die Gemeinschaft mit den Brüdern, die zugleich die Gemeinschaft mit dem Vater und dem Sohn ist, preisgegeben haben, erweist sich, daß sie grundsätzlich nicht zu den erwählten Gotteskindern gehört haben, sondern aus dem Kosmos sind (2,19; 4,5). Weil das wahre Licht nur in der Gemeinde leuchtet, haben sie sich durch ihr Verhalten vom Licht selbst ausgeschlossen. Indem sie durch ihre Sezession aber den Ort des wahren Lichts verworfen haben, haben sie auch geleugnet, daß Jesus der Christus sei, und mit dem Sohn zugleich den Vater verworfen (2,22f.), ja ihn zum Lügner gemacht (5,10). Weil sie mit dem Anspruch

[22] G. Klein, a.a.O. (Anm. 7), 288: »Die Übertragung der Lichtprädikation auf Gott ... will die Lichtterminologie im Rahmen der johanneischen Sprachentwicklung geschichtlich tradierbar erhalten.«

auftraten, die johanneische Christusbotschaft zu bringen, und in Wirklichkeit gerade Jesus als den Christus zunichte machten, sind sie die endzeitliche Verkörperung des Antichrists und seiner falschen Propheten. Daran erkennen der Schreiber und seine ihm treu verbundene Gemeinde, daß die letzte Stunde vor dem Ende da ist (2,18; 4,3).

Das ist aber nur ein Teil des Gesamtbildes. Es treten weitere Aussagen hinzu, die der Verfasser zwar nicht immer deutlich als Polemik gegen die Abtrünnigen formuliert, die aber dennoch erst auf Grund des durch sie vollzogenen Bruches und anläßlich ihres verführerischen Einwirkens auf die Gemeinden zur Sprache kommen.

Nur in der Gemeinde und unter den Bedingungen der Gemeinschaft untereinander reinigt das Blut Jesu, des Gottessohnes, die Glaubenden von aller Sünde (1,7). Die Behauptung grundsätzlicher Freiheit von der Sünde wie auch jede Negierung des faktischen Sündigens wären eine Selbsttäuschung, durch welche schließlich Gott zum Lügner gemacht würde (1,8–2,2). Es würde damit ja die Erlösungstat Jesu Christi, nämlich sein sühnender Tod für die Sünden aller (2,2; vgl. 4,9.14) verworfen. Zwar gilt, daß die nicht sündigen, welche in Christus bleiben, wie er selbst keine Sünde in sich hat, und daß die, welche sündigen, ihn weder gesehen noch erkannt haben (3,5f.; vgl. 3,9f.; 5,18). Das kann aber nur im Blick auf die Glaubenden in der Gemeinde gesagt werden, die den Kampf gegen die Sünde auf Christus hin aufgenommen haben und dabei auch gelegentlich unterliegen können (2,1f.; 5,16f.). Die Gegner scheinen durch ihr Verhalten und durch ihre Behauptungen deutlich gemacht zu haben, daß ihnen weder an dem Ort der gewirkten und wirksamen Sühnung (2,1f.; 5,16f.) noch am sühnenden Sterben des Gottessohnes selbst liegt. Den Tod Jesu Christi erfahren die Glaubenden ja als Zeichen der Liebe Gottes, auf welche sie mit der Hingabe ihres eigenen Lebens für die Brüder antworten (3,16; vgl. 4,9f.). Durch ihre Trennung von der Gemeinde leugnen die Dissidenten aber die Liebe Gottes, die in der Sendung des einzigen Sohnes des Vaters in den Kosmos (4,8f.) und zur Rettung des Kosmos (4,14) erfahren werden konnte.

Damit hängt für den Verfasser direkt zusammen, daß die Angegriffenen sich durch ihren Auszug als Menschen des Kosmos erwiesen haben, was sie dann auch schon von jeher waren. Während der Kosmos die Gotteskinder nicht als solche erkennt, weil er Gott nicht erkannt hat (3,1; vgl. 3,13), hört er sehr wohl auf die Dissidenten, denn sie sprechen seine Sprache (4,5). Dagegen können für den Verfasser die nicht aus Gott sein, die nicht auf ihn und seine Gemeinden hören (4,6). Hatten die Gegner etwa durch besondere Missionserfolge den Kosmos bereits für sich eingenommen (4,3)? Oder sind sie durch Herkunft, Bildung und gesellschaftliche Stellung den wahrhaft Glaubenden im Bereich des Kosmos überlegen, was man auch hinter 2,15–17; 3,17 und 4,20 wiederfinden könnte? Beides ist denkbar, und zudem ergabe sich für den Verfasser das eine aus dem anderen. Dann wäre aber der Auszug der Dissidenten nicht ein einseitiger oder willkürlicher Akt gewesen, sondern er hätte seinen Grund in einer internen Auseinandersetzung im johanneischen Kreis gehabt, durch welche die Gegner des Verfassers als Weltmenschen zunehmend aus diesem Kreis hinausgedrängt wurden.

In eine ähnliche Richtung weisen die Texte des 1 Joh, in welchen in je verschiedenen Formulierungen Gemeinschaft mit Gott (1,6f.), Erkenntnis Gottes (2,3f.; vgl. 4,6f.12f.), Sein in Gott (2,5c–8) bzw. Sein im Licht (2,9f.) in einen untrennbaren Zusammenhang mit dem Wandel im Licht, dem Halten der Gebote Gottes, dem Wandel nach dem Vorbild (2,6[23]) und Gebot Jesu (2,7f.) und schließlich mit der Bruderliebe als dem (einzig möglichen) Bleiben im Licht gebracht wird. Da man das eine nur in der Gestalt des anderen haben kann, sollen die Gemeinden hieran sich selbst beurteilen und alle anderen messen. Verwandte Aussagen, die letztlich das Halten der Gebote Gottes bzw. des Gebotes Jesu zum Prüfstein jedes christlichen Selbstanspruchs machen, lassen sich leicht hinzufügen: 3,6.7f.10.17f.21f.23; 4,7f.12f.16.20f.; 5,18.20. Sie repräsentieren insgesamt die Vorwürfe des Verfassers, daß seinen Gegnern am rechten Wandel, am Gebot und am Tun der Gerechtigkeit nichts gelegen sei.

Was könnte der Anlaß für eine so vernichtende Kritik sein? Es ist ja kaum anzunehmen, daß die Abtrünnigen nicht auch selbst gemeint hätten, in irgendeiner Weise dem Willen Gottes zu entsprechen. Daß sie ausgesprochene Libertinisten seien, kann der Schreiber gerade nicht behaupten. Ein Lasterkatalog ist in 2,16 zwar angedeutet. Er hängt dort aber mit der grundsätzlichen Ermahnung an die Leser zusammen, nicht den Kosmos zu lieben (2,15).

Hier führt die Beobachtung weiter, daß für den Verfasser die Gebote Gottes[24] nur im Gebot Jesu[25] zur vollen Geltung kommen. Das Gebot Jesu ist der Inbegriff der Gebote überhaupt, und ohne dieses Gebot hätten die Leser mit Gottes Geboten nichts zu tun[26]. Deshalb wissen für den

---

[23] καθὼς ἐκεῖνος περιεπάτησεν ... [οὕτως] περιπατεῖν.

[24] Plur. ἐντολαί in 2,3f.; 3,22.24; 5,2f. Sing. nur in 3,23a, hier jedoch bedingt durch den direkt angeschlossenen Verweis auf Jesu Gebot der Bruderliebe in v. 23b.

[25] Stets Sing.: 2,7f.; 3,23b; 4,21.

[26] Es wäre verfehlt, daraus zu schließen, daß die Gegner letztlich auf einem jüdischen Hintergrund die Messianität Jesu als des Mittlers Gottes geleugnet hätten und ihnen der Verfasser *deshalb* vor Augen gehalten hätte, daß die Gebote Gottes allein im Gebot Jesu erfüllt seien, wie z.B. J. A. T. Robinson, a.a.O. (Anm. 7), 60ff., und J. M. Lieu, a.a.O. (Anm. 20), 221ff., vermuten. Die Kontroverse zielt vielmehr darauf, daß die Dissidenten deshalb den Gottesgeboten fern sind, weil sie das Jesusgebot nicht als das Gebot der gegenseitigen Liebe bis hin zur Preisgabe des eigenen Lebens oder wenigstens des eigenen Vermögens für die notleidenden Brüder (3,16f.) halten wollen. Liegt ihnen nichts an der Liebe Jesu, wie kann dann die Liebe Gottes in ihnen sein (3,17)? Dagegen ist nicht zu bezweifeln, daß der Verfasser und seine Leser der alttestamentlich-jüdischen Tradition

Verfasser die Leser, die in Tat und Wahrheit Liebe üben (3,18), auch in ihrem Herzen, daß sie das Urteil Gottes über sie selbst nicht zu scheuen haben (3,21), sie halten ja letztlich *seine* Gebote (3,22). Damit bleiben sie in Gott und er in ihnen (3,24). Das Gottesgebot besteht in nichts anderem, als an Jesus Christus, den Gottessohn zu glauben und dessen Gebot der gegenseitigen Liebe zu erfüllen (3,23). In 4,21 wird dies zu einem, den synoptischen Texten von ferne vergleichbaren »Doppelgebot der Liebe« verdichtet (vgl. Mk 12,28–31 par.), aber auch hier geht es im Zusammenhang darum, daß nach dem Gebot Jesu nur die Gott lieben können, die die Brüder lieben. Das Gebot Jesu allein erschließt also den Willen Gottes. Deshalb sind für die, welche in der Gemeinde von der Liebe Gottes her leben, auch die Gebote Gottes nicht schwer (5,3): Die gegenseitige Liebe der Glaubenden ergibt sich von selbst aus ihrer gemeinsamen Herkunft aus Gott. Wie die Gottesliebe die Bruderliebe bedingt (4,21), so ist zugleich die Bruderliebe nur die andere Seite der Gottesliebe, und zwar in einem solchen Maß, daß die Liebenden sich nicht mehr fragen müssen, ob ihre Liebe wirklich solchen gilt, die es verdienen, nämlich wahren Brüdern; die Liebe selbst als die Erfüllung der Gebote Gottes wird nur solche finden, die als Glaubende ebenfalls aus Gott und damit wahrhaft Brüder sind (5,1–2)[27]. Das Bleiben in Gott entscheidet sich also schlicht an einem Wandel, der dem Wandel wie dem Gebot Jesu entspricht (2,6; vgl. 3,3.7.17) und hierin letztlich die liebende Zuwendung Gottes zum Kosmos (4,8–10) abbildet.

Da der Verfasser mit diesen Aussagen sowohl die Dissidenten treffen will als auch Besorgnisse seiner Leser um ihr eigenes Heil zerstreuen will, die durch das Auftreten der Abtrünnigen erst entstanden sind, wird man

---

nicht fremd gegenüberstehen, wie aus der Anspielung auf Kain in 3,12 und aus dem in 3,4 als vertraut vorausgesetzten Terminus ἀνομία zu ersehen ist. Daß aber ἀνομία für die Sprache der Gegner typisch sei, läßt sich kaum behaupten. Es könnte entweder in das endzeitliche Denken des Verfassers hineingehören, vgl. K. Wengst, a.a.O. (Anm. 1), 133, oder (wahrscheinlicher) zum Ausdruck bringen sollen, daß Sünde den Widerspruch zum Willen Gottes schlechthin bedeutet. Wenn dann nach 3,5f. der geoffenbarte Christus alle Sünde ausschließt, ergibt sich für den Verfasser, daß der Wille Gottes allein durch Christus erfüllt wurde und weiterhin erfüllt werden kann.

[27] S. dazu bes. R. Kittler, Erweis der Bruderliebe an der Bruderliebe?! Versuch der Auslegung eines »fast unverständlichen« Satzes im 1. Johannesbrief, KUD 16, 1970, 223–228. Daß im johanneischen Verständnis des Liebesgebotes die durch das Wort gestiftete Einheit der Gemeinde der Liebe grundsätzlich vorgeordnet ist und somit allgemeine Aussagen über Nächsten- oder Feindesliebe gar nicht formuliert werden können, hat vor allem E. Käsemann, Jesu letzter Wille nach Johannes 17, [3]1971, 118ff., mit Nachdruck herausgestellt. Auch der 1 Joh ist durchgehend dieser Konzeption verpflichtet, ja geradezu ihr reflektierter Ausdruck, was sich besonders deutlich in 3,17 zeigen mag. Die Gegner des Verfassers haben aber diesen Ansatz in zweifacher Weise durchbrochen: Sie lieben die Brüder nicht, und sie suchen die Verbindung zum Kosmos.

den Anlaß solcher Reflexionen über die Gebote und das Gebot am ehesten darin suchen, daß die Gegner gerade den Druck der ethischen Forderung innerhalb des johanneischen Kreises als zu große Belastung empfunden haben und damit schließlich auch die Gemeinden unsicher machen. Diese Sicht stimmt mit den bisher gewonnenen Erkenntnissen zusammen, denn die Dissidenten wenden sich ja der Welt wieder zu und glauben, nicht mehr auf die Vergebung der Sünden durch den sühnenden Tod Jesu angewiesen zu sein. Sie haben wohl ein freieres und offeneres Leben im Kosmos gesucht, als dies die Botschaft der Lebenszeugen zuließ. Deshalb tadelt sie der Verfasser einerseits und versucht andrerseits zugleich, seine Leser zu überzeugen, daß für die wahrhaft Glaubenden und von der Liebe Gottes Getragenen alle Gebote Gottes leicht sind und voll erschlossen im Jesusgebot der gegenseitigen Liebe und in der vorbildhaften Erfüllung dieses Gebotes durch Jesus selbst zutage liegen. Die so leben, sind Gottes Kinder und damit von der Welt getrennt (3,1). Die aber gegen das Jesusgebot verstoßen und damit sündigen, ohne in ihrem Selbstverständnis ihr Verhalten überhaupt als Sünde wahrzunehmen – sie verzichten ja auf die Sündenvergebung –, die handeln wider den Willen Gottes (3,4), tun die Gerechtigkeit nicht (2,29; 3,7) und sind damit nicht Kinder Gottes, sondern des Teufels (3,8.10). Wer durch sein gesamtes Verhalten und konkret durch den Auszug aus der Gemeinde die Bruderliebe verweigert, wird notwendig zum Hasser der Brüder nach dem Muster Kains, des Brudermörders (3,12ff.).

Wahrscheinlich haben die Dissidenten mit ihrer freieren Ethik und Welthaltung auch die Gerichtsaussagen des johanneischen Kreises nicht mehr akzeptiert, weswegen der Verfasser seine gesamte Auseinandersetzung und Mahnung unter den endzeitlichen Aspekt stellt und so seinen Lesern einmal den Ernst der Stunde klarmacht (2,28), zum anderen sie aber auch damit tröstet, daß ihnen als den wahren Gotteskindern allein eine heilvolle Zukunft offensteht, in der sie in ihrem wahren Sein auch endgültig offenbar werden sollen (3,2f.). Daher fürchten sie weder jetzt die Anklage ihres Herzens (3,19–21[28]) noch dann im Gericht das Urteil über sich selbst, denn wie ihr Herr ist, leben auch sie in dieser Welt (4,17f.). Alles, was sie vom Vater erbitten, wird ihnen gegeben werden (3,22; 5,14f.16; vgl. 2,1).

Bruderliebe, nicht nur im Wort, sondern in der Tat (3,17f.), ist also allein das Kriterium für die Zugehörigkeit zum Sohn und zum Vater und damit letztlich zu der Gemeinde der Gotteskinder. Das wissen die Glaubenden mit dem Gebot Jesu (Joh 13,34f.) von Anfang an. Dieser λόγος (1 Joh 2,7) bzw. diese ἀγγελία (3,11) haben als johanneische Botschaft ihr Christentum begründet. Hieran gibt es nichts zu erneuern; es ist nur neu

---

[28] Vgl. hierzu W. Pratscher, Gott ist grösser (sic!) als unser Herz. Zur Interpretation von 1. Joh. 3,19f., ThZ 32, 1976, 272–281.

zu begreifen, daß das Gebot Jesu in ihm und in den Glaubenden wahrhaft gültig ist, denn allein am Ort der Bruderliebe setzt sich schon das wahre Licht gegen die Finsternis durch (2,8). Deswegen ist das »alte« Gebot Jesu ein der Finsternis der Welt gegenüber schlechthin neues Gebot. In ihm steht, gültig offenbar in Jesus und den Glaubenden, die Liebe Gottes selbst zugunsten des Kosmos gegen die Finsternis des Kosmos. Also ist die Liebe der Glaubenden untereinander nichts als die Antwort auf die Liebe Gottes, »denn er hat uns zuerst geliebt« (4,19).

Haben die Dissidenten weder das Sterben Jesu als die liebende Dahingabe des guten Hirten für die Seinen begreifen können noch seine Erhöhung als das Voranschreiten auf einem Weg, den die Glaubenden noch vor sich haben (2,28–3,3), so ist abschließend nach ihrem Christusverständnis überhaupt zu fragen. Beziehen sich die Warnungen des Verfassers vor neuer und falscher Lehre (2,27) und seine beruhigende Zusicherung, die Leser hätten das χρῖσμα von dem Heiligen und seien alle Wissende (2,20; vgl. v. 27), wirklich auf eine spezifische christologische Konzeption? Eher ist doch anzunehmen, daß die Dissidenten die in der überlieferten johanneischen Christologie beschlossenen Spannungen einseitig aufgelöst hatten, ohne ausdrücklich ein neues Christusbekenntnis zu formulieren oder gezielt das Bekenntnis der Gemeinden zu verwerfen. Erst der Verfasser brächte dann das Christusbekenntnis des johanneischen Kreises gegen sie ins Spiel! Er könnte ihren antichristlichen Widerspruch zum johanneischen Bekenntnis Jesu als des Christus sowohl aus ihren Behauptungen als auch aus ihrem gesamten Verhalten erschlossen haben. Vor allem dürfte hierbei sein Vorwurf ausschlaggebend gewesen sein, daß sie das Vorbild und die Niedrigkeit Jesu nicht ernst nahmen und sich damit von der Liebe Gottes, die in Jesus als dem Christus wirkte und wirkt, losgesagt haben.

Was ergeben hierfür die christologischen Verwerfungen in 2,22f. und 4,2f., die mit den nicht ausdrücklich polemischen christologischen Feststellungen in 4,15; 5,1.5 zusammenzusehen sind? Zunächst bedient sich der Verfasser in 2,2f. und 4,2f. der geläufigen Bekenntnisterminologie: ὁμολογεῖν/ἀρνεῖσθαι (2,22f.) bzw. ὁμολογεῖν/μὴ ὁμολογεῖν (4,2f.; vgl. weiter 4,15; 2 Joh 7)[29]. Hier stehen sich nicht zwei christologische Auffas-

[29] Aus dem Evangelium sind Joh 1,20; 9,22; 12,42 mit heranzuziehen. Daß in 1 Joh 4,3 μὴ ὁμολογεῖν eine glättende Ersetzung des nur sehr schwach bezeugten λύειν sei, könnte u. a. damit begründet werden, daß v. 3 in der Textüberlieferung auch hinsichtlich der übrigen Formulierungen oft an v. 2 angeglichen worden ist, vgl. R. Schnackenburg, a. a. O. (Anm. 1), 222; K. Wengst, a. a. O. (Anm. 20), 17f. mit Anm. 14. Es müßte dann allerdings eine im gesamten NT völlig singuläre Verwendung von λύειν (Beziehung auf eine Person und in einem christologischen Zusammenhang) angenommen werden, was wiederum neue Schwierigkeiten mit sich brächte. Ein Nebeneinander von »Bekennen« und »Nicht-Bekennen« bzw. »Leugnen« entspricht dagegen der Absicht des Verfassers in 4,2f. wie auch in 2,22f.

sungen gegenüber, die einander noch angenähert werden könnten, sondern es geht alternativ um Bekennen und Nicht-Bekennen bzw. Bekennen und Leugnen. Nur wer Jesus bekennt bzw. ihn als den im Fleisch gekommenen Christus bekennt, bekennt mit dem Sohn auch den Vater und hat den Geist Gottes. Die Bekenntnissprache dient nicht dazu, ein falsches Christusbekenntnis zu zitieren, sondern dazu, einen falschen Christusglauben zu verwerfen.

Eine vollkommene »Leugnung« des von ihm vertretenen johanneischen Christusbekenntnisses konnte der Verfasser bei seinen Gegnern aber im Grunde nur dann voraussetzen, wenn er es mit Juden zu tun hatte, die Jesus nicht als Messias anerkannten, oder allenfalls mit Judenchristen, die aus Furcht vor der synagogalen Verfolgung kein öffentliches Christusbekenntnis wagten[30]. Weder die einen noch die anderen hatte er jedoch wirklich im Blick, denn die Gegner kamen zum einen aus dem johanneischen Kreis und hielten sich für Christen und sind zum anderen für den Schreiber nicht deshalb gefährlich, weil sie ihr Bekenntnis verschwiegen, sondern weil sie nach seiner Sicht Lüge für Wahrheit hielten und auch noch im Kosmos verbreiteten. Also ist vorauszusetzen, daß er das volle Gewicht des johanneischen Christusbekenntnisses in erster Linie als »Waffe« gegen seine Gegner einsetzte. Er könnte ihnen beispielsweise ein rein menschlich-profanes Jesusverständnis unterstellt haben, so daß ihnen aus diesem Grund der Christus fehlte. Als »Jesusanhänger« sind aber die Gegner sonst im 1 Joh nicht zu erkennen, wird ihnen doch im Gegenteil der johanneische Jesus kritisch vor Augen gehalten (vgl. 2,6; 3,3.7.16; 4,17). Eher schon könnte man die Verwerfungen unter der Voraussetzung zu erklären versuchen, daß für den Schreiber das Christusbild seiner Gegner dualistisch-gnostisch geprägt sei. Er würde ihnen dann das Gekommensein des Christus oder des Gottessohnes im Fleisch, d. h. in menschlicher Seinsweise, entgegenhalten, weil sie selbst die Auffassung vertreten hätten, daß der Christus oder Gottessohn nicht in eine irdische Gestalt eingehen könne. Der Verfasser hätte sie also auf einem Weg gesehen, den wir z. B. aus der antidoketischen Polemik des Ignatius von Antiochien oder aus der späteren antignostischen Polemik gegen Kerinth noch einigermaßen rekonstruieren könnten.

Allerdings versucht der Verfasser nirgends in seinem Brief nachzuweisen, daß der Christus in Jesus wirklicher Mensch geworden sei, nach dem Fleisch aus dem Geschlecht Davids, wirklich geboren von der Jungfrau Maria, daß er aß und trank und wirklich unter Pontius Pilatus und dem Tetrarchen Herodes für uns im Fleisch an das Kreuz genagelt wurde (Ign., Trall. 9,1; Smyrn. 1,1) und nicht nur zum Schein (τὸ δοκεῖν) gelit-

---

[30] Vgl. dazu Joh 9,22; 12,42 und 16,1–4, wo schließlich die jüdischen Verfolger der Judenchristen im gleichen Licht erscheinen wie die johanneischen Dissidenten im 1 Joh: Sie haben den Vater und den Sohn nicht erkannt (Joh 16,3; vgl. 1 Joh 2,22f.; 5,20).

ten habe (Smyrn.2), sondern wirklich von den Toten auferweckt wurde (Trall. 9,2) usw. Auch muß der schwierige Abschnitt 5,5–10 nicht zwingend als Auseinandersetzung mit einer Christologie interpretiert werden, nach welcher der bloße Mensch Jesus nur für die Zeit seit seiner Taufe und bis hin zu seiner Passion mit dem geistigen Christus verbunden gewesen sei, der selbst nicht leiden könne, wie sie besonders durch Irenaeus (haer. I 26,1) dann als Häresie des Kerinth bekämpft wurde[31].

In 5,4ff. geht es um die grundsätzliche Überlegenheit des Glaubens bzw. der Glaubenden gegenüber dem Kosmos. Sie gründet auf dem Glauben, daß Jesus der Sohn Gottes ist (5,5). Er ist dies als der durch bzw. mit Wasser und Blut Gekommene, wobei der Aor. ἐλθών durchaus nicht auf die Damaligkeit oder Einmaligkeit Jesu zu beziehen ist, sondern eher komplexiv die Geschichte Jesu Christi mit seiner gegenwärtigen Bedeutung zusammenfaßt. Ähnlich sind die unterschiedlichen Tempora von ἔρχεσθαι in 4,2; 5,20 (Perf.) und 2 Joh 7 (Präs.) zu verstehen. Dieser Jesus Christus macht die an ihn Glaubenden zu Überwindern des Kosmos, was ihnen der Geist (in ihnen) verläßlich bezeugt (5,6 mit v. 10). Daß dieses Geistzeugnis die Wahrheit ist, bestätigen als Zeugnis Gottes insgesamt der Geist, das Wasser und das Blut, denn ihr Zeugnis stimmt überein (5,7f. mit v. 8–10). Also sind Wasser und Blut Zeugnisse Gottes, die das vom Geist in den Glaubenden begründete Wissen um den weltüberlegenen Christusglauben fest machen. Daß Jesus Christus in Verbindung mit Wasser und Blut gekommen ist, erfahren die Glaubenden daraus, daß sich ihr Wissen um Jesus mit ihrem Glauben an ihn als Christus und Gottessohn verbindet.

Nur annäherungsweise kann erschlossen werden, woran der Verfasser mit der sonst in den johanneischen Schriften nur noch in Joh 19,34 (in umgekehrter Reihenfolge) bezeugten Zusammenstellung von Wasser und Blut konkret gedacht hat. Die traditionelle Deutung auf Taufe und Kreuzigung Jesu findet besonders hinsichtlich der Taufe nur geringen Anhalt in den johanneischen Texten, aber immerhin könnte der Verfasser vor Augen haben, daß der zum Zeichen für Israel mit Wasser getaufte Jesus für den Täufer von Anfang an der Gottessohn (Joh 1,34) und zugleich das Lamm war, das die Sünde des Kosmos wegtragen würde (Joh 1,29; vgl. 1 Joh 3,5). Von Joh 4,10ff. und 7,37ff. her ließe sich auch an Wasser als Symbol für Heil oder Lebensgabe denken, was dann in Verbindung mit 19,34 dahin zu interpretieren wäre, daß die Heilsgabe Jesu für die Seinen mit seinem blutigen Tod untrennbar zusammengehört. Jedenfalls wären Joh 19,34 und 1 Joh 5,5–10 durch den Zeugnisbegriff eng miteinander verbunden[32].

[31] Vgl. zum einzelnen K. Wengst, a.a.O. (Anm. 20), 24–38.

[32] S. hierzu bes. J. Heer, Der Durchbohrte. Johanneische Begründung der Herz-Jesu-Verehrung, 1966; W. Thüsing, Die Erhöhung und Verherrlichung Jesu im Johannesevangelium, NTA 21, 1/2, ²1970, 160f. 172; H.-J. Venetz, »Durch Wasser und Blut gekom-

Die Annahme, daß in 1 Joh 5,6.8 direkt auf Joh 19,34 angespielt sei, setzt allerdings voraus, daß der Verfasser die Meinung seiner Gegner, Jesus sei als der Christus nur im Wasser gekommen (5,6b), gleichsam wörtlich zitiert, was wiederum den gesamten Zusammenhang sehr unwahrscheinlich machen würde, denn er müßte ihnen ja unterstellen, daß sie Joh 19,34 bewußt aufgegriffen hätten, um dann erst das Miteinander von Blut und Wasser in diesem Text bewußt auseinanderzureißen. Wie sollte dies angesichts dessen vorstellbar sein, daß doch in Joh 19,34 Blut und Wasser aus der Lanzenwunde des Gekreuzigten zunächst einmal als Zeichen für den wirklichen Tod Jesu unbedingt zusammengehörten! Deshalb spricht, auch aufgrund der Reihenfolge von Wasser und Blut, mehr dafür, daß der Schreiber von Taufe und Kreuzigung Jesu sprechen will, die ihm jedoch nicht als einzelne historische Geschehnisse bedeutsam sind, sondern als die entscheidenden Stationen des irdischen Weges des einzigen Sohnes des Vaters (1 Joh 4,9), an denen er als Gottessohn offenbar wurde und bleibend offenbar ist, nämlich einmal als der zur Wegnahme der Sünden der Welt gesandte und zum anderen als der diesen Auftrag bis zur Hingabe seines Lebens für die Seinen vollendende Sohn. Wer einen nur einseitig begründeten und damit auch nicht weltüberwindenden Christusglauben so vertritt und vor allem so lebt, daß dabei grundsätzlich das Kreuz Jesu an den Rand rückt oder gar die Heilsbedeutung des Sühnetodes Jesu Christi ausgeklammert wird – was nach dem Voranstehenden die Dissidenten gar nicht wörtlich als »Gegenbekenntnis« behauptet haben müssen –, der hat das dreifache Zeugnis Gottes für den wahren Glauben nicht auf seiner Seite und damit auch letztlich nicht den Geist, der die Wahrheit ist, in sich.

Die Gegner müssen also auch nach 5,5–10 nicht »Doketen« oder Gnostiker gewesen sein, die eine spezifische Christologie vertreten hätten, in welcher Jesus und der Christus grundsätzlich oder zeitweise voneinander getrennt wurden. Vielmehr hat sich bestätigt, daß der Verfasser auch in seinen christologischen Verwerfungen auf den Auszug, die gesamte Lebenshaltung und das Selbstverständnis der Dissidenten zielt, die sich *ihren* Christus nicht von der Realität Jesu, seines vorbildhaften und gehorsamen Dienens und vor allem seines in Erfüllung der Liebe Gottes zum Kosmos getragenen Sterbens für die Seinen vorzeichnen ließen. Im Zentrum der Auseinandersetzungen des 1 Joh steht nicht die christologische Lehre, wie dies aus dem Horizont der späteren Lehrauseinandersetzungen allzuleicht eingetragen werden kann, sondern die für den Schreiber unfaßliche Tatsache, daß johanneische Christen den Ort des Lichtes, der Liebe Gottes und der durch den Sohn gewirkten Sündenvergebung und Bruderliebe verlassen konnten. Daß sie für ihn letztlich nicht Jesus als den Christus bekennen, heißt, daß sie das im Leben und Sterben Jesu beschlossene Rettungs-

---

men«. Exegetische Überlegungen zu 1 Joh 5,6, in: Die Mitte des NT. Einheit und Vielfalt neutestamentlicher Theologie, Festschrift für E. Schweizer, 1983, 345–361.

handeln Gottes zunichte machen und damit schließlich Gott selbst als Lügner hinstellen. Demgegenüber muß festgehalten und bekannt werden, daß der Christus und Gottessohn nur in der Konkretheit und Niedrigkeit der σάρξ Jesu gekommen ist und bleibend wirkt.

*

Hat der Verfasser seine Gegner letztlich mißverstanden und ins Unrecht gesetzt, wenn er ihnen den Gottesgeist absprach, sie aus den Gotteskindern ausschloß und schließlich in Überbietung aller denkbaren innergemeindlichen Alternativen als die Antichriste der letzten Stunde brandmarkte? Für ihn hatten sie das zerstört, wovon die johanneischen Gemeinden gerade lebten, nämlich die vollkommene Solidarität untereinander als Zeichen der aller menschlichen Liebe zuvorkommenden und in Jesus, dem Christus, vollgültig verwirklichten Liebe Gottes. Was die Verworfenen wirklich von sich gedacht und wie sie ihren Auszug begründet haben, kann wohl nur andeutungsweise erschlossen werden. Wahrscheinlich haben sie den vollmächtigen und verherrlichten Christus über den in Niedrigkeit dienenden und gekreuzigten gestellt und von daher auch ihr eigenes christliches Leben im Sinne einer unverlierbaren und Gott direkt zugewandten Frömmigkeit verstanden. Wahrscheinlich haben sie sich auch aufgrund ihrer Gottesbeziehung für die »Starken« gehalten, worunter andere dann als »Schwache« zu leiden hatten. Ihre »Ethik« wird von Offenheit für den Kosmos und womöglich Liberalität geprägt gewesen sein, was wohl auch durch ihre Herkunft und soziale Stellung unterstützt wurde. Sie werden eine zunehmende Isolierung der johanneischen Gemeinden im Kosmos nicht mitvollzogen haben und sich vielleicht um die Rettung des Kosmos in einer Weise bemüht haben, die ihnen schließlich das Verdikt eintrug, daß sie die entscheidende und bereits geschehene Tat Gottes zur Rettung des Kosmos zunichte machten.

Für den Verfasser des 1 Joh sind jedenfalls unter dem Aspekt der »letzten Stunde« johanneische Theologie und Ethik in ihrer immer schon untrennbaren Einheit neu zum gültigen Kriterium für johanneisches Christentum geworden, und er weiß dabei das allein wahre Christusbekenntnis auf seiner Seite, das der Geist der Wahrheit in den Glaubenden weckt und bestätigt. Er verwirft, um zu retten und zu bewahren, und er hält dabei als untrügliches Kriterium für alle christliche Rede von Gott fest, daß Gott Licht ist und Finsternis in ihm keine ist, was schon in seiner Zeit leicht zu sagen, aber nicht für alle leicht zu leben war[33].

---

[33] Oder um es mit den Worten von H. Greeven, Das Hauptproblem der Sozialethik in der neueren Stoa und im Urchristentum, NTF III/4, 1935 (Nachdruck 1983), 159, zu sagen: »Das individual-ethische Ideal des Weisen macht eine wirkliche Gemeinschaft von Mensch zu Mensch unmöglich. Der christliche Glaube faßt alle zusammen, die sich retten lassen wollen, zu einer Gemeinschaft des Dienens und der Liebe.«

Old Testament history according to Stephen and Paul

by C. K. Barrett

(8 Princes Street, Durham DH1 4RP, England)

The Old Testament is frequently cited in the New, which claims to present the fulfilment of the promises spoken in the past to Israel. There are also allusions, and not infrequently the use of language which in its vocabulary, and sometimes in its syntax, calls to mind themes of the Old Testament. It is relatively seldom that any New Testament writer stands back to present a survey of any substantial part of Old Testament history. This is done, however, twice in Acts, in speeches attributed to Stephen when he appears before the Council (7,2–53) and to Paul when he preaches in the synagogue at Pisidian Antioch (13,16–41). It may be profitable to consider what one New Testament writer[1] made of the Old Testament as a historical narrative. The discussion of the matter falls into three parts. The first will deal with textual questions; the second will compare divergent accounts of historical events; the third will consider the view or views of Old Testament history and its significance that are set forth.

I.

The question of text is not easy to handle. If there is anything in the historical settings that Luke has provided for the two discourses it would be too much to expect scholarly accuracy of quotation from a man on trial for his life, or even from one invited on the spur of the moment to preach an extemporary sermon. These excuses are in fact superfluous; even when writing in favourable circumstances New Testament authors do not always display an itch for strict accuracy of quotation. It follows from this that a number of apparent variants are not variants in the proper sense at all; that is, they do not represent a divergent textual tradition. Thus (to take the first example) when Stephen at 7,3 quotes the words ἔξελθε ἐκ τῆς γῆς σου καὶ ἐκ[2] τῆς συγγενείας σου, καὶ δεῦρο εἰς τὴν γῆν ἣν ἄν σοι δείξω,

[1] I do not raise in this paper the question of the historical accuracy of the narratives in Acts; whether or not Stephen and Paul uttered the words attributed to them we may be confident that Luke approved of the opinions he ascribed in this book to these noted Christian leaders.

[2] ἐκ is omitted by B D.

we are not to suppose that he had a LXX text differing from others in that it omitted καὶ ἐκ τοῦ οἴκου τοῦ πατρός σου; still less should we consider the omission of מבית אביך from the Hebrew text. The speaker, or writer, either forgot the words in question or perhaps thought that they were adequately covered by the two parallel phrases and could be dropped without loss. Other examples of the same kind are the following:

7,32, ὁ θεὸς Ἀβραὰμ καὶ Ἰσαὰκ καὶ Ἰακώβ. Both Ex 3,6 and 3,15 (LXX) repeat θεός before each name (with the Hebrew)[3].
7,33, λῦσον τὸ ὑπόδημα ... ἐφ' ᾧ ἕστηκας. At Ex 3,5 the LXX has λῦσαι (Hebrew של) ... ἐν ᾧ (Hebrew עליו).
7,35, Stephen omits the ἐφ' ἡμῶν of Ex 2,14. It was quoted at 7,27 and was not thought necessary here[4].
7,37, προφήτην ὑμῖν ἀναστήσει ὁ θεὸς ἐκ τῶν ἀδελφῶν ὑμῶν ὡς ἐμέ. This differs from Dtn 18,15 (LXX) only in the order of the words. The LXX agrees with the Hebrew; the different order in Acts is due simply to loose quotation.
7,40, ὁ γὰρ Μωυσῆς οὗτος ... ἐκ γῆς Αἰγύπτου ... τί ἐγένετο[5] ... The LXX has οὗτος ὁ ἄνθρωπος ... ἐξ Αἰγύπτου ... τί γέγονεν. The words occur at both Ex 32,1 and 32,23. Again, there is nothing more serious here than failing memory.
7,42, ἔτη τεσσεράκοντα ἐν τῇ ἐρήμῳ. The LXX of Am 5,25 has ... ἐν τῇ ἐρήμῳ τεσσεράκοντα ἔτη.
7,49. The position of λέγει κύριος varies, and Acts has τίς τόπος where the LXX of Isa 66,1 has ποῖος τόπος[6].

These passages may all be placed with the following where there is identity between Acts and the LXX.

7,18: Ex 1,8[7].
7,27: Ex 2,14.
13,33: Ps 2,7[8].
13,35: Ps 15,10 (Hebrew 16,10).

A few other variations may be more significant. Here may be included:

---

[3] D E and many others harmonize with the Old Testament.

[4] The short text is that of P^{45} P^{74} A B P al.

[5] D E Ψ and many others have γέγονεν.

[6] D has ποῖος τόπος; h has qualis domus.

[7] There is a slight difference in that in Acts the words are placed in a temporal clause beginning ἄχρι οὗ. There is also evidence for the omission of ἐπ' Αἴγυπτον, and for ἐμνήσθη in place of ἤδει.

[8] D sy^{hmg} mae add to the quotation.

7,6: Here a slight difference from Gen 15,13 in word order and the omission of τετρακόσια ἔτη are probably unimportant. Trivial in itself but textually suggestive is the fact that where the LXX has ἐν γῇ οὐκ ἰδίᾳ Stephen has ἐν γῇ ἀλλοτρίᾳ. The Hebrew has בארץ לא להם. Luke's Greek is neater and more idiomatic, but it probably arises from memory of the sense rather than the wording of the Greek Bible.
7,7 seems to combine Gen 15,14 and Ex 3,12. The interesting variation is ἐν τῷ τόπῳ τούτῳ, where Ex 3,12 has ἐν τῷ ὄρει τούτῳ. The Hebrew has על ההר הזה, of which the LXX is a correct rendering (though it has not chosen the best preposition). The appearance of significant variation is misleading. The context is determined by the reference to Abraham, and whereas the verse in Exodus means that the people will leave Egypt and worship God on Mount Sinai, Stephen refers to worship in the land of Israel[9].
7,34. Here we have a combination of Ex 3,7.8.10. The one possibly significant point is that Stephen has τοῦ στεναγμοῦ αὐτῶν ἤκουσα in place of τῆς κραυγῆς αὐτῶν ἀκήκοα. The tense of the verb (Hebrew שמעתי) is not significant[10], and the LXX's κραυγή is as near to the Hebrew (צעקתם) as στεναγμός, perhaps nearer. There is no reason in the context why στεναγμός should have been substituted for κραυγή and it may be that we should regard it as an alternative reading[11].
7,50. Isaiah's statement (66,2) is turned into a rhetorical question (with the same meaning) by the prefixing of οὐχί: Did not my hand make all these things? Again, it is quite probable that we have here nothing more than a slightly inaccurate quotation from memory; a variant is not impossible[12].
13,41. This quotation of Hab 1,5 is interesting because in two respects the LXX differs from the Hebrew. Instead of the Hebrew בגוים we have οἱ καταφρονηταί, which presumably renders בוגדים (or הבוגדים), and after ἐπιβλέψατε (הביטו) and θαυμάσατε θαυμάσια (התמהו תמהו) the LXX adds ἀφανίσθητε. Stephen drops ἐπιβλέψατε, but shows acquaintance with the rendering καταφρονηταί and the addition of ἀφανίσθητε. The latter makes it probable that Stephen was using the LXX, but the use of καταφρονηταί, though consistent with this does not demand it, since בוגדים seems to have been in the Hebrew text used at Qumran (4QHab). It is unfortunate that the verse itself has been lost at the foot of Column 1, but the interpretation, which appears in Column 2, uses the word three

[9] Josephus has τόπος in Antiquities 2,269.
[10] Cf. 7,40 (p. 58).
[11] The cause of the confusion may be found in a recollection of Ex 2,24; 6,5.
[12] The second half of the verse is in the LXX a question; has this affected the Acts form of the first?

times (lines 1.3.5). Of this καταφρονηταί is not the most natural equivalent, so that it is still probable that Paul is using the LXX rather than the Qumran Hebrew.

A few passages remain for consideration.

7,43, quoting Am 5,26f., provides a famous and interesting puzzle. There is no textual problem in the first thirteen words, identical in Acts and the LXX[13]. In the next clause the two differ in wording though not in sense. Acts has τοὺς τύπους οὓς ἐποιήσατε προσκυνεῖν αὐτοῖς; the LXX, τοὺς τύπους αὐτῶν οὓς ἐποιήσατε ἑαυτοῖς. The last three words of the LXX correspond exactly with the Hebrew אשר עשיתם לכם, but the first three (in English, their images) either misrepresent צלמיכם (your images) or represent צלמיהם. Luke's text cannot be regarded as a divergent translation of the Hebrew, though it may involve the mistaking of לכם for להם. This however provides no explanation for the insertion of προσκυνεῖν[14]. It would be wrong to waste much ingenuity on this text; what did the Israelites make the images for if not to worship them? If however Stephen (Luke) was using a non-LXX text it might be easier to explain his surprising substitution of Damascus for Babylon at the end of the quotation. I do not know any satisfactory explanation of this change in terms of Luke's own interests. The most ingenious is undoubtedly that of W. L. Knox[15]. "The effect of this alteration is that this section of the speech is made to end not, as Amos does in the LXX, with the worst possible rhetorical ending, the end of a hexameter (ἐπέκεινα Δαμάσκου), but with the best possible; for ἐπέκεινα Βαβυλῶνος gives a cretic with the second long syllable resolved and a trochee." But does Luke care for cretics?

13,22 is hardly a quotation so much as a freshly constructed sentence based on Ps 88,21 (LXX) and 1 Sam 13,14. We need not consider it here.

13,34, δώσω ὑμῖν τὰ ὅσια Δαυὶδ τὰ πιστά is close to but not identical with Isa 55,3, διαθήσομαι ὑμῖν διαθήκην αἰώνιον, τὰ ὅσια Δαυὶδ τὰ πιστά. The opening words of the LXX are close to the Hebrew (ואכרתה לכם ברית עולם), much closer than Paul's δώσω, and no better explanation is on hand than that Paul has been influenced by the occurrence, in association with the adjective ὅσιος, of the verb διδόναι which occurs in the next verse in the quotation of Psalm 15,10 (LXX), οὐ δώσεις τὸν ὅσιόν σου

[13] That is, if we read them as they are printed in NA^{26} and in Rahlfs. In Acts ὑμῶν is omitted by B D (with other authorities) – a combination that must be taken seriously; and the name of the god is variously given: Ῥαιφάν; Ῥεφάν; Ῥομφά; Ῥομφάν; Ῥεμφάμ; Ῥεμφάν all have some serious support, and there are other forms.

[14] This is naturally represented in Delitzsch's Hebrew as להשתחות – far too long a word to be accounted for as due to mere confusion of letters.

[15] W. L. Knox, Some Hellenistic Elements in Primitive Christianity, Schweich Lectures 1942, 1944, 14f.

ἰδεῖν διαφθοράν. Again, we cannot arrive at a special Lucan form of Old Testament text.

13,47. Here the same comment must be made. Paul follows Isa 49,6 (LXX) precisely except that he omits εἰς διαθήκην γένους, which would not suit his purpose in justifying his turning from the γένος, the Jews, to the ἔθνη.

Thus on the whole Luke appears to be following a familiar LXX text, not always quoting it accurately and occasionally altering it to suit his own purposes, but not consistently following an aberrant tradition.

II.

Under the heading of History the brief sketch contained in Ac 13 is hardly worth considering. In Stephen's speech however a number of points arise. Some of them are slight and need not be discussed in this paper[16]. Such are, for example, the place in which Abraham received God's call (according to Ac 7,2 while he was in Mesopotamia, before he lived in Haran; according to Gen 11,31; 12,1, in Haran) and the number of persons whom Joseph summoned to Egypt with his father Jacob (according to Ac 7,14, seventy five; according to Gen 46,27, seventy). I shall mention two matters that seem to me to be of some interest.

We may note first a number of passages where it is possible that there is some connection between Stephen's account of Old Testament history and Samaritan traditions.

In 7,4 Stephen says expressly that Abraham's departure took place μετὰ τὸ ἀποθανεῖν τὸν πατέρα αὐτοῦ. According to Gen 11,26 Terah was 70 when Abraham was born, and according to Gen 12,4 Abraham was 75 when he left Haran for Canaan; Terah was thus 145. He lived altogether 205 years (Gen 11,32), and thus had another 60 years to live after Abraham moved into the promised land. In these figures the LXX agrees with the Hebrew. The Samaritan Pentateuch, however, cuts 60 years off Terah's life, giving in 11,32 not 205 but 145 years. Was Stephen following Samaritan tradition? Possibly, but I do not think that the matter is proved. Anyone reading Genesis with less than full attention notes the statement in 11,32 that Terah died in Haran; in 12,1 that God called Abram to leave his home; and in 12,4 that Abram obediently departed from Haran. If the reader does not do the arithmetic carried out above he will assume that these events happened in the order described. Philo shows independently the same innumeracy as Luke: Abraham migrated from Chaldea and dwelt in Haran, and τελευτήσαντος αὐτῷ τοῦ πατρὸς ἐκεῖθε he removed from that country also (de Mig. Abr. 177).

[16] They are discussed in all the standard commentaries.

The question at issue in 7,15f. is set out with great clarity by J. Jeremias[17], in three points. (1) The end of v. 16 contains a simple error. Abraham is mentioned instead of Jacob. It was Jacob who bought (Gen 33,19) from the sons of Hamor, Shechem's father, for 100 pieces of silver the piece of land on which he had pitched his tent. This passage has been confused with Gen 23,3–20: ... Abraham agreed with Ephron; and Abraham weighed out for Ephron the silver which he had named in the hearing of the children of Heth, 400 shekels of silver ... Abraham buried Sarah his wife in the cave of the field of Machpelah east of Mamre (that is, Hebron) in the land of Canaan. The field and the cave that is in it were made over to Abraham as a possession for a burying place by the children of Heth. That Jeremias is right in seeing confusion here cannot be doubted. (2) Ac 7,15f. may at first sight suggest that Jacob and all his sons were buried at Sichem. This would be a further error, for according to Gen 49,30; 50,13 Jacob was buried at Hebron. One should however take the subject of μετετέθησαν and ἐτέθησαν (in 7,16) to be οἱ πατέρες ἡμῶν (7,15), that is, the patriarchs other than Jacob. The Old Testament does not say where the sons of Jacob were buried. Some Jewish sources maintained that Joseph's brothers were buried not at Shechem, as Joseph was (Jos 24,32), but at Hebron, in the piece of land that Jacob had bought. So Jubilees 46,9[18]; also Testament of Reuben 7,2[19]. The same tradition appears in Josephus, War 4,532[20] and Antiquities 2,199[21]. This tradition is however by no means unanimous. Hebron was originally Kiriath Arba, קרית ארבע, the City of Four. From this name it was deduced that four men (and their wives) were buried there; of these, three were Abraham, Isaac, and Jacob, and the most favoured candidate for the fourth place was Adam. The twelve sons of Jacob were thus excluded. (3) This (according to Jeremias) leaves us with the question whether Stephen is simply expanding the tradition about Joseph (Jos 24,32) to cover the remaining patriarchs, or depends upon some local, presumably a Shechemite tradition. Jeremias chooses the latter alternative, and adds that the Shechemite tradition will be Samaritan. For this conclusion however his supporting evidence is weak. He quotes two passages from Jerome. In Epistle 57,10 Je-

---

[17] J. Jeremias, Heiligengräber in Jesu Umwelt, 1958, 37f.

[18] The children of Israel brought forth all the bones of the children of Jacob save the bones of Joseph, and they buried them in the double cave in the mountain. According to 46,8 Joseph had been buried in Egypt.

[19] ἔθαψαν αὐτὸν ἐν Χεβρών. There are similar statements in T. Issachar 7,8; T. Symeon 8,2; T. Levi 19,5; T. Judah 26,4; T. Zebulun 10,7; T. Dan 7,2 (si v. 1.); T. Naphtali 9,1.3; T. Gad 8,5; T. Asher 8,2; T. Benjamin 12,1(3).

[20] Τὰ μνημεῖα μέχρι νῦν ἐν τῇδε τῇ πολίχνῃ (Hebron) δείκνυται.

[21] Τούτων μὲν τὰ σώματα κομίσαντες μετὰ χρόνον οἱ ἀπόγονοι [καὶ οἱ παῖδες] ἔθαψαν ἐν Νεβρῶνι.

rome writes, duodecim autem patriarchae non sunt sepulti in Arboc (= Hebron), sed in Sychem; and in the Peregrinatio Paulae (Epistle 108,13), atque inde (Jacob's well) devertens vidit duodecim patriarcharum sepulchra. By Jerome's time it is quite possible that local residents were showing Christian pilgrims tombs whose existence, or identification, was based solely on Ac 7. The only additional evidence comes from the Ἐκλογὴ Χρονογραφίας of Georgius Syncellus (A.D. 806–810) who after recounting that the bones of Joseph were buried at Sichem adds φασὶ δ'ὅτι καὶ τῶν λοιπῶν πατριαρχῶν[22]. Jeremias argues that it is this established Shechemite tradition that explains why the early Jewish belief that the Patriarchs were buried in Hebron fails to appear in the rabbinic and patristic literature; and if it is asked why the Shechemite, Samaritan, tradition does not appear in the Samaritan literature he answers that written Samaritan material comes from the 14th century and later and that the site in question had been in Mahometan hands since long before that time.

This reconstruction is possible, but not compelling. If the Samaritan tradition was so strong as to inhibit the rise and spread of the alternative Hebron tradition it would surely have left more traces than those we have. Stephen's references to the burial of the Patriarchs contains at least one confusion (where he puts Abraham for Jacob), and it may well contain others. Whether any Samaritan influence has been at work will probably turn on other alleged Samaritanisms. These are few and amount to little, but must be reviewed.

It was pointed out above that at 7,32 the text of Acts refers to ὁ θεὸς Ἀβραὰμ καὶ Ἰσαὰκ καὶ Ἰακώβ, whereas the Hebrew and the versions of Ex 3,6.15.16 repeat θεός before each name. It is also to be noted that in the first part of the verse Stephen says, ἐγὼ ὁ θεὸς τῶν πατέρων σου. At Ex 3,6 the Hebrew, the LXX, the Vulgate, and the Peshitto all have father in the singular; the Samaritan Pentateuch however has, like Stephen, The God of thy fathers (plural). Was Stephen affected by the Samaritan tradition? Again one has to answer: This is possible, but by no means necessary. At Ex 3,15.16 the Hebrew, the LXX, the Vulgate, the Syriac, and the Samaritan all have fathers (plural). How easy to assimilate the one passage to the other!

In 7,37 Dtn 18,15.(18) is quoted; the same passage is used at 3,22, so that if there is Samaritan influence it must have been more than a personal contact of Stephen's (or of the Hellenists'). The two passages in Acts are sufficient to show that the passage in Deuteronomy was given a messianic interpretation by at least some Christians of the first century. It was long remarked, with some surprise, that it seemed not to have been so used in Judaism. "Dtn 18,15 u. 18 wird in der rabbinischen Literatur äußerst

[22] 284 (Dindorf).

selten erwähnt"[23] and when they are mentioned it is not with a messianic interpretation. It is now a familiar fact that Dtn 18,18–19 was so used at Qumran. In 4Qtest it is combined with Dtn 5,28–9, thus[24]:

The Lord spoke to Moses saying: You have heard the words which this people have spoken to you; all they have said is right. O that their heart were always like this, to fear me and to keep my commandments always, that it might be well with them and their children for ever! (Dtn 5,28–9). I will raise up for them a Prophet like you from among their brethren. I will put my words into his mouth and he shall tell them all that I command him. And I will require a reckoning of whoever will not listen to the words which the Prophet shall speak in my name (Dtn 18,18–19).

The relation of these quotations to those that follow in the Testimonia is an important and difficult question, but we need not discuss in here. What is for us more important is that the same two passages are combined in an expansion in the Samaritan Pentateuch inserted after Ex 20,21. The words are almost identical, though the quotation of Dtn 18 is taken further. The combination of the two passages makes it impossible to believe that there is no connection between the Samaritan and Qumran traditions. To investigate the connection that must exist would go beyond the limits of this paper, and of my competence; and as far as the New Testament is concerned the combination of the two texts cuts in the other direction, for there is as far as I know no trace of Dtn 5,28–9 in Acts or indeed anywhere in the New Testament. There are three possibilities: (1) Stephen derived the use of Dtn 18,15 or 18 from Qumran by way of Samaria, dropping Dtn 5 on the way. (2) Stephen derived the use of Dtn 18,15 or 18 from Samaria by way of Qumran, dropping Dtn 5 on the way. (3) Stephen derived Dtn 18,15 or 18 directly from the Old Testament, the Christians selecting it as a useful messianic testimony. We could reach a firm decision on this matter only if we knew more than we do about the diverse messianic beliefs of first-century Judaism. But (a) the absence of Dtn 5,28–9 from the New Testament and (b) the occurrence in various parts of the New Testament (especially Ac 3,22) of references and allusions to Dtn 18 make it probable that Christians, though not the first to give a messianic interpretation to Dtn 18, did not draw their use of it directly from either Qumran or Samaria.

It is hard to avoid the conclusion that none of the evidence we have surveyed is sufficient to establish the belief that Stephen (Luke) was in any way connected with Samaria.

The second topic arises out of the references to Moses. There are some features in which Stephen is in disagreement with the Old Testament.

---

[23] Str. B. 2,626.

[24] I quote the translation of G. Vermes, The Dead Sea Scrolls in English, 1962, 245.

At 7,22 he declares that Moses was δυνατὸς ἐν λόγοις. This conflicts with Ex 4,10–16 (I am not eloquent ... I am slow of speech and of tongue), which is not to be dismissed as mock modesty on Moses's part, since in the end God agrees that Aaron shall do the talking. It is sometimes said that in this matter Stephen has a parallel in Josephus, Antiquities 2,271–2, but this is not so. Josephus paraphrases the Old Testament; God promises αὐτὸς παρέσεσθαι καὶ οὗ μὲν ἂν δέῃ λόγων, πειθὼ παρέξειν ... Philo, like Josephus, has every reason to magnify the figure of Moses but writes similarly; in de Vit. Mos. 1,21–30 he fills out in detail Stephen's claim that Moses was instructed in the wisdom of the Egyptians but does not claim that he was eloquent. Ezekiel, the Jewish tragic poet[25], makes Moses describe his inability to speak effectively:

οὐκ εὔλογος πέφυκα, γλῶσσα δ'ἐστί μοι
δύσφραστος, ἰσχνόφωνος, ὥστε μὴ λόγους
ἐμοὺς γενέσθαι βασιλέως ἐναντίον.
(lines 113–15).

God replies simply that Aaron will speak on Moses's behalf.

'Ἀάρονα πέμψον σὸν κασίγνητον ταχύ,
ᾧ πάντα λέξεις τἀξ ἐμοῦ λελεγμένα,
καὐτὸς λαλήσει βασιλέως ἐναντίον,
σὺ μὲν πρὸς ἡμῶν, ὁ δὲ λαβὼν σεθεν πάρα.
(lines 116–19).

It should be noted that Stephen's words (δυνατὸς ἐν λόγοις καὶ ἔργοις) are a Lucan expression; cf. Lk 24,19, δυνατὸς ἐν ἔργῳ καὶ λόγῳ. Stephen (Luke) is undoubtedly concerned to give Moses an exalted position and the Lucanism slips in, perhaps thoughtlessly.

From 7,23 Stephen develops the theme of Moses as the deliverer of his people, in many respects heightening the picture given in Exodus. Thus Moses determined to visit, ἐπισκέψασθαι, his brothers in Egypt. The word is not in Ex 2,11; it is the word of Lk 1,68 (ἐπεσκέψατο καὶ ἐποίησεν λύτρωσιν). 78, used of God's action in delivering his people (and similarly in the LXX, e.g. Ex 3,16). In v. 25, Moses supposed that his brothers would understand that God was giving them σωτηρία by his hand. They did not understand this; one, whom Moses sought to reconcile to a fellow Israelite whom he was ill-treating, thrust Moses away[26] with the words[27], Who made you an ἄρχων and δικαστής over us? Here the language is taken from Ex 2,14. It was however fear of his fellow Jews,

[25] Eusebius, Praeparatio Evangelica, 2,29,10. I take the line references from the edition by H. Jacobson, The Exagoge of Ezekiel, 1983, 56.

[26] ἀπώσατο – a stronger word, according to Conzelmann, than those used in Exodus; see note 30.

[27] See above p. 58.

rather than fear of Pharaoh (as in Ex 2,15), that led to Moses's flight. In v. 35 the words of rejection, ἄρχων and δικαστής, are taken up and developed in that God sends Moses to his people as ἄρχων and λυτρωτής. ἄρχων is a common LXX word[28] but λυτρωτής occurs only twice (Ps 18(19),14(15) = גאלי; 77(78),35 = גאלם), each time of God. Moses was in the assembly of God's people[29] in the wilderness, and received λόγια ζῶντα for transmission to them. Nevertheless they continued to reject him[30] and fell back into idolatry, but Moses was responsible for the tent – the only kind of earthly dwelling that God chose to have (v. 44). He was also, as the quotation of Dtn 18 shows, the type of the eschatological prophet, whom Acts takes to be the final redeemer.

So far Acts goes, but no farther. Stephen represents an early stage in the development of thought about Moses. We do not hear, for example, of the ascent into heaven, based upon Ex 20,21 and developed by Philo. In De Vit. Mos. 1,158 Philo points out that Moses was given the titles θεός and βασιλεύς. He is not said to be God, but Philo[31] is not far from this: εἴς τε τὸν γνόφον, ἔνθα ἦν ὁ θεός, εἰσελθεῖν λέγεται, τουτέστιν εἰς τὴν ἀειδῆ καὶ ἀόρατον καὶ ἀσώματον τῶν ὄντων παραδειγματικὴν οὐσίαν. For Stephen, Moses is a human redeemer, a human conveyer of living oracles, called by God and aided in his mission by an angel. But in his initial rejection and subsequent vindication and saving work he is an exact type of Jesus. It is the more striking that Stephen does nothing to point this out. There is, I believe, only one possible explanation of these facts. The speech that we read in Ac 7 is not Luke's composition, for Luke was a Christian; it was a Hellenist Jewish work; the sort of synagogue sermon that Hellenist Jewish Christians (such as Stephen is represented as being) could, and no doubt did, take over with a minimum of modification[32].

III.

The interpretation of the Old Testament put by Luke into the mouths of Stephen and Paul can be treated briefly because some points have already been hinted at. The two speeches under consideration present the two fundamental aspects of Luke's understanding of the Old Testament.

The synagogue sermon of Ac 13 contains what may be called Luke's Jewish understanding of the Old Testament – for it is Jewish, with the one

[28] Nine columns in Hatch-Redpath.

[29] The ἐκκλησία, v. 38.

[30] ἀπώσαντο, v. 39; cf. v. 27 (note 26).

[31] There is a summary account of Moses's "mystic ascents" in W. A. Meeks, The Prophet-King, Supplements to Nov. T. 14, 1967, 122–5.

[32] Paul's Areopagus speech (Ac 17,22–31), which also becomes specifically Christian only at its end, may come from a similar source. For the Christian modification in Stephen's speech see p. 68.

additional conviction that Jesus of Nazareth was the promised Messiah. It does not call for long discussion. It begins (v. 17) with the fundamental conviction that God, who is the God of Israel, chose our fathers – *our* fathers. Paul speaks as a Jew to Jews. God then, by what he did rather than by anything he said, proceeded to manifest his purpose. He delivered his people from Egypt; and at this point comes the one surprising omission, omitted perhaps because it had already been fully treated in ch. 7. There is nothing about Moses and the Law. God himself was the mighty λυτρωτής, and he took thought for the organization of the people in the land in which he settled them by dispossessing its former inhabitants. He gave them judges and then gave them a king, Saul. But Saul was displaced and David became king. Here the history stops, for the essential factors have all been disclosed: gracious election, deliverance, organized society, and a human king whose reign puts into effect the reign of God. David could only foreshadow and foretell the true king, but he did truly foreshadow and foretell him, and the resurrection, to which there are trustworthy witnesses, establishes his identity – Jesus, in whom not only specific promises, such as Isa 55,3, but the whole story from the beginning, find fulfilment. This is the point, says Paul, at which Jews must either accept or deny the destiny to which their history points.

With this Stephen's speech is, up to a point, in agreement. Again we have the gracious election of the fathers. Again we have deliverance from Egypt, and this time not only is the human λυτρωτής named as Moses, a surprisingly full account of his life is given. The law he received through angels is described as λόγια ζῶντα, and it is he, not David, who is the type of the Coming One, the Latter Redeemer[33] – for if Moses could be λυτρωτής as well as προφήτης, so also could his successor. It is here that a second difference between Stephen and Paul appears. Stephen points out that after the time of Moses the story took a turn for the worse. Indeed already in the time of Moses the people had shown their perversity by making and worshipping a golden calf, and Amos (5,25–7) accuses them of offering sacrifices in the wilderness to strange gods. David was a good king; he found favour with God and planned to make him a σκήνωμα, a word that is used occasionally for the tabernacle[34]. At this point the decisive rot set in. Solomon built God a house, οἶκος. This was contrary to God's will, declared (according to Stephen) in Isa 66,1.2. Stephen, as we have seen, quotes these verses in substantial agreement with the LXX. The original sense of the oracle is disputed, and will not be discussed here. Perhaps the best view is that it is an oracle of comfort. The Temple has been destroyed; there is no Temple; yet God has no need of one, for he

33 "As was the first Redeemer (Moses), so is the latter Redeemer." The saying occurs frequently; see Str. B. 1,69.

34 3 Kdms 2,28.

dwells in heaven and at the same time is ready to make himself available to him that is poor and of a contrite spirit and that trembles at his word (66,2). The next verse however does seem to include a polemical note: He that kills an ox is as he that slays a man; he that sacrifices a lamb, as he that breaks a dog's neck; he that offers an oblation, as he that offers swine's blood; he that burns frankincense, as he that blesses an idol. Some think that this was addressed against the proposal to rebuild the Temple in Jerusalem, others against a schismatic Temple. Rightly or wrongly, Stephen took it to be against the whole notion of a dwelling house for God: The Most High does not dwell in human constructions (ἐν χειροποιήτοις, 7,48). How did Judaism in the first century understand Isaiah's words? The Temple polemic of Qumran is not relevant here; the Qumran sect did not object to the Temple in principle but to its mismanagement (as they deemed it) by the priests in possession. Nor should we look to material that originated after A.D. 70, that is, from the period when no Temple existed and Jews, willy nilly, had to do without one. The fact seems to be that we have virtually no evidence; the most we can do is pick up a few moral maxims, such as Aristeas 234[35], though this is hardly consistent with earlier passages which praise the Temple and its ordering. It is not so much on the basis of specific evidence as in terms of general probability that one must affirm H. Braun's conclusion regarding Stephen's use of Isa 66,1.2: "Hier spricht ... eine *hellenistische* Kritik am Tempel, weil der Tempel mit Händen gemacht ist"[36]. This presumably was the theological reason assigned, but one may suspect that sour grapes played some part in the feelings of Hellenistic Jews. "The Temple is inaccessible; we have to practise our religion without it; it cannot therefore be indispensable."

It was suggested above[37] that Stephen's speech was taken from a Hellenistic Jewish synagogue sermon. If this hypothesis is correct, the synagogue must have been both liberal and radical, for the sermon asserts that the record of Israel is one of almost unbroken apostasy. Moses gave living oracles, but his contemporaries and successors worshipped idols. God chose a movable tent for his home, but Solomon insisted on building him a house. God sent prophets to instruct his people, but they were persecuted and killed. The reference (v. 52) to Jesus brings no offer of penitence and forgiveness; only a climax of condemnation. It may be that the original Jewish sermon ended with the acceptance of Moses as ἄρχων and λυτρωτής, and the implication that if dispersed Israelites would repent

---

[35] "What is the highest form of glory? To honour God, and this is done not with gifts and sacrifices but with purity of soul and holy conviction, since all things are fashioned and governed by God in accordance with his will."

[36] Theologische Rundschau 29, 1963, 167.

[37] p. 66.

and observe the living oracles of Torah God would send the prophet like Moses as a new deliverer[38].

In these two reviews of Old Testament history, Luke, through the mouths of Stephen and Paul, has shown (a) that Christianity is the fulfilment of the Old Testament, and (b) that it is the exclusive fulfilment of the Old Testament, since the Jewish establishment has crowned the sins of its ancestors by bringing about the death of Jesus.

Whether this is a satisfactory interpretation of the Old Testament is another question.

[38] Cf. the sermon in Ac 3,12–26.

John 12,31–32: The Eschatological Significance of the Lifting up of the Son of Man

by George R. Beasley-Murray

(193 Croydon Road, Beckenham, Kent BR3 3QH)

Now is the judgment of this world,
Now the ruler of this world shall be overthrown,
And I, if I be lifted up from the earth will draw all to myself.

The title may be queried: Where does the expression "Son of Man" appear in the saying above cited? It does not, of course, but the response of the hearers to it in v. 34 assumes that the subject of the last line is "the Son of Man". Since the two related "lifting up" sayings in 3,14–15 and 8,28 explicitly refer to the Son of Man, and the context of vv. 31–32 is controlled by 12,23 ("The hour has come that the Son of Man be glorified") we may view 12,31–32 as a Johannine Son of Man saying.

It is generally acknowledged that the three sayings in question are related to the synoptic predictions of the passion. This is most apparent in comparing 3,14–15 ("The Son of Man must be lifted up ...") with Mk 8,31 ("The Son of Man must suffer much ... and be killed, and after three days rise")[1]. The startling difference between the lifting up sayings of the Fourth Gospel and the synoptic passion predictions is the condensation of the references to death and resurrection in the latter into a single term: ὑψοῦν, or passive ὑψωθῆναι. But the rationale behind the synoptic passion predictions and the Johannine lifting up sayings is virtually identical: the event depicted in both groups of sayings is the eschatological action of the Son of Man in relation to the kingdom of God. The passion predictions are formulated on a common pattern, embodied in the varied concepts of the Righteous Man who suffers and is delivered by God (cf. especially Wisd. chs 2–5), the Servant of the Lord, whose innocent suffering leads to his being "lifted up and glorified" (Is 52,13), the Martyr for God's cause, who is set by God at his right hand (e.g. Test Job 41,3–4; Apoc Elijah 37,3; Test Benj 10,6), and the Rejected Prophet, whose word and ministry

---

[1] The parallel with Mk 9,31 is not materially different, for the future tenses show that παραδίδοται also relates to the future, while Mark's δεῖ παθεῖν represents a Semitic future, with probably no more difference of meaning than the emphatic future tenses in the translation of J 12,32 that stands at the head of this article (they could have been rendered unemphatically, "*will* be overthrown ... *shall* draw").

are alike vindicated by God (cf. Lk 13,31–35). In the synoptic tradition these models are gathered up in the eschatological figure of the Son of Man, who fulfils their functions in his service of the kingdom of God; his suffering of death and being raised from death form the climax of his mediation of the kingdom of God in the present time. The Johannine lifting up sayings provide a closely related concept in their representation of the Son of Man being lifted up as the climax of his ministry of bringing to the world *zoe* and *krisis*. Inevitably, however the employment of the term ὑψοῦν, aided by the equally characteristic Johannine δοξάζειν, entails special reflection on the nature of the event so described.

The extent to which this reflection was aided by the Semitic linguistic background has long been debated, but that this was a material factor seems to me to be reasonably clear. Significantly, the idea of death and lifting up occurs in a variety of expressions. The old Aramaic *zeqaph* means set up, lift up, hang up, and could be used on the one hand of raising a criminal on a stake for his execution and on the other for lifting up one who is bowed down; it occurs in Ezr 6,11 of impaling an offender, and in the Old Syriac and Peshitta of the Markan passion narrative of the crucifixion[2]. Bertram draws attention to the use of רום in Ps 9,14, where מְרוֹמְמִי מִשַּׁעֲרֵי מָוֶת is rendered in the LXX ὁ ὑψῶν με ἐκ τῶν πυλῶν τοῦ θανάτου, an expression which Bertram thought may have helped to establish the rising belief in resurrection; the same term appears in 1QH 6,34; 11,12 of raising from death for resurrection, while in Aramaic ארים means "take away"[3]. M. McNamara was attracted to C. C. Torrey's suggestion that the term *slq* used reflexively lay behind 12,32; its reflexive form (*'stlq*) meant "be raised up", but more commonly to go away, depart, die (the same range of meanings is evident in the Hebrew use of the term: Hithpael, Nithpa. = be dismissed, removed; rise; especially be called away from this world, die; the reflexive Aramaic occurs in the Palestinian Targum to the Pentateuch in the sense of "die")[4]. Dodd was impressed with the use of the expression נָשָׂא רוֹשׁ in Gen 40,13.19, in connection with the

---

[2] See the illuminating discussion of G. Kittel, אִזְדְּקֵף = ὑψωθῆναι = gekreuzigt werden. Zur angeblichen antiochenischen Herkunft des vierten Evangelisten, ZNW 35 (1936) 282–285. Many have been persuaded to follow Kittel, e.g. G. Bertram, TDNT VIII 610 n. 38; M. Black, An Aramaic Approach to the Gospels and Acts, ^{2}1946, 103; E. Schweizer, Erniedrigung und Erhöhung, 1955, 118; C. Colpe, TDNT VIII 466; E. M. Sidebottom, The Christ of the Fourth Gospel, 1961, 80 n. 7; H. T. Wrege, Jesusgeschichte und Jüngergeschick nach Joh 12,20–33 und Hebr 5,7–10, in: Der Ruf Jesu und die Antwort der Gemeinde, Festschrift J. Jeremias 1970, 271 n. 38; C. K. Barrett, The Gospel according to St. John, ^{2}1978, 214.

[3] Bertram, op. cit. 606–7.

[4] The Ascension and the Exaltation of Christ in the Fourth Gospel, Scripture, XIX (1967) 66–69. See also C. C. Torrey, "When I am Lifted up from the Earth", John 13,32, JBL 51 (1932) 320–22.

dreams of the baker and the butler imprisoned with Joseph; "lifting up the head" meant for the former his execution, but for the latter his restoration to office[5].

More important than the linguistic precedents are intimations that the concept embodied in the Johannine use of ὑψοῦν was adumbrated in the primitive church. On the assumption that 1 Tim 3,16 should be viewed as a stanza containing three couplets it is possible that the clause ἀνελήμφθη ἐν δόξῃ combines the thought of death and exaltation, in a similar manner to the unusual use of ἀνάλημψις in Lk 9,51. The echo of Is 52,13 in the hymn citation, Phil 2,9, διὸ καὶ ὁ θεὸς ὑπερύψωσεν αὐτόν marks the ascent of the Christ from the death on the cross to the throne of God. So also the exordium of Hb 1,3, which may also embody early confessional language, speaks of Christ as καθαρισμὸν τῶν ἁμαρτιῶν ποιησάμενος ἐκάθισεν ἐν δεξιᾷ τῆς μεγαλωσύνης ἐν ὑψηλοῖς. In this passage there is no suggestion of Christ's death as entailing humiliation, rather there is conveyed a sense of majestic progression of events: the Son of God, who is the effulgence of God's splendour, the stamp of his being and who sustains the universe by his word of power, brought about a purgation of sins and took his seat at the right hand of the Majesty on high. The recognition of the greatness and sublimity of the willing offering of himself in death was a prime factor in leading the Fourth Evangelist to associate the cross with the divine glory and to bracket the death and the ascent in the single word ὑψωθῆναι. Behind the terminology and literary expressions which he inherited lay the conviction that the death of the Son of Man is unique alike by reason of who he is and why he dies. From his incarnation on he is the mediator of the saving sovereignty of God, and his mediatorial role in its coming for humanity reaches its apex in the death on the cross and exaltation to the throne of God. One work it is, for in life and in death he is the instrument of the kingdom of God, i.e. of God exercising his saving, sovereign power; that sovereign action is operative in the death on the cross and raising to Lordship in the kingdom that has come for the world. Fundamentally that is the faith embodied in the primitive kerygma and in the varied traditions of the synoptic writers, but the Fourth Evangelist has given it a special expression through his ὑψωθῆναι-δοξασθῆναι language. Contrary to the notion that this evangelist does not develop a theology of the cross[6], his representation of the death of Christ as a lifting up to the throne of God via the cross indicates a meditation which enhances its significance. It is no accident that the two clearest expressions of this view of the cross fall in the central kerygmatic section J 3,14–21, one of the most

---

[5] The Interpretation of the Fourth Gospel, 1953, 377; the thought was communicated orally at a seminar by D. Daube.

[6] Cf. e. g. S. Schulz, "It is in no way a ruling feature of the Johannine proclamation", Das Evangelium nach Johannes, NTD Band 4, 1978, 237.

important statements of Johannine theology, and in J 12,20–36, which expounds the meaning of the death of Jesus in the context of his last message to his people[7]. Admittedly the concept of the death which is a passage to enthronement appears to overlook the tradition of a resurrection on the third day. Yet this cannot really be the case, since the Evangelist narrates the Easter appearances (ch. 20), gives emphatic expression to the authority of the Christ to lay down his life and take it again (10,17–18), and refers to the Easter resurrection in terms that associate it with the glorification of Jesus. J. Blank draws attention to the Evangelist's comments in J 2,22 ("When he was *risen from the dead* his disciples remembered ...") and in 12,16 ("When Jesus was *glorified* they remembered ..."), and he drew the conclusion, "It is thereby proved once for all that the glorification of Jesus includes his resurrection"[8]. Bertram further maintained that there is no antithesis between exaltation and resurrection, though logically priority seems to belong to the former: "Whether the NT references be to awakening, resurrection, reception, ascent, rapture (*diastasis,* Lk 24,29f.), enthronement (Mt 26,64; Ps 110,1) or royal dominion (Lk 22,29f.; 1 Cor 15,25), all these can be summed up in the one word 'exaltation'"[9]. The Evangelist's concern in using the term ὑψωθῆναι appears to be to emphasize the unity between the death on the cross and the ascent to rule. The key to it is the eschatological action of God in and through the Son of Man whereby his "lifting up" becomes his installation to sovereign rule.

This element of divine action is to the fore in J 12,31–32. "If I be lifted up" is a so-called divine passive, as is indicated in the prayer, "Glorify your name" and the response from heaven, "I have glorified it and will glorify it again" (12,28). Both the context and content of vv. 31–32 show that the ὑψωθῆναι denotes more than a simple return via death to the heavenly home of the Son of Man; in this event the judgment of this world takes place, the prince of this world is dethroned, and the Son of Man assumes the position of lordship within the saving sovereignty under which all humanity may now come. The peculiar significance of the "lifting up" of the Son of Man in death and exaltation is set forth in the three statements of vv. 31–22, which we must briefly consider.

"The judgment of this world" is frequently interpreted in the light of 3,19–21 as a process whereby mankind separates itself, in faith or revulsion, before the enthroned Son of Man. Or, in the endeavour to take into account the nature of the judgment as an event, it is viewed as a decision

---

[7] In the view of A. Corell the drama of redemption is the central theme of the Fourth Gospel and the "lifting up" or exaltation of Jesus the key that gives significance to all that he does and says, Consummatum Est, Eschatology and Church in the Gospel of St John, 1958, 12–13.

[8] Krisis. Untersuchungen zur johanneischen Christologie und Eschatologie, 1964, 266 n. 5.

[9] Op. cit. 611.

of God against "this age" and its sinful ways. Rather we should see it as a decision of God with reference to mankind as it exists in this age, characterized by rebellion against God and readiness to follow the "prince of this world". But the "rebellion" is not merely general but concrete; the "now" of v. 31 relates to its ultimate expression in the rejection of the Son of Man and putting him to death. Since the Son of Man is sent by God into the world as his representative and revealer, rejection of the Son of Man is rejection of God himself. Therein sin is exposed in its most naked form. Insofar as the judgment of this world is a revelation of its sin and occasion of its condemnation, the death on the cross with its corollary of divine exaltation is that moment. But it is more than that; *in that event God gave his Son,* that the condemned world might not perish but live. Here we would urge that we must beware of divorcing 12,31–32 from other equally distinctive utterances of the Evangelist relating to the activity of God in and through the Redeemer. The Evangelist deliberately set 3,14–15 in juxtaposition with the kerygmatic 3,16–17, and as deliberately set 12,31–32 alongside the sayings *he* brought together in 12,23–28. Moreover his Lamb of God concept was almost as distinctive as his lifting up sayings ("almost", because this was shared by his friends in the Johannine school). He and they knew perfectly well the origin of the Lamb of God in Jewish apocalyptic as the Leader of God's flock who delivers the flock by powerful acts of destructive judgment (in Rev 5,6 the Lamb has *seven* horns – powerful to kill!); in the Johannine reinterpretation the Lamb brings the deliverance of the kingdom of God by his fulfilling the role of the Passover Lamb (so J 19,31–37; Rev 5,9–10; in the Revelation judgment and redemption are perpetually represented in terms of the second Exodus). If therefore we relate J 12,31–32 with the Evangelist's general outlook we must understand that the sentence of judgment passed on "this world" is endured by the One whom this world murders – the Son of Man. This it is that turns the awful news of judgment at the cross into the good news of deliverance from judgment through the Son of Man exalted on and from the cross. It is an eschatological event in the fullest sense of the term – God acting in sovereign (= Kingdom!) power in and through the Son of Man[10].

The assertion "Now the prince of this world shall be thrown out" manifests a use of apocalyptic imagery unusual for the Evangelist; the fact that he employs it in relation to the central event of his kerygma is to be observed. Naturally exegetes recall Lk 10,18 in this connection: "I watched Satan fall, as lightning, out of heaven", indicating a defeat of Satan through the ministry of Jesus. In view, however, of the link between

[10] On the objective aspect of the judgment of this world that brings redemption see especially A. Schlatter, Der Evangelist Johannes ^{2}1948, 270–71; J. Blank, Krisis, 282; also R. Schnackenburg, The Gospel according to St John II, 1980, 390–91.

the Lamb of God in the gospel and in the Book of Revelation it is yet more natural to recall the vision of Satan's fall in Rev 12. This is the more plausible in that the passage is plainly a previously existing isolated apocalyptic prophecy which the Seer has adopted and made it yield a "Johannine" meaning. The original was a version of the ancient combat myth, wherein a "woman" gave birth to one destined to slay the dragon and who was rapt to heaven before the dragon could harm him. In the myth the "man child" was the slayer of the dragon, but a Jewish apocalyptist, seeing in the myth a signal likeness to the Messianic hope, introduced Michael and his angels as the instruments of the dragon's conquest; the Christian seer acknowledged the likeness, but added a hymnic postscript which transformed its meaning: the fall of the dragon marked the arrival of "the salvation and the power and the sovereignty of our God and the authority of his Christ", and the followers of the Lamb "overcame him *on account of the blood of the Lamb*". The Dragon was overthrown then through the death and exaltation of the Christ to reign with God. The details in the mythical picture are ignored by the Seer in the interest of the theological tenet that in the death and resurrection of the Christ the eschatological event has taken place whereby the power of the devil has been broken in heaven and the rule of God in Christ has begun, which is to be shortly followed by the final victory and revelation of the Jerusalem from above. The Evangelist is not an apocalyptist, but it is difficult to believe that his assertion "the prince of this world shall be thrown out" is *not* linked with the Apocalyptist's picture through the common traditions of the Johannine school. No interpretation of the "throwing out" of Satan is offered by the Evangelist; the ejection from the presence of God is an image of the judgment that the evil one shares with the world he has led in rebellion against God (cf. 16,11), and emphasizes the changed situation for humanity, since the exalted Son of Man now exercises rule over the world for which he died[11].

The two statements on judgment are followed by a third that emphasizes the redemptive purpose of the dying and rising of the Son of Man: "I, if I be lifted up from the earth, will draw all to me". Clearly the lifting up of the Son of Man is not simply six feet above earth, but to a position from

[11] T. Preiss' idea that the place of the Accuser in heaven is taken by the exalted Son of Man in his role as Paraclete-Intercessor is attractive but uncertain (Life in Christ, Studies in Biblical Theology 13, 1952, 19). It is adopted by Blank (Krisis, 284). It undoubtedly suits the representation in the Fourth Gospel of the Spirit as *another* Paraclete, and the notion of "the Friend from Court" balancing the activity of "the Friend in Court", but it entails a fairly complete adoption of the Apocalyptist's picture by the Evangelist and expects the original readers to fill in more than they were likely to know. Perhaps it is sufficient to recall the fundamental tenet, enunciated by E. Percy in his discussion of Mt 12,28, "Where Satan is driven back, the rule of God begins" (Die Botschaft Jesu, 1953, 179).

where he can draw all to himself – to his throne in heaven. The thought is not that the Son of Man will draw all *to his cross,* but that he will draw all to *himself as the crucified-exalted Redeemer* (cf. the NEB rendering of Rev 5,6, "a Lamb with the marks of slaughter upon him"). It is in virtue of the total action of the dying and the rising that the saving sovereignty comes to the world, and the exalted Lord exercises his sovereignty by drawing all to him. The result is the same as in 3,15: "that everyone who believes may have eternal life in him". The "drawing" entails a "coming", and the coming denotes believing. The process envisaged is that depicted in 6,37 and 44: the Father "gives" to the Son those whom he "draws", and those who come are not "thrown out" (cf. ἐκβληθήσεται of 12,31!). The πάντας of v. 32 accordingly expresses the universal scope of the eschatological event disclosed in ὑψωθῆναι; the saving sovereignty is for all mankind (the kingdom of God cannot be for less!). Yet, as Schnackenburg remarked, "There is no limit to Jesus' saving power – *except the resistance of unbelief*"[12]. If the Evangelist does not explicitly state that, it is because he has sufficiently indicated it in the rest of his gospel. So also while he has not mentioned it here, he assumes that the reader understands that the Father's "drawing" all to the Son is through the agency of the Paraclete, whom God sends in virtue of the ὑψωθῆναι (cf. 7,39; 16,7). The Paraclete is the Spirit of the new age, sent to bear witness to the Exalted Christ (c. 15,26–27; 16,8–15). Those who respond to the witness are united by him to form the eschatological community in Christ, participating through their exalted Lord in the life of the saving sovereignty.

The lifting up of the Son of Man, accordingly, denotes the eschatological action of God whereby the saving sovereignty manifested in the ministry of Jesus accomplishes deliverance and salvation for all mankind. The kingdom has come for all nations! If that be so a question urgently thrusts itself forward: does this eschatological action of God through the Son of Man *exclude* or *demand* further like eschatological action in the future? Bultmann's answer is well known: "The turn of the ages results now . . . No future in this world's history can bring anything new, and all apocalyptic pictures of the future are empty dreams"[13]. The first sentence is impeccably correct; it expresses a conviction that the Fourth Evangelist sought to make plain through his entire gospel. But does the second sentence logically follow from the first? Is it self-evident that the incursion of the saving sovereignty into this world's history means that nothing new can happen in history? Is not the reverse true, namely that because the saving sovereignty has come, all history is to be made new through that same Son of Man? And does that not signify further eschatological action of God through the Son of Man?

---

[12] Op. cit. 39.

[13] The Gospel of John, A Commentary, Eng. tr. 1971, 431.

It is the present writer's conviction that Bultmann made the same mistake with regard to the Fourth Gospel as Dodd made with respect to the other three. Dodd's insight into the synoptic representations that the kingdom of God came in the ministry of Jesus led him to assert that no future coming of the kingdom of God was anticipated by Jesus, and that sayings and parables indicating the contrary were due in part to misunderstanding of the tradition and in part through failure to perceive the function of eschatological language to convey the notion of the finality of the divine intervention in history[14]. By contrast Bultmann undeviatingly rejected the idea that the synoptic gospels portray Jesus as teaching the presence of the kingdom of God in his word and action, and that doubtless contributed to his viewing the Johannine eschatology as a radical repudiation of the synoptic eschatology, and so justifying critical elimination of elements of traditional eschatology within the gospel as alien to the Evangelist's thought. It seems not to have occurred to these two notable scholars that Jesus may have understood the eschatological event taking place in his ministry as *the inauguration of eschatological action that leads to ultimate eschatological fulfilment,* and that the synoptic tradition, reflecting the earliest expection of the Church, emphasized the element of hope (the ultimate eschatological fulfilment) and that the Johannine emphasized the inauguration of the eschatological action of God in the Son of Man, while neither tradition excluded the reality of the other element.

It is instructive to compare Bultmann's comment on J 12,32, "The turn of the ages results now . . . no future in this world's history can bring anything new" with Bertram's assertion relating to this issue: "Exaltation is . . . the presupposition of his coming again"[15]. In this statement Bertram was confessedly influenced by W. Thüsing's investigation of this theme, which Thüsing regarded as of crucial importance for the understanding of early Christology[16]. In Thüsing's view the expection of the returning Lord at his parousia was most intense in the earliest period of the Church, but it was always the parousia of the *risen* Lord that was in mind, and so despite the eschatological intensity of hope there was always a holding together in faith of the Risen One and the Coming One at the parousia. This I believe to be reflected in various ways, some more and some less explicitly, throughout the evangelic traditions. One sees it implied even in so markedly an eschatological utterance as Mk 14,62, for therein it is not said that the Son of Man will *become* enthroned with God at his parousia, but

---

14 See especially the lecture "Eschatology and History", in: The Apostolic Preaching and its Developments, ^{2}1944, 79–96.

15 Op. cit. 612.

16 See his Erhöhungsvorstellung und Parusieerwartung in der ältesten nachösterlichen Christologie. Stuttgarter Bibelstudien 42, 1969, first published in BZ NF 11, 95–108, 205–222 and 12, 54–80, 223–240.

that he will at the parousia be *revealed* as the enthroned One[17]. That leads one to ask what eschatological expectation is implied in the hymn of Phil 2,6–11. The Redeemer has been "highly exalted" and given the name that is above every name; i.e. he has been enthroned in heaven, the turn of the ages has occurred. But when does the universal confession of Jesus as Lord take place? The same question is posed yet more vividly in the vision of heaven in Rev 4–5: the Lamb has conquered and, in accord with the oriental coronation pattern, is represented as enthroned, so that all angelic hosts and the entire creation, living and dead, render glory to God and the Lamb. Here there is no time division; the turn of the ages has happened and all creation acknowledges it. It gives the same interpretation of the redemptive event as that in Phil 2,9–11 (and in J 12,31–32!), but by means of apocalyptic pictures of the present. If we possessed nothing more from its author we might well assume that he had no concept of a future parousia; as it is, the Seer works out through apocalyptic pictures of the future what in his view must come to pass to bring about the universal acknowledgement of the Lamb, as Paul does with much greater sobriety in his letters (e.g. 1 Cor 15,20–28). What we must ungrudgingly acknowledge is that both the Seer and the Apostle set forth with greatest clarity the eschatological significance of the redemptive action of God in Christ in the paschal death and resurrection, but in their distinctive ways they unite in seeing the Exalted One pressing on to his parousia.

We have no interest in equating the theological outlooks of the Fourth Evangelist with that of the Seer of the Revelation. Without doubt J 12,31–32 is the strongest single utterance in the Bible of the eschatological action of God in and through the incarnate Redeemer, and it is in harmony with his entire representation of the incarnate life. Nevertheless the Evangelist makes it very plain that he does not look on the world after the exaltation of the Christ with rose tinted spectacles. The world persists in its evil, and goes on opposing the disciples with the virulence that it opposed the Lord (chs. 14–17), and Jesus prays that the disciples will be kept from the power of the Evil One (ch. 17). As Jesus had his "hour" of suffering, so his followers will have theirs in the world's "hour" – the time of the world's power. How long will that condition last? For all time? Or till the world changes? Neither answer is justified on Johannine premises. In the light of the "world's" continued rejection of the message of the crucified-exalted Revealer it is entirely comprehensible that Jesus is represented as saying, "He who rejects me and does not receive my sayings

---

17 Such is the implication of P. Vielhauer's exegesis of Mk 14,62: "What those addressed will see is not two actions, enthronement and coming, but an already existing circumstance – Jesus sitting at the right hand of God – and an event – Jesus coming as Son of Man on the clouds of heaven", Erwägungen zur Christologie des Markusevangeliums, in Zeit und Geschichte, Festschrift R. Bultmann, 1964, 160–61.

has a judge; the word that I have spoken will be his judge *on the last day*" (12,48). It is significant that this saying is set in a paragraph shortly after the shattering eschatological word of 12,31, and it is wholly consistent with it, since the judgment of the end is a revelation of the action of God in accordance with the judgment at the lifting up of the Son of Man.

The Lord who uttered 12,31–32 bade his disciples in their time of tribulation to maintain faith in the Father and in him, for he goes to prepare a place for them; "And if I go and prepare a place for you I will come again and welcome you to myself, that where I am you may be also" (14,1–3). None can deny that that is parousia language. The question is whether the Evangelist reproduced it in order to give it a transformed meaning, consonant with his predominantly realized eschatology. It is implausible to relate the words to the believer's departure at death; that idea belongs to days when eschatology was not understood in the Church[18]. Nor is it likely that the Evangelist wished to interpret the language as relating to the coming of the Paraclete. Admittedly the first Paraclete promise (14,15–16) is followed by the words, "I will not leave you desolate, I will come to you" (14,18), but a comparison of 14,18–20 with 16,16–24 shows what the Evangelist has in mind in the former passage: the grief of the disciples for "a little while" is to be swallowed up in the joy of meeting Jesus in the Easter resurrection, when the perplexities of the present will be understood. The coming of Jesus at Easter is not the coming of the Spirit, but the condition of the Spirit's coming. Certainly the Easter reunion and the sending of the Spirit will make possible the dwelling of the Father and the Son with the believer through a kind of private parousia (14,23), but this cannot be thought to exhaust the meaning of 14,3. It would seem that in ch. 14 the Evangelist sets forth in pictorial but non-apocalyptic imagery the hope of the kingdom of God consummated in the parousia of the Redeemer, prior to which the disciples are to know his conquest of death in the revelation of Easter and in fellowship with him through the Spirit; that is a genuinely eschatological foretaste of the ultimate fellowship which they will enjoy with all the redeemed in the Father's "house". There is no confusion in such a formulation of the parousia hope: Paul has virtually the same, but expounded in epistolary contexts instead of gospel narrative.

The affirmations of resurrection and eternal life in the gospel bear a comparable interpretation. The emphasis in the gospel on the present gift of life is remarkable; it is the great lesson of the signs, beginning with the first and coming to a climax in the last, it is reiterated in the discourses, is set forth in symbolic action at Easter (20,22), and its appropriation is de-

---

[18] R. H. Charles long ago stated, "According to the N.T. death translates believers to Christ (2 Cor 5,8; Phil 1,23) but nowhere is he said to come and fetch them", Eschatology, A Critical History of the Doctrine of a Future Life, ^{2}1913, 422.

clared to be the purpose of the gospel (20,31). Nevertheless, just as 12,32 speaks of an immediately impending future ("if I be lifted up") with a prospect on a more distant future ("I will draw all to myself"), so the promises of life under the divine sovereignty portend a consummation of that life in a future resurrection. That is most clearly set forth in the discourse on the Bread of Life; note especially v. 40: "This is the will of my Father, that everyone who sees the Son and believes in him may have eternal life, and I will raise him in the last day". Why should it be thought that the last clause of that sentence must be editorial, not least in view of the essentially corporate nature of resurrection to the kingdom of God? It affirms a present participation in the saving sovereignty (eternal life) which anticipates fulness of participation in the consummation of that sovereignty (resurrection). The same concept is set forth in 6,44, in terms closely similar to those of 12,32; and it appears to me that the famous 11,25 embodies a like understanding. One is aware that the latter is commonly viewed as modifying the traditional concept of resurrection, voiced by Martha, but in the light of our discussion a different interpretation may be called for. "I am the Resurrection (and the Life)" may be understood as a declaration, comparable to 5,17.21–22, that the resurrection for which the Jews hope and which Martha awaits is vested by God in Jesus; from that two conclusions follow, first that by his power the believer in him shall "live" after death, and so shall surely rise; secondly that "he who lives and believes" in him shall never die, for he possesses the life of the divine sovereignty that Jesus brought, and so the future is *confirmed* through the reality of the Redeemer's present eschatological action. This language is by no means unique. It is in harmony with Jesus' deduction from the revelation to Moses at the bush: "I am the God of Abraham ..." shows that the God of the fathers is the God of *the living,* who therefore *shall rise* (Mk 12,26–27). Paul in 2 Cor 5,15 makes a statement with the same curious ambiguity as that in J 11,26: the NEB renders οἱ ζῶντες in the former, "men while still in life", but it surely means, "they who live through the resurrection of Christ", i.e. in the καινὴ κτίσις; so also in J 11,26 πᾶς ὁ ζῶν καὶ πιστεύων εἰς ἐμέ most likely means, "he who has the life of the divine sovereignty now, namely he who believes in me ...". The statement is a powerful affirmation of life through the Risen One, now and in the future until the resurrection in the likeness of Christ[19].

We conclude that the Fourth Gospel from beginning to end is shot through with eschatology, a remarkable thing to assert of a work in which the expression "kingdom of God" occurs in one saying only (3,3 and 5,

---

[19] Such is the interpretation of J. H. Bernard, A Critical and Exegetical Commentary of the Gospel according to St. John, I.C.C., II, 319; Schlatter, op. cit. 253; Dodd, Interpretation, 36; R. E. Brown, The Gospel according to John, Anchor Bible, 1966, 425; F. F. Bruce, The Gospel of John, 1983, 244.

but cf. 18,36). It is the most thoroughgoing New Testament exposition of the sovereignty of God that has appeared in Jesus, whom the Evangelist prefers to call the Son of God and Son of Man. That sovereign action of God is seen as embracing the whole work of the incarnate Son. Its most critical revelation is in the "lifting up" of the Son of Man, but it is not ended there, for the exalted Lord continues his work of judgment and salvation in the world through the Paraclete-Spirit. As the death of the Son of Man marked his return to the glory that he had with the Father before the foundation of the world, so the end of the process will be the uniting of all whom the Father has given the Son in the glory of the divine sovereignty[20].

This is less a radical departure from the earliest traditions of the teaching of Jesus than a profound exposition of their real meaning. Its radicality is magnified when the synoptic teaching is interpreted in terms of an exclusively future expection of the kingdom of God, but that is increasingly recognized as a false interpretation. The element in Jesus' proclamation of the kingdom of God, distinguishing it from that of Israel's prophets and apocalyptists, was his reiterated assertion of the presence of the kingdom of God in his word and action, his mediation of its reality to his people, and his advance to death that it might come in power to all nations. But at all times the kingdom proclaimed as present was that which is to come in fulness in the future. W. G. Kümmel's conclusion of his review of the eschatological teaching of Jesus in the synoptic gospels is noteworthy:

> "The inseparable union of hope and present experience demonstrates the fact that the true meaning of Jesus' eschatological message is to be found in its reference to God's action in himself, that the essential content of Jesus' preaching about the kingdom of God is the news of the divine authority of Jesus, who has appeared on earth and is awaited in the last days as the one who effects the divine purpose of mercy"[21].

Extraordinarily enough, the intent of that statement is more transparently plain in the Fourth Gospel than it is in the synoptics. While the last clause is more emphatically expressed in the synoptics, it is the merit of the Johannine presentation of Jesus that it makes luminous the truth of the sentence as a whole. That perhaps is an indication that the two modes of presentation of Jesus – the synoptic and the Johannine – are complementary, and that both are needed.

---

[20] So E. C. Hoskyns: "The conclusion of the prayer (of J 17) is therefore pure eschatology, the prayer that the *Ecclesia Militans* may become the *Ecclesia Glorificata,* and that the *Theologia Crucis* may be transformed into the *Theologia Gloriae*", The Fourth Gospel ²1947, 506.

[21] Promise and Fulfilment, The Eschatological Message of Jesus, Studies in Biblical Theology 23, 1957, 155.

Die Erwählung der Völker durch das Evangelium

Theologiegeschichtliche Erwägungen zum 1 Thess

von Jürgen Becker

(Rönner Weg 15, 2313 Raisdorf üb. Kiel)

Der 1 Thess darf in der Regel zu drei Themen der paulinischen Theologie etwas beisteuern: Zum frühen Typ einer Heidenmissionspredigt (1,9f.), zur christlichen Auferstehungshoffnung (4,13–18) und zur paulinischen Auseinandersetzung mit dem Judentum (2,14–16). Das ist für diesen kleinen Brief zwar nicht wenig, jedoch kommt er wegen dieser selektiven Benutzung kaum dazu zu zeigen, daß er ein klar umrissenes theologisches Gesamtkonzept sein eigen nennt. Gesetzt den Fall, man wird bei der Suche nach einem solchen Schatz fündig, dann wäre sein Wert kaum zu überschätzen, blickte man dann doch nicht nur auf die älteste, literarisch faßbare Gestalt der paulinischen Theologie, sondern könnte zugleich sicher sein, Rückschlüsse auf die letzten Jahre paulinisch-antiochenischer Geschichte ziehen zu können. Man hätte also zum einen einen entscheidenden Ansatzpunkt für die Frage nach einer möglichen Entwicklung der paulinischen Theologie. Man gewönne zum anderen einen wichtigen Querschnitt innerhalb der Gemeindegeschichte Antiochias, da Paulus, der den 1 Thess ca. 2 Jahre nach seinem Fortgang aus Antiochia schreibt, in ihm sicherlich noch große Nähe zu Antiochia aufweist.

*

Wer den 1 Thess für eine solche Untersuchung benutzen will, muß vorweg einige strittige Fragen klären. Dabei wird man ohne erneute Begründung davon ausgehen dürfen, daß der 2 Thess kein echter Paulusbrief ist[1]. Auch setzt die folgende Untersuchung voraus, daß die traditionelle Chronologie die besseren Argumente auf ihrer Seite hat, d. h., daß Paulus nach dem Zusammenstoß mit Petrus in Antiochia ca. 48/49 n. Chr. dieser Stadt den Rücken kehrt und ca. 50 n. Chr. von Korinth aus den 1 Thess an die neugegründete Gemeinde in Thessaloniki schrieb, die er fluchtartig verließ und noch nicht wieder besuchen konnte[2].

---

[1] Vgl. Ph. Vielhauer: Geschichte der urchristlichen Literatur, 1975, 95–100.

[2] M. E. hängt die chronologische Neugestaltung der Vita des Apostels bei G. Lüdemann: Paulus der Heidenapostel I, FRLANT 123, 1980, von zu vielen hypothetischen Konstruktionen ab, als daß man ihr folgen sollte. Sie führt zu mehr neuen Problemen, als sie

Schwieriger gestaltet sich die literarkritische Frage. Doch hat der kleine und älteste Paulusbrief keine so harten Brüche wie z. B. der 2 Kor. Die Doppelungen und Wiederholungen bleiben auch bei Zergliederung des Briefes zum Teil erhalten. Die neu zusammengestellten Briefkorpora setzen nicht nur recht komplizierte Operationen voraus[3], sondern ermangeln auch oft an vielen Stellen einer einsichtigen inneren Kohärenz. Umgekehrt zeichnet sich der 1 Thess durchgängig und im Unterschied zu den anderen Paulusbriefen dadurch aus, daß er von dem Stilmittel der Dreiergruppierung von Wörtern[4] geprägt ist, von den schon genannten vielen Doppelungen und Wiederholungen[5] wie auch von den häufigen eschatologischen Abschlüssen[6]. Vor allem aber scheint die Trias Glauben, Liebe, Hoffnung, die gleich eingangs auftritt (1,3; vgl. 5,8) die Stichworte für den Briefaufbau abzugeben, indem jeweils zwei Abschnitte unter verschiedenen Gesichtspunkten einem dieser Stichworte zugeordnet werden können[7]. Nicht selten werden auch Übergänge von einem zum anderen Abschnitt durch Stichwortanschluß mitbestimmt[8]. So ist es ratsam, von der Einheitlichkeit des Briefes auszugehen. Dieses Urteil ist ausdrücklich auch auf solche Versuche zu beziehen, die Teile des Briefes wie z. B. 2,15f. oder 5,1–11 als unpaulinische Nachträge kennzeichnen wollen[9].

Für unsere Untersuchung ist endlich noch die Feststellung bedeutsam, daß der Brief nur zwei aktuelle Themen behandelt: In 1,2–3,13 ist

vorhandene löst, so sicher sie zu manchen Einzelfragen beachtliche Beobachtungen enthält.

3 Dies gilt insbesondere von den Ergebnissen bei W. Schmithals: Die Thessalonicherbriefe als Briefkomposition, in: Zeit und Geschichte, Dankesgabe an R. Bultmann, 1964, 295–315, und bei H.-M. Schenke, in: Ders. – K. M. Fischer: Einleitung in die Schriften des Neuen Testaments I, 1978, 65–71.

4 Vgl. dazu G. Friedrich: 1 Thess 5,1–11, der apologetische Einschub eines Späteren, ZThK 70 (1973) 298 = Ders.: Auf das Wort kommt es an, 1978, 261.

5 Ein großer Teil ist anschaulich gesammelt bei R. Pesch: Die Entdeckung des ältesten Paulus-Briefes, HerBü 1167, 1984, 24–32.

6 Vgl. z. B. 1,10; 2,12.16; 3,13; 4,17; 5,10.23f.

7 Vgl. das Stichwort: »Glaube« als Annahme des Evangeliums bestimmt 1,2–2,16; »Glaube« als treues Festhalten am Heilsstand 2,17–3,13. Beide Abschnitte haben 3 Unterteile (1,2–10; 2,1–12; 2,13–16 und 2,17–20; 3,1–5; 3,5–13). Alle enden eschatologisch. Mit 4,1–12 folgt der erste Abschnitt zum Stichwort »Liebe« (im Alltag der einzelnen Christen). Die beiden Abschnitte 4,13–18; 5,1–11 stehen unter dem Stichwort »Hoffnung« (das besondere Problem verstorbener Christen, die Festigung aller in der Hoffnung). 5,12–24 ist wieder dem Stichwort »Liebe« zuzuordnen (mit besonderer Betonung der institutionellen Gemeindefragen).

8 Vgl. 1,9 und 2,1 (»Zugang«); 2,9f. und 2,13 (»Evangelium/Wort Gottes« und »Glaubende«); 3,12f. und 4,3.9 (»Heiligung« und »Liebe«) usw.

9 Vgl. H.-M. Schenke (Anm. 3) 70; G. Friedrich (Anm. 4) passim. Zur gesamten literarkritischen Diskussion vgl. noch: W. G. Kümmel: Einleitung in das Neue Testament [21]1983, 224–226.

immer wieder auf die historische Situation abgehoben, und in 4,13–18 wird das aktuelle Problem aufgegriffen, das durch die entschlafenen Christen gestellt ist. Beides geschieht so, daß viel Typik und generell für heidenchristliche Gemeinden Geltendes zu erkennen ist. Dies muß nun auch im besonderen Maße für die anderen Partien des Briefes reklamiert werden. Dabei gilt dieses Urteil um so eindeutiger, als der Gemeinde nachdrücklich und betont oft bescheinigt wird, sie stehe fest in Glaube, Liebe und Hoffnung und bedürfe darum keiner Belehrung[10], sondern nur der Ermunterung, in der christlichen Existenz noch mehr Fortschritte zu machen[11]. Weil die Gemeinde so intakt ist und problemlos (Ausnahme: 4,13ff.) ihren Weg geht, redet Paulus zu ihr in einer Weise, die überhaupt typisch ist für seine Theologie in dieser Zeit. So hat es Sinn, mit Hilfe des 1 Thess die Theologie des (noch) antiochenischen Paulus zu erheben.

*

Läßt man den 1 Thess einmal für sich ohne die Einrede aus anderen Paulusbriefen sprechen und ihn dabei alles so vortragen, wie es bei ihm gewichtet steht, ohne z. B. sofort ein dem Römerbrief entlehntes Raster der paulinischen Theologie als Vorgabe zu benutzen, so springt förmlich in die Augen, daß der Zusammenhang von Evangelium und Erwählung schlechterdings grundlegend ist. Sofort in 1,4f. konstatiert der Apostel: »Wir wissen, von Gott geliebte Brüder, um eure Erwählung, denn unser Evangelium für euch geschah nicht durch Worte allein, sondern auch in Kraft, d. h. durch den heiligen Geist und in großer Zuversicht.« Dieses theologische und geschichtliche Urdatum der Gemeinde, gekennzeichnet durch das Stichwort der Erwählung, steht nicht nur gleich eingangs des Briefes als Kern der für das Briefformular typischen Danksagung, sondern wird vielmehr ebenfalls am Schluß des Briefes nochmals betont herausgestellt, wenn es dort heißt (5,23f.): »Er selbst aber, der Gott des Friedens, heilige euch durch und durch und bewahre euch Geist, Seele und Leib vollkommen, daß sie untadelig seien bei der Parusie unseres Herrn Jesu Christi. Getreu ist der, der euch berufen hat, er wird es auch vollenden.«

Etwa gleichmäßig über den kleinen Brief verteilt stehen noch dreimal einschlägige Aussagen zum Thema. So schließt Paulus die Schilderung seines »Zugangs« (1,9; 2,1) zur Gemeinde ab mit der Mahnung in 2,11f.: »Ihr wißt, daß wir jeden einzelnen von euch wie ein Vater seine Kinder ermahnt, ermuntert und beschworen haben, des Gottes würdig zu wandeln, der euch berufen hat zu seiner Herrschaft und Herrlichkeit.« Ebenso deutlich reden die beiden ganz gleich strukturierten Grundsätze in 4,7 und 5,9, die jeweils an formal analoger und sachlich gleich bedeutungsvoller

---

[10] Vgl. 1,5–7.8f.; 2,1.13f.19f.; 3,3f.6.9; 4,1.9f.; 5,1f.11.

[11] Vgl. 3,2; 4,1.10; 5,11.

Stelle die Paränese bzw. den Stand in der Hoffnung begründen: »Denn Gott hat uns nicht berufen (zum Leben) in Unreinheit, sondern in Heiligung.« »Denn Gott hat uns nicht bestimmt zum Zorn, sondern zur Erlangung des Heils.« Beide Grundsätze bilden abschließende Begründungen, aus denen dann jeweils eine letzte Folgerung gezogen wird. Sie sind syntaktisch bis hin zur Wortfolge gleich gebaut und definieren in typischer Weise die göttliche Erwählung durch Abgrenzung vom Unheilszustand (»Denn nicht erwählte uns Gott zu/in ...«) und setzen diesen adversativ zum positiven Berufungsziel (»... sondern zu/in ...«).

Die Kenntnisnahme dieser fünf zentralen Stellen führt zu der Feststellung: Der 1 Thess ist durch eine Erwählungstheologie geprägt, die deutliche Konturen besitzt und die dabei das ordnende Koordinatensystem abgibt, in das alle anderen Aussagen des Briefes eingetragen werden können. Um dies näher in den Blick zu nehmen, soll zunächst die Auffassung von der Erwählung näher beschrieben werden.

Durchweg und ausnahmslos ist Gott der Berufende (nie Christus). Diese Tat entspringt seiner Souveränität. Darum kann die partizipiale Wendung »der euch Berufende« (2,12) nicht nur Gott kennzeichnen, sondern sogar als selbständige Gottesbezeichnung dienen (5,24)[12]. Die abgrenzenden Formulierungen in 4,7; 5,9 machen dabei deutlich, Erwählung geschieht durch Herausnahme aus einem allgemeinen Unheilszustand. Dieser wird gekennzeichnet durch den negativ qualifizierten Wandel und die Folgen der göttlichen Reaktion. Positiv zielt die Berufung auf die »Erlangung der (endzeitlichen) Soteria« (5,9). Gott beruft »zu seiner Herrschaft und Herrlichkeit« (2,12). Diese durchaus noch formal jüdischen Aussagen werden christlich interpretiert, indem der Endzustand beschrieben wird als Zusammensein der Gemeinde mit ihrem Herrn (4,17; 5,10), der der Retter vom Zorn ist (1,10). Der göttliche Zorn ist dabei die aggressive und penetrant nahe Reaktion Gottes auf den Zustand der Menschheit (2,16; 5,9), die dadurch zu einer solchen wird, die »keine Hoffnung« hat (4,13).

Aus diesen Beobachtungen ergibt sich: Gottes Berufung ereignet sich unmittelbar vor dem Ende der Geschichte. Sie ist endzeitliche Gnadenwahl, indem sie unmittelbar vor dem nahen Endgericht zum endzeitlichen Heil beruft. Die Berufenen werden nicht mit der massa perditionis dem Zorn verfallen sondern endgültig Rettung erfahren. Als jetzt endzeitlich Berufene sind sie Kirche, Ekklesia (1,1), also Endzeitgemeinde, die mit Ausnahme weniger Toter fast alle als Lebende bei der Parusie des Herrn dabeisein werden (4,15–17). Die Kirche ist die unmittelbar vor dem Ende gesammelte Schar, die dem kommenden Zorn entgehen soll und die von der Parusie ab immer mit dem Herrn zusammensein wird

[12] Vgl. dazu G. Delling: Partizipiale Gottesprädikationen in den Briefen des Neuen Testaments, StTh 17 (1963) 28–31.

(4,17; 5,10). Von dieser Funktion her definiert sie sich. Erwählung ist somit ausgelegt als Bestimmung der Endzeitgemeinde unmittelbar vor dem nahen Gericht, damit so am »Tag des Herrn« (5,2) ein Teil der sonst insgesamt verlorenen Menschheit gerettet wird. In der kurzen Zeitspanne bis zum Ende steht das Leben der Kirche unter der bewahrenden Heiligung des seinem Berufungshandeln gegenüber treuen Gottes (5,23f.); jedes Glied derselben steht unter dem Anspruch, seiner Berufung durch Heiligung im Wandel aktiv zu entsprechen (4,7).

Die Berufung vollzieht sich durch das Evangelium (1,4f.). Dabei ist das Verb desselben Stammes noch im alltäglichen Sinn mit der Bedeutung »gute Nachricht bringen« geläufig (3,6). Paulus benutzt es wenige Jahre später aber auch als terminus technicus für die Ausrichtung des Evangeliums (1 Kor 1,17). Das Substantiv jedoch dient schon im 1 Thess nur als feststehender Ausdruck für die Kennzeichnung der christlichen Botschaft. Vorherrschend ist die Bezeichnung »das Evangelium Gottes« (2,2.8.9), weil darin der berufende Gott wirkt und seine Berufung an die Adressaten der Botschaft ausrichten läßt. Damit ist Paulus betraut (2,4), so daß er von »unserem (d. h. meinem) Evangelium« sprechen kann (1,5). So kennzeichnet er es als das von ihm verkündigte Evangelium (vgl. Gal 1,8f.). Auch Timotheos ist »Mitarbeiter Gottes am Evangelium Christi« (1 Thess 3,2). Endlich kann auch in absoluter Weise vom »Evangelium« gesprochen werden (2,4). Neben »Evangelium« wird ohne Unterschied vom »Wort Gottes« (2,13 zweimal) und vom »Wort des Herrn« (1,8)[13] geredet. Auch hier begegnet absoluter Gebrauch (1,6). Die Erwählung Gottes durch das Evangelium ist also worthaft. Ebenso entscheidend ist die Beobachtung, daß der beschriebene Gebrauch von »Evangelium« und »Wort« nur in 1 Thess 1,2–2,16; 3,2 begegnet, also im thematischen Umfeld der missionarischen Ursprungssituation des Glaubens der Thessalonicher. Darum ist die These aufzustellen: »Evangelium« ist Begriff der Missionssprache.

Die Adressaten dieses Evangeliums sind die Heiden, die den einen und wahren Gott bisher nicht kannten (4,5), die jedoch durch diese Botschaft zu ihm und weg von den Göttern umkehren sollen (1,9). Ihre Umkehr ist als Annahme des Evangeliums Glaube an Gott (1,8). Damit werden sie versetzt aus der Bestimmtheit durch den endzeitlichen Zorn (1,10; 5,9) und dem Verderben (5,3), also aus der objektiven Hoffnungslosigkeit

---

[13] 1 Thess 4,15 ist das Wort des Herrn ein Einzelwort (vgl. Joh 21,23), also nicht Ausdruck der Verkündigung überhaupt. Im Sinne der Verkündigung ist diese Wendung bei Paulus singulär, jedoch in Apg 8,25; 12,24; 13,49; 15,35f. usw. als Missionsbegriff für die nachpaulinische Zeit belegt. Liegt 1 Thess 1,8 vielleicht Septuagintasprache vor wie 4,6 (vgl. Ps 94,1); 5,2 (vgl. Am 5,18.20; Joel 2,1 usw.), so daß in allen drei Fällen mit dem Herrn auf Gott verwiesen wird? Jedenfalls folgen in 1,8f. »euer Glaube zu Gott« und die Umkehr »zu Gott«.

(4,13), in die neue Bestimmung endzeitlicher Heilserwartung (1,10; 5,9). Die, die Gott bisher nicht kannten (vgl. 4,5), kennen ihn nun. Darum sind sie vorbereitet für den Tag des Herrn. Sie halten nichts von gängigen Friedens- und Sicherheitsparolen, die in Unkenntnis des nahen Endes abgegeben werden (5,2 f.); sie sind wachsam und nüchtern, angetan mit dem Panzer des Glaubens und der Liebe und mit dem Helm der Hoffnung und des Heils (5,6–8).

Der Zusammenhang von Erwählung und Evangelium wäre unvollständig beschrieben, käme nicht noch die damit verwobene Existenz des Apostels zur Sprache. Mag Paulus im Präskript auf den Aposteltitel verzichten, mag er in 2,7.11 zur Kennzeichnung seines Verhältnisses zur Gemeinde lieber aus der elterlichen Beziehung zu Kindern Metaphern wählen, er weiß sich dennoch grundsätzlich ermächtigt, »mit dem Gewicht als (einer der) Apostel Christi aufzutreten« (2,7; vgl. 2 Kor 11,13), wie er – wohl in antiochenischer Sprache – formulieren kann. Diese Ermächtigung beruht darauf, daß er »von Gott als tauglich befunden wurde, mit dem Evangelium betraut zu werden« (2,4), so daß nun dies Evangelium sein Evangelium ist (1,5). Diese Tauglichkeitsprüfung ist natürlich keine Feststellung seiner Qualitäten, sondern göttlicher Akt erwählender Approbation, der Ruf der Gnadenwahl Gottes in den apostolischen Dienst (1 Kor 15,9 f.; Gal 1,15), der dem Inhalte nach Betrauung mit dem Evangelium an die Völker ist. So wie einst Gott Israel mit seinen Worten betraute (Röm 3,2), so betraut er Paulus zu diesem speziellen Dienst. Dieses Betrautsein mit dem Evangelium an die Unbeschnittenen (Gal 2,7) war auf dem Apostelkonvent von Petrus und den anderen Aposteln für die Person des Paulus ausdrücklich festgestellt worden. In diesem Sinn ist er gesamtkirchlich einer der anerkannten Apostel Christi. Das Evangelium, durch das Gott die Völker in seine Erwählung ruft, ist also gebunden an den Apostel, als dem in besonderer Weise berufenen Boten Christi.

*

Die Adressaten des Evangeliums nehmen allerdings nicht einfach eine neue Belehrung über Gott und die Endzeit, also eine neue religiöse Orientierung, zur Kenntnis, sondern sie werden mit der Botschaft durch den heiligen Geist bestimmt: »Denn unser Evangelium an euch geschah nicht nur mit Worten, sondern in Kraft, im heiligen Geist ...« (1,5). Im Wort wirkt der heilige Geist zur Annahme der Botschaft in Freude (1,6). Wer das Evangelium annimmt, nimmt nicht ein Menschenwort an, sondern das Wort Gottes, das sich an den Glaubenden als wirksam erweist (2,13). Diese Wirksamkeit bezieht sich sicherlich auch auf die inhaltliche Überzeugungskraft des Wortes selbst (1,6 f.; 2,13). Aber es wäre vorschnell, sie auf diesen Gesichtspunkt zu beschränken. Davor sollten schon solche Aussagen des Apostels warnen, die wie 2 Kor 12,12; Gal 3,5; Röm

15,18f. von Zeichen, Wundern und Krafttaten reden, die das paulinische Evangelium begleiten. Ebenso »wirken« Gott bzw. der Geist durch die Charismen in der Gemeinde (1 Kor 12,6.11). Weil Paulus auf dem Apostelkonvent darlegen kann, wie Gott durch ihn unter den Völkern »wirkte«, so wie er bisher durch Petrus unter den Juden »gewirkt« hatte (Gal 2,7f.), kommt sein gesetzesfreies Evangelium zur Anerkennung. In seiner antiochenischen Zeit wird Paulus ekstatisch in den dritten Himmel versetzt (2 Kor 12,1ff.). Vor diesem Hintergrund muß man die Aufforderung des Apostels in 1 Thess 5,19–21: »Den Geist unterdrückt nicht! Prophetie verachtet nicht! Prüfet alles, das Gute behaltet!« so deuten, daß er solche pneumatischen Phänomene bewußt fördern will. Die Endzeitgemeinde ist eine geistgeleitete, – wenn man so will – enthusiastische Größe. Auch angesichts der pneumatischen Turbulenzen in Korinth wird Paulus den Geist nicht einschränken, den geistlichen Reichtum vielmehr loben, jedoch die Korinther aus dem Himmel der Ekstase in die irdische Wirklichkeit der Gemeinde und der Welt zurückrufen.

Allerdings ist auch mit diesen Hinweisen auf das pneumatische Wirken Gottes in der Gemeinde das Entscheidende am Geist noch nicht in den Blick gekommen. Dieses wird erst thematisiert, wenn die Erwählung als endzeitliche Neukonstitution der glaubenden Personen begriffen wird. So sind die »von Gott geliebten Brüder« (1,4) durch die Geistbegabung unmittelbar »von Gott belehrt«, ihre »Heiligung« (4,3.4.7) als Bruderliebe zu vollziehen (4,8f.). Dabei wird dieses das Innere der Glaubenden verwandelnde Geschehen, aufgrund dessen sie zur Liebe befähigt und berufen sind, beschrieben als Einlösung der endzeitlichen Geistbegabung, wie sie Ezechiel (Ez 36,26f.) verheißt. Also: durch die Erwählung aufgrund des Evangeliums, in dem der Geist wirkt, löst Gott die durch die alttestamentliche Prophetie erwartete schöpferische Veränderung des menschlichen Innern am Ende der Tage ein. Was z. B. in 1QS 4,20–22 erst für die ausstehende Endzeit noch erwartet wird, ist für Paulus schon endzeitliche Gegenwart. Es besteht kein Zweifel, daß dieser Zusammenhang, den Paulus hier auf der Linie von Evangelium und Geistbegabung beschreibt, im frühen Urchristentum sonst durch den Zusammenhang von Taufe, Geist und Neuschöpfung präsent ist. Diese Taufauffassung wird man, da sie gerade von Paulus als vorgegebene Tradition benutzt wird, primär dem antiochenisch-syrischen Raum zuweisen dürfen (vgl. 1 Kor 7,19; 12,13f.; 2 Kor 5,17; Gal 3,26–28; 5,6; 6,15)[14]. Daß Paulus dabei von der Missionsbotschaft her denkt, mag nicht zuletzt damit zusammenhängen, daß er sich ausdrücklich zur Verkündigung des Evangeliums und nicht zum Taufen berufen wußte (1 Kor 1,17; indirekt 1 Thess 2,1–12). So spiegelt der 1 Thess diesen Grundentscheid klar wider: Taufe und Her-

[14] Vgl. dazu J. Becker: Geschöpfliche Wirklichkeit als Thema des Neuen Testaments, in: Schöpfungsglaube und Umweltverantwortung, zur Sache, 1985, 45–84.

renmahl sind in ihm ganz zugunsten der Wortverkündigung zurückgedrängt.

Aber wie er z. B. in 2 Kor 5,11–6,2 unter Vorrangstellung des Wortes von der Versöhnung dieses Verkündigungsgeschehens mit Hilfe seinshaft-eschatologischer Taufaussagen interpretieren kann[15], so deutet er in 1 Thess 5,1–11 die Erwählung durch das Evangelium (5,9f. ist von Kp 1–2 her zu verstehen) durch analoge seinshafte Aussagen (v. 4–8), deren Wurzelboden die eben skizzierte Tauftradition ist: Christen sind Söhne des Lichtes und des Tages. Sie sind nicht mehr in Finsternis, nicht mehr Nacht oder Finsternis. Verwandte Seinsaussagen mit Abgrenzung zu »den Übrigen« (v. 6), d. h. Ungetauften, sind ebenfalls für Tauftraditionen wie Gal 3,26–28 usw. typisch. Das neue Sein kann z. B. ebenfalls Gal 3,27; Röm 13,12 durch die Gewandsymbolik erfaßt werden: Was der Mensch (dauerhaft) angezogen hat, ist Ausdruck seines Wesens. Man ist, was man trägt: Wer Christus angezogen hat, ist neue Kreatur. So wird 1 Thess 5,8 in Aufgriff von Jes 59,17 der Christ in der Dienstkleidung eines Wachsoldaten beschrieben, um sein durch den Geist neubegründetes Sein zu kennzeichnen, indem – sicherlich bewußt – die Trias Glaube, Liebe, Hoffnung aus dem Anfang des Briefes (1,3) Verwendung findet: »Wir aber, die wir des Tages sind, wollen nüchtern sein, (sind wir doch) angezogen mit dem Panzer des Glaubens und der Liebe und mit dem Helm der Hoffnung und des Heils.« Erwählung erweist sich als endzeitliche Neuschöpfung, sie ist endzeitliche Existenz in Glaube, Liebe und Hoffnung. Wie die Heiligung Gabe und Aufgabe ist, so ist diese Trias schützender Mantel und persönlicher Existenzvollzug in einem. Endlich kann in den Taufaussagen die Sohnschaft das neue Sein beschreiben (Gal 3,26). Ob die Rede von den »Söhnen des Lichts« und den »Söhnen des Tages« (1 Thess 5,5) eine Variante dazu darstellt, bedingt durch die kontrastierende Sprache der Erwählung, die in Licht und Finsternis klassifiziert? Jedenfalls wird man noch – über 1 Thess 5,1–11 hinausblickend – konstatieren dürfen, daß die für Paulus typische Ausdrucksweise »in Christus« (2,14; 4,16; 5,18) und »im Herrn« (3,8; 4,1; 5,12) eine im 1 Thess schon erstaunlich festgeprägte Verwendung findet und nicht zuletzt ebenfalls in dieser Tauftradition (Gal 3,28; 2 Kor 5,17) einen Haftpunkt hat. Daß sich auch in diesem Fall Erwählungsaussagen und Tauftradition verbinden können, beweist 1 Kor 1,26–31. So ergibt sich: Im 1 Thess ist Erwählung als endzeitliche Neuschöpfung durch den im Evangelium wirkenden Geist verstanden.

Aufgrund dieser Einsicht kann nun besser gewürdigt werden, daß Paulus im 1 Thess als Regelfall voraussetzt, die Erwählten, die dann noch leben, werden bei der nahen Ankunft des Herrn mit diesem – so wie sie

[15] Vgl. U. Schnelle: Gerechtigkeit und Christusgegenwart, GTA 24, 1983, 47–50.

sind – immer zusammensein (4,17; 5,10). Man muß dazu zunächst beachten: Paulus spricht – obwohl dazu 4,13 ff. Gelegenheit gewesen wäre – nirgends davon, daß Christen sich für das Endheil einer Verwandlung unterziehen müßten (so 1 Kor 15,51). Gesichtspunkte wie dieser, daß »Fleisch und Blut die Gottesherrschaft nicht ererben können« (1 Kor 15,50), sind ihm im 1 Thess noch fremd. Daraus ist zu folgern: Die nie mehr endende (»immer« 4,17) Gemeinschaft mit dem Kyrios ist durch die den Glaubenden seinshaft neu konstituierende Erwählung bereits anthropologisch so vorbereitet, daß die grundlegende und notwendige Veränderung des Menschen bereits geschehen ist. Oder, was dasselbe meint: Gott gibt im Evangelium seinen neuschaffenden Geist endgültig. Gerade auch in diesem Sinn ist die Ekklesia Endzeitgemeinde, gelten die Erwählten als dem Gericht enthoben, ist die kurze Zeit zwischen Erwählung und Parusie unter dem Doppelaspekt der göttlichen Treue (5,24) und der menschlichen Bewährung in der Heiligung (4,1 ff.) gesehen. Vielleicht erklärt es sich von hier aus auch, daß Paulus im 1 Thess den Begriff des »(ewigen) Lebens« (noch) nicht verwendet, offenbar erst seit 1 Kor 15 von »diesem Leben« in stillschweigender Abgrenzung vom zukünftigen redet (v. 19) und dann 2 Kor 5,4 auf dem Hintergrund der 1 Kor 15 neu erarbeiteten Unterscheidung vom Leben vor dem Tod und vom Leben nach der Vernichtung des Todes vom zukünftigen Endzustand als »Leben« spricht, das dann das Sterbliche verschlingen wird. Diesen Zusammenhang vor Augen, wird man fragen müssen, ob die Korinther nicht Paulus nur etwas enthusiastischer ausgelegt haben, als er zugestehen konnte, so daß die zur theologia crucis umgearbeitete Erwählungstheologie (vgl. besonders 1 Kor 1,18–31 unter Beachtung der voranstehenden Verse 1,4–9 und 1 Kor 15) nicht nur die Korinther zur Korrektur veranlaßte, sondern auch Paulus selbst zwang, seine Theologie neu zu bedenken.

Diese Neukonstitution des Menschen darf nun allerdings nicht naturalistisch mißverstanden werden. So sicher das neue Sein eine grundlegende, seinshafte Veränderung des Menschen in seinem Personzentrum beinhaltet, so sicher macht jedenfalls Paulus deutlich, daß hierbei personale Gesichtspunkte im Vordergrund stehen: Nicht grundlos ist für ihn das neue Sein in die Linie von Evangelium und Glaube (1,4–9) eingefügt, so daß die Christen als »die Glaubenden« bezeichnet werden (1,7; 2,10.13) und die Hoffnung aus dem Glaubensstand begründet ist (4,14). Die schöpferische Kraft des Geistes, der im und mit dem Evangelium wirkt, verändert den Menschen nur ausnahmslos über den Glauben. Auch ist es nicht zufällig, daß der Geist den Menschen als Handelnden anspricht, indem er Bruderliebe lehrt und Willigkeit zur Liebe schafft (4,9 f.). Endlich ist mit der glaubenden Annahme des Evangeliums die Neukonstitution nicht unverbindliche Gegenwart, die nicht verpflichtet. Paulus weiß vielmehr sehr genau von einem Doppelaspekt der christlichen Existenz, dem Aspekt des erstmaligen »Zugangs« (1,9; 2,1) und der immer wieder geltenden Aufforderung »Gott zu gefallen« und darin »zuzunehmen« (4,1.10). So kennt er den Glauben als Annahme der Botschaft (1,8) wie auch die Glaubenstreue (3,2.5–7). Er weiß, daß Glaube, Liebe und Hoffnung Dauerbestimmungen im Existenzvollzug zu sein haben (1,3; 5,8). Heiligung ist die Bestimmung (4,7; vgl. 3,13) und der Vollzug (4,3f.) der Berufung während der Zeit, in der man noch auf den kommenden Herrn wartet. Evangelium und Geist, die den Menschen verändern, verändern ihn also im Status des Glaubens und in der Heiligung. Den zur Endzeitgemeinde Berufenen ist dieser Stand zwar kraft der Treue Gottes zugesichert (5,23f.), aber ebenso selbstverständlich gehört die normative Beanspruchung der menschlichen Existenz zum Wesen der Erwählung (4,1–12). Der Geist und das Ich des Menschen gehen also eine solche intime und enge Verbindung ein, daß er selbst und alle seine Lebensäußerungen neu sind.

Damit ist schon der Ansatz der Paränese im 1 Thess in den Blick geraten. Sie ist Vollzug der neu konstituierten Existenz im Glauben. Erwählt durch das Evangelium (1,4f.) und – wie Paulus wenige Jahre später in alter traditioneller Sprache sagen kann – geheiligt im einmaligen Taufakt (1 Kor 6,11), so ist die Zugehörigkeit zu Gott in der Endzeitgemeinde und die Trennung von der Welt vollzogen. Diese konstitutive Vorbedingung für die Erlangung der Soteria (1 Thess 5,9) ist Werk des Gottesgeistes, dessen Belehrung nun normativ die Glaubenden lenkt und sie zur Liebe treibt (4,8f.). Mahnung ist darum kein von außen an den Menschen herangetragenes Gesetz mehr, daß er sich durch Internalisierung erst zu eigen machen müßte, sondern ist Explikation der Geisterfahrung jedes Christen und dient der gemeinsamen fortschreitenden Einübung in der Liebe, die jeder in sich spürt (4,1f.8f.10): Heilig geworden, vollzieht man die Heiligung, womit das entscheidende Stichwort genannt ist, unter dem der Wandel steht (3,13; 4,3.4.7). Darum sind in diesem Zusammenhang das atl. Gesetz wie auch die Worte des Herrn keine selbständigen Normen. Die Forderung der Einehe (4,4) mag sachlich der alten Jesustradition entsprechen, die egoistische Vorteilsnahme dem Genossen gegenüber (4,6) mag sachlich auch im Alten Testament gerügt sein, entscheidend ist jedoch: »Gott hat uns (durch seine endzeitliche Gnadenwahl im Evangelium) nicht berufen zur Unreinheit sondern (zum Leben) in Heiligung« (4,7). Geistgeleitete Heilige müssen heilig leben.

Geordnet wird in der Mahnung vor allem das Verhältnis der Glieder der Endzeitgemeinde untereinander: Nicht Weltverantwortung, sondern Bruderliebe (4,9) ist die Grundbestimmung[16]. Das Außenverhältnis wird nur als Konfliktvermeidung durch Wohlanständigkeit beschrieben (4,12). Sollte eine Endzeitgemeinde, die allein sich aus dem allgemeinen göttli-

---

[16] Vgl. J. Becker: Feindesliebe – Nächstenliebe – Bruderliebe, ZEE 25 (1981) 10f.

chen Zorn herausgenommen weiß und nur noch auf das alsbaldige Kommen ihres Herrn wartet, um mit ihm immer zusammenzusein, sich anders orientieren?

*

Der Inhalt des Evangeliums ist soteriologisch ausgerichtet, betrifft die Rettung der Völker (2,16a) und muß vor allem konzentriert durch die Christologie bestimmbar sein, insofern das Evangelium als »Evangelium von Christus« bezeichnet wird (3,2). Wobei sowohl diese letzte Stelle (Timotheos ist »Mitarbeiter Gottes am Evangelium von Christus«) wie auch die erste (die in 2,15f. überhaupt typisierte Judenpolemik betreibt) keine Neuformulierungen des Apostels darstellen. Da weiter der Apostel »mit dem Evangelium betraut« ist (2,4) und sich dabei selbst zu den »Aposteln Christi« zählt (2,7), kann diese Aussage die christologische Bestimmung des Evangeliums bestätigen. Mehr ist durch die Danksagung 1,2–10 zu erfahren: Hier wird u. a. ausgeführt, daß die Thessalonicher das paulinische Evangelium (1,5) als Wort »angenommen« haben (1,6). Diese Annahme ist ihr Glaube (1,7), genauer »ihr Glaube an den Gott« (1,8), so daß Paulus seinen »Zugang« zu ihnen (1,9) durch die bekannte Kurzfassung des Inhaltes einer Heidenmissionspredigt (1,9f.) angeben kann[17]. Sie beschreibt die Hinwendung zu dem alleinigen Schöpfer und Richtergott[18], der Jesus von den Toten auferweckte, so daß dieser nun als sein Sohn erwartet werden kann, der vom kommenden Zorn errettet. Durch das paulinische Evangelium erwählt Gott also die Völker, indem er im Evangelium sich als lebendigen und wahren Gott und Weltenrichter zu Gehör bringt, der vor dem Endgericht seinen Sohn von den Toten auferweckte, so daß dieser nun Rettung im sonst ausweglosen Gericht sein kann.

Diese Weise, das Evangelium durch geprägte Tradition zu bestimmen, ist Paulus auch sonst geläufig, so daß man annehmen darf, Paulus war solche »Definition« sehr früh nach seiner Berufung vertraut. Die individuelle und biographisch besondere Berufung des Apostels ist eine Berufung unter dasjenige Evangelium, das allgemein bei allen Christen dasselbe ist. So versteht es Paulus selbst, wenn er 1 Kor 15,1ff. – also zeitlich im nächsten Dokument seiner Korrespondenz nach dem 1 Thess – nicht nur dies, sondern überhaupt die Beobachtungen zu den sprachlichen Stich-

---

[17] Vgl. zur Diskussion: G. Friedrich: Ein Tauflied hellenistischer Judenchristen, 1 Thess 1,9f.; ThZ 21 (1965) 502–516; Cl. Bussmann: Themen der paulinischen Missionspredigt auf dem Hintergrund der spätjüdisch-hellenistischen Missionsliteratur, EHS.T 3, 1971, 38–56; J. Becker: Auferstehung im Urchristentum StB 82, 1976, 32–41; T. Holtz: »Euer Glaube an Gott«, in: Die Kirche des Anfangs (FS H. Schürmann) 1977, 459–488.

[18] Es ist vorausgesetzt, daß die Gottesaussagen in v. 9b sprachliche Signale für diese Doppelaussage sind, vgl. dazu Cl. Bussmann (Anm. 17) 174–186.

worten in 1 Thess 1,2–10 bestätigt. Spricht er doch hier von dem Evangelium, das er den Korinthern verkündigte, das sie annahmen, durch das sie gerettet werden und das er selbst empfangen hat, um es dann mit einer geprägten Doppelformel zum Heilssinn des Geschickes Jesu Christi inhaltlich zu beschreiben. Ganz analog verfährt er im Präskript des Römerbriefes (Röm 1,1–7)[19]. Man wird also davon ausgehen dürfen, daß 1 Thess 1,9f. im Sinne des Apostels geeignet ist, den Inhalt des Evangeliums im Kern zu erfassen. Darum lohnt es sich, bei diesem Text noch etwas zu verweilen.

Dabei soll es nicht zur Aufgabe gemacht werden, die Mischung von paulinischer Diktion und typischer Formulierung abermals zu entwirren. Es reicht hier die Feststellung, daß der Sache nach Paulus so in Thessaloniki missioniert hat und auch den anderen Gemeinden (1,9a!) diese Art der Missionspredigt bekannt war. Die Umkehrforderung angesichts der Nähe des kommenden Zorns, mit der v. 9b beginnt, hat über Johannes den Täufer Eingang in die christliche Verkündigung gefunden (Mt 3,7–12 par). Umkehren sollen danach die Israeliten, damit sie dem Zorn des Gottes Abrahams entgehen. Jesus übernimmt diese an der Gerichtsandrohung orientierte Umkehrpredigt (z. B. Lk 13,1–5). Jedoch ist sie nicht mehr das Zentrum seiner Botschaft. Er wie vielleicht auch der Täufer lassen dabei den Menschensohn Vollstrecker des Gerichtes sein (z. B. Lk 17,24.26–30 par; Mt 3,11 par). Jesus bestimmt jedoch die Gegenwart vorrangig durch die nahe Gottesherrschaft, die den Umkehrenden jetzt schon Heil zuspricht (Lk 6,20f. par.; 11,2–4 par.; 11,20 usw.). So ruft er – zugespitzt – nicht unter das Mosegesetz, sondern unter die Güte des Schöpfers[20].

Die frühe judenchristliche Gemeinde glaubte Jesus aufgrund seiner Auferstehung zum alsbald kommenden Menschensohn eingesetzt (1 Kor 16,22) und richtete daraufhin die Bußpredigt in veränderter Form an Israel. Diese wird vor allem neu gestaltet durch die Verchristlichung des deuteronomistischen Geschichtsbildes, so daß nun Israel speziell wegen der Tötung Jesu unter die Gerichtsandrohung gestellt wird[21]. Auch das Geschick der christlichen Israelboten wird dabei integriert. Buße ist Umkehr zum schuldhaft getöteten Jesus, der als Endrichter in Bälde kommt.

---

[19] Zwei weitere Beispiele der inhaltlichen Bestimmung des Evangeliums durch geprägte Aussagen kann man, etwas indirekter in ihrer Art, finden: In dem geprägten Text Röm 4,24f. geht es um die Zurechnung der Gerechtigkeit, die nach 1,14–17 Inhalt des Evangeliums ist. In Gal 1,1b.4 beschreibt Paulus Gottes Heilshandeln formelhaft, das dann 1,6–9 als Evangelium zur Sprache kommt.

[20] Vgl. zu Johannes und Jesus: J. Becker: Johannes der Täufer und Jesus von Nazareth, BSt 63, 1972.

[21] Vgl. zur Diskussion: M.-L. Gubler: Die frühesten Deutungen des Todes Jesu, OBO 15, 1977, 10–94.

Mit der Heidenmission, wie sie in Antiochia unter Mitwirkung des Paulus begann, muß sich diese Umkehrpredigt Veränderungen gefallen lassen, richtete sie sich doch nun nicht mehr an Israel, mit dem man denselben Gott verehrte, aber über Jesu Geschick und seine Bedeutung zerstritten war, sondern an Nichtjuden, die der heidnischen Götterwelt anhingen und an Jesu Tod unbeteiligt waren. Der Hellenen Schuld mußte vielmehr beschrieben werden als Perversion der Religion und des Ethos (Röm 1,18–32). Nun kannte die hellenistische Synagoge längst vor der christlichen Heidenmission die Umkehrpredigt an Heiden in zweifacher Gestalt: Einmal als nichteschatologisch motivierte Umkehrpredigt weg von den Göttern zu dem allein wahren Gott mit den Folgen der Eingliederung des Lebens unter das Gesetz des Mose. Das Ziel ist dabei die Inkorporierung in die Synagoge durch Beschneidung (illustratives Beispiel: JA). Zum zweiten als eschatologische Umkehrpredigt unter Aufkündigung der Vielgötterei und Lasterhaftigkeit angesichts des einen Schöpfers und Weltenrichters, um so dem baldigen Gericht zu entgehen und die Zeit der Langmut Gottes als Chance der Rettung zu ergreifen (z. B. OrSib Prooemium, Buch III–IV). Dieses zweite Modell griffen die Antiochener auf, wie Paulus, ihr Kronzeuge, mit Röm 1,18–2,29 belegt. Sie mußten die vorgegebene Umkehrpredigt an Israel und diesen Predigttyp nur in folgender Weise aufeinander abstimmen: Gott, den man neu erfahren hatte als den, der Jesus von den Toten auferweckte, blieb der eine Gott, der als Schöpfer und Richter im Gegensatz zu den Göttern und dem Leben unter ihnen stand. Jesus wurde kraft seiner Auferweckung der alsbald kommende Retter angesichts des göttlichen Gerichtes. Da die Synagoge als der Ort der Gesetzespredigt von den antiochenischen Christen indessen wegen des Streites um das Gesetz verlassen war, fehlt Mose in dieser Predigt absichtlich: Christus rettet, nicht der Gesetzesweg. Damit ist das Doppelthema aus 1 Thess 1,9b–10 als ein geschlossener Zusammenhang in seiner geschichtlichen Entstehung erklärt. Zugleich kann festgestellt werden: Die beiden Themen, das Angebot zur Umkehr wie die Aufrichtung der Hoffnung auf Christus, die sich wie zwei Seiten einer Medaille zueinander verhalten, sind das Evangelium, wie es Paulus nach dem 1 Thess versteht. In diesem Schema konnte der Aufweis der Schuld der Juden am Tod Jesu, wie er die Israelpredigt bestimmte, keinen Platz mehr haben. Aber es konnte daraus eine Anklage gegen die Juden vor heidenchristlichem Auditorium werden, wobei die Juden nun auch als die gelten mußten, die das Evangelium für die Heiden behinderten. Aufgefüllt mit typischer hellenistisch-römischer Judenpolemik und im Horizont des nahen Gerichtes belassen, ist 1 Thess 2,15f. dafür Zeuge. Im Blick auf diese theologiegeschichtliche Entwicklung sind also 1 Thess 1,9b–10 und 2,15f. gar nicht so fern voneinander.

Die typische Heidenmissionspredigt eingangs des 1 Thess akzentuierte vor allem die futurische Retterfunktion Jesu. Dies harmoniert nicht von ungefähr mit der futurischen Ausrichtung der Berufungsaussagen im 1 Thess. Daß diese futurisch-christologische Aussage vorrangig für das christologische Konzept des 1 Thess ist, belegt der Brief auch sonst: Kein literarisches Zeugnis des Urchristentums ist so konzentriert auf die Parusie des Kyrios ausgerichtet wie der 1 Thess. Thematisch beherrscht sie nicht nur die beiden Abschnitte 4,13–18 und 5,1–11, die ausdrücklich die nahe Parusie des Herrn zum Inhalt haben, vielmehr blitzt diese Hoffnung ebenso gleich eingangs in der Danksagung auf (1,3.10) wie in dem abschließenden Segenswunsch (5,23f.). Dazwischen stehen weitere Hinweise auf sie wie leuchtende Signale (2,19; 3,13). Ohne Zweifel belegen diese Stellen einhellig, wie stark die Verkündigung von dieser Hoffnung bestimmt ist und wie der Ausdruck »Parusie des Kyrios« indessen ein feststehender Begriff geworden ist. Daß er in dieser Funktion die Erwartung des Gottesreiches abgelöst hat, kann man an 2,12 studieren: Nach dieser mit typischer Selbstverständlichkeit formulierten Stelle beruft Gott »zu seinem Reich und zu seiner Herrlichkeit«. So sicher diese Aussage nicht ohne den Wurzelboden jesuanischer Gottesreichsbotschaft erklärt werden kann und also belegt, daß auch die antiochenische Gemeinde diese Jesustradition einmal pflegte, so deutlich ist auch, daß indessen die Rede von der Parusie des Herrn diese Aussageform verdrängt hat (vgl. nur 2,12 mit 3,13). Diese sprachliche Neubestimmung der Hoffnung ist erklärbar: Seit der Ostererfahrung erwartete die Gemeinde den auferweckten Herrn als personalisierten Inbegriff des von Jesu angekündigten Gottesreiches zunächst in Gestalt der Menschensohnchristologie (1 Kor 16,22; vgl. 1 Thess 1,10), sodann im griechischen Sprachbereich als Kyriologie, so daß Formulierungen wie »immer mit dem Herrn zusammensein« (1 Thess 4,17) oder »mit ihm leben« (5,10) zum Hoffnungsinhalt schlechthin wurden.

Dabei lassen sich Differenzen in der Funktion Gottes und des Kyrios erkennen. Damit soll nicht nur auf die vorherrschende »subordinatianische« Anlage der Christologie überhaupt verwiesen werden, wie sie etwa auch für die anderen Paulusbriefe gilt, sondern speziell auf den Umstand, daß Gott als Schöpfer und Herr der Welt ihr Richter ist (1,9f.), der Kyrios jedoch der endzeitliche Retter derer, die Gott durch das Evangelium erwählt hat (1,4f.10; 2,12f.19f.; 4,13–18; 5,9f.23f.)[22]. Der Weltbezug ist also durch die Gottesaussagen gegeben: Zu dem einen Gott muß sich der

[22] Nach 2,19 wird der Kyrios das paulinische Missionswerk beurteilen, aber dies ist eine Belobigung unter der Voraussetzung, dem allgemeinen Gericht enthoben zu sein. Falls in 4,6 Jesus als Kyrios gemeint sein sollte (vgl. dagegen Anm. 13), geht es um Züchtigung durch den Herrn vor der Parusie, ohne daß der Status der Erwählung tangiert ist (vgl. W. H. Schmidt–J. Becker: Zukunft und Hoffnung, KTB 1014, 1981, 142). Falls endlich der Tag des Herrn (5,2) Jesu Tag meint (vgl. dagegen Anm. 13), dann ist so im Blick auf die positive Hoffnung der Gemeinde gesprochen und nach 5,9f. auszulegen.

Nichtchrist bekehren (1,9), so daß er zum Glauben an ihn kommt (1,8). Ihn kennen die Völker nicht (4,5), ihm können die Juden nicht gefallen (2,15). Unter seinem Zorn steht die Menschheit (1,10; 2,16; 5,9). Vom Kyrios Jesus fehlen analoge Aussagen. Natürlich wird man es nicht überbewerten dürfen, daß in einem so kleinen Brief keine auch sonst bei Paulus seltene christologische Schöpfungsmittleraussage begegnet (vgl. 1 Kor 8,6) und daß die Herrenstellung des Kyrios über die mythischen Repräsentanten der Welt, wie sie der Philipperhymnus beschreibt (Phil 2,10f.; vgl. auch 1 Kor 15,20–28), nicht ausgesagt ist. Jedoch darf nicht unbeachtet bleiben, daß in jedem Fall die strenge Konzentration der Christologie auf die soteriologische Funktion gegenüber der durch das Evangelium erwählten Endzeitgemeinde eindeutig und offenbar gewollt ist. Christus ist die Personifikation des Heilsangebotes im Evangelium Gottes, das allen Völkern gilt (2,16a), das aber nur dort seine Erwählungsaufgabe wahrnimmt, wo man zum Glauben kommt. Auch diese Funktion des Herrn wird in bestimmter Weise akzentuiert: Nirgends ist auch nur ansatzweise diese Heilsperson als präexistenter Sohn beschrieben, den der Vater sandte (z. B. Gal 4,4f.), auch nicht als die Erfüllung heilsgeschichtlicher Zusagen an das Gottesvolk. Alle christologischen Aussagen sind auf die Parusie gerichtet und von der Erwählung der Endzeitgemeinde für dieses Ereignis her zu verstehen. Darum begegnet Christologie vornehmlich und betont als Erwartung des kommenden Herrn. Tod (4,14; 5,10) und Auferstehung Jesu (1,10; 4,14) sind dieser Linie eingeordnet. Sie haben nicht wie z. B. schon im 1 Kor einen eigenständigen Sinn. Das Geschick Jesu dient vielmehr als Hilfe, Gesichtspunkte des Endheils zu beschreiben. Im übrigen ist längst nicht so häufig von diesem geredet wie von dem Umstand, daß die Endzeitgemeinde durch die Annahme des Evangeliums »im Herrn« (1,1; 3,8; 4,1; 5,12) bzw. »in Christus« (2,14; 5,18; vgl. 4,16) lebt und »durch den Herrn« (4,2) Mahnung erfährt, also jetzt schon im Heilsbereich des Kommenden lebt und auf ihn bezogen ist.

Im übrigen wird auch das Verhältnis Gottes zur Endzeitgemeinde vom Weltbezug Gottes unterschieden: Nur im ersten Zusammenhang ist Gott »Vater« (1,1.3; 3,11.13). Alle Stellen haben dabei in unmittelbarer Nachbarschaft eine Aussage zum Kyrios Jesus (Christus). Keine Stelle meint Gott als Vater der Welt (vgl. 1 Kor 8,6; 15,24; Phil 2,11) oder als Vater Jesu Christi. Bis auf den Beleg im Präskript reden alle von »unserem Vater«. Über die Entstehung dieser Paulus im 1 Thess schon längst geläufigen Aussage, kann man folgende Vermutungen anstellen: Sollten Röm 8,14–16; Gal 4,6 die besten Hinweise abgeben, dann gilt: Die Sohnschaft ist israelitischer Erwählungsbegriff (Röm 9,4). Christen werden durch den Empfang des Geistes zu Söhnen. So wird Gott ihr Vater[23],

[23] Man muß dabei die beliebte Redeweise der »Adoption« in die Sohnschaft zurückstellen: Die Sohnschaft ist als ein Sein beschrieben, verursacht durch den Empfang des schöpferi-

so daß er mit Abba angeredet werden kann. Das würde mit der Erwählungstheologie des 1 Thess gut harmonieren. Es fände auch eine Stütze in dem unpaulinischen, jedoch keineswegs spät zu datierenden Stück 2 Kor 6,14–7,1, wenn hier die Gemeinde geistlicher Tempel Gottes ist (v. 16), und dann in dem langen atl. Mischzitat Gott für sie als Vater (v. 18) da ist. Dieser Gesamtzusammenhang würde auch erklären, daß die Gemeindeglieder sich selbstverständlich als »Brüder« anreden (vgl. 1 Thess 1,4; 2,1.9.14; 4,1.6.10; 5,1.4.26f. usw.): Das neue Sein der Sohnschaft ordnet die Gemeinde als Bruderschaft.

*

Das theologische Konzept des 1 Thess wurde bisher beschrieben, ohne die geschichtlichen Antagonismen und Konkurrenzen zu Wort kommen zu lassen. Jedoch die Synagoge behindert das Evangelium (2,14–16) wie auch die Griechen dasselbe tun (2,14). Letztere können den kompromißlosen Monotheismus ohne Kult nicht verstehen (1,9; 4,5), haben für die enge Verbindung von Gottesverehrung und Ethos (4,1ff.) kaum Verständnis und können sich auch der Eschatologie nur mühsam nähern[24]. Auch die Erwählung ist trotz aller Öffnung zu den Völkern ein jüdisches Thema. Eben das war es ja: Diese anstößigen Auffälligkeiten waren ihnen immer noch eine fremde Welt, wenn auch ein bereits entschränktes Judentum. Da ging es der Synagoge anders: Sie konnte sich über den Monotheismus und den ethischen Ernst eigentlich freuen. Doch diese Christen hatten die Trias Vätergott, Bund, Gesetz durch das Evangelium ersetzt und in ihm Jesus Christus zur soteriologischen Zentralfigur erhoben. Eine Wahl zwischen dem Ethos aus dem Geist oder aus dem Gesetz fiel den Juden nicht schwer. Die Neufassung des Erwählungsgedankens war für sie ein übles Plagiat, das sie als Heilsvolk tief traf: Proselyten machen, wollten sie schon, aber selbst sich durch das Evangelium erst erwählen lassen, so daß Gesetz und Beschneidung bedeutungslos wurden, das konnte nicht ihre Sache sein! So war das Christentum für sie ein illegitimer Ableger ihrer Religion.

Beide Positionen können den Blick für die Eigenart des 1 Thess schärfen: Er ist ganz selbstverständlich heidenchristlich orientiert und vertritt diese Ausrichtung als geschlossene und in sich ruhende Position, die sich nicht mehr ständig direkt auf ihren ehemaligen jüdischen Ursprung bezieht und davon abgrenzt: Die Diskussion um das Gesetz und seine Geltung ist überhaupt kein Gegenstand der Erörterung mehr. Der Zwang,

---

schen Geistes der Sohnschaft. Zu analogen Seinsaussagen vgl.: 1 Kor 1,30; 6,11; Gal 3, 26–28 usw., sowie oben S. 89.

24 Man kann immerhin z. B. auf die OrSib verweisen oder auf Cicero, Ad Polybium de Consulatione I 1).

sich als legitime Fortsetzung israelitisch-heilsgeschichtlicher Erwählung zu verstehen, ist nirgends zu finden. Gottesaussagen, Christologie und Ekklesiologie bedürfen nicht der heilsgeschichtlichen Bestimmung. Man darf diese Feststellung und mögliche weitere nicht durch einen Verweis auf die Kürze und Zufälligkeit des Briefes relativieren, denn es geht nicht darum, ob Paulus im 1 Thess seine theologischen Gedanken vollständig entfaltet hat (Antwort: natürlich nicht), sondern um die Beobachtung, daß er imstande ist, die theologische Selbständigkeit des Heidenchristentums durch eine in Umrissen gut erkennbare, in sich geschlossene Position zu entfalten – und das so kurze Zeit nach dem Apostelkonvent. Kaum sind wesentlich mehr Jahre verflossen, seitdem die bis dahin ausschließlich judenchristliche Christenheit sich in Antiochia erstmals anschickte, getrennt von der Synagoge zu existieren und programmatisch Heidenmission zu betreiben. Mag man mit Recht die Rede des Paulus beim Zusammenstoß mit Petrus (Gal 2,11–21) mehr zu den Galatern gerichtet, als an der historischen Situation orientiert ansehen, der Paulus des 1 Thess konnte damals kaum anders reagieren, als Petrus zu widerstehen.

Und dennoch: Die Erwählungstheologie des 1 Thess trägt versteckt, ohne daß es auf ihrer Visitenkarte offen ausgedruckt ist, ein eigentümliches Verhältnis der Nähe und Distanz zum Judentum bei sich. Das wird sofort sprachlich deutlich: »Erwählung« (1,4) ist schon nach Ausweis von Röm 9,11; 11,5.7.28 für Paulus von Haus aus ein israelitischer Erwählungsbegriff. Daß Gottes Erwählung durch das Verb »rufen« beschrieben wird (1 Thess 1,12) und er der »Rufende« ist (5,24), ist Israel vor allem durch Deuterojesaja (vgl. nur Jes 45,3) bekannt. Auch »betrauen mit« (1 Thess 2,4) gehört nach Paulus selbst (Röm 3,2) zur Beschreibung israelitischer Erwählung. Die Erwählten heißen die von Gott »Geliebten« (1 Thess 1,4; vgl. Röm 10,28; PA 3,14) und sind untereinander Brüder (so z. B. TPatr passim). Ihr Erwählungsstand gründet in der Treue Gottes, die in der formelhaften Wendung »treu ist Gott, der ...« (1 Thess 5,24; vgl. noch 1 Kor 1,9; 10,13; 2 Kor 1,18) zur Geltung kommt und atl.-jüdische Vorgänger hat (Dtn 32,4; Jes 49,7; PsSal 14,1; 17,10). Daß es aber darum geht, Gott zu gefallen bzw. ihm nicht zu gefallen (2,4.15; 4,1), oder ihm zu dienen und ihm würdig zu wandeln (2,12), zu ihm umzukehren (1,9) und so seinem Zorn zu entgehen (1,9), muß nicht nochmals als jüdische Sprache nachgewiesen werden. Auch strukturell sind die Zusammenhänge zwischen dieser paulinischen Erwählungstheologie und vor allem der hellenistisch-jüdischen Synagoge gut erkennbar. Vor allem drei Grundpositionen seien aufgezählt: 1. Die Predigt von dem einen Gott, der Israel erwählt hat und die Völker als Proselyten hinzukommen läßt, aber der in den anderen die Verlorenen sieht (vgl. für den Diasporapharisäer Paulus: Röm 2,17–20; 3,2; 9,4). 2. Das Verständnis der Erwählung als Bund zum Leben und zugleich als Gehorsam (ebd.) im Gegensatz zum Ungehorsam der Völker in Götzendienst und Lasterhaftigkeit (Röm

1,18–32). 3. Die Verantwortung aller vor Gott in seinem kommenden Gericht, dem niemand entrinnt (Röm 2,1–11), in dem aber das erwählte Volk nicht verlorengehen kann (Röm 9,6a; 11,1f.26).

Diese drei Grundpositionen bergen nun aber zugleich bei näherem Zusehen die Differenzen in sich, ohne daß diese noch explizit gemacht werden: 1. Entscheidend ist dabei natürlich die christologische Orientierung des 1 Thess, d. h. die Ausrichtung am kommenden Herrn, der durch sein Geschick von Kreuz und Auferstehung bestimmt ist. Da dies eine Veranstaltung Gottes ist, ist damit Gott selbst neu definiert. Der Gott der Väter wird zu dem Gott in Christus. 2. Bedeutsam ist sodann das neue Geschichtsverständnis: Der im Evangelium Angesprochene ordnet sich nicht in eine lange Heilsgeschichte ein, sondern orientiert sich am nahen Gericht, am kommenden Herrn, am Geist der Endzeit. Das weitest zurückliegende Ereignis von Bedeutung ist das Geschick Jesu, das aber gar nicht Vergangenheit ist, vielmehr durch die gegenwärtige Bestimmtheit »im Herrn« Gegenwart. Der Weltenrichter sammelt unmittelbar vor dem Endgericht die Erwählten, das ist entscheidend. 3. Wichtig ist sodann die neue Option für die Adressaten der Erwählung. Das Evangelium ergeht unmittelbar an alle Völker. Die Partikularerwählung Israels ist kein Orientierungspunkt mehr. Man muß nicht zum Abrahambund, zum Sinaigesetz hinzukommen, sondern ist durch den Geist unmittelbar erwählt – vorbei am Gesetz, das nicht mehr erwähnt wird[25]. 4. Auch das Ethos der Erwählten ist neu begriffen: Man liebt nicht die Menschen, indem man sie zur Tora bringt und damit zu den ersten der drei Dinge, auf denen die Welt steht (PAboth 1,2.12). Der Mensch ist nicht mehr geschaffen, um die Tora auszüben und sich so das Leben der zukünftigen Welt zu erwerben (PAboth 2,7f.). Vielmehr schafft der Geist den Menschen so neu, daß sein Handeln in der Bruderliebe besteht und er mit der Parusie des Herrn immer mit ihm zusammenleben kann. 5. Das Selbstverständnis des Judentums beruht auf der Trias Väterbund – Gesetz – Leben, das des Christentums nach dem 1 Thess auf der Trias Glaube – Liebe – Hoffnung.

*

[25] Paulus geht von dem Ergebnis des Apostelkonvents aus, d. h. die Beschneidungsforderung und damit das Gesetz gilt für die Heidenchristen nicht. Auch der Kampf aus Gal 2,11 ff. ist für Paulus selbstverständlich zuungunsten des Judenchristentums entschieden. Die Auflage aus Apg 15,28f. im Sinne von Lev 17f. ist für ihn undiskutabel. Das jüdische Reinheitsgesetz, das auch gerade die Diaspora prägte (vgl. Dan 1,8ff.; Tob 1,10–12; Josephus, Antiquitates 4,137; 13,243; JA 7,1 usw.), ist irrelevant für seine Gemeinden. So kann er z. B. den ursprünglich rituell-kultisch gemeinten Gegensatz von Unreinheit und Heiligung (1 Thess 4,7) ganz selbstverständlich unkultisch gebrauchen. Wenig später wird der Apostel in 1 Kor 8; 10 für einen so freien Umgang mit dem Opferfleisch eintreten, wie sonst niemand im Urchristentum.

In Umrissen ist damit die Erwählungstheologie des 1 Thess skizziert. Es hat sich gezeigt, daß dieser erste Brief des Apostels aus sich heraus so gedeutet werden kann, daß er eine in sich geschlossene Theologie enthält. Mag man durch traditionsgeschichtliche Analyse und historische Rückschlüsse aus dem corpus Paulinum und der Apg die theologiegeschichtliche Entwicklung von Ostern bis zum Apostelkonvent noch durch einige weitere Aspekte aufhellen können, in jedem Fall bietet der 1 Thess als erste ausführliche literarische Hinterlassenschaft des Urchristentums die unschätzbare Möglichkeit, ein ganzes theologisches Konzept quellenmäßig unmittelbar zu erkennen. Aus diesem Befund lassen sich Folgerungen ableiten.

Wenn der Antiochener Paulus im 1 Thess nicht so eigenständig geredet hat, daß er ganz atypisch für Antiochia wurde, vielmehr auch die Antiochener für ihre Heidenmission eine analoge Erwählungstheologie ihr eigen nannten, da zwischen Paulus und ihnen ein Geben und Nehmen stattfand, dann lassen sich Spuren dieser Theologie als Reflex antiochenischer Wirkung suchen. Solche Spuren sind aufweisbar: Kann man nicht 1 Petr 1,1–2,10; 5,10 als Fortentwicklung dieser Erwählungstheologie verstehen? Wie ja der 1 Petr überhaupt eher als Fortsetzung syrisch-antiochenischer Theologie deutbar ist als unter paulinischem Einfluß stehend. Doch wird man nicht z. B. auch an die erste Deutung der Parabel vom sog. ungerechten Richter und der Witwe in Lk 18,6–8a denken dürfen, wenn hier von den Auserwählten Gottes die Rede ist, die fortwährend (wie 1 Thess 5,17) zu ihm schreien und denen er alsbald Rettung zukommen lassen wird? Oder wie ist es um die Allegorie der Einladung zum Endheil in Mt 22,1–14 bestellt? Damit steht man vor der umfassenderen Frage, wieweit überhaupt synoptische Tradition aufgrund dieser Theologie neu interpretiert wurde.

Natürlich bedeutet dies auch für die Interpretation der Briefe des Apostels, daß der 1 Thess nur eine erste Stufe der paulinischen Entwicklung darstellen wird. Deutlich ist dies zunächst an der korinthischen Korrespondenz: Paulus setzt z. B. in 1 Kor 1,1–9 mit der theologischen Konzeption des 1 Thess ein. An 1 Kor 7 kann man z. B. dann sehr schön studieren, wie er die Erwählung zum Glied der Endzeitgemeinde bemüht, um konkrete Lebenspraxis zu klären. Doch viel bedeutsamer ist es, wie er 1 Kor 1,18–31 die Erwählungstheologie zur theologia crucis umprägt und diese so zugespitzte Auffassung dann für seine korinthische Korrespondenz überhaupt charakteristisch wird. Also wird die theologia crucis, in die die Erwählungstheologie aufgegangen ist, zum neuen ordnenden Rahmen der theologischen Äußerungen des Paulus. Auch im Gal und Röm ist das Thema der Erwählung mit seinen Ausführungen aus dem 1 Thess nicht einfach verschwunden (vgl. nur Gal 1,1–12; 5,8.13; Röm 1; 8), jedoch nun auf dem Hintergrund der theologia crucis als Rechtfertigungsbotschaft entfaltet. Natürlich muß in diesem Zusammenhang noch an

Röm 9–11 erinnert werden, wenn Paulus hier das Schicksal Israels von dem Erwählungsgedanken und der Rechtfertigungsbotschaft her neu und anders als 1 Thess 2,14–16 bedenkt. Damit sind die Folgerungen für die Interpretation der paulinischen Korrespondenz angedeutet. Wenn sich die Ergebnisse dieser Untersuchung zum 1 Thess als valide erweisen, ist eine entscheidende Basis gewonnen, Einblick in die Entwicklung der paulinischen Theologie zu nehmen.

The geographical and cultural origin of the Codex Bezae Cantabrigiensis: a survey of the *status quaestionis,* mainly from the palaeographical standpoint

by J. Neville Birdsall

(1 Bideford Drive, Selly Oak, Birmingham B29 6QG (England))

Heinz Greeven's revision of Huck's Synopsis bears witness to his text-critical interests. Those who have the privilege of personal knowledge will be aware that the evidence given there is based on first hand acquaintance with Greek manuscripts and with the versions each in its own tongue. He sets us an awesome example in undertaking, for instance, the study of Georgian, at an age when many other scholars have ceased to labour. His interest has been attested too in his regular participation within *Studiorum Novi Testamenti Societas* in the Seminar concerned with text-critical questions (for much of its life, with the Diatessaron in particular) of which I had the honour to be convenor for a number of years. The support and interest of Heinz Greeven in that Seminar were greatly valued by me throughout the years of my convenorship. I am accordingly happy to publish this paper, of which that Seminar heard the first draft, to honour Heinz and in the hope that it will further the study and understanding of one of the most ancient and most intriguing of the documents of the Greek New Testament.

The Codex Bezae Cantabrigiensis has been the focus of scholarly interest and investigation since the days of Beza himself. Its study up to the third decade of this century is well summarized in the work of J. H. Ropes[1]: while the views of the Latinist A. C. Clark[2], published shortly afterwards, provide an important argument for a contrary view.

Since these major studies, little has been produced: they were moreover within the context of the textual criticism of the Acts of the apostles, so that the preliminary questions of palaeography, codicology, language and origin, although dealt with in some detail, are not the major object of

[1] The Beginnings of Christianity. Part I. The Acts of the Apostles. Edited by F. J. Foakes Jackson and Kirsopp Lake. Vol. III. The Text of Acts. by James Hardy Ropes. London 1926.

[2] The Acts of the Apostles. A critical edition with introduction and notes on selected passages by Albert C. Clark. Oxford 1933.

the investigation. Clark's work was followed by a searching criticism by Kirsopp and Silva Lake in a relatively short article[3].

In attempting a critical survey of the present position, I cannot claim to speak in the role of an expert. The palaeography and codicology of Latin manuscripts and the history of the Latin language which are major aspects of the study of this (and other) Graeco-Latin bilinguals are areas which a student of Eastern versions can rarely visit. Yet I hope that we may observe some factors which may help us to make advances in the location of this manuscript in the history and geography of Christian antiquity, and thus in casting some light upon its text.

Two studies of importance are the work of R. C. Stone on the Latin of Codex Bezae[4] and the pages devoted to the manuscript in the survey of ancient translations, patristic quotations and lectionaries edited by Kurt Aland in 1972: the author of these pages was Bonifatius Fischer[5]. On the Greek side the work of James Yoder is clearly significant: we have his concordance of the peculiar Greek passage[6], and a summary of work on Semitisms in Codex Bezae[7]. Stone gave us a lexicon of the Latin of the manuscript[8].

In relation to the Latin side, the palaeographer E. A. Lowe made a number of contributions to our understanding, which are now conveniently gathered together in his Palaeographical Papers 1907–1965 (edited by Ludwig Bieler in 1972. This is a rich treasure store.)[9] In the field of Greek palaeography, the study of majuscule (as we are enjoined to call what to most of us was uncial) is dominated by the work of Guglielmo Cavallo, Ricerche sulla maiuscola biblica[10]. (He has extended his work to other types of majuscule elsewhere – this may be relevant to the supplementary leaves of our codex and their dating and ascription to Florus of Lyon, but Cavallo has not considered those leaves).

---

[3] Kirsopp and Silva Lake. "The Acts of the Apostles". JBL. vol. 53. (1934) pp. 34–45.

[4] Robert C. Stone. The Language of the Latin of Codex Bezae. (Illinois Studies in Language and Literature. Vol. XXX. Nos. 2–3.) Urbana 1946.

[5] Die alten Uebersetzungen des Neuen Testaments, die Kirchenväterzitate und Lektionare. (ANTT. Band 5) Berlin– New York 1972. pp. 1–92. Bonifatius Fischer. Das Neue Testament in lateinischer Sprache. esp. pp. 39–49. V. Der Codex Bezae und verwandte Probleme.

[6] Concordance to the distinctive Greek text of Codex Bezae. compiled by James D. Yoder. (NTTS vol. II) Leiden 1961.

[7] "Semitisms on Codex Bezae". JBL vol. 78 (1959) pp. 317–21 cp. "The language of the Greek Variants of Codex Bezae". NT vol. III (1959) pp. 241–8.

[8] op. cit. (fn. 4) pp. 71–199. Index verborum.

[9] E. A. Lowe. Palaeographical Papers 1907–1965. Edited by Ludwig Bieler. 2 Volumes. Oxford 1972.

[10] Guglielmo Cavallo. Ricerche sulla maiuscola biblica. (STP 2) Firenze 1967.

In accordance with codicological practice, I propose in my survey to try to move up the stream of the transmission of the manuscript from the point at which it first enters our ken, giving a résumé of positions reached and assumptions made, confirming or criticizing these as may be necessary and possible. Beza found it in 1562, it having come from the monastery of St. Irenaeus at Lyon. In 1546 it was used in argument at the council of Trent by the bishop of Clermont. These are proven facts[11]. We now go back seven centuries to the next point at which scholars have attempted to plot the presence of the manuscript, still at Lyon. This attempt links the codex with Florus Diaconus whose *floruit* was about AD 785–860[12]. He was a scholar and controversialist of great importance in his day. He worked entirely in Lyon. (Lowe – I 228 – seems to be in error when he says that "Florus had travelled much"). His links with the Codex Bezae are deduced from the identification of various critical signs with which a number of Lyonnais manuscripts are furnished. This identification stems from Tafel (a German palaeographer who was killed in the First World War and whose work was published in a summary form by W. M. Lindsay):[13] it was taken further by Lowe in his study and collection of facsimiles of Manuscripts of Lyon[14]. Up to that date, it must be pointed out, this assumption was an assumption made with many a "possibly", on the basis that the annotations "pointed to an erudite ecclesiastic interested in Biblical, patristic and legal works and particularly familiar with the works of St. Augustine". (Lowe I 322). A proof as definitive as possible seems to have been subsequently provided by Célestin Charlier in the Mélanges Podechard (1948)[15] where the link between such annotations and the precise passages, especially of St. Augustine, excerpted by Florus in his catena-like commentaries and other works, is demonstrated. (The edition of the *inedita* of Florus, there proposed by Dom Célestin, does not seem to have been accomplished).

In the paper of Lowe just referred to, dated 1931, it is further stated that "the added pages (viz. of Codex Bezae) in ninth century uncial, are probably by Florus". cp. II 474 "perhaps even partially restored." (earli-

---

[11] Ropes. op. cit. (fn. 1) pp. lvif.

[12] DSp 5 (1964) columns 514–25 (C. Charlier); DHGE 17 (1971) columns 648–54 (M. Cappuyns).

[13] Palaeographia Latina Part. II (St. Andrews University Publications XVI: Oxford 1923) pp. 66–7. "The Lyons Scriptorium." by the late S. Tafel: id. Part. IV (eadem XX: ibid. 1925) pp. 40–70. (continuation).

[14] E. A. Lowe. Codice Lugdunenses Antiquissimi. Lyons 1924. Plates II. VIII. IX. XIV. XVI. XVII. XVIII. XXIV. XXXI. XXXIII. XXXIV. XXXV. XXXVII. cp. RBen. t. 57 (1947) pp. 132–67.

[15] Mélanges E. Podechard (Lyons 1948) pp. 71–84 "Les manuscrits personnels de Florus de Lyon et son activité littéraire".

er, (1927), (I 228), this was "there is some ground for believing that the added leaves were written by Florus himself"). This seems to be based on the use of a mark of interrogation shaped like an Arabic numeral "three" (3) in the additional leaves; Lowe gives an example from fol. 169* (1.15 "quem quaeritis" Jn. 18.4): and on the use of blue ink (see the colophon to the gospel of Mark fol. 348* v, on the Greek side). The former point is amongst the critical signs which we have referred to: the latter is confirmed for Lowe from the ms. Lyon 484 (414) containing excerpts from St. Augustine on the Pauline Epistles made by Florus: the palaeographer Delisle regarded it as the autograph of Florus, on which Lowe comments "for part of it at least this may very easily be true". In this ms. blue ink is used where normally red would be (see Lowe's article "The Codex Bezae and Lyons", JThS 25 (1924) 270–274). = I. 182–186).

The other evidence for linking the history of Codex Bezae with Florus was gathered by Dom Henri Quentin from the quotations and allusions to the New Testament and especially the Acts of the Apostles in the Martyrology of Ado made in the ninth century. His article[16] is well summarized by Ropes pp. lx–lxii. A number of these allusions contain Latin renderings which are peculiar to Codex Bezae while others have a text akin to that of the Codex Gigas. Some of them are conflates of Bezae and Gigas and even of the Vulgate as well. From this Quentin deduced that Ado took them from a copy of Acts (akin in text to the Gigas) which had marginal notes derived from Codex Bezae. Such a work he ascribes to Florus. It is known from Florus' work against Eriugena that he knew the Greek text of Acts and Romans[17].

In sum, although the proof is through the amassing of circumstantial evidence, we seem to have a cogent case here. Some questions are left unresolved. For instance, a study of the Greek hand of the supplementary leaves might be of interest if they are indeed by Florus. This is not *known,* of course. The ms. Lyon 484 (414), of which Lowe gives a photograph to show the sign of interrogation characteristic of Florus, is a minuscule: a further search is necessary if we are to find a facsimile of Latin uncials written by him. The Latin hand of the supplementary leaves is defined by Lowe elsewhere as Q uncial: this is a hand in which alone of the letters Q has the capital form. This type of hand came into use, according to him, when "uncial had ceased to be a normal bookhand and became a display script"[18]. A thorough search of the mss. ascribed to Florus would be necessary to determine if this was the uncial he used for headings, colophons, etc. Once this was established, the Greek hand of codex Bezae supple-

---

[16] RBen. t. XXXIII (1906) pp. 1–23. "Le *Codex Bezae* à Lyon au IXe siecle? Les citations du nouveau Testament dans le martyrologe d'Adon" cp. Ropes op. cit. (fn. 1) pp. lx–lxii.

[17] PL CXIX (Liber adversus Joannem Scotum ch. XIV) coll. 183f.

[18] Palaeographical Papers vol. II. pg. 404 fn. 2 and pg. 405.

ment could tell us what Greek mss. (if any) he knew: certainly, it would not seem that he was copying the hand characteristic of the original leaves.

Whence then did Codex Bezae come to Lyon before the ninth century? A number of scholars have entertained the notion that Florus may have had it brought (as I have remarked, Lowe's suggestion that he travelled himself and may have brought it back, seems erroneous). On the basis of correspondence of Florus with an Italian abbot, Quentin suggested that this might have been the case with Codex Bezae. (loc. cit.) This notion was put forward as plausible by Ropes (op. cit.). For them, it was from Italy that the manuscript came to Gaul: for Ropes, at any rate, it was in Italy that it originated.

But when we look at the letter in question we find that Florus had sent the ms. there referred to to Italy for collation: and asks that it be safely returned. Thus, this provides no evidence for a practice of Florus to seek mss. for his collection from abroad[19].

This hypothesis brings us to a field of discussion, as complex as that to do with Lyons and Florus, but apparently much more difficult to resolve. Textual, linguistic, liturgiological and palaeographical considerations enter into the debate. Stone gives a rather rambling account: to Fischer belongs the merit of clarity. All who have dealt with the ms. would agree in general with Lowe in his discussion of the Latin hand in Codices latini antiquiores vol. II. (no. 140): it "has a provincial look and can hardly be a product of a great centre of calligraphy; ... the scribe is not expert: he writes the Latin in the Greek manner, but his Greek too is peculiar and unlike usual Oriental uncial". Cavallo says that the execution of the ms. shows "scarsa cura calligrafica". But he thinks it is "probabilmente di origine occidentale": such origin in his view is "in ogni caso sicura". But in making so decided a remark he appears to be introducing many factors other than the palaeographical, referring to a well known article of Cardinal Mercati, in which he took Lowe to task for an early note suggesting (in JThS 14. (1913) pp. 385–389) that Codex Bezae originated in a non-Italian centre, where Greek tradition prevailed, and was preserved until about AD 800 in a centre where Greek was the literary and ecclesiastical language. (Lowe's "The Codex Bezae and Lyons", already referred to, was a partial recantation, on his part, of these opinions). Fischer's summary of the case for the West is largely based on Mercati: he mentions (op. cit. fn. 131) that the signatures of the gatherings are on the last folium (although Greek letters are used.): that the style of the colophons and the presence of abbreviated titles on each page are a Western style unknown in Greek manuscripts: and that an abbreviation for *denariis* is present which is unknown to Greek scribes but is used for δηναρίων in the Greek.

[19] MGHEp Tom. V. Epistolae Variorum 26 (Epistolae Karolini Aevi III) 1898–99, pp. 340–343.

(see however footnote 28) On the other hand, Fischer indicates the Greek text dominates (he means, I think, that the Latin is a translation of the Greek and has not influenced it), and the Greek hand is normal whereas the Latin uncial is archaic and abnormal. Signs of omission in the form of an arrow are very rare in the West[20]. (On this see Lowe. "The oldest omission signs in Latin mss." II. 349–380). F. C. Burkitt made the point that the pen of the scribe was cut to write Greek (i. e. cut straight, not slanting), which Lowe later confirmed[21].

Cavallo dates the Greek hand in the earlier part of the fifth century; Lowe the Latin hand as fifth century. Fischer, however, declares that the fourth century is more likely, and quotes Wilmart and Mallon in support of this earlier date. He also states that both Lowe and Bischoff in conversation had each intimated that he would be prepared to accept such a dating[22].

Much turns, as I see it, on the palaeography of the Latin. The Codex is written in the hand called "b–d uncial" by Lowe, this signifying that b and d are half-uncial forms in an otherwise uncial hand. There are a number of hints in Lowe's writings that he was interested in this hand and might have given us a definitive study of it: but we are left with adumbrations only from which we must deduce his total view[23]. The latest reference comes from 1961 (Festschrift for Albareda) (= II 466–474) where on the last page we find "this b-d-type, as I hope to show elsewhere, usually occurs in manuscripts with definite Greek connections, as in the Graeco-Latin manuscript of the Pauline epistles, and in papyri coming from Egypt and probably originating there". A survey and discussion are also to be found in H. J. Frede's Altlateinische Paulus-Handschriften[24] in a section which Fischer suggests is based on his own views and discussion with his colleague (*art. cit.* pg. 41 fin. 131)[25]. There, the closest similarities to the hand of Codex Bezae are said to be seen in the Seneca palimpsest, Vatic. Palat. lat. 24 (foll. 10,15,39–40, 43–4), (= Lowe Codices rescripti CIX 187), and the papyrus fragment of Livy, Bodleianus lat. Class. f. 5 (P); these are of the third-fourth century and the fourth-fifth century respectively, which are closely linked in calligraphy with the epitome of Livy (BM pap. 1532), which is dated in the 3–4 century, the hand of which is defined as "half-uncial" since not only *b* and *d* but *r* and *m* are in minus-

[20] E. A. Lowe. Palaeographical Papers II. "The oldest omission signs in Latin manuscripts" pp. 349–380.

[21] F. C. Burkitt. "The Date of Codex Bezae" (JThS vol. III (1901–2) pp. 501–13): E. A. Lowe op. cit. I. pg. 227.

[22] Op. cit. (fn. 5) pg. 41 fn. 133.

[23] See the Index to Palaeographical Papers vol. II pg. 627 sn. "bd uncial".

[24] Freiburg (1964) (AGLB 4) pp. 17–20.

[25] Op. cit. pg. 41 fn. 131.

cule. The two latter are mss. found at Oxyrhynchus: the former, which Lowe at first considered of uncertain origin, was later (Codices rescript p. 73 = II 486) *viz.* in 1964, deemed to have been used in Italy on the grounds of the uncial writing of the upper text (Old Test. Vg.). Later examples of the same and related styles are mainly from Italy: but the b–d style continued to be used in the East as the papyrus PSI 1182 shows: this is a ms. of the Institutions of Gaius in uncial of the 5–6 century: its marginalia in Greek show it to have come from a great centre of calligraphy, probably Byzantium. The Latin words in the marginal notes are in b–d uncial form.

The b–d uncial is discussed more systematically in the recent survey by Bernhard Bischoff, Paläographie des römischen Altertums und des abendländischen Mittelalters (Berlin 1979)[26]. Here he emphasises that all examples of the earliest form of this script come from Egypt, and that it never became a conventional form in the West. He advances the hypothesis that it is in the East that we should seek the origin of semi-uncial hand: and suggests the Latin Law School of Berytus, which at least played a part in the spread of this style.

He names the Codex Bezae and the Seneca written by Nicianus (CLA I. 69 = Vat. Palat. Lat. 24 fols. 10,15,39–40, 43–4 = Lowe Codices Rescripti CIX. 187) as calligraphic examples of the script which fit into a Greek setting (fügen sich in den griechischen Rahmen ein) while in a footnote on pg. 243 (fn. 34) he states specifically that the Codex Bezae is of Eastern origin. I have now had the privilege of the opinion of the leading English authority on Latin palaeography, Professor T. J. Brown,[27] who says that he agrees with almost every word of Bischoff on b–d uncial and goes on to develop a view of the origin of Codex Bezae which accepts Eastern origin as a starting point. This view may be summarized as follows. "The scribe was a specialist hack, technically competent but poorly educated, who had been engaged in the more or less exclusive copying of texts in Roman law, which he did in 'early half uncial' somewhere in the Roman East. He sometimes had to copy some Greek as part of his job."

Such a background would account for some of the features on which Mercati laid stress and which have continued to influence the conclusions of scholars such as Fischer and Cavallo. The abbreviation for "denarius" would clearly be a feature of the scribe's professional practice,[28] and orna-

---

[26] (Grundlagen der Germanistik 24) Berlin 1979. I am indebted to Dr. Bruce Barker-Benfield, of the Bodleian Library, for knowledge of this monograph.

[27] In private letters of 23 July, 28 July and 12 August 1983. My warm thanks to Professor Brown must be here publicly expressed: he spared no pains to survey and assess the matter for me, and has put all interested parties in his debt.

[28] It has become clear, since this paper was originally given, that the sign * for *donarius* has been known as an abbreviation on Greek sources since the time of Montfaucon (Palaeo-

mentation and the form of colophon might be too, although we lack evidence at present. The encroachment of Latin forms of abbreviation in the headlines or running titles is perhaps the most difficult datum to explain: and I have no completely satisfactory resolution at present.

A contrary feature is the presence, in the hands of a later corrector, of liturgical notes which Brightman long ago showed belong to a primitive stage of the Greek lectionary system.[29] This too we have to bear in mind. We shall be helped in our analysis by the emphasis of Fischer that there are three clearly demarcated periods in the history of the manuscript, which he calls the bilingual period, the purely Greek period and the purely Latin period.[30] It is with the last of these that we have already dealt. It dates from about AD 800 when the Greek correctors cease activity. Just as that discernible period in the manuscript's history indicates a change of place, so the explanation of the other periods may be due to a change of place, although it might also indicate a change of conditions (cultural, political or ecclesiastical) in one and the same place. The bilingual period and the Greek period may thus be successive phases of the history of the place of origin (this would be the argument of those who see the West as the place of origin as well as the eventual home of the Codex): but a geographical movement of the manuscript between the bilingual period and the Greek period may also meet the data. This I consider is a necessary part of any hypothesis which sees the East as the place of origin. On the palaeographical evidence which I have set out, and the specialist opinions which confirmed my own initial impression (which was based largely on the work of Lowe as gathered together in his collected works), I have reached the conclusion that the East must be the place of origin.

The Western origin was argued forcefully in the past. Harris attempted, with his customary bravura, a philological argument based on the phonology of the Latin, which he believed pointed to Gaul.[31] It should suffice to say that the advances of comparative Romance philology in the present century have shown the utterly untenable nature of Harris's arguments on this point. All arguments on the basis of the Latin need to be

---

graphia graeca, Paris 1708, pg. 359) who describes it as "frequentius". More recent remarks, which confirm that early observation, may be found in the article "Siglae" by F. Bilabel (Pauly-Wissowa RE 2te Reihe 2te Bd. (1923) columns 2286 and 2306): and in M. Avi-Yonah. Abbreviations in Greek Inscriptions (The Near East, 200 B. C.–A. D. 1100) London 1940 (The Quarterly of the Department of Antiquities in Palestine. Supplement to vol. IX) pg. 114.

[29] F. E. Brightman "On the Italian origin of Codex Bezae. The marginal notes of lections" JThS vol. I. (1899–1900) pp. 446–54.

[30] Op. cit. pg. 40.

[31] J. Rendel Harris. A Study of Codex Bezae. (TaS vol. II no. 1) Cambridge 1891 especially chapters IV, V, XII and XIII.

updated: even Stone's study has some latent faults, although its amassing of evidence does for *d* what no one has done for any other Latin biblical ms. Roensch[32] is invaluable but out of date. Hoogterp's monograph of the Latin of the Codex Bobbiensis[33] is the only other study of the same kind as Stone's which I know, but I am uncertain whether his lists are meant to be exhaustive. For the gospels specifically we possess "Itala",[34] and a full study of the Latin of the Vetus Latina tradition would have to utilize all the riches of the Beuron material. When we make comparison of Stone's figures for features which he claims to be characteristic of *d*, we find that he has made no comparison with the other biblical mss. as we can now do, due to "Itala". One such feature is the change of conjugation of verbs from third to second conjugation.[35] Of thirty-one (31) instances, only twelve prove to be, in fact, peculiar to *d*. To take the study further, we should need to analyze other biblical manuscripts in themselves and against the whole tradition, and to peruse a considerable literature on the history of Latin. I claim no expert knowledge in this field. I have mainly laid under contribution the posthumously published work of Einar Loefstedt, "Late Latin" (1955),[36] and on some specific points, Sven Lundstroem "Uebersetzungstechnische Untersuchungen auf dem Gebiete der christlichen Latinitaet" of the same date[37]. The conclusion of this type of research seems clearly to be that at the present stage of our knowledge of Late Latin, local differentiations cannot be made. Thus Stone's allegation that the *Peregrinatio Aetheriae* is proven to be a product of Gaul cannot stand.[38] In another matter, also adumbrated by Harris, the writers I have named help us to see the data with more understanding. There are occasional common features between the Latin of *d* and the Latin of the translation of Irenaeus' *Adversus Haereses*. Lundstroem's discussion shows that the influence of the Greek original upon the Latin translation is the cause of the data which have been adduced.[39] They cannot be used to prove a

---

[32] Hermann Rönsch. Itala und Vulgata. Das Sprachidiom der urchristlichen Itala und der katholischen Vulgata unter Berücksichtigung der römischen Volkssprache. 2te Auflage. Marburg 1875.

[33] P. W. Hoogterp. Étude sur le Latin du codex Bobiensis (k) des Évangeles. Akademisch Proefschrift. Wageningen 1930.

[34] Itala. Das Neue Testament in altlateinischer Ueberlieferung nach den Handschriften, herausgegeben von Adolf Jülicher. I, Matthäusevangelium. 2te verb. Auflage. Berlin 1972. II. Marcusevangelium. 2te verb. Auflage. ibid. 1970. III. Lucasevangelium. 2te verb. Auflage. ibid. 1976. IV. Johannesevangelium. ibid. 1963.

[35] Op. cit. (fn. 4) pg. 39.

[36] Institutet for Sammenlignende Kulturforskning. Serie A. Forelesninger. XXV. Einar Löfstedt. Late Latin. Oslo 1955.

[37] Lunds Universitets. Årsskrift. N. F. Avd. 1. Bd. 51. Nr. 3. Lund 1955.

[38] Stone op. cit. pg. 66; Löfstedt op. cit. pp. 44–48.

[39] Löfstedt op. cit. pg. 91; Lundström op. cit. pg. 259. The earlier work of Lundström (Stu-

Gaulish or Western origin for *d*. If the *Verzeichnis* of *Vetus Latina*[40] is correct in being so specific in its dating of between AD 380 and 395, this common feature might help to date *d*: Lundstroem's dating is much wider, giving bounds of AD 200 and AD 400.

It is often repeated, for instance by Lowe (Palaeographical Papers I. 227), that "neither Greek nor Latin seem to have been the native tongue of the scribe". Such views are not any longer tenable: they go back to a day when these languages as found in ancient manuscripts were judged against the artificially rigid canons of classical schooling. The discoveries and researches of the present century should exclude their repetition. The Latin is a normal late Latin: and furthermore, as Fischer observes on the basis of Stone's wordlist, the orthography of the Latin is relatively good.[41] This is so especially in Greek loan words and in aspiration, while prepositions are unassimilated in composita.

Fischer also draws our attention to the analogous data of the Greek as discussed by our colleague, now Cardinal Martini,[42] in his work on p 75 and B, especially his pages 91 to 95 and pages 99, where assimilation and gemination are discussed. The orthography of the Greek of *D* is archaic and even archaizing. We need a discussion of the Greek of *D* against the numerous recent works on the Greek of the papyri of the Roman period. (Mayser is of course indispensable: but that we have had previously to rely upon his work alone should not make us unmindful that he deals with Ptolemaic papyri). Two recent works are Francis Gignac "A grammar of the Greek papyri of the Roman and Byzantine periods", which has now reached its second volume[43] and Basil G. Mandilaras, "The verb in the Greek non-literary papyri" (who claims that his data covers a millenium).[44] Such knowledge as these monographs provide has not yet been assimilated into the study of New Testament Greek. In the light of Yoder's conclusions, I anticipate that, when it is, the normality of the Greek of *D* will be further emphasised. We can tell nothing about the origin of codex Bezae from its languages.

---

dien zur lateinischen Irenäusübersetzung. Lund 1943, pp. 15–43 esp. pg. 25) is referred to by Löfstedt and should be consulted.

40 VL 1/1. Hermann Josef Frede. Kirchenschriftsteller. Verzeichnis und Sigel. Freiburg 1981. pg. 404 s. siglo IR. As Dr Frede informs me, the dating turns on the use of "graecitas", in the sense of "the Greek language", apparently a neologism, created by Hilarius of Poitiers, and thus postdating his anti-Arian writings. See Bertrand Hemmerdinger, JThS n.s. 17 (1966) pp. 308–326, and M. C. Díaz y Díaz RET t. 14 (1954) pp. 393–395.

41 Op. cit. pp. 40, 41 fn. 131.

42 Carlo M. Martini, S. I. Il problema della recensionalità del codice B alla luce del papiro Bodmer XIV. (AnBib 26) Roma 1966.

43 Milano. vol. 1. n. d.; vol. 2, 1981. (Testi e documenti per lo studio dell'antichità. LV).

44 Athens 1973.

Ropes's arguments for a Sicilian origin were for long the most coherent.[45] Greek was there the native language in the Imperial and post-Imperial periods but there was social dominance of Latin-speaking landlords and at one period most of the clergy were Latin. Later, Greek came to dominate and the church became more closely Eastern in its affiliations. This would provide the background for a Greek codex with a Latin translation, and the features on which Mercati and Brightman respectively laid stress would meet with plausible explanations. To this theory I adhered until the present task stimulated me to take a fresh look at the data. As I have already declared, the palaeographical data of the Latin led me – and have led the current experts too, which carries far more conviction for our purposes – to move to the hypothesis of an Eastern origin. (I might mention at this point, that before I had the benefit of expert advice, I looked at the possibility of African origin which Lowe once declared to have some palaeographical plausibility.[46] On the data which we now possess, this must now be dismissed. Even if it had been a possibility for the Latin[47], palaeographically and textually (as the case might have been made), it would in any case be difficult to envisage the circumstances which, on such an hypothesis, gave rise to the production of the codex).

The suggestion of Eastern origin, when formerly made, was based on somewhat shaky grounds. Clark, for instance, although he once thought of Jerusalem, eventually proposed Alexandria, basing himself very largely on Tischendorf's belief that codex Claromontanus came from Alexandria, on the fact that a number of bilinguals are of Egyptian origin, and on the evidence that in Acts we find that the text of *D* is paralleled in Egyptian papyri and in the manuscripts which Thomas of Harkel used at the Enaton.[48] As I have said, he once thought of Jerusalem, and his view is revived by Stone. The basis of this opinion is that Aetheria (or Egeria) tells us that sermons and lections in Greek were rendered into Latin and Syriac for the

---

[45] Op. cit. pp. lxviif.

[46] Lowe. Palaeographical papers I. 227.

[47] It appears from Lowe (ibid. 129–132) and from scattered references in Bischoff that the codex Bobbiensis of the Gospels (Turin. Bibl. Naz. G. VII. 15) and a number of early manuscripts of Cyprian are representative examples of African productions. Not even Lowe, in spite of the remark referred to in footnote 46, attempted to link the hand of codex Bezae with these examples by any rigorous manner of comparison.

[48] Op. cit. (fn. 2) pp. lxiiff. It may also be added that Clark's remarks about the three letter form of *nomina sacra* in the codex Bezae, which have often been adduced as due to Latin influence, are fully justified by more recent study. The forms are found in Greek papyri from the earliest point in the first five centuries of A. D., decreasing in frequency with the passage of time. (see A. H. R. E. Paap, Nomina sacra in the Greek papyri of the first five centuries A. D. The sources and some deductions. Leiden 1959). If anything, it would seem that these forms are archaisms in codex Bezae, called by Paap a "conservative manuscript".

comprehension of pilgrims who spoke no Greek[49]. This would give the raison-d'être of such a bilingual. The text would be that read in Jerusalem in the fourth or fifth century. The rendering is independent of, but akin to, the Vetus Latina: the study made by Bakker on the codex Bobbiensis claimed to find affinities with *d*. Such a view seems to me not implausible. Here as elsewhere we are challenged to investigate a number of things still to some degree unknown, for example, the relation of the Greek text of *D* to quotations by writers in Jerusalem in the relevant period, the relation of *d* to the Old Latin in general, textual affinities (if any) between codex Bezae and the Jerusalem lectionary which latter is now better known than hitherto.

My conclusion has been reached on mainly palaeographical grounds. Is there any evidence, other than that latent in the desired investigations just listed, to support it elsewhere? Very little, but two crumbs may be for our comfort. The hymnodist and homilist Andreas, later Archbishop in Crete, was of Damascene birth, and as a young monk and deacon was in Jerusalem. In his homilies on the raising of Lazarus and the triumphal entry[50] there are some distinctive variants otherwise singular to *D*. He might have known these in his youth: the date of his homilies is not precisely known. He later served in Constantinople: I have not attempted to link codex Bezae with that city, although it should be noted that some instances of b–d uncial in legal documents come from there[51].

The other slight indication of the correctness of the Jerusalem hypothesis is in a datum upon which Lake laid some emphasis,[52] although we cannot accept his interpretation. The text of the Pericope Adulterae in *D* is closely paralleled in one manuscript only, namely Gregory-Aland 1071 (Athos Lavra A 104). This manuscript is probably of Calabrian origin, and Lake suggested that it derived its text of the pericope from *D*, in Calabria, before it was taken to Athos. This falls down on palaeographical and codicological grounds. 1071 is dated in the twelfth century by palaeography. We have seen that it is proven that, by about AD 800, codex Bezae

49 Itinerarium Egeriae XLVII, 3, 4 (CChr.SL CLXXV. pg. 89 11.13–24: SC 296 pg. 314).

50 In lazarum quatriduanum: PG 97.960–85. In ramos palmarum: ibid. 985–1017. There is now a new edition on the basis of the rich manuscript tradition, prepared by Mary Cunningham, and presented successfully in 1984 as a Ph. D. thesis of the University of Birmingham, as yet unpublished. ("Andreas of Crete: homilies on Lazarus and Palm Sunday: a critical edition and commentary").

51 There are marginalia in b–d uncial in the Codex Pisanus (Firenze, Laurent. S. N.), one of the oldest manuscripts of the second edition of the Digest of Justinian, a Latin manuscript assigned to Constantinople. See Bischoff op. cit. pg. 233 and Lowe Palaeographical Papers II. 466–74 (The manuscript's designation in terms of discussion of it in Lowe's Codice Latini Antiquiores, by which reference is sometimes made, is CLA III. 295).

52 SBEc. V. (Oxford 1892) Part II. Texts from Mount Athos by Kirsopp Lake esp. pp. 148f.

was amongst the manuscripts of Florus in Lyons. However, it could be argued that this textual affinity in the Pericope Adulterae betokens a link in the ancestry of 1071 which could be brought into an argument for a Jerusalemite origin for codex Bezae. 1071 is amongst those manuscripts which contain the "Jerusalem colophon", alleging that a collation has been made with Jerusalemite manuscripts "in the holy mountain". It would be rash to adduce this slenderest of links with Jerusalem as any kind of proof. It may however just hint at the plausibility of this hypothesis for codex Bezae, somewhat less strongly than the evidence of Andreas of Crete. (Here once more, we may indicate a topic on which research has stood still: the manuscripts containing this intriguing colophon have not been investigated since 1911, in the work of Schmidtke[53]).

On my hypothesis, the "bilingual period" of codex Bezae lasts while it lies in its homeland of Jerusalem: it is taken to South Italy in the seventh century by refugees fleeing from the Persian or Arab invasions of Syria and Palestine.[54] There lies its Greek period in which the addition of lectionary references, liturgical notes and chapter titles took place. The Sortes in Mark[55] are undateable by palaeography: but they might well come from this period too, in regions whose history is unsettled. Thence, although we do not know how, to Florus in Lyons, and a more certain, though still occasionally murky, path to where it rests today.

[53] Alfred Schmidtke. Neue Untersuchungen zu den judenchristlichen Evangelien (TU 37. Band. Heft 1. [3. Reihe 7. Band., Heft 1]) Leipzig 1911.

[54] Schmidtke op. cit. pg. 16: H. G. Beck. Kirche und theologische Literatur im byzantinischen Reich (Byzantinisches Handbuch im Rahmen des Handbuchs der Altertumswissenschaft. 2ter Teil, 1ter Bd., München 1959) pp. 227f.

[55] For these we must still rely, it appears, on the materials gathered by Rendel Harris, that paragon of "curious learning", in his Annotators of the Codex Bezae (London 1901) pp. 45–74 (the Bezan series is given on pp. 59–64) and 113–184 (appendices A–E). A new edition of the Sortes Sangallenses (discussed by Harris op. cit.) has been made by Alban Dold (Die Orakelsprüche im St. Gallen Palimpsestcodex 908, die sogenannten ‚Sortes Sangallenses': SÖAW 225 Bd. 4 Abt.) Wien 1948, with discussion, mainly linguistic, by Richard Meister, in the same volume of Sitzungsberichte (viz. 225 Bd. 5 Abt.) Wien 1951. Other material and bibliography can be found in F. Drexl. Ein griechisches Losbuch. ByZ Bd. 41. (1941) pp. 311–318.

The apostolic decree of Acts 15

by F. F. Bruce

('The Crossways', Temple Road, Buxton, Derbyshire/England)

I.

The apostolic decree, laying down certain conditions to be complied with by Gentile converts to Christianity, is set out in Ac 15,28.29, at the end of a letter sent by "the apostles and elder brothers" at Jerusalem to "the brothers from the Gentiles in Antioch and Syria-and-Cilicia". Its terms are anticipated in Ac 15,20, where James proposes them to his colleagues at the so-called Council of Jerusalem; they are repeated in Ac 21,25, where Paul, visiting Jerusalem for the last time, is informed or reminded of them.

Apart from the distinctive readings of the Western text (which are studied in another contribution to this volume), the textual phenomena of the decree need not detain us. In place of εἰδωλόθυτα (εἰδωλόθυτον) of Ac 15,29 and 21,25, the more wide-ranging ἀλισγήματα τῶν εἰδώλων appears in Ac 15,20 (among various "pollutions" of this kind the eating of the flesh of animals sacrificed to idols is most relevant to the immediate occasion); and the order in which the prohibited things are mentioned changes from one passage to another. It might be said that in Ac 15,29 Luke gives the verbatim content of the decree, as embodied in the apostolic letter, while 15,20 and 21,25 present a freer report. But Luke is given to variations of this kind whenever he reproduces a theme two or three times, and the Lukan factor cannot be excluded from the wording of the letter.

Antioch, to which the letter was carried, was at that time the seat of government of the united Roman province of Syria-Cilicia. The senders of the letter refer to certain persons who have upset the Gentile Christians of that province with "words" for which they had received no authorization. What the "words" were is spelt out in the Byzantine text (on the basis of Ac 15,5): "saying that you should be circumcised and keep the law" (15,24). They go on to tell how they have met together to consider the matter, and conclude the letter with the decree:

> "The Holy Spirit and we ourselves have resolved to impose on you no further burden than these necessary things: you are to abstain from food sacrificed to idols, from blood, from strangled meat, and from fornication. If you guard yourselves from these, you will do well."

The decree clearly marks a compromise between two contrasted positions on the terms for admitting Gentile believers to the fellowship of the church. There was the position of those who maintained that Gentile converts should conform to the law of Moses and, in particular, that the males among them should be circumcised. This is attested not only in Luke's narrative but also in Paul's admonition to the churches of Galatia. When Paul warns the Galatian Christians that, if they get themselves circumcised, Christ will be of no use to them[1], he makes it plain that those Christians were under pressure to accept circumcision, if not as something necessary for salvation itself, then certainly as necessary for recognition by their Jewish fellow-believers as members of the saved community. On the other hand there was Paul's position, which refused the law any status in reference to salvation or to church fellowship. From this point of view it was through faith in Christ alone that Gentiles and Jews alike received salvation and were admitted to the new common life in him: in this realm the distinction between Jews and Gentiles was as irrelevant as that between slaves and free persons or that between men and women. Paul may not have been the only Christian leader to take this position, but he was assuredly its most articulate spokesman.

The decree implied rather than affirmed that circumcision was not required on the part of Gentile believers. But certain things were expressly required, not for entrance into salvation indeed but for practical Christian fellowship – abstention from certain kinds of forbidden food and from illicit sexual relations. The body that issued the decree was not an inter-church council but the church of Jerusalem, acting through its leaders, "the apostles and elder brothers".

The church of Jerusalem, or its leadership, takes it for granted that it exercises authority over other churches, including the mainly Gentile church of Antioch and others in that area. It has been argued, e.g. by F. J. A. Hort, that "the New Testament is not poor of words expressive of command, ... yet none of them is used"[2] in the apostolic decree. True: but the terms of the resolution, invoking the authority of the Holy Spirit as well as that of the Jerusalem leaders, are stringent enough, and so is the statement that abstention from the things specified is "necessary" – not to say "compulsory" (ἐπάναγκες). It may seem odd to western readers today that ethical and non-ethical restrictions (as they would regard them) should be lumped together as they are in the decree; but this would not have seemed so odd to the authors of the decree, or even (perhaps) to its recipients.

The compromise character of the decree is emphasized in Luke's record by his bringing together to the meeting from which it was issued the

---

[1] Gal 5,2.

[2] F. J. A. Hort, The Christian Ecclesia, London: Macmillan, 1897, p. 82.

representatives of different viewpoints. The terms of the decree are proposed by James, who seems to regard them as logically involved in Peter's argument. The extremists on one side were present, insisting that Gentile converts should bc circumcised and directed to keep Moses' law. At the other extreme Paul and Barnabas, missionaries to the Gentile world, were present – but they do not stand so far out at the other extreme as might have been expected. Although they play no part in the drafting of the decree or in the composition of the letter embodying it, Paul and Barnabas evidently acquiesce in it; indeed Paul (along with his new colleague Silas) is said to have "delivered" the decree not only to the churches of Syria and Cilicia to which it was explicitly addressed but also to the churches more recently planted in Derbe, Lystra and other cities of South Galatia[3].

That Paul should have done any such thing is virtually ruled out by the unambiguous evidence of his own letters. In them he deals with the issues of idolatry, fornication and the eating of forbidden kinds of food, but he never invokes the authority of the Jerusalem decree. He urges the Christians of Corinth to flee from fornication (1 Cor 6,18) and idolatry (1 Cor 10,18), but on the ground that these practices are wrong in themselves, fundamentally incompatible with Christian faith and life, not because the Jerusalem authorities have so decreed. As for food restrictions, he lays down none: Christians are free to eat any food for which they can with a good conscience thank God, even the flesh of animals which have been sacrificed to pagan divinities. The one restriction which he does urge is a voluntary restriction on the eating of food in circumstances where one's example would have a harmful effect on the conscience of an unenlightened fellow-Christian[4]. So Paul, on the one hand, supports the ethical abstentions of the apostolic decree, but independently, by an appeal to first principles; on the other hand, he ignores its non-ethical abstentions and gives his friends quite different advice – advice which, in fact, runs counter to them. It has indeed been argued that Ac 16,4, where Paul and Silas are said to have handed over the terms of the decree to the churches of South Galatia, is no part of Luke's original text[5]: whether that is so or not, its statement cannot be squared with Paul's own testimony.

II.

The question arises whether or not the decree has any direct bearing on controversies which surface in Paul's letters. It is held by some that Paul was first made aware of the decree during his last visit to Jerusalem,

3 Ac 15,30; 16,4.

4 1 Cor 8,7–13; Rom 14,13–15,2.

5 A. S. Geyser, Paul, the Apostolic Decree and the Liberals in Corinth, in Studia Paulina in honorem Johannis de Zwaan septuagenarii, ed. J. N. Sevenster and W. C. van Unnik, Haarlem: De Erven F. Bohn, 1953, pp. 136–138.

when the elders of the church told him of it (Ac 21,25)[6]. If this is so, then we need not expect to find its influence reflected in any of the capital letters. But the reference to the decree in Ac 21,25 is incidental; it has almost the character of a footnote[7]. Paul is urged to take some public action to put an end to rumours that he taught *Jewish* believers to give up circumcision and other ancestral customs. "As for *Gentile* believers," the elders added, "you know that we have refused to impose circumcision and similar requirements on them; we have simply let them know our decision that they should beware of food sacrificed to idols, blood, strangled meat and fornication". This is added, however, by way of an afterthought: the context does not give the impression that Paul is being told something for the first time; rather, he is being reminded of something he already knows.

The eating of the flesh of animals sacrificed to pagan divinities is the chief of the "idolatrous pollutions" from which the decree directed Gentile Christians to abstain. When the Corinthian church sent its questionnaire to Paul in Ephesus about A.D. 54 or 55, this was one of the points on which they sought a ruling from him; and he answered their question at some length. As we have said, he makes it plain that such meat is unobjectionable in itself, and that a Christian may thank God for it and eat it with a good conscience. In certain circumstances it would be better to refrain from it, not only if an immature Christian's conscience might be harmed by the example of another Christian eating it, but also if the setting in which it was taken might compromise one's public witness as a Christian – for instance, if it were taken at a banquet in a pagan temple, under the nominal patronage of the divinity worshipped there[8]. From his handling of the Corinthians' question it is evident that, if Paul by this time knew of the Jerusalem decree (as he probably did), he did not feel himself bound by it, nor did he expect his converts to be bound by it: he simply ignored it.

Did the Corinthian Christians raise the matter spontaneously in their letter to Paul, or had something happened in their church to make it a live issue? Paul refers to the recent emergence of a "Cephas" party in the Corinthian church[9]. What were the special characteristics of this party? We can only speculate, but it is likely that Cephas/Peter had paid a visit to Corinth not long before Paul wrote 1 Corinthians. It may well be supposed that, remembering the trouble at Antioch when Jewish and Gentile believers had to eat at separate tables, Peter recommended the observance

[6] Cf. A. Strobel, Das Aposteldekret als Folge des antiochenischen Streites, in Kontinuität und Einheit: für Franz Mussner, ed. P.-G. Müller and W. Stenger, Freiburg: Herder, 1981, p. 94.

[7] H. Conzelmann (Apg., HNT, *ad loc.*) and E. Haenchen (Apg., KEK, *ad loc.*) treat it as redactional.

[8] 1 Cor 8,10; 10,14–22.

[9] 1 Cor 1,12.

of the Jerusalem decree to the Corinthian Christians[10]. If so, those of their number who set high store by Paul's guidance would certainly ask him what his mind on this subject was.

Peter must have been well content with the Jerusalem decree: the compromise which it embodied delivered him from the dilemma in which he found himself at Antioch when the men who came from James persuaded him to discontinue enjoying table fellowship with Gentile Christians[11]. We could wish that we had Peter's account of this occasion as well as Paul's: as it is, we must be content with Paul's account and try to read between the lines.

III.

But what is the relation of the decree to Paul's narrative in Galatians – whether to his account of the Jerusalem conference at which he was present (Gal 2,1–10) or to his account of the confrontation with Peter at Antioch? The question is a complicated one. There is certainly no explicit reference to the decree in Galatians. This might mean that the decree had not yet been issued when Galatians was written (this is my own view); but it might simply mean that Paul ignores the decree, as he does elsewhere when he is dealing with subjects covered by its terms. Why, for example, does he not silence the demand that the Galatian Christians should be circumcised by pointing out that the Jerusalem leaders had agreed that circumcision should not be required from Gentile converts? Probably (*me iudice*) because that agreement had not yet been reached – but then, even if it had already been reached, would Paul have been disposed to invoke it and thus give the impression that he was appealing to the authority of Jerusalem?

Some scholars have understood Peter's *volte-face* at Antioch to have been the result of James's messengers informing him or reminding him of the Jerusalem decree[12]. It is most improbable that Peter had to be informed of the decree; there is no reason to doubt Luke when he represents Peter as being a party to the decree. Even if the decree was (by Luke's account) formulated and proposed by James, it went far to meet Peter's position. One scholar, accepting the reading τινα instead of τινας in Gal 2,12, treats it not as masculine singular ("a certain person") but as

---

[10] For the view that Peter brought the decree to Corinth see H. Lietzmann, Geschichte der alten Kirche, 1. Die Anfänge, Berlin/Leipzig: Walter de Gruyter, 1932, p. 155; C. K. Barrett, Things Sacrificed to Idols, NTS 11, 1964–65, p. 150.

[11] Gal 2,12–14. Lietzmann (op. cit., p. 107) suggests that the men who came from James were Judas and Silas (cf. Ac 15,22.27).

[12] Cf. D. R. Catchpole, Paul, James and the Apostolic Decree, NTS 23, 1976–77, pp. 428–444; see also J. D. G. Dunn, The Incident at Antioch, JSNT, issue 18, June 1983, pp. 3–57.

neuter plural ("certain things") and takes it to refer to the contents of the decree[13]. This is not likely: Paul's allusive language is intelligible if it refers to some person or persons whom he may not care to name; but it would be strange to call the contents of the decree "certain things".

If, however, Peter was reminded by James's messengers of the apostolic decree, it is suggested, he attempted to impose it on the church of Antioch, and withdrew from table fellowship with Gentile Christians until it was accepted. But if he knew of it already, why did he not insist on the Antiochenes' acceptance of it even before the message came from James?

Another possibility is that the decree was not intended to facilitate table fellowship between Jewish believers and uncircumcised Gentile Christians: rather, it laid down the conditions for recognizing Gentile Christians as fellow-members of the church, but still envisaged separate tables. Peter, however, assuming that it gave him *carte blanche* to enjoy table fellowship with Gentile Christians, went ahead at Antioch and acted accordingly, until James's messengers assured him that the decree was never meant to allow table fellowship with Gentiles as long as they remained uncircumcised[14]. If so, Peter and James had understood its terms differently – which is unlikely, if Peter was present when it was drawn up. Although the decree does not expressly state what benefits the Gentile Christians would derive from observing its terms, one may wonder why Luke should represent the Antiochene congregation as rejoicing when the decree was read (Ac 15,31). Was it because Jerusalem recognized them as believers on the ground of their acceptance of the gospel, albeit only second-class believers so long as they remained uncircumcised? Then, if the decree implied that circumcision was not essential for salvation, it contained a further, hidden implication that circumcision was still necessary for recognition as first-class believers. This hardly gave cause for rejoicing.

Luke's eirenic and reconciling tendency must be borne in mind, and his representation of events is not necessarily determinant for our understanding of a conflict which is attested mainly by Paul's correspondence. At the same time, Luke is our only witness for the terms of the apostolic decree and some attempt must be made to relate the setting in which he places it to the situation reflected in Paul's correspondence. The Antiochene congregation, I suggest, did rejoice when the decree arrived: it rejoiced because the decree promised to relieve the embarrassment which it experienced as a result of Peter's withdrawal from table fellowship with Gentile Christians.

---

[14] See the important discussion "Apostles in Council and in Conflict" in C. K. Barrett, Freedom and Obligation: A Study of the Epistle to the Galatians, London: SPCK, 1985, pp.

[13] D. W. B. Robinson, The Circumcision of Titus, and Paul's Liberty, Australian Biblical Review 12, 1964, pp. 40f.

91–108.

At the council of Jerusalem the leaders of the mother church decided not to impose circumcision and other traditional Jewish requirements on Gentile Christians. But this decision, welcome as it was, left many practical questions unanswered. There was disagreement on the question of table fellowship between Jewish and Gentile believers. At Antioch, in the early days, this question had not surfaced. Barnabas (and Paul, of course) ate freely with uncircumcised Gentile Christians; so did Peter when he first came to Antioch. As Paul put it, Peter in the society of Gentile Christians lived ἐθνικῶς and not ἰουδαϊκῶς (Gal 2,14). It can readily be understood that some stricter Jewish believers were scandalized when news of Peter's free and easy way of life reached them: no doubt reports of his behaviour created difficulties for their mission among their fellow-Jews, but they disapproved of it on principle and not simply because of the difficulties it caused. Hence the peremptory message from James that made Peter change his practice and eat with Jews only, saying in effect to the Gentile Christians, "If you wish to go on having table fellowship with me, you must 'judaize'" (Gal 2,14) – i.e. you must live ἰουδαϊκῶς and no longer ἐθνικῶς. There is the further possibility that the renewal of Zealot activity in Judaea about this time, in which Jews who fraternized with Gentiles were targets for attack, added urgency to James's expostulation[15], but the logic of the situation (as the stricter party saw it) was plain enough even apart from that consideration.

The resultant split in the Antiochene congregation is described by Paul. Paul seems to have been isolated among the leaders of the congregation – even Barnabas sided with Peter – and there is no evidence that the cleavage between him and his fellow-leaders was healed; it was still there when he wrote to the Galatians. But not only was Paul isolated from the other leaders; the church of Antioch was itself divided, and this state of affairs could not be allowed to continue. If (as all sides now apparently agreed) circumcision was not a requirement for salvation, what were the conditions which would enable Jewish and Gentile Christians to meet in table fellowship and other forms of social intercourse? This was a situation which called for debate and decision at the highest level. No one had a greater concern for a satisfactory settlement on the issue than Peter. No doubt it was with reluctance that he had withdrawn from table fellowship with Gentile Christians at Antioch: he had, in fact, been placed in a most embarrassing position. He did not want to appear illiberal and reactionary, but the representations made by James's messengers could not be ignored.

It is probable, then, that Luke in Ac 15 conflates two separate meetings at Jerusalem – an earlier one (at which Paul was present), which re-

[15] See R. Jewett, The Agitators and the Galatian Congregation, NTS 17, 1970–71, pp. 198–212.

fused to require circumcision from Gentile converts, and a later one (at which Paul was not present), where the apostolic decree was drawn up[16]. Having decided on the earlier occasion that circumcision was not to be imposed, the Jerusalem leaders now had to consider the terms on which practical day-to-day fellowship could be tolerated in mixed churches (like the church of Antioch).

It may be that this second meeting, like the first, was attended by delegates of the church of Antioch. By this time, however, Paul's standing in that church was not such that he would have been chosen as a delegate. He had failed to carry any of his colleagues with him: all the other Jewish Christians in the church followed Peter's example. Indeed, Antioch seems to have ceased to provide a missionary base for Paul from then on.

IV.

As for the compromise decree, it bears marks of Peter's inspiration. From the traditional Jewish point of view, it is an extremely liberal document: those who had insisted that Gentile converts should be circumcised must have felt that their "pillar" apostles had sold the pass in settling for such easy terms as these. Martin Hengel does not exaggerate when he says that the apostolic decision "bears witness to an astounding magnanimity that can hardly be explained on other grounds than the sense of obligation felt even by the 'pillars' at Jerusalem (Gal 2,9) to follow the intent of Jesus' message"[17]. Such magnanimity was characteristic of Peter. There is a hint of the Petrine inspiration of the decree in Luke's narrative, where James introduces his proposal to adopt it with a reference to "Symeon's" argument. "Symeon's" argument was that, since God had manifestly made no distinction between Jewish and Gentile believers, they for their part should follow the divine example. James finds this argument confirmed by prophetic testimony, which tells how all the nations over which the name of Yahweh has been called will be brought back into their allegiance to the house of David (now represented by Jesus, the son of Da-

---

[16] For an argument that the apostolic decree did not originate in the Jerusalem meeting of Ac 15,6 see M. Dibelius, Das Apostelkonzil, in Aufsätze zur Apostelgeschichte, ed. H. Greeven, Göttingen: Vandenhoeck & Ruprecht, 1951, pp. 84–90. Cf. T. W. Manson, Studies in the Gospels and Epistles, ed. M. Black, Manchester: Manchester University Press, 1962, pp. 186f.; F. Hahn, Das Verständnis der Mission im Neuen Testament, WMANT 13, Neukirchen-Vluyn: Neukirchener Verlag, 1963, pp. 70–74. Hahn thinks that the council and the decree were already associated in a pre-Lukan Antiochene source.

[17] M. Hengel, Gewalt und Gewaltlosigkeit: Zur "politischen Theologie" in neutestamentlicher Zeit, Calwer Hefte, ed. G. Hennig, 118, Stuttgart: Calwer Verlag, 1971, trans. D. E. Green, Victory over Violence, London: SPCK, 1975, p. 87.

vid). In the LXX version of Amos 9,11f., put in James's mouth in Ac 15,16f., the oracle has already been spiritualized so as to point to religous rather than political submission; how likely James is to have quoted it in this sense, if not in this form, is a matter for debate.

Peter, being a man of decent feeling, no doubt felt real distress at the dismay which his withdrawal from table fellowship with them had created among the Gentile Christians of Antioch. Since it was a message from James that prompted his withdrawal, then the problem must be sorted out with James. Against the insistence of the circumcision party, but without going so far as Paul, Peter succeeded in having an acceptable compromise sponsored by James himself and embodied in the decree. It may well be believed that the news of this decision brought as much relief to the church of Antioch as Luke says it did. Then, when Peter embarked on a wider ministry, he recommended the terms of the decree as a reasonable *modus vivendi* for mixed churches in other places, including (in all probability) Corinth. Hence came the Corinthians' question to Paul about meat offered to idols, and his reply to them.

As for Peter, the bridge-builder among the apostles[18], the decree must have been welcomed by him not only because it would relieve his personal embarrassment but also because it provided a bridge between the church of Jerusalem and the Gentile churches. Paul too was conscious of the need for bridge-building, but the bridge which he undertook to build was "the collection for the saints"; it is doubtful, however, if the collection did succeed in bringing the church of Jerusalem and Paul's Gentile mission any closer together.

Even after the dispersal of the mother-church and the fall of Jerusalem, when the situation which called forth the decree had lost its urgency, the decree continued for long to be observed by Gentile Christians around the Mediterranean. There was some resistance to it in the churches of Asia later in the first century: the seer of Patmos insists on submission to it, and classes those who try to relax its terms with Balaam and Jezebel, who in Old Testament times seduced the Israelites into wrong ways, teaching them to practise fornication and to eat food sacrificed to idols (Rev 2,14.20). He refers to such people as Nicolaitans (Rev 2,6.15); if the tradition is accepted which associates them with Nicolaus of Antioch (Ac 6,5), then we can well understand that one of Stephen's colleagues might have taken the same attitude to controversial food as Paul took.

The churches of the Rhone valley were daughter-congregations of the churches of proconsular Asia: the letter which describes the persecution which they endured in A.D. 177 makes it clear that among them the

[18] See J. D. G. Dunn, Unity and Diversity in the New Testament, London: SCM Press, 1977, p. 385.

eating of blood was banned (Eusebius, *HE* 5.1.26). In North Africa, a little later in the second century, we find the same situation: Christians, according to Tertullian (*Apol.* 9.13), do not even include animals' blood in their ordinary diet, and therefore avoid the flesh of strangled animals. In the early church, as at the present day, the majority of Christians probably preferred to have a ruling on such matters from an acknowledged authority than to have the decision left to their own conscience and sense of what is fitting. To such people "tell me my duty and I will do it" is more congenial than the gospel liberty for which Paul contended.

V.

These desultory reflections are offered as a tribute, imperfect but none the less sincere, to Heinrich Greeven in admiring gratitude for the many great services that he has rendered to New Testament scholarship. One of his early services was to edit and publish the collection of Martin Dibelius's *Aufsätze zur Apostelgeschichte.* The appearance of this volume in 1951 was eagerly welcomed by students of Acts (not least, by the present writer): it seems appropriate, therefore, that some observations on an episode in Acts should be presented to Professor Greeven on this happy occasion. *In multos annos*!

The Purpose and Construction of a Critical Apparatus to a Greek New Testament

by J. K. Elliott

(The University of Leeds, Department of Theology and Religious Studies, Hopewell House, 173 Woodhouse Lane, Leeds LS2 3AR, England)

The critical apparatus in Greeven's *Synopse* is a model of compactness. After only a little practice it yields to the diligent reader much valuable information. *Multum in parvo* indeed. Another praiseworthy feature of this apparatus is that the range of variation units selected is deliberately circumscribed. In his Introduction p. XI Greeven states that his apparatus includes all the variants from his text to be found in six other editions as well as variants which some textual critics claim to be original. Also, he includes variants which have the effect of assimilating the text of the synoptic parallels. Just as the range of variants is thereby deliberately controlled so too is the number of mss. chosen for special attention. The Introduction pp. XXVIIIff. draws attention to the thirty-seven papyri, one hundred and sixty-six uncials, sixty-one cursives and one lectionary regularly used in the preparation of the apparatus as well as the fifty-one Old Latin manuscripts consulted and the other versional evidence used. Although many other manuscripts turn up from time to time in this apparatus, those listed in the Introduction have been controlled consistently[1] with the result that even those not explicitly cited may have their readings inferred. Thus the absence of Old Latin n from the apparatus does not mean its readings are ignored; at Mark 9,3 for example the apparatus shows that στίλβοντα is omitted by, among others, the Old Latin k[e]l. Insofar as p. XXIV shows that n is extant for this verse we infer that n includes the equivalent of στίλβοντα. Likewise the absence of a fragmentary papyrus from the apparatus should indicate that this ms. does not reveal or support a *v. l.* that is included in this edition.

These three features of Greeven's apparatus, its compactness, control over variants, and comprehensiveness of citation of certain selected mss., should be heeded as desiderata for any select apparatus. But, before any editor attempts to compile an apparatus, certain principles need to be established and certain queries answered.

---

1 See my 'The Citation of Manuscripts in Recent Printed Editions of the Greek New Testament', *NovT* XXV (1983), pp. 97–132.

I.

Several basic questions arise when a critical apparatus is to be appended to a printed text:

(i) What is the need for a critical apparatus at all? Unless one follows in the footsteps of Palmer, Westcott and Hort, Tasker or Kilpatrick's diglott fascicles in whose editions the reader is expected to accept editorial decisions without being able to check on the basis for such decisions, except in minimal notes, a critical apparatus is deemed normal in a scholarly edition of the Greek New Testament[2].

Even the most confident editor is confronted from time to time with alternative readings whether his textual principles are based on internal or external evidence or on a combination of both, either because the arguments for selecting one variant over another are inconclusive, or the mss. selected as authoritative elsewhere are themselves divided in their attestation. In such circumstances an editor of a Greek New Testament text finds it expedient to expose his dilemma. This publicising of alternatives is particularly necessary when the editor is himself not certain which reading is original and which secondary. Another reason for displaying alternative readings in the margin is when the editor wishes to show a reading that has been deemed important in other printed editions or in the history of the church. Occasionally a reading may be in an apparatus either because it is found in a ms. in which the editor is interested, or because it is of some interest or importance; such seems to be the reason why several readings peculiar to a papyrus are to be found in the apparatus to Nestle-Aland *Novum Testamentum Graece* 26th edition (N-A[26]).

(ii) One decision that must be reached is over the comprehensiveness of the apparatus. For normal purposes, especially for a pocket edition, an exhaustive apparatus is unthinkable. If 'exhaustive' means the inclusion of every viable variant in every accessible ms. then this is clearly an impossibility. Even so full an apparatus as the International Greek New Testament Project's (IGNTP) edition of Luke is limited in the number of mss. it uses (see II below). Therefore some selection is needed both in terms of the number of mss. cited and the *v. ll.* included. The question concerns the control of an editor over any selection. In several editions of the Greek New Testament published in the last fifty years it would seem as if the selection of both variants and manuscripts is both arbitrary and haphazard. All too often one is subjected to editorial whim and, in the absence of clearly defined principles, an apparatus in such an edition is dangerously unhelpful.

---

[2] See I. A. Moir's justification for a critical apparatus in his basic 'A Mini-Guide to New Testament Textual Criticism', *BibT* 36 (1985) 122–9.

The nature of the readings to be included in an apparatus ought to be discussed by an editor. A selective apparatus by definition is always going to disappoint but the editor of a pocket edition ought to be aware of the limitations and therefore try to mitigate the effects. If one is investigating a theological feature such as the virgin birth tradition, one needs to know how often Mary and Joseph are described as Jesus' parents. In a variant reading at Luke 2,22 they are so described but this is not given in the select apparatus of, say, N-A^{26}, UBS, Bover–O'Callaghan or Vogels. Similarly, if one's interest is grammatical or linguistic, as full an apparatus as possible is required. For example, a few years ago I tried to determine the original form of the name 'Jerusalem' in various parts of the New Testament[3]. For the purpose I needed to collect evidence of firm instances, undisputed in our available stock of mss., of both forms of the name. A pocket edition and a select apparatus could not be relied on. Similarly, one inevitably reaches an impasse with a select apparatus if one wishes to follow through the firmness of a text while investigating, say, diminutive nouns, word-order, tense fluctuations, presence or absence of certain particles etc. A good grammar of New Testament Greek or of an individual author's style should not be made on the basis of one printed text or even one printed text with a select apparatus. For such purposes only a comprehensive assemblage of readings is satisfactory.

Although the number of variant readings given in a pocket edition such as N-A^{26} is normally adequate for general teaching purposes, certain safeguards are needed: the range of the variant readings needs to be spelt out in an introduction so at least the reader is aware how the selection has been carried out. This is done in *The Greek New Testament according to the Majority Text* (= GNTMT), UBS and (as we have seen) in Greeven's *Synopse.*

(iii) If it is agreed that an apparatus displaying certain alternative readings is essential in an edition of the Greek testament a subsidiary question follows. That is: Why cite mss. in support of the reading? If the purpose in printing an apparatus is to exhibit alternative readings that have been important in the history of the church or have been influential in other editions or readings which the editor has relegated to the margin only reluctantly, then in theory it could indeed be argued that there should be no obvious requirement to append to the reading the mss. in support. (If one is presenting in the apparatus the rejected readings of certain chosen mss. then of course such a practice would not be considered.) But the absence of supporting evidence for any reading would be a dangerous omission and it has not usually been the practice of New Testament scholars to quote readings without at least giving a selection of the available supporting evidence. To be confronted in an apparatus by a 'disembodied'

[3] 'Jerusalem in Acts and The Gospels', *NTS* 23 (1976–77), pp. 462–9.

reading could lead one to conclude that the reading may be a mere conjecture. To have a general statement such as one finds in the footnotes to modern translations that says 'Some ancient authorities here add . . .' or 'Some mss. omit these words . . .' or the like is unsatisfactory in a critical Greek text. To have at least some of the ms. support printed allows one (a) to be able to check on the accuracy of the evidence from a microfilm, facsimile or collation of the ms. in question, (b) to evaluate the range of support for the reading: this latter is an activity beloved of those textual critics who require a certain weight or spread of evidence before they countenance the reading as original, and (c) to relate the reading to a ms. that at one time and in one place was at least its possessor's bible. If one can date a reading or at least establish the earliest extant record of its existence, and if one can see the geographical spread of the reading from the provenance of the support for it (insofar as that can be determined), then these may be of importance in discussing the originality or the history of the reading. Even the most radical of thoroughgoing eclectic critics, whose regard for external evidence is scant, has to recognise that certain mss. are prone to certain types of reading. To identify scribal idiosyncrasies in particular mss. enables him to disregard such aberrations when they are included in a variation unit; knowledge of a ms. precedes a decision on the originality of its readings – at least to that extent! A ms. that is known uniquely, regularly and automatically to expand the *nomina sacra* is unlikely to be a seriously considered supporter for a variant expanding the divine names found in another ms. that has betrayed no such proclivity elsewhere (cf. III B (b) below). In such cases one needs to identify in the apparatus which mss. support the readings.

(iv) This leads on to our next question: How many mss. ought to be cited in support? The United Bible Societies' (UBS) text has an apparatus limited to only one thousand four hundred variation units, the theory behind this selection being that only variants deemed important for translators (the market for which this text was originally conceived) would be shown[4]. For such a readership one might have contemplated an apparatus with readings printed without supporting evidence, especially as Metzger's companion volume discusses each of these variation units (together with six hundred more) but, for the reasons given above (iii) the display of unattributed readings is undesirable. In fact the UBS apparatus has such a full range of ms. evidence supporting each reading that one pities the translator who is not a textual critic as he wades through the lines of cursive numbers, possibly overwhelmed and unduly influenced by the sheer quantity of mss. in support of a reading. UBS^3 brings the evidence of over nine hundred Greek mss. into its edition. By contrast in $N\text{-}A^{26}$ five

[4] Criticism of the actual selection is to result in a slightly revised selection of variants in a fourth edition currently being prepared.

hundred are included (excluding those under M = majority text). Not only is the number of mss. in N-A[26] smaller but it is more carefully controlled: some mss. are identified in the Introduction and Appendix as being cited consistently throughout the New Testament or a part of it or only for particular readings. No such help is offered in UBS[3].

Whatever the range and quantity of mss. an editor chooses for his edition this selection needs to be determined and indicated even if an occasional ms. has been cited only for a particular section of the text (e.g. the Comma Johanneum, the longer or shorter endings to Mark etc.) If this is not done then one is inevitably left with the impression that the editor has picked up ms. support casually here and there from earlier apparatuses such as von Soden's or Tischendorf's to bolster a reading that he finds important for inclusion in his apparatus. The apparatuses to the editions of Bover, Merk and Vogels seem to suffer from this defect.

II.

The need for an exhaustive or at least a comprehensive apparatus is obvious for a professional textual critic and exegete. Such are satisfied only when as full a range of readings and mss. is available. The IGNTP Luke[5] purports to be such a comprehensive apparatus. It is not a new text nor was it ever intended to be[6]. Within the range of mss. (all papyri and nearly all uncials of Luke, forty-one lectionaries and one hundred and twenty-eight cursives (selected by the Claremont Profile Method)) and the self-imposed limitations it is as full as may be expected. It certainly is the most extensive collection of information on the text of Luke ever assembled. In the (unpublished) words of one early reader:

> The plan of the work is revolutionary in that at every point where a variant, however small, occurs, the evidence of all the hundreds of authorities used in the edition is quoted in full, either explicitly or

---

[5] *The Gospel According to St Luke* edited by the American and British Committees of the International Greek New Testament Project, Part I, chapters 1–12 (Oxford, 1984), Part II (forthcoming).

[6] It has been wrongly criticised for not attempting to create a definitive text, e.g. K. Aland 'Bemerkungen zu Probeseiten einer großen kritischen Ausgabe des Neuen Testaments', *NTS* 13 (1965–6), pp. 176–85. The launch of another major apparatus was trumpeted in the 1967–8 *Bericht* of the Institut für neutestamentliche Textforschung (Münster). Despite lavish external funding, work on this 'new Tischendorf' unfortunately seems to have been shelved and the later issues of the biannual *Bericht* quietly dropped all reference to the Editio Maior Critica although the 1985 *Bericht* still anticipates a 'Große Ausgabe' (by which it now seems to be referred to) in the very far distant future – and apparently without regret for the delay (p. 65). This leaves the IGNTP Luke as the sole beacon of achievement and accomplishment in this area.

> implicitly, whereas in all previous editions quotation has been more or less selective, and one always has the feeling that information which to the editor seems unimportant is being omitted. When one turns from one of these editions to the IGNTP edition the effect is electric: it is like coming out of a fog. Suddenly everything is before one and one no longer has the feeling of being under the control of the editor.

In IGNTP a decision was taken to record only the divergences from the Textus Receptus in the apparatus. It would, of course, be a great convenience, for each variant, to be able to quote both the authorities which support the variant and those which do *not*; but of course this would have resulted in an enormous increase in the size of the work and consequent difficulty in securing publication. It is in fact possible, if one wishes, to work out a full list of the authorities which do *not* support a variant by taking the list of all authorities used, printed in the Introduction, deleting those which are defective at this particular point[7], and then deducting those supporting the variant. This would be a laborious process, and I am not sure of the circumstances in which it would be required: it is far more likely that the reader would be interested in the affiliations of a particular manuscript or group of manuscripts, and for such a restricted group the process of subtraction would provide little difficulty.

In IGNTP it was (wisely) decided to delete certain types of variant to be found in the Greek material from the apparatus. Nonsense readings and scribal blunders (including examples of dittography) and sheer orthographical errors and itacisms which do not affect the sense were omitted, but, obviously, where an 'itacistic' reading could be construed as a genuine variant this is retained, for instance we record ἴδητε / εἰδῆτε at Luke 21,31 and εἴχετε / ἔχετε at Luke 17,6 and διέλιπε / διέλειπε at Luke 7,45. Other orthographical exceptions are set out in the Introduction but within these parameters an attempt was made to retain every variant in every ms. used for the edition.

III.

In addition to the continuous text mss. in Greek other material is commonly found in a critical apparatus to a Greek New Testament, namely Greek lectionaries, early versions and patristic citations. Each creates particular problems for an editor.

---

[7] Lacunae in each ms. are recorded in the edition. This meets F. C. Grant's plea (in *New Testament Manuscripts Studies* ed. M. M. Purvis and A. Wikren (Chicago, 1950) p. 93) that this information ought to be given in a critical apparatus, otherwise silence would be mistakenly taken for support.

A. *Lectionaries*

As far as lectionary evidence is concerned this is seldom cited with any degree of consistency in an apparatus, partly because of the difficulty of obtaining collations of the material. Although there are some two thousand[8] lectionaries registered in the Aland list very few have been analysed in detail[9]. Greeven's apparatus actually includes the readings of over one hundred and forty lectionaries but most of the material is unchecked and second-hand. The worst problem with this material in the average apparatus is that, even when it is included, it is inadequately displayed. D. W. Riddle states[10] 'The essential secret of the lectionaries, and the necessary principle of their proper use, is the recognition that the lectionary text is heterogeneous with reference to its several parts. It follows that if parts are discriminated and the individual lections identified, a published collation or citation of lectionary readings in an apparatus becomes a genuinely scientific instrument. The full report of lection incipits is likewise necessary'. The IGNTP Luke is the only edition known to me that tries to satisfy these requirements: the individual lections are identified by day and date, and the incipits are shown[11]. This edition shows in full the evidence of thirty-one lectionaries that deviate from the dominant text, and a consortium of ten as representing the dominant text[12].

---

[8] Cf. K. Junack 'Zu den griechischen Lektionaren und ihrer Überlieferung der Katholischen Briefe' in K. Aland (ed.) *Die Alten Übersetzungen des Neuen Testaments, die Kirchenväterzitate und Lektionare* = ANTF 5, (Berlin, New York, 1972) pp. 498–590, esp. p. 500.

[9] Over fifty years ago the lack of research into and understanding of the lectionaries was noted by E. C. Colwell and D. W. Riddle in their *Prolegomena to the Study of the Lectionary Text of the Gospels* (Chicago, 1933). Little has changed since then.

[10] 'The Use of Lectionary Manuscripts in Critical Editions and Studies of the New Testament Text' in Colwell and Riddle, *Prolegomena* op. cit. pp. 67–77. Quotation from p. 77.

[11] Greeven's *Synopse* does indicate if a lectionary that repeats a given lection agrees only in part with a *v. l.*

[12] In a review article in *Gnomon* 56 (1984), pp. 481–97, prepared with the help of the Mitarbeiter of the Institut für neutestamentliche Textforschung, its retired director, K. Aland, complains on p. 485 that he is unaware of the method used for selecting these lectionaries. This is surprising because in the case of both minuscules and lectionaries the Introduction refers the reader to an article in *JBL* that describes the selection (p. vi). It is even more surprising because extensive selections of and comments on that *JBL* article appear with special reference to the selection process of lectionaries in IGNTP in K. Aland's own edition *Die Alten Übersetzungen des Neuen Testaments, die Kirchenväterzitate und Lektionare* (*op. cit.* pp. 491–3)!

B. *Versions*

As the compiler of the IGNTP apparatus I found that my greatest problems concerned the versions and fathers. I soon came to appreciate why the evidence from these two sources in so many critical editions is haphazard, irrelevant, useless or just plain wrong. So often such material has been lifted from earlier editions without being checked. No wonder that the Münster Institut with its resources of personnel and finance is undertaking an examination of all such material for UBS⁴ (and, one hopes, for N-A also)[13].

Before we look in detail at some of the problems associated with citing the versions we may well pause to ask how necessary it is to include in the critical apparatus to a *Greek* NT such material, even though nearly all critical editions, including IGNTP, do indeed include this evidence.

The justification is usually given that such evidence can genuinely support the Greek manuscript tradition and in some cases may even preserve readings which have either virtually disappeared from all Greek sources, or which are unknown in extant Greek mss. Some of the early versions in particular depend on Greek mss. that antedate surviving Greek evidence and therefore could preserve older and more reliable material than that found in the later and possibly corrupted Greek tradition.

In some respects versional evidence can be ambiguous in a Greek apparatus or reflect a purely inner-versional variant, but at other times the reading in a version can unambiguously support one or other variant in the Greek, the most obvious example being where the issue is a longer against a shorter text. Wikgren writing on versions in the volume *New Testament Manuscript Studies*[14] reminded us that sometimes originally peculiar readings in a version have subsequently been found to have Greek support. The vagaries of survival need always to be kept in mind. However, powerful arguments are required before scholars are convinced that the original reading has been preserved only in translation. This might have happened occasionally as G. D. Kilpatrick argued[15] with reference to the introductory formula at Rev. 2,1.8.12.18; 3,1.7.14 τῷ ἀγγέλῳ τῷ ἐν. At 3,14 this formula has survived only in the Armenian and Harklean Syriac versions (cf. also 3,7 where the Syriac and Armenian have patristic support from Primasius and Cassiodor). A more dubious use of versional evidence is where the editors of the UBS³ (and N-A²⁶) texts are prepared to cite the evidence of two medieval versions (the Provençal and Old Dutch) to support their conjectural Greek reading at Acts 16,12.

---

13 Some preliminary spadework has been done and is evident in UBS^3A. See my review in *NovT* XXVI (1984), pp. 337f.

14 *Op. cit.* p. 103.

15 'Professor J. Schmid on the Greek Text of the Apocalypse' VC 13 (1959) pp. 1–13.

In less extreme – but nonetheless important – circumstances, versional evidence can bolster material that would otherwise be described in some quarters as inadequate, and may alter not only the age but also the geographical extent of a given variant.

Accuracy is obviously required for all material in an apparatus. Where versional citations are concerned, accuracy needs to be accompanied by relevance. B. M. Metzger in *The Early Versions of the New Testament* drew our attention to the special problem of the versions: in his subchapters on particular languages, scholars such as S. P. Brock on the Syriac and J. M. Plumley on the Coptic outlined the hazards to be faced when matching the Greek to a version.

Let us take examples from the Syriac, the Ethiopic and the Latin:

(a) Syriac has a syntax that in many ways runs counter to the Greek and this inevitably creates many readings that are unlikely to reflect on the Greek original. I am thinking here in particular of word order changes necessitated by the syntax of the Syriac and also of καί and δέ as introductory particles, which are often freely treated in the Syriac. These, in general, should be ignored, unless there is Greek evidence for the variants, when it might be proper to include the Syriac. For instance at Luke 19,22 many Greek mss. omit δέ. The old Syriac, the Peshitta and the Harklean likewise have no particle here and thus it seems permissible to add their testimony to that of the Greek even though it could be argued that their evidence gives no real clue to the Greek text they were translating. To ignore their evidence might by implication be tantamount to adding them to the Greek mss. supporting the inclusion of δέ.

Many readings by both the Syriac, and other versions for that matter, could be added to the apparatus and would be formally correct, but if the purpose of citing versions in an apparatus to the Greek testament is to throw light on the *Greek* does the inclusion of a version for such a reading really add anything? Such a question has regularly been in my mind during the compilation of the Luke apparatus. Often a fine editorial judgement is required, a judgement that I fear I have not always exercised consistently. But one factor that has sometimes swayed me in favour of inclusion is the weight of ms. support, and indeed the support of other versions. So, occasionally, the Syriac, for example, will be found in the IGNTP apparatus supporting a variant that happens to agree with the natural word order of that version because it is arguable that if such a word order is known to have existed in several Greek mss. then the translators *might* have used such a text and found it fitted naturally with their native idiom anyway. When such evidence is ambiguous I have generally tended, as in the case of the particles, to err in favour of including the evidence of a version rather than excluding it. One does not want to mislead a reader by overwhelming him with evidence that is irrelevant, ambiguous or meaningless but on the other hand it has sometimes seemed wisest to present the reader with the chance to accept, or indeed to reject, the editorial judgement; and this is easier for the reader if such evidence is placed before him rather than when it is omitted. Such omitted material would then have to be sought, in some cases laboriously, in outside sources.

(b) The Ethiopic, because of its close links with the Semitic and Coptic versions, is an important source of material in the apparatus, but most extant mss. are late and we lack a good critical edition of this version. N-A[26] and the IGNTP Luke were obliged to rely heavily on Pell Platt and Pretorius's edition of 1899, although for the Project we also had access to some unpublished material.

Coupled with the lack of a modern critical edition of the Ethiopic[16], one has to cope with the distinctive problems of this version. One observes many times in Luke just how free a translation the Ethiopic is; thus in a collation many variants come to light that have no outside support. One tendency of the Ethiopic is to paraphrase and another is to translate with duplicate expressions. In general such variants were deemed not to be relevant in our apparatus. Other idiosyncrasies were observed: for instance, one ms. always prefaced the name Jesus with 'Lord'. Such a liturgical addition is unlikely to throw light on the underlying Greek. Hence, even when one finds a Greek *v. l.* + κύριος one would hesitate before adding this Ethiopic ms. to the support for κύριος: to do so would be formally correct but would be meaningless in our search for the original Greek.

(c) For the Latin, once one has decided which ms. belongs to the Old Latin and which Vulgate (given the sizable penumbra of mss. whose attribution as witnesses to a pre-Jerome text is disputed)[17] the relevance of all the variants within the Latin that can be observed in, among other sources, the Wordsworth and White, Stuttgart or Jülicher texts has to be assessed.

First the accuracy of these texts has itself to be established before their readings can be accepted! Let us take a few examples: at Luke 10,24 for ἤκουσαν Wordsworth and White say gat reads capierunt against Heer's edition of this ms. that claims gat reads audierunt (= ἤκουσαν). At Luke 10,34 Jülicher² does not clearly show if r¹ omits eius². At Luke 20,33 Jülicher² implies that ff² reads uxorem, whereas Wordsworth and White say ff² *omits* uxorem (Wordsworth and White are wrong here). But at Luke 20,47 Jülicher² is wrong and Wordsworth and White correct in distinguishing between the readings of c on the one hand and fs on the

[16] For the Harklean Syriac the situation is worse: the latest printed edition is 1778!

[17] The ambiguity of some mss. has led different editors in different directions, e.g. see the way in which g¹ (Sangermanensis), gat (gatianus), δ and Armagh are treated in my 'Old Latin Manuscripts in Printed Editions of the Greek New Testament', *NovT* XXVI (1984), pp. 225–48.

other. Part of the problem there is that Jülicher[2] cites c twice – for different readings! (cf. also in Jülicher[2] the double reading for d at Luke 23,6 (autem)). Jülicher[2] includes the evidence of aur at Luke 21,23 even though it also reports a lacuna in aur from 21,8 to 21,30! These, and other, oddities need to be sorted out before an editor can borrow evidence, even from such modern critical editions.

But after having ascertained the accuracy of the evidence, the question of its relevance for inclusion in an apparatus designed principally to illuminate the history of the Greek text needs to be considered. In the following examples from Luke the Latin variants, interesting though they are and significant though they may be for an apparatus to the Latin text, are probably to the excluded from a Greek apparatus because they all seem to be inner-Latin alternatives:

(i) 15,23.27.30 saginatum vitulum *v. l.* vitulum illum saginatum *v. l.* illum vitulum saginatum *v. l.* vitulum saginatum. Is the change in word order relevant? Do the variants with illum reflect an attempt to render the definite article in Greek? The answer to both seems to be 'No'.

(ii) 18,3. The context requires ἤρχετο to be part of the verb ἔρχομαι. The Latin translators were confused, some taking it to be from ἔρχομαι (and rendering it venit or veniebat), others taking it from ἄρχομαι (as coepit), and ff[2] rendering the two (veniens coepit)!

(iii) 23,33. Only quidem in a seems to render μέν, but insofar as there is no regular Latin equivalent of μέν this reading of a is probably of no help in our unearthing the underlying Greek.

(iv) 21,26. The variety of rendering of ἀποψυχόντων in Latin merely reflects the translators' ignorance of the verb; only d gets it right.

(v) 12,37 ἀνακλινει. The Greek is ambiguous unaccented, hence some Latin mss. render it as future, others as present. The context requires the future.

Of a rather different type is the rendering of ἐλαιων at Luke 19,29; 21,37. If this is ἐλαιῶν then olivarum read by δ at 19,29, and by e at 21,37 is worth recording; if it is ἐλαιών (= ἐλαιῶνος) then olivetum or oliveti is the correct rendering. As the Greek here is ambiguous it seems worthwhile to indicate in an apparatus how at least some early translators understood, or read, the Greek (cf. Luke 19,37; 22,39).

It has been a convention in some editions to print the peculiar readings, especially of the Latin versions, in Latin in the apparatus. In IGNTP Luke we have in general preferred to represent the versional reading by retroverting it into Greek: such a practice is usually desirable even though it obviously requires care. Care is also required for both the Latin and other versions even when the variant seems to have Greek ms. support. Sometimes, for instance, it is impossible to determine which of several synonyms in a version belongs to which Greek variant, and, conversely, which of several Greek synonyms in a variant is supported by a version. In such instances it is wiser not to risk retroverting lest one misleads a reader by suggesting only one of several possible Greek words is intended.

More controversial is the attempt to preserve grammatical features that belong to the Greek idiom when one is retroverting. *Lvt* (b) and LUC consistently make ἡ μνᾶ in Lk. 19 'talent' = *το* τάλαντον. If one retroverts the Latin to the neuter noun in Greek, is one not obliged in 19,20 to alter the related feminine particle ἀποκειμένην later in the sentence to a purely illusory [ἀποκειμένον] to preserve the concinnity? Here no Greek is ever presumed to read ἀποκειμένον but such a reading would have to be invented if the reading of the version were shown in Greek.

C. *Fathers*

The significance of patristic citation in an apparatus has long been recognised even though the manner of citation and the relevance of all such evidence are sometimes open to question in several of our printed editions. On one level it is important to be able to see how certain texts were interpreted at different times in church history and that can indeed be established to a certain extent in the known writings of particular church fathers. Metzger in his presidential address to SNTS[18] pointed out how E (Acts) and Bede often agree and this is because E was once located in Jarrow. Patristic evidence needs to be taken into account not only when assessing the originality of the text but (perhaps of even greater importance) when discussing the date of a reading insofar as it enables us to provide a *terminus a quo* for its appearance.

Another important advantage of including the evidence of the fathers in an apparatus is that it enables the investigation into which theologically significant variants were known to which father. For instance it is of interest to see who supports readings favourable to the virginal conception in variants in Luke 1–2. Other significant passages where patristic testimony is of importance include John 1,3–4,18, or the endings to Mark.

Certain readings may in fact be preserved only in patristic citations. Fee[19] draws our attention to the reading πολλαὶ μοναὶ παρὰ τῷ πατρί at John 14,2 against the normal ἐν τῇ οἰκίᾳ τοῦ πατρός μου μοναὶ πολλαί εἰσιν. This variant is found in about sixteen Greek and several Latin fathers but not, it seems, in any Greek ms. Such a reading deserves to be heard even if it is rejected as secondary.

---

[18] 'Patristic Evidence and the Textual Criticism of the New Testament', reprinted in B. M. Metzger *New Testament Studies* (Leiden, 1980), pp. 167–88 (= NTTS 10).

[19] G. D. Fee 'The Text of John in the Jerusalem Bible: A Critique of the Use of Patristic Citation in New Textual Criticism' *JBL* XC 1971, 163–173, esp. pp. 171ff.

I have written elsewhere[20] of the readings χωρίς θεοῦ and χάριτι θεοῦ at Heb. 2,9. I argue for the originality of the former (despite the alleged weakness of the Greek support), but, quite independent of the question of the originality of the text here, it is significant to see in an apparatus who knew and quoted Heb. 2,9 in one form or the other. The evidence from the fathers shows that more of them seem to quote χωρίς than χάριτι. Indeed Origen on Jn. 1,35 (GCS 4,45) assumed χωρίς was the normal reading in his day. Both Origen and Jerome, alert as they were to variants in mss., can be instructive about how the text was understood. The explicit references to variants in the fathers deserve special attention. We learn, for example, that Jerome[21] knew in several mss. the longer text after Mark 16,14: Greek ms. evidence for this has been found only recently in the Freer Codex. Origen knew of several mss. with the reading at Luke 14,19 διό οὐ δύναμαι ἐλθεῖν found now only in D *Lvt* (d)[22]. Similarly at Rom. 3,5, Origen knew κατὰ τῶν ἀνθρώπων in several mss.: today due to the vagaries of survival this reading is represented only in 1739 mg *Cs*[23]. Such statements ought to serve as a warning to those who are suspicious of accepting as original a reading that is supported by only a few extant witnesses. An instructive lesson may be had from Westcott and Hort's appendix on suspected readings where they express their high regard for the text of Clement of Alexandria at Heb. 11,4 αὐτῷ τοῦ θεοῦ against the normal αὐτοῦ τοῦ θεοῦ (which they printed although suspecting this was a secondary text to be found in the corrupted ms. tradition). Today Clement has the support of P[13]!

In 1965[24] G. D. Kilpatrick argued in favour of υἵος θεοῦ at Acts 7,56. Additional support for that reading was provided in a supplementary article[25] from patristic citations. For those scholars for whom ms. weight and geographical spread are important such additional testimony can be of crucial importance in deciding on the originality of a variant.

The presentation of patristic material in the apparatus ought however to be there in its own right and not just to bolster those readings that seem

---

[20] 'When Jesus was Apart from God': an Examination of Hebrews 2,9' *ExpT* LXXXIII (1972) pp. 339–341.

[21] Cf. B. M. Metzger 'St. Jerome's Explicit References to Variant Readings in Manuscripts of the New Testament', reprinted in B. M. Metzger, *New Testament Studies* (Leiden, 1980), pp. 199–210 (= NTTS 10).

[22] Cf. Basil the Great's statement that the majority of mss. read ἄρει at Luke 22,36. Today only D *Lvt* (d) have this text.

[23] For further examples see B. M. Metzger 'Explicit References in the Works of Origen to Variant Readings in New Testament Manuscripts', reprinted in B. M. Metzger *Historical and Literary Studies* (Leiden, 1968), pp. 88–103 (= NTTS 8).

[24] 'Acts 7,56: Son of Man?' *TZ* 21 (1965), p. 209.

[25] 'Again Acts 7,56: Son of Man?' *TZ* 34 (1978), p. 232.

to require additional support to make them look convincing to those for whom additional testimony is a requirement before such a reading merits attention.

But the selection and the presentation of this patristic material is problematic.

The conventional way in which patristic citation has been shown in an apparatus is, in general, less than satisfactory. The mere name of a father in an apparatus, followed as it sometimes is (e.g. in Souter and UBS) by an indication if patristic testimony is divided in itself in the way it supports the variant in question, tells us very little. That is why IGNTP has provided for each verse an index detailing all the fathers who quote the verse. Lachmann seems to have been the first to cite in an apparatus the fathers with volume and page of the edition. Tischendorf[8] often added text and context. IGNTP gives not only the extent of the quotation for each verse from which the citation comes[26] but the references both to the patristic work itself and to the latest accessible printed edition of that work. In this way the reader is enabled to locate the quotation in the context of the father's writing and this can of course be significant for the way in which a father might introduce or even cite the quotation.

The problems of the patristic quotations are well-known. Unless the father is providing a commentary on a Biblical book and citing each verse consistently one cannot always be confident what he is quoting from. In the Synoptic Gospels in particular one is not always sure if he is quoting from Luke where a parallel exists or from the parallel itself[27]. Thus in IGNTP we tended to err on the side of caution by including the citation as if it came from Luke but also by giving cross-references to the parallels.

But even if the location of the passage is unambiguously from one gospel or from any one Biblical book for that matter, one has to assess the accuracy with which the father quotes. Often the father may be citing from memory, and any variation between the quotation and the collating base

---

26 A firm decision about the precise length of the text of certain quotations is not always possible; a short citation in a father may be in accord with a ms. variant displaying a shorter text and one could therefore add that patristic witness as a support for this shorter text: on the other hand, the short citation may mean nothing of the sort – it could be taken as evidence that the father is independently and deliberately using only part of the verse, and that what he read or knew was the longer text. IGNTP, however, makes the extent and content of each patristic citation clear. Aland, in his review of IGNTP in *Gnomon* (*op. cit.* p. 484, cf. *ThRev* 80 (1984) col. 445) allows himself the gratuitous criticism that access to the quotation itself is limited by the practice in IGNTP of giving only the first and last words of each citation in the Index. In fact these are the words of the collating base in order to describe the extent of the quotation as is made clear in the Introduction: it therefore follows that the patristic citation agrees with that collating base unless the apparatus indicates otherwise.

27 This is especially true for the Syriac fathers.

may not reflect a genuine variant such as one finds in the New Testament mss.[28]. And even if a father is referring to a ms. of the New Testament he may well be adapting the quotation to suit his argument. Where the type, number or variety of such variants exist in a patristic citation, the wise convention in IGNTP has been to index such quotations as 'adaptations' (this implies a free quotation by the author): mere references or allusions to a passage are usually ignored.

Such decisions are of course easier to reach when one is dealing with the Greek fathers than with those who wrote in Latin or Syriac, but even within the Greek a quotation displaying several variants most, if not all, of which agree with existing variants in the mss. of the New Testament, raises the question if the quotation ought legitimately be listed as an adaptation. But even if such a citation is so labelled, such a device does not preclude our including in IGNTP the variant of an 'adaptation' in support of a variant in the apparatus, although, in general, a loose quotation found in a patristic citation and given as an adaptation in the IGNTP index usually means that one does expect to find details of its variants in the apparatus. Again, a fine editorial decision is often required. The policy has been that if a striking variant exists that has support elsewhere then even if the citation as a whole is deemed to be an adaptation, nonetheless that support is included in the apparatus. For instance, IGNTP records the support of Bachiarius and Paulinus of Nola at Luke 13,8 for κόφινον κόπριων (a reading found in D *Lvt*, Ambrose, Augustine and Pseudo-Augustine) even though the citation of this verse in these fathers is in the nature of a free adaptation. Similarly an adaptation by Marcion of Luke 21,11 gives the order λοιμοὶ καὶ λιμοί. This agrees with B *Lvg Lvt* and for this reason its support is included.

What has been said about the Greek fathers is doubly problematic with the citations in Latin and Syriac. Here the issue whether a quotation is dependent on a ms. of the New Testament is more pronounced. As a result of this problem it will be noted in the index to IGNTP Luke that many more Latin and Syriac citations are shown as adaptations than is the case with the Greek fathers. The citations attributable to Marcion and Irenaeus bring with them yet another set of problems that needs to be tackled by an editor: these important sources of our knowledge of the second century text are accessible to us only through quotations or allusion by others (in the case of Marcion) or in translations and excerpts (in the case of Irenaeus).

---

[28] See J. Suggs 'The Use of Patristic Evidence in the Search for the Primitive New Testament Text', *NTS* 4 (1958) pp. 139–47 and see J. Duplacy and J. Suggs 'Les Citations Grecs et la Critique du Texte du Nouveau Testament' in *La Bible et les Pères* (ed. A. Benoit and P. Prigent) (Paris, 1971) pp. 187–213.

With all these patristic citations IGNTP was of course dependent on those who slipped the references from the printed editions of each father: some editions aid those undertaking such slipping by the provision of footnotes or a list of Biblical quotations or allusions, whereas other editions do not provide such cribs. Those slipping from the editions with the Biblical passages identified in some way have doubtless depended to some extent on the accuracy and, more particularly, the comprehensiveness of the editor concerned, but in many cases subsequent investigation has revealed deficiencies in the printed editions – not only deficiencies of omission, but also of reference. Many editors tend overconfidently to label a Biblical citation found in both Matthew and Luke as Matthaean rather than Lukan. Other editors treat all citations, whether precise or free, on the same footing.

A good critical edition of a father wisely consulted by those slipping citations is essential but not always available. Another requirement – not always fulfilled – is that variants within the patristic material itself ought to be located in the apparatus of that edition. Those working on patristic material need to have undertaken the textual criticism of that father's work. For this reason, where possible (i.e. where such a critical printed edition of the father exists) one should not rely only on the editor's judgement but should cull from the apparatus to the patristic text relevant variants. This we have tried to do for the IGNTP Luke apparatus.

However, such a possibility does not exist in the case of most patristic texts. All too often one still has to depend on the old Migne editions, but, as more and more modern editions are prepared, further variants might come to light that ought to be inserted in an apparatus to the Greek New Testament.

In addition to limitations imposed on anyone searching a patristic text one further qualification is the extent to which one can trust the extant mss. of a father's work to represent his original text, especially in the case of the Biblical citations. How far have these quotations been contaminated in all existing patristic mss., especially as most witnesses are late? If a scribe copying a patristic work came across an obvious Biblical quotation then there would be a temptation for him to alter the wording to a version of the citation with which he was familiar. This is sometimes difficult to prove and that is why the textual criticism of each father is a necessary and important precondition of work on the citations. In some of the Latin fathers the temptation of scribes working in areas dominated by the Vulgate to assimilate Biblical quotations to the wording of the Vulgate would have been strong.

For this reason IGNTP states that quotations in a father which consistently agree with the Vulgate are, in general, ignored. This was laid down as a policy when the principles of the edition were being established.

In theory that seemed a sensible precaution but in practice it is an inheritance that has led to some editorial headaches.

Although the principle, as expressed in the Introduction to IGNTP Luke, leads the reader to expect to find no references to fathers whose text consistently agrees with the Vulgate, I must confess that this statement has been the cause of problems. What, for instance, is the Vulgate? For such a principle to apply, agreement with only the Stuttgart edition, for instance, would be insufficient. And does 'consistent agreement' mean that that father has to be consistent in *never* diverging from the Stuttgart edition (or from any other edition for that matter)? What is one to do when the Vulgate and the Old Latin are in either full or partial agreement for a verse, as for example in Luke 17,21?

With Augustine *De Consensu Evangelistarum,* the citations in which seem to be regularly in agreement with printed editions of the Vulgate, are we to assume that most of the citations in this work will be ignored? And if so, what of the exceptions? If a father cites a verse six times, five equivalent to the Vulgate and one disagreeing with the Vulgate, we should, on the basis of the principle enunciated above, include that exception, but to do so would give the wrong impression to the reader who may assume that is the *only* time the father cites the verse in question. In IGNTP I have tended to treat the original principle somewhat liberally and have therefore included many references in the index that should be dismissed as mere Vulgate readings, but, by so doing, I have at least presented the evidence to the reader.

A related policy decision in IGNTP, but one which has to be tackled by any editor of a Greek New Testament, was to limit the citations by imposing a cut-off date. We decided to cite only from those fathers whose work can be dated before 500 A.D. This was partly necessitated on pragmatic grounds insofar as the number of citations had to be limited if the work was to see light of day, but, more important, it seems as if the decision was taken on textual grounds in that an increasing number of fathers who wrote after 500 would (if writing in Greek) have used a Biblical text conforming to the Majority Byzantine text and (if in Latin) to Jerome's Vulgate, but the cut-off date at 500 may be seen as somewhat arbitrary: fathers later than 500, the printed editions of which contain Biblical citations not in accord with either the Byzantine Greek text or the Latin Vulgate text, are excluded. It would have been interesting to see just how many exceptions there would have been: each exception would, of course, have been of great significance. A different policy therefore, extending the range of patristic citations, would be desirable.

Even if one has a good critical edition of a father in which the citations and allusions are confidently and accurately shown, and variants from these citations given, and even where such precise quotations are in agreement with a version of the Biblical text differing from the TR and the

Vulgate, another problem remains. That is the way in which a quotation is exhibited in both an index of patristic quotations and in the apparatus. Inevitably many citations are closely influenced by their contexts: sermons or letters often use introductory formulae that necessitated changes within the citation. Where those are identifiable they are obviously of no value in assessing the underlying Greek New Testament text. Ideally, every alleged variant in an apparatus referring to a father's testimony should be investigated within the context of that father. Maybe much patristic support for say, a particle in the apparatus should be expunged as due to nothing more than the context in which the father places that quotation. At least the IGNTP index enables readers to pursue such enquiries.

IV.

Once an editor has decided on the range of mss. and of readings to be included in his text his next task is to present this material in a convenient form in the footnotes. The drafting of an apparatus is obviously of prime importance if the clarity of the material is to shine through. Many editors seem to prefer to take a large unit as a lemma and to include within it all variants, be they of omission, transposition, addition or substitution under that head. Greeven frequently does this and that is why his apparatus seems complicated at first glance. But there are often compelling reasons to treat variants within the larger unit of variation. For instance at Luke 14,5 instead of ὄνος ἢ βοῦς of the Textus Receptus some mss. substitute one or other of these nouns with υἱός or πρόβατον, others add υἱός in various positions, also one or more of these nouns has the postpositional αὐτοῦ in some mss. To display the variants for ὄνος separately from the variants for βοῦς would be confusing unless one first disposed of the variants for ὄνος ἢ βοῦς together. Thus one needs to display first ὄνος ἢ βοῦς (if that is the text printed) before giving the variants from that complete unit: e.g. ὄνος ἢ βοῦς:

v. 1. υἱὸς ἢ βοῦς ἢ ὄνος
v. 1. βοῦς ἢ ὄνος
v. 1. βοῦς αὐτοῦ ἢ ὄνος αὐτοῦ
v. 1. βοῦς ἢ ὄνος αὐτοῦ
v. 1. υἱὸς αὐτοῦ ἢ βοῦς αὐτοῦ ἢ ὄνος αὐτοῦ

then one can exhibit the *v. 11.* that belong exclusively (a) to ὄνος (namely the substitutions υἱός, ὁ υἱὸς, υἱὸς αὐτοῦ, πρόβατον; the additions + υἱός, + αὐτοῦ) and (b) to βοῦς (*v. 1.* + αὐτοῦ).

A related problem in drafting concerns transpositions that also involve the omission of a word or words. Our question is whether we repeat the omission in a separate lemma. In general the policy adopted in IGNTP is not to repeat the reading of a ms. even where a substantial number of other mss. supports only the omission, it being assumed that readers will peruse the apparatus carefully to check if any preceding lemma is also giving evidence to support the omission. But there are exceptions and, as with certain other cases of apparent inconsistency, my policy as editor of this apparatus has been pragmatic, with an eye to the reader in haste. I have assumed that many who consult the edition of Luke will do so to check the support for an occasional variant in which he is interested. If, in the case of an omission, the evidence for which could be displayed in more than one lemma, then I have repeated the evidence if the lemmata are separated by several lines. It should not confuse anyone if such evidence is displayed twice, once under a transposition *v. l.*, and once under the *v. l.* showing the shortening of the text, whereas to exclude the evidence on the second occurrence may mislead the hasty reader.

The care required in drafting is shown in the corrections to UBS^3 and in the 4th and 7th printings of N-A^{26} [29]. Even with these corrections many of the errors noted by Larson in his review of N-A^{26} [30] still remain. He claimed there that some witnesses are missing from an apparatus, some mislabelled, some misplaced and some misrepresented. All these, and other pitfalls, are encountered by those who try to assemble an apparatus[31]. Another pitfall, especially if one is culling ms. evidence to support a *v. l.* from an early apparatus such as Tischendorf^8 is to fail to convert the siglum to the Gregory-Aland system. I have found[32] several examples in the apparatuses to Merk, Bover–O'Callaghan, Souter and in Metzger's commentary on UBS^3 where a ms. number is taken from the old Tischendorf or Hoskier system: such information is at best confusing, at worst misleading.

* * *

In honouring the long-lasting and valuable contribution Professor Greeven has made to the study of the Greek New Testament text, we recognise and acknowledge that the issues and problems outlined in this paper are ones which he has attempted to tackle and which he has been conspicuously aware of. This all-too-rare talent in an editor of an apparatus is a shining example to all of us who labour in the textual vineyard.

---

29 Cf. my review of UBS^{3A}, *NovT* XXVI (1984), pp. 377f.and of N-A^{26} 7th printing in *Bib Trans* 36 (1985) pp. 143f.

30 S. Larson 'The 26th Edition of Nestle–Aland, *Novum Testamentum Graece*: A Limited Examination of its Apparatus', *JSNT* 12 (1981), pp. 53–68.

31 Some errors in Huck-Greeven are to be found in my 'An Examination of the Text and Apparatus of Three Recent Greek Synopses', *NTS* (forthcoming, October 1986).

32 In 'The Citation of Greek Manuscripts in Six Printed Texts of the New Testament', *Rev Bib* 92 (1985) pp. 539–56, and in 'The Citation of Greek Manuscripts in Recent Printed Editions of the Greek New Testament', *NovT* XXV (1983), pp. 97–132.

KAI HN META TΩN ΘHPIΩN (Mk 1,13b)

Ansätze einer theologischen Tierschutzethik

von Erich Gräßer

(Ev.-Theol. Fakultät, Am Hof 1, 5300 Bonn 1)

I

Λέγει κύριος· »ἰδού, ποιῶ τὰ ἔσχατα ὡς τὰ πρῶτα«. (Barn 6,13b) Das bekannte Zitat aus einer uns unbekannten apokryphen Schrift[1] gibt der in einen breiten Traditionsstrom eingebetteten eschatologischen Erwartung klassischen Ausdruck, daß Urzeit und Endzeit einander *entsprechen* werden[2]. Δευτέραν πλάσιν ἐπ' ἐσχάτων ἐποίησεν = eine zweite Schöpfung hat er (sc. der Herr) in der Endzeit gemacht. (Barn 6,13a)

»Die Schöpfung der Endzeit nach der Schöpfung der Urzeit ist ein überraschend klarer und glücklicher Ausdruck«, heißt es dazu kommentierend bei Hans Windisch[3]. Über der Schöpfung der Urzeit hatte Gott einst das טוֹב מְאֹד (= sehr gut) gesprochen. Es galt allen seinen geschaffenen Werken (Gen 1,31), einer Schöpfung, die »in Ordnung« war[4], die ihrem Sinn entsprach, gut war für das, was Gott mit ihr vorhatte[5], in der »nichts Störendes« war[6], in der es noch kein Blutvergießen gab:

---

[1] H. Windisch, Der Barnabasbrief, HNT ErgBd., 1920, 337; K. Wengst, Didache (Apostellehre), Barnabasbrief, Zweiter Klemensbrief, Schrift an Diognet, SUC 2, 1984, 155 Anm. 104.

[2] H. Gunkel, Schöpfung und Chaos in Urzeit und Endzeit. Eine religionsgeschichtliche Untersuchung über Gen 1 und Apk 12, ²1921; G. Fohrer, Die Struktur der alttestamentlichen Eschatologie, in: H. D. Preuß (Hg.), Eschatologie im Alten Testament, WdF 480, 1978, 147–180, bes. 171–178. Mit Recht lehnt Fohrer die einfache Gleichsetzung »Urzeit = Endzeit« – τὰ ἔσχατα ὡς τὰ πρῶτα – ab. »Statt dessen ist genauer zu sagen: Die Entsprechungsmotive drücken aus, daß das künftige, eschatologische Handeln Jahwes wie sein früheres und bisheriges Handeln und die eschatologischen Erfahrungen des Menschen wie die früheren und bisherigen geschichtlichen Erfahrungen sein werden« (178). Vgl. auch H. Schwantes, Schöpfung der Endzeit. Ein Beitrag zum Verständnis der Auferweckung bei Paulus, AzTh R. 1, H. 12, 1963. Kritisch dazu H. Hegermann, ThLZ 92, 1967, 667f.

[3] A.a.O. 337.

[4] I. Höver-Johag, Art. טוֹב (ṭôb), in: ThWAT 3, 1982, 315–339, dort: 324.

[5] C. Westermann, Schöpfung, ThTh 12, ²1976, 88f. Der Schwerpunkt liegt auf dem funktionalen Aspekt, nicht auf einem Gutsein, das sich nach objektiven Maßstäben bemißt.

[6] W. H. Schmidt, Die Schöpfungsgeschichte der Priesterschrift. Zur Überlieferungsgeschichte von Genesis 1,1–2,4a und 2,4b–3,24, WMANT 17, ³1973, 62.

Dann sprach Gott: Hiermit übergebe ich euch alle Pflanzen auf der ganzen Erde, die Samen tragen, und alle Bäume mit samenhaltigen Früchten. Euch sollen sie zur Nahrung dienen. Allen Tieren des Feldes, allen Vögeln des Himmels und allem, was sich auf der Erde regt, was Lebensatem in sich hat, gebe ich alle grünen Pflanzen zur Nahrung. So geschah es. Gott sah alles an, was er gemacht hatte: Es war sehr gut. (Gen 1,29–31a. Einheitsübersetzung)

Dieses »sehr gut« einer »schönen Welt«[7], in die erst durch das Handeln des ungehorsamen Menschen der *Bruch* hineinkam[8], wird als Prädikat einst auch über der Schöpfung der Endzeit stehen:

Wolf und Lamm weiden zusammen, der Löwe frißt Stroh wie das Rind. (Jes 65,25)

Der nachexilische Zusatz Jes 11,6–9 zeichnet das Bild von einem der Urzeit entsprechenden endzeitlichen Friedensreich, in dem totaler Friede zwischen den Tieren sowie zwischen Mensch und Tier herrschen soll:

Dann wohnt der Wolf beim Lamm,
der Panther liegt beim Böcklein.
Kalb und Löwe weiden zusammen,
ein kleiner Knabe kann sie hüten.
Kuh und Bärin freunden sich an,
ihre Jungen liegen beieinander.
Der Löwe frißt Stroh wie das Rind.
Der Säugling spielt vor dem Schlupfloch der Natter,
das Kind streckt seine Hand
in die Höhle der Schlange.
Man tut nichts Böses mehr
und begeht kein Verbrechen
auf meinem ganzen heiligen Berg;
denn das Land ist erfüllt von der Erkenntnis des Herrn,
so wie das Meer mit Wasser gefüllt ist[9].

Die Hoffnungsgewißheit, daß der durch Adams Sünde gebrochene Schöpfungsfriede (vgl. IV Esr 7,11 f.; ApkMos 10 f.)[10] in der messianischen Zeit

---

[7] C. Westermann, Genesis, BK.AT I/1, 1974, 229.

[8] P »erklärt« das Zustandekommen des Bruches nicht. Doch heißt es unter betontem Rückgriff auf die Sprache der Billigungsformel (bes. Gen 1,31) in Gen 6,12: »Und Gott sah (= überschaute) die Erde, und siehe, sie war verdorben; denn alles Fleisch hatte seinen Wandel auf der Erde verdorben.« Vgl. W. H. Schmidt, a.a.O. 62f.

[9] Zur Idee des ewigen Friedens in Menschen- und Tierwelt vgl. auch Jes 2,4; 9,4; 35,9; 65,25; Hos 2,20; Ez 34,25; Sach 9,10; Ps 46,10. Auch sonst bestimmen Paradiesvorstellungen die Verhältnisse der kommenden Heilszeit: Jes 27,6; 30,23–25; Am 9,13; Joel 4,18; Sach 14,8. Dazu vgl. G. Fohrer, a.a.O. 173; ferner W. Eichrodt, Die Hoffnung des ewigen Friedens im alten Israel. Ein Beitrag zu der Frage nach der israelitischen Eschatologie, 1920; G. Fohrer, Glaube und Welt im Alten Testament, 1948, 230–358; H. Groß, Die Idee des ewigen und allgemeinen Weltfriedens im alten Orient und im Alten Testament, TThSt 7, 1956.

[10] Vgl. Bill., III 247ff.

wieder hergestellt wird, pflanzt sich fort ins Frühjudentum hinein. In aller Regel wird dabei auch dem Frieden zwischen Mensch und Tier Erwähnung getan:

> Und einst wird es geschehen, wenn er alles erniedrigt hat, was in der Welt besteht, und sich gesetzt auf seiner Königsherrschaft Thron in ewigem Frieden, daß Freude dann geoffenbart und Ruhe erscheinen wird. Gesundheit wird im Tau herniedersteigen, die Krankheit wird verschwinden, und Angst und Trübsal und Wehklagen gehen vorüber an den Menschen, und Freude wird umhergehen auf der ganzen Erde. Und niemand wird vorzeitig sterben, und nicht wird plötzlich mehr ein Mißgeschick erscheinen. Urteile und Verurteilung und Streitigkeit und Rachetaten und Blut und Gier und Neid und Haß und alles Ähnliche verfallen dann der Verdammung und werden ausgerottet sein. Denn diese sind es, die die Welt erfüllt haben mit Bosheiten, um ihretwillen ist der Menschen Dasein noch in größere Verwirrung gekommen. Die wilden Tiere werden aus dem Walde kommen und den Menschen dienen, aus ihren Höhlen werden Ottern dann und Drachen kommen, um einem Kinde sich zu unterwerfen. Die Weiber werden keine Schmerzen mehr leiden, wenn sie gebären, nicht werden Pein sie leiden, wenn sie zur Welt die Früchte ihres Schoßes bringen. (syrBar 73)[11]

Wenn Gott »ein Königreich für alle Zeiten über alle Menschen« aufrichten wird (Sib III 767), dann werden wieder paradiesische Zustände herrschen:

> Er wohnt in deiner Mitte
> und so hast du unsterblich Licht.
> Und auf den Bergen fressen Wölfe
> mit Lämmern im Vereine Gras.
> Und Panther weiden mit den Böcklein.
> Und Bären lagern mit den Kälbern auf der Weide.
> Der Löwe, der sonst Fleisch verzehrt,
> frißt Stroh aus einer Krippe, wie ein Ochs,
> und kleinste Knaben führen ihn an Stricken.
> Er macht die wilden Tiere auf der Erde zahm.
> Es schlafen Drachen, Ottern
> mit Säuglingen zusammen,
> beschädigen sie nicht;
> denn Gottes Hand wird über ihnen sein. (Sib III 787–795)[12]

Schließlich ist jener Text aus den Zwölfertestamenten zu nennen, mit dem wir möglicherweise die traditionsgeschichtliche Brücke betreten, die unmittelbar zu unserem Markustext 1,13 hinüberführt[13]:

---

[11] Übersetzung nach A. F. J. Klijn, Die syrische Baruch-Apokalypse, in: JSHRZ V/2, 1976, 103–191, dort: 171.

[12] Übersetzung nach P. Rießler, Altjüdisches Schrifttum außerhalb der Bibel, 1928, 1037f.

[13] J. Gnilka, Das Evangelium nach Markus, EKK II/1, 1978, 57: »Diese umrätselte Bemerkung stimmt mit TestNaph 8,4 überein, weil dort die wilden Tiere die Gerechten fürchten.«

Wenn ihr das Gute tut:
werden euch Menschen und Engel segnen,
und Gott wird durch euch unter den Völkern verherrlicht werden,
und der Teufel wird von euch fliehen,
und die (wilden) Tiere werden euch fürchten,
und der Herr wird euch lieben,
und die Engel werden sich euer annehmen...
Den jedoch, der das Gute nicht tut:
den werden sowohl Engel als auch Menschen verfluchen,
und Gott wird durch ihn unter den Völkern verachtet werden,
und der Teufel wird ihn bewohnen wie sein eigenes Gefäß,
und jedes (wilde) Tier wird ihn beherrschen,
und der Herr wird ihn hassen,
⟨und die Engel werden ihn verschmähen.⟩ (TestNaph 8,4–6)[14]

In diesem Text finden wir die Motivkombination Tiere/Engel[15], die in den synoptischen Versuchungsgeschichten nur dem Markustext eigen ist und die es unmöglich macht, Mk 1,13 mit Mt 4,1–11 par. Lk 4,1–13 in Einklang zu bringen[16]. Der Aussagesinn in TestNaph 8,4–6, zu dem noch TestIss 7 zum Vergleich heranzuziehen wäre, ist klar und wird durch ApkMos 10f. vollends erklärt: Der Tiere Herrschaft ist erst durch des Menschen Sünde entstanden (ἡ ἀρχὴ τῶν θηρίων ἐκ σοῦ ἐγένετο).

Das Umgekehrte, daß der Mensch wieder im ursprünglichen Sinne von Gen 2,19 über die Tiere »herrscht« – in solidarischer Gemeinschaft und nicht in tödlicher Feindschaft –, wird dann der Fall sein, wenn er sich nicht mehr vom Geist Beliars leiten läßt, sondern vom Geist Gottes[17]. Jürgen Becker hat das richtig erkannt, wenn er zu dem in TestNaph 8,4.6 vorausgesetzten Verhältnis Mensch-Tier neben Jes 11,6–8; Hos 2,18f.; Ps 91,11f.; Hi 5,22f.; syrBar 77,20ff.; ApkMos 10f.; TestBenj 3,5; 5,2 auch auf Mk 1,13 verweist[18]. Damit ist ein ausreichender traditionsgeschichtlicher Hintergrund der Stelle aufgewiesen: die Wiederherstellung der ursprünglichen Gerechtigkeit macht den Riß, der jetzt durch die gefallene Schöpfung geht, wieder heil. Mensch und Tier leben dann wieder wie im Paradies in vertrauter Gemeinschaft mit- und nicht gegeneinander.

---

14 Übersetzung nach J. Becker, Die Testamente der zwölf Patriarchen, JSHRZ III/1, 1974, 105.

15 Dagegen ist VitAd 4 kein Beleg für die Motivkombination und eine entsprechende typologische Verbindung zu Mk 1,13. So mit H.-G. Leder, Sündenfallerzählung und Versuchungsgeschichte. Zur Interpretation von Mk 1,12f., ZNW 54, 1963, 188–216, dort: 206f., gegen J. Jeremias, Art. 'Ἀδάμ, in: ThWNT 1, 1949, 141–143, dort: 141, 18ff. und L. Goppelt, Typos. Die typologische Deutung des Alten Testaments im Neuen, BFChTh.M 43, 1939 (= Darmstadt 1973), 118.

16 So richtig E. Fascher, Jesus und die Tiere, ThLZ 90, 1965, 561–570, dort: 564, der im übrigen mit seinem Aufsatz die Aussichtslosigkeit entsprechender Bemühungen darlegt.

17 F. Spitta, Beiträge zur Erklärung der Synoptiker, ZNW 5, 1904, 303–326, dort: 324.

18 A.a.O. 105 Anm. 4d. – Zu den genannten Stellen wäre noch Jes 65,25 hinzuzufügen.

Jedoch ist es in der Forschung nach wie vor umstritten, ob das wirklich auch der Sinn von Mk 1,12f. ist.

II

Zwischen Mk 1,9 und 1,14 mit ihren geschichtlich und geographisch klaren Angaben schiebt Markus »jenes seltsame, Ort und Zeit völlig ausschaltende Geschehen von 1,12f.«[19]:

Und sogleich führte ihn der Geist in die Wüste hinaus.
Er weilte vierzig Tage in der Wüste,
vom Satan versucht;
er lebte mit den wilden Tieren zusammen,
und die Engel bedienten ihn.

Das Dunkel der traditions- und literarkritischen Probleme des Textes hat sich als undurchdringlich erwiesen[20]. Ein weiterer Versuch der Aufhellung wird hier gar nicht erst gemacht. Der immer wieder angestellte Vergleich mit der ausführlichen Versuchungslegende in Mt 4,1–11 par. Lk 4,1–13 (nach Q) hat das »Eigenleben« unseres Textes eher verhüllt als aufgedeckt[21]. Daß Mk 1,12f. für sich betrachtet werden muß, ist daher eine Erkenntnis, die sich in der modernen Exegese mehr und mehr durchsetzt. Dabei ist die Szene von ihren drei »Hauptmotiven« in V. 13 aus zu deuten: 40 Tage Wüstenaufenthalt, Gemeinschaft mit den Tieren, Bedienung durch die Engel. Ihnen ist die »Versuchung« partizipial als »Nebenmotiv« nur beigeordnet[22]. Bei den drei Hauptmotiven fällt dem mittleren – καὶ ἦν μετὰ τῶν θηρίων – die hermeneutische Schlüsselfunktion zu. Denn je nachdem, wie es gedeutet wird – paradiesisch, diabolisch oder neutral –, fällt das Gesamtverständnis der Szene aus. Vier Grundmuster lassen sich unterscheiden[23]:

1. *Die Tiere sind Zeichen des natürlichen Umfeldes,* sie sind »malerischer Zusatz« (de Wette) bzw. »Staffage der menschenlosen Wüste« (Wellhausen)[24]. Wäre dies die Meinung, würde man den Zusatz »er war

[19] E. Fascher, a.a.O. 567.

[20] Vgl. bes. H. Mahnke, Die Versuchungsgeschichte im Rahmen der synoptischen Evangelien. Ein Beitrag zur frühen Christologie, BBE 9, 1978 (Lit.). Zuletzt W. Popkes, Art. πειράζω κτλ., in: EWNT 3, 1983, 151–158, dort: 155.

[21] Vgl. E. Haenchen, Der Weg Jesu. Eine Erklärung des Markus-Evangeliums und der kanonischen Parallelen, STö.H 6, 1966, 63.

[22] So richtig W. Schmithals, Das Evangelium nach Markus. Kapitel 1–9, 1, ÖTK 2/1, 1979, 90. Anders H. Mahnke, a.a.O. 23f.

[23] Überblicke über die jeweiligen Vertreter bei E. Fascher, Jesus und die Tiere, 562ff. und H.-G. Leder, Sündenfallerzählung, 203f., der die Auslegungsgeschichte bis zur Väterexegese zurückverfolgt (188ff.).

[24] W. M. L. de Wette, Das Neue Testament griechisch, mit kurzem Commentar, Teil I, 1887, 180; J. Wellhausen, Das Evangelium Marci, 1903, 7.

mit den Tieren« viel näher bei dem Motiv »er war in der Wüste« suchen[25]. Auch wird bei dieser Exegese das Nebenmotiv πειραζόμενος ὑπὸ τοῦ σατανᾶ zum Hauptmotiv, weswegen sie schwerlich im Recht sein dürfte.

2. *Die Tiere sind Zeichen des Schreckens.* Sie unterstreichen »den feindlichen Charakter der Wüste und des Satans«[26]. Dabei rücken die Tiere als »des Satans Verbündete«[27] in einen Gegensatz zu den Engeln, was diese Exegese jedoch scheitern läßt. Denn der Text spricht von *Dienst-* und nicht von *Schutz*engeln.

3. *Die Tiere sind Jesu Feinde,* die er jedoch sicher beherrscht. Bei dieser Auslegung wird regelmäßig auf Ps 91,11–13 und Hi 5,22 als Vorstellungshintergrund verwiesen. Die Semantik unseres Textes weist jedoch in eine ganz andere Richtung: Einmal drückt μετά mit Genitiv die *Gemeinschaft* aus: Jesus war »unter« bzw. »bei« den Tieren[28]. Für Markus ist es ein Ausdruck »engere(r), freundschaftliche(r) Gemeinschaft«[29], wie andere Stellen zeigen: Nach Mk 3,14 sind es die Jünger, die »mit Jesus waren«; 5,18 bittet der geheilte Dämonische, mit Jesus zusammenbleiben zu dürfen; und 14,67 wird Petrus als derjenige identifiziert, der mit Jesus zusammen war. »Alle drei Male ist dieses Zusammensein ein so enges und positives, daß es schwer verständlich ist, Mk. sollte es in 1,13 anders gemeint haben. Mt. 12,30 und Lk. 11,23 bestätigen diese Deutung.«[30] Sodann: aus dem Imperfektum ἦν geht hervor, daß Jesus einen *dauernden* Umgang mit den Tieren hatte (»durative Aktion«).[31] Schließlich spricht gegen das feindschaftliche Verhältnis, daß ganz allgemein von *den* Tieren die Rede ist. Θηρία sind nach der LXX wildlebende Landtiere[32], z. B. jene Tiere des Feldes, die nach Gen 2,19 dem Adam zugeführt werden, daß er sie benenne. Daß es sich in Mk 1,13 um besonders bösartige oder sata-

---

[25] So richtig D. Fr. Strauß, Das Leben Jesu. Kritisch bearbeitet, 1835, I 402.

[26] J. M. Robinson, Das Geschichtsverständnis des Markus-Evangeliums, AThANT 30, 1956, 25.

[27] E. Lohmeyer, Das Evangelium des Markus, KEK 1/2, [14]1957, 27f. So auch W. Marxsen, Der Evangelist Markus. Studien zur Redaktionsgeschichte des Evangeliums, FRLANT 67, [2]1959, 28; E. Haenchen, Der Weg Jesu, 65; A. Strobel, Art. θηρίον, in: EWNT 2, 1981, 367–369, dort: 368.

[28] Bl-Debr-R, § 227,2. Vgl. auch U. Holzmeister, »Jesus lebte mit den wilden Tieren.« Mk 1,13, in: Vom Wort des Lebens. FS M. Meinertz, NTA.E 1, 1951, 85–92, bes. 86f.; H. Mahnke, a.a.O. 25f.

[29] G. Wohlenberg, Das Evangelium des Markus, KNT 2, [3]1930, 48; vgl. auch E. Fascher, Jesus und die Tiere, 567; R. Pesch, Das Markusevangelium. I. Teil. Einleitung und Kommentar zu Kap. 1,1–8,26, HThK II/1, 1976, 95. – Zum Thema »Der Zaddik und die Tiere« und damit auch zu unserem Thema der Gemeinschaft Jesu mit den wilden Tieren vgl. auch R. Mach, Der Zaddik in Talmud und Midrasch, 1957, 114–117.

[30] E. Fascher, Jesus und die Tiere, 567.

[31] Vgl. Bl-Debr-R, § 325ff.; E. Fascher, Jesus und die Tiere, 565.

[32] A. Strobel, Art. θηρίον, 368.

nische Tiere handelt, ist von einem falschen Verständnis der Geschichte her in den Begriff eingelesen.[33] So hat auch diese Auslegung wenig Wahrscheinlichkeit für sich.

4. *Die Tiere stehen in typologischer Beziehung zu Gen 2f.* Der erste Adam zerstörte den Tierfrieden, der zweite stellt ihn wieder her, indem er das messianische Reich heraufführt. Es sind gleich mehrere Gründe, die für diese Adamtypologie sprechen[34]:

- Adam lebte im Paradies in Gemeinschaft mit den Tieren (Gen 2,19f.). Nach seiner Gebotsübertretung stehen die Tiere gegen ihn auf (ApkMos 24); sie kämpfen gegen Seth (VitAd 37–39; ApkMos 10–12).
- Adam wurde von der Schlange verführt, die später mit dem Teufel identifiziert wurde (ApkMos 16; Bill., I 136–138f.).
- Dienstengel haben den ersten Menschen Nahrung gebracht (bSan 59b).

Auch wenn die typologische Bezugnahme im einzelnen ungewiß bleiben sollte[35], dürfte doch die übergreifende Entsprechung von Endzeit und Urzeit der Auslegungsschlüssel unseres Textes sein und seine Interpretation im Sinne der Adam-Christus-Typologie rechtfertigen.

Das religionsgeschichtliche Material der Vorstellung von den beiden Adam-Anthropoi »als gegensätzlich entsprechenden Universalgestalten« ist vor allem durch Egon Brandenburger bereitgestellt worden.[36] Danach finden wir besonders im IV Esr und im syrBar die Vorstellung breit entfaltet, daß Adams Sünde nicht nur für ihn und seine Nachkommen den Tod brachte (vgl. IV Esr 3,7; 3,21; 7,118; syrBar 17,3; 23,4; 48,42f.; 54,15; 56,6), sondern die ganze Schöpfung ins Verderben riß:

> Der Herr sagte zu mir: So verhält es sich auch mit Israels Erbteil. Denn ihretwegen habe ich die Welt erschaffen. Als aber Adam meine Gebote übertrat, wurde das Geschaffene gerichtet: Da wurden die Zugänge in dieser Welt eng, leidvoll und beschwer-

---

[33] Vgl. E. Fascher, Jesus und die Tiere, 567.

[34] Das folgende nach J. Gnilka, Das Evangelium nach Markus, 58.

[35] Vgl. dazu vor allem H.-G. Leder, Sündenfallerzählung, 198–201, dem J. Jeremias in einigen Punkten zustimmen mußte: Nachwort zum Artikel von H.-G. Leder, ZNW 54, 1963, 278f. Die Typologie als solche ist jedoch kaum zu bestreiten. Vgl. P. Lengsfeld, Adam und Christus. Die Adam-Christus-Typologie im Neuen Testament und ihre dogmatische Verwendung bei M. J. Scheeben und K. Barth, Koin. 9, 1965, 32f.

[36] E. Brandenburger, Adam und Christus. Exegetisch-religionsgeschichtliche Untersuchung zu Röm. 5,12–21 (1. Kor. 15), WMANT 7, 1962, 68–157. Zu vergleichen ist auch der Art. »Adam« in seinen verschiedenen Teilen I. Altes Testament, Neues Testament und Gnosis; II. Judentum; III. Religionsgeschichte; IV. Systematisch-theologisch, in: TRE 1, 1977, 414–437 (Lit.!).

lich, wenig und böse, voll von Gefahren und mit großen Nöten behaftet. (IV Esr 7,10–12)[37]

Daß es vor allem auch die Tiere sind, die unfreiwillig durch Adams Schuld ins Verderben gerissen wurden – wir kennen diese Vorstellung aus Röm 8,20 –, schildert eindrücklich die Apokalypse des Moses. Hier wird erzählt, daß Eva mit Seth auf dem Weg in die Paradiesesgegend ist. Da wird ihr Sohn von einem Tier angefallen und bekämpft. Eva schilt das Tier, weil es keine Furcht habe, »das Abbild Gottes zu bekämpfen«:

Da rief das Tier:
Eva! Nicht uns trifft deine Anklage,
dein Weinen.
Nur dich allein!
Ist doch der Tiere Herrschaft erst durch dich entstanden.
Weswegen tat dein Mund sich auf,
vom Baum zu essen?
Gott hat dir strengstens untersagt,
von ihm zu essen.
Auch unsere Natur hat sich dadurch verwandelt.
Du kannst dich nicht rechtfertigen,
wenn ich beginn, dich anzuklagen. (ApkMos 11)[38]

Adam (und Eva) ist also verantwortlich für die »Depravation der Schöpfung«[39]. Entsprechend geht die eschatologische Erwartung dahin, von diesem Unheilsverhängnis in der messianischen Zeit endgültig wieder befreit zu werden (vgl. nur syrBar 28,5; 43,2; 51,9.17; 85,5). *Et requiescet saeculum,* heißt es PsPhilo 3,10. Daß der zweite Adam die ganze Schöpfung heil machen wird, ist neutestamentliche Erwartung (Röm 5,12–21; 1 Kor 15,21f.45–50; Röm 8,18ff.)[40], während die ältere rabbinische Literatur die Bezeichnung des Erlösers als ἔσχατος Ἀδάμ nicht kennt.[41]

[37] Übersetzung nach J. Schreiner, Das 4. Buch Esra, JSHRZ V/4, 1981, 342. – Zur Interpretation dieses Textes vgl. bes. W. Harnisch, Verhängnis und Verheißung der Geschichte. Untersuchungen zum Zeit- und Geschichtsverständnis im 4. Buch Esra und in der syr. Baruchapokalypse, FRLANT 97, 1969, 106ff.

[38] Übersetzung nach P. Rießler, Altjüdisches Schrifttum, 141.

[39] W. Harnisch, a.a.O. 108.

[40] Röm 8,18ff. zählt man normalerweise nicht zur neutestamentlichen Adam-Christus-Typologie. Der Sache nach aber ist er ihr verwandt. Denn den religionsgeschichtlichen Kontext für die paulinische Aussage in Röm 8,20, daß die Ktisis *unfreiwillig* in die Knechtschaft der Vergänglichkeit geriet, bilden jüdische Spekulationen über Schöpfung und Fall wie bSan 108a; GenR 5 [5a]; 65 [41e] sowie die oben zitierten apokalyptischen Aussagen über die auf die ganze Schöpfung durchschlagende Schuld Adams. Vgl. dazu H. R. Balz, Heilsvertrauen und Welterfahrung. Strukturen der paulinischen Eschatologie nach Römer 8,18–39, BEvTh 59, 1971, 41–45. Zur Diskussion vgl. P. Lengsfeld, a.a.O. 31.

[41] Wohl aber die spätere kabbalistische Literatur! Vgl. Bill., III 477f.; J. Jeremias, Art. Ἀδάμ, 143f., der darauf hinweist, daß das Frühjudentum die Vorstellung vom Urmen-

Aber der für Mk 1,13 vorauszusetzenden Tradition scheint sie doch zugrunde zu liegen. Schon Justin hat sie aufgegriffen: »Wie er (Satan) nämlich Adam betrogen hatte, so meinte er auch mit Jesus verfahren zu können« (Dial. 103,6). Jedenfalls beginnt die typologische Exegese unseres Textes bereits in der Alten Kirche.[42] Und in der neuesten Markus-Exegese ist sie zur Standardauslegung geworden.[43] Sie läßt sich dahingehend zusammenfassen: Den ersten Adam weisen die Engel aus dem Paradies, dem zweiten dienen sie. Der erste Adam reißt durch seine Schuld die Tiere ins Verderben (Jub 3,28; VitAd 37f.; ApkMos 11; 24; slHen B 58,3ff.; Apk 19,17f.; Just Dial 88,4) und macht sie sich dadurch zum Feind (Gen 3,15; ApkMos 24), der zweite Adam lebt mit ihnen wieder in paradiesischem Frieden. Der erste Adam will selbst sein wie Gott und zerreißt damit den Schöpfungsfrieden: Des Bruders Hüter ist er nicht mehr (Gen 4,9), und Furcht und Schrecken legen sich vor ihm auf alle Tiere der Erde (Gen 9,2). Der zweite Adam dagegen übt Gehorsam und stellt so den Schöpfungsfrieden wieder her, alles im Himmel und auf Erden versöhnend (Kol 1,20).

Kurz: Das Sein Jesu bei den Tieren in Mk 1,13 ist ein Hinweis auf den Paradieszustand der Endzeit. »Jesus erschließt das Paradies neu, das sich der erste Mensch verscherzt hatte.«[44]

---

schen als idealen Menschen kannte »sowie die Lehre von der Wiederherstellung seiner infolge des Sündenfalles verlorenen Herrlichkeit durch den Messias« (ebd. 143,1f.). Herkunft und Entstehung dieser typologischen Bezüge von Adam und Christus sind jedoch noch nicht hinreichend geklärt. Vgl. B. Schaller, Art. Ἀδάμ, in: EWNT 1, 65–67, dort: 66.

42 K.-P. Köppen, Die Auslegung der Versuchungsgeschichte unter besonderer Berücksichtigung der Alten Kirche, BGBE 4, 1961; vgl. auch U. Holzmeister, a.a.O. 87f.

43 Ich verweise nur auf die neuen Markus-Kommentare von J. Gnilka, R. Pesch und W. Schmithals. Von daher ist zu revidieren, was H.-G. Leder, Sündenfallerzählung, 190 schreibt: »Bemerkenswerterweise hat sich die typologische Deutung von Mk 1,12f. aber weder vor noch nach JEREMIAS wirklich durchsetzen können.« Recht hat Leder dagegen mit seiner Feststellung, daß es zu keiner Auseinandersetzung zwischen den Interpretationsrichtungen gekommen ist. »Mit anderen Worten: Diese uneigentliche ›Diskussion‹ um die Interpretation von Mk 1,12f. zeigt entgegen dem sonst Üblichen in der Auseinandersetzung über exegetische Fragen eine auffallende Sterilität.« (191) Sicher hängt das mit dem grundsätzlichen theologischen Desinteresse am Thema »Tier« zusammen. Siehe dazu unten.

44 J. Jeremias, Art. Ἀδάμ, 141, 24. Die Kritik von H.-G. Leder, Sündenfallerzählung, passim, ist nicht durchschlagend, wie schon E. Fascher, Jesus und die Tiere, 568 feststellte (er bezog sich dabei auf H.-G. Leders umfangreiche Dissertation »Die Auslegung der zentralen theologischen Aussagen der Paradieseserzählung«, Greifswalder Diss. 1961, 814–832, die mir nicht zugänglich war). Im übrigen bestreitet Leder gar nicht, daß es in Mk 1,12f. um den Tierfrieden der messianischen Zeit und damit die Wiederherstellung paradiesischer Zustände geht (206). Nur »den Umweg über die pseudepigraphische Literatur« hält er für verfehlt. In den alttestamentlichen Aussagen Jes 11,6–8; 65,25; Hos

Die Entsprechung von Urzeit und Endzeit ist auch darin gewahrt, daß am Satan als dem Widersacher Gottes kein Weg vorbeiführt.[45] Es muß entschieden werden, wer herrscht. Durch den ersten Adam konnte Satan sein Reich bauen, durch den zweiten verliert er es (Lk 10,18; 11,18–22; Joh 12,31; Apk 12). Die Trias: wirkungslose Versuchung durch den Satan – Verweilen bei den wilden Tieren – Dienst der Engel proklamiert in der Tat Jesus als den »Weltvollender«.[46]

Mk 1,12f. ist also gar keine Mt und Lk vergleichbare »Versuchungsgeschichte«, schon gar nicht die gekürzte von Q.[47] Sondern der πειρασμός zielt auf den Gehorsam Jesu, dessen Preisgabe ihn als den eschatologischen Proklamator der Gottesherrschaft disqualifizieren würde. »Indem Jesus widersteht, gewinnt er das Paradies zurück.«[48] Insofern ist Mk 1,12f. die gedrängte Darstellung des Herrschaftswechsels und damit des eschatologischen Umschwungs, der Gottes gesamter Schöpfung den Frieden wiederbringt. In diesem Sinne ist dann auch im sekundären Mk-Schluß 16,15 die *gesamte Schöpfung* der Adressat der Verkündigung des Evangeliums (vgl. auch Kol 1,23).[49]

Ob der *Evangelist Markus* um die apokalyptische Tradition weiß und bewußt von ihr Gebrauch macht, kann man fragen.[50] Denn den spezifi-

2,18 findet er einen ausreichenden traditionsgeschichtlichen Hintergrund für Mk 1,13 umrissen (205). Zur Kritik an Leder vgl. H. Mahnke, a.a.O. 37f.

[45] Vgl. J. Jeremias, Nachwort, 279: Es spricht »eine große Wahrscheinlichkeit dafür, daß auch der 1. Satz (Versuchung durch den Satan) das Urzeit-Endzeit-Schema im Auge hat«. Vgl. auch H. Mahnke, a.a.O. 32f.

[46] J. Jeremias, ebd. Nach H. Mahnke, a.a.O. 34–37, fügt sich auch der 40tägige Wüstenaufenthalt Jesu nahtlos in die paradiesische Deutung: »in der Wüste als der dem Paradies diametral entgegengesetzten Stätte verwirklicht sich das eschatologische Geschehen. Jesus bleibt trotz satanischer Angriffe mit Gott verbunden in einem paradiesischen Verhältnis, das in der Gemeinschaft mit den Tieren und dem Engeldienst sichtbaren Ausdruck findet. So wurde die ›Wüste‹ zum ›Paradies‹« (36f.).

[47] Anders S. Schulz, Q. Die Spruchquelle der Evangelisten, 1972, 182. Für ihn ist es »mehr als deutlich«, warum Markus »so radikal« gekürzt hat: »Weil die Q-Gemeinde gerade gegen die Wundermann-Christologie im Sinne des θεῖος ἀνήρ polemisiert und diese als teuflisch ablehnt. Da Markus selbst – das beweisen ja die überaus zahlreichen Wundergeschichten seines Evangelienbuches – aber gerade darin ein besonderes Zeugnis der Evangeliumsverkündigung sah, mußte er diese Tradition drastisch kürzen und völlig umarbeiten. So blieb kein Stein mehr auf dem anderen, denn bei Markus ›erfährt man weder, worin die Versuchungen bestanden haben, noch welchen Sinn es hat, daß Jesus μετὰ τῶν θηρίων ist‹« (Zitat im Zitat von R. Bultmann, Die Geschichte der synoptischen Tradition, FRLANT 29, ^{3}1957, 271).

[48] W. Popkes, Art. πειράζω, 155. Damit erledigen sich auch Überlegungen, ob Mk 1,12f. ein unvollständiges Stück ist, dessen Ausgang später (3,27) nachgetragen wird (ebd.).

[49] E. Fascher, Jesus und die Tiere, 568; G. Petzke, Art. κτίζω κτλ., in: EWNT 2, 1981, 803–808, dort: 806.

[50] E. Schweizer, Das Evangelium nach Markus, NTD 1, 1967, 22; vgl. auch L. Goppelt, Typos, 118.

schen Sinn *seiner* Eingangskomposition erfaßt man nur anhand der Verknüpfung von Täufer-Taufe-Versuchung mittels des Geistes (Mk 1,8.10.12). Damit markiert er die ἀρχὴ τοῦ εὐαγγελίου, das ist die Überwindung des Satans durch die Herbeiführung der Königsherrschaft Gottes.[51] Seiner christologischen Grundkonzeption folgend und im Verbund mit den rahmenden Erzählungen sieht Markus in unserer knappen Szene Mk 1,12f. das Leitmotiv für seine Wundergeschichten überhaupt: Jesus ist Sieger über den Satan und sein Reich (3,24ff.).[52] Aber das verdrängt nicht die zugrundeliegende apokalyptische Adam-Christus-Typologie. Beides verträgt sich miteinander: Im Gegensatz zu Adam ist Jesus vom Geist Gottes geleitet, bricht des Teufels Herrschaft und richtet die Gottesherrschaft auf.[53] Die Vernichtung des Teufels stellt den wesentlichen Teil der eschatologischen Erwartung dar. »Nur in diesem Sinne, d. h. als integrierender Bestandteil für die Erfüllung der Johannes-Weissagung auf das messianische Zeitalter, können wir das Handeln des Geistes verstehen, wenn er – wie Markus es schildert – Jesus in die Wüste hinaus treibt; und nur so können wir überhaupt verstehen, warum die Versuchungsgeschichte gerade in der Einleitung ihren Platz gefunden hat.«[54] *Die Geschichte ist in ihre Krise geraten.* Es muß sich *jetzt* entscheiden, wer herrscht, Satan oder Christus. Die Christusherrschaft aber stellt den Schöpfungsfrieden wieder her. In ihm ist der Tierfriede kein Nebenmotiv, sondern zentraler Bestandteil.

III

Diese eschatologische Erwartung bekommt vor dem Hintergrund der in verschiedenen alttestamentlichen Traditionen überlieferten positiven Mensch-Tier-Beziehung, die sich auch und gerade in der zerstörten Schöpfung durchhält, ihr Gewicht. Theologisch getragen wird sie vom Gedanken der solidarischen Gemeinschaft *aller* Geschöpfe vor Gott: sie teilen das gleiche Geschick und die gleiche Hoffnung. Dazu im folgenden nur einige Hinweise.[55]

Tierrechte und Tierschutz sind in der *Tora* verankert. Wie der rechtsschwache Mensch steht das Tier unter dem Schutz des Gesetzes, das es vor Ausbeutung und Hunger bewahrt. Aus diesem Grunde wird die Sabbatru-

---

51 Zur »sachlich-theologische(n) Dichte« in der Komposition des Markusanfanges vgl. bes. W. Marxsen, Der Evangelist Markus, 32.

52 Vgl. J. M. Robinson, Geschichtsverständnis, 25–32. 42; K. Kertelge, Die Wunder Jesu im Markusevangelium. Eine redaktionsgeschichtliche Untersuchung, StANT 23, 1970, 32 Anm. 15.

53 J. Schniewind, Das Evangelium nach Markus, NTD 1, [6]1952, 49.

54 J. M. Robinson, a.a.O. 26.

55 Im wesentlichen verdanke ich sie Marie-Louise Henry, Das Tier im religiösen Bewußtsein des alttestamentlichen Menschen, SGV 220/221, 1958.

he auch auf die Tiere ausgedehnt (Ex 23,12; vgl. Ex 20,10). Nach Ex 23,11 sollen in jedem Sabbatjahr die Wildtiere ungehindert auf den Feldern grasen dürfen. Zwischenmenschliche Feindschaften setzen das Gebot der Tierliebe und des Tierschutzes nicht außer Kraft:

> Wenn du deines Feindes Ochsen oder Esel begegnest, daß er irret, so sollst du ihm denselben wieder zuführen. Wenn du des, der dich haßt, Esel siehest unter seiner Last erliegen, hüte dich und laß ihn nicht, sondern versäume gerne das Deine um seinetwillen. (Ex 23,4f.)

Jahwe gehört das Wild auf den Bergen, er kennt die Vögel des Himmels; was sich auf dem Feld regt, ist sein eigen (Ps 50,10f.). Aus diesem Grunde auch schließt Gott seinen Bund nicht nur mit Noah und seiner Familie, sondern ausdrücklich auch mit allen Geschöpfen, die mit ihm in der Arche waren (Gen 9,10ff.). Insofern war der Prophet Jona gottlos, als ihm mißfiel, daß Gott gegenüber Ninive Gnade vor Recht ergehen ließ. Gott sprach zu ihm:

> Mir aber sollte es nicht leid sein um Ninive, die große Stadt, in der mehr als einhundertzwanzigtausend Menschen leben, die nicht einmal rechts und links unterscheiden können – und außerdem so viele Tiere? (Jon 4,11)

Seinen markantesten Ausdruck hat das Bewußtsein der nahen Zusammengehörigkeit von Mensch und Tier alttestamentlich im Bereich kultischer und zivilrechtlicher Gesetzgebung gefunden.[56] In der gleichen Weise wie dem Menschen werden dem Tier in Ex 21,28ff. Schuldmaß und Rechte zuerkannt. Dem arbeitenden Rind z. B. darf nicht verwehrt werden, sich von der eingebrachten Ernte nach seinem Gutdünken zu nehmen, was es braucht:

> Du sollst dem Ochsen zum Dreschen keinen Maulkorb anlegen. (Dtn 25,4; vgl. 1 Kor 9,9; 1 Tim 5,18)

Josephus gibt dazu die Begründung: »Denn es ist nicht recht, diejenigen (tierlichen Erntearbeiter), die sich bei der Erzeugung der Früchte mitabmühen, vom Mitgenuß derselben abzuhalten«. (Ant IV, 8,21) Alttestamentlich empfängt so das Tier »als ein dem Menschen nahverwandtes Wesen auch im Gemeinschafts- und Rechtsleben seine Stätte an dessen Seite.«[57]

Der Gedanke, daß Gerechtigkeit als Gemeinschaftstreue die Mitgeschöpfe nicht aus-, sondern einschließt, setzt sich vom Alten Testament ins Neue hinein fort, wenngleich er hier nicht so stark ausgeprägt ist (vgl. Mt 6,26.28; 10,29; Lk 14,5 par. Mt 12,11f.). Mk 1,13 ist in den Evangelien und Röm 8,18ff. im Apostolos ein Einzeltext geblieben. Sie deswegen für theologisch unwichtig zu halten, ist um so weniger gerechtfertigt, als

---

[56] Marie-Louise Henry, a.a.O. 26ff.

[57] Marie-Louise Henry, a.a.O. 27f.

man damit eine Hoffnungsgewißheit ignorieren würde, die in der alttestamentlichen, der frühjüdischen und der neutestamentlichen Eschatologie ihren festen Platz hat. In den frühchristlichen Heiligenlegenden lebte sie noch lange fort. Es wird von nicht wenigen Heiligen berichtet, daß sie mit den wilden Tieren im Frieden lebten (z. B. Hieronymus) oder überhaupt einen freundschaftlichen Verkehr mit der Tierwelt unterhielten (z. B. Franz v. Assisi).[58]

IV

In seinem Albert Schweitzer zum 90. Geburtstag gewidmeten Artikel »Jesus und die Tiere« schrieb Erich Fascher schon 1965: »Es wäre ein sehr verengtes ›christliches Weltbild‹, wenn wir theologisch bloß über das Gott-Menschverhältnis oder über das Verhältnis von Mensch und Mitmensch diskutieren wollten und alle übrige ›Kreatur‹ säkularen Organisationen wie dem Naturschutz oder dem Tierschutz überließen.«[59]

Nun, das tun wir in der Tat! Eine nüchterne Bestandsaufnahme dessen, was heute in der Exegese, der theologischen Ethik und christlichen Verkündigung betrieben wird, kommt um die Feststellung nicht herum, daß das *verengte* »christliche Weltbild« noch immer das Denken in Kirche und Theologie beherrscht.[60] Dem Bekenntnis, daß die Erde, und was sie füllt, *dem Herrn* gehört (Ps 24,1; 1 Kor 10,26), entspricht ethisch nichts.

Erst ganz allmählich und unter dem Druck der ökologischen Krise und der immer stärker werdenden Tierschutzbewegung beginnt sich die anthropozentrisch verengte Ethik zu weiten. Wir fangen an, den »Frieden

---

[58] Vgl. J. Bernhart, Heilige und Tiere, ArsSac, München 1937; W. A. Schulze, Der Heilige und die wilden Tiere. Zur Exegese von Mc 1,13b, ZNW 46, 1955, 280–283. – Nicht darum geht es, Mk 1,13 von den Heiligenlegenden her zu deuten, sondern es geht umgekehrt darum, ob die Heiligenlegenden sich als Wirkungsgeschichte von Mk 1,13 verstehen lassen (gegen H. Mahnke, a.a.O. 25–27). – Im übrigen kennt auch die rabbinische Tradition die Vorstellung, daß zwischen dem Zaddik und den Tieren »der urzeitliche Zustand des friedlichen Zusammenlebens fortbestehen« bleibt. Vgl. R. Mach, a.a.O. 115.

[59] A.a.O. 568.

[60] Zwei charakteristische Beispiele: J. Becker, Feindesliebe – Nächstenliebe – Bruderliebe. Exegetische Beobachtungen als Anfragen an ein ethisches Problemfeld, ZEE 25, 1981, 5–18 redet der Öffnung des »verengten christologischen Ansatz(es)« für die Ethik durch den ersten Artikel, also durch Schöpfungsaussagen, das Wort. »Dies würde die notwendige Gesprächsoffenheit zum nichtchristlichen Gesprächspartner ganz anders konstituieren, doch auch die brennenden Probleme von Verantwortlichkeit in Naturwissenschaft, Medizin und Technik auf eine angemessene Basis stellen« (17). Daß jene Öffnung auch eine Ausweitung der anthropozentrischen Ethik zu einer *mitgeschöpflichen* bringen könnte, wird nicht gesagt. – Das andere Beispiel: M. Honecker hat in einem großen Forschungsbericht »Tendenzen und Themen der Ethik« vorgestellt (ThR 47, 1982, 1–72; 48, 1983, 349–382). Zum Thema Tierschutzethik ist darin nichts zu lesen, weil es im Berichtzeitraum nichts gibt (mündliche Auskunft).

mit der Natur« als *theologische* Aufgabe zu begreifen.[61] Dabei könnte Mk 1,12f. einer dringend benötigten theologischen Tierschutzethik[62] als ein möglicher Ansatz unter anderen denkbaren biblischen Ansätzen[63] dienen.

---

[61] Ich nenne als wichtige kirchliche Verlautbarungen aus der jüngsten Zeit: Landwirtschaft im Spannungsfeld zwischen Wachsen und Weichen, Ökologie und Ökonomie, Hunger und Überfluß. Eine Denkschrift der Kammer der Evangelischen Kirche in Deutschland für soziale Ordnung. Herausgegeben vom Kirchenamt im Auftrag des Rates der Evangelischen Kirche in Deutschland, 1984, bes. 56ff. (»Das Verhältnis des Menschen zur Natur«). Schließlich sei verwiesen auf G. M. Teutsch, Lexikon der Umweltethik, 1985, bes. den Art. »Biblische Schöpfungsethik« (12–15, Lit.!); ferner: W. Lohff/H. Chr. Knuth (Hg.), Schöpfungsglauben und Umweltverantwortung. Eine Studie des Theol. Ausschusses der VELKD, 1985 und die vielleicht wichtigste Veröffentlichung zur Sache von dem Physiker und Philosophen K. M. Meyer-Abich, Wege zum Frieden mit der Natur. Praktische Naturphilosophie für die Umweltpolitik, 1984. – Dagegen einen Rückfall in die falsche Anthropozentrik stellen dar: Verantwortung wahrnehmen für die Schöpfung. Gemeinsame Erklärung des Rates der Evangelischen Kirche in Deutschland und der Deutschen Bischofskonferenz. Herausgegeben vom Kirchenamt der Evangelischen Kirche in Deutschland und dem Sekretariat der Deutschen Bischofskonferenz, 1985 (»Der Mensch und seine Mitgeschöpfe«). Zur Kritik vgl. G. Orth, Verantwortung übernehmen für die Schöpfung – nicht für die Marktwirtschaft, JK 46, 1985, 581–585.

[62] Dafür, daß auch die *Juristen* darauf warten, vgl. R. Stober, Rechtsfragen zur Massentierhaltung. Rechtsgutachten zur Verfassungs- und Gesetzmäßigkeit des Entwurfs einer Hennenhaltungsverordnung, Monographien zur rechtswissenschaftlichen Forschung 10, 1982. Darin heißt es im Schlußteil »Ergebnisse« unter 5.: »Das Tierschutzrecht ist nach dem Willen des Gesetzgebers ethisch und damit sittlich ausgerichtet. Deshalb sind die Tiere in den Schutzkreis des Sittengesetzes im Sinne des Art. 2 Abs. 1 GG einbezogen. Da es sich bei der Massentierhaltung und der Käfighaltung um neue technische Entwicklungen handelt, konnte sich bislang noch keine allgemein verbindliche Meinung über die Sittenhaftigkeit der Käfighaltung herausbilden. Die jüngsten Stellungnahmen der beiden großen christlichen Kirchen zum Verhältnis Mensch und Tier scheinen für eine Ablehnung der Massentierhaltung zu sprechen. *Eine abschließende Beurteilung der Sitten- und Verfassungswidrigkeit ist derzeit aber noch nicht möglich, da sich die Kirchen noch nicht allgemein gegen bestimmte Formen der Massentierhaltung ausgesprochen haben« (87. Sperrung von mir).*

[63] Vgl. dazu O. H. Steck, Welt und Umwelt, Kohlhammer TB 1006, 1978; G. Friedrich, Ökologie und Bibel. Neuer Mensch und alter Kosmos, 1982; E. Gräßer, Neutestamentliche Erwägungen zu einer Schöpfungsethik, WPKG 68, 1979, 98–114; ders., Zum Thema Tierversuch. Erwägungen aus der Sicht einer theologischen Ethik, PTh 72, 1983, 466–478; ders., Kirche und Tierschutz – eine Anklage, in: Ursula M. Händel (Hg.), Tierschutz. Testfall unserer Menschlichkeit, Fischer »Informationen zur Zeit« Bd. 4265, 1984, 59–70; J. Schreiner, Der Herr hilft Menschen und Tieren (Ps 36,7), TThZ 94, 1985, 280–291.

Ist das textkritische Problem von 2 Kor 1,17 lösbar?

von Ferdinand Hahn

(Institut f. Neutestamentliche Theologie, Schellingstr. 3, 8000 München 40)

Im Jahre 1973 habe ich in der Festschrift für Herbert Braun einen Aufsatz veröffentlicht, in dem ich mich unter anderem mit dem textkritischen Problem von 2 Kor 1,17c befaßt habe und eine Konjektur in Vorschlag brachte[1]. Heinrich Greeven hat mir unter dem Datum vom 20. 5. 1974 einen ausführlichen Brief geschrieben und zu meiner in Erwägung gezogenen Textänderung Stellung genommen. Seine Argumente sind so wichtig und beachtenswert, daß ich anläßlich seines 80. Geburtstages auf das Problem nochmals eingehen will. Ich möchte auf diesem Wege verspätet meinen Dank zum Ausdruck bringen und hoffe, dem Jubilar damit eine kleine Freude zu machen.

I.

Der handschriftliche Befund ist eindeutig und läßt keine weitreichenden Schlüsse im Sinne der äußeren Textkritik zu. Mehrheitlich lautet der Text: ἢ ἃ βουλεύομαι κατὰ σάρκα βουλεύομαι, ἵνα ᾖ παρ᾽ ἐμοὶ τὸ ναὶ ναὶ καὶ τὸ οὒ οὔ; nur wenige Zeugen haben den abschließenden Finalsatz verkürzt und lesen: . . . τὸ ναὶ καὶ τὸ οὔ (so P^{46} 0243 6 pc lat)[2].

---

[1] Ferdinand Hahn, Das Ja des Paulus und das Ja Gottes. Bemerkungen zu 2 Kor 1,12–2,1, in: Neues Testament und christliche Existenz (Festschrift für Herbert Braun), Tübingen 1973, S. 229–239, dort S. 234–237.

[2] Vgl. Nestle-Aland, Novum Testamentum Graece ^{26}1983. Nach freundlicher Auskunft von Frau Prof. Barbara Aland, Münster, sind weitere Zeugen für den Kurztext: 424^{C} (in Nestle-Aland ^{25}1963 = 424^{2}), 1739 und Origenes. Der Korrektor (= zweite Hand) der Handschrift 424 »ist ein interessanter und als selbständig zu wertender Zeuge«, weil er die reine Koine-Handschrift 424 bei Paulus und den Katholischen Briefen »in Richtung alter Texte verbesserte«; das kann »nur nach einer Vorlage geschehen sein, die einen relativ guten alten Text enthielt« und möglicherweise mit einem Vorfahren der Minuskel 6 in Verbindung steht (Brief vom 25. 10. 1985). Die Handschrift 1739 muß beim Mehrheitstext weggelassen und ebenfalls als Zeuge für den Kurztext angeführt werden; außerdem ist aufgrund einer Randglosse in Minuskel 1739 auch Origenes als Zeuge zu nennen (ebd. im Anschluß an Kirsopp Lake – Silva New, Six Collations of New Testament Manuscripts [Harvard Theol. Studies XVII], Cambridge/Mass.-London 1932, S. 207f, mit Verbesserung nach Neukollationierung). – Für den mehrheitlich bezeugten Text sind die

Man hat den Eindruck, daß keine der beiden Lesarten ursprünglich sein kann. Der mehrheitlich bezeugte Text ist Reminiszenz an ein Jesuswort, jedoch im Zusammenhang schwer verständlich; die schwach bezeugte Lesart ergibt zwar einen Sinn, fügt sich aber ebenfalls nur mühsam in den Gedankengang ein. Deshalb sind in der Exegese mehrfach Konjekturen vorgeschlagen worden. Die bekanntesten sind: ἵνα ᾖ παρ' ἐμοὶ τὸ ναὶ οὔ καὶ τὸ οὔ ναὶ (Markland)[3] oder: ἵνα μὴ ᾖ παρ' ἐμοὶ τὸ ναὶ ναὶ καὶ τὸ οὔ οὔ (Nissen)[4].

Eine Lösung des Problems ist nur zu gewinnen, wenn einerseits der Argumentationszusammenhang von v. 17–20 überzeugend aufgezeigt werden kann und wenn andererseits der traditionsgeschichtliche Befund berücksichtigt wird, da v. 17c in seiner überlieferten Fassung unverkennbar mit dem Logion vom Schwören in Mt 5, (33–)37 bzw. Jak 5,12 in Beziehung steht. Unter dieser Voraussetzung habe ich in meinem früheren Aufsatz zunächst die Auffassung vertreten, daß vom Kontext her ναί und ναὶ καὶ οὔ die Alternativbegriffe sind, wie sich aus v. 18–20a ergibt; und zwar geht es im besonderen um das ναὶ ἐν αὐτῷ (sc. Ἰησοῦ Χριστῷ). τὸ ναί wird schließlich in v. 20b mit τὸ ἀμήν aufgenommen, hier aber, da es um das Responsorium der Gemeinde geht, als τὸ ἀμὴν τῷ θεῷ δι' αὐτοῦ erläutert. Geht man davon aus, ergibt v. 17c keinen klaren Sinn, vielmehr müßte dort vorausgesetzt werden: ἵνα ᾖ τὸ ναὶ ναὶ καὶ οὔ, was ich meinerseits als Konjektur vorgeschlagen habe[5]. Die jetzige mehrheitlich vertretene Lesart erklärt sich dann durch eine frühe Einwirkung von Mt 5,37 bzw. Jak 5,12, während die ursprüngliche Formulierung des Apostels damit wohl gar nichts oder nur sehr indirekt zu tun hatte[6].

Es kann kein Zweifel daran bestehen, daß überlieferungsgeschichtlich Jak 5,12 der Urfassung des Logions vom Schwören sehr viel näher steht als Mt 5,33–37, was unverkennbar eine erweiterte und umgestaltete

ältesten Zeugen die Majuskeln ℵ, B, A, C, D sowie die sehr beachtenswerten Minuskeln 33 und 81.

[3] Vgl. W. Bowyer, Critical Coniectures and Observations on the New Testament, collected from various Authors, London ^{3}1782, S. 351.

[4] Vgl. Theodor Nissen, Philologisches zum Text des Hebraeer- und 2. Korintherbriefes, in: Philologus 92 (1937) S. 247f.

[5] Das ναὶ καὶ οὔ ist hier ebenso wie in v. 18 Prädikatsnomen. ἵνα hat in v. 17 keinen finalen, sondern konsekutiven Sinn; vgl. Rudolf Bultmann, Der zweite Brief an die Korinther (KEK Sonderband), Göttingen 1976, S.43. Nach Blaß-Debrunner-Rehkopf, Grammatik des neutestamentlichen Griechisch, Göttingen ^{14}1976, § 391,5 (mit Anm. 9) kann für den Inf. der Folge ἵνα bei gedachter Folge eintreten.

[6] W. C. van Unnik, Reisepläne und Amen-Sagen. Zusammenhang und Gedankenfolge in 2. Korinther i 15–24, in: ders., Sparsa collecta I, Leiden 1973, S. 144–159, sagt S. 147 mit Recht: »Zusammenhang mit dem Jesuswort in Matth. v 37 ist ausgeschlossen, denn die Situation ist ganz verschieden«. Vgl. auch Jean Héring, La seconde épître de Saint Paul aux Corinthiens (CNT VIII), Neuchâtel-Paris 1958, S. 26.

Fassung des ursprünglichen Logions ist[7]. Einmal abgesehen von der antithetischen Eingangsformulierung in 5,33.34a und der Erweiterung in 5,34b–36 ist die Verdoppelung des ναί und des οὔ in ἔστω δὲ ὁ λόγος ὑμῶν ναὶ ναί, οὒ οὔ 5,37a gleichsam ein Schwurersatz, und 5,37b ist ein sekundärer Zusatz. Nun enthält auch Jak 5,12c einen offensichtlich sekundären Zusatz, aber wichtig ist neben der Einleitung 5,12a das einfache ἤτω δὲ ὑμῶν τὸ ναὶ ναὶ καὶ τὸ οὒ οὔ in 5,12b. Nur von dieser Textfassung her ist eine Beeinflussung von 2 Kor 5,17c überhaupt möglich gewesen.

Natürlich stellt sich auch die Frage, ob und wie sich das Zustandekommen verschiedener Lesarten erklären läßt. Geht man von der meinerseits vorgeschlagenen Konjektur aus, dann wäre, möglicherweise durch falsche Abtrennung, die Aussage von v. 17c irrtümlich als verkürzte bzw. verstümmelte Zitation des Herrnworts vom Schwören angesehen und dementsprechend bei der Mehrheit der Textzeugen bzw. ihres Archetyps ergänzt worden[8]. Der von der Minderheit vertretene Text hat dies teilwei-

---

[7] Vgl. Martin Dibelius, Der Brief des Jakobus (KEK 15), Göttingen [6]1984, S. 294–299; auch Franz Mußner, Der Jakobusbrief (HThK XIII/1), Freiburg i. Br. [4]1981, S. 213–216; Peter Davids, The Epistle of James (NIC), Exeter 1982, S. 188–191; ferner Georg Strecker, Die Antithesen der Bergpredigt, in: ZNW 69 (1978) S. 36–72, dort S. 56–63; ders., Die Bergpredigt, Göttingen 1984, S. 80–84; Gerhard Dautzenberg, Ist das Schwurverbot Mt 5,33–37; Jak 5,12 ein Beispiel für die Torakritik Jesu?, in: BZ NF 25 (1981) S. 47–66, bes. S. 50ff. 61ff.

[8] Zu dieser Textfassung gibt es verschiedene Erklärungsversuche:
a) Das zweite ναί und das zweite οὔ ist ebenso wie in Jak 5,12 Prädikat. So z. B. Johann Christian Konrad von Hofmann, Die heilige Schrift neuen Testaments II/3: Der zweite Brief des Paulus an die Korinther, Nördlingen [2]1877, S. 24f. Dagegen, weil in dieser Form kein Vorwurf, Philipp Bachmann, Der zweite Brief des Paulus an die Korinther (KNT VIII), Leipzig [3]1918, S. 61f. Vgl. auch Paul Wilhelm Schmiedel, Die Briefe an die Thessalonicher und an die Korinther (HC II/1), Freiburg i. Br. [2]1892, S. 214f, der deshalb die Konjektur τὸ ναὶ οὒ καὶ τὸ οὒ ναί vorzieht.
b) Es handelt sich um eine Verdoppelung von ναί und οὔ (im Sinne des nachdrücklich betonten einfachen Ja und Nein; vgl. Blaß-Debr-R § 493,1 mit Anm. 2), wobei καὶ τὸ οὒ οὔ als Prädikat anzusehen ist und καί die Bedeutung von »auch« hat. So gelegentlich in älterer Exegese; dagegen Adolf Schlatter, Paulus, der Bote Jesu. Eine Auslegung seiner Briefe an die Korinther, Stuttgart 1934 = [2]1956, S. 479.
c) Es handelt sich um eine Verdoppelung von ναί und von οὔ, wobei καὶ τὸ οὒ οὔ grammatikalisch als koordiniert und angereiht zu verstehen ist. Damit ist aber das Auslegungsproblem nicht erledigt; hierauf verweist Schlatter, a.a.O. S. 479: »Der für diese Deutung wesentliche Gedanke, die Gleichzeitigkeit von Ja ja und Nein nein, bekommt keinen sprachlichen Ausdruck«. Vgl. die gezwungene Deutung bei Bachmann, a.a.O. S. 63: »καί ist aufs stärkste betont, es schweißt einen kontradiktorischen Gegensatz zusammen ... ᾖ an betonter Stelle in 17b weist darauf hin, daß hier etwas als existierend gesetzt wird, dessen Existenz doch unmöglich und unberechtigt ist«. In der Regel wird deshalb ein »zugleich« oder »zusammen« eingetragen; so z. B. Georg Heinrici, Das zweite Sendschreiben des Apostels Paulus an die Korinthier, Berlin 1887, S. 112; Hans Windisch,

se wieder rückgängig gemacht, aber das Nebeneinander substantivierter Formen bei τὸ ναί und τὸ οὔ belassen. Während nun τὸ ναὶ ναὶ καὶ τὸ οὔ οὔ am ehesten noch mit Windisch als eine vulgäre Ausdrucksweise erklärt werden kann, die aber nirgendwo sonst belegt ist[9], lenkt τὸ ναὶ καὶ τὸ οὔ zu dem vermutlich ursprünglicheren τὸ ναὶ ναὶ καὶ οὔ in gewisser Weise zurück, nur daß jetzt mit τὸ ναί nicht das ναὶ καὶ οὔ als Prädikatsnomen verbunden ist, sondern καὶ τὸ οὔ, wodurch das betonte καί den Sinn von »auch« oder »zugleich« erhält[10].

II.

Heinrich Greeven hat nun zunächst im Blick auf 2 Kor 1,18–20 darauf hingewiesen, daß ναὶ καὶ οὔ für ein unzuverlässiges oder falsches Versprechen »nicht gerade der nächstliegende Ausdruck« sei. Da Paulus diese Wendung aber in v. 18f verwendet, müsse sie ihm »als Ausdruck der Unzuverlässigkeit« vorgegeben gewesen sein. Da sie weder mit Mt 5,37 noch mit Jak 5,12 etwas zu tun hat, ist nach ihrer Bedeutung zu fragen. Es könnte sich um eine Kurzformel für (λέγει) ναὶ καὶ οὐ (ποιεῖ) handeln, was zur Folge hätte, daß ου ursprünglich nicht als »nein«, sondern als »nicht« zu verstehen wäre. »Die Verdeutschung ist etwas mühsam: ›Ja‹ und – nicht. Aber das wirkt im Griechischen nicht so ungelenk, da ου nicht nur Verneinung eines Begriffes, sondern auch das (absolute) ›Nein‹ ausdrückt«. Greeven verweist dazu auf ein wichtiges Sach-Paradigma im Sondergut des Matthäusevangeliums, das Gleichnis von den beiden Söhnen. Der erste sagt nach Mt 21,29 οὐ θέλω und geht dann doch, als es ihn reut, zur Arbeit in den Weinberg. Vom anderen Sohn dagegen heißt es in v. 30: ἐγώ (statt ναί), κύριε, καὶ οὐκ ἀπῆλθεν.

Der zweite Korintherbrief (KEK 6), Göttingen 1924 = 1970, S. 65; Heinz Dietrich Wendland, Die Briefe an die Korinther (NTD 7), Göttingen ^{12}1968, S. 170f; C. K. Barrett, A Commentary on the Second Epistle to the Corinthians (BNTC), London 1973, S. 75f (»at the same time«). Wilhelm Bousset, Der zweite Brief an die Korinther, in: Johannes Weiß (Hrsg.), Die Schriften des Neuen Testaments II, Göttingen ^{2}1908, S. 170f, erklärt, daß »das Ja, Ja und das Nein, Nein dicht beieinander lägen«, und übersetzt: »so daß es bei mir bald Ja Ja und bald Nein Nein heißt«. Demgegenüber zu beachten ist das nüchterne Urteil von Hans Lietzmann, An die Korinther I/II (HNT 9), Tübingen ^{4}1949, S. 103: »aber die Hauptsache ›zugleich‹ ist nicht gesagt«.

d) Es handelt sich um eine Verdoppelung von ναί und οὔ, die nach semitischem Sprachgebrauch eine iterative Bedeutung hat. So van Unnik, a.a.O. S. 147, im Anschluß an A. J. Wensinck: »immer wieder ja und immer wieder nein«. Das ist ganz unwahrscheinlich, da Paulus griechisch denkende Leser voraussetzt.

Weitere Erklärungsversuche sind in Anm. 12 und 13 erwähnt.

9 Hans Windisch, a.a.O. S. 65: »Aber vielleicht hat sich P. einer vulgären, in Kor. auf ihn angewandten Redeweise bedient«.

10 In diesem Fall ist die Bedeutung von καί im Sinne von »auch« oder »zugleich« eindeutig. Vgl. Anm. 8b.

Ob man nun das ου im Sinn von »nicht« oder »nein« versteht, in jedem Falle wäre ein Zusammenhang mit v. 18–20 gegeben, wenn meine Konjektur für v. 17c akzeptiert wird, zumal dieser Vorschlag noch den Vorzug hat, »daß er die sturmflutartige Wirkung des Mehrheitstextes besser erklärt, der das Eidesverbot (allerdings in der Jakobus-Form) hier einträgt«. Immerhin ergeben sich zwei Bedenken:

a) Die vorgeschlagene Textverbesserung enthält eine Härte, das Aufeinanderstoßen von ναί und ναί, »das ein stilbewußter Autor wie Paulus leicht hätte vermeiden können (z. B. ἵνα παϱ' ἐμοὶ τὸ ναὶ ᾖ ναὶ καὶ οὔ)«.

b) Zu der stilistischen kommt eine textgeschichtliche Erwägung: »Hätte der Mehrheitstext die gleiche Form an unserer Stelle wie er sie in Mt 5,37 hat (ναὶ ναί, οὒ οὔ), so wäre die Überflutung eines abweichenden Originaltextes hinreichend verständlich. Daß aber diese Verdrängungskraft von Jak (5,12) ausgegangen sein soll, der noch bei Euseb zu den Antilegomena gehört, das ist schwer begreiflich. Dagegen ist die Glättung durch P^{46} 424^{2} vg nur zu naheliegend«.

Angesichts dieser Bedenken ist Heinrich Greeven eher zu einer anderen Konjektur bereit und findet Nissens Vorschlag, der ein μή eingefügt hat, gar nicht so schlecht. Er hat dafür ein sehr beachtliches textkritisches Argument: »MHHΠ mit den acht aufeinanderfolgenden Hasten bietet dem abirrenden Auge eine hinlänglich glatte Rutschbahn, an deren Ende nur der nach dem ἵνα zu erwartende Konjunktiv ᾖ samt dem vor APEMOI nicht entbehrlichen Π erfaßt wurde«. Deshalb will er Nissens Konjektur einen leichten Vorzug vor der meinigen geben, weil ihm »ein optisches Versehen eher denkbar erscheint als die fast einmütige Korrektur nach Jakobus. Freilich müßte das optische Versehen bereits für den Archetyp des Corpus Paulinum angenommen werden«. Sachlich läßt sich Nissens Konjektur gut verstehen, denn es ergibt sich ein tadelloser gedanklicher Zusammenhang: »Paulus bezieht sich auf das bei Jakobus in seiner Urform erhaltene Herrnwort«.

III.

Heinrich Greeven hat am Ende seines Briefes die Hoffnung ausgesprochen, daß seine Stellungnahme meine Erwägungen ein wenig vorantreiben könne. Wenn ich erst nach über zehn Jahren die Problematik wieder aufgreife, dann hat das seinen Hauptgrund in der Schwierigkeit des Sachproblems. »Konjekturen haben im Neuen Testament – mit Ausnahme weniger Schriften – immer etwas Verzweifeltes«, schrieb der Jubilar. So stellt sich auch die Frage, ob das textkritische Problem von 2 Kor 1,17c überhaupt lösbar ist.

Wenn ich Greevens Argumente im einzelnen aufnehme, so ist zu dem Vorschlag, das ναὶ καὶ οὔ im Sinn von (λέγει) ναὶ καὶ οὒ (ποιεῖ) zu verstehen, festzustellen, daß dies durchaus den Hintergrund der Wendung verständlich machen kann (einschließlich des Hinweises auf Mt 21,29f), aber wohl kaum die von Paulus aufgegriffene Formulierung erklärt, die sehr viel eher den Eindruck einer bereits erstarrten Formel macht[11].

Das stilistische Argument verdient Beachtung, denn in der Tat wäre eine von Paulus vorgenommene Umstellung des ᾖ nach τὸ ναί sprachlich besser und zudem eindeutiger gewesen. Aber es muß berücksichtigt werden, daß die Briefe des Apostels diktiert worden sind und gerade im gesprochenen Satz die Wortstellung ἵνα ᾖ παρ᾽ ἐμοὶ τὸ ναὶ ναὶ καὶ οὔ wegen der Betonung durchaus verständlich ist[12].

Die Erwägung, es könne mit einer sehr früh anzusetzenden fehlerhaften Lesung des Paulustextes und einer Auslassung des μή gerechnet werden, geht von der Prämisse aus, daß bei Paulus selbst bereits eine Anspielung auf das Herrnwort vom Schwören vorliegt. Letzteres entspricht natürlich dem mehrheitlich überlieferten Text. Aber schafft diese negierte Fassung wirklich einen Übergang zu den Aussagen von v. 18–20? Dort geht es ja nicht um die Alternative von »Ja« und »Nein«, sondern um die von »Ja« und »Ja und Nein«. Man kann die Konjektur Nissens allenfalls so deuten, daß der Streit um ein eindeutiges »Ja« oder ein zweideutiges »Ja und Nein« vorweg durch eine unmißverständliche Bestätigung der Aussage Jesu über ein klares »Ja« oder »Nein« in die rechte Bahn gelenkt werden soll[13].

Das zweifellos gewichtigste Argument Greevens gegen die von mir vorgeschlagene Konjektur ist nun aber sein Hinweis auf den sehr unterschiedlichen Rang des Matthäus- und des Jakobustextes in der Frühge-

---

[11] So schon Heinrich August Wilhelm Meyer, Kritisch exegetisches Handbuch über den zweiten Brief an die Korinther, Göttingen ^{5}1870, S. 28: »Der Artikel bezeichnet das ναὶ ναί und das οὒ οὔ als bekannte und solenne Formeln der bejahenden und verneinenden Betheuerung (wie sie es auch im Judentum waren)«. Gustav Stählin, Zum Gebrauch von Beteuerungsformeln im Neuen Tesatament, in: NovTest 5 (1962) S. 115–143, dort S. 130 (vgl. auch S. 118–120) lehnt zu Unrecht die Verwendung einer geläufigen Redeweise ab und rechnet mit einer direkten Beziehung auf das Jesuswort.

[12] Die gelegentlich erwogene Betonung von παρ᾽ ἐμοί (im Sinne von παρ᾽ ἐμοί ἐστιν, »es steht bei mir«), so daß hier der Vorwurf aufgenommen sei, Paulus habe selbstherrlich und nicht aus Gottes Antrieb heraus gehandelt, scheidet aus. Vgl. Bachmann, a.a.O. S. 62; anders allerdings Schlatter, a.a.O. S. 479. Der Ton der Aussage liegt eindeutig auf dem Schlußglied.

[13] Diese Auffassung wird gelegentlich auch anhand des Mehrheitstextes vertreten, indem hinter κατὰ σάρκα βουλεύομαι ein Fragezeichen gesetzt und eine Brachylogie angenommen wird, und zwar derart, daß ἵνα ᾖ κτλ. in v. 17c ein adversativer Gedanke sei. So Luther in seiner Textübersetzung seit 1522: »... oder sind meyne anschlege fleyschlich? Nicht also/sondern bey mir ist ia/ia un neyn ist neyn«. Doch das erfordert eine nicht gerechtfertigte Einfügung. In der Revision des Luthertextes von 1956 und 1984 lautet die Stelle: »Oder ist mein Vorhaben fleischlich, so daß das Ja Ja bei mir auch ein Nein Nein ist?«

schichte der Kirche und damit auch in der Textgeschichte[14]. Kann überhaupt eine nur bei Jakobus belegte Fassung eines Herrnwortes einen Einfluß auf die Textgestalt des Corpus Paulinum haben? Das ist sicher nicht vorauszusetzen. Hier wäre nur an eine Beeinflussung durch Mt 5,37 zu denken; eine solche liegt jedoch nicht vor. Bei Paulus selbst würde es sich, wenn er unter Umständen doch auf das Herrnwort vom Schwören Bezug genommen haben sollte, um einen anderen Sachverhalt handeln, weil dann mit einer mündlichen Tradition zu rechnen ist, auf die er zurückgreift. Es bleibt aber die methodische Frage, ob diese Alternative: Abhängigkeit von mündlicher Tradition bei Paulus – Abhängigkeit von der schriftlichen Gestalt des Matthäusevangeliums, in der Textgeschichte ohne weiteres anwendbar ist. Es zeigt sich bei 2 Kor 1,17c, daß fast alle Handschriften eine einheitliche Überlieferung haben und daß die durch eine Minderheit vertretene Variante als davon abgeleitet angesehen werden muß[15]. Ist das aber der Fall, dann kann die erwogene Veränderung des Paulus-Textes nur in eine ganz frühe Zeit zurückreichen, eine Zeit, in der die mündliche Überlieferung des Herrnwortes durchaus noch lebendig und von nicht geringem Einfluß war[16]. Wenn wir die vermutete sekundäre Angleichung an das Herrnwort vom Schwören noch in das ausgehende 1. Jahrhundert setzen, was durchaus erwägenswert ist, dann ist das dieselbe Zeit, in der die mündliche Überlieferung der Herrnworte auch noch auf die Gestaltung des Matthäus- und Lukasevangeliums, aber ebenso auf den Jakobusbrief erheblichen Einfluß genommen hat, einmal ganz abgesehen von den nach- und außerneutestamentlichen Dokumenten. Eine sekundäre Abänderung des vermuteten ursprünglichen Paulus-Textes braucht also durchaus nicht von den bereits verschriftlichten Evangelien ausgegan-

---

[14] Zur Verbreitung des Jakobusbriefes in den ersten Jahrhunderten ist außer den Kommentaren und Einleitungen zu vergleichen: Arnold Meyer, Das Rätsel des Jacobusbriefes (BZNW 10), Gießen 1930, S. 8–108.

[15] Daß die Lesart ἵνα ᾖ παρ᾽ ἐμοὶ τὸ ναὶ καὶ τὸ οὔ von dem mehrheitlich vertretenen Text abzuleiten ist, ist überwiegend wahrscheinlich, da hier weder eine Anlehnung an das Herrnwort noch eine konsequente Eingliederung in den Kontext vorliegt. Wohl aber läßt sie sich als vorsichtige Angleichung an v. 18 verstehen.

[16] Hierbei ist dann mit einer Fassung zu rechnen, die Jak 5,12 nahesteht, aber nicht damit identisch gewesen ist. Interessant ist in diesem Zusammenhang die Fassung des Herrnworts vom Schwören bei Justin, Apol. I 16,5: μὴ ὀμόσητε ὅλως· ἔστω δὲ ὑμῶν τὸ ναὶ ναὶ καὶ τὸ οὔ οὔ· τὸ δὲ περισσὸν τούτων ἐκ τοῦ πονηροῦ. Dabei ist v. 5a an Mt 5,34a angelehnt, v. 5b entspricht Jak 5,12b (nicht Mt 5,37a!), und v. 5c ist Wiedergabe von Mt 5,37b. Nun hat Justin nachweislich die Evangelien gekannt; ob ihm der Jakobusbrief zur Verfügung stand, ist dagegen äußerst zweifelhaft. So läßt sich sein Text eigentlich nur aus einer mündlichen Tradition erklären, die weder mit Matthäus noch mit Jakobus voll übereinstimmt. Vgl. hierzu noch Paul S. Minear, Yes and No: The Demand for Honesty in the Early Church, in: NovTest 13 (1971) S. 1–13.

gen zu sein, sondern kann in die Frühzeit gehören, in der die mündliche Traditionsweitergabe noch eine erhebliche Rolle spielte.

Unter diesen Umständen halte ich es nach wie vor für wahrscheinlich, daß aufgrund des Zusammenhangs mit 2 Kor 1,18–20 der ursprüngliche Text von 1,17c gelautet hat: ἵνα ᾖ παρ' ἐμοὶ τὸ ναὶ ναὶ καὶ οὔ, und daß erst sekundär eine Angleichung an das Herrnwort vom Schwören erfolgt ist. Ich freue mich deshalb, daß Heinrich Greeven, mein verehrter Vorgänger auf dem Kieler Lehrstuhl, den ich von 1964–1968 innehatte, die von mir vorgeschlagene Konjektur für sehr erwägenswert hält und der Konjektur Nissens ihr gegenüber nur »einen leichten Vorzug« gegeben hat. Auch wenn Textprobleme, die eine Konjektur erfordern, nie abschließend gelöst werden können, dürfte die vorgeschlagene Textänderung von 2 Kor 1,17c vielleicht doch ernsthaft in Betracht gezogen werden.

Zur Ethik der Sapientia Salomonis

von Hans Hübner

(Vereinigte Theol. Seminare der Universität Göttingen, 3400 Göttingen)

Daß dieser Beitrag zur Festschrift des Jubilars die Sapientia Salomonis zum Gegenstand hat, ist zwar u. a. auch durch die augenblickliche Beschäftigung des Verfassers mit diesem Buch bedingt. Und daß die Thematik Bezug zur Ethik hat, hängt mit dem Themenhorizont der Festschrift zusammen, der dem wissenschaftlichen Werk des Geehrten entsprechen soll. Doch ist darüber hinaus der Bezug des Themas zum Jubilar noch spezieller: In der Einleitung eines der heute immer noch wichtigsten Kommentare zur Sap, nämlich dem von Johannes Fichtner[1], lesen wir: »Für manchen wertvollen Rat in sprachlichen und textkritischen Fragen bin ich meinem Kollegen Lic. H. Greeven (z. Zt. Heidelberg) zu Dank verpflichtet.«[2]

In dieser Studie soll es um die Ethik der Sap gehen. Ist aber eine solche Studie überhaupt sinnvoll? Ist Ethik ein konstitutives Element der Ausführungen in der Sap? Ein nur sehr flüchtiger Blick in die Bibliographien bis zum heutigen Tage zeigt bereits, daß die Ethik des Buches kaum monographisch behandelt oder in einem Aufsatz thematisiert wurde. Gewiß, über Gerechtigkeit oder den Gerechten in Sap wird viel gesagt.[3] Aber dabei geht es meist um die Frage, welche alttestamentlichen Traditionen hier ihre Wirkungsgeschichte zeitigen, etwa ob der leidende Gerechte in Kap. 2ff. mit den Farben von Jes 53 oder denen bestimmter Psalmen gezeichnet wird. Man diskutiert über ihn im Rahmen der eschatologischen Problematik des Buches.

Interessant wird die Frage, warum die Autoren der ethischen Komponente der Sap so wenig Aufmerksamkeit schenken, vor allem im Blick

[1] J. Fichtner, Weisheit Salomos (HAT II,6). Tübingen 1938.

[2] Ib. 11.

[3] Ich nenne hier zunächst nur L. Ruppert, Der leidende Gerechte, Eine motivgeschichtliche Untersuchung zum Alten Testament und zwischentestamentlichen Judentum (fzb 5), Würzburg 1972, vor allem 70–105, zitiert als Ruppert I; K. Th. Kleinknecht, Der leidende Gerechtfertigte, Die alttestamentlich-jüdische Tradition vom ›leidenden Gerechten‹ und ihre Rezeption bei Paulus (WUNT II/13), Tübingen 1984, vor allem 101–110. Die Fortsetzung des genannten Werkes von Ruppert, nämlich *ders.*, Der leidende Gerechte und seine Feinde, Eine Wortfelduntersuchung, Würzburg 1973, ist jedoch für unsere Thematik weniger ergiebig. Weitere relevante Publikationen werden in späteren Anmerkungen genannt.

auf den unleugbaren Einfluß stoischen Denkens auf dieses Buch. Sicher war die stoische Philosophie mehr als Ethik. Aber unleugbar ist die Ethik eine ihrer tragenden Säulen. Und was der Stoa die damalige Weltgeltung verschaffte, war doch wohl a parte fortiori ihre ethische Stärke. Um nur einen Philosophiehistoriker für viele zu zitieren: Charles Werner sagt mit Recht: »Doch die Stärke der Stoa liegt in ihrer Moral.«[4] Aber gerade bei der Frage, inwieweit Sap vom stoischen Geiste beeinflußt ist, geht es zumeist kaum um Ethik. Paul Heinisch, der das immer noch grundlegende Werk über die griechische Philosophie im Buche der Weisheit[5] geschrieben und dabei zumindest im Grundsätzlichen den Unterschied des Denkens des Autors der Sap zum griechisch-philosophischen Denken überzeugend herausgearbeitet hat, behandelt beim Vergleich Stoa – Sap in der Hauptsache das Wesen der Weisheit im Blick auf die Frage, ob in Sap Pantheismus vorliege, und das Problem der Vorsehung, der πρόνοια[6]. Nur sozusagen anhangsweise geht er auf 2 (!) Seiten[7] auf die ethische Komponente des Verhältnisses Stoa – Sap ein, indem er nachzuweisen versucht, daß in Sap 8,7, wo die vier Kardinaltugenden genannt werden, direkte Abhängigkeit weder von Plato noch von der Stoa vorliege. »Was aber die Zahl und Namen der Kardinaltugenden anlangt, so waren sie in jener Zeit des Eklektizismus Gemeingut aller Gebildeten.«[8] Das Fazit: »Daher kann man auch nicht auf Grund von Sap 8,7 behaupten, daß der Verfasser des Buches der Weisheit an ein bestimmtes philosophisches System sich anlehnte oder mit einem solchen sich näher beschäftigt hatte.«[9] Wenn nun im Folgenden die Sap unter der anvisierten Fragestellung untersucht wird, dann geschieht das, weil angesichts der genannten Forschungslage die Ethik einer dringenden Aufarbeitung bedarf.[10] Das kann im Rahmen eines Aufsatzes natürlich nur äußerst fragmentarisch geleistet werden. Zunächst erfolgt ein z. T. etwas ausführlicherer, z. T. – um diese Studie nicht zu umfangreich werden zu lassen – ein reichlich kursorischer Durchgang durch das Buch. In diesem ersten Abschnitt geht es vor allem um eine Problemanzeige, wobei freilich schon erste Konturen einer theologischen Antwort deutlich werden. Im zweiten Abschnitt soll dann, vor allem im Blick auf Kap. 1–6, eine Fundierung des bereits Herausgearbei-

---

4 Ch. Werner, Die Philosophie der Griechen, Herder-Bücherei 251, Freiburg/Basel/Wien 1966, 197.

5 P. Heinisch, Die griechische Philosophie im Buche der Weisheit (ATA I 4), Münster 1908.

6 Ib. 99–112.

7 Ib. 113f.

8 Ib. 114.

9 Ib. 114.

10 Selbst C. Larcher, Études sur le livre de la Sagesse (EtB), Paris 1969, hat auf mehr als 400 Seiten der Ethik der Sap nur am Rande Aufmerksamkeit geschenkt (s. Anm. 66!).

teten, hauptsächlich im Blick auf dort zugrundeliegende alttestamentliche Traditionen, versucht werden.

*

Der Abschnitt 1,1–15, die Eingangsrede an die Herrscher der Welt, beginnt mit der Aufforderung, die Gerechtigkeit zu lieben, ἀγαπᾶτε δικαιοσύνην, οἱ κρίνοντες τὴν γῆν, und schließt 1,15 mit einer theologisch programmatischen Aussage über die Gerechtigkeit. Diese Eingangsrede ist somit durch den Hinweis auf die Gerechtigkeit gerahmt – wohl ein deutliches Zeiches dafür, wie wichtig sie für die Gesamtkonzeption des Buches ist.[11] In rhetorischer Sicht liegt hier die »Wiederholung als Klammer«, die redditio[12], vor, wobei freilich die Theorie der antiken Rhetorik den einzelnen Satz vor Augen hat, während der Begriff hier einmal ausnahmsweise auf eine größere rhetorische Einheit, nämlich Sap 1,1–15, angewendet werden soll.

Welche Funktion hat die Aussage über die δικαιοσύνη in 1,15, wenn von ihr gesagt wird, sie sei unsterblich, ἀθάνατος? Daß diese Aussage begründenden Charakter besitzt, geht schon aus dem bezeichnenden γάρ hervor. Was aber soll begründet werden? Es ist die Warnung, die an die Könige der Welt ergeht. Sie sollen sich nicht auf den Weg des Todes, θάνατος, und des Verderbens, ὄλεθρος, einlassen, 1,11 ff. Und sofort erscheint auch der theologische Bezug: Gott hat nämlich den Tod nicht gemacht; er hat alles geschaffen, damit es sei. Was aber Gott in der Welt geschaffen hat, das ist vom göttlichen Heil erfüllt, σωτήριοι; in der Schöpfung gibt es an sich kein Gift des Verderbens, keine Herrschaft des Todesreiches, des Hades. Warum? Eben weil die Gerechtigkeit unsterblich ist. Damit ist aber, wie bereits gesagt wurde, der Anfang des Abschnitts 1,1–15 thematisch aufgegriffen: Liebt und übt die Gerechtigkeit; denn sie ist der Weg Gottes, der Leben und nichts als Leben will! Das heißt aber, daß den Weg des eigenen *Todes* und des eigenen Verderbens geht, wer *ungerecht* ist. Und so wird bereits am Ende des Eingangsabschnitts deutlich, daß die drei Imperative in 1,1 inhaltlich verbunden sind. Über Gott in Güte, ἐν ἀγαθότητι[13], nachzusinnen und ihn in der Einfalt des

[11] Ich setze mit den meisten Autoren die Einheitlichkeit und Integrität der Sap voraus, ohne dies hier zu begründen. Damit ist nicht die Möglichkeit ausgeschlossen, daß der Vf. der Sap auf bereits literatisch vorliegende Einzelstücke zurückgegriffen hat. Eine solche Möglichkeit einzuräumen bedeutet aber nicht, daß die formale und inhaltliche Einheitlichkeit des Buches zu bestreiten wäre. Um diese formale und inhaltliche Konsistenz geht es aber in der hier vorgelegten Studie.

[12] H. Lausberg, Handbuch der literarischen Rhetorik, Eine Grundlegung der Literaturwissenschaft, München ^{2}1973, § 625; *Quintilian,* Inst. 9,3,34.

[13] P. Heinisch, Das Buch der Weisheit (EHAT 24), Münster 1912, 1, übersetzt »in guter Gesinnung«; ib. 5: Die Wendung »bezeichnet die *Gesinnung,* mit welcher der Mensch

Herzens zu suchen heißt zugleich, die Gerechtigkeit zu lieben (nicht nur in einem äußerlichen Gehorsamsakt). Wer die Gerechtigkeit wirklich liebt, zu dem kommt die Weisheit (worüber »Salomo« später noch Genaueres sagen wird). Ist diese aber als heiliger Geist ein Geist der Menschenfreundllichkeit, φιλάνθρωπον πνεῦμα, 1,5f., so dürfte diese Menschenfreundlichkeit in den Augen des Verfassers der Sap ein konstitutives Element der vom Menschen geforderten Gerechtigkeit ausmachen. Und in an stoische Terminologie angelehnter Formulierung heißt es dann 1,7, daß der Geist des Herrn die Erde erfüllt und, da er das All umfaßt, τὸ συνέχον τὰ πάντα (cf. SVF II, 439), allwissend ist.

Bereits durch dieses Eingangsstück ist also inhaltlich und zugleich in *theologisch* relevanter Weise Entscheidendes über die δικαιοσύνη gesagt worden: Gerechtigkeit *übt,* wer Menschen liebt und danach handelt; Gerechtigkeit *kann üben,* wem die Weisheit und damit Gottes Geist zuteil geworden ist. Gerechtigkeit ist danach nicht nur Aufgabe, sie ist vor allem erst einmal Gabe, Gabe Gottes. *Der Imperativ des Gerecht-sein-sollens gründet also im Indikativ des Gerecht-sein-könnens.* Wenn hier von Indikativ und Imperativ die Rede ist, so mag das sicher sofort an ein Grundproblem paulinischer Theologie erinnern. Doch soll nicht unnötig eine Parallelität von paulinischer Theologie und der der Sap – soviel ist allerdings schon jetzt deutlich, daß es in Sap um *Theo*logie geht, in welchem Zusammenhang und aus welcher Intention auch immer sie gedacht sei – strapaziert werden; aber in Sap 1,1–15 geht es eben unbestreitbar um das Verhältnis von Indikativ und Imperativ.

Bei Paulus steht – es sei um der Verdeutlichung willen gesagt – dieses Verhältnis im Kontext der für ihn zentralen Christologie und in der Polemik gegen einen christliche Theologie im Kern treffenden und daher a limine abzulehnenden Judaismus. Für Paulus ist christliche Theologie per definitionem antijudaistisch, wobei antijudaistisch natürlich nicht antijüdisch heißt, sondern die radikale Ablehnung jener Auffassung meint, nach der Christentum in sektiererischer und nationalistischer Verengung nur ein messianisch vollendetes Judentum ausmachen soll. Das ist jedoch innerster Grund jeglicher christlicher Theologie: Sie muß antijudaistisch sein und sie darf nicht antijüdisch sein. Die Theologie der Sap ist freilich durch und durch jüdisch – und insofern ihrem Wesen nach nicht christlich. Aber sie eröffnet ihre Diskussion im Horizont weltweiter Paränese. Und insofern sie diesen weltweiten Horizont aufweist, nimmt sie etwas von dem vorweg, was für Paulus später essentiell sein sollte.

Sap 1,16 ist bereits Übergang zur Rede von Gottlosen, ἀσεβεῖς (Plural!), über den Gerechten (Singular!). Wohlgemerkt, es sind Gottlose (undeterminiert!), die hier sprechen, nicht, wie man vielleicht erwarten würde, Könige – ein Indiz dafür, daß die Stilisierung der Sap als Rede des Königs Salomo an Könige nicht auf die wirklichen Adressaten schließen läßt. Diese sind vielmehr Juden im ägyptischen Alexandrien, die in gewis-

---

über Gott reflektieren muß. Dies ergibt sich aus der parallelen Wendung ἐν ἁπλότητι καρδίας ›in Aufrichtigkeit, Geradheit des Herzens‹.«

ser Pression leben, vielleicht sogar auch durch abgefallene Volksgenossen.[14] Diese Gottlosen also haben einen Bund mit dem Tod geschlossen – ob sie ihn gemäß Jes 28,15 willig eingingen oder ob der Autor der Sap meint, der Bund sei die notwendige Implikation ihres gottlosen Verhaltens, kann hier auf sich beruhen. Als so dem Tode Verfallene sprechen sie 2,1–5 zunächst resignierend und überaus pessimistisch vom Leben: Es ist kurz, dem baldigen Tode unwiderruflich preisgegeben – für sie als im Bund mit dem Tode »Lebende« bedeutet dieser die ihre Existenz bestimmende und dominierende Macht (vgl. Sap 2,24 mit Röm 5,12!). Die Konsequenz heißt für sie exzessiver Lebensgenuß, 2,6–9. Ihr Motto lautet, 2,6: »Laßt uns genießen, ἀπολαύσωμεν« (Dieser Abschnitt erinnert wiederum an Paulus, nämlich an 1 Kor 15,32, wo Jes 22,13 zitiert ist. Daß dieser Sap gut kannte, ist m. E. sicher.) Die Frage ist, ob, wie Dieter Georgi annimmt, 2,10–20 ein satirisches Redestück ist, das der »Autor« zum ursprünglichen Klagelied hinzugefügt hat[15], oder ob mit Lothar Ruppert 2,10f. gedanklich eindeutig zu 2,6–9 zu rechnen ist[16]. Es hätte nun in der Tat seine eigene Logik, wollte man 2,1–9 als inhaltlich in sich geschlossene Einheit sehen: Zunächst Selbstbemitleidung und dann Überkompensierung durch grenzenlosen Lebensgenuß. Diese Sequenz braucht im Grunde nichts mit der Unterdrückung des Gerechten zu tun zu haben (übrigens ist die 2,1–9 geschilderte Haltung nicht königsspezifisch!, s. o.). Es fallen aber die parallelen Kohortative auf: ἀπολαύσωμεν und χρησώμεθα 2,6, πλησθῶμεν und μὴ παροδευσάτω 2,7, στεψώμεθα 2,8 ἔστω und καταλίπωμεν 2,9, καταδυναστεύσωμεω, μὴ φεισώμεθα und ἐντραπῶμεν 2,10, ἔστω 2,11, ἐνεδρεύσωμεν 2,12. Formal zumindest liegt also kein Bruch zwischen 2,9 und 2,10 vor. Und es hat *auch* seine eigene Logik, wenn der, der sich höchsten Lebensgenuß zum Lebensprinzip gemacht hat, auch über Leichen geht, wenn es nur für ihn von Vorteil ist. Die höhnische, ja menschenverachtend-sarkastische Aussage 2,11 – Unsere Stärke, sie allein soll bestimmen, was für uns das »Gesetz der Gerechtigkeit« ist! – fügt sich bestens zu einer Lebenshaltung, die nur Genuß und somit nur sich selbst kennt. Wurde in 1,1 aufgefordert, Gerechtigkeit zu lieben, so wird nun gerade diese Gerechtigkeit auf perfideste Weise pervertiert.

Lothar Ruppert hat, wie bereits in Anm. 16 gesagt, aufgrund einiger interessanter Beobachtungen die Hypothese vorgetragen, 2,12*–20 und

---

[14] Der These Dieter Georgis, Weisheit Salomos (JSHRZ III/4), Gütersloh 1980, 391–397, die Entstehung der Sap sei in Ägypten möglich, hingegen spräche das meiste für Syrien, kann ich mich nicht anschließen, auch nicht seiner Charakteristik des Buches als ältester gnostischer Schrift, die wir besäßen.

[15] Ib. 405.

[16] Ruppert I, 75ff., spricht allerdings die Autorschaft für 2,12–20 dem Vf. der Sap ab; dieser habe 2,12–20 und 5,1–7, das »Diptychon«, aus einer literarischen Vorlage herausgenommen und neu in seinem Geiste kommentiert.

5,1–7 hätten dem Verfasser der Sap bereits in größerem Zusammenhang vorgelegen.[17] Seine Gründe scheinen mir zumindest nicht durchschlagend; doch ist für unsere Überlegungen, die der Sap als ganzer gelten, eine Entscheidung in dieser Frage nicht unbedingt erforderlich. Auch unabhängig von einer literarkritischen Entscheidung läßt sich fragen, wie der Autor der Sap den Gerechten in 2,12–20 verstanden hat. Die Gottlosen von 1,16 planen seine physische Beseitigung, da er ihnen durch seine Vorhaltungen, ja schon durch seinen Lebenswandel gefährlich wird. βαρύς in 2,14 meint doch wohl Gravierenderes, als die Übersetzungen von Fichtner[18] – »lästig« –, Dieter Georgi[19] – »belastend« – und anderen zum Ausdruck bringen. Richtig sieht Ruppert, daß es sich in 2,14 um Vorhaltungen des Gerechten gegenüber den Gottlosen wegen ihrer Gesetzesübertretungen handelt[20], zumal in 2,12 eindeutig von Verfehlungen gegen das Gesetz, ἁμαρτήματα νόμου, die Rede ist. Somit ist der Gerechte, der sich als Sohn Gottes[21] ausgibt (2,13.18), ein gesetzestreuer Jude, der andere – doch wohl Juden! – wegen ihres gesetzlosen Lebens anschuldigt.

Das Bild dieses gesetzestreuen und deshalb leidenden Juden wird mit Farben gezeichnet, die z. T. Jes 53, z. T. bestimmten Psalmen, z. T. vielleicht auch der Josephsgeschichte entnommen sind. M. Jack Suggs hat Sap 2,10–5,23 als Homilie interpretiert, die hauptsächlich auf Jes 52,13–53,12 Bezug nimmt.[22] Daß Jes 53 hier im Hintergrund steht, dürfte unbestritten sein und wird auch in der Forschung kaum bestritten. Doch ist die These von Suggs genauso überspitzt wie die von Georg Ziener, wonach der Autor der Sap nach Jes 53 »an 2. Stelle wohl am ausführlichsten ... für die Zeichnung des Gerechten auf Ps 88 (LXX) zurückgegriffen« habe.[23] »Eine Reihe von Übereinstimmungen zwischen Ps 88 und Wsh 2,12ff. zeigen (sic!), daß Züge des davidischen Königs auf den Gerechten übertragen wurden.«[24] An keiner Stelle des Alten Testaments werde der Offenbarungsfortschritt innerhalb des Alten Testaments so deutlich wie beim Vergleich von ψ 88, 48b–49b und Sap 2,23f.31a, wo Sap die pessimistischen Anschauungen des Psalmisten bewußt korrigiere.[25] Patrick W. Skehan vergleicht Abschnitt für Abschnitt der Sap mit dem Psalter und

---

[17] Ihm hat sich Kleinknecht, a.a.O. 104ff., angeschlossen.

[18] Fichtner, a.a.O. 16.

[19] Georgi, a.a.O. 408.

[20] Ruppert I, 79.

[21] Daß in 2,13 παῖδα κυρίου im Sinne von »Sohn Gottes« zu verstehen ist, ist heute opinio communis der Interpreten.

[22] M. J. Suggs, Wisdom of Solomon 2,10–5: A Homily Based on the Fourth Servant Song, JBL 76 (1957), 26–33.

[23] G. Ziener, Die Verwendung der Schrift im Buche der Weisheit, TThZ 66 (1957), (138–151)139.

[24] Ib. 140.

[25] Ib. 141.

verweist jeweils auf Parallelen.[26] Seine Ergebnisse sind weithin überzeugend. Man wird auch dem Fazit in seiner Substanz zustimmen können: "We conclude, therefore, that the author of Wisdom was well acquainted with the Psalms in Greek, and used them in that form by preference and habitually."[27] Aber Skehan hat doch einiges übersehen, was gerade für unsere Thematik von großer Wichtigkeit ist. C. Larcher schwächt die Bedeutung der Psalmen für Sap etwas ab. Trotz der Anspielungen auf eine Reihe von Psalmstellen sei der Psalter keine primäre Quelle.[28]

Für die Frage nach dem Gerechten, wie ihn sich der Autor der Sap denkt, und somit für die Frage, welche ethischen Grundüberzeugungen hier vorliegen, ist aber, wie noch zu zeigen ist, der Sachverhalt von entscheidender Bedeutung, daß bei der Darstellung des Gerechten der Psalter eine erhebliche Rolle spielt. Doch schauen wir erst auf den weiteren Gang der Ausführungen in Sap.

In 2,21–24 wird das Urteil über die törichte Rede der Gottlosen gesprochen, die sich sehr getäuscht haben. Ihre Bosheit hat sie verblendet. Sie, die sich anmaßten, die ethische Qualität (ἐπιείκεια) des Gerechten zu prüfen und so zu erkennen (2,19: ἵνα γνῶμεν), bekommen nun bescheinigt, daß sie die Geheimnisse Gottes nicht verstanden haben (2,22: οὐκ ἔγνωσαν μυστήρια θεοῦ). Sie hofften nicht auf den Lohn (μισθός) der Frömmigkeit, ihr Urteil über den himmlischen Ehrenpreis der untadeligen Seelen (γέρας ψυχῶν ἀμώμων) war falsch. Halten wir hier unbedingt fest: Der Gerechte ist der *Untadelige (ἄμωμος)*, also der, der *keines Verstoßes gegen das Gesetz schuldig* ist. Wer aber gesetzestreu lebt, erhält *himmlischen Lohn.* Der Hinweis auf den Lohn des Endgerichts erfolgt in einem noch erweiterten eschatologischen Kontext: Nach 2,23 hat Gott den Menschen zur Unvergänglichkeit (ἐπ' ἀφθαρσίᾳ) erschaffen, ihn zum Bilde seines eigenen göttlichen, also unvergänglichen Wesens erschaffen[30].

Fichtner[31] überschreibt Sap 3,1–5,23 mit »Vergleich des zeitlichen und ewigen Geschickes der Gerechten und der Gottlosen.« Allerdings zeigt dieser Abschnitt markante Zäsuren. Wir müssen jedoch aus Platzgründen auf eine genauere Analyse verzichten. Gesagt werden soll nur,

---

[26] P. W. Skehan, Borrowings from the Psalms in the Book of Wisdom, CBQ 10 (1948), 384–397.

[27] Ib. 397.

[28] Larcher, a.a.O. 96: «le Psautier n'apparaît pas avoir été, pour Sag., une source de premier plan.»

[29] Falls mit Joseph Ziegler, Göttinger Septuaginta, τῆς ἰδίας ἰδιότητος zu lesen ist.

[30] Sollte, wie es z. B. Fichtner, a.a.O. 16, und Georgi, a.a.O. 409 und 409, Anm. 23c, mit Rahlfs, LXX-Ausgabe, tun, doch ἀϊδιότητος zu lesen sein – nach Georgi fordert der Parallelismus membrorum diese Lesart –, so ändert sich dadurch soviel gar nicht. Denn die ἰδιότης Gottes impliziert wesentlich seine ἀϊδιότης!

[31] Fichtner, a.a.O. 18.

daß in Kap. 3 und 4 in belehrender Form ausgeführt wird, daß die Seelen der Gerechten nach all ihrer Bedrängnis in Gottes Hand sind, 3,1. Gott selbst hatte sie versucht und geprüft, 3,5f. Die Gottlosen aber werden (im Endgericht) bestraft, 3,10. Im Spiegel ihrer Gesetzlosigkeit läßt sich einiges über das Leben der Tugend (ἀρετή!, in unserem Abschnitt 4,1 und 5,13 – ein typisch griechischer Begriff, der in LXX 31mal[32] vorkommt, und zwar nur in späteren Schriften des Alten Testaments[33]) aussagen. Die Gottlosen kümmern sich nicht um den Gerechten, sie fallen vom Herrn ab, 3,10, sie verachten Weisheit und Zucht (παιδεία[34]), 3,11. Konkret werden 3,16 Ehebruch und gesetzloser Beischlaf genannt. Geradezu unalttestamentlich heißt es 4,1: »Besser ist Kinderlosigkeit mit Tugend.« Und auch die bezeichnende alttestamentliche Vorstellung, erst nach einem langen erfüllten Leben alt und lebenssatt zu sterben[35], wird 4,7ff. umgebogen: Gott läßt den Gerechten womöglich frühzeitig sterben, damit nicht Bosheit sein Denken verändere oder List seine Seele betrüge; er könnte ja Opfer der herumstreifenden Begierde (ἐπιθυμία) werden!

Auf die Parallele Jes 53 – Sap 5,1ff. wurde immer wieder aufmerksam gemacht, nämlich auf das Eingeständnis der Schuldigen hinsichtlich ihres fatalen Irrtums. Freilich besteht ein bezeichnender Unterschied: In Jes 53 bekennen sie, daß sie den Knecht Gottes für einen von Gott Geschlagenen hielten, daß dieser jedoch ihre Schuld zu ihrem *Heil* getragen hat. In Sap 5 hingegen bekennen die Gottlosen in ihrer eschatologischen *Heillosigkeit,* daß sie den Gerechten für eine lächerliche Gestalt und sein Leben für Irrsinn gehalten haben. Und gerade dieser kontradiktorische Gegensatz von Heil und Heillosigkeit der Bekennenden zeigt, daß die Parallele nicht den Kern der jeweiligen Darstellung betrifft. Für unsere Fragestellung ist innerhalb des Bekenntnisses von Sap 5 vor allem v. 6 wichtig: »Wir sind also vom Weg der Wahrheit abgeirrt, und das Licht der Gerechtigkeit schien uns nicht.« Diese Menschen bekennen ihren Verstoß gegen die Gerechtigkeit, wobei Gerechtigkeit als gerechtes und rechtmäßiges Handeln gegenüber anderen verstanden ist. Ungerechtigkeit wird in v. 7 als Verflechtung in Gesetzlosigkeit gewertet, eine Einstellung, die, wie sie damals in ihrer Torheit (v. 4: οἱ ἄφρονες!) nicht erkannt hatten, ins Verderben führte. Der Gerechte ist aber dann der Kluge, der sein Leben in Gerechtigkeit führt. δικαιοσύνη ist als ἀρετή die Verwirklichung des Menschen als δίκαιος – ein Gedanke, der nahe bei der ethischen Auffassung des *Aristoteles* zu stehen scheint. Aus dessen Nikomachischer Ethik sei hier nur auf die wichtige Stelle V,5,1134a, hingewiesen: καὶ ἡ

32 Sofern man ἀρετή in Prov 1,7 und 4 Macc 17,17 als sekundär ansieht.

33 Von 31 Vorkommen 24 in Büchern, die nur in der LXX, nicht im MT stehen: 3mal in Sap, 4mal in 2 Macc, 1mal in 3 Macc, 16mal in 4 Macc!

34 Georgi, a.a.O. 411, übers.: Bildung.

35 H. Hübner, Art. Leben II, Der L.-Begriff der Bibel, in: HWPh 5,56–59.

μὲν δικαιοσύνη ἐστὶ καθ' ἣν ὁ δίκαιος λέγεται πρακτικὸς κατὰ προαίρεσιν τοῦ δικαίου. Der Gerechte, der nach Aristoteles so handelt, daß er das Gerechte wählt, strebt nach der vollendeten Tugend, der τελεία ἀρετή, V,1,1129b. Mit diesem Hinweis auf Aristoteles soll nicht gesagt sein, daß der Autor der Sap bewußt auf diesen Gedanken des Stagiriten rekurrierte. Es sollte nur die Frage aufgeworfen werden, ob nicht der philosophische Eklektiker, der der Autor der Sap nun einmal war, auch Gedanken aufgegriffen hat, die wir bei Aristoteles verifizieren können. Diese Frage soll aber jetzt noch nicht beantwortet werden. Schauen wir erst weiter auf die folgenden Ausführungen in Sap!

In 6,1–11 sehe ich mit einer Reihe von Forschern den Abschluß des ersten Teils des Buches. Wurden die Herrscher 1,1 aufgefordert, die Gerechtigkeit zu lieben, so wird nun in der Anrede an sie festgestellt, daß sie, denen von Gott die Herrschaft gegeben wurde, das Gesetz nicht befolgt haben, οὐδὲ ἐφυλάξατε νόμον, 6,4, was konkret bedeutet: Ihr habt die Gerechtigkeit nicht geliebt und nicht geübt. Aber der Autor der Sap gibt anscheinend die Herrscher der Welt noch nicht auf. Beschwörend ermahnt er sie 6,9: »An euch, ihr Herrscher, richte ich mein Wort, damit ihr die Weisheit lernt und nicht (weiterhin) versagt!« (Insofern hier die folgende Belehrung über die Weisheit eingeleitet wird, hat 6,1–11 sicherlich auch seine Funktion für die nachstehenden Ausführungen und folglich ein gewisses Janusgesicht, so daß der Abschnitt nicht nur Abschluß des 1. Teils des Buches ist.) Die Begründung für die Aufforderung erfolgt 6,10a in einer Art »Satz heiligen Rechts«, in dem das negative οὐδὲ ἐφυλάξατε von 6,4 durch das positive οἱ φυλάξαντες aufgegriffen wird: »Die auf heilige Weise das Heilige (sc. Gottes Gesetz!) bewahrt haben, werden geheiligt werden (pass. divinum).«

Mit 6,12 beginnt der Lobpreis der Weisheit. Wir müssen uns hier auf wenige Charakteristika beschränken. Die Weisheit läßt sich von denen finden, die sie suchen, 6,12 (cf. 1,1f.: ζητήσατε ... εὑρίσκεται!). Für unsere Fragestellung ist vor allem der Kettenschluß 6,17ff. wichtig, von dem hier nur die ersten Glieder zitiert werden: »Ihr Anfang ist das aufrichtige Begehren nach ›Bildung‹ – παιδεία natürlich verstanden als Wissen um den Willen Gottes (cf. 6,4: τὴν βουλὴν τοῦ θεοῦ) und somit um die Gerechtigkeit –, das überzeugte Streben (φροντίς) nach ›Bildung‹ ist aber Liebe, Liebe ist aber das Halten ihrer (!) Gesetze ...« Deshalb sollen die Herrscher die Weisheit begehren. »Ehret die Weisheit, damit ihr für alle Zeiten herrscht!«

6,22 ist sozusagen Überschrift über alles Folgende: »Was die Weisheit ist und wie sie entstand, will ich berichten.« Daß dieses Ich das Ich des weisen Königs Salomo ist, geht aus Kap. 7 hervor, obwohl gemäß der Konzeption der Sap, keine Namen zu nennen, auch der seinige nicht genannt wird. Aber die bibelkundigen jüdischen Leser in Alexandrien wußten natürlich sofort Bescheid.

In Kap. 7 berichtet also »Salomo«, wie er Gott um die Weisheit gebeten hat und sie ihm auch gegeben wurde. Wir lesen 7,7: »Deshalb betete ich, und Einsicht (φρόνησις) wurde mir gegeben. Ich rief (Gott an), und der Geist der Weisheit (πνεῦμα σοφίας) kam zu mir.« Recht eigentümlich ist aber nun die Art der Erkenntnis, die »Salomo« erlangte. Auf einmal ist ihm gar nicht mehr die Gabe der Gerechtigkeit, die er doch zum Regieren brauchte, verliehen, sondern ein geradezu *philosophisches Wissen,* 7,17: »Er gab mir die untrügliche Kenntnis von allem Seienden, τῶν ὄντων γνῶσιν, das Wissen vom Aufbau der Welt und Wirken der Elemente, σύστασιν κόσμου καὶ ἐνέργειαν στοιχείων.« Hier liegt nicht nur stoische Terminologie vor (SVF II, 527 u. 555), sondern auch eindeutig stoisches Gedankengut. Haben wir eben noch die Frage gestellt, ob möglicherweise ein gewisser Einfluß aristotelischen Denkens hinsichtlich der δικαιοσύνη vorliege, so bleibt hier nur die unbestreitbare Feststellung: Der Autor der Sap denkt an dieser Stelle stoisch, freilich im Rahmen seines Eklektizismus. Diese eindeutig stoische Denkweise zeigt sich auch 7,22f. bei der »Definition« der Weisheit als πνεῦμα mit ihren 21 (= 3 × 7!) Attributen. Wenn es dabei zu Beginn πνεῦμα νοερόν heißt, so ist die stoische Parallele SVF III, 1009, frappierend: Ὁρίζονται δὲ τὴν τοῦ θεοῦ οὐσίαν οἱ Στωικοὶ οὕτως· πνεῦμα νοερόν ... Und wenn dann 7,24/8,1 von der Weisheit gesagt wird διήκει δὲ καὶ χωρεῖ διὰ πάντων ... καὶ διοικεῖ τὰ πάντα χρηστῶς, so muß auf SVF II, 416, verwiesen werden: τὸ διῆκον διὰ πάντων πνεῦμα, ὑφ᾽ οὗ τὰ πάντα συνέχεσθαι καὶ διοικεῖσθαι.

Es kommt in unserem Zusammenhang gar nicht so sehr auf den Tatbestand an, *daß* massiver stoischer Einfluß vorliegt. Was vielmehr für unsere Thematik von Bedeutung ist, ist, daß dem »Salomo« zunächst Auffassungen der stoischen Physik als Wissen durch die Weisheit zuteil werden. Aber dann kommt – im Aufbau des Ganzen unvermittelt – in 8,7 doch noch der ethische Aspekt zum Tragen. Hier werden die vier Kardinaltugenden genannt. Freilich läßt, wie Fichtner[36] mit Recht feststellt, ihre Nennung nicht auf Vertrautheit mit einem bestehenden System schließen. In der Tat verrät die Art ihrer Einführung und Aufzählung weder Gespür für platonische noch stoische Auffassung. Der Autor der Sap kannte sie, weil sie eben Allgemeingut der damaligen gebildeten griechischen Welt waren. Eigentümlich ist auch die logische Inkonsequenz in v. 7: Die Mühen der Gerechtigkeit sind die Tugenden. Als diese Tugenden werden die vier Kardinaltugenden aufgezählt, also auch die Gerechtigkeit, δικαιοσύνη, die somit als Ober- und Unterbegriff fungiert! Und auch die Einsicht, φρόνησις, erscheint zweimal: in v. 6 wirkt sie mehr als Nachklang von 7,7.16, in v. 7 hingegen wird sie als eine der vier Tugenden aufgezählt. In 7,7 aber steht φρόνησις im synonymen Parallelismus mit πνεῦμα σοφίας – ganz im Gegensatz zu 8,7, wo sie lediglich als eine der vier

[36] Fichtner, a.a.O. 34.

Tugenden mit die Frucht der Gerechtigkeit ist. Wir kommen also nicht um das Urteil herum, daß hier starke terminologische Unstimmigkeit vorliegt.[37] Was aber theologisch von entscheidender Relevanz ist, ist die *Einbettung der ethischen Thematik in die übergeordnete Weisheitskonzeption!* In diese Konzeption ist aber des weiteren integriert, daß »Salomo« durch die Weisheit mit intellektuellen Fähigkeiten begabt wurde, z. B. mit Scharfsinnigkeit beim richterlichen Urteil, 8,11, oder mit staatspolitischer Klugheit und strategischem Können, 8,14.

Deshalb betet er um die Gabe der Weisheit, Kap. 9. Gott hat den Menschen mit der Weisheit ausgestattet, damit er über die Geschöpfe herrsche – soweit eine Aufgabe, die nach Gen 1,26–28 für alle Menschen gilt – und in Frömmigkeit und Gerechtigkeit die Welt verwalte – wegen des Verbs διέπω, als terminus technicus in der hellenistischen Königsliteratur verwendet,[38] eine Aufgabe für Könige, 9,2f. Doch sei noch einmal darauf hingewiesen, daß die eigentlichen Adressaten nicht die Könige sind. James M. Reese hat Recht, wenn er unter Hinweis auf die 32 Vorkommen von ἄνθρωπος in Sap vom Autor dieses Buches sagt: "He wants his ideal king, his just and wise 'man', to be understood not as the individual King Solomon but rather as the type of everyman ..."[39]

»Salomo« bittet deshalb 9,4: »Gib mir die Weisheit, die mit dir auf deinem Throne residiert.« Sie ist nach 9,5 für ihn unverzichtbar, denn »ich bin dein Knecht und der Sohn deiner Magd, ein schwacher und kurzlebiger Mensch, und zu gering im Verständnis von Recht und Gesetzen, ἐλάσσων ἐν συνέσει κρίσεως καὶ νόμων.« Also ohne die Gabe der Weisheit Gottes muß »Salomo« bei seiner Aufgabe als König intellektuell versagen. In diesem Vers ist allerdings nicht ausdrücklich davon die Rede, daß er ohne die Gabe der Weisheit sein Amt in Schuld und Sünde ausüben mußte. Selbst die Wendung ἄνθρωπος ἀσθενής in v. 5 ist, isoliert gesehen, keine eindeutige Umschreibung des Sünderseins. Aber man wird wohl im Gesamtduktus der Argumentation in dem »schwachen Menschen«, der ohne genügende Einsicht ist, auch einen Sünder sehen müssen, da er ja ohne rechte Einsicht in das Gesetz gegenüber Gottes ausdrücklichem Willen, der sich nun einmal im Gesetz dokumentiert, schuldig wird. Wer ohne wirkliche Gesetzeskenntnis regiert, sündigt, weil er so notwendig gegen das Gesetz verstößt. Er vermag ja ohne Besitz der Weisheit nicht in Gerechtigkeit, also gemäß der Grundforderung des Gesetzes,

---

[37] Fichtner, a.a.O. 34. Ein nicht geglückter Harmonisierungsversuch liegt bei G. Ziener, Das Buch der Weisheit (WB), Düsseldorf 1970, 57, Anm. 24, vor: »›Gerechtigkeit‹ ist in 8,7a biblisch als Rechtschaffenheit, in 8,7d nach griechischer Ethik als Kardinaltugend der Gerechtigkeit zu verstehen.«

[38] J. M. Reese, Hellenistic Influence on the Book of Wisdom and its Consequences (AnBibl 41), Rom 1970, 76, Anm. 195.

[39] Ib. 76.

zu regieren (v. 5!); mit ihrem Besitz kann er jedoch erkennen, was Gott wohlgefällig ist (εὐάρεστον παρὰ σοί, v. 10, cf. Sap 4,10 und Röm 12,1f.!). Für den Stoiker Kleanthes war das Gute identisch mit dem Gerechten, dem Frommen und dem Wohlgefälligen: τἀγαθὸν ἐρωτᾷς μ' οἷον ἔστ', ... δίκαιον, ὅσιον, ... εὐάρεστον, ... ἄμεμπτον (SVF I, 557). Überhaupt bringt das ganze 9. Kap. im Grunde nur eine rhetorische Explikation des Gedankens, daß »Salomo«, also der Mensch schlechthin, auf die Weisheit total angewiesen ist, um vor Gott bestehen zu können. Nur so sind seine Werke vor Gott angenehm, προσδεκτά, v. 12! Nur dann weiß er um den Willen Gottes, wenn dieser ihm die Weisheit und den heiligen Geist geschickt hat, v. 17! Nur dann, wenn die Menschen (von Gott) über das Gott Wohlgefällige, τὰ ἀρεστά σου, belehrt sind, sind sie durch die Weisheit gerettet, ἐσώθησαν, v. 18!

Aus dem letzten Teil der Sap, der Kap. 10–19 umfaßt, wird vor allem das 13. Kap. wegen des dort ausgesprochenen Theologumenons der Erkennbarkeit Gottes aus der Schöpfung diskutiert. Für unsere Überlegungen ist dieses Kap. jedoch nur von sekundärer Bedeutung. Wichtig ist für unsere Thematik, daß an der frühen Geschichte Israels bis zum Exodus und vor allem im Blick auf den Exodus – freilich wird, wie schon erwähnt, kein Name genannt – gezeigt wird, wie die Gerechten durch Gott in aller Not und Unbill und aus aller Not und Unbill geleitet und gerettet werden. Während im ersten Teil des Buches der eschatologische Akzent gesetzt ist, geht es nun hauptsächlich um das Wirken Gottes in der Geschichte (Israels). So hat die Weisheit den *gerechten* Noah »durch ein armseliges Holz« (die Arche) geleitet, den *gerechten* Abraham untadelig vor Gott bewahrt (im Blick auf Gen 22 gesagt) und den *gerechten* Lot bei der Katastrophe von Sodom und Gomorrha aus dem Verderben gerettet, 10,4–6. Sie hat den *gerechten* Jakob (!) vor dem Zorn Esaus auf geradem Wege geleitet, 10,10, sie hat den *gerechten* Joseph nicht im Stich gelassen, 10,13. Die hier vorkommenden Verben sind u. a. κυβερνέω, τηρέω, ῥύομαι, ὁδηγέω. Von den Einzelpersonen geht in 10,15 der Blick auf das Volk Israel: Die Weisheit hat ein heiliges Volk, λαὸν ὅσιον (ὅσιος steht in Sap geradezu synonym für δίκαιος), samt fehlloser Nachkommenschaft, σπέρμα ἄμεμπτον, vor dem Volk der Bedränger (gemeint sind die Ägypter) bewahrt (wiederum ῥύομαι; v. 17 wiederum ὁδηγέω). Wie in Kap. 1–6 geht es um den Gegensatz von Gerechten und Gottlosen, δίκαιοι und ἀσεβεῖς, z. B. 10,20. Die Gottlosen sind die zugleich Ungerechten, ἄδικοι, 16,24, und Gesetzlosen, ἄνομοι, 17,2. In 18,7 erscheinen sie als Feinde (der Gerechten), ἐχθροί. Das Volk der Gerechten hingegen ist – hier wird das individuelle Verständnis des Sohnes von 2,13.18[40] auf das Volk Israel ausgeweitet – Gottes Sohn, 18,13: θεοῦ υἱὸν λαὸν εἶναι.

---

[40] J. Jeremias, Art. παῖς θεοῦ in: ThWNT 5, 682,24ff., überspitzt, wenn er bereits in 2,13 die kollektive Deutung von Jes 53 annehmen möchte. Natürlich ist der Gerechte in Kap.

Georg Ziener macht mit Recht darauf aufmerksam, daß δίκαιος, obwohl es 30mal in Sap vorkommt, nur einmal, nämlich 12,15, ausdrücklich von Gott ausgesagt wird.[41] Doch gerade hier handelt es sich um eine Schlüsselstelle für das Verständnis der Gerechtigkeit in Sap: Gott ist gerecht und in gerechter Weise verwaltet er das All, δίκαιος δὲ ὢν δικαίως τὰ πάντα διέπεις.[42] Diese Aussage ist insofern besonders interessant, als hier eine an 8,1 (διοικεῖ τὰ πάντα χρηστῶς) erinnernde Formulierung vorliegt, also an eine Aussage im Horizont der stoischen Physik. Dann aber ist für den Autor der Sap die *Gerechtigkeit Gottes in seiner Weltregierung begründet.* Stoisch gesprochen, greifen hier Physik und Ethik ineinander. Das »Verwalten«, besser: »Durchwalten« (Fichtner), also das διοικεῖν bzw. διέπειν Gottes, manifestiert sich in seinem Gerechtsein bzw. gerechten Wirken, wie es dann unmittelbar nach 12,15a in 12,15bc.16 ausgesagt wird. Fichtner[43] übersetzt gut: »Da du aber gerecht bist, durchwaltest du das All gerecht; den, der keine Strafe verdient hat, zu verurteilen hältst du für deiner Macht nicht würdig. Denn deine Macht ist die Quelle der Gerechtigkeit, und daß du aller Herr bist, läßt dich alle schonen.« Diese Stelle wirft aber Licht auf den bereits genannten eigentümlichen Tatbestand, daß die von »Salomo« erbetene Weisheit ihm zunächst eine Erkenntnis gibt, die in stoischer Terminologie die stoische Physik betrifft, und ihn erst dann zur Erkenntnis des Gesetzes und der Gerechtigkeit führt.

Daß die Gerechtigkeit der Angelpunkt zwischen »Physik« und Ethik ist, läßt aber nun die Glaubenslosigkeit in einem neuen Horizont sehen. Jetzt bekommt auch das bereits genannte 13. Kap. seine theologisch-ethische Relevanz. Wer aus den sichtbaren Gütern dieser Welt Gott, den eigentlich Seienden, τὸν ὄντα, nicht zu erkennen vermag, 13,1, wer so zum Götzendiener pervertiert, der wird auch in ethischer Hinsicht versagen. So ist das »Sinnen auf Götzenbilder« (Fichtner) der Anfang der Unzucht, 14,12 – ein Gedanke, den Paulus in Röm 1,18ff. aufgreifen wird. Die Verehrung der Götzen ist der Anfang eines jeglichen Bösen, sie ist dessen Ursache und schließliche Vollendung, 14,27. Sie führt in die rasende Manie des (wohl orgiastisch verstandenen) Freudentaumels und in ein Leben, das durch Ungerechtigkeit erfüllt ist, ζῶσιν ἀδίκως, 14,28. Kurz: Gottlosigkeit im strengen Sinne des Wortes führt in die Ungerechtigkeit hinein.

1ff. auch »Typ des Gerechten« (Z. 35). Aber zunächst ist doch wohl der Einzelne angesprochen! Auf Jeremias beruft sich u. a. B. L. Mack, Logos und Sophia, Untersuchungen zur Weisheitstheologie im hellenistischen Judentum (StUNT 10), Göttingen 1973, 86.

[41] G. Ziener, Die theologische Begriffssprache im Buch der Weisheit (BBB 11), Bonn 1956, 65f.

[42] Reese, a.a.O. 76, Anm. 194, will τὰ πάντα als Adverb fassen und mit »in every way« übersetzen – m. E. nicht möglich.

[43] Fichtner, a.a.O. 46.

Der Verstoß gegen die Erste Tafel des Dekalogs führt unweigerlich und unaufhaltsam zum Verstoß gegen die Zweite Tafel. Ethisches Versagen ist im Glaubensversagen impliziert. Der *Gott-Lose ist ungerecht.* Positiv heißt das in 15,3: »Dich zu kennen ist vollkommene Gerechtigkeit und « – jetzt folgt der eschatologische Ausblick – »um deine Macht zu wissen ist Wurzel der Unsterblichkeit.« Was aber heißt konkret Gerechtigkeit? Die Antwort gibt 12,19 als von Gott gegebene Lehre: »Der Gerechte muß menschenfreundlich sein, δεῖ τὸν δίκαιον εἶναι φιλάνθρωπον« (cf. 1,6; 7,23). Sicher soll sich der Leser hier im Sinne des Autors der Sap an 7,23 – die »Definition« der Weisheit als des menschenfreundlichen Geistes – erinnern. Damit ist aber zum Ausdruck gebracht, daß die Verpflichtung zur Gerechtigkeit als Menschenfreundlichkeit durch die Gabe des Geistes der Weisheit, 7,7, ermöglicht ist. *Die Aufgabe gründet also in der Gabe.* Am Rande sei darauf aufmerksam gemacht, daß in Kap. 10–19 σοφία nur viermal in Kap. 10 und zweimal in Kap. 14 vorkommt. Eine Deutung dieses eigentümlichen Sachverhalts kann hier nicht erfolgen.

Das negative Prinzip der Gerechtigkeit bzw. das Prinzip der Gerechtigkeit als der strafenden Gerechtigkeit ist in Kap. 10–19 vor allem in 11,16 ausgesprochen: »Womit einer sündigt, damit wird er bestraft.« Dieses Prinzip wird dann in den folgenden Kap. an vielen Beispielen von immanenter Sanktion exemplifiziert. Und 14,31 heißt es: »Die Bestrafung derer, die sündigen, folgt stets der Übertretung durch die Ungerechten.«

*

Bei Aussagen über Ethik geht es nicht nur um ethische Prinzipien und Gehalte, sondern auch um die jeweilige Situation, in die hinein derartige Aussagen gesprochen sind. Im Blick auf die israelitische Weisheitsliteratur bedeutet das, den didaktischen Charakter etwa der Sprüche Salomos, weitgehend in der Tradition der gemeinorientalischen Weisheit stehend, von der Trostintention der Sap zu unterscheiden. Mit Recht sprach Fichtner vom weiten Weg, den die israelitisch-jüdische Weisheit von ihren Ursprüngen bis in das erste vorchristliche Jahrhundert zurückgelegt, und vom grundsätzlichen Wandel, den sie erlebt hatte.[44] So ist der »Sitz im Leben« der Sap ein völlig anderer als der älterer Weisheitsbücher. Man vergleiche nur einmal den didaktisch-ethischen Charakter von Prov 22,17–23,12 mit Sap. Dieser Abschnitt der Sprüche Salomos, bekanntlich bis ins Detail von der um ca. 1000 v. Chr. entstandenen ägyptischen Weisheitslehre des Amenemope abhängig, will zum guten Tun ermahnen und vor bösem Tun warnen. Das ist aber nicht die Intention der Sap! Nach

---

[44] J. Fichtner, Zum Problem Glaube und Geschichte in der israelitisch-jüdischen Weisheitsliteratur, in: Ders. Gottes Weisheit, Gesammelte Studien zum Alten Testament, hg. K. D. Fricke (AzTh II/3), Stuttgart 1965, (9–17)12.

Fichtner ist Sap als »eine echt hellenistisch-jüdische Propagandaschrift« zu beurteilen, die sich an fromme und verweltlichte Juden und an hellenistische Heiden wende und ihnen die Überlegenheit der jüdischen Weisheit über alle heidnische Religion und Philosophie verkünde.[45] Nach Otto Eißfeldt besteht die Absicht des Autors der Sap darin, den jüdischen Gottesglauben mit den Mitteln der hellenistischen Bildung gegen abtrünnig gewordene Volksgenossen und gegen seine heidnische Umgebung zu verteidigen.[46] In dieser Charakterisierung durch Fichtner und Eißfeldt ist sicher ein nicht geringes Wahrheitsmoment ausgesprochen. Aber entscheidender ist m. E. die Absicht des Autors der Sap, die wohl in Pression, vielleicht sogar unter Verfolgung stehenden Juden der ägyptischen Diaspora Alexandriens, die treu am religiösen Erbe ihrer Väter festhalten, zu trösten und zu stärken. Von daher wird man seine Intention weniger darin sehen, daß er primär Ungerechte zur Gerechtigkeit bewegen will, sondern daß er Gerechte, also Untadelige in der Gesetzesbefolgung, die ungerecht leiden, stärken möchte.[47] Bezeichnend ist die Differenz zwischen Jesus Sirach und Sap, auf die Fichtner selbst aufmerksam macht: Sir idealisiere im allgemeinen durchaus nicht die Gestalten und Ereignisse der Geschichte Israels.[48] »Dagegen sieht das Bild des Volkes Israels und seiner Großen in der Weish. wesentlich anders aus ... Die Möglichkeit, daß Gottes Volk sündigen könnte, wird zwar erwogen (12,19; 15,2), aber 15,2 unmittelbar danach festgestellt: ›Wir werden aber nicht sündigen, weil wir wissen, daß wir zu dir gerechnet sind!‹«[49] Also: »Aufs Ganze gesehen ist *Israel schlechthin* das *Volk der Gerechten,* die Ägypter sind das Volk der Gottlosen; ihr Geschick wird unter dem Gesichtspunkt der Strafe für die Gottlosen und der Wohltaten für die Gerechten miteinander verglichen ...«[50] *Das Volk der Gerechten braucht aber keine Paränese!* Das Volk der Gerechten braucht im Unglück Trost, es braucht in der Verfolgung Stärkung. Und genau das tut der Autor der Sap.

Er tut es als einer, der ganz im Alten Testament zu Hause ist, genauer: in der alexandrinischen Übersetzung des Alten Testaments in die griechische Sprache. Er lebt und denkt aus der Septuaginta. Es wurde bereits darauf aufmerksam gemacht, daß in der wissenschaftlichen Diskussion unterschiedliche Hypothesen aufgestellt wurden, aus welchen Teilen des Alten Testaments er hauptsächlich schöpfe, ob aus Jes 53, ψ 88 oder anderen Stellen. Vielleicht ist die Frage so nicht ganz angemessen formuliert. Man wird eher fragen müssen, *unter welchem Gesichtspunkt der Au-*

---

[45] Ders., Art. Salomo-Weisheit, in: ^{3}RGG V, 1344.

[46] O. Eißfeldt, Einleitung in das Alte Testament (NTG), Tübingen ^{4}1976, 816.

[47] S. dazu Ruppert I, 104.

[48] Fichtner, Zum Problem Glaube und Geschichte, 13.

[49] Ib. 13.

[50] Ib. 13; Hervorhebung durch mich.

tor der Sap das Alte Testament liest und *wie er sich von da aus auf unterschiedliche Partien der Schrift bezieht.* Aus dem Gesamtduktus seiner Argumentation läßt sich klar erkennen, daß er das Alte Testament unter dem leitenden Gesichtspunkt liest, wie in ihm Gott Anwalt des leidenden Gerechten ist. Das ist für ihn geradezu der hermeneutische Schlüssel des Alten Testaments. Um sein zentrales Theologumenon von Gott, der sich des leidenden Gerechten annimmt – sei es im Endgericht (der eschatologische Teil Kap. 1–6), sei es in der Geschichte (der »historische« Teil Kap. 10–19) –, zum Ausdruck zu bringen, bedient er sich sowohl der Sprache hierfür in Frage kommender Psalmen und zentraler Vorstellungsgehalte von Jes 53 als auch vieler Details aus dem Exodusschicksal Israels. *Die Schrift* ist für ihn *eine Ganzheit, die in ihren einzelnen Büchern theologisch gleiches aussagt.*

Die zu Ehren des Jubilars hier publizierte Studie kann als Problemskizze nur fragmentarischen Charakter haben.[51] Deshalb möchte ich das zuletzt Gesagte lediglich im Blick auf Sap 1–6 und einige Psalmen veranschaulichen. Wenn ich in diesem Zusammenhang vor allem ψ 36 heranziehe, so dürfte es sich aufgrund der bisherigen Darlegungen von selbst verstehen, daß dieser Psalm nicht als die »wichtigste Quelle« für die theologische Absicht des Autors der Sap hingestellt werden soll. Auf ψ 36 soll jedoch vor allem deshalb aufmerksam gemacht werden, weil er in der bisherigen Diskussion zu geringe Aufmerksamkeit gefunden hat. Skehan hat mehr en passant auf v. 12–14 für Sap 2,10–12 und auf v. 13 für Sap 4,18b, überhaupt auf ψ 36 für Sap 4,7–18 aufmerksam gemacht.[52] Georgi verweist lediglich »zu der jetzigen Ironie« des Klageliedes Sap 2,1 ff. auf diesen Psalm.[53] Nach Larcher hat sich der Psalm, der das Schicksal des Gerechten dem des Ungerechten gegenüberstelle, dem Autor der Sap als »une ambiance et un stimulant« für seine Überlegungen angeboten; er nennt als mögliche Bezüge v. 13 für Sap 4,18b, v. 28 für Sap 3,16b und 12,11a und v. 18 für Sap 2,22.[54] Ruppert verweist lediglich für δίκαιος und πένης in Sap auf die entsprechenden Vorkommen in dem Psalm.[55] Kleinknecht, der auf Ruppert aufbaut, nennt den Psalm im Zusammenhang mit Sap nicht.

Richtig wurde also gesehen, daß für ψ 36 wie für Sap der Gegensatz von Gerechtem und Sünder konstitutiv ist. Während es in Sap 1–6 zu-

---

[51] Ausführlich werde ich in meiner in Arbeit befindlichen Monographie »Weisheit als Theologie, Zum Schriftverständnis und Schriftgebrauch in der Sapientia Salomonis« eine möglichst umfassende Antwort auf den theologischen Umgang des Autors der Sap mit dem Alten Testament zu geben versuchen.

[52] Skehan, a.a.O. 386f.

[53] Georgi, a.a.O. 406.

[54] Larcher, a.a.O. 94f.

[55] Ruppert I, 215, Anm. 294 zu S. 75.

meist um den Gegensatz von δίκαιος/δίκαιοι und ἀσεβεῖς geht, ist es in ψ 36 der von δίκαιος/δίκαιοι und ἁμαρτωλός/ἁμαρτωλοι (ἁμαρτωλός in Sap nur 4,10 und 19,13; hingegen kommt ἀσεβής in ψ 36 dreimal vor: v. 28.35.38). Für unsere Frage nach der Ethik der Sap ist nun erheblich, daß in ψ 36 der *Gesetzesgehorsam des Gerechten* die *vorausgesetzte Situation* ist. Der Beter des Psalms fleht zu Gott, weil er als der Gesetzesfromme verfolgt wird, v. 31: »Das Gesetz Gottes ist in seinem Herzen.« Das für den Gesetzesgehorsam konstitutive ethische Verhalten wird also für den Gerechten weder in ψ 36 noch in Sap erst angestrebt. In Sap wird der Gerechte in seiner Hoffnung bestärkt, freilich in der Form des Indikativs, 3,4: »Ihre Hoffnung ist voll von Unsterblichkeit.« Im Psalm wird der Beter aufgefordert, auf den Herrn zu hoffen, v. 3.5, bzw. er selbst bekennt, daß Gott die Gerechten retten wird, weil sie auf ihn gehofft haben, v. 40. Der Unterschied zwischen der im Psalm und der in Sap zum Ausdruck kommenden Hoffnung ist, daß es in ersterem um eine Hoffnung geht, die hier und jetzt in Erfüllung geht bzw. in Erfüllung gegangen ist, in Sap 3–5 jedoch um eine Hoffnung, die in jenseitiger Glückseligkeit ihre Erfüllung findet (3,4: ἀθανασίας πλήρης; über das Problem der Eschatologie in Sap kann hier nichts gesagt werden).[56] Das Aussagegefälle von beiden Schriften läßt jedoch nicht zu, die irdische Hoffnung des Psalms und die eschatologische Hoffnung der Sap als Zweck des Gesetzesgehorsams zu verstehen. Der Gerechte tut nicht das vom Gesetz Gebotene, um vor Gott als gerecht dazustehen und sich so durch das Tun der Gebote des Gesetzes die Gerechtigkeit vor Gott zu verdienen. Das, was in späterer theologischer Terminologie Verdienstdenken genannt wurde, läßt sich weder in ψ 36 noch in Sap finden. Vollends ist eine solche Einstellung für Sap ausgeschlossen, da ja der Weisheitsbesitz, also Gottes wichtigste Gabe, erst die Ermöglichung des wahren Gesetzesgehorsams schafft.[57] In etwa liegt hier eine Parallele zwischen der Denkart der Sap und der des Paulus vor: Der Lohn durch Gott ist die *Konsequenz* des guten Tuns, *nicht* dessen *Intention*.[58] (Daß gerade die letzten Ausführungen die Differenz der Sap zur Nikomachischen Ethik des Aristoteles (s. o.) augenfällig werden lassen, braucht wohl kaum bewiesen zu werden.)

Vielleicht ist ψ 36,30 mit ein Grund, warum der Autor der Sap gerade diesen Psalm besonders heranzieht. Man lese diesen Vers einmal mit

---

56 Die Auffassung von Georgi, a.a.O. 410, Anm. 4a, daß Unsterblichkeit und Hoffnung Gegenwartsgut seien, teile ich nicht. Eine Auseinandersetzung mit ihm muß ich auf spätere Zeit verschieben.

57 Daß »Salomo« erst um die Weisheit bittet, 7,7, und so ein »synergistisches« Moment für die theologische Konzeption der Sap zu verzeichnen wäre, bedeutet die anachronistische Eintragung späterer Denkkategorien in eine Schrift des 1. Jh. v. Chr.

58 H. Hübner, Das Gesetz des Paulus, Ein Beitrag zum Werden der paulinischen Theologie (FRLANT 119), Göttingen ³1982, z. B. 101f.

seinen Augen: »Der Mund des Gerechten wird Weisheit sprechen und seine Zunge wird Gerechtigkeit, κρίσιν, reden.«! Das Dreieck »Gerechter – Weisheit – Gerechtigkeit« ist doch auch für jenen alexandrinischen Juden unübersehbar.

Doch listen wir nun die weiteren Parallelen zwischen ψ 36 und Sap 1–6 auf, wobei wir nach der Reihenfolge der Psalmverse vorgehen. Natürlich ist nicht jede Parallele, vor allem, wenn es nur um einzelne Begriffe geht, von gleich starker Beweiskraft. Aber es kommt ja auch gar nicht so sehr auf die einzelene Parallele an, sondern vor allem auf die Gesamtheit der Parallelen. (Die bereits genannten Entsprechungen werden nicht mehr genannt; eine vollständige Auflistung ist hier nicht beabsichtigt.)

	ψ 36		Sap
1	τοὺς ποιοῦντας τὴν ἀνομίαν	5,7	ἀνομίας ἐνεπλέχθημεν τριβόλοις (so Göttinger LXX mit Konjektur Bretschneider)
6	ἐξοίσει ὡς φῶς τὴν δικαιοσύνην σου	5,6	τὸ τῆς δικαιοσύνης φῶς οὐκ ἔλαμψεν ἡμῖν
7	ἐν ἀνθρώπῳ ποιοῦντι παρανομίας	3,16	ἐκ παρανόμου κοίτης σπέρμα
10	ἔτι ὀλίγον καὶ οὐ μὴ ὑπάρξῃ ὁ ἁμαρτωλός	2,1 f.	᾿Ολίγος ἐστὶν . . . ὁ βίος ἡμῶν . . . καὶ μετὰ τοῦτο ἐσόμεθα ὡς οὐχ ὑπάρξαντες
10	καὶ ζητήσεις τὸν τόπον αὐτοῦ καὶ οὐ μὴ εὕρῃς	2,2–5	inhaltliche, nicht verbale Parallele
13	ὁ δὲ κύριος ἐκγελάσεται αὐτὸν		Umkehrung des Gedankens in
		5,4?:	Οὗτος ἦν, ὃν ἔσχομέν ποτε εἰς γέλωτα
14	τοῦ καταβαλεῖν πτωχὸν καὶ πένητα, τοῦ σφάξαι τοὺς εὐθεῖς τῇ καρδίᾳ	2,10.20	καταδυναστεύσωμεν πένητα δίκαιον . . . θανάτῳ ἀσχήμονι καταδικάσωμεν αὐτόν
16	κρεῖσσον ὀλίγον τῷ δικαίῳ ὑπὲρ πλοῦτον ἁμαρτωλῶν πολύν	5,8	τί πλοῦτος μετὰ ἀλαζονείας συμβέβληται ἡμῖν;

	ψ 36		Sap
18	γινώσκει κύριος τὰς ὁδοὺς τῶν ἀμώμων	2,22	γέρας ψυχῶν ἀμώμων
20	οἱ δὲ ἐχθροὶ τοῦ κυρίου ... ἐκλιπόντες ὡσεὶ καπνὸς ἐξέλιπον (καπνός in ψψ sonst nur noch 3mal!, in LXX 29mal)	2,2 5,14	καπνὸς ἡ πνοὴ ἐν ῥισὶν ἡμῶν (im Zusammenhang des Todes gesagt!) ὅτι ἐλπὶς ἀσεβοῦς ... ὡς καπνὸς ὑπὸ ἀνέμου διεχύθη
27 (!)↓	ποίησον ἀγαθόν	3,15 (!)↓	ἀγαθῶν γὰρ πόνων καρπὸς εὐκλεής
28	σπέρμα ἀσεβῶν ἐξολεθρευθήσεται	3,16	ἐκ παρανόμου κοίτης σπέρμα ἀφανισθήσεται
31	ὁ νόμος τοῦ θεοῦ αὐτοῦ ἐν καρδίᾳ αὐτοῦ	6,4	οὐδὲ ἐφυλάξατε νόμον
32 ↓	κατανοεῖ ὁ ἁμαρτωλὸς τὸν δίκαιον καὶ ζητεῖ τοῦ θανατῶσαι αὐτόν	2,17–20,	vor allem 20: θανάτῳ ἀσχήμονι καταδικάσωμεν αὐτόν (= τὸν δίκαιον)
33	ὁ δὲ κύριος ... οὐδὲ μὴ καταδικάσηται αὐτόν	s. 2,20	unmittelbar zuvor
35 f.	εἶδον ἀσεβῆ ... καὶ παρῆλθον, καὶ ἰδοὺ οὐκ ἦν	1,16–2,5	inhaltliche Parallele
38	οἱ δὲ παράνομοι ἐξολεθρευθήσονται	3,16	ἐκ παρανόμου κοίτης σπέρμα ἀφανισθήσεται
39 (!)↓	σωτηρία δὲ τῶν δικαίων παρὰ κυρίου	5,2 (!)↓	ἐπὶ τῷ παραδόξῳ τῆς σωτηρίας (sc. τοῦ δικαίου)
39	ὑπερασπιστὴς αὐτῶν ἐστιν ἐν καιρῷ θλίψεως	5,1	κατὰ πρόσωπον τῶν θλιψάντων αὐτὸν
40	κύριος ... ῥύσεται αὐτοὺς καὶ ἐξελεῖται αὐτοὺς ἐξ ἁμαρτωλῶν	2,18	ῥύσεται αὐτὸν ἐκ χειρὸς ἀνθεστηκότων

Für die übrigen Kap der Sap sei hier nur noch auf 10,13 verwiesen: αὕτη (sc. ἡ σοφία) πραθέντα δίκαιον οὐκ ἐγκατέλιπεν. Der inhaltliche Bezug geht natürlich auf Gen 37–50, aber als sprachliche Parallele ist ψ 36,28 zu erwägen: οὐκ ἐγκαταλείψει τοὺς ὁσίους αὐτοῦ.

Aufschlußreich wäre auch ein detaillierter Vergleich von Sap 1–6 mit einigen Psalmen, die im LXX-Psalter in der Nähe von ψ 36 stehen. Hier soll aber nur auf wenige Übereinstimmungen hingewiesen werden. Für Sap 2,1 οὐκ ἔστιν ἴασις ἐν τελευτῇ ἀνθρώπου fällt die Parallele in ψ 37,4.8 auf: οὐκ ἔστιν ἴασις ἐν τῇ σαρκί μου (ἀπὸ προσώπου τῆς ὀργῆς σου). In Sap 2,1 ist es die Selbstaussage des – freilich reuigen – Sünders. Die Wendung οὐκ ἔστιν ἴασις (ἐν) begegnet in den Psalmen nur hier, in LXX, von Sap abgesehen, insgesamt nur 6mal. Für Sap 5,14 ἐλπὶς ἀσεβοῦς ὡς φερόμενος χνοῦς ὑπὸ ἀνέμου sei auf ψ 34,5 verwiesen: γενηθήτωσαν ὡσεὶ χνοῦς κατὰ πρόσωπον ἀνέμου, zumal in unmittelbarer Nähe beider Verse (Sap 5,20; ψ 34,3) ῥομφαία begegnet. Und könnte nicht das Eingeständnis der Gottlosen Sap 5,6, daß ihnen das Licht der Gerechtigkeit nicht geschienen hat, ein Nachklang von ψ 34,6 sein: γενηθήτω ἡ ὁδὸς αὐτῶν σκότος?

Genug der Beispiele, die sich leicht vermehren ließen! Nochmals: Die einzelne Parallele besagt oft wenig, da zuweilen auch andere alttestamentliche Parallelen zu den betreffenden Sap-Stellen aufweisbar sind. Ihre Kumulation in ψ 36 und benachbarten Psalmen sollte aber zu denken geben.

Folgendem Sachverhalt sollte man auch Beachtung schenken: Ps 37 (ψ 36) ist ein Weisheitspsalm, der den Tun-Ergehen-Zusammenhang deutlich ausspricht. Die Gegenüberstellung von v. 20 und v. 25 möge hier genügen: »Denn die Gottlosen kommen um, und die Feinde Jahwes – wie die Pracht der Auen vergeh'n sie, vergehen wie Rauch ... Ich war jung, wurde alt, doch nie sah ich einen Gerechten verlassen noch seine Kinder betteln um Brot.«[59] Der weisheitliche Autor der Sap hat also bezeichnenderweise einen Weisheitspsalm so stark herangezogen. Was jedoch im Psalm direkter Ausdruck festesten Vertrauens ist, geboren aus der Erfahrung des Beters, – Hans-Joachim Kraus sagt mit Recht, daß im Zentrum des Ps 37 nicht »die Gerechtigkeit« oder »die Vergeltung« liege, sondern das Zeugnis vom lebendigen Ergreifen Jahwähs in das Leben der Menschen, und daß nirgendwo ein Prinzip der Gerechtigkeit oder eine Idee der Vergeltung zu erkennen sei, sondern zum Vertrauen auf Jahwäh aufgerufen werde[60] – wird in Sap mehr zur demonstrierenden Darlegung. Mag auch das Vertrauensmoment hier sicherlich nicht fehlen, so ist doch der Tun-Ergehen-Zusammenhang an dieser Stelle eher im Sinne eines Prinzips ausgesagt als in unserem Weisheitspsalm. In Sap dürfte das theoretische Moment eine etwas größere Rolle spielen als im Psalm. Allerdings ist die Form der Darlegung des »Prinzips« aufgrund ihrer narrati-

[59] Übersetzung des hebräischen Textes nach H.-J. Kraus, Psalmen I (BK XV/1), Neukirchen ^{2}1961, 286.

[60] Ib. 291.

ven, zuweilen fast dramatischen Züge nicht die einer theoretischen Abhandlung.

Kommen wir noch einmal auf den *Einfluß stoischer Gedanken in Sap* zurück. Es war von der Fundierung der Ethik in der stoischen Physik die Rede. Der Autor der Sap hat jedoch bei aller bereits zugestandenen Übernahme stoischer Terminologie und Gedanken die stoische Physik mit ihrem zweifellos pantheistischen Charakter (z. B. SVF II, 1022: Οὐσίαν δὲ θεοῦ ... τὸν ὅλον κόσμον καὶ τὸν οὐρανόν ...) entscheidend modifiziert. Oder besser gesagt: Er hat sie in den biblischen Monotheismus *integriert.* Aber gerade diese Integration behält die genannte Fundierung der Ethik in der Physik bei. Kann man deshalb das stoische Grundprinzip der Ethik, wie es Kleanthes mit seinem ὁμολογουμένως τῇ φύσει ζῆν (SVF III, 12) formulierte, auch für Sap annehmen? Insofern sicherlich nicht, als die Gabe der Weisheit im Sinne des Autors der Sap nicht zum Bereich der Physis gehören dürfte. Trotzdem läßt sich eine gewisse Analogie zwischen dem Denken des jüdisch-alexandrinischen Theologen und dem der Stoa an diesem Punkte schlecht leugnen, da die »übernatürliche« Weisheit den »Salomo« lehrt, was die »natürliche« Weltstruktur in ihrem Innersten ausmacht (Sap 7,15ff.!).[61] Insofern die Ethik und gerade ihre Hauptforderung, das Gesetzesgebot der Gerechtigkeit, in der Schöpfungsordnung gründen, läßt sich zumindest mit einem gewissen Vorbehalt die Formel des Kleanthes »monotheistisch integrieren«. Martin Hengel formuliert den Vergleich zwischen dem Stoiker und dem rabbinischen Frommen wie folgt: »So betrachtet war der fromme Jude rabbinischer Prägung wie der Stoiker stets darauf bedacht, in ›Übereinstimmung mit dem Weltgesetz zu leben‹, nur daß er diesem Gesetz nicht so sehr als einer inneren Norm, sondern in Gestalt einer Unzahl minutiös fixierter Einzelforderungen begegnete.«[62] Der Unterschied zwischen dem frommen Autor der Sap und dem rabbinischen Frommen ist, daß in Sap der Akzent nicht auf »eine Unzahl minutiös fixierter Einzelforderungen« gelegt ist. Deshalb steht Sap dem ethischen Denken der Stoa etwas näher als das rabbinische Denken.

Insofern gerade durch die Rezeption stoischer Denkfiguren das theoretische Moment in Sap an Gewicht gewonnen hat, erlangte das Buch auch theo*logischen* Charakter. Seine theologische Wirkungsgeschichte können wir im Neuen Testament verfolgen. Es sei hier nur an Paulus erin-

---

[61] Die Begriffe »Natur und Übernatur« sind zugegebenerweise etwas anachronistisch verwendet.

[62] M. Hengel, Judentum und Hellenismus, Studien zu ihrer Begegnung unter besonderer Berücksichtigung Palästinas bis zur Mitte des 2. Jh. v. Chr. (WUNT 10), Tübingen ^{2}1973, 315. Daß »in Übereinstimmung mit dem Weltgesetz zu leben« und »in Übereinstimmung mit der Natur zu leben« nahezu identisch sind, braucht wohl kaum näher begründet zu werden.

nert. Bereits 1892 hat Eduard Grafe in seinem heute noch lesenswerten Aufsatz »Das Verhältnis der paulinischen Schriften zur Sapientia Salomonis« gesagt: »Und noch eins hat Paulus mit diesem eigenthümlichen Buche gemein. Wie Sap jüdische und hellenische Elemente in sich vereinigt, und zwar in einer Weise, daß nicht immer die völlige Ausgleichung der disparaten Elemente gefunden ist, so ringen auch in der christlichen Brust des Apostels diese beiden Mächte mit einander.«[63] Sicherlich ist das Ergebnis dieses Ringens in entscheidenden Punkten anders ausgegangen als in Sap. Darauf hat der Jubilar, dem unsere Festschrift gewidmet ist, in seiner Habilitationsschrift »Das Hauptproblem der Sozialethik in der neueren Stoa und im Urchristentum«[64] energisch hingewiesen. Die Symbiose von alttestamentlichem und griechischen Geist ist nicht, wie es Adolf von Harnack annahm, der Abfall vom Evangelium; nicht erst das altkirchliche Dogma ist das Werk des griechischem Geistes auf dem Boden des Evangeliums.[65] Die Aufgabe, das Zueinander von Altem Testament, Neuem Testament und griechischem Geist zu klären, steht weithin noch vor uns. Sap dürfte uns für diese Aufgabe einige wichtige Denkmuster anbieten.[66]

---

[63] E. Grafe, Das Verhältnis der paulinischen Schriften zur Sapientia Salomonis, in: Theologische Abhandlungen, Carl von Weizäcker zu seinem siebzigsten Geburtstag 11. December 1892, gewidmet von Adolf Harnack u. a., Freiburg 1892, (251–286)286; s. auch H. Hübner, Das ganze und das eine Gesetz, Zum Problemkreis Paulus und die Stoa, KuD 21 (1975), 239–256.

[64] H. Greeven, Das Hauptproblem der Sozialethik in der neueren Stoa und im Urchristentum, Gütersloh 1935.

[65] So vor allem die Tendenz von A. von Harnack, Lehrbuch der Dogmengeschichte, 3 Bde., Tübingen 1983 (= 1909/10).

[66] Auf die gerade erst erschienene Publikation C. Larcher, Le livre de la Sagesse ou la Sagesse de Salomon, 2 Bde. (EtB), Paris 1984/85, werde ich erst in der angekündigten Monographie (s. Anm. 51) eingehen.

The Two Texts of Acts

by G. D. Kilpatrick

(27 Lathbury Road, Oxford, England)

Professor H. Greeven and I have known each other for nearly forty years and it gives me particular pleasure to acknowledge our indebtedness to him in the study of the Gospels and in the textual criticism of the New Testament. His fundamental revision of Huck's *Synopse* of 1981 is a concentrate of learning and doctrine that rewards those who apply themselves to it. For example at a time when pressures were great to use Nestle–Aland^{26} (the so-called 'Standard Text') he has produced an independent recension of the text which has a proper value. A comparison of this text with that of N-A^{26} for the Synoptic Gospels is to be found in Neirynck and van Segbroeck, *New Testament Vocabulary,* 451–461 (1984).

If he has produced a text of the Gospels, he has left something to be done with the rest of the New Testament. In particular despite the many labours of previous scholars something remains to be treated in the text of Acts. Whatever our starting point there is much unfinished business.

We have a recent reminder of this in an article by M.-E. Boismard in Epp and Fee (editors) *New Testament Textual Criticism* (1981) 147–157 "The Text of Acts: A Problem of Literary Criticism?" in variations "where problems of textual criticism and literary criticism can be closely linked" (157). I have since learnt that Boismard is preparing a book on this subject, but I have only been able to use his article.

Boismard is not the first to discuss the two forms of text which we encounter in Acts. These forms, the General and the Western, were early recognised, the General being the kind of text found in most witnesses from the third century, and the Western found principally in D, the Latin, and some Coptic. Most students of the text of Acts regarded the GT (= General Text) as being for the most part original (e.g. Ropes, *The Beginnings of Christianity* III *The Text,* 1926), but some have preferred the Western text (= WT) (e.g. A. C. Clark, *The Acts of the Apostles,* 1933). Some of us have decided to pick and choose, as I have in my paper, "An Eclectic Study of the Text of Acts" in *Biblical and Patristic Studies in Memory of Robert Pierce Casey* (ed. Birdsall and Thomson, 1963).

Blass, *Acta Apostolorum,* 1895, and Zahn, *Die Urausgabe der Apostelgeschichte bei Lucas,* 1916, propounded a more complicated hypothesis: both forms of Acts proceeded from the author. Blass argued that WT represented a first edition and GT a second edition, both the work of the author. This hypothesis exercised great influence on subsequent scholars but did not convince them, cf. Ropes, *The Text,* ccxxvii–ccxxxi, Kenyon–Adams, *The Text of the Greek Bible,* 238f. (1975).

Boismard approaches the problem independently. He examines two passages, 11,2 and 19,1 and argues that as both Western and General texts show distinctively features of the style of the author, they must both be his work.

Boismard is right in including linguistic considerations in his discussion, and any difference from him may for the most part be a difference, not in principle, but in detail. As an example of this let us take the conjecture in WT at 11,2 κατήντησεν ⟨αὐτοῦ⟩ instead of κατήντησεν αὐτοῖς. We are told that "κατήντησεν αὐτοῖς is impossible" (149) but is αὐτοῦ possible?

If we look αὐτοῦ up in the concordances we find it at six passages:

Mt 26,36 ὧδε 33 700; omit S (* 61 300
Mk 6,33 προῆλθον αὐτούς] συνῆλθον αὐτοῦ D 565 cf. *L* ff[2] 1 r[1]
L 9,27 αὐτοῦ P[75vid] S B L Ξ 1 1582 Cyra, Orig] ὧδε ceteri
A 15,34 αὐτούς C D *L*] αὐτοῦ 33 614 1739 al; uersum omittunt *P*[75] S A B E Ψ ω; πρὸς αὐτούς D *L* g l w vg(pt)
A 18,19 αὐτοῦ B Ψ 0120 ω] ἐκεῖ P[74vid] S A D E *33al*
21,4 αὐτοῦ S B C*al*] αὐτοῖς A L ω.

We see at once that in none of these passages is αὐτοῦ textually secure. In addition we notice that the presence of αὐτοῦ in many witnesses at Mt 22,36 may be due to an assimilation to Gen 22,5; Mk 6,33 presents several variants, but the reading of D looks like an attempt to avoid repetition as may be seen from the synopsis. At L 9,27 we have a straight choice: either αὐτοῦ or ὧδε. ὧδε appears some 63 times in the NT. It is part of the vocabulary of the NT but we have not proved that αὐτοῦ is. The same consideration applies to A 18,19. ἐκεῖ occupies some two columns in Moulton and Geden's *Concordance.* Both words occur in Luce-Acts: ὧδε L 14–15 A 2; ἐκεῖ L 16 A 6. At 15,34 (if the longer text is right) and 21,4 the pronoun or adverb depends on ἐπιμένειν. ἐπιμένειν is construed with a dative R 6,1; 11,23; Phl 1,24; 1 T 4,16 and with πρός and the accusative 1C.16.17, G.1.18. If we read πρὸς αὐτούς at A 15,34 this is another example of this construction.

The result of our examination is that the adverb αὐτοῦ does not appear too certain anywhere in the NT. This conclusion is supported by other considerations. αὐτοῦ does not occur in the Apostolic Fathers. In the LXX it seems to be certain in the Pentateuch Gn 22,5; Exod 24,14; Nu 9,8; 22,8,19; 27,6; Dt 5,31. Elsewhere it is questionable: Jd 16,9, A G 108, 2 K 20,4 ἐνταῦθα Luc, Tob 8,20 S La, Ju 12,1 αὐτοῦ 126, Ezk 44,14 αὐτοῦ A?, 48,20 αὐτούς V. We may infer that after the translation of the Pentateuch αὐτοῦ went out of use and like ἐνταῦθα is not a NT word.

We must admit that there seems to be no parallel for the construction αὐτοῖς with καταντᾶν. One argument in favour of αὐτοῖς may be that it is repeated after ἀπήγγειλεν and our author likes repetitions. Otherwise for αὐτοῖς we would expect εἰς αὐτούς. We may regard αὐτοῖς as a corruption not of αὐτοῦ but of some expression which could be construed with καταντᾶν. *L* d has *obuiauit eis,* but for αὐτοῖς *C* G67 seems to have rendered εἰς ιλημ.

After ἐπιστηρίξας αὐτούς the Western witnesses other than D seem to translate ἐξῆλθεν and this may be right. If it is, D has omitted the verb through inadvertence. On the evidence of the mistake αὐτοῖς and the omission of ἐξῆλθε we are reminded that D may present us with a faulty text.

This reminder may be pertinent in two respects. First, we notice the variation, Ιερουσαλημ (ιλημ) in GT against Ἱεροσόλυμα, not abbreviated. Ιερουσαλημ is by far the commoner form in the LXX, representing a transliteration from the Hebrew (ed. S. Jellicoe, *Studies in the Septuagint,* 422 f.). Ἱεροσόλυμα, the non-Jewish form, occurs in Mark, Matthew (except for 22,37), rarely in Luke, and in John. Ιερουσαλημ appears regularly in Luke and the Epistles (except Gal 1,17,18; 2,1), and at Rev 4,12; 21,2,10.

In Acts we find both forms. Ἱεροσόλυμα may come only twice in Luke (2,22; 23,7) but may appear some thirty three times in Acts. Ιερουσαλημ occurs some twenty six times in Luke including 18,34/Mt 23,27, but some forty times in Acts. Sometimes both forms are variants as at 15,4; 20,16.

Is there any explanation of the presence of both forms in Acts? In A 25,26 Ἱεροσόλυμα occurs in a non-Jewish context, often on the lips of the Roman governor. In the rest of Acts Ἱεροσόλυμα is used where there is a contrast of Jerusalem with the outside world. We may notice that where the author would use ἔθνος of the Jews he would also employ the form Ἱεροσόλυμα, A 26,4.

In 11,2 it is customary to print Ιερουσαλημ, but we must notice that Ἱεροσόλυμα is read by E H L P S Ψ ω. This may be right as there is implied a contrast between Jerusalem and the outside world. Ἱεροσόλυμα of WT would be in keeping with this.

Another distinction appears in A 11,2. WT has the article with Πέτρος, but GT (we should probably read καὶ ὅτε ἀνέβη) lacks it. WT here follows the general practice of the Gospels and Acts. This is that proper names normally have the article. There are exceptions to this: a proper name which occurs in a list or one that has an expression in apposition usually lacks the article. Acts follows the rule though there are some exceptions. If this is so, WT is regular and GT is out of line. We can suggest that the text of our General witnesses is corrupt and that originally it had the article. This is not impossible. For example in GT the article is lacking with Πέτρος at 3,4 but D has the article.

Boismard has shown that WT is as much in the idiom of Acts as GT. Beyond this we may suspect that at several places our text is corrupt, αὐτοῖς and the omission of ἐξῆλθε in D and Πέτρος without the article in GT.

Secondly, Boismard examines the textual variation at 19,1 and shows that WT, for which we have in Greek *P*38 as well as D, is in the idiom of Acts. WT begins with a genitive absolute which is resumed by a dative αὐτῷ, a practice which occurs elsewhere in Acts (cf. N. Turner *A Grammer of New Testament Greek* III *Syntax,* 322).

ἔρχεται in WT presents a problem. Except for 10,11 θεωρεῖ and 10,27 εὑρίσκει historic presents in Acts are all from verbs of saying, cf. *ZNW*. lxviii (1977), 258–262. We would expect ἦλθεν corresponding to the ἐλθεῖν of GT. In contrast to Hellenic style the historic present could be a stylistic improvement, an imitation of Attic usage. On the other hand, while GT has Παύλου without the article, WT has τοῦ Παύλου which is what we would expect.

This introduces us to another problem. In *JBL*. lxxxix (1970) 77 I have suggested that in Acts the form of the proper name is Ἀπελλῆσ and in the Epistles Ἀπολλῶς. At 19,1 GT has Ἀπολλῶ and WT does not use the name at all. Has WT suppressed the name entirely?

There is the contrary suggestion made by Boismard: that the reference to the story of Apollos in GT is an intrusion. This is important as indicating a substantial difference between WT and GT. Boismard argues that not only is there a difference in substance between WT and GT, but that, while GT appears Lucan in style, there is in GT "a subtle difficulty" (150). ἐγένετο "is followed either (*a*) by ἐν τῷ and the infinitive or (*b*) by the accusative and infinitive". (*a*) is commoner in the Gospel, (*b*) in Acts. Only here are constructions (*a*) and (*b*) combined. This irregular feature is removed "if we assume that ἐν τῷ τὸν Ἀπολλῶ εἶναι ἐν Κορίνθῳ is a Lucan interpretation". If this is granted GT is subsequent to WT.

Boismard in effect argues differences both in style and in substance distinguish WT and GT and that these differences reflect editorial revision. WT of 19,1 lacks a reference to Apollos. According to Boismard this may suggest that WT lacked 18,24 also. Once we consider suggestions of this kind we are in the area, not of textual, but of literary criticism.

We have three considerations to bear in mind. First, as we have seen D, sometimes our only Greek witness for WT, occasionally presents a corrupt text. Secondly, the differences between WT and GT are often differences of style. Thirdly, we have differences of substance between GT and WT.

Let us begin with a matter of style. As has been pointed out elsewhere (e.g. *Theologische Zeitschrift* XXI (1965) 209) the author of Acts shows himself remarkably insensitive to repetition. We may have an example of this at Acts 3,3–5 as can be seen from the following table:

4 ἀτενίσας	*cet.*	ἐμβλέψας	D *L* h p^2 vg
ἀτένισον	D	βλέψον	*cet.*
5 ἀτενίσας	D (cf. *L* d h)	ἐπεῖχεν	*cet.*

Here the variation can be explained if the original text had at all three places some form of ἀτενίζω and at all three places scribes sought to avoid the repetition.

This consideration encourages us to look at 3,3 ὅς ἰδὼν] οὗτος ἀτενίσας τοῖς ὀφθαλμοῖς αὐτοῦ καὶ ἰδὼν D *L* h *O* m. For the association of ἀτενίζειν and οἱ ὀφθαλμοί we may compare Lk 4,20. The longer text seems to present a tautology, ἰδών repeating more briefly what has already been said.

3,5 ἀτενίσας D presents a problem as the reading does not construe. *L* d has *adtendebat* and *L* h *contemplatus e[st]*. A. G. Clark, *The Acts of the Apostles* 16 suggested ἀτενίσας ἦν. The order ἦν ἀτενίσας may seem more probable, but there is a greater difficulty in this suggestion. ἦν etc. with the present participle is frequent in the Gospels and Acts though the copyists did not like it (cf. Mk 2,4; A 10,6), but εἶναι with the aorist participle is very uncommon (Blass–Debrunner, *Grammatik des Neutestamentlichen Griechisch* § 355) in the New Testament, though not unknown in the old language. We are tempted to suspect that the original form of the text has not survived in Greek but lies behind *L* d h.

There is another consideration bearing on the reading ἐπεῖχεν. Elsewhere in Luke-Acts the verb does not seem to be used in this way. In A 19,22 ἔπεσχεν χρόνον is "spent time". At L 14,7 ἐπέχων is "observing" with an indirect question following. L 4,42 ἐπεῖχον is "restrained" (κατεῖχον *cet.*). Ph 2,16 ἐπέχοντες is "holding fast" and 1 T 4,16 ἔπεχε κτλ. is "attend to yourself and to the teaching". Only here is ἐπέχειν again used with the dative. All these instances seem to be out of line with A 3,5 ἐπεῖχεν.

Style comes into the problem of text. On our suggestion ἀτενίζω occurs some twelve times in Acts (1,10; 3,3 D,4,4 D,5 D,12; 6,15; 7,55; 10,4; 11,6; 13,9; 13,9; 14,9; 23,1) and is construed with εἰς seven times, 1,10; 3,4,4 D; 6,15; 7,55; 11,6; 13,9 with the following variants: 10,4 αὐτῷ] εἰς αὐτὸν 88 915 1311 *L* g p 5963 vg (6) and 14,9 αὐτῷ] εἰς αὐτόν 296 467 vg (1). At 3,3 D ἀτενίσας is used absolutely. On this evidence the readings we prefer in 3,3–5 are in keeping with the style of Acts.

If the suggestions about ἀτενίζειν in Acts 3,3–5 are right, the variation is not to be explained on literary grounds but on the assumption of an original form of the text which has suffered stylistic alterations in our witnesses. At one point we have to argue that our evidence is defective.

We may notice ἰδού at 2,2 in D Cyr Al. *C* m and at 3,2 D* *S* p *C* m. At the quotation from Is 49,6 in Ac 13,47, ἰδού D E 314 1838 *L* d e Cypr may represent assimilation to the LXX, but as ἰδού occurs in the previous verse, 13,46, the shorter text in 13,47 may represent an attempt to avoid repetition. Apart from these three instances ἰδού occurs some twenty three times in Acts, but at 20,25 it is absent from E 218 337 431 460 1814 *L* g. We have to recognize that ἰδού is characteristic of the style of Acts and may well be genuine at 2,2; 3,2 and 13,47.

We can produce many other examples of variation between GT and WT. In this connexion Boismard has cited my paper, "An Eclectic Study of the Text of Acts" in Biblical and Patristic Studies in Memory of Robert Pierce Casey (ed. J. N. Birdsall and R. W. Thomson) 64–77. In this paper I tried to show not only that WT is sometimes right, but also that GT in part or whole showed such rewriting of the text as we usually associate with WT.

We may now add some instances where the older text has survived partly in WT and partly in GT. For example at 2,1 GT reads ἐν τῷ συμπληροῦσθαι τὴν ἡμέραν τῆς πεντηκοστῆς ἦσαν πάντες ὁμοθυμαδὸν (or ὁμοῦ) ἐπὶ τὸ αὐτό, but D gives us ἐγένετο ἐν ταῖς ἡμέραις ἐκείναις τοῦ συμπληροῦσθαι τὴν ἡμέραν τῆς πεντεκοστῆς ὄντων αὐτῶν πάντων ἐπὶ τὸ αὐτό. Ropes preferred the text of D, but WT and GT each contain elements that seem more plausible. The genitive absolute ὄντων αὐτῶν πάντων may seem secondary against the finite clause ἦσαν πάντες. We may compare L 24,44 ἐν ᾧ ἤμην, D cf. *L*, which is probably right against ἔτι ὤν GT. Again, we may think GT ὁμοθυμαδὸν ἐπὶ τὸ αὐτό more likely to be original than ἐπὶ τὸ αὐτό alone in WT. On the other hand ἐγένετο ἐν ταῖς ἡμέραις τοῦ συμπληροῦσθαι seems to be original as Ropes saw (10). It is easy to contrast WT as a whole with GT as Ropes does, but when we look at each piece of the variation sometimes WT seems right and sometimes GT.

If we look at 11,2 and 10,1, the two passages discussed by Boismard, we notice features in which WT may be right. For example in 11,2 WT seems right with ὁ Πέτρος and Ἱεροσόλυμα against GT Πέτρος and Ἰερουσαλημ. Likewise in 19,1 we have in GT τὸν Ἀπολλῶ but Παῦλον without the article. WT has τοῦ Παύλου and Ἱεροσόλυμα. If at 19,1 we prefix 19,1 a WT θέλοντος δὲ τοῦ Παύλου . . . τὴν Ἀσίαν To GT ἐγένετο δὲ κτλ., we may avoid some of our difficulties by assuming that part of the original text survives in WT and part in GT. There are however difficulties which prevent us from carrying this through consistently.

In his suggestion that the reference to Apollos in 19,1 GT is secondary, Boismard calls our attention to the possibility that in this variation we may see a substantial development of the text. There are differences between WT and GT which are differences of substance. Before we consider such a difference in Acts 15 we may recall that at certain points Hort's Syrian text went beyond GT as at 8,37; 15,34; 24,6–8; 28,16,29. Ropes was persuaded that WT had preserved the original at 20,15 (with the agreement of the Syrian witnesses), 21,1; 27,5.

We may consider such substantial differences as evidence of editorial activity and as taking us beyond textual criticism into literary criticism. There are however other possibilities. First, we may notice a few passages where an author has slipped up:

(i) 4,25 ὁ τοῦ πατρὸς ἡμῶν διὰ πνεύματος ἁγίου στόματος Δαυιδ παιδός σου εἰπών. The witnesses vary about the text, but the seems to lie behind the variations. Would an author, revising his work, have left such a text unaltered?
(ii) 8,7 πολλοὶ τῶν ἐχόντων πνεύματα ἀκάθαρτα βοῶντα φωνῇ μεγάλῃ ἐξήρχοντο is faulty.
(iii) 12,25 ὑπέστρεψαν εἰς Ιερουσαλημ; we may ask the same question: Would not an author have altered this text on revision?
(iv) 13,33 τοῖς τέκνοις ἡμῶν; this looks like an author's mistake; would he not have eliminated it in a revision?

Second, we may refer to some passages where the evidence of our witnesses is deficient. We may remember 11,2 where αὐτοῖς is faulty and 3,5 where ἀτενίσας D must be a mistake. We may infer from Latin evidence that ἠτένισε was the original WT.

Next we must discount in general readings which are the product of a scribal mistake, for example the absence of τῶν κυμάτων in many witnesses at 27,41. Another instance may be detected at 4,32. After μία D adds καὶ οὐκ ἦν διάκρισις ἐν αὐτοῖς οὐδεμία. Here we have a recurrent group of letters ΜΙΑΚΑΙΟΥ, ψυχὴ ΜΙΑΚΑΙΟΥ κ. ἦν and οὐδε ΜΙΑΚΑΙΟΥ δέ which would make an omission easy. We may have a similar mistake at the bottom of 4,10.12 (cf. "An Eclectic Study", 68f.).

We may notice the influence of the LXX in forms with θ, οὐθείς, 15,9; 19,27 (n b. D), 20,33; 26,26 (not Syrian witnesses), μηθείς 27,33 (A B Σ$) ανδ περηαπσ ιν τηε ωαριατιον ϐετςεεν ἀναγγέλλειν and ἀπαγγέλλειν.

With ἀναγγέλλειν and ἀπαγγέλλειν we may enter another world. ἀπαγγέλλειν is the Attic compound, ἀναγγέλλειν is home in Hellenistic Greek though the relation between the two words in the LXX has not been sorted out (Jellicoe, "Studies in the Septuagint", 425). In Acts ἀπαγγέιλλειν occurs without variant some fourteen times but ἀναγγέλλειν only twice, 20,20.27. At six places the text is in dispute. We may be dealing with a variation in the author's usage whereby he has been influenced by the LXX. Have we here traces of more than one stage in the author's language?

We may detect stylistic revision in the manuscript tradition. For example, at 23,22 ἐκέλευσεν may have been corrected in various directions to avoid a bad Greek construction. In the same way at 23,10 εὐλαβηθείς may have been corrected to the better Greek φοβηθείς. Other instances of such changes can be detected up and down Acts.

This is made more complicated by the probability that we can detect differences in language in the various parts of Luke-Acts. I have made some suggestions about this, Böcher and Haacker (edd.), *Verborum Veritas* 83–88, "The Gentiles and the Strata of Luke". A. C. Clark, *The Acts of the Apostles.* 393–405 has listed differences between the language of Luke and that of Acts. Between Ac 1–15 and Ac 16–28 we may notice πνεῦμα ἀκάθαρτον 5,16; 8,7 but πνεῦμα πονηρόν 19,12.13.15.16.

There remain the passages where an important piece of evidence for the text has been lost as we have noted above at p. 194. It is easy to go from this recognition to conjectural emendation and in principle we cannot exclude conjecture. It is debatable however whether this can provide the solution of our problem.

We are indebted to Boismard that he has called our attention to the complexities of Ac 11,1; 19,2. We have also seen that 2,1 has its problems. Anyone who sets out to construct a text of Acts discovers a number of passages where the text is recalcitrant, even when every allowance is made for sheer mistakes and for deliberate changes, be they stylistic or not. Boismard would explain those difficulties as being the product of deliberate editorial revision and would seek a solution not in the area of textual but of literary criticism. If we find difficulty in accepting his solution, we must at least recognize the difficulty which he has brought to our attention and seek diligently for another solution. Meanwhile we await his book with high expections.

Werkruhm und Christusruhm im Galaterbrief und die Frage nach einer Entwicklung des Paulus

Ein hermeneutischer und exegetischer Zwischenruf

von Günter Klein

(Potstiege 12, 4400 Münster)

1. In der gegenwärtigen Paulusforschung haben entwicklungsgeschichtliche Rekonstruktionen einzelner theologischer Themenbereiche, wenn nicht der Theologie des Apostels im ganzen, wieder einmal[1] beachtliche Konjunktur[2]. Solches Interesse an der Identifikation biographischer Streckenabschnitte zum Aufweis eines individuellen Denkweges bedarf historisch natürlich keiner Legitimation; entsprechende Perspektiven erscheinen um so weniger entbehrlich, je komplexer sich die Denkleistung eines Autors darstellt. Gleichwohl sind, insbesondere auf bibeltheologischem Arbeitsfeld, mit solchem Ansatz unvermeidlich auch erhebliche hermeneutische Risiken zur Stelle, so selten sie merkwürdigerweise erörtert zu werden pflegen. Kann die Gesamtproblematik hier unmöglich ausgebreitet werden, so sei doch an zwei der sperrigsten Störfaktoren wenigstens erinnert.

1.1. Zum einen bedarf die Fixierung auf individualgeschichtliche Reflexionsphasen jedenfalls der Ausbalancierung durch die Einsicht, daß

---

[1] Daß es sich der Sache nach um ein altes Problem handelt, betont U. Luz (Rez. H. Hübner, Das Gesetz bei Paulus, Göttingen 1978, ThZ 35, 1979, 121–123), 121 zu Recht.

[2] Beispiele: C. Buck–G. Taylor, Saint Paul. A Study of the Development of his Thought, 1969 (Gesetzeslehre, Eschatologie, Christologie); G. Klein, Apokalyptische Naherwartung bei Paulus, in: H. D. Betz–L. Schottroff (Hg.), Neues Testament und christliche Existenz. FS H. Braun, 1973, 241–262; Ders., Art. Eschatologie IV. Neues Testament, TRE 10 (270–299), 279f. (Naherwartung); G. Strecker, Befreiung und Rechtfertigung. Zur Stellung der Rechtfertigungslehre in der Theologie des Paulus, in: J. Friedrich–W. Pöhlmann–P. Stuhlmacher (Hg.), Rechtfertigung. FS E. Käsemann, 1976, 479–508 (von der »ontologischen Befreiungslehre« zur »juridischen Rechtfertigungslehre«); W. Schmithals, Zur Herkunft der gnostischen Elemente in der Sprache des Paulus, in: B. Aland (Hg.), Gnosis. FS H. Jonas, 385–414: »Paulus wurde zu dem ›gnostisierenden‹ ... Christentum bekehrt, trat dann in die antiochenischen Traditionen ein und bildete auf dieser doppelten Basis ... seine heidenchristliche Theologie, besonders die Rechtfertigungslehre (im engeren Sinne) aus« (413); H. Hübner, Das Gesetz bei Paulus. Ein Beitrag zum Werden der paulinischen Theologie (FRLANT 119), ³1982; U. Wilckens, Zur Entwicklung des paulinischen Gesetzesverständnisses, NTS 28, 1982, 154–190.

»der wirkliche Sinn eines Textes ... eben nicht von dem Okkasionellen ab(hängt), das der Verfasser und sein ursprüngliches Publikum darstellen«, wenn denn »nicht nur gelegentlich, sondern immer ... der Sinn eines Textes seinen Autor (übertrifft)«[3]. Anders droht zumindest tendenziell die Gefahr, daß der für die herauszupräparierende Entwicklungsstufe ausgewertete Text im Hinblick auf das von seinem Autor durchmessene Curriculum bloß noch als eines seiner Bestandteile vor Augen kommt, transitorisch durch und durch, und daß umgekehrt die Denkentwicklung im ganzen nurmehr als Reihe von lauter Übergängen, als Prozeß ständiger Wandlung erscheint, dessen Abgeschlossenheit nur eine scheinbare wäre, weil nur sein zufälliger Abbruch seine prinzipiell unendliche Mutationsfähigkeit verdecken würde. Wo das Einzelne wie das Ganze derart in den Sog einer Relativierung zu geraten drohen, kann der Interpret, wie ungewollt auch immer, leicht zum Voyeur werden[4]. Er hat sich dann »gleichsam aus der Situation der Verständigung zurückgezogen. Er selber ist nicht antreffbar. Indem man den Standpunkt des anderen von vornherein in das miteinrechnet, was er einem zu sagen beansprucht, setzt man seinen eigenen Standpunkt in eine sichere Unerreichbarkeit[5].« So gerät das Interesse an individueller Entwicklung auf eine eigentümliche Weise in eine Problemzone, die der Debatte um universal-, heils- oder seinsgeschichtliche Kolossalgemälde seit langem vertraut ist. Was dort kritisch einzuschärfen war und bleibt[6]: die unverrechenbare Dignität des widerständigen Einzelzeugnisses, das sich einer umstandslosen Einspeisung in übergreifende Sinnzusammenhänge widersetzt – anders gesagt: der Vorrang des Objektivums »Text« gegenüber den textverschlingenden Konstrukten integralistisch gestimmter Subjekte –, muß in individualgeschichtlichem Horizont nicht minder zu denken geben.

1.2 Aber selbst bei Vernachlässigung der angedeuteten Grundlagenproblematik behält die entwicklungsgeschichtliche Fragestellung mit einer erheblichen hermeneutischen Schwierigkeit zu tun. Diese tritt spätestens dann zutage, wenn es um die theologische Gewichtung der rekonstruierten Denkbewegung geht. Denn welches der herausgearbeiteten Ent-

---

3 H.-G. Gadamer, Wahrheit und Methode. Grundzüge einer philosophischen Hermeneutik, 1960, 280.

4 Zum kompromittierenden Charakter der Situation der »Besichtigung« vgl. A. R. Bodenheimer, Warum? Von der Obszönität des Fragens, 1984, 247–250.

5 Gadamer (s. o. Anm. 3) 287.

6 Vgl. etwa G. Klein, Individualgeschichte und Weltgeschichte bei Paulus. Eine Interpretation ihres Verhältnisses im Galaterbrief (Rekonstruktion und Interpretation. Gesammelte Aufsätze zum Neuen Testament, 1969, 180–224), 219ff.; Ders., Bibel und Heilsgeschichte. Die Fragwürdigkeit einer Idee (ZNW 62, 1971, 1–47), bes. 27f. 46f. (Lit!); Ders., Rudolf Bultmann (in: M. Greschat, Theologen des Protestantismus im 19. und 20. Jahrhundert II, 1978, 400–419), 404f.

wicklungsstadien soll für das Verständnis der vom Autor durchmessenen Gesamtbahn ausschlaggebend sein? Die Frage wird jedenfalls dann unabweisbar, wenn es – wie im Falle des paulinischen Vermächtnisses – nicht bloß um Verschiebungen im weltbildlichen Vorstellungsrahmen[7], sondern um vermeintliche Modulationen im Verständnis des Evangeliums geht, auf deren bloßen Nachvollzug sich die Interpretation doch unmöglich zurückdämmen lassen darf.

1.2.1. Soll dann – um das Problem an einigen repräsentativen Beispielen einzuschärfen – eine angeblich in die Frühzeit des Apostels zurückweisende Konzeption, sofern er in seiner Spätphase darauf zurückgriff, zu einem »›zeitlosen‹ und insofern ...›grundsätzlichen‹ Modell« avancieren[8]? Sieht man schon nicht ein, wieso die biographische Konstanz einer Denkweise deren Zeitlosigkeit und Grundsätzlichkeit verbürgen könnte, so ist ferner die umgekehrte Möglichkeit, daß eine ältere Ausarbeitung durch die Einstellung in einen neuen literarischen Kontext tiefgreifend re-interpretiert wird, doch jedenfalls nicht von vornherein auszuschließen. Auch kann, was »zeitlich ... voraus« geht, doch wohl nicht eo ipso auch »sachlich voraus« gehen[9], so gewiß bei entwicklungsgeschichtlicher Betrachtungsweise grundsätzlich damit zu rechnen bleibt, daß Früheres biographisch auch obsolet werden kann und dann als Wurzelgrund für das Spätere schwerlich in Frage käme.

1.2.2. Aber auch die gegenläufige Perspektive, die demjenigen, was sich als spätere »Revision« einer früheren »Kampfposition« darzustellen scheint, daraufhin die größere theologische »Tiefe und Kraft« beimißt[10], erscheint wenig plausibel, da sich in derartigen Werturteilen offenkundig mitgebrachte Idealvorstellungen von persönlicher Reifung, theologischer Sublimierung oder von Reduktion polemischer Disposition auswirken, deren Subjektivität offenkundig ist[11].

---

[7] Wie m. E. im Falle der paulinischen Naherwartung: TRE 10, 279–286.

[8] So W. Schmithals, Die theologische Anthropologie des Paulus (UB 1021), 1980, 174, mit Bezug auf Röm 8,18–30.

[9] So G. Strecker (s. o. Anm. 2), 508.

[10] So Wilckens (s. o. Anm. 2), 180. 285.

[11] Das Problem meldet sich auch auf heuristischer Ebene. Einerseits wird dem Früheren ein Prae zuerkannt: »Frühere Briefe zur Hilfe bei der Exegese späterer heranzuziehen, ist ungleich weniger problematisch als umgekehrt, da Erfahrungen, die Paulus in konkreten Situationen gemacht hat ..., nicht ohne weiteres schon in früheren Briefen vorausgesetzt werden dürfen« (W. Marxsen, Einleitung in das Neue Testament. Eine Einführung in ihre Probleme, [4]1978, 25). Nun wäre gewiß einzuwenden, ob für den objektiven Gehalt und die sachliche Reichweite einer Aussage die subjektive Erfahrung ihres Autors überhaupt ausschlaggebend sein kann und frühe Gedanken hinsichtlich ihrer Valenz sich nicht u. U. erst vom später Gedachten her voll aufschließen mögen. Doch bleibt auch davon abgesehen die Warnung vor einer »entwicklungsgeschichtliche(n) Darstellung« zu hören, die, da

1.3. So wenig die angedeuteten Probleme den entwicklungsgeschichtlichen Aspekt der Paulusforschung historisch auszumanövrieren vermögen, so wenig empfiehlt sich ihnen gegenüber, die wir noch längst nicht ausgestanden haben, die übliche Nonchalance. Jedenfalls sind sie dazu angetan, die Hemmschwelle vor einer Projektion der paulinischen Theologie auf prozessuale Verläufe kräfig anzuheben. Zumindest sollte die Regel gelten: Was nicht unabweislich zur entwicklungsgeschichtlichen Zerdehnung zwingt, bleibe vor ihr bewahrt.

2. Im Zuge seines ebenso interessanten wie herausfordernden Versuchs, die paulinische Rechtfertigungslehre und insbesondere die darin wirksame Auffassung vom Gesetz als einen »Prozeß« verständlich zu machen, der »das Werden der paulinischen Theologie« zur Erscheinung bringe und der erst im Römerbrief »durch das endgültige Gesetzesverständnis die endgültige Rechtfertigungslehre des Apostels ihre Gestalt« habe finden lassen, bemüht sich Hans Hübner[12], eine »theologische Entwicklung« des Paulus auch daran abzulesen, »wie er die Thematik des Sich-Rühmens bzw. des Ruhms in unterschiedlicher Weise in seinen Briefen behandelt«[13].

2.1. Ausgehend von der Frage, ob »der Verzicht des Sich-Rühmens der eigenen Werke vor Gott« als eines »entscheidende(n) Charakteristikum(s) christlicher Existenz«, wie es der Römerbrief als eine »ins Zentrum der paulinischen Theologie hineinreichende Aussage« bezeuge, auch schon für den Galaterbrief zu belegen sei[14], gelangt er zu dem Ergebnis, daß hier der »Ruhmverzicht vor Gott« noch nicht als Merkmal christlichen Selbstverständnisses zum Ausdruck komme[15]. Ausschlaggebend für diese überraschende Feststellung ist die Interpretation von Gal 6,4: τὸ δὲ ἔργον ἑαυτοῦ δοκιμαζέτω ἕκαστος καὶ τότε εἰς ἑαυτὸν μόνον τὸ καύχημα ἕξει καὶ οὐκ εἰς τὸν ἕτερον. Hier werde, wenn auch nur als »Randgedank(e)«, die Möglichkeit eines »echten Anspruch(s) des Christen auf Ruhm aufgrund eines gerichtsrelevanten Lebenswerkes« klar ausgesprochen[16], als »grundsätzlich« nicht einmal »durch eigenes Versagen relati-

---

sie »den Ausgang allemal schon kennt«, Gefahr läuft, »die jeweils vorangehenden Ereignisse auf eben diesen Ausgang zusteuern zu lassen« (so, im Blick auf die Barth-Interpretation, E. Jüngel, Barth-Studien, 1982, 64). Müßte also umgekehrt »zunächst einmal der Ausgang, das Telos der Geschichte zur Darstellung kommen . . ., um von da aus dann in die vorangegangene Geschichte zurückzufragen« (ebd.)? Nur: inwiefern ist solcher heuristischer Ansatz nicht einfach einer inversen entwicklungsgeschichtlichen Perspektive verpflichtet?

12 (S. o. Anm. 2); das Zitat S. 15.

13 Ebd. 81.

14 Ebd.

15 Ebd. 91.

16 Ebd. 87f.

viert« verstanden und nur im Falle »des Vergleichs mit anderen« für hinfällig erklärt[17]. Das werde durch v. 14 (Ἐμοὶ δὲ μὴ γένοιτο καυχᾶσθαι εἰ μὴ ἐν τῷ σταυρῷ τοῦ κυρίου ἡμῶν Ἰησοῦ Χριστοῦ) keineswegs konterkariert, denn während es in v. 4 um »den vor Gott geltenden Ruhm« gehe, stehe in v. 13f. der allerdings unzulässige »Akt des Sich-Rühmens vor anderen« im Blick[18].

2.2 Dieses aufregende Verständnis von v. 4, das in der Tat dazu nötigt, das »Christenleben« insgesamt als »›Werk‹« zu verstehen[18a], knüpft faktisch in eigenständiger Weise an ältere Auslegungstradition an[19] und hat zweifellos das Verdienst, indirekt darauf aufmerksam zu machen, wie wenig exegetische Probleme dadurch geklärt werden, daß man auslegungsgeschichtliche Positionen, weil man sich ihrer dogmatisch geniert, einfach dem Vergessen überantwortet. Denn freilich kann keine Rede davon sein, daß die darüber hinauszielenden Interpretationsangebote, wie sie heute das Feld beherrschen, so sehr sie den Anstoß mindern oder vermeiden mögen, dem Text wirklich gerecht würden. Sie operieren vielmehr in auffallendem Maße mit textfernen Konjekturen, stehen häufig im Zeichen stärkster innerer Spannungen und verweisen damit auf die theologische Verlegenheit, aus der sie hervorgegangen sind.

2.2.1. Das gilt zunächst von dem anspruchslosen Versuch, den positiven Gehalt des Ruhmmotivs quantitativ zu beschränken. Demnach soll hier zum Ausdruck kommen, daß der Ruhm »ein sehr mäßiger sein wird«, bzw. daß er nur »gegebenenfalls«, nämlich bei Vorhandensein »etwaiger rühmlicher Bestandteile« eines Lebenswerks sich einstelle[21]. Beide Auffassungen scheitern schon daran, daß sie die Antithese εἰς ἑαυτὸν μόνον – καὶ οὐκ εἰς τὸν ἕτερον nicht wirklich als Pointe von v. 4b zur Geltung kommen lassen können, die zweite wird zusätzlich dadurch falsifiziert, daß sich für den Apostel der »Ruhm« ja nicht bloß möglicherweise, sondern auf alle Fälle einstellen wird.

---

[17] Ebd. 90f.

[18] Ebd. 91.

[18a] Hübner ebd. 88.

[19] Vgl. etwa W. Bousset, SNT, II, ^{3}1917, 72: »Paulus verwehrt den sittlichen Stolz nach einer guten Tat nicht. Was er verwehrt, das ist, daß man diesen Stolz den andern merken läßt ...«; ähnlich noch Lietzmann (s. u. Anm. 53), 39. Etwas anders, aber hinsichtlich der angeblichen Konzession legitimen Werkruhms gleichlaufend F. Sieffert, Kritisch exegetisches Handbuch über den Brief an die Galater, KEK 7, ^{6}1880, 320: »... dann wird er lediglich in Betracht des selbsteigenen Guten, welches er etwa bei dieser Prüfung findet sich zu rühmen Ursach haben, und nicht im Hinblick auf den Andern, mit welchem er andernfalls zu seinem Vortheil sich vergleichen würde.«

[20] B. Weiß, Die paulinischen Briefe und der Hebräerbrief im berichtigten Text, ^{2}1902, 36

[21] A. Oepke, Der Brief des Paulus an die Galater, ThHK IX, ^{2}1957, 149f.

2.2.2. Um die theologisch reflektierteren Bemühungen, bei festgehaltener Positivität des Ruhmmotivs dieses mit der paulinischen Rechtfertigungslehre zu vermitteln, steht es leider nicht besser. Sie laufen allemal darauf hinaus, den Ruhm zur gloria aliena zu verfremden. Dazu wird entweder der καύχημα- oder der ἔργον-Begriff meditativ extrapoliert. So läßt man, für den Fall eines begründeten καύχημα, »das Rühmen zugleich ein Danken«[22], »ein dankbares καυχᾶσθαι ἐν θεῷ«[23] sein. Oder das als rühmlich ausgemachte Werk soll die Gnade widerspiegeln, die dem Glaubenden »für sein Tun und Leben gewährt wird«[24], bzw. es soll als »Frucht des Geistes« verdankt werden[25].

Die Brüchigkeit derartiger Interpretationen zeigt sich aber schon daran, daß sie, je sorgsamer sie um Nuancierung bemüht sind, um so anfälliger für innere Spannungen, ja Widersprüche werden. Bezeichnet das ἔργον das *geforderte* christliche Tun[26], kann es dann, strenggenommen, noch als Gegenstand einer »Selbst*prüfung*« in Frage kommen, von der ja in der Tat gelten muß, daß sie nie »eindeutig, unfehlbar und definitiv« ausfallen kann[27]? Läuft der als Möglichkeit zugestandene Werkruhm auf den Ruhm Gottes bzw. Christi hinaus[28], kann dann das geforderte δοκιμάζειν den Sinn haben, »unweigerlich die eigene Sünde vor Augen« zu führen und so »alle vor Gott gleichzumachen«[29]? Definiert sich das καύχημα als die göttliche Gnade[30], kann dann unser Vers als Ausnahme von der Regel gelten, daß Paulus einzig den Ruhm des Herrn zulasse[31]?

---

[22] R. Bultmann, ThWNT III 651, Z. 37f.

[23] E. Synofzik, Die Gerichts- und Vergeltungsaussagen bei Paulus. Eine traditionsgeschichtliche Untersuchung, GTA 8, 1977, 44.

[24] H. Schlier, Der Brief an die Galater, KEK 7, [11]1951, 201; vgl. H.-D. Betz, Galatians (Hermeneia), 1977, 303; auch F. Mußner, Der Galaterbrief, HThK IX, [3]1977, 400 (mit Betonung der Alternative, »daß das ›Werk‹ des Menschen entweder böse ... ist oder durch die Gnade des Herrn gut«).

[25] J. Becker, NTD 8, [14]1976, 75 und beiläufig selbst Hübner (s. o. Anm. 2) 85, der damit freilich in stärkste Spannung mit seiner Gesamtauffassung gerät, der zufolge »gerade« der Gedanke, daß die Prüfung des Werks die darin waltende Gnade erkennen lasse, »aus 6,1ff. *nicht* erhoben« werden könne (ebd.; Sperrung von mir). Entsprechend ebd. 87: »... *dein* Werk *allein* ist's, wodurch du im Gericht bestehen wirst – oder eben nicht« (Sperrungen von Hübner). Vgl. auch u. Anm. 67. Nach W. Schrage ist bereits durch den Singular ἔργον sichergestellt, daß es sich um die »Bezeichnung des geforderten christlichen Tuns« handelt (Die konkreten Einzelgebote in der paulinischen Paränese. Ein Beitrag zur neutestamentlichen Ethik, 1961, 54; vgl. Ders., Ethik des Neuen Testaments, GNT 4, 1982, 177).

[26] Schrage (s. o. Anm. 25), Einzelgebote.

[27] Ebd. 85 (Sperrung von mir).

[28] Synofzik (s. o. Anm. 23).

[29] Ebd.

[30] Betz (s. o. Anm. 24).

[31] Ebd. 371 Anm. 55.

Hat die geforderte Selbstprüfung auf die doppelte Möglichkeit gefaßt zu sein, daß sich das »Werk« als Ausgeburt der Sünde oder der Gnade erweisen kann[32], wie kann dann die apostolische Anweisung zugleich einsinnig als Ausdruck »tiefe(r) Resignation« angesichts »der eigenen, täglich erfahrenen Sündhaftigkeit« verstanden werden[33]?

2.2.3. Solchen Schwierigkeiten ist kaum dadurch zu entgehen, daß man unsern Textzusammenhang pointiert »die Zweideutigkeit des eigenen Handelns« einschärfen läßt[34]. Denn zunächst ist nicht einzusehen, wie überhaupt von Zweideutigkeit die Rede sein kann, wenn sich nach Meinung des Paulus »wohl auch immer herausstellen« soll, »daß nicht alles nur glänzend ist«, sondern auch seine »negativen Seiten« hat[35]. Sofern sich negative und positive Handlungszüge unterscheiden lassen, waltet ja gerade Eindeutigkeit! Hinzu kommt, daß solche Auslegung den καύχημα-Begriff faktisch zur »vox media« neutralisieren muß[36], wozu es im paulinischen Sprachgebrauch keine Parallele gibt[37].

3. Kann also angesichts der verworrenen Interpretationslage zu dem Vorstoß von Hübner nur resigniert vermerkt werden, daß Gal 6,4 eben »eine singuläre Stelle« bleibe[38], oder läßt sich die Frage, ob hier tatsächlich der Ausgangspunkt eines tiefgreifenden apostolischen Lernprozesses zum Vorschein komme, womöglich doch exegetisch diskutieren und zur Entscheidung bringen?

3.1. Zunächst ist der Aufbau des Kontextes zu beachten. Unabhängig davon, wohin man 5,25f. orientiert sein läßt[39], und ob es möglich ist, eine »innere Ordnung« bis hin zu 6,10 aufzuzeigen[40], gibt sich jedenfalls das Gefüge 6,1–5 durchaus als gegliederte Sequenz zu erkennen. Auch wenn einzuräumen ist, daß sich von v. 2 an die einzelnen Sätze wie selbständige

---

32 Mußner (s. o. Anm. 24).

33 Ebd. 401.

34 D. Lührmann, Der Brief an die Galater, ZBK 7, 1978, 97.

35 Ebd.

36 So K. Weiß, ThWNT IX 88 Anm. 9, während sich Lührmann zu dem Begriff nicht äußert.

37 Weiß ebd. beruft sich auf 1 Kor 5,6 (οὐ καλὸν τὸ καύχημα ὑμῶν), aber schon der Zusammenhang mit πεφυσιωμένοι ἐστέ (v. 2) zeigt die negative Färbung des Begriffs; vgl. H. Conzelmann, Der erste Brief an die Korinther, KEK 5, [12]1981, 126.

38 So Luz (s. o. Anm. 1), 123.

39 Zog man diese Verse früher nicht selten zum Vorigen (vgl. Sieffert [s. o. Anm. 19], 314; E. de Witt Burton, A Critical and Exegetical Commentary on the Epistle to the Galatians, ICC, 1921, 290), so ist heute die Zuordnung zum Folgenden die Regel; vgl. insbesondere Becker (s. o. Anm. 25), 74; G. Ebeling, Die Wahrheit des Evangeliums. Eine Lesehilfe zum Galaterbrief, 1981, 324. Völlig unannehmbar angesichts der die beiden Verse zusammenhaltenden 1. Pers. Pl. dürfte es sein, den Schnitt mit Mußner (s. o. Anm. 24), 391. 395, zwischen v. 25 und v. 26 zu legen.

40 So Ebeling (s. o. Anm. 39), 347.

»Maximen« lesen lassen[41], und eine geradezu »systematische Ordnung« einem paränetischen Text von vornherein nicht abzuverlangen ist[42], geht es doch entschieden zu weit, den Apostel hier rein »as a gnomic poet« am Werk zu sehen[43].

Nicht einmal v. 1 steht unverbunden für sich. Zwar ist die strukturelle Parallelität mit dem Folgenden überzeichnet, wenn Schlier[44] urteilt: So wie das σκοπῶν σεαυτόν v. 1c die voranstehende Mahnung begründe, »so begründen die Verse 3–5 die Mahnung, gegenseitig die Lasten zu tragen, mit der Erwägung, daß Selbstkritik notwendig ist«. Denn während das Begründungsverhältnis zwischen v. 2 und v. 3ff. allerdings unverkennbar ist (γάρ; v. 3a!), läuft die Mahnung v. 1 mit der (einem Adverbialsatz gleichwertigen[45]) partizipialen Schlußwendung nicht eigentlich in eine Begründung, sondern in eine modale Bestimmung aus. Doch so viel ist jedenfalls richtig, daß sich beiderseits Außen- und Innenperspektive charakteristisch verschränken, sofern nämlich durchgehend »das Verhältnis zu sich selbst und das Verhältnis zum anderen immer wieder auf ihr Ineinander-Verflochtensein hin bedacht werden. Wer den andern wahrnehmen und richtig einschätzen soll, der muß auch sich selbst allererst wahrnehmen und richtig einschätzen[46].« Nur die Gewichtung der beiden Aspekte ist in v. 1 und v. 2ff. deutlich verschieden: stellt dort das Selbstverhältnis ein Nebenthema dar, so hat es hier, breit entfaltet in v. 3–5, das Hauptgewicht. – Alles in allem läßt sich die Beziehung der Eingangsmahnung zur Fortsetzung so umschreiben: Das, was v. 1 einleitend am Einzelfall vor Augen rückt, erscheint in v. 2ff. mit gewisser Akzentverlagerung ins Grundsätzliche erhoben.

Erst recht stellen v. 2–5 sich als sachliche Einheit dar. Keine Rede kann davon sein, daß v. 2 und v. 3–5 durch eine rein »äußerliche« Stichwortverbindung ad vocem βαστάζετε – βαστάσει zusammengehalten wären; dazu sind die beiden Verbformen doch viel zu weit auseinander[47]. Vielmehr weisen eben diese den Zusammenhang, dessen Dekomposition sich zudem durch das zwischen v. 2 und v. 3 waltende Begründungsverhältnis verbietet, als ringförmige Kompostion aus. Dann gilt: "The paradoxical antithesis" zwischen Einsatz und Abschluß dieser Texteinheit "is doubtless conscious and intentional"[48].

---

[41] Vgl. Betz (s. o. Anm. 24), 298ff. Daß dies auch schon für v. 1c gelte (ebd. 298), leuchtet freilich nicht ein.

[42] Zu Lührmann (s. o. Anm. 34), 95.

[43] Zu Betz (s. o. Anm. 24), 298.

[44] (s. o. Anm. 24), 201.

[45] Bl. D. 418. [46] Ebeling (s.o. Anm. 39), 347f.

[47] Gegen M. Dibelius–H. Greeven, Der Brief des Jakobus, KEK 15, [11]1964, 22.

[48] Burton (s. o. Anm. 39), 334. Von einer »eigentümlich paradox anmutenden Mahnung« spricht im Blick auf den offenkundigen Spannungsbogen auch Ebeling (a.a.O. Anm. 39), 349.

3.2. Die Frage nach der sachlichen Bedeutung jener Paradoxie leitet zu den inhaltlichen Problemen des Textes über, die im folgenden nur in Engführung auf die hier zur Prüfung anstehende Spitzenthese hin bedacht werden können.

3.2.1. Bereits mit der Auslegung von v. 1 sind bei Hübner die Weichen für sein Verständnis des Folgenden gestellt. Halte das hier zum Zuge gebrachte Moment der Selbstkritik die πνευματικοί dazu an, »nicht in ähnliche Schuld« wie der bei einer Übertretung betroffene ἄνθρωπος zu geraten, so werde zwar »die Versuchlichkeit der Christen warnend vor Augen« geführt, dies jedoch gerade solchen gegenüber, die »Sünde *noch nicht* getan« haben. Damit aber sei über die Fortsetzung entschieden. Da es nämlich »kaum wahrscheinlich« sei, »daß schon im nächsten Vers ... *jedem* Christen Sündetaten (sic!) unterstellt« würden, müsse v. 2 den komplexen Sinn haben: »Tragt euch gegenseitig als solche, die nur allzu leicht wegen ihrer Versuchbarkeit in Sünde geraten können; tragt euch aber selbst dann gegenseitig, *wenn* ihr der Versuchung nachgegeben habt«[49]. Daß nur bei solchem Interpretationsansatz, dem zufolge der Bedeutungsgehalt von τὰ βάρη zwischen Realität und Potentialität changiert und sich »nicht grundsätzlich« auf »die Sündentaten« eingrenzen läßt[50], in v. 4 die Konzession eines immerhin möglichen Werkruhms gefunden werden kann, ist von vornherein deutlich.

Nun ist gewiß nicht zu bestreiten, daß die Warnung v. 1c lediglich auf die Möglichkeit abhebt, der Versuchung zu erliegen. Wohl aber läßt sich bezweifeln, daß damit das Verständnis von v. 2 festgelegt ist. Schon die in der formalen Analyse erhobenen Gewichtsverlagerungen lassen es nicht ratsam erscheinen, den Befund zu v. 1 ohne weiteres für den Kontext fortzuschreiben. Massiv gegen solche Interpretation spricht mehreres. Zunächst ist unter ihrer Direktive der enge Zusammenhang von v. 2 mit v. 5 nicht mehr zu wahren. Denn in dem Satz: ἕκαστος γὰρ τὸ ἴδιον φορτίον βαστάσει, wie immer man ihn im einzelnen versteht, kann der Begriff der »Last« schlechterdings nicht auf eine u. U. bloß virtuelle Größe gehen, wie er denn für Hübner[51] »das gesamte Lebenswerk« bezeichnet, also durchaus eine Gegebenheit. Es wäre ferner mehr als seltsam, wenn die einschränkungslose Mahnung zum gegenseitigen Tragen »der« Lasten nicht nur zum Ertragen des Bruders in seiner Sünde, sondern auch in seiner bloßen »Disposition zur Sünde« aufriefe[52] und dabei den Glücksfall eines begründeten Werkruhms vor Augen hätte, der dann doch wohl unter keinen Umständen »den« Lasten zuzuschlagen wäre. Vor allem aber

---

[49] Hübner (s. o. Anm. 2), 82 (Sperrungen von H.).

[50] Ebd. 86.

[51] Ebd. 87.

[52] So Hübner ebd. 83.

spricht gegen solches Verständnis von v. 2, daß der Stellung dieser Mahnung im Kontext so nicht gerecht zu werden ist. Denn unverkennbar weist der Apostel der von ihm angemahnten Selbstkritik in v. 1c und in v. 3f. jeweils verschiedene Bezugspunkte an, und v. 2 hat in diesem Gefüge eine Scharnierfunktion.

Gerade nach Hübner, der hier richtiger sehen dürfte als viele Ausleger[53], steht in v. 1c die Gefahr im Blick, einer dem παράπτωμα jenes »Menschen« vergleichbaren Verfehlung zu verfallen, während v. 4 eindeutig auf die Gefährdung durch einen der eigenen Korrektheit gewissen Vergleich mit anderen zielt. Mit der Erhebung der Paränese ins Grundsätzliche geht also eine Radikalisierung in der Sache einher, und es deutet sich in der Abfolge von v. 1 nach v. 2 ein qualitativer Sprung an: indem Paulus, in einer bei ihm nicht seltenen Denkbewegung[54], ein zunächst moralisch geprägtes Sündenverständnis hinter sich läßt, steuert er die gerade für Christen stets aktuelle Einsicht an, daß Sünde sich nicht in der Untat (dem aufweisbaren παράπτωμα von v. 1) erschöpft, ja erst dort endgültig triumphiert, wo sie nicht bloß einzelne Taten, sondern das Sein des Menschen entstellt. Dieser, den Abgrund zwischen defektivem und intaktem Dasein noch überwölbenden Einsicht arbeitet v. 2 mit der Mahnung zur allgemeinen gegenseitigen Entlastung vor[55], wie sich aus dem begründenden Anschluß v. 3a deutlich ergibt. Der Terminus τὰ βάρη hat also als Oberbegriff zu gelten, der die unmoralische zusammen mit der moralischen Spielart der Sünde unter sich befaßt. Auf diese Weise läßt der Apostel seine Leser dessen inne werden, daß sie allesamt der Belastung durch eine Gegenmacht ausgesetzt sind, deren Zeitigungsweisen sich bei weitem nicht in gelegentlichen παραπτώματα erschöpft. Seine Mahnung zum wechselseitigen Lastentragen hat dann im Kontext den Sinn, über die Fürsorge für jenen eklatant sündigen »Menschen« hinaus in eine umfassende

---

53 Der Leser von v. 1 kann doch schwerlich darauf kommen, daß er vor einer ganz anderen Verfehlung auf der Hut sein soll, nämlich vor dem »Zorn des selbstvergessenen Hochmutes« (Schlier [s. o. Anm. 24], 199); ähnlich Betz (s. o. Anm. 24), 298 u. a. Das καὶ σύ führt ihn doch auf eine ganz andere Fährte. Das Richtige sehen z. B. auch H. Lietzmann, An die Galater, HNT 10, ²1923, 38; Mußner (s. o. Anm. 24), 397.

54 Vgl. z. B. den Übergang von Gal 3,10 nach v. 11f., dazu G. Klein, Sündenverständnis und theologia crucis bei Paulus (in: C. Andresen–G. Klein [Hg.], Theologia crucis und Signum crucis. Festschrift E. Dinkler, 1979, 249–282), 270ff., oder den Argumentationsduktus in Röm 2,12–29 (dazu ebd. 253ff.).

55 Daß bereits von v. 2 an das in v. 6 thematisierte »Verhältnis von Katechumen und Katechet« anvisiert sei (Ebeling [s. o. Anm. 39], 349), ist m. E. schon deshalb ausgeschlossen, weil unter solcher Annahme zumindest v. 4 nicht mehr interpretiert werden kann. Das gilt erst recht für die seltsame These von J. G. Strelan, Burden-bearing and the Law of Christ: A Re-examination of Galatians 6:2, JBL 94, 1975, 266–276, schon von v. 2, eventuell gar von v. 1 an gehe es um einen Finanzausgleich.

Solidarität einzuweisen, die in dem Wissen um die stets sprungbereite Gewalt menschlicher Eigenmächtigkeit gründet[56].

3.2.2. Das Profil von v. 3 zeichnet sich damit bereits ab. Für Hübner muß gelten, daß »in v. 3 nicht alle galatischen Christen angesprochen« sind und Paulus hier »nur auf die mögliche Gefahr der Selbsttäuschung aufmerksam« macht[57]. Freilich sieht er richtig, daß , wenn nach v. 3 »*jeder* Glaubende« sich »als völliges Nichts« zu betrachten habe, der behauptete Skopus von v. 4 – »die Möglichkeit echten Ruhms« – »sinnlos« werde[58]. Doch läßt sich v. 3 unter keinen Umständen anders verstehen. Das ergibt sich einmal aus dem Begründungszusammenhang mit v. 2. Höbe v. 3 kasuistisch nur auf einen partikularen Tatbestand ab, hätte also das μηδὲν ὤν konditionalen Sinn, so ergäbe sich aus diesem Satz im Umkehrschluß, daß derjenige, auf den das μηδὲν εἶναι *nicht* zutrifft, mit der Selbsteinschätzung, εἶναί τι, sich *nicht* betrügt, – und das würde heißen: solche Christen blieben aus der Begründung der vorangegangenen Mahnung ausgeschlossen. Es ist aber unmöglich, daß eine Mahnung, die allen Christen gilt, nur einem Teil von ihnen begründend eingeprägt wird. Dies um so mehr, als doch wohl gerade derjenige, der sich eines tatsächlichen εἶναί τι erfreuen dürfte, die Mahnung benötigte, die Lasten der weniger Glücklichen mitzutragen!

Daß v. 3 in Wahrheit unkonditioniert gilt und das μηδὲν εἶναι eine Grundbefindlichkeit bezeichnet, die den Christen wie jeden Menschen prägt[59], legen formale[60] und terminologische[61] Indizien weiter nahe; es

---

[56] Der im Begründungsgefüge von v. 2f. aufscheinende Sachzusammenhang ist in einer Predigt von E. Jüngel über Gal 6,2 bewegend zur Sprache gebracht: »der Wolf in uns ... profitiert von der Überbelastung, die den Menschen unter Druck setzt ... deshalb kann uns nichts Heilsameres widerfahren, als von einem anderen Menschen entlastet zu werden ... Fremde Lasten kann man freilich nur dann auf sich nehmen, wenn man nicht selber unter dem eigenen Gewicht zu leiden hat. Dieses Gewicht aber, will heißen: das Übergewicht, das wir uns selber geben, um vor Gott und der Welt gewichtig zu sein, ... ist dem Christenmenschen ein für allemal abgenommen« (Der Mensch dem Menschen kein Wolf, in: Ders., Der Wahrheit zum Recht verhelfen, ^{2}1977, 70–77, das Zitat S. 76).

[57] (S. o. Anm. 2), 83; sachlich gleichlaufend schon Lietzmann (s. o. Anm. 53), 39.

[58] Ebd. Vorsichtiger, aber grundsätzlich gleichgerichtet Becker (s. o. Anm. 25), 75: »Die unkritische Selbstbeurteilung ... führt allzu schnell« zu realitätsfremder »Selbstwertbestimmung«. Daher gilt es zu erkennen, »daß der Realität viel eher (!) der Normalfall entspricht ...« (Interjektion von mir).

[59] Daß solches universale Verständnis den Satz »faktisch auf den Menschen außerhalb der Gnade« beziehe (Hübner [s. o. Anm. 2] 85), trifft nicht zu. Freilich gilt er *auch* für ihn, wie denn das Nichtsein coram deo paulinisch überhaupt keine differentia specifica zwischen Christen und Nichtchristen markiert. Es ist ja als solches auch keineswegs böse, wie Betz (s. o. Anm. 24), 301, mit Recht festhält.

[60] Der Satz hat dieselbe Struktur wie die apodiktischen Feststellungen 1 Kor 3,18; 8,2; 10,12, die allesamt auch dann nicht zu kasuistischen würden, wenn sie noch um eine das

ergibt sich aber vor allem aus dem Zentrum des paulinischen Denkens mit überwältigender Evidenz. Wie sollte der Apostel, der in der Rechtfertigung des Gottlosen den creator ex nihilo walten sieht (Röm 4,17), der deshalb die Christusgemeinde als τὰ μὴ ὄντα begreift, welches sein Dasein allein der göttlichen Gnadenwahl verdankt (1 Kor 1,28), der schließlich über sich selbst sogar in seiner apostolischen Funktion das οὐδέν εἰμι spricht (2 Kor 12,11), – wie sollte ausgerechnet er ein frommes εἶναί τι aufgrund eines »als ›Werk‹ verstandene(n) Christenleben(s)«[62] als Möglichkeit zulassen können! Die Durchschlagskraft jenes Fundamentalmotivs der paulinischen Theologie ließe sich keineswegs entwicklungsgeschichtlich abfangen, so gewiß es auch der Galaterbrief in voller Ausprägung bezeugt. Denn was ist es anderes als Schöpfung aus dem Nichts, wenn das Geschöpf, auf daß es seinem Schöpfer lebe, mit Christus gekreuzigt wird und so seiner alten Daseinsverfassung abstirbt (2,19)? Gilt von dieser neuen Kreatur das ζῇ ἐν ἐμοὶ Χριστός (2,20) und bleibt sie beständig darauf angewiesen, daß Christus in ihr Gestalt gewinnt (4,19), so ist es nur die Kehrseite solchen eschatologischen Umbruchs, wenn das davon ereilte Subjekt seines eigenen μηδὲν εἶναι gewahr wird und sich dessen sogar zu freuen vermag.

3.2.3. Akzeptiert also der Apostel kein aus der Daseinsverfassung des Frommen gespeistes εἶναί τι, so kann man ihn nur unter Voraussetzung einer heillosen Bewußtseinsspaltung in v. 4 den möglichen Ruhm eines gerichtsrelevanten Lebenswerkes zugestehen lassen[62a]. Dies um so mehr, als die bestrittene Interpretation nicht ohne kräftige Umbiegung von Wortlaut und Aussagegefälle auskommt.

Indem sie eine »wirklich (!) kritisch(e)« Selbstbeurteilung zur Voraussetzung des Ruhmanspruchs erhebt[63], führt sie unter der Hand einen

---

Gegenteil der jeweiligen Selbsteinschätzung konstatierende partizipiale Wendung angereichert wären.

[61] Man vergleiche, mit welch unüberhörbar sarkastischem Unterton Paulus in demselben Galaterbrief die den »Säulen« beigelegte Autorität als ein εἶναί τι apostrophiert (2,6)! Unverkennbar hält diese Wendung in dem Fächer der die Kontrahenten bezeichnenden Ausdrücke im Kontext die negative Spitzenstellung: Zwar bleibt in dem durchgehaltenen οἱ δοκοῦντες die innere Reserve des Apostels überall beredt genug, doch läßt er sich zum Schluß (v. 9) immerhin auf den tatsächlichen Titel des Triumvirats, οἱ στῦλοι, ein. Eine Mittelstellung markiert der in seiner Isoliertheit ebenso vieldeutige wie kalte appositionslose Ausdruck (v. 3. 6c), während in der Verbindung mit εἶναί τι die Distanzierung kaum von einer Disqualifizierung zu unterscheiden ist.

[62] Hübner (s. o. Anm. 27), 88.

[62a] Es sei denn, man läßt mit Betz (s. o. Anm. 24), 302, v. 4 gegen eine ganz andere Illusion gerichtet sein, was sich aber doch schon aufgrund des Sachzusammenhangs zwischen dem δοκεῖν εἶναί τι und dem Ruhmmotiv verbietet.

[63] Ebd. (Interjektion von mir).

mit der angeblichen Anspruchsvoraussetzung, dem ἔργον, konkurrierenden Rechtsgrund ein.

Sie muß ferner dem Text entnehmen, »daß der Blick auf andere zum Verlust des Ruhms führt«[64], was eine Eintragung ist und sich mit der Apodiktik der Ruhmansage stößt[65].

Sie ist darüber hinaus genötigt, den unverbrüchlichen Zusammenhang von v. 4a und 4b ein zweites Mal konditional zu erweichen, indem sie nur »bei einem positiven Ergebnis« der Selbstprüfung den Anspruchsfall eintreten läßt[66]. Dem Text zufolge stellt sich aber nach dem δοκιμάζειν in *jedem* Fall das καύχημα ein[67]!

Schließlich muß sie der doppelten εἰς- Bestimmung einen Sinn geben, der mit dem einschlägigen paulinischen Sprachgebrauch robust kollidiert, indem sie jene nämlich faktisch so auffaßt, als bezeichne sie den jeweiligen Gegenstand und Grund, das Woraufhin des Ruhmanspruchs[68]. Demgegenüber ist daran zu erinnern, daß das Woraufhin des Ruhms vom Apostel sonst, solange er sich präpositionaler Wendungen bedient, in verbalem Sprachgebrauch durchweg mit ἐν[69], in substantivischem mit ἐν oder ὑπέρ, jedoch nie mit εἰς wiedergegeben wird[70].

Umgekehrt läßt der einzig einschlägige Beleg Phil 2,16 (καύχημα εἰς ἡμέραν Χριστοῦ) den Sinn der Wortverbindung deutlich erkennen. Daß hier nicht das Woraufhin des Ruhms benannt wird, versteht sich von

64 Ebd. 83; vgl. 91.

65 Paulus sagt ja nicht, daß der Ruhm beim Blick auf andere dahinsinkt, sondern er qualifiziert mit der doppelten εἰς-Bestimmung den jeglicher Selbstprüfung unbedingt gewissen Ruhmanspruch.

66 Ebd. 88.

67 Dies ist im übrigen einer der stärksten Einwände gegen die Bestimmung des ἔργον als Frucht des Geistes, der Hübner im Vorübergehen inkonsequenterweise selbst zuneigt (vgl. o. Anm. 25).

68 Das wird freilich nirgendwo gesagt. Stattdessen wird das εἰς fast durchweg mit »im Blick auf« wiedergegeben (ebd. 83. 86. 88. 91), doch läuft die Auslegung der Sache nach darauf hinaus, daß das καύχημα εἰς τὸν ἕτερον das gegenstandslose, das κ. εἰς ἑαυτόν das durch seinen Gegenstand begründete ist; vgl. ebd.: »Nicht durch Vergleich mit anderen« ist der Ruhmanspruch festzustellen, »sondern nur ... durch Vergleich des je eigenen ›Werks‹« mit der göttlichen Forderung.

69 Röm 5,2 ist keine Ausnahme, denn hier bezeichnet das ἐπί gegen manche Ausleger nicht den Gegenstand, sondern den Modus des Rühmens. Doch ist diese Frage in unserm Zusammenhang unerheblich.

70 Vgl. die Belege bei Bauer, WB^4 772f. Zu 2 Kor 10,16 vgl. W. G. Kümmel, HNT 9, ^{4}1949, 209: »εἰς τὰ ἕτοιμα ist neben ἐν ἀλλοτρίῳ κόπῳ schwerlich auch noch direktes Objekt zu καυχήσασθαι« (in Korrektur von Lietzmanns Auslegung). In 2 Kor 11,10 geht das εἰς ἐμέ nicht auf den Gegenstand des Ruhms (der ist vielmehr der Unterhaltsverzicht des Paulus), sondern auf dessen Träger. 2 Kor 10,13.15 sind unvergleichbar, denn zufolge der geographischen Bestimmung des μέτρον (vgl. v. 13b) hat das εἰς τὰ ἄμετρα geradezu lokalen Sinn; zu Betz (s. o. Anm. 24), 303 Anm. 101.

selbst. Es handelt sich auch nicht eigentlich um eine Zeitangabe (»am Tage Christi«)[71]. Vielmehr wird so der für den Ruhm maßgebliche Relationszusammenhang bestimmt[72]. Das καύχημα gilt vor dem Forum des Gerichtstages[73]. Kein anderer Sinn eignet dem Sprachgebrauch in Gal 6,4. Indem der Apostel das καύχημα εἰς τὸν ἕτερον nicht etwa verbietet, sondern objektiv ausgeschlossen sein läßt, und indem er das καύχημα εἰς ἑαυτόν nicht etwa anempfiehlt, sondern als die notwendige und vom Ergebnis gänzlich unabhängige Folge jeglicher Selbstprüfung ankündigt, gibt er seinen Lesern zu verstehen, mit wem es derjenige, dem es um sein καύχημα geht, zu tun hat: einzig mit sich selbst. Sein »Ruhm« zählt nur vor der Instanz seines Ich und vor keiner anderen, natürlich auch nicht vor der göttlichen, auf die mit der Antithese εἰς τὸν ἕτερον – εἰς ἑαυτόν ja gar nicht reflektiert ist[74]. Das aber heißt, da jeglichem Ruhm ein externes Forum wesentlich ist: Unabhängig vom konkreten Ergebnis winkt grundsätzlich keiner Selbstprüfung ein wahres καύχημα[75], bzw., auf v. 3 gewendet: ein frommes εἶναί τι bleibt allemal imaginär.

So schließt sich denn auch v. 5 nahtlos an. Dem Christen, dem kein ἔργον je ein wirkliches καύχημα verschafft, dessen Selbstprüfung daher allemal des eigenen μηδὲν εἶναι inne werden wird, erwächst aus seinen eigenen Beständen wie jedem Menschen stets eine Last[76]. Eben darum bleibt er darauf angewiesen, daß der Nächste sie ihm solidarisch tragen hilft, wie es nach v. 2 die Lebensordnung der Gemeinde erheischt. Der Kompositionsring ist geschlossen; der Gedankenfortschritt zwischen v. 2 und v. 5 aber liegt darin, daß am Ende klargestellt ist, wie wenig die »Lasten« sich in »Übertretungen« nach Art der in v. 1 erwähnten erschöpfen[77].

---

[71] Gegen manche Ausleger ist daran zu erinnern, daß Paulus in solchem Falle ἐν verwendet; vgl. 1 Kor 5,5; (Röm 2,16), auch wenn er andererseits nach Art der Koine diese Präposition für εἰς im Sinne von »für« einsetzen kann: E. Käsemann, HNT 8a, 1973, 52 zu Röm 2,5; vgl. auch 1 Kor 1,8.

[72] Das καύχημα ist ja als solches keine ausstehende, sondern eine gegenwärtige Größe, wie schon der anschließende ὅτι-Satz zeigt, der seinerseits im Lichte von v. 17 sich eindeutig als Aussage über die Gegenwart erweist. Auch findet sich in Phil 1,10 – dem einzigen weiteren paulinischen Beleg für ἡμέρα + εἰς – derselbe Sprachgebrauch: als ἀπρόσκοποι sollen die Philipper ja nicht erst am Jüngsten Tage dastehen, wie wiederum die Fortsetzung v. 11 sicherstellt.

[73] Die nicht seltene Übersetzung »für den Tag« scheint das zur Geltung bringen zu sollen. Noch eindeutiger wäre forensisches »vor«.

[74] Gegen Hübner (s. o. Anm. 2), 91.

[75] Die alte ironische Auffassung des Stichworts (vgl. Sieffert [s. o. Anm. 19], 321), war auf richtiger Fährte.

[76] Die geistreiche Deutung von φορτίον auf die Last der καυχήματα (Lietzmann [s. o. Anm. 53], 39), scheitert an der Irrealität der καυχήματα.

[77] Die eschatologische Deutung von v. 5 ist also tatsächlich abzulehnen; mit Betz (s. o. Anm. 24), 304 gegen Hübner (s. o. Anm. 2), 87 u. a. Wenigstens erwogen sei, ob sich für den

4. Nach alledem dürfte das auf dem Prüfstand stehende Interpretationsangebot abzuweisen sein. Doch sind die einzelexegetischen Gegengründe nicht die einzigen.

4.1. Daß Paulus wenige Sätze später, in v. 14, jeglichen anderen Ruhm als den des Kreuzes Christi für den Glaubenden strikt ausschließt, kann unmöglich mit der Auskunft bewältigt werden, in v. 4 gehe es um den Ruhm coram deo, in v. 14 um denjenigen coram hominibus[78]. Denn einmal steht in v. 4 Gott als Forum des Ruhms ja gar nicht im Blick[79]. Zum andern ist solche Unterscheidung der Sache nach überhaupt haltlos. Äußert sich im Ruhm »das tragende Existenzverständnis«[80] und ist speziell mit dem Motiv des Selbstruhms »das ontologische Phänomen« im Blick, »daß der Mensch sein Leben auf das abstellt, was in seiner Tatmacht liegt«[81], so dürfte es evident sein, daß ich, wenn ich mich schon vor Menschen allein des Gekreuzigten rühmen kann, vor Gott erst recht keinen anderen Ruhm geltend zu machen vermag.

4.2. Vollends der kühne Versuch, sogar noch den 1. Korintherbrief ein Durchgangsstadium in der paulinischen Verarbeitung der Ruhmthematik dokumentieren zu lassen, ist zum Scheitern verurteilt. Nach Hübner wird zwar in 1 Kor 1,29–31 »Gal 6,14 theologisch weiterentwickelt«, jedoch »die Frage nach dem Ruhm des ›Werkes‹ nicht grundsätzlich disqualifiziert«[82]. Die erstaunliche Auskunft, der weder 1 Kor 3,13ff. noch 2 Kor 5,10 Schützenhilfe geben[83], muß v. 29 dahingehend erweichen, daß es hier nur »um die Abwertung jener menschlichen Qualitäten« gehe, »die außerhalb des Bereiches ›in Christus‹ vorweisbar sind. Insofern darf man vielleicht die Wendung ›kein Fleisch‹ im strengen Sinn des Wortes verstehen: Keiner soll sich, insofern er nur Fleisch ist, vor Gott rühmen.

äußerlich abrupten Übergang von v. 5 nach v. 6 nun nicht eine einleuchtende Erklärung anbietet. Will Paulus, nachdem er so energisch jedwede Leistung als Ruhmbasis ausgeschlossen hat, nun sicherstellen, daß die (Dienst-)Leistung der Wortverkündigung sehr wohl einen Anspruch εἰς τὸν ἕτερον begründet?

[78] Hübner (s. o. bei Anm. 18).

[79] S. o. bei Anm. 74.

[80] Käsemann (s. o. Anm. 71), 124.

[81] H. Weder, Gesetz und Sünde. Gedanken zu einem qualitativen Sprung im Denken des Paulus, NTS 31, 1985, 357–376, 371.

[82] Vgl. a.a.O. 91f.

[83] Gegen Hübner a.a.O. 92. An beiden Stellen fehlt die Ruhm-Terminologie. Zudem würde die erste, die von den Wortverkündigern handelt, allenfalls im Motivfeld des apostolischen Ruhms zu erörtern sein, was ein Thema für sich ist und auch von Hübner (a.a.O. 92f.) mit guten Gründen ausgespart wird. Was die zweite Stelle, die das Gericht nach den Werken ansagt, für die Ruhmthematik austragen soll, ist vollends nicht ersichtlich, zumal dieses Motiv ja auch im Römerbrief, und dort sogar mit gesteigerter Intensität, zum Zuge gebracht wird (2,2–11).

M. a. W., rühmen kann sich keiner, der sich noch im Bereich ›des Fleisches‹ aufhält, sondern nur der, der schon im entgegengesetzten Bereich lebt, nämlich ›in Christus‹ «[84]. Aber bekanntermaßen bezeichnet der Ausdruck πᾶσα σάρξ gar keinen Bereich, sondern »den Menschen überhaupt«[85], unterfängt also mit allen zwischenmenschlichen Unterschieden auch denjenigen zwischen Christen und Nichtchristen[86]. In der Tat: »Damit ist *jede* ... Möglichkeit menschlichen Selbstruhmes zerstört«[87].

4.3 Zum Abschluß sei auf eine interne Schwierigkeit der zur Debatte stehenden Auslegung hingewiesen. Sie steht nämlich in starker Spannung zu der entwicklungsgeschichtlichen Gesamtanschauung des paulinischen Gesetzesverständnisses, zu deren weiteren Fundierung sie angeblich doch gerade gereicht[88]. Denn einerseits soll gemäß der Hauptthese in der Abfolge vom Galater- über den 1. Korinther- bis zum Römerbrief eine Entradikalisierung der Gesetzeslehre zum Vorschein kommen, der entsprechend der Apostel von schroffem Antinomismus über eine Position der »Toleranz«[89] endlich zu der Einsicht herangereift wäre, daß dem »Gesetz des Mose« positives theologisches Gewicht zukäme[90]. Andererseits aber soll der Lernprozeß vom christlichen Ruhm der Werke zur grundsätzlichen Destruktion allen Werkruhms fortgeschritten sein. Wie diese beiden Linien konvergieren könnten, sehe ich nicht.

5. Fazit: Ein Curriculum in Sachen Ruhmthematik war dem Apostel nach Ausweis unserer Quellen fremd. Daß Paulus nämlich zeit seiner uns erkennbaren Wirksamkeit jedwedem Ruhm der Werke als dem Gipfel der Blasphemie widerstanden hat, wird durch Gal 6,4 nicht dementiert, sondern bestätigt.

---

[84] A.a.O. 92.

[85] Bultmann, NT § 22.2.

[86] Auch in Röm 3,20 ist das πᾶσα σάρξ ja nicht auf den Unglauben zu beschränken, sondern schließt es die Christen ein!

[87] Conzelmann (s. o. Anm. 37), 72 (Sperrung von mir).

[88] Vgl. Hübner a.a.O. 81.

[89] A.a.O. 132.

[90] Vgl. a.a.O. 75. Daß von einer solchen Entwicklung des paulinischen Gesetzesverständnisses tatsächlich keine Rede sein kann, steht auf einem anderen Blatt; dazu vgl. meinen Art. Gesetz III. Neues Testament, TRE 13, 58–75, bes. 65.

Zur explikativen Redeweise im neutestamentlichen Griechisch

von Helmut Krämer

(Offenburger Str. 14, 4800 Bielefeld 12)

Die griechische Sprache hat die Fähigkeit entwickelt, die Realitätsgehalte von Aussagen zu differenzieren. Den geringsten Realitätsgrad besitzt beim Verbum der Infinitiv, der zunächst nur die Verbalbedeutung als solche einschließlich des Aspekts bzw. der Aktionsart angibt. Eine besondere Rolle spielt der Infinitiv im Gegensatz zum Verbum finitum bei den sog. *Konsekutivsätzen*. Nach ὥστε steht eine finite Verbform, wenn es sich um eine tatsächliche Folge handelt, d. h. wenn Haupt- und Nebensatz je ein Faktum enthalten und das zweite Faktum als die Folge des ersten, der Ursache, hingestellt wird. Nur dieses Satzgefüge ist konsekutiv im strengen Sinne. Steht aber nach ὥστε ein Infinitiv, so ist die Folge nur gedacht; das kann bis zur Vorstellung einer beabsichtigten Folge gehen, so daß eine Annäherung an einen Finalsatz bis hin zur Identität stattfindet. In der Koine und im ntl. Griechisch ist dieser Ausgleich bis auf wenige Ausnahmen vollzogen[1]. Das bringt den Exegeten in Schwierigkeiten; Übersetzer pflegen sich mit »auf daß ...«, Lexika und Grammatiken mit der Schrägstrichangabe »final/konsekutiv« aus der Affäre zu ziehen.

Bei der nur gedachten Folge handelt es sich also nicht um ein zweites Faktum, das als Folge des erstgenannten hingestellt wird, sondern mehr um eine wichtige Ergänzung des Satzes. Der weitaus häufigste Fall liegt da vor, »wo eine Wirkung oder Folge angegeben wird, welche in dem *Wesen*, in der *Qualität* oder *Quantität (Intensität)* eines Gegenstandes oder in der *Qualität* oder *Quantität (Intensität)* einer Handlung begründet ist«[2]. Diese präzise und hilfreiche Definition ist leider nicht weiter tradiert worden. Für ihre Gültigkeit bietet das NT u. a. bei den sog. Pronominaladjektiven zwei singuläre, treffende Beispiele. *Qualität*: 1 Kor 5,1 ἀκούεται ἐν ὑμῖν... τοιαύτη πορνεία ... ὥστε γυναῖκά τινα τοῦ πατρὸς ἔχειν »man hört von einer Unzucht bei euch, die darin besteht, daß jemand die Frau seines Vaters hat«; *Quantität*: Mt 15,33 ἄρτοι τοσοῦτοι ὥστε χορτάσαι

---

[1] Vgl. die Übersicht in meiner Einführung in die griechische Sprache II 1978, 132 Nr. 7; ebd. 131 Nr. 5 zur o. a. Differenzierung der Realitätsgrade.

[2] R. Kühner–B. Gerth, Ausführliche Grammatik der griechischen Sprache, Satzlehre II ^{4}1955, 501; Hervorhebungen im Original.

ὄχλον τοσοῦτον »Brote in so großer Menge, daß wir damit so viele Leute sättigen können«[3]. In Übereinstimmung mit der lateinischen Grammatik[4] sollte man diese (im Grunde nicht konsekutive) Redeweise »explikativ« nennen. Andere Vorschläge sind »deskriptiv«[5] oder »illustrierend«[6]; doch treffen sie nicht so genau die gemeinte Sache wie »explikativ«. Zu eng ist der Terminus »epexegetisch«, den die Grammatik des ntl. Griechisch von Blaß-Debrunner-Rehkopf verwendet, weil Epexegese per definitionem[7] parataktische Beifügungen bezeichnet (Appositionen, καί epexegeticum[8], τοῦτ' ἔστιν u. ä.) und damit Nebensätze (z. B. mit ἵνα) ausschließt; andrerseits gehen die dort[9] gemachten Angaben – »in freier Weise«, »lose Verbindung«, »(sehr) lockere Verbindung« u. ä. – einer präzisen Bestimmung aus dem Wege und sind deshalb wenig hilfreich.

Als Grundübersetzung explikativer Redeweise ins Deutsche empfiehlt sich zunächst »von der Art daß«, »in der Weise daß«, »was darin besteht daß « u. ä. Ihre griechischen Ausdrucksmöglichkeiten sind im NT folgende[10]:

1. Infinitiv[11]. Außer den Fällen, wo ein Demonstrativum expliziert wird (Jak 1,27 θρησκεία καθαρὰ ... αὕτη ἐστίν, ἐπισκέπτεσθαι ὀρφανοὺς καὶ χήρας »reiner Gottesdienst ... ist von der Art, daß man ein Au-

---

3 So übersetzen ὥστε χορτάσαι zu Recht E. Klostermann HNT 4, ^{2}1927, und ihm folgend E. Schweizer NTD 2, $^{14(2)}$1976. Während Luther mit »daß wir sättigen« die Frage final/konsekutiv in der Schwebe gehalten hatte, hat sich die Revision 1975 für das finale »um zu sättigen« entschieden, ähnlich wie vorher Weizsäcker, Zürcher Bibel, Menge, Wilckens, später die Einheitsübersetzung, und die Revision 1984 ist bedauerlicherweise dabei geblieben.

4 Vgl. J. B. Hofmann–A. Szantyr, Lateinische Syntax und Stilistik (HAW II 2,2) 1965, 645f. über »explikative ut-Sätze«. Schon J. Weiß hatte in seinem Kommentar zu 1 Kor (KEK 5, ^{9}1910) 125 das ὥστε von 5,1 und 241 Anm. 1 das ἵνα von 9,18 als »rein explikativ« bezeichnet. Präzise verwendet diesen Begriff auch P. Lampe in seinem ἵνα-Artikel EWNT II (1981) 460–466.

5 T. Muraoka, Purpose or result? ὥστε in Biblical Greek, NovTest 15, 1973, 205–219, bes. Kap. II: Descriptive use.

6 So mündlich mein Lehrer H. Fränkel in Göttingen 1930 in einer Lateinübung.

7 J. B. Hofmann–H. Rubenbauer, Wörterbuch der grammatischen und metrischen Terminologie, ^{2}1963, 35: »Epexegese: parataktische Ergänzung oder Erläuterung eines Satzteils, z. B. lat. *hīc in Ephesō*.«

8 Nur hier hat, soweit ich sehe, F. Rehkopf in seiner Neubearbeitung (seit 1976 § 442,6a) »oder explicativum« hinzugefügt; er gebraucht anscheinend die beiden Termini promiscue.

9 §§ 390 Anm. 5; 391,4; 400,8.

10 Die angegebenen Beispiele sind unter dem Gesichtspunkt ausgewählt, daß bei ihnen die Vorstellung finaler oder »konsekutiver« Bedeutung möglichst ausgeschlossen werden kann. Auf Auseinandersetzung mit Sekundärliteratur ist im allgemeinen verzichtet.

11 Bl.-Debr.-Rehk. §§ 394; 391,4 mit Anm. 8.

ge hat auf Waisen und Witwen« u. ä.)[12], Lk 1,54 ἀντελάβετο Ἰσραὴλ παιδὸς αὐτοῦ, μνησθῆναι ἐλέους »er hat sich seines Knechtes Israel angenommen, was dadurch bestimmt war, daß er seines Erbarmens gedachte.« Hebr 6,10 οὐ γὰρ ἄδικος ὁ θεὸς ἐπιλαθέσθαι τοῦ ἔργου ὑμῶν: Eine Ungerechtigkeit Gottes würde wesentlich darin bestehen, daß er vergäße, was ihr getan habt. Apk 16,9 οὐ μετενόησαν δοῦναι αὐτῷ δόξαν: Die Umkehr »wird vollzogen, indem man Gott die Ehre gibt«[13].

2. ὥστε + Infinitiv[14]. Außer den o. a. Stellen (1 Kor 5,1; Mt 15,33) 1 Kor 13,2 πᾶσαν τὴν πίστιν ὥστε ὄρη μεθιστάναι »allen Glauben von einer Intensität und einem Ausmaß, daß er (bzw. ich?) Berge versetzen könnte.« Mt 27,1 συμβούλιον ἔλαβον . . . κατὰ τοῦ Ἰησοῦ ὥστε θανατῶσαι αὐτόν »sie faßten gegen Jesus einen Beschluß des Inhalts, ihn zu töten.«

3. τοῦ + Infinitiv (substantivierter Infinitiv im Genitiv des Sachbetreffs)[15]. Act 7,19 ἐκάκωσεν τοὺς πατέρας [ἡμῶν] τοῦ ποιεῖν τὰ βρέφη ἔκθετα αὐτῶν »er (der Pharao) mißhandelte unsre Väter in der Weise, daß er ihre kleinen Kinder aussetzen ließ«[16]. Mt 21,32 ὑμεῖς δὲ ἰδόντες οὐδὲ μετεμελήθητε ὕστερον τοῦ πιστεῦσαι αὐτῷ »ihr aber, nachdem (obwohl) ihr es gesehen habt, habt nicht einmal später euren Sinn geändert, was darin bestanden hätte, ihm Glauben zu schenken«[17]. Röm 1,24 παρέδωκεν αὐτοὺς ὁ θεὸς . . . εἰς ἀκαθαρσίαν τοῦ ἀτιμάζεσθαι τὰ σώματα αὐτῶν ἐν αὐτοῖς: Die Unreinheit besteht in der Schändung des eigenen Leibes durch die Menschen.

4. ἵνα + Konjunktiv, auch Ind. Fut.[18] (am häufigsten im johanneischen Schrifttum). Außer den zahlreichen Fällen, wo ein Demonstrativum

---

[12] Eph 3,8f. ἐμοὶ . . . ἐδόθη ἡ χάρις αὕτη, . . . εὐαγγελίσασθαι . . . καὶ φωτίσαι gehört nicht zu dieser Gruppe, wie Bl.-Debr.-Rehk. § 394 Anm. 1 angeben, da αὕτη nicht auf die folgenden Infinitive hinweist, sondern Rückbezug auf den vorhergehenden Text v. 2 u. 7 ist; die Infinitive sind Explikation von χάρις.

[13] E. Lohse NTD 11, 8(1)1960. 84 z. St.

[14] Bl.-Debr.-Rehk. § 391.

[15] Ebd. § 400, bes. 7.8; so wichtig der in 7 gegebene Hinweis auf das Hebräische ist (vgl. dazu auch H.-P. Stähli, Hebräisch. Kurzgrammatik 1984, 79), so unsinnig ist es, vom Griechischen her gesehen, τοῦ als »abundierend« zu bezeichnen.

[16] Grammatisch unmöglich ist die Überlegung von E. Haenchen, KEK 3, 12 1959, 232 Anm. 1, τοῦ ποιεῖν final »damit sie aussetzten« zu verstehen, weil dann der Subjektswechsel durch ein αὐτούς o. ä. ausgedrückt sein müßte. – Für die textkritische Entscheidung über ἡμῶν ist zu beachten, daß der griechische Artikel nach dem Zusammenhang als Ausdruck der possessiven Beziehung genügt (vgl. Mk 7,11; Mt 19,19).

[17] Klostermann a.a.O. 171 spricht vom »schwierigen τοῦ πιστεῦσαι αὐτῷ«. – Luther hat ὕστερον zu diesem Infinitiv gezogen; nur die inzwischen verfemte Revision 1975 hatte im Luthertext diesen Irrtum beseitigt.

[18] Bl.-Debr.-Rehk. §§ 391,5; 394,3; Lampe a.a.O. passim.

expliziert wird (1 Joh 5,3 αὕτη ... ἐστὶν ἡ ἀγάπη τοῦ θεοῦ, ἵνα τὰς ἐντολὰς αὐτοῦ τηρῶμεν »die Liebe zu Gott besteht darin, daß wir seine Gebote halten«), Apk 13,13 ποιεῖ σημεῖα μεγάλα, ἵνα καὶ πῦρ ποιῇ ἐκ τοῦ οὐρανοῦ καταβαίνειν εἰς τὴν γῆν »es (das Tier) vollbringt große Zeichen von einer Qualität, daß es sogar Feuer vom Himmel herabfahren läßt auf die Erde«[19]. 1 Kor 9,18 τίς ... μού ἐστιν ὁ μισθός; ἵνα εὐαγγελιζόμενος ἀδάπανον θήσω τὸ εὐαγγέλιον »Was ist mein Lohn? Er besteht darin, daß ich, wenn ich verkündige, die Heilsbotschaft zu etwas mache, das keine Kosten verursacht«.

5. εἰς τό + Infinitiv[20]. Wenigstens den Versuch explikativer Deutung erlaubt die exegetisch umstrittene Stelle Röm 3,26 πρὸς τὴν ἔνδειξιν τῆς δικαιοσύνης αὐτοῦ ..., εἰς τὸ εἶναι αὐτὸν δίκαιον καὶ δικαιοῦντα ...[21] »zum Erweis seiner Gerechtigkeit ..., deren Wesen es ist, daß er gerecht ist und gerecht macht ...«. Ebenso 2 Thess 1,5 ἔνδειγμα τῆς δικαίας κρίσεως τοῦ θεοῦ, εἰς τὸ καταξιωθῆναι ὑμᾶς τῆς βασιλείας τοῦ θεοῦ »ein Anzeichen der gerechten Entscheidung Gottes, deren Gerechtigkeit darin bestehen wird, daß ihr des Gottesreichs gewürdigt werdet«[22].

6. πρὸς τό + Infinitiv[23]. Nur Mt 5,28 ὁ βλέπων γυναῖκα πρὸς τὸ ἐπιθυμῆσαι αὐτήν ... Für eine finale Auffassung von πρός[24] müßte entweder ein Verbum konkreteren Inhalts dastehen oder αὐτήν Subjekt zu ἐπιθυμῆσαι sein[25] (»wer eine Frau ansieht mit der Absicht, daß ihr Begehren rege wird«, neudeutsch »um sie anzumachen«), was jedoch durch den Text des Dekalogs Ex 20,17 bzw. Dtn 5,21 ausgeschlossen ist. Der

---

19 Der Hinweis ebd. § 391,5 »vgl. Mt 24,24« (δώσουσιν σημεῖα μεγάλα καὶ τέρατα ὥστε πλανῆσαι, εἰ δυνατόν, καὶ τοὺς ἐκλεκτούς) ist irreführend; er läßt den unbefangenen Leser vermuten, es handle sich um eine sachliche Parallele; aber die Mt-Stelle hat wie auch ihre Vorlage Mk 13,22 (πρὸς τὸ ἀποπλανᾶν, εἰ δυνατόν, τοὺς ἐκλεκτούς) schon wegen des εἰ δυνατόν eindeutig finalen Sinn »um womöglich sogar die Auserwählten irrezuführen«.

20 Bl.-Debr.-Rehk. § 402,2.

21 Die Wiederaufnahme von εἰς ἔνδειξιν τῆς δικαιοσύνης αὐτοῦ (v. 25) geschieht in v. 26 durch πρὸς τὴν ἔνδειξιν τῆς δ., wie auch der jetzt hinzugesetzte Artikel (»die eben schon genannte« ἔνδειξις) zeigt.

22 Die genaue Erklärung folgt in v. 6f. – Beabsichtigt die Streichung des Kommas vor εἰς τὸ εἶναι im Nestle-Aland [26]1979 gegenüber den früheren Ausgaben eine ganz andere grammatische Lösung, etwa »Hinweis des gerechten Gerichts (gen. subj.) Gottes darauf, daß ihr ... gewürdigt werdet«?

23 Bl.-Debr.-Rehk. § 402,4.

24 Ausdrücklich vertreten z. B. von Billerbeck I 301; Zürcher Bibel; W. Grundmann ThHK I [2]1971, 160, im Grunde aber von allen, die wortwörtlich »sie (ihrer) zu begehren« übersetzen.

25 So K. Haacker, Der Rechtssatz Jesu zum Thema Ehebruch (Mt 5,28), BZ 21, 1977, 113–116.

Passus kann nur explikativ[26] verstanden werden »wer eine Frau ansieht in einer Art und Weise, daß das Begehren nach ihr in ihm rege wird«, und so trifft die Paraphrase »mit begehrlichem Blick«[27] die Sache genau.

Die genannten Beispiele zeigen, daß es sinnvoll ist, jeweils zu prüfen, ob nicht der Terminus »explikativ« den vom Autor des Textes gemeinten Sachverhalt genauer bezeichnet als andere grammatische Bestimmungen.

---

[26] So Rehkopf a.a.O. § 402 Anm. 5 sachlich treffend (natürlich in seiner Terminologie »epexegetisch«), während sich Debrunner § 402,5 noch mit dem recht allgemeinen »mit Rücksicht auf« begnügt hatte.

[27] Z. B. H. Greeven, Ehe nach dem NT, in: Theologie der Ehe, 1969, 72; Grundmann a.a.O. 160f.; U. Wilckens in seiner Übersetzung (»mit begehrlichen Augen«).

Die Entstehung von Gemeindeverbänden

von Heinrich Kraft

(Theologische Fakultät der Universität Kiel, Olshausenstraße, 2300 Kiel)

Einleitung

Kirche und Einzelgemeinde finden sich im Neuen Testament mit demselben Ausdruck »Ekklesia« bezeichnet. Die Einzelgemeinde ist dadurch als Teil oder Abbild der endzeitlichen oder himmlischen – im Erscheinen begriffenen – Kirche gedeutet. Erst Ignatios von Antiochien vermag die Ecclesia und die Ecclesia catholica zu unterscheiden (Sm 8,2); wir wissen nicht genau, ob er die irdische oder die himmlische Gesamtkirche »katholisch« nennt. Daß Ignatios der erste ist, der diesen Unterschied macht, ist kein Zufall; Ignatios ist auch der erste, der das Wesen der Einzelgemeinde dadurch erfaßt, daß er sie als Abbild der idealen Kirche deutet. Für ihn besteht die Kirche wesentlich im Bischof mit dem Klerus. Die irdische Hierarchie erhält dadurch ihre Legitimation, daß sie die himmlische Hierarchie abbildet. Der Bischof erweist sich dabei, weil er in dieser Konfiguration Abbild Gottes ist, als der alleinige und allein berechtigte Repräsentant seiner Gemeinde. Des Ignatios beständige Forderung, daß alle Christen sich zum Bischof halten müssen, findet auf diese Weise ihre Begründung.

Dieser Gedanke des Ignatios setzt die auf der Realität des Abbildes beruhende Mysterientheologie voraus. Ignatios denkt in ihren Bahnen. Aber die Gemeindeverfassung, die er fordert, ist für seine Zeit (nach Eusebs Kirchengeschichte 3,36,1–3 die Zeit Trajans, etwa das zweite Jahrzehnt des zweiten Jahrhunderts) überraschend fortschrittlich. Die Vorstellungen des Ignatios sind grundverschieden von der aus dem Sukzessionsprinzip entwickelten Begründung des geistlichen Amtes im Clemensbrief (42.44). Der Clemensbrief ist sicher auf die letzten Monate des Jahres 96 datierbar; er ist rund 20 Jahre vor dem für die Ignatiosbriefe überlieferten Datum geschrieben. Auf der Amtstheorie des Ignatios beruht die Meinung, die Gesamtkirche sei der Numerus episcoporum. Tertullian kennt diese Deutung; als Montanist lehnt er sie ab (pud. 21,17). Auch dem Cyprian ist sie nicht fremd; seine Theorie vom Wesen der katholischen Kirche berücksichtigt die Entwürfe des Clemens und des Ignatios.

Die Vorstellungen vom geistlichen Amt in den Briefen des Ignatios eilen ihrer Zeit weit voraus. Erst zu Ende des zweiten Jahrhunderts finden wir Gemeinden von der Gestalt, wie Ignatios sie fordert; Gemeinden, die an ihrer Spitze den dreistufigen Klerus von Bischof, Presbytern und Diakonen haben. Nach der Mitte des zweiten Jahrhunderts ist die katholische Kirche dadurch entstanden, daß die Gemeinden sich in Glauben und Sitte aneinander anpaßten. Die Regula fidei, die bischöfliche Verfassung und der Kanon der Heiligen Schrift wurden überprüfbare Merkmale der Katholizität. Von da an können wir für katholische Gemeinden die Struktur voraussetzen, die Ignatios zwei bis drei Generationen früher beschreibt und fordert. Auf die Dauer wird die Forschung nicht vermeiden können, sich mit den unbequemen Ergebnissen Rius-Camps' auseinanderzusetzen, auch wenn sie dadurch gezwungen sein sollte, große Partien der anfänglichen Verfassungsgeschichte der Kirche neu zu schreiben. (J. Rius-Camps, The four authentic letters of Ignatius, the martyr. XPICTIANICMOC 2, Rom 1979. Rius-Camps sieht die entsprechenden Partien der Ignatiosbriefe für das Werk eines Compilators vom Anfang des 3. Jhs. an. Wir setzen einstweilen die konventionelle Auffassung von der Entstehung der Briefe voraus, um die folgenden Ausführungen nicht durch fremde Hypothesen zu belasten. Doch rechnen wir, daß diese Hypothesen sich großenteils als zutreffend erweisen werden.)

Der römische Clemens und Ignatios sind die ersten, die eine Begründung für das kirchliche Amt als Institution angegeben haben. Beide setzen die Existenz von Gemeindeverbänden voraus. Gemeindeverbände können durch Untergliederung der Gesamtkirche und Zusammenfassung von Einzelgemeinden entstanden sein. Die Vorstellungen der Gesamtkirche und der Einzelgemeinden haben verschiedenen Ursprung. Die Gesamtkirche wurzelt in der Enderwartung des palästinensischen Judentums, nämlich in der Selbstdeutung der hebräischen Urgemeinde, die sich als das aus Israels heiligem Rest erwachsende Gottesvolk verstand. Anders die Einzelgemeinde; sie setzt die um die Heimkehr der Zerstreuten kreisende Enderwartung der jüdischen Diaspora voraus. Dementsprechend erwartet sie auch nicht, daß in ihrer Struktur die Gestalt des endzeitlichen Gottesvolks vorgegeben sei. Das bedeutet, daß diese Struktur der Einzelgemeinde nur in geringem Maße durch alttestamentliche Weissagungen bestimmt ist und sich leichter an die wirtschaftlichen und sozialen Gegebenheiten der Zeit anpassen kann. Diese Elastizität wird freilich zur Unsicherheit, wo man den Gedanken festhält, die endzeitliche Gemeinde sei in ihrer Gestalt durch alttestamentliche Weissagungen bestimmt. Lukas in der Apostelgeschichte und der römische Clemens haben Mühe, alttestamentliche Stellen zu finden, in denen das Bischofsamt geweissagt ist. Solche Mühe hat Ignatios nicht. Für ihn hat die Prophetie keine über ihre Erfüllung durch Christus hinausreichende Bedeutung. Besonders deutlich zeigt sich das Dilemma bei dem Apostel Paulus und seiner Suche nach alttestamentlichen Weissagungen auf die kirchliche Organisation. Denn Paulus schreibt für Einzelgemeinden, aber seine Vorstellung vom Wesen der Kirche wird von der Idee der Gesamtkirche beherrscht. Darum muß er auch seinen Anspruch auf Leitung des von ihm geschaffenen Gemeindeverbandes ohne alttestamentliche Begründung lassen.

Die Gestalt der Urgemeinde

Die Urgemeinde ist in Jerusalem gegründet. Im Augenblick ihrer Gründung besteht sie aus Jüngern und Anhängern Jesu, die hierher zurückgekehrt waren, wo sie in Kürze das Ende der alten und den Anbruch der neuen Weltzeit zu erleben erwarteten. So besteht die Urgemeinde im Augenblick ihrer Gründung ausschließlich aus Galiläern. Als solche konnten die Jünger benannt werden, und der Name blieb ihnen noch lange erhalten. Kaiser Julian konnte ihn noch nach der Mitte des 4. Jhs. als verächtliche Benennung gebrauchen.

Die Urgemeinde setzte die Organisationsform fort, zu der sich Jesus und seine Jünger verbunden hatten. Die Jüngergemeinde befand sich vor Ostern auf beständiger Wanderschaft und war für ihren Unterhalt auf Spenden und Beiträge angewiesen. Die wurden von den Anhängern aufgebracht, die einstweilen in ihrem Eigentum verblieben waren und sich noch nicht dem armen Leben Jesu angeschlossen hatten. Die besitzende Randgemeinde unterhielt die besitzlose Kerngemeinde. Diese Lebensform erfuhr durch die Niederlassung der Jünger in Jerusalem keine Veränderung. Die wirtschaftliche Existenz der Urgemeinde beruhte auf den Beiträgen ihrer auswärtigen Anhänger, und diese Abhängigkeit wurde noch fühlbarer, als man die Beitrittswilligen unter Hingabe ihres Besitzes in die Kerngemeinde aufnahm.

Der Name »Galiläer« für die Glieder der Urgemeinde verweist nicht allein auf die galiläischen Jünger, die sich in Jerusalem niedergelassen hatten, sondern auch auf die galiläischen Anhänger, die die Urgemeinde unterhielten. Er setzt regelmäßigen Verkehr zwischen Jerusalem und Galiläa voraus. Weil die Urgemeinde durch ihre auswärtigen Anhänger unterhalten wurde, war sie bestrebt, den Kreis der beitragenden Mitglieder zu vergrößern. Die Beamten, die in Galiläa die Beiträge einzogen, hatten zugleich die Aufgabe, in Judäa und Galiläa für die Gemeinde zu werben. Sie konnten darauf verweisen, daß den Unterhalt leistenden Anhängern dieselben Verheißungen wie den Gliedern der Kerngemeinde galten. Die Werbung richtete sich nur an Juden, die in Judäa oder Galiläa ansässig waren. Missionserfolge unter Samaritanern werden nicht eindeutig berichtet, und die Evangelien erwecken den Eindruck, solche Bemühung sei grundsätzlich unterblieben. Hingegen traten hellenistische Juden, die sich als Pilger in Jerusalem aufhielten, von Anfang an in die Urgemeinde ein.

Die Urgemeinde deutete sich als das endzeitliche Gottesvolk; demgemäß hielt sie sich mit ihren Jerusalemer und auswärtigen Mitgliedern für eine einzige Gemeinde. An ihrer Spitze stand das in sich hierarchisch gegliederte Apostelamt aus den drei Säulenaposteln, den Zwölfaposteln und den Aposteln schlechthin. Die Qualifikation für den Apostolat lag in einer Vision des Auferstandenen. Die Apostel fungierten als Repräsentanten der Gemeinde. Die mit der Werbung und dem Einsammeln der Beiträge beauftragten Apostel haben das Bild des Amts für die älteste Kirche bestimmt. Nach diesem Bild hat sich besonders der Apostel Paulus bei der Vorstellung von seinem eigenen Apostolat gerichtet. Neben den Aposteln kannte die Urgemeinde die charismatischen Ämter der Propheten und Lehrer. Diese drei Ämter fand sie zweifelsfrei im Alten Testament geweissagt.

Außerhalb Jerusalems gab es keine selbständigen Gemeinden. Innerhalb wie außerhalb der Stadt gab es jedoch Gruppen von Tisch- und Gebetsgemeinschaften. An deren Spitze standen jeweils Älteste, Presbyter. Die Existenz solcher Hausgemeinden ist für Jerusalem durch die Apostelgeschichte unmittelbar bezeugt; Lukas setzt sie jedoch auch außerhalb Jerusalems voraus. Darüber hinaus gibt es Gründe, aus denen auf sie geschlossen werden muß. Wir erfahren beispielsweise, daß bei der Einführung der Taufe 3000 Mitglieder auf einmal in die Gemeinde eintraten, und daß deren Zahl täglich weiter zunahm. Hätten diese Mitglieder sämtlich ihren Wohnsitz in Jerusalem gehabt, so wäre die tägliche Versammlung der Gemeinde im Tempel oder Tempelbezirk unvorstellbar. Die Neophyten dürften zum großen Teil auswärtige Mitglieder gewesen sein. – Ferner ist anzunehmen, daß die Apostel, die die Beiträge einsammelten und die auswärtigen Mitglieder geistlich versorgten, nicht jeden Anhänger einzeln aufsuchten, sondern Anlaufstellen im Lande hatten, an denen sich der Kontakt zwischen den Aposteln und den örtlichen Gemeindegliedern zusammenfassend bewerkstelligen ließ. Solche örtlichen Gesellschaften waren keine Gemeinden im theologischen Sinn, konnten aber die organisatorischen Funktionen von Einzelgemeinden wahrnehmen. – Lukas kennt als Apostel nur die Zwölfapostel. Darum vermischen sich bei ihm für die Anfangszeit die Aufgaben der Apostel und der Presbyter. Er meint, ursprünglich hätten geistliche und wirtschaftliche Funktionen gleichermaßen in den Händen der Apostel gelegen. Erst nachträglich sei zwischen beiden Aufgaben durch die Einrichtung eines Verwaltungsamtes unterschieden worden (Apg 6,2 ff.). Darum erscheinen in der Apostelgeschichte zunächst die Apostel, von 11,30 an jedoch die Presbyter als die Empfänger der Beiträge und Spenden.

Die Gemeindeleitung lag nach der Apostelgeschichte zu Anfang allein bei den Aposteln. Von Apg 15,4 an üben Apostel und Presbyter die Leitung gemeinsam aus, und von Apg 21,18 an erscheinen nur noch der Herrenbruder Jakobus und die Presbyter als Leiter der Gemeinde. Somit sind die Presbyter nach Meinung der Apostelgeschichte in der Urgemeinde die Nachfolger der Apostel. Lukas möchte den Eindruck erwecken, der Übergang der Leitung von den Aposteln auf die Presbyter sei gleitend gewesen. Zumindest einen Sprung muß diese Entwicklung jedoch aufgewiesen haben. Er ist durch die Spaltung der Urgemeinde in Hebräer und Hellenisten verursacht und erlangte kirchengeschichtliche Bedeutung durch den kräftigen Impuls, den die Heidenmission durch die Vertreibung der Hellenisten aus Jerusalem erhielt. Denn die aus Jerusalem vertriebenen Hellenisten warben keine Mitglieder für die Urgemeinde, sondern gründeten Einzelgemeinden. Diese Einzelgemeinden litten von Anfang an unter Mangel an Charismatikern, so daß die Gemeindeleitung dem institutionellen Amt zufallen mußte. Dementsprechend groß ist von Anfang an die Bedeutung des institutionellen Amtes für die Diasporagemeinden, auch wenn noch Jahrzehnte vergehen, bis es dem charismatischen Amt den Rang abgelaufen hat.

Während in der Diaspora sich das institutionelle Amt als das normale Gemeindeamt etabliert, wächst auch in der Urgemeinde die Bedeutung des institutionellen Amtes. Die charismatitischen Ämter der Apostel, Propheten und Lehrer sind und bleiben gesamtkirchliche Ämter. Die Nachfolger der Apostel, die Presbyter, sind aber in der Urgemeinde und dort, wo das Vorbild der Urgemeinde wirksam wird, Beamte von Teil- oder Einzelgemeinden. Zwar gibt es eine Reihe von Versuchen, das Presbyteramt – als das Amt der Apostelschüler und -nachfolger – gesamtkirchlich und charismatisch zu deuten. Bis auf Irenaeus und Tertullian läßt sich erkennen, daß mit dem Amt des als Apostelnachfolger verstandenen Presbyters gesamtkirchliche Aufgaben und Ansprüche verbunden gedacht werden konnten. Der in der zweiten Hälfte des zweiten Jahrhunderts aufkommende monarchische Episkopat drängte aber solche Ansprüche zurück, und mit dem Montanismus wurden sie endgültig aus der Kirche ausgeschieden. (Bei Ignatios ist der Zusammenhang zwischen Aposteln und Presbytern noch nicht gelöst. Die Bischöfe sind bei ihm noch nicht die Apostelnachfolger, und ihre Autorität ist noch nicht in der Apostelnachfolge begründet.)

Die Gestalt der hellenistischen Gemeinde

Die Abspaltung der Hellenisten und die Entstehung des institutionellen Wirtschaftsamtes sind von Lukas zu einem einzigen Vorgang zusammengezogen worden. Er behauptet, der Anlaß seien Versorgungsschwierigkeiten der Kerngemeinde gewesen. Man habe sie dadurch zu beheben versucht, daß man die Verpflegung der hellenistischen Hausgemeinden unterließ. Aus allem, was wir über die Geschichte des Urchristentums wissen, geht jedoch als eigentlicher Grund die laxe Handhabung der gesetzlichen Reinheitsvorschriften durch Hellenisten hervor; sie verbot den gesetzesstrengen Mitgliedern die Tischgemeinschaft mit ihnen.

Dennoch wird die Begründung zutreffen, die die Apostelgeschichte angibt. Dann wurden bis zur Spaltung die hellenistischen Glieder der Kerngemeinde mit den andern durch die Beiträge aus Palästina unterhalten. Weil diese aber nicht für die ganze Gemeinde ausreichten, legte man den Griechen nah, für ihren Unterhalt eigene Quellen in den palästinensischen Griechenstädten oder der Diaspora zu erschließen, aus der sie hergekommen waren. Das Problem der Tischgemeinschaft löste sich auf diese Weise von selber. Die Spaltung nötigte die Hellenisten zum Aufbau einer eigenen Verwaltung, die nach Lage der Dinge vor allem eine Wirtschaftsorganisation sein mußte. An deren Spitze traten sieben Männer, die auch in der Apostelgeschichte als Charismatiker bezeichnet werden. Über vier von ihnen gibt es Nachrichten, aus denen hervorgeht, daß sie Propheten waren; der Besitz dieses Charismas kann darum bei allen sieben vorausgesetzt werden. Diakone waren sie nicht. Diese Sieben waren gleicherweise für die geistliche und die wirtschaftliche Leitung des hellenistischen Gemeindeteils zuständig. Als Amtstitel wird für sie Apg 21,8 »Evangelist« angegeben; der Titel wird auch durch den paulinischen Epheserbrief bezeugt. 2. Tim 4,5 verweist auf die geistlichen und wirtschaftlichen Aufgaben dieses Amtes. Der Begriff bezeichnet, wie Apostolos, einen mit der Verkündigung des Gottesreiches beauftragten Heilspropheten (nach Jes 52,7; Nah 2,1; Mal 1,1).

Synonym ist der Amtstitel des »Angelos«, der nach den Sendschreiben der Johannesapokalypse an der Spitze der Gemeinden in der Asia steht. Ignatios nennt zwei Jahrzehnte danach diese Beamten jedoch »Bischöfe«. Folglich muß es sich um dasselbe Amt handeln, dessen Inhaber hier als »Episkopos« und dort als »Angelos« bezeichnet wird. Als Titel eines mit der Verkündigung des Evangeliums beauftragten Propheten ist der Begriff auch Apg 6,15 auf Stephanos angewandt. Lukas hat mithin »Angelos« und »Euangelistes« für gleichwertig und für den Vorgänger des institutionellen Bischofsamtes angesehen.

Somit war der Angelos/Evangelist ein von Gott mit der Verkündigung des Evangeliums, von der Gemeinde mit Verwaltungsaufgaben betrauter Charismatiker. Beim Übergang des Amtes auf einen von der Gemeinde gewählten Nichtcharismatiker erhielt dieser den Titel Episkopos, der ihn nach seinen Verwaltungsaufgaben bezeichnete.

Die Vertreibung der Hellenisten bedeutete nicht, daß es hinfort keine hellenistischen Christen in Jerusalem und der Urgemeinde gegeben hätte. Verschwunden war lediglich der besondere hellenistische Gemeindeteil mit den hellenistischen Hausgemeinden. Doch führte die Vertreibung der Hellenisten zu vermehrter Gründung hellenistischer Gemeinden in der Diaspora. Für diese Gemeinden waren die Apostel nicht zuständig, und darum nehmen die Amtsnachfolger der Sieben nicht den Titel »Presbyter« an, der die Schüler und Nachfolger der Apostel bezeichnet. Die nach ihren Wirtschaftsaufgaben benannten Bischöfe und Diakone treten an die Spitze dieser Gemeinden. Das Bischofsamt wird damit charakteristisch für die im Anschluß an die Vertreibung entstandenen hellenistischen Gemeinden. Viel Zeit vergeht noch, bis die Bischöfe sich als Amtsnachfolger der Apostel verstehen können, und weil das Bischofsamt aus einem Verwaltungsamt hervorgegangen ist, haben die Bischöfe noch größere Mühe als die Presbyter, den geistigen Charakter ihres Amtes zu beweisen. Während der ganzen Kirchengeschichte finden sich Beispiele dafür, daß man den Bischöfen den charismatischen Charakter ihres Amtes bestritten und das Charisma bei andern gesucht hat.

Die Vertreibung der Hellenisten beschleunigte einen Prozeß, der vorher schon in Gang gekommen und Ursache der Vertreibung geworden war. Die Fluktuation von Pilgern zwischen der jüdischen Diaspora und Jerusalem führte zur Entstehung von christlichen Gemeinden in der Heimat der Pilger und entlang der Verkehrswege.

In diese Gemeinden wurden nicht bloß Juden und Proselyten, sondern auch unbeschnittene Gottesfürchtige aufgenomen. Die aus Jerusalem vertriebenen Hellenisten hatten anfänglich die Grundsätze der Urgemeinde befolgt und sich mit ihrer Werbung ausschließlich an Juden in den Griechenstädten Phöniziens und Syriens gewandt. Als diese Art der Ausbreitung Antiochien erreichte, fand sie dort ein auch den Heiden geöffnetes Christentum vor, das sich auf dem Seeweg über Alexandrien, die Kyrenaika und Zypern ausgebreitet hatte. In Antiochien flossen die beiden Ströme in einander, ohne daß es dort zum Streit gekomen wäre. Die antiochenische Christengemeinde wurde zu einer Gemeinde aus Juden und Heiden. Währenddessen erinnerte sich die Urgemeinde, daß ihre Enderwartung mit der Bekehrung der Heiden rechnete. Ihre Abhängigkeit von auswärtigen Spenden wird mitgewirkt haben, daß sie sich dem Gedanken der Heidenmission nicht weiter verschließen wollte. Sie sandte zunächst den aus Zypern stammenden Apostel Barnabas nach Antiochien; der berichtete von einer lebendigen, im Wachsen begriffenen Gemeinde. Daraufhin forderte sie durch Propheten die Antiochener auf, mit Spenden zu ihrem Unterhalt beizutragen. Die Christen in Antiochien erwarteten, gleich allen anderen, daß das Gottesreich auch für sie in Jerusalem anbrechen werde. Sie fühlten sich der Urgemeinde verpflichtet und entsprachen ihrem Wunsch. Beide Seiten scheinen darauf geachtet zu haben, daß die Zahlung nicht als Eingliederung der antiochenischen Gemeinde in die Urgemeinde gedeutet werden konnte. Die Gabe wurde nicht von Jerusalem durch Apostel eingezogen, sondern durch charismatische Boten der antiochenischen Gemeinde nach Jerusalem gebracht. Man war sich bewußt, daß Heiden – die Form der Übergabe bringt es zum Ausdruck – ihr Geld nach Jerusalem gebracht hatten. In derselben Weise ist hernach auch die Kollekte der heidenchristlichen Gemeinden übergeben worden, die der Apostel Paulus gegründet hatte.

Dennoch kommt in der Spende – ihrer Anforderung, Aufbringung und Annahme – das Bewußtsein der Zusammengehörigkeit zum Ausdruck. Wenn die Urgemeinde antiochenische Heidenchristen zu ihrem Unterhalt beitragen ließ, so erkannte sie das Christentum in Antiochien als solches an. Dabei zeigte sich jedoch ein Wandel in ihrem Selbstverständnis. Die Urgemeinde konnte zwar auch weiterhin die endzeitliche Kirche repräsentieren, aber sie war nicht mehr mit ihr identisch. Die eine Kirche aus Heiden und Juden war nun zum endzeitlichen Heilsgut geworden. Erscheinung und Verwirklichung dieser Kirche lagen nicht mehr in der Gegenwart, sondern in der Zukunft; sie waren zusammen mit der Wiederkehr Jesu Christi und dem Anbruch der Gottesherrschaft zu erwarten.

Die antiochenische Mission

Die Gemeinde in Antiochien war zu dieser Zeit noch von Charismatikern – Propheten und Lehrern – geleitet. Einige darunter wurden durch die Anerkennung der Urgemeinde und das Vorbild ihrer Organisation veranlaßt, die Ausbreitung des Christentums in die Diaspora zu ihrer Aufgabe zu machen. Man war überzeugt, das Ende der Zeit und das Gottesreich könnten nicht kommen, bevor das Evangelium der ganzen Welt verkündigt war. Wenn man sich entschloß, die Werbung zunächst auf Zypern und im südlichen Kleinasien aufzunehmen, so wird die Zielsetzung auf die beiden Missionare zurückgehen, die man mit dem Vorhaben betraute. Barnabas stammte aus Zypern, Paulus aus Tarsus in Kilikien. Man wußte zudem, da das Christentum auch über Zypern nach Antiochien gekommen war, daß es auf der Insel Christen gab, die aber in keiner organisatorischen Beziehung zur antiochenischen Gemeinde standen.

Zudem hatte das Christentum in Antiochien eine Fortentwicklung gegenüber dem älteren hellenistischen Christentum erfahren, das auf der Insel vertreten war. In Antiochien war man dazu übergegangen, die von allen Christen erwartete Wiederkehr des auferstandenen Herrn als Ankunft des Messias zu deuten, in dem man den Führer bei der Heimkehr der Zerstreuten sah. Die neue Deutung fand in einem neuen Bekenntnis zu Jesus als dem »Messias, dem Sohn des lebendigen Gottes« ihren charakteristischen Ausdruck. Das ältere hellenistische Christentum war mit der Deutung Jesu als Gottesknecht ausgekommen. Diesem älteren hellenistischen Christentum ist auch der, seinem Namen nach aus Libyen stammende Prophet Elymas – Bar Jesus zuzurechnen, der auf Zypern missionierte. Der Zusammenstoß der antiochenischen Missionare mit ihm ist, nach dem Bericht der Apostelgeschichte durch die unterschiedliche Deutung der Person Jesu veranlaßt. (Zum Verständnis der Stelle ist zu berücksichtigen, daß »Weg Gottes« in der Apostelgeschichte eine technische Bezeichnung für die Deutung der Person Jesu ist, daß Lukas, ähnlich wie Josephus, die von ihm abgelehnten Propheten »Zauberer« nennt, und daß Elymas einen Prophetennamen als Beinamen trägt.)

Die Heftigkeit des Zusammenstoßes zwischen Elymas und den antiochenischen Missionaren verlangt eine Erklärung. Lukas hat sie in der Eifersucht des Elymas auf die Gunst des Prokonsuls und seinem Festhalten an der älteren Jesusdeutung gesehen. Wahrscheinlicher ist ein anderer Grund, nämlich daß Elymas mit dem antiochenischen Bekenntnis auch Primatsansprüche der antiochenischen Gemeinde zurückwies. Als Apollos hernach in den Dienst der paulinischen Mission trat, mußte er eben dieses antiochenische Bekenntnis übernehmen. Gegen seinen Inhalt war kaum etwas einzuwenden; gegenüber der älteren hellenistischen Jesusdeutung stellte es eine Bereicherung dar. Elymas mußte aber befürchten, mit der Übernahme der antiochenischen Gemeinde eine ähnliche Bedeutung zuzuerkennen, wie sie die Urgemeinde für die Juden in Palästina besaß. So wies er die Gemeinschaft mit den Sendboten aus Antiochien zurück. Die Arbeit des Paulus und Barnabas auf Zypern hat man sich ebenso vorzustellen, wie sie hernach für Pisidien und Lykaonien mitgeteilt wird: sie predigten, gründeten Gemeinden und setzten in ihnen Leiter ein, die in der Apostelgeschichte Presbyter heißen, weil die Nachfolger der Apostel grundsätzlich Presbyter sind.

Das Problem, wessen Autorität die neugegründeten Gemeinden unterstanden, scheint sich erst auf oder nach der ersten Missionsreise gestellt zu haben. Paulus hat auch in Syrien und Kilikien missioniert, hat aber über die Gemeinden dort keine Autorität beansprucht, weil sie nicht von ihm gegründet waren. Ebenso scheint er Zypern ohne eigene Autoritätsansprüche dem Barnabas überlassen zu haben, weil er die Insel als dessen Missionsgebiet ansah. Dafür betrachtete er die Gemeindegründungen in Pisidien und Lykaonien als sein Werk, für das er sich zuständig glaubte. Als es hernach zum Streit mit Barnabas kam, ließ er diesen so nach Zypern gehen, wie er selber sich für das südliche Kleinasien entschied. Es könnte sein, daß die antiochenische Gemeinde den Primat auch über diese Gemeinden beanspruchte, weil sie von Barnabas und Paulus gemeinsam in ihrem Auftrag gegründet waren. Die sogenannte »südgalatische Hypothese« über die Adressaten des Galaterbriefs ist zwar in einem andern Zusammenhang entworfen, könnte aber durch die vorgetragene Überlegung eine Stütze erfahren.

Die Verselbständigung der paulinischen Mission

Die Frage, ob der antiochenischen Gemeinde der Primat über die von hier aus gegründeten Gemeinden zustand, scheint nicht von Anfang an abgesprochen, sondern erst nachträglich erkannt worden zu sein. Die antiochenische Gemeinde sah jedenfalls die Mission in der Diaspora, in den Ländern der Heiden, grundsätzlich als ihre Aufgabe an, mit der sie neben die auf die Werbung unter den Juden in Palästina beschränkte Urgemeinde trat. Die stand inzwischen der Heidenmission ebenfalls nicht mehr völlig ablehnend gegenüber. Es gab Grund genug, die Missionsaufgaben gegeneinander abzugrenzen. Nach einigen Auseinandersetzungen über die Tischgemeinschaft zwischen gesetzesstrengen Judenchristen, gesetzeslaxen Judenchristen und Heidenchristen begaben sich Paulus und Barnabas als Vertreter der antiochenischen Mission nach Jerusalem, um mit den Führern der Urgemeinde die wichtigsten Fragen zu klären: die Verpflichtung der Heidenchristen durch das Gesetz und die Abgrenzung der Missionsaufgaben. Grundsätzlich einigte man sich dahin, daß die Mission unter den Juden von Jerusalem, unter den Heiden von Antiochien aus betrieben werden solle. Ungeklärt blieb jedoch die Frage, ob die Missionierung der Juden in der Diaspora Jerusalemer oder antiochenische Aufgabe sei. Desgleichen blieben unterschiedliche Auffassungen über die Reinheitsvorschriften bestehen, die Juden- und Heidenchristen den Umgang mit einander ermöglichen sollten. Paulus sah sich mit seiner Verkündigung eines gesetzesfreien Evangeliums an die Heiden darum veranlaßt, sein Missionsunternehmen von Antiochien zu lösen und zu verselbständigen. Er wählte Kleinasien, wo er seine Arbeit erfolgreich begonnen hatte, als Missionsgebiet und schuf sich in Ephesus einen Missionsstützpunkt. Das Christentum war nicht erst durch ihn in die Stadt gekommen, aber er konnte sich hier eine Basis für die Weiterführung seiner Arbeit schaffen. Von hier aus reiste er zunächst nach Antiochien und Jerusalem, vermutlich, um die Geltung der Absprache zwischen beiden Gemeinden auf seine eigene Unternehmung auszudehnen und sich bestätigen zu lassen.

Aus der Wahl von Ephesus als Basis ergab sich zuerst das westliche Kleinasien als Bereich der paulinischen Mission. Danach dehnte der Apostel sein Unternehmen auf Makedonien und Achaia aus. Später, von den Pastoralbriefen an, wurde auch Kreta dem paulinischen Missionsgebiet zugerechnet. So stellten die Länder um die Ägäis den Missionsbezirk des Paulus dar. Wir wissen nicht, ob diese Erweiterung zu Lebzeiten des Paulus oder erst nach seinem Tod Platz gegriffen hat. Es könnte sein, daß für die Abrundung ein Mann veantwortlich ist, der stärker als der Apostel griechisch empfand und die Länder um die Ägäis als Einheit ansah.

Die Briefe des Paulus reden von der Autorität, die er über die von ihm gegründeten Gemeinden beanspruchte. Er mußte sich aber damit auseinandersetzen, daß das Christentum schon vor ihm sich entlang der Verkehrswege in sein Missionsgebiet ausgebreitet hatte und weiterhin unabhängig von seiner Bemühung ausbreitete. In Ephesos fand er Reste des älteren hellenistischen Christentums vor (die von uns häufig »Johannesjünger« genannt werden, weil Lukas ihre Taufe durch seine Vorstellung von der Vorläufigkeit der Johannestaufe erklärt.) Der wahre Unterschied lag jedoch im Taufbekenntnis; die Jünger kannten noch nicht das antiochenisch-paulinische Taufbekenntnis zu Jesus als dem Messias. Ebenso mußte Apollos, der aus Alexandrien nach Ephesos gekommen war und bis dahin nur die ältere Jesusdeutung der Hellenisten kennengelernt hatte, zuerst für das paulinische Christentum und das paulinische Christusbekenntnis gewonnen werden. – Noch stärker wirkte sich die spontane Ausbreitung des Christentums in Korinth aus, wie Ephesus einer Hafenstadt mit starkem Verkehr. Der Anteil der Christen, die ihren Glauben nicht dem Apostel Paulus verdankten, war erheblich. So kommt es zum Parteienstreit, zur Anfechtung der Autorität des Paulus aus der Gemeinde und zu der energischen Verteidigung, die uns im zweiten Korintherbrief erhalten ist. Zur Aufrechterhaltung seiner Autorität hatte Paulus mit der Versendung von Hirtenbriefen begonnen und diese Literaturgattung dadurch ins Leben gerufen. Die Gefangenschaft am Ende seines Lebens hinderte ihn am Besuch seiner Gemeinden, ließ ihm aber die Möglichkeit, durch Briefe Einfluß auf ihre Leitung zu nehmen. Versendung und Inhalt dieser Briefe wurden als charakteristische Äußerungen des Apostels empfunden. Die unter dem Namen des Paulus von andern geschriebene Briefliteratur zeigt als Meinung ihrer Verfasser, daß Paulus seine Briefe schrieb, um seine Autorität in seinem Missionsgebiet aufrecht zu erhalten.

Innerhalb der unter dem Namen des Paulus gehenden Literatur ändert sich die Vorstellung des Apostels vom geistlichen Amt und von der Bedeutung, die er für die Gemeinden in seinem Missionsgebiet besitzt. Von Anfang an besteht für ihn das regelmäßige geistliche Amt aus der Trias der Apostel, Propheten und Lehrer. Diese Ämter fand er im Alten Testament und deutete dies als Weissagungen auf die endzeitliche Gemeinde und damit als verbindliche Vorschrift für ihre Gestalt. Wie die endzeitliche Kirche nur aus einer einzigen Gemeinde besteht, sind ihre Ämter gesamtkirchliche, nicht einer Einzelgemeinde zugeordnete Ämter. Ihre Funktion ist, daß sie die Kirche erbauen, ihre Glieder vor der endzeitlichen Versuchung bewahren und ins vollendete Gottesreich geleiten. Das regelmäßige charismatische Amt ist somit eine Veranstaltung Gottes, nicht das Ergebnis menschlichen Organisationstalents. Die institutionellen Ämter, die die Ortsgemeinden tatsächlich verwalten, haben keine vergleichbare Begründung und gelten dem Paulus als dementsprechend zufällig. Diese Sicht der Dinge bringt er im ersten Korintherbrief dadurch zum Ausdruck, daß er die Bischöfe und Diakone nicht bei ihrem Amtstitel nennt, sondern sie als »Regierer und Helfer« in der Wolke von Charismen sucht, durch die der Heilige Geist die Gemeinden leitet und durch die Christen einander dienen. Eine Änderung bringt der Philipperbrief, gegen Lebensende geschrieben, in dem Paulus mit der Möglichkeit rechnet, daß sein Tod dem Ende zuvorkommen könne. So berücksichtigt er in der Adresse die tatsächlich vorhandenen Bischöfe und Diakone. Danach sind im Epheserbrief die Gemeindeämter feste Institutionen, und in den Pastoralbriefen ist die institutionelle Trias von Bischof, Presbytern und Diakonen etabliert.

Von seinem Amtsverständnis aus fiel es Paulus schwer, seine Bedeutung für die von ihm gegründeten Gemeinden zu artikulieren. Sein Apostolat bezog sich auf die ganze Kirche, und die geistliche Vaterschaft, die ihn mit seinen Gemeinden verband, war eine persönliche Beziehung und keine Institution. Epheserbrief und Pastoralbriefe setzen hingegen einen Apostel voraus, der die Leitung seines Missionsgebietes als festes Amt versteht, seine Amtsaufgaben auf Schüler und Assistenten delegiert und so seine Kirchenprovinz einrichtet. Die Sicht des Lukas in der Apostelgeschichte zeigt da keinen grundsätzlichen Unterschied. Als Paulus in Milet von den Presbytern Abschied nimmt, ist Ephesos als Vorort der Gemeinden in der Asia verstanden; die Vorsteher (»Bischöfe«) dieser Kirche sind die ephesinischen Presbyter. Für die Apostelgeschichte ist Ephesus der Vorort einer Kirchenprovinz, die Paulus eingerichtet und geleitet hat. Vor den Bischöfen dieser Provinz leistet er darum auch seinen Rechenschaftsbericht und übergibt ihnen sein geistliches Vermächtnis.

Die Anfänge des römischen Primates

Für die zweite Hälfte des ersten Jahrhunderts weist unsere Kenntnis der Kirchengeschichte eine Lücke von mehr als einem Menschenalter auf. Die Nachrichten von der Urgemeinde enden vor dem Ausbruch des jüdischen Krieges. Die spärlichen Andeutungen über Christen und Christentum in Ägypten sind nicht datierbar. Über Syrien und Kleinasien herrscht Schweigen. Am auffälligsten, wenn auch erklärbar, ist das Fehlen von Nachrichten über die römische Gemeinde. Mit der neronischen Verfolgung, von der uns nur heidnische Quellen Einzelheiten mitteilen, reißen die Nachrichten ab und setzen erst nach der Zeit Domitians wieder ein. Nach der domitianischen Verfolgung ist der Clemensbrief geschrieben. Er stellt uns vor die Frage, warum ihn die römische Gemeinde geschrieben und darin der korinthischen autoritative Weisung erteilt hat, und warum sich die Korinther dieser Weisung gefügt haben.

Das Briefpräskript gibt einen Hinweis. Der Apostel Paulus hat in seinen Briefen das übliche Präskript auf eine eigentümliche Weise um Bestandteile erweitert, durch die er sich als Sendboten Jesu Christi bezeichnete, um seine Autorität von dem Herrn herzuleiten, der ihn gesandt und beauftragt hatte. Dieses Präskript wird hernach von allen Verfassern geistlicher Briefe nachgeahmt, die sich dem Apostel verpflichtet glauben, und vor allem von denen, die seine Autorität fordern. Dies ist im Clemensbrief der Fall. Die römische Gemeinde verlangt mit der Zusendung des Briefes die Autorität über die korinthische Gemeinde, die Paulus einst besessen hatte. Der Anspruch findet seine Begründung durch die Theorie des geistlichen Amtes, die in dem Brief entfaltet und auf das Verhältnis der römischen zur korinthischen Gemeinde angewandt wird. Ebenso wie das in der deuteropaulinischen Literatur geschieht, deutet der Verfasser die Leitung der Gemeinden im paulinischen Missionsgebiet als institutionelles Amt. Der Brief führt aus, daß Gott das geistliche Amt gestiftet und Jesus Christus damit betraut habe; der habe seine Apostel ausgesandt, und die hätten in den Gemeinden ihre Vertreter und deren Nachfolger eingesetzt. – Paulus hat während seiner Gefangenschaft seine Gemeinden beaufsichtigt und durch Briefe geleitet, und diese Aufgabe kommt nun in der Nachfolge des Apostels der römischen Gemeinde zu. Aus dem Hirten des Hermas erfahren wir, daß es das Amt eines römischen Christen – eines Presbyters nach der Terminologie des Hermas – namens Clemens ist, die Korrespondenz mit den auswärtigen Gemeinden zu führen, und der Clemensbrief hat seinen Namen davon, daß die Überlieferung seine Abfassung einem römischen Bischof Clemens zuschreibt.

Die Korinther haben der römischen Gemeinde diese von ihr beanspruchte Autorität zugestanden. Dionysios von Korinth, der selber geistliche Autorität im paulinischen Missionsgebiet in Anspruch nimmt, teilt uns (um 170) mit, daß die Korinther den Clemensbrief in Ehren gehalten und liturgisch gebraucht haben (Eus.h.e. 4,23). Er deutet allerdings dabei auch an, daß die Liebesgaben der römischen Gemeinde den Korinthern die Anerkennung ihrer Autorität erleichtert haben. Dionysios zeigt uns, daß er das paulinische Missionsgebiet, wie es die Pastoralbriefe voraussetzen, als Einheit empfand. In seiner eigenen Sammlung katholischer Briefe hat er sich an dessen Grenzen gehalten; zwei Briefe sind nach Achaia, zwei nach Kleinasien und zwei nach Kreta gerichtet, und der siebte Brief ist ein Römerbrief. Die Briefe des Dionysios fallen in die Zeit zwischen den beiden Osterstreitigkeiten, in denen die römische Gemeinde als ihr Recht verlangte, den Kleinasiaten Datum und Art der Osterfeier vorzuschreiben. (Später dienen Osterfestbriefe nicht nur dazu, das Datum der Osterfeier bekanntzugeben, sondern vor allem, oberhirtliche Autorität zu demonstrieren). Im zweiten Osterstreit berief sich der römische Bischof Victor auf die Autorität der Apostel Petrus und Paulus, um seine Weisungsrechte gegenüber den Kleinasiaten zu begründen. Wir erfahren das aus dem Antwortschreiben des Polykrates von Ephesus. Polykrates verweist in seiner Antwort aber nicht auf die eigenen Paulustraditionen seiner Gemeinde, sondern auf Johannes, den zweiten Apostel, der in Ephesus gewirkt hatte. Man sieht daraus, daß die Gemeinden in Kleinasien der römischen Gemeinde die Begründung ihrer Autorität auf der des Paulus zugestanden haben. Ihre besondere Überlieferung war durch ihre johanneischen Traditionen besser zu begründen, weil das Recht der Römer, sich auf Paulus zu berufen, unanfechtbar war.

Die Gemeinden in Kleinasien

Paulus hatte die Leitung der Gemeinden in seinem Missionsbezirk nicht als institutionelles Amt verstanden. Jedoch ist in Rom daraus ein übergemeindliches Leitungsamt der römischen Gemeinde geworden, lang bevor ein monarchischer römischer Bischof dieses Amt für sich forderte. Jerusalem, Antiochien und Rom sind sämtlich Vororte von Gemeindeverbänden; doch sind die Primatsansprüche auf unterschiedliche Weise zustandegekommen. Die Urgemeinde war ursprünglich die einzige Gemeinde; ihre Leitungsaufgaben verblieben bei ihr, als neben ihr ein von ihr unabhängiges Christentum entstand. Nach dem Vorbild Jerusalems nahm Antiochien als Muttergemeinde die Aufsicht über die von ihr aus gegründeten Tochtergemeinden in Anspruch. Die römische Gemeinde geht hingegen von dem Gedanken aus, daß ein übergemeindliches Leitungsamt zum Wesen der Kirche gehöre, von den Aposteln ausgeübt und von Paulus auf sie gekommen sei. Gut ein Jahrhundert nach dem Clemensbrief hat die römische Gemeinde diese Vorstellung erweitert; sie beruft sich nicht nur auf Paulus, sondern noch mehr auf Petrus und beansprucht den Primat über alle Gemeinden, die mit Petrus verwandt sind, nämlich wie Kinder mit ihren Eltern. – Im übrigen dürften die römischen Ansprüche auch von dem hauptstädtischen Bewußtsein in einem zentralistisch verwalteten Staat und dem Empfinden für die sakrale Bedeutung Roms unterstützt worden sein.

In Kleinasien ist die Entwicklung einen ganz anderen Weg gegangen. Die Gemeinden bleiben gleichrangig; die Begründung durch einen Apostel oder sein Wirken geben der Gemeinde keine Prärogative. Ephesus genießt unter den Gemeinden in der Asia das größte Ansehen. Sein Bischof kann – wie Polykrates – als Sprecher aller Gemeinden auftreten. Aber daneben ist es möglich, daß ein anderer, beispielsweise Polykarp von Smyrna, für alle das Wort ergreift und in ihrem Namen und Auftrag mit dem römischen Bischof verhandelt. Man kann vermuten, diese Verfassung sei der bürgerlichen Verfassung der Städte nachgebildet, die gewohnt waren, ihre Angelegenheiten auf einem Landtag gemeinsam zu ordnen. Nötig ist die Annahme nicht, so wenig, wie sich der römische Primat vollständig auf die Bedeutung der Stadt Rom für das Reich zurückführen läßt.

In den Sendschreiben der Offenbarung finden wir zum ersten Mal – es sei denn, daß die Apostelgeschichte mit dem Abschied des Paulus in Milet älter ist – die Gemeinden in der Asia als Einheit zusammengefaßt. Wenn es gerade sieben sind, dann darum, weil die Apokalypse durch die Siebenzahl Vollständigkeit ausdrückt. Später ist man dazu übergegangen, durch Zusammenstellung von sieben Briefen zu einem Corpus Vollständigkeit und allgemeine Geltung auszudrücken; die Sendschreiben können das Vorbild für diese Sitte abgegeben haben. Man darf jedenfalls aus der Siebenzahl nicht schließen, es habe in der Asia nur sieben, oder nur sieben rechtgläubige Gemeinden gegeben; vielmehr handelt es sich um ein Stilelement.

Die Gemeinden haben an ihrer Spitze einen Angelos, an den die Briefe gerichtet sind. Man sieht dem Wort allein nicht an, ob es sich um einen himmlischen oder irdischen Beauftragten Gottes handelt. Aber die bisweilen vertretene Annahme, Christus habe durch einen menschlichen Propheten einen Brief an einen himmlischen Engel geschrieben, ist absurd; der Angelos ist ein Beamter der Gemeinde, und der Brief behandelt ihn als den leitenden und verantwortlichen Beamten. Fünfzehn oder zwanzig Jahre danach haben – sagt Ignatius – die Gemeinden Bischöfe an ihrer Spitze. Man wird darum in dem Angelos den Bischof der Gemeinde zu sehen haben. Wenn der Verfasser der Sendschreiben ihn mit einem Amtstitel nennt, der auf seinen Verkündigungsauftrag und nicht seinen Verwaltungsauftrag hinweist und darüber hinaus im Alten Testament begegnet, so erinnert man sich, daß auch Paulus Bedenken hatte, von den Bischöfen als Bischöfen zu sprechen, und daß es für die Gemeinden der Didache nicht selbstverständlich ist, daß die Bischöfe ein geistliches Amt versehen.

Der Verfasser der Sendschreiben versteht sich als einen Propheten, den Christus mit einem gemeinsamen Auftrag an die sieben Gemeinden gesandt hat. Er bezeichnet sich nicht als Propheten; das tut kein wahrer Prophet. Stattdessen berichtet er, um sich auszuweisen, wie die alttestamentlichen Propheten von seiner Berufung. Das gemeinsame Anliegen aller Briefe ist die Warnung vor Synkretismus, vor Nachlässigkeit im Umgang mit dem heidnischen Kult. Die Gefahr droht den Gemeinden durch Apostel, die sich selber so nennen und darum keine sind (Paulus ist nicht von allen Briefverfassern als Vorbild angesehen worden), durch eine Prophetin, die ebenfalls von sich behauptet, eine zu sein und darum keine sein kann, und durch die Nikolaiten. Die alle verführen die Gemeinden dazu, Götzenopfer zu essen und zu huren, das heißt, sich auf Kompromisse mit dem heidnischen Kult einzulassen. Der Name »Nikolaiten« kann sich nur auf den Proselyten Nikolaos aus Antiochien beziehen, einen der Sieben; die Urgemeinde dürfte gegen ihn dieselbe Abneigung gehabt haben, wie der Verfasser der Sendschreiben gegen die Nikolaiten.

Der Titel, mit dem er sich einführt, ist »Adelphos kai Koinonos«. Damit drückt er aus, daß er keinen höheren Rang als die Adressaten beansprucht und daß er ihnen gemeinsam und gleichmäßig zugeordnet ist. Daß er Charismatiker ist und deshalb Autorität fordert, sagt er durch seinen Auftrag. Sein Dienst gilt weder einer einzelnen Gemeinde, noch allen überhaupt, sondern den Gemeinden in der Asia. Er hält sich in keiner der Gemeinden auf, an die er schreibt; man kann ihm glauben, daß er sich zum Empfang seiner Visionen auf die Insel Patmos begeben hat.

Die Sendschreiben entwerfen das Bild einer Kirche, die im Übergang von der charismatischen zur institutionellen Leitung steht. Die Führung der einzelnen Gemeinden liegt in den Händen des institutionellen Amts, aber ein Charismatiker erteilt ihnen gemeinsam Weisungen. Dieser Charismatiker befindet sich nicht auf der Wanderschaft, aber in der Einöde; beide Lebensweisen können als gleichwertig angesehen werden. Er setzt voraus, daß er den Gemeinden bekannt ist, und fordert Gehör. Eine ähnliche Situation besteht auch für den Verfasser des zweiten und dritten Johannesbriefs. Er ist ein außerhalb der Gemeinde lebender Charismatiker und gibt sich den Amtstitel »Apostelschüler« (Presbyter). Allerdings hat er erfahren müssen, daß seine Briefe nicht angenommen werden und seine Autorität damit abgelehnt wird. Aber wer weiß, ob der Verfasser der Sendschreiben bei den Gemeinden in der Asia Anerkennung seiner Autorität gefunden hat!

An Gemeinden in der Asia hat ebenfalls Ignatius geschrieben. Vier der sieben Ignatiusbriefe sind an Orte adressiert, an die sich auch die Sendschreiben gewandt hatten. Die Situation der Gemeinden ist so ähnlich, daß die 15 bis 20 Jahre Abstand zwischen der Apokalypse und Ignatius eher zu viel als zu wenig scheinen; vielleicht sind die Sendschreiben in der Zeit des Ignatius nachträglich vor den Hauptteil der Apokalypse gesetzt worden. An der Spitze der Gemeinden, an die sich Ignatius wendet, stehen Bischöfe, und Ignatius schreibt in erster Linie, um die bischöfliche Monarchie für die allein zulässige Gemeindeverfasung zu erklären. Das ist sehr früh für seine Zeit, selbst wenn die Entwicklung der Verfassung in Antiochien weiter gediehen gewesen sein sollte als in der übrigen Kirche; Grund genug, Rius-Camps Interpolationshypothesen ernst zu nehmen. In jedem Fall gewinnt man aus den Briefen den Eindruck, der Zustand, den der Verfasser anstrebt, sei in der Asia noch lange nicht erreicht.

Ignatius schreibt nicht als Bischof von Syrien in die Asia, denn dahin erstreckt sich seine bischöfliche Autorität nicht. Er macht allerdings den vorsichtigen Versuch, die Gemeinden von Philadelphia und Smyrna zur Entsendung eines Diakons nach Antiochien und damit zur Anerkennung des antiochenischen Primates zu bewegen. Aber sein Epheserbrief an die Symmysten des Paulus zeigt wenig Hoffnung, Autoritätsansprüche in Kleinasien auf Institution und Tradition zu begründen.

Die Begründung liefert ihm sein Charisma. Das Märtyrercharisma besitzt er zweifelsfrei; es sichert ihm Gehör in Rom und Ephesus, den Gemeinden, die am wenigsten geneigt sind, eine auswärtige Autorität anzuerkennen. Ignatius will aber dem Umstand Rechnung tragen, daß in einigen Gemeinden nur die Prophetie und nicht das Bischofsamt Ansehen genießt. So deutet er sein Recht, den Gemeinden Weisung zu erteilen, durch den Beinamen »Theophoros« an, den er an Stelle eines Amtstitels in der Intitulatio seiner Briefe anbringt. Der Name besagt, daß der Schreiber des Briefes Träger des Heiligen Geistes ist und für ihn Autorität fordert. Wer sich Theophoros nennt, der deutet damit an, daß er das prophetische Charisma besitzt, sagt aber, als wahrer Prophet, nicht von sich selber, daß er ein Prophet sei. Der Heilige Geist, der durch Ignatius als Propheten spricht, tritt nicht für die Gemeindeleitung durch das Prophetenamt, sondern durch die bischöfliche Monarchie ein. In jeder Gemeinde gibt es einen Bischof; der soll die Leitung ausüben. Die Alternative der Gemeindeleitung durch Propheten oder durch den Bischof hat hernach zum montanistischen Schisma geführt. Zwischen Ignatius und dem Schisma liegen nach den überlieferten Daten zwei Generationen. Doch konnte der Gegensatz zwischen Charisma und Institution zu jeder Zeit der Kirchengeschichte aufbrechen. In jedem Fall zeigen die Briefe, daß die Verfassung der adressierten Gemeinden sich im Übergang vom Charisma zur Institution befand.

Was aber hat den Ignatius veranlaßt, gerade an die Gemeinden in der Asia zu schreiben? Er ist auf dem Landweg durch Kleinasien gereist, und das Land war vom Christentum durchdrungen. Auch vorher schon, bevor er auf dem Weg von Antiochien in die Asia kam, müßte er durch christliche Gemeinden gekommen sein. Warum hat er nicht an diese geschrieben? – Der Grund läßt sich nur vermuten. Am wahrscheinlichsten ist, daß er dort kein Gehör gefunden hätte, wenigstens nicht für sein Hauptanliegen, die Durchsetzung der bischöflichen Monarchie. Bischöfe gab es in jeder Gemeinde, weil jede bereits wegen der Eucharistiefeier und der Armenpflege Einkünfte zu verwalten hatte. Doch können die Bischöfe östlich der Asia derart ausschließlich untergeordnete Verwaltungsbeamte gewesen sein, daß es nicht denkbar war, für sie die Gemeindeleitung zu fordern. Der Montanismus ist östlich der Asia in Phrygien entstanden und in Gemeinden, die wohl Bischöfe besaßen, aber in ihnen nicht ihre Leiter sahen.

Der monarchische Episkopat hat sich nicht in der Zeit des Ignatius oder unmittelbar danach durchgesetzt. Antiochien kann dabei vorangegangen sein, weil Mangel an Charismatikern und Akzentuierung der Eucharistiefeier hier die Gemeindeleitung den Bischöfen zuwies, und weil die Gemeinde die Heidenmission nach dem organisatorischen Vorbild der Urgemeinde in Angriff nahm und darum die Aufsicht über die Tochtergemeinden anstrebte. – Im Westen haben sich in Rom, vielleicht nach syrischem Vorbild, mit der Entstehung der altkatholischen Kirche ähnliche Verhältnisse herausgebildet. Der monarchische Bischof erlangt nicht nur die Leitung seiner Gemeinde, sondern zugleich der zuvor entstandenen, von der hauptstädtischen Gemeinde beaufsichtigten Kirchenprovinz. – Vom Ende des zweiten Jahrhunderts an kann man auch Ägypten zum Vergleich heranziehen. Hier steht der Primat des hauptstädtischen Bischofs über die Gemeinden von der Formierung der katholischen Kirche an im allgemeinen – sehen wir von der Kyrenaika ab – nicht in Frage. Aber der Bischof hat bis ins vierte Jahrhundert hinein Mühe, der alexandrinischen Presbyter Herr zu werden. Seine Monarchie ist nicht durch die Bischöfe in der Provinz, sondern durch die Kleriker in der Hauptstadt in Frage gestellt. Charismatiker im eigentlichen Sinn, deren Autorität mit der des Bischofs konkurrieren konnte, spielen hier keine Rollc. Statt ihrer befriedigten Asketen die Bedürfnisse der Frömmigkeit, und sie erhoben keinen Anspruch auf die Leitung der Kirche. Überall geht die Entwicklung der Gemeindeverfassung und der übergemeindlichen Verbände Hand in Hand. Nicht der Kampf gegen die Gnostiker treibt sie voran, sondern die Ausscheidung des Montanismus.

Die montanistische Verfassung

Die bischöfliche Monarchie ist vom Montanismus als Neuerung bekämpft worden. Im Kampf gegen die Gnosis ergab sich für die kirchlichen Gemeinden die Notwendigkeit, Merkmale der Katholizität zu suchen und sich in diesen Merkmalen aneinander anzupassen. Als solche Merkmale fanden sich die im Taufbekenntnis formulierte Regula fidei und die bischöfliche Monarchie. Nach der Mitte des zweiten Jahrhunderts reisen Christen aus dem Osten nach Rom, um sich der Übereinstimmung ihrer Tradition mit der römischen zu vergewissern, und solche Vergleiche konnten zu Anpassungen und Korrekturen führen. So reiste Hegesipp nach Rom, um die Diadoche in der Leitung der römischen Gemeinde seit den Aposteln zwar nicht auf-, aber doch festzustellen. Was er »angefertigt« hat, wird eine Abschrift der römischen Liste gewesen sein. Irenaeus und Tertullian deuten beide an, daß die römische Tradition als Norm diente. Die Angleichungen mußten nicht völlige Übereinstimmung zur Folge haben. Polykarp von Smyrna sah keinen Grund, die Osterpraxis der römischen Kirche zu übernehmen. Nur in der Regula fidei scheint man zu wirklicher Übereinstimmung gekommen zu sein. Wenn Irenaeus behauptet, man werde Übereinstimmung finden, wenn man den Glauben aller katholischen Gemeinden mit einander vergleiche, so ist er seiner Sache darum sicher, weil man solche Vergleichungen tatsächlich vorgenommen hat.

Bei diesen Anpassungen erhielt auch die Vereinheitlichung der Gemeindeverfassung einen kräftigen Impuls. Doch haben die altkatholischen Väter noch nicht die bischöfliche Monarchie, sondern die lückenlose Sukzession seit den Aposteln als Argument der Katholizität angeführt. Der erste, der den Zusammenhang zwischen der bischöflichen Gemeindeverfassung und der Katholizität herausgearbeitet hat, war Cyprian; die altkatholischen Väter stehen dem monarchischen Episkopat eher indifferent gegenüber; als Verteidiger der bischöflichen Monarchie lassen sie sich nicht ansehen.

Die Bischöfe erscheinen beim montanistischen Schisma zum ersten Mal als Vertreter der Kirche in der Geschichte. Der Kampf gegen den Montanismus wird ganz überwiegend von Bischöfen geführt. Die Männer, die zur Feder greifen, sind größtenteils Bischöfe. Sie teilen mit, daß sie von Bischöfen zur Abfassung ihrer Streitschriften aufgefordert und ermutigt werden; sie berichten von Diskussionen, bei denen Bischöfe im Streitgespräch mit den Montanisten auftreten, von Bischofsversammlungen, die der Verständigung und dem Zusammenschluß gegen die Montanisten dienen, und von Bischöfen, die an den montanistischen Prophetinnen Exorzismen versuchen. Eine solche Häufung von Bischöfen hat es bisher noch nicht gegeben; neu ist auch die Hervorhebung ihres Ranges, daß es gerade Bischöfe sind, die in dieser Weise Stellung nehmen. Wie ungewöhnlich eine Konfiguration ist, in der auf der einen Seite nur Bischöfe stehen, auf der andern Seite keine, zeigt der Vergleich mit dem Kampf gegen die Gnosis. Allein ein Bischof ist als Antignostiker hervorgetreten, Irenaeus von Lyon, und der gilt zwar der Überlieferung als Bischof, dürfte aber der bischöflichen Monarchie eher ablehnend gegenüber gestanden haben; sein Eintreten für die Prophetie bedeutet in seiner Zeit ein Eintreten für den Montanismus und gegen die bischöfliche Monarchie.

Wenn man sich in dieser Zeit auf die Tradition beruft, so beruft man sich damit noch nicht auf das Bischofsamt. Die Bischöfe beginnen erst, ihre künftige Rolle als Hüter der Tradition zu übernehmen. Die Montanisten als Verteidiger der älteren Verfassung konnten zeigen, daß zwar nicht das Bischofsamt, wohl aber die bischöfliche Monarchie eine Neuerung war, und daß die Tradition eher für als gegen sie sprach. Es geht dabei nicht um die Frage, ob Bischöfe oder Presbyter die apostolische Überlieferung bewahrt hätten; der Gegensatz ist der zwischen charismatischem und institutionellem Amt. Doch setzt sich im Verlauf der Streitigkeiten der Bischofstitel für das gemeindeleitende Amt durch, und der Presbytertitel verliert in der Großkirche diese Bedeutung. Den Vorgang kann man am Vergleich der Amtstitel beobachten, die Irenaeus von Lyon und Polykrates von Ephesus, beide Kleinasiaten, gebrauchen. Irenaeus redet den römischen Bischof als Presbyter an, gerade um hervorzuheben, daß dieser in der Tradition der Apostel stehe. Polykrates betont, um auf seine eigenen apostolischen Traditionen zu verweisen, daß es sich bei seinen Gewährsleuten und Vorfahren um Bischöfe handelt. Beidemale soll der Amtstitel den Hüter der apostolischen Tradition kennzeichnen. Nach der Ausscheidung des Montanismus wird das leitende Amt nicht mehr mit dem Presbytertitel benannt. Die Presbyter, die es hernach noch in der Kirche gibt, sind die dem Bischof unterstellten Presbyter im Gemeindedienst und die Doctor-Presbyter. Die Montanisten sind im Gebrauch des Titels der Kirche gefolgt.

Die montanistische Krise ist eine der Auseinandersetzungen zwischen charismatischem und institutionellem Amt, wie es sie während der ganzen Geschichte des Glaubens und der Frömmigkeit gegeben hat. Will man für eine ständig schwelende Krise ein Datum nennen, muß man den Zeitpunkt des Aufflammens angeben, nämlich die Zeit, für die Montanus die Herabkunft des himmlischen Jerusalems erwartete und einen neuen Exodus veranstaltete. Dafür sind verschiedene Daten überliefert. Für das frühere Datum könnte die Neigung der kirchlichen Polemik sprechen, die Entstehung von Häresien so spät wie möglich anzunehmen; auch der große Zeitabstand in der Sukzessionsliste der montanistischen Propheten zwischen Quadratus und den Prophetinnen des Montanus könnte das frühere Datum empfehlen. Entscheidend für die Spätdatierung ist jedoch ein anderes Argument. Zur Zeit des Lyoner Martyriums im Jahre 177 war für den römischen Bischof die Aufhebung der Kirchengemeinschaft mit den

Montanisten noch keine beschlossene Sache, und in Karthago scheint sich die Spaltung der Gemeinde in Katholiken und Montanisten erst nach der Jahrhundertwende vollzogen zu haben. So wird das Datum 170/1 festzuhalten sein.

Als Entstehungsort nennen die Montanisten ein Dorf Ardabau oder die Orte Pepuza und Thymion. (Zur Lokalisierung s. A. Strobel, Das heilige Land der Montanisten, RVV 37, 1980). Die antiken Polemiker betonen durchweg die Bedeutungslosigkeit dieser Örtlichkeiten. Ardabau, wo Montanus geboren oder erweckt wurde, gilt als Dorf oder Bauernhof. Pepuza und Thymion sind allenfalls kleine Städte. Auf die Dauer ist von Ardabau und Thymion nicht mehr die Rede. Als Zentrum der montanistischen Bewegung bleibt in der kirchlichen Berichterstattung nur Pepuza übrig, die Ortschaft selber oder ein nahe gelegener Platz, den die Montanisten »Jerusalem« nennen. Der Ort wird regelmäßig als einsam, öde oder wüst angegeben. Thymion läßt sich gar nicht lokalisieren. Der Ortsname verweist wahrscheinlich nur auf die grünen Kräuter des Feldes, auf dem man das himmlische Jerusalem erwartete. Auch Ardabau war kein geographischer, sondern ein mythischer Ortsname für ein Feld, auf dem noch kein Haus gestanden hatte.

Anlaß der montanistischen Unruhen war die Überzeugung, das himmlische Jerusalem werde demnächst sichtbar in Erscheinung treten. Montanus muß selber oder durch Propheten eine Offenbarung empfangen haben, die ihm einen öden Platz bei Pepuza als das Ardabau bezeichnete, wo sich das himmlische Jerusalem offenbaren werde. Somit ist Ardabau nicht zu lokalisieren. Selbst die Suche nach Pepuza ist problematisch. Augustin (haer. 27) zitiert: »Andere sagen schließlich, Pepuza sei keine Stadt, sondern ein Gutshof des Montanus und seiner Prophetinnen gewesen. Weil sie dort gelebt hätten, habe der Ort verdient, Jerusalem zu heißen.« Auszüge aus der Welt, um dem himmlischen Jerusalem entgegenzugehn, folgen in der alten Kirche regelmäßig auf Verfolgungen. Die Mißachtung der trajanischen Regelung des Christenprozesses unter Mark Aurel, die kaina dogmata der Regierung, werden den Auszug unmittelbar veranlaßt haben, den Montanus proklamierte.

In dem Ort, an dem man das himmlische Jerusalem erwartete, fand die Bewegung ihr Zentrum. Um sie zu unterhalten, brauchte man Geld. Der Montanismus war auf die Spenden seiner Anhänger angewiesen. Menschen, die die Bewegung unterstützten, ohne sich persönlich am Auszug zu beteiligen, fanden sich reichlich, zuerst in Phrygien und östlich und westlich davon, in Kappadokien und Asien. Bald breitete sich die Bewegung auch nach Europa aus, nach Makedonien und Thrakien. Später gibt es Montanismus in Africa, Numidien und Gallien. Zum Einsammeln der Spenden wurden Propheten ausgesandt, die zugleich die Nähe der Gottesstadt verkündigten. Die kirchliche Polemik hat – wie zu erwarten – den montanistischen Propheten vorgeworfen, sie hätten Geschenke angenommen und die Beiträge der Anhänger auf Gelagen verpraßt. Doch waren die Spenden für den Unterhalt derer bestimmt, die im Dienste der Bewegung standen. Ein Jahrhundert zuvor waren auch in der Kirche nach Möglichkeit Propheten als Empfänger und Verwalter der Spenden gebraucht worden, die den Armen und Besitzlosen zugedacht waren. Wo es keine Propheten gab, mußten Bischöfe und Diakone an deren Stelle treten.

Bei den Montanisten gab es von Anfang an Bischöfe und Propheten neben einander. Die Gemeinden waren nicht durch Bischöfe geleitet, aber das heißt nicht, daß die Montanisten keine Bischöfe gehabt hätten. Sie bestritten aber den geistlichen Charakter des Bischofsamtes. Geistliche waren bei ihnen die Propheten und die Christen mit prophetischen Fähigkeiten, die Offenbarungen empfangen konnten. Darüber hinaus hatten die Märtyrer geistlichen Rang. Die Martyrien der Lyoner und der Perpetua veranschaulichen die Rangordnung. Dementsprechend rühmen sich die Montanisten der Menge ihrer Märtyrer. »Sie suchen Zuflucht bei ihren Märtyrern und behaupten, die vielen Märtyrer, die sie hätten, seien ein deutlicher Beweis für die Kraft ihres sogenannten prophetischen Geistes« (h. e. 5,16,21).

Später haben die Montanisten ihre Organisation an die der Großkirche angeglichen, haben aber an der Geringschätzung des institutionellen Amtes festgehalten. Die Mißachtung des Bischofsamtes bei den Montanisten wird zum Topos der kirchlichen Ketzerpolemik. Hieronymus kennt ihn, verbindet aber keine Vorstellung damit, wie ein unbeholfener Erklärungsversuch in seinem Brief 41,3 an Marcella zeigt: »Bei uns nehmen die Bischöfe den Platz der Apostel ein; bei ihnen kommt der Bischof an dritter Stelle. Als erste haben sie nämlich die Patriarchen aus Pepusa in Phygien, als zweite diejenigen, die sie Koinonen nennen, und so sinken die Bischöfe auf den dritten, das heißt beinahe den letzten Platz ab.« Wenn die Koinonen der Montanisten den Platz der Metropoliten in der katholischen Kirche einnehmen, dann stehen die Bischöfe in beiden Organisationen an derselben Stelle. – Die Angleichung der montanistischen an die katholische Organisation bezeugt auch ein Gesetz Kaiser Justinians a. d. J. 530 (Cod. Iustiniani ed. Krüger 1,5,20,3): »Besonders wegen der gottlosen Montanisten verkündigen wir, daß keinem ihrer sogenannten Patriarchen, Koinonen, Bischöfe, Presbyter, Diakone oder sonst einem Kleriker – soweit man sie mit diesem Namen überhaupt nennen darf – erlaubt werde, sich in dieser glücklichen Stadt (Konstantinopel) aufzuhalten.«

Es ist nicht allein das bischöfliche, sondern das ganze institutionelle Amt, das bei den Montanisten weniger hoch geschätzt wird als bei der katholischen Kirche; doch fällt der Unterschied beim Bischof besonders deutlich ins Auge. Eine Nachricht des Kirchenhistorikers Sokrates, geschrieben zwischen 440 und 450, hilft uns zu einem deutlicheren Bild. Sie setzt voraus, daß der Bischof der Großkirche seinen Sitz in einer Stadt hat, und die Dörfer der Umgebung zu seinem Sprengel gehören. Die Montanisten haben auch auf den Dörfern Bischöfe (h. e. 7,19,2): »Es ist nicht möglich, in jeder Hinsicht gleiche Überlieferungen zu finden, auch wenn die Menschen denselben Glauben haben. Skythien besteht bekanntlich aus vielen Städten, hat aber nur einen einzigen Bischof. Es gibt aber andere Völker, wo auch in den Dörfern Bischöfe geweiht werden, wie ich das bei den Arabern und Kyprioten erfahren habe und bei den Novatianern und Montanisten in Phrygien.« Arabien, Phrygien und Zypern sind Landschaften, in die sich das Christentum von Anfang an vor jeder organisierten Mission ausgebreitet hatte. Die Gemeinden waren hier durch – möglicherweise wandernde – Charismatiker geistlich versorgt. Für ihre Verwaltungsaufgaben und besonders für die tägliche Eucharistiefeier hatten sie sich aber, wie die Didache es für ähnliche Verhältnisse empfiehlt, Bischöfe gewählt. Die Christen in den genannten Landschaften und besonders die Montanisten in Phrygien waren bei dieser Organisation geblieben, die ihnen gleichermaßen die Abhaltung ihrer Eucharistiefeiern und die Gemeindeleitung durch den Heiligen Geist ermöglichte. Beim Ausbruch des montanistischen Schismas blieben die städtischen Bischöfe der Bewegung fern, während die von Dorfgemeinschaften gewählten und ihnen verantwortlichen Dorfbischöfe mit den Gemeinden an ihrem Herkommen festhielten. – Daß die Montanisten im Bischof in erster Linie den Gemeindebeamten sehen, der für die Eucharistiefeier verantwortlich ist, belegt auch die Rüge, die Bischof Optatus im Perpetuamartyrium erfährt.

Geringschätzung des Bischofsamtes im besonderen und des institutionellen Amtes im allgemeinen zeigen die Lyoner Märtyrer. Ihr uralter Bischof Potheinos, der im Kerker an den Strapazen der Haft stirbt, wird als der bezeichnet, »der mit der Diakonie des Bischofsamtes betraut war«: der Bischof ist in ihren Augen eine Art Diakon, der vor den andern Christen nichts voraushat und weniger bedeutet als die Bekenner, aus denen der Heilige Geist spricht. Dem Irenaeus geben sie ein Empfehlungsschreiben an den römischen Bischof mit und nennen ihn darin: »Presbyter der Kirche«; der Titel ist hier noch als Apostelnachfolger verstanden. Zugleich sprechen sie aber aus, daß sie die institutionelle Seite des Amtes als Belanglosigkeit ansehen.

Der Presbytertitel scheint bei den Montanisten denselben Wandel wie in der katholischen Kirche erfahren zu haben. Sie waren daran nicht besonders interessiert, weil sie das Charisma nicht aus der apostolischen Sukzession herleiteten. Tertullian gilt der Überlieferung als montanistischer Presbyter; damit entsteht ein falsches Bild. Er dürfte bereits in seiner katholischen Zeit Doctor-Presbyter geworden sein und dafür die Presbyterweihe empfangen haben. Daß er den Presbytertitel auch gegen Ende seines Lebens noch in der älteren Bedeutung »Apostelnachfolger« gebrauchen konnte, zeigt sich Pud. 21,5; dort redet er dem Episcopos episcoporum ironisch »Apostolice!« an; zu ergänzen ist nicht ›episcope‹, denn das gab es nicht, sondern ›presbyter‹ (Als apostolischer Herr konnte übrigens nicht der karthagische, sondern nur der römische Bischof angeredet werden.)

Die Geringschätzung des institutionellen Amtes führte dazu, daß es in Kleinasien noch Laienlehrer gab, während sonst die Lehrer in der ersten Häfte des dritten Jahrhunderts in der Regel bereits als Doctor-Presbyter in den Klerus aufgenommen (und der bischöflichen Aufsicht unterstellt) waren. Die Bischöfe Alexander von Jerusalem und Theoktist von Cäsarea suchten nach Präzedenzfällen, um das Predigen des Laien Origenes in ihren Sprengeln zu rechtfertigen (Eus. h. e. 6,19,17–19). Das kam in Ägypten nicht vor, und aus ihren eigenen Diözesen konnten sie ebenfalls nichts beibringen, hingegen ließen sich aus Kleinasien gleich drei Beispiele für diese Praxis anführen.

An der Spitze der montanistischen Kirche steht der in Pepuza residierende Patriarch. Der Titel wird nach katholischem Vorbild entstanden sein. In der Großkirche gibt es seit der zweiten Hälfte des vierten Jahrhunderts oberhalb der Metropoliten, deren Sprengel sich nach der staatlichen Provinzeinteilung richtete, Oberbischöfe, deren Amtsbereich kirchlich-historischen Gesichtspunkten entsprach. Der Titel ist zu Anfang des Jahrhunderts noch nicht in der Kirche üblich, aber das Oberhaupt der Juden wurde schon seit zwei Jahrhunderten Patriarch genannt.

Der erste Leiter der montanistischen Kirche ist Montanus selber. Daß er Neophyt und vorher Kybelepriester gewesen sei, sagt die kirchliche Ketzerpolemik; darauf beruht der Versuch, den Montanismus aus dem phrygischen Kult abzuleiten. Er gilt – der Gedanke lag nah – Katholiken wie Montanisten als Prophet. Dennoch haben ihn die Montanisten nicht in die Sukzessionsliste ihrer Propheten eingeordnet. In der katholischen Kirche entstanden zwischen 160 und 170 Bischofslisten, die die Lückenlosigkeit der Tradition seit den Aposteln nachweisen sollten. Ursprünglich wollte man damit ein Argument gegen die Gnosis gewinnen, doch scheint man das Argument auch in der antimontanistischen Polemik gebraucht zu haben. Die Montanisten wollten ihrerseits zeigen, daß die Kirche von Anfang an Propheten, ebenfalls in lückenloser Sukzession gehabt habe. Sie beriefen sich zunächst auf die im Neuen Testament genannten Propheten, Agabos, Judas/Bar-Sabbas und Silas (Apg 15,32) und dazu die Töchter des Philippos. Von denen hatte man eigene Überlieferung; zwei hatten ihr Grab im phrygischen Hierapolis, das Grab der dritten wurde in Ephesos verehrt. In Kleinasien war man stolz auf sie; Polykrates von Ephesos nannte sie Träger apostolischer Überlieferung. Nach diesen ging der Geist auf die Ammia in Philadelphia über. Die Zeit ihres Wirkens geht daraus hervor, daß weder die Johannesoffenbarung noch Ignatius eine Andeutung von ihr machen, obwohl beide sich für die Prophetie in Philadelphia interessieren. Sie hat somit nach Ignatius – unter Traian und Hadrian – prophezeit. Nach Ammia empfing Quadratus, der eine Apologie an Kaiser Hadrian gerichtet hat, den Prophetengeist. Er muß seine Apologie vor 138 geschrieben haben. Danach geht der Geist auf die Prophetinnen des Montanus über (Eus. h. e. 5,17,4). Das ist ein relativ großer Sprung, und hier wäre Platz für die Einfügung des Montanus in die Liste gewesen. Das ist nicht geschehen; der Antimontanist bei Euseb hätte es uns mitgeteilt, weil er damit den Montanismus hätte diskreditieren können. Montanus hat folglich in der Anfangszeit zwar als Verkünder der Prophetie, aber nicht als Prophet im eigentlichen Sinn gegolten; er ist erst in der Überlieferung dazu geworden.

Wer waren schließlich die montanistischen Koinonen? Bei Hieronymus und Iustinian entsprechen sie den Metropoliten, Oberbischöfen, die ihren Platz zwischen dem Patriarchen und den Bischöfen haben. Dergleichen paßt nicht in die Anfangszeit. Metropoliten gibt es erst seit Nikaia. Betrachtet man den beißenden Spott, mit dem Tertullian den Episcopus episcoporum bedenkt, so erkennt man, wie schlecht sich Oberbischöfe mit der montanistischen Vorstellung vom geistlichen Amt vertragen. – Ihres Namens wegen hat man sie mit der Eucharistie oder der Finanzverwaltung in Zusammenhang gebracht; der Name, meinte man, enthalte einen Hinweis auf die Gemeinschaft am Sakrament oder an den irdischen Gütern. Beides ist unwahrscheinlich. Das Sakrament hat bei den Montanisten geringere Bedeutung als bei den Katholiken, und daß ein dem Bischof an Rang überlegener Gemeindebeamter dazu ausersehen gewesen wäre, die vom Bischof geweihten Apophoreta auszutragen, kann man sich gar nicht vorstellen. Eher könnte man sich denken, die von den Propheten eingesammelten Gaben und Beiträge seien durch ein übergeordnetes geistliches Amt verwaltet worden. Der hätte dann eine Art Oberprophet sein müssen, und wir kommen auf diesem Wege zu einer Art Hierarchie innerhalb des montanistischen Prophetenamtes, die auch nicht viel für sich hat.

Henning Paulsen hat (Die Bedeutung des Montanismus etc., Vigiliae Christianae 32/1978 19–52, speziell 48–50) auf eine Textstelle hingewiesen, an der ein Koinonos mit Namen genannt wird. Irenaeus wird im Empfehlungsschreiben der Lyoner als Adelphos kai Koinonos bezeichnet, und Paulsen fragt dazu, ob damit nicht auf das Koinonenamt hingewiesen werde. Irenaeus gilt der kirchlichen Überlieferung als Bischof von Lyon. Man muß aber im Auge behalten, daß er nie für die bischöfliche Monarchie eingetreten ist. Die Märtyrer nennen »Presbyter« als seinen Amtstitel, und er bezeichnet seinen verehrten Lehrer Polykarp als »apostolischen Presbyter«; wenn er seiner Zeit Sprecher der Kirche Galliens war, so war er damit noch nicht ihr Oberbischof oder Metropolit.

Gelegentlich des Osterstreits fanden allenthalben in der Oikumene Bischofsversammlungen statt, zu denen der römische Bischof Victor aufgerufen hatte. Sie sollten die kirchliche Überlieferung zur Frage des Osterdatums feststellen. Abschriften der Synodalbriefe sind in die Bibliothek von Cäsarea gelangt. Aus Eusebs Referaten und Regesten geht hervor, daß die Bischöfe, die die Antwortschreiben verfaßten, in ihren Provinzen unterschiedliche Autorität genossen. Die Bischöfe von Rom, Korinth, Cäsarea in Palästina und Jerusalem können danach Oberbischöfe gewesen sein. Polykrates von Ephesus wehrt sich gegen eine übergeordnete Autorität seines Amtes, ebenso Palmas von Amastris, der als Senior der Bischöfe von Pontus antwortet. In derselben Weise tritt auch Irenaeus als Sprecher der gallischen Bischöfe auf. Die Bischöfe der Osroene haben sich nicht durch einen einzelnen Amtsbruder vertreten lassen, sondern gemeinsam geantwortet. Insgesamt zeigen sich zwei Typen von Zuordnungen nebeneinander; im einen Fall hierarchische Gliederung der Bischöfe unter einem Oberbischof, im andern Fall Gleichrangigkeit. Der Koinonos könnte damit der Sprecher einer Gruppe gleichrangiger, charismatisch geleiteter Gemeinden gewesen sein. Da die charismatische Gemeindeleitung aus der Kirche verschwand und nur bei den Montanisten erhalten blieb, hat sich auch der Amtstitel des Koinonos nur bei diesen erhalten.

Wenn die Lyoner Märtyrer Irenaeus Adelphos kai Koinonos nannten, so haben sie Apk 1,9 zitiert. In den Apokalypsetext ist an dieser Stelle Koinonos eingedrungen und hat das ältere synkoinonos verdrängt. Man könnte erwägen, ob Ursache der Variante nicht das Amt des Koinonos gewesen sei und ob die Textänderung nicht in Gemeinden vorgenommen wurde, die in Johannes den Koinonos der sieben Gemeinden in der Asia sahen.

Die biblischen Toragebote und die paulinische Ethik

von Andreas Lindemann

(An der Rehwiese 38, 4800 Bielefeld 13)

I.

Die Frage, welche Bedeutung die biblische Tora für das theologische Denken des Paulus besitzt, gehört nach wie vor zu den zentralen Diskussionsthemen neutestamentlicher Exegese[1]. Dabei sind zwei Fragehorizonte sorgfältig voneinander zu unterscheiden: Einmal das Problem des Gesetzes im Kontext der paulinischen Rechtfertigungslehre, also die Frage nach der »soteriologischen« Funktion der Tora; zum andern das Gesetzesproblem im Kontext der Ethik des Apostels, also die Frage nach der »ethisch-moralischen« Bedeutung der Toragebote. Bedeutet das Nein des Paulus zur Tora als Heilsweg zugleich auch, daß die inhaltlichen Forderungen der biblischen Gebote außer Kraft gesetzt sind[2]? Oder trennt der Apostel zwischen der (in Christus an ihr Ende gelangten) Tora als Heilsweg und der (auch für Christen bleibend gültigen) Tora als Quelle der sittlichen Forderungen Gottes[3]?

In der Forschung wird vielfach auf diejenigen paulinischen Aussagen hingewiesen, die positiv von der Geltung des νόμος für Christen spre-

---

[1] Vgl. zuletzt G. Klein, Art. Gesetz. III. Neues Testament, TRE 13, 1984, 58–75 (zu Paulus a.a.O. 64–72); R. Mohrlang, Matthew and Paul. A comparison of ethical perspectives, MSSNTS 48, 1984, vor allem 33–42. Vgl. zur Sache auch U. H. J. Körtner, Rechtfertigung und Ethik bei Paulus. Bemerkungen zum Ansatz paulinischer Ethik, WuD NF 16, 1981, 93–100.

[2] So etwa J. Becker, in: Handbuch der christlichen Ethik 1, 1978, 259: Das Alte Testament sei »seines verbindlichen Charakters als lebensgestaltender Norm entbunden«; eine Durchsicht der paulinischen Mahnungen zeige, daß das Gesetz »nirgends mehr autoritative Norm« ist. Ähnlich V. P. Furnish, Theology and Ethics in Paul, 1968, 33: »Paul never quotes the Old Testament in extenso for the purpose of developing a pattern of conduct«, und er mache ausgesprochen selten Gebrauch vom Dekalog.

[3] So beispielsweise R. Bultmann, Theologie des Neuen Testaments (hg. von O. Merk), [9]1984, 261; vgl. W. Schrage, Die konkreten Einzelgebote in der paulinischen Paränese. Ein Beitrag zur neutestamentlichen Ethik, 1961, 238: »Die Freiheit *vom* Gesetz als Heilsweg ist zugleich eine Freiheit *zum* Gesetz als inhaltlichem Gebot.« Ähnlich E. P. Sanders, Paul and Palestinian Judaism. A Comparison of Patterns of Religion, 1977, 513: Die Norm für das konkrete Verhalten der Christen, paulinisch gesprochen »die Frucht des Geistes«, »coincides materially with the ethical elements of the Old Testament«.

chen[4]: Gal 6,2 (ὁ νόμος τοῦ Χριστοῦ), Röm 3,27 (νόμος πίστεως) und Röm 8,2 (ὁ νόμος τοῦ πνεύματος κτλ.) scheinen von der durch Christus erneuerten Tora zu sprechen; und in Röm 13,8–10 werden sogar einzelne Dekaloggebote ausführlich zitiert. Indem Paulus in Röm 13,10 (und schon zuvor in Gal 5,14) die ἀγάπη zum höchsten ethischen Wert erkläre und indem er dabei ausdrücklich den biblischen Ursprung des Liebesgebots markiere, zeige er, daß für ihn die inhaltlichen Weisungen der Tora nach wie vor uneingeschränkt in Geltung stünden[5]. Die paulinische Kritik an der Toraobservanz beschränke sich also ganz allein auf den Mißbrauch des Gesetzes als eines Mittels zur Selbstrechtfertigung des Menschen; daß das biblische Gebot mit seinen sittlichen Forderungen vom Menschen das Tun des Gotteswillens verlange, stehe für den Apostel außer Frage[6], und er unterstreiche dies dadurch, daß er seine Argumentation ja Heidenchristen gegenüber vortrage[7].

Nun sind natürlich die erwähnten Beobachtungen zu Röm 13,8–10; Gal 5,14 zweifellos zutreffend; die Frage ist aber, ob die daraus gezogenen Konsequenzen richtig sind. Steht es für Paulus wirklich fest, daß die ethischen Normen der Tora unverändert in Geltung stehen, ja, daß sie womöglich überhaupt erst »in Christus«, d. h. für Christen ihre volle Wirksamkeit entfalten[8]? Im folgenden sollen, um auf diese Frage eine Antwort zu finden, nicht diejenigen Texte untersucht werden, wo Paulus explizit und gleichsam »systematisch« vom νόμος spricht; vielmehr soll es um eine Interpretation derjenigen Texte gehen, die auf aktuelle ethische Konflikte Bezug nehmen. Solche Konflikte werden am klarsten im Ersten Korintherbrief sichtbar, auf den sich die folgenden Überlegungen deshalb vor allem konzentrieren sollen[9]. Beruft sich Paulus, wenn er in diesem Brief der Gemeinde in Korinth konkrete Weisungen erteilt, auf Gebote oder

---

[4] So etwa O. Michel, Paulus und seine Bibel, ^{2}1972, 158f.; P. von der Osten-Sacken, Das paulinische Verständnis des Gesetzes ..., EvTh 37, 1977, 569f.

[5] So vor allem W. Schrage, Ethik des Neuen Testaments, GNT 4, 1982, 198: In Gal 6,2 wolle Paulus »wahrscheinlich« sagen, »daß die Thora im ›Gesetz Christi‹ ihrer eigentlichen Intention nach erfüllt wird«. Ähnlich T. Holtz, Zur Frage der inhaltlichen Weisungen bei Paulus, ThLZ 106, 1981, 396: Das Liebesgebot ist ein »konkretes Gebot, das, indem durch es Liebe konkret verwirklicht wird, sich als identisch mit der Thora erweist«.

[6] Schrage a. a. O. 195: Paulus kämpfe nicht »gegen das Halten der Gebote, sondern dagegen, diese als Heilsbedingung gesetzlich zu verdrehen«; freilich werde die alttestamentliche Ethik von ihm »selektiv und also kritisch rezipiert« (a. a. O. 197).

[7] Schrage a. a. O. 196.

[8] So U. Wilckens, Zur Entwicklung des paulinischen Gesetzesverständnisses, NTS 28, 1982, 159 unter Verweis auf 1 Kor 7,19.

[9] Auf 2 Kor und auf die Paränese des Röm kann aus Raumgründen nur kurz eingegangen werden; s. u. S. 261 ff.

Normen der Tora? Orientiert er sich zumindest an den entsprechenden Traditionen – möglicherweise auch ohne explizite Zitate?

Man könnte gegen diesen Ansatz einwenden, daß im Ersten Korintherbrief die Gesetzesthematik (noch) kaum eine Rolle spielt und daß dieser Brief als Prüffeld für die genannte Fragestellung ungeeignet ist. Bisweilen wird ja die These vertreten, die paulinische Theologie, insbesondere sein Urteil über die Tora, habe sich erst allmählich entwickelt[10] und sei jedenfalls nicht schon mit dem »Damaskus-Erlebnis« gleichsam fertig dagewesen. Gehört möglicherweise auch der Erste Korintherbrief noch in diejenige Phase der theologischen Entwicklung des Paulus, in der die Reflexion des Gesetzesthemas noch nicht voll ausgeprägt war?

Sicherlich läßt sich über die spezifischen Inhalte der paulinischen Theologie in der Zeit bis zur Abfassung des Ersten Thessalonicherbriefes kaum etwas sagen[11]; auch in diesem Brief selbst fehlt eine ausdrückliche Auseinandersetzung mit dem Gesetzesthema. Doch dies bedeutet nicht, daß für Paulus das Problem noch nicht aktuell gewesen wäre[12]. Denn zweierlei fällt auf: (1) In der in 1 Thess 4,1–12 formulierten Paränese fehlt jeder (und sei es auch nur indirekte) Hinweis auf die Tora. Ist es denkbar, daß der ehemalige Pharisäer Paulus bei den Themen περιπατεῖν καὶ ἀρέσκειν θεῷ (v. 1) bzw. θέλημα τοῦ θεοῦ (v. 3) die Aussagen der Tora »vergessen« haben könnte? Wahrscheinlicher als dies ist jedenfalls die Vermutung, daß Paulus schon hier die Kriterien für die inhaltlichen Weisungen der Paränese nicht mehr aus der Tora gewinnt, sondern daß er sie aus dem Christusgeschehen ableitet (vgl. ἐν κυρίῳ Ἰησοῦ v. 1; διὰ τοῦ κυρίου Ἰησοῦ v. 2). Diese Vermutung könnte (2) unterstützt werden

---

[10] So etwa G. Strecker, Befreiung und Rechtfertigung. Zur Stellung der Rechtfertigungslehre in der Theologie des Paulus, in: Eschaton und Historie. Aufsätze, 1979, 229–259. »Eine Reflexion über die Bedeutung des Gesetzes und der Rechtfertigung findet sich erst im Galaterbrief, veranlaßt durch judenchristliche Gesetzeslehrer« (a.a.O. 231). – Ein Problem liegt m. E. von vornherein darin, daß Strecker 1 Thess der frühen Phase des Paulus zurechnet, Gal – der nach seiner chronologischen Rekonstruktion als nächster Brief folgt – dagegen bereits der Spätphase; dabei setzt Strecker 1 Thess durchaus »spät« an – etwa 15–17 Jahre nach der Bekehrung des Paulus (a.a.O. 230). Dann müßte sich in dem verhältnismäßig kurzen Zeitraum zwischen 1 Thess und Gal eine sehr grundsätzliche Wandlung des theologischen Denkens des Paulus vollzogen haben.

[11] Das in Gal 2,11 ff. geschilderte Ereignis liegt zeitlich vor der Abfassung des 1 Thess; aber Paulus formuliert jedenfalls aus späterer Sicht, so daß man die Gal-Stelle nicht ohne weiteres als Zeugnis für das theologische Denken des »frühen« Paulus in Rechnung stellen darf. – Anders verhielte es sich, wenn G. Lüdemann, Paulus, der Heidenapostel I. Studien zur Chronologie, FRLANT 123, 1980 mit seiner Frühdatierung des 1 Thess recht hätte; das aber ist m. E. ganz unwahrscheinlich (vgl. meine Rezension in ZKG 92, 1981, 344–349).

[12] Strecker a.a.O. 231: »Die Gesetzesproblematik [ist] bis in die Zeit des 1. Thessalonicherbriefes durch Paulus noch nicht voll durchdacht worden.«

durch die Beobachtung, daß Paulus in 1 Thess 1,3 im Rahmen der Trias πίστις – ἀγάπη – ἐλπίς vom ἔργον τῆς πίστεως spricht[13]; das Stichwort ἔργον bzw. dessen Plural τὰ ἔργα wird in den späteren Briefen meist mit νόμος verknüpft, bis Paulus schließlich im Römerbrief πίστις und ἔργα (νόμου) in einen direkten Gegensatz zueinander stellt (Röm 3,27f.; 9,32). Es ist m. E. jedenfalls nicht undenkbar, daß Paulus in 1 Thess 1,3 πίστις bewußt an die Stelle von νόμος gesetzt hat, um anzuzeigen, daß der Glaube das Gesetz abgelöst hat.

Auch der Befund im Ersten Korintherbrief ist differenzierter, als es nach dem seltenen Vorkommen von νόμος zunächst scheinen mag. Die Annahme, die Gesetzesproblematik sei dem Apostel bei der Abfassung des Briefes (noch) nicht klar oder für ihn jedenfalls hier nicht aktuell gewesen[14], erweist sich als zumindest sehr fragwürdig angesichts von 1 Kor 15,56; denn hier wird deutlich, daß Paulus durchaus bereits in diesen Kategorien denkt – und daß er vor allem bei seinen Lesern glaubt voraussetzen zu können, sie würden seine stark verkürzte Redeweise ohne weiteres verstehen. Paulus interpretiert nämlich das für seine Argumentation in 1 Kor 15 wichtige Zitat von v. 55 (eine Mischung aus Jes 25,8 [nicht LXX] und Hos 13,14 LXX[15]) im Sinne seiner spezifischen Theologie: Der »Stachel«, dessen sich der Tod gegenwärtig bedient, ist die Sünde; die Sünde ihrerseits aber praktiziert ihre Macht mittels der Tora (v. 56); durch das Christusgeschehen werden »wir« (v. 57) dieser verhängnisvollen Verstrikkung entrissen. Wer Gal 3,10ff.; Röm 5,12ff.; 6,12ff.; 7,7ff. kennt, vermag diese kurzen Sätze natürlich von daher zu interpretieren; die Korinther aber kannten keinen dieser Texte. Wenn Paulus sich gleichwohl mit einer so knappen Anmerkung meint begnügen zu können, so scheint der Schluß erlaubt, daß er das Thema in Korinth offenbar mündlich erörtert hat[16]. Die theologische Reflexion des Toraproblems war also zum Zeit-

[13] Den Hinweis auf die nur hier bei Paulus begegnende Wendung verdanke ich J. A. Fitzmyer; er interpretiert sie allerdings anders, als ich es im folgenden tue.

[14] Bei einer solchen Annahme wäre ohnedies vorausgesetzt, daß 1 Kor zeitlich vor Phil (jedenfalls früher als Phil 3,2ff.) verfaßt wurde. Nimmt man jedoch an, daß Phil zeitlich früher liegt als 1 Kor (wofür zumindest unter Zugrundelegung der Ephesus-Hypothese zum Phil einiges spricht), so erledigt sich die Annahme, zur Zeit der korinthischen Korrespondenz sei die Rechtfertigungsthematik für Paulus noch unwichtig gewesen.

[15] Paulus ändert allerdings ᾅδη in θάνατε; es geht ihm nicht um das (räumlich vorzustellende) Toten- oder Todesreich, sondern um den Tod selbst.

[16] v. 56 wird gelegentlich als sekundäre Glosse angesehen (so z. B. W. Schmithals, Die Briefe des Paulus in ihrer ursprünglichen Form, 1984, 32). Aber diese Annahme hat wenig für sich: Die Sprache in v. 56 ist paulinisch, die Argumentationsweise (exegetische Bemerkung zum zitierten Bibeltext in Form eines Kettenschlusses) ist paulinisch, und inhaltlich paßt die Aussage im Kontext ausgezeichnet. Vgl. dazu H. Conzelmann, Der erste Brief an die Korinther, KEK V, ^{2}1981, 361f.

punkt der Abfassung des Ersten Korintherbriefs deutlich ausgeprägt[17]; es ist deshalb methodisch zulässig, sich bei der Frage nach der Geltung der ethischen Gebote der Tora für Paulus auf diesen Brief zu beziehen.

II.

Der Erste Korintherbrief, vor allem von 1 Kor 5 an, enthält eine sonst bei Paulus so nicht begegnende Aufzählung konkreter ethischer Probleme, die jeweils ausgelöst sind durch aktuelle Konflikte in der korinthischen Gemeinde. Das Thema von 1 Kor 5 ist πορνεία, und zwar in einer Form, wie sie Paulus zufolge nicht einmal ἐν τοῖς ἔθνεσιν als sittlich tolerierbar gilt[18]. »Die Frau des Vaters«, mit der ein korinthischer Christ – offenkundig mit Billigung der Gemeinde[19] – in ehelicher (oder eheähnlicher?) Gemeinschaft zusammenlebt, ist vermutlich nicht dessen eigene Mutter, sondern die Stiefmutter, die selbst offenbar keine Christin ist[20]. Paulus ordnet an, daß sich die Gemeinde von diesem Mann zu trennen habe (v. 5); sein bildhafter Hinweis auf den Sauerteig setzt, insbesondere in v. 7, bei den Korinthern die Kenntnis der jüdischen Passa-Sitte voraus. Paulus schließt (v. 13b) mit einem nicht ausdrücklich markierten biblischen Wort, das u. a. in Dtn 17,7[21], darüber hinaus aber noch mehrfach im Deuteronomium belegt ist[22]; es handelt sich um eine in vielen Zusammenhängen verwendbare und jedenfalls nicht speziell auf die sexualethische Konfliktsituation bezogene Aussage[23]. Aus welchem Grunde ist nun eigentlich das Verhalten des betreffenden korinthischen Gemeindegliedes nach dem Urteil des Paulus so verwerflich[24]? Es ist durchaus denkbar, daß Paulus das Kriterium dafür aus der Tora bezieht (Lev 18,8; Dtn

---

[17] Für die Wahrscheinlichkeit dieser Annahme spricht im übrigen auch die intensive Benutzung des AT in diesem Brief.

[18] Der Relativsatz in 5,1a enthält kein Verb (zahlreiche Handschriften haben sekundär ὀνομάζεται ergänzt). Gemeint ist wohl nicht, solche πορνεία »komme bei den Heiden nicht vor«; zur Diskussion steht die Frage, ob das von Paulus als πορνεία gewertete Verhalten von den Heiden üblicherweise verurteilt wird oder nicht.

[19] Darauf deutet v. 2 hin.

[20] Jedenfalls geht Paulus auf ihr Verhalten nicht weiter ein. Die theoretisch denkbare Vermutung, daß für Paulus die Frau gar nicht als eigene handelnde Person in den Blick kommt, ist angesichts der sonstigen Aussagen im 1 Kor wenig wahrscheinlich.

[21] Der einleitende Imperativ ist von Paulus kontextbedingt in den Plural gesetzt worden; ansonsten entspricht der Text der LXX-Fassung.

[22] Dtn 19,19; 21,21; 22,21.24; 24,7; vgl. 17,12; 22,22.

[23] Immerhin aber begegnet die Wendung gehäuft innerhalb von Dtn 22,13–29, wo es um Weisungen für den Bereich der Sexualsphäre geht.

[24] Im deutschen Eherecht bestand bis 1976 das »Ehehindernis der Geschlechtsgemeinschaft« (§ 4 Abs. 2 EheG); diese Bestimmung wurde am 1. 7. 1976 aufgehoben

27,20 und vor allem Dtn 23,1[25]). Aber gerade dann fällt auf, daß er diesen Sachverhalt nicht erwähnt, sondern mit der Wendung οὐδὲ ἐν τοῖς ἔθνεσιν die Korinther vielmehr an das selbst unter Heiden, d. h. bei Nichtchristen[26], geltende Unwerturteil[27] erinnert. Hinweise auf die hier einschlägige Torabestimmung fehlen; und Paulus wird kaum stillschweigend annehmen, die Korinther seien mit dieser Bestimmung vertraut gewesen – zumal der von ihm explizit gegebene Hinweis auf die Rechtsordnung bzw. die sittliche Anschauung der Heiden durchaus korrekt ist.

In 1 Kor 6,1–11 kritisiert Paulus, daß korinthische Christen Rechtsstreitigkeiten vor heidnischen Gerichten austragen. »Die zeitgeschichtliche Voraussetzung« für diese Kritik ist nach H. Conzelmann »die jüdische Schiedsgerichtsbarkeit«, derzufolge Juden nicht bei Nicht-Juden Recht suchen dürfen[28]. Die heidnischen Richter werden von Paulus polemisch als ἄδικοι (v. 1) und als ἄπιστοι (v. 6) bezeichnet. ἄπιστοι sind sie, weil sie nicht an Christus glauben; ἄδικοι sind sie als »Verächter des göttlichen Rechtes«[29]. Das Ziel der paulinischen Argumentation ist nicht die Errichtung einer eigenen christlichen Gerichtsbarkeit[30] nach jüdischem Modell; vielmehr geht es Paulus letztlich um den Verzicht auf Rechtsprozesse unter Christen überhaupt[31]. Dafür aber gibt es – auch im Bereich jüdischer Tradition – gar kein Vorbild[32].

In 1 Kor 6,12–20 wird das Thema πορνεία erneut aufgenommen. Hier geht es konkret um den sexuellen Umgang mit der πόρνη. Vor der

---

[25] Sollte Paulus diese Stelle vor Augen gehabt haben, dann hätte er das Zitat in 5,13 vermutlich aus Dtn 22,24b gewonnen.

[26] In diesem Sinne ist τὰ ἔθνη jedenfalls in 1 Kor 12,2 (und vermutlich auch in 2 Kor 11,26) gebraucht; denkt Paulus an Heiden im Gegenüber zu Juden, so sagt er das im 1 Kor ausdrücklich (1,23).

[27] Vgl. Conzelmann, 1 Kor, 123 (mit Anm. 29 zum Römischen Recht). G. Delling, Art. Ehehindernisse, RAC IV, 1959, 685–687 (zu Rom: Die Ehe zwischen Stiefeltern und Stiefkindern war nicht möglich.).

[28] Conzelmann, 1 Kor, 133 mit Anm. 13. Vgl. Bill II 362f.

[29] G. Schrenk, Art. ἄδικος κτλ., ThWNT I, 1933, 151,43. – Es handelt sich nicht um einen traditionellen Terminus zur Bezeichnung von Heiden; Paulus hat ihn offenbar gewählt, um ihre Untauglichkeit für die ihnen von den Christen zugestandene Rolle zu unterstreichen.

[30] Als »Notordnung« wäre Paulus damit freilich einverstanden (v. 5b).

[31] Vgl. E. Dinkler, Zum Problem der Ethik bei Paulus. Rechtsnahme und Rechtsverzicht (1 Kor 6,1–11), in: Signum Crucis. Aufsätze zum Neuen Testament und zur Christlichen Archäologie, 1967, 204–240.

[32] Bei Plato (Gorgias 509 C) formuliert Sokrates den Grundsatz, Unrechtleiden (ἀδικεῖσθαι) sei das geringere Übel gegenüber Unrechttun (ἀδικεῖν); das ist aber etwas anderes als das von Paulus angestrebte Ziel (vgl. Conzelmann, 1 Kor, 135). – In der Sache liegt eine Parallele vor in Mt 5,39; dort erscheint die Forderung des Rechtsverzichts ausdrücklich in Form einer Antithese zur Tora.

πόρνη warnen das Proverbienbuch (5,3[33] und vor allem der Abschnitt 6,20–7,27[34]) und Jesus Sirach (9,6[35]; 19,2[36]). Doch keiner dieser Texte klingt in der paulinischen Argumentation auch nur an. Paulus zitiert jedoch in 6,16b – ausdrücklich durch φησίν hervorgehoben – Gen 2,24 LXX. Ist das ein Beleg dafür, daß der Apostel der Tora eben doch letzte Autorität in der hier diskutierten und zu entscheidenden Frage zumißt? Die Verwendung von Gen 2,24 durch Paulus ist freilich in jeder Hinsicht ungewöhnlich; denn der Apostel beruft sich auf diese Stelle ja nicht etwa, um die (monogame) Ehe zu rechtfertigen bzw. als gottgewollte Ordnung zu erklären[37]. Vielmehr dient das biblische Zitat als Warnung vor der Geschlechtsgemeinschaft mit der πόρνη, d. h. es verweist aus paulinischer Sicht auf eine mit der Schöpfungsordnung selbst gegebene Gefährdung des Menschen, die in einem bestimmten Fall unweigerlich wirksam wird. Die negative Wertung wird noch dadurch unterstrichen, daß Paulus dem ἓν σῶμα (bzw. dem εἰς σάρκα μίαν des biblischen Zitats) im Blick auf die πόρνη ein betontes ἓν πνεῦμα mit Blick auf den κύριος entgegenstellt (v. 17). Die geschlechtliche Bindung an die πόρνη gefährdet, ja beendet die Bindung an Christus. Der von Paulus dafür gewählte biblische Belegtext hatte aber ursprünglich und auch in der Tradition die Funktion gehabt, die eheliche Sexualität als schöpfungsgemäß zu werten, und er ist – diese Stelle ausgenommen – offenbar nie anders verstanden worden[38]. Paulus benutzt ihn nun allein dazu, das auf das σῶμα bezogene Einssein im Geschlechtsakt biblisch zu belegen; als Kriterium für seine konkrete Entscheidung spielt weder dieser noch ein anderer biblischer Text eine Rolle.

Besonders wichtig für das hier erörterte Thema ist 1 Kor 7[39]. Paulus sezt sich im ersten Teil (v. 1–7) mit der vermutlich in Korinth propagierten Parole auseinander, daß es für den Mann gut sei, keinen (sexuellen) Umgang mit Frauen zu haben (v. 1b[40]); diese Parole enthält zwar ein

[33] Der hebräische Text spricht von der »fremden« Frau; vgl. Prov 5,20.

[34] Hier geht es um den Umgang mit der Hure und um Verführungskünste einer verheirateten Frau (vgl. H. Ringgren, Sprüche, ATD 16/1, ^{3}1980, 35–37).

[35] Sir 9,1–9 warnt freilich generell vor dem Kontakt zu Frauen.

[36] Der hebräische Text warnt allgemein vor »Wein und Frauen«, die das Herz leichtfertig werden lassen (vgl. G. Sauer, Jesus Sirach, JSHRZ III/5, 1981, 551); die LXX-Fasssung von v. 2b lautet: ὁ κολλώμενος πόρναις τολμηρότερος ἔσται.

[37] Das ist die Funktion des Zitats in Eph 5,31 und in Mk 10,6/Mt 19,5.

[38] Dies ist auch in den halachischen Interpretationen von Gen 2,24 vorausgesetzt (Bill I 802f.), auch wenn es dort primär um Detailfragen zu gehen scheint, die nach unserem Verständnis dem Text offenbar fernliegen.

[39] Vgl. dazu vor allem W. Schrage, Zur Frontstellung der paulinischen Ehebewertung in 1 Kor 7,1–7, ZNW 67, 1976, 214–234; ferner H. Merklein, »Es ist gut für den Menschen, eine Frau nicht anzufassen«. Paulus und die Sexualität nach 1 Kor 7, in: Die Frau im Urchristentum, QD 95, 1983, 225–253.

[40] Für die Annahme, daß in v. 1b die korinthische Position zu Wort kommt, spricht der Sprachgebrauch: Hier ist ἄνθρωπος im Sinne von »der Mann« gebraucht; in v. 2–5 wird

(Un-)Werturteil, sie formuliert aber nicht eine das Verhalten bindende Norm[41]. Paulus interpretiert im Gegenzug in v. 2–7.8f. die Ehe und dabei speziell das Sexualverhalten innerhalb der Ehe als eine Zulassung (v. 6); er lehnt sie also, gegen v. 1, nicht ab, doch er versteht sie, entgegen der biblisch-jüdischen Tradition, auch nicht als ein Pflichtgebot[42]. Auffallend ist, daß seine Anweisungen in v. 2–5 stark die Reziprozität im Verhältnis von Mann und Frau betonen; überraschend ist ferner die einseitige Interpretation der Ehe ausschließlich vom Bereich der Sexualität her, wobei für ihn – anders als in der jüdischen Diskussion[43] – die Fortpflanzung offenbar überhaupt keine Rolle spielt[44]. Bemerkenswert ist schließlich, daß Paulus auf religiös zu nennende Begründungen für seine Ratschläge gänzlich verzichtet[45].

In 7,10f. verwirft Paulus unter Berufung auf den κύριος die Ehescheidung (vgl. Mk 10,11f. par) – im klaren Widerspruch zur biblischen Tora, die ja durchaus Regeln für den Vollzug der Ehescheidung formuliert[46]. Zwar macht Paulus in v, 11a ein dem unbedingten Scheidungsverbot nicht entsprechendes Zugeständnis; doch dazu verweist er nicht etwa auf die von der Tora eingeräumte Möglichkeit, sondern er bezieht sich einfach auf einen möglicherweise gegebenen Sachverhalt (ἐὰν δὲ καὶ χωρισθῇ; ähnlich v. 15). Der in 7,10.11b formulierte Widerspruch zur Tora wird – anders als in der synoptischen Jesusüberlieferung – nicht ausdrücklich erwähnt; der Hinweis auf die Weisung des κύριος, keiner der Ehepartner solle die Scheidung suchen[47], reicht als autoritative Basis völ-

---

dagegen von ἀνήρ gesprochen, bevor dann in v. 7 mit ἄνθρωποι tatsächlich alle Menschen gemeint sind. S. auch die folgende Anm.

[41] Darauf verweist W. Wolbert, Ethische Argumentation und Paränese in 1 Kor 7, MSS 8, 1981, 78f. Enthielte v. 1b ein von Paulus formuliertes verpflichtendes Urteil, so würde schon v. 2 wieder dessen Aufhebung bedeuten; handelte es sich um ein verpflichtendes Urteil der Korinther, so wäre die Fortsetzung sinnlos: »Warum sollte nämlich der die Unzucht vorziehen wollen (v. 2), für den jedes Berühren einer Frau sündhaft ist?«

[42] Vgl. dazu Bill II 372f. (zu Joh 2,1). Textgrundlage im Judentum ist vor allem Gen 1,28.

[43] Vgl. A. Lindemann, Die Kinder und die Gottesherrschaft. Markus 10,13–16 und die Stellung der Kinder in der späthellenistischen Gesellschaft und im Urchristentum, WuD NF 17, 1983, 84f. und die dort genannten Belege.

[44] Das läßt sich nicht damit erklären, daß Paulus in gespannter Naherwartung der Parusie lebte; der Apostel argumentiert hier ja ganz von der Körperlichkeit des Menschen her und läßt jeden Hinweis auf seine Eschatologie vermissen.

[45] Als Ausnahme könnte man allenfalls den Hinweis auf das Gebet (v. 5) werten. Paulus sagt aber nicht, daß Gebet und Praktizierung der Sexualität einander ausschließen (etwa weil Sexualverkehr den Menschen kultisch verunreinigen könnte); er räumt lediglich ein, daß die Eheleute, sofern sie sich einig sind, eine Zeitlang enthaltsam leben können.

[46] Vgl. Mt 5,31f., wo das Ehescheidungsverbot als Antithese zu Dtn 24,1 formuliert ist.

[47] Vorausgesetzt ist das hellenistische Eherecht, das auch die von der Frau ausgehende Trennung kennt; die vom Mann ausgehende Scheidung wird im Nachsatz (v. 11b) lediglich gestreift.

lig aus – eines Hinweises darauf, daß die Tora etwas anderes sagt, bedarf es offenbar gar nicht.

Das in 7,12–16 erörterte »Mischehenproblem«, zu dem es – verständlicherweise – eine Weisung des κύριος nicht gibt, war für Korinth vermutlich von besonderer Bedeutung. Paulus setzt von vornherein voraus (v. 14), daß der heidnische Ehepartner den Christen nicht etwa gefährdet oder ihn in irgendeiner Weise »verunreinigt[48]; vielmehr gilt umgekehrt der Nichtchrist als in der Ehe mit dem Christen »geheiligt«[49]. Dies gilt auch für die (jedenfalls nicht getauften) Kinder aus solchen Ehen: Sie sind ἅγια durch den christlichen Elternteil. Im ganzen Abschnitt geht es wohl nicht um die Eheschließung mit einem heidnischen Partner[50], sondern um den Fall, daß einer der beiden Partner später Christ geworden ist. Im Judentum war die Ehe mit Nichtjuden generell illegitim[51]; der Übertritt nur eines Ehepartners zum Judentum war aus diesem Grunde rechtlich unmöglich. Die Argumentation des Paulus in 7,12–16 setzt also Verhältnisse voraus, die es im Kontext des damaligen Judentums so gar nicht geben konnte[52].

Innerhalb des Abschnitts 1 Kor 7,17–24 bezeichnet Paulus die τήρησις ἐντολῶν θεοῦ explizit als einen der Beschneidung wie der »Vorhaut« gleichermaßen übergeordneten Wert. Eine solche Argumentation wäre im Kontext eines noch irgendwie von der Tora bestimmten Denkens nicht möglich; denn gerade die Beschneidungsforderung war eines der zentralen Toragebote Gottes und nicht etwa nur eine kultisch-rituelle Norm, auf die man auch hätte verzichten können. Zwar hat es im Diaspora-Judentum eine gewisse Diskussion über Notwendigkeit und Bedeutung der Beschneidung im Zusammenhang der Mission gegeben[53]; aber auch

---

[48] Paulus urteilt hier also anders als in dem in 6,12–20 erörterten Fall. Er steht damit im Gegensatz zur jüdischen Anschauung, die die »Mischehe« verwirft und diese letztlich mit πορνεία gleichsetzt (vgl. F. Hauck/S. Schulz, Art. πόρνη κτλ. ThWNT VI, 1959, 589).

[49] Dabei ist kein »dingliches« Verständnis von Heiligkeit vorausgesetzt, wie gelegentlich angenommen wird; sonst wäre v. 16 sinnlos. Paulus meint offenbar, daß der Christ den nichtchristlichen Partner als jemanden behandeln soll, der – wie er selbst – von Gott her »geheiligt« ist (ἡγίασται weist auf Gott als Urheber der Heiligung).

[50] v. 39b fordert jedenfalls, eine Witwe solle, wenn sie denn wieder heiraten wolle, μόνον ἐν κυρίῳ die Ehe eingehen; das dürfte nicht allein für diesen speziellen Fall gegolten haben, doch läßt sich darüber Näheres nicht sagen.

[51] Bill IV/1, 378f.

[52] Die Aussage von v. 15b, daß im Fall der Auflösung einer »Mischehe« der Christ »nicht gebunden« sei, widerspricht Mk 10,11f., wo eine neue Ehe nach der Scheidung als Ehebruch gilt. 1 Kor 7,15 setzt freilich voraus, daß der Christ jedenfalls nicht der aktive Teil beim Scheidungsbegehren ist.

[53] In der Regel gilt als Beleg die Debatte über den Übertritt des Königs Izates von Adiabene zum Judentum (Josephus Ant XX 40–48). Der jüdische Kaufmann Ananias erklärt, Izates könne Gott (τὸ θεῖον) auch ohne Beschneidung verehren, denn wichtiger als diese

dort hätte die περιτομή keinesfalls für οὐδέν erklärt werden und die τήρησις ἐντολῶν gar als eine Alternative zu ihr bezeichnet werden können[54]. Besagt v. 19 damit also doch, daß Paulus zwischen kultischen Geboten und ethischer Tora differenziert, daß nach seinem Urteil für Christen zwar nicht mehr das kultisch-rituelle Toragebot der Beschneidung gilt, wohl aber die von Gott geforderten sittlichen Handlungsnormen[55]? Paulus beginnt seine Erörterung in v. 17 mit dem Hinweis auf Christi bzw. Gottes Tat: Die Praxis christlichen Existierens, das περιπατεῖν, soll sich vollziehen in dem Status, den der Betreffende bei seiner Berufung durch Christus bzw. Gott hatte; dies, so betont Paulus, ordne er »in allen Kirchen« an[56]. In der Tat sind auch nach dem Galaterbrief »Beschneidung« und »Vorhaut« im Blick auf das Heil bedeutungslos; als übergeordnete Alternative nennt Paulus dort die πίστις δι' ἀγάπης ἐνεργουμένη (5,6) bzw. die καινὴ κτίσις (6,15)[57]. In 1 Kor 7,19 verweist er stattdessen auf das Halten der Gebote Gottes[58]. Diese Aussage wirkt zunächst etwas zusammenhanglos; denn weder zuvor noch später ist in 1 Kor 7 der Sache nach oder gar explizit von den ἐντολαί Gottes die Rede. Paulus will offen-

---

sei das Bewahren der jüdischen Tradition (ζηλοῦν τὰ πάτρια τῶν Ἰουδαίων). Dann aber tritt der gesetzeskundige Eleazar auf und kritisiert dies scharf: Es genüge nicht, die Torabestimmungen nur zu lesen, man müsse sie auch einhalten; unbeschnitten zu leben sei ἀσέβεια (§ 44f.). Daraufhin läßt sich der König sofort beschneiden, und zwar ohne daß die von Ananias befürchteten politischen Probleme eintreten, wie Josephus durchaus befriedigt konstatiert.

54 Die »Gottesfürchtigen«, die den Monotheismus und einen Teil des Zeremonialgesetzes akzeptierten, jedoch nicht die Beschneidung auf sich nahmen, waren eben deshalb keine Juden; es gab vielmehr »eine scharfe Trennung zwischen den σεβόμενοι oder φοβούμενοι τὸν θεόν einerseits und den προσήλυτοι andererseits als zwei völlig verschiedenen Kategorien« (K. G. Kuhn/H. Stegemann, Art. Proselyten, PRE Suppl IX, 1962, 1260; vgl. 1264–1267).

55 Nach Wilckens a.a.O. (Anm. 8) macht Paulus in 1 Kor 7,19 die Gebote der Tora für Heiden- wie für Judenchristen verbindlich; niemals sonst spreche er so »ungeschützt jüdisch« wie an dieser Stelle. Auch Schrage, Ethik, 195 nennt 1 Kor 7,19 als Beleg dafür, daß der Christ vom Halten der Gebote nicht dispensiert sei; ebenso H. Räisänen, Paul and the Law, WUNT 29, 1983, 68: "The observation that this statement sounds very much Jewish and very little specifically Christian is quite correct. It should not be harmonized with the Galatians statements; it differs markedly from them in content." "The law ... can thus be used ... as a norm of behaviour."

56 J. Weiß, Der erste Korintherbrief, KEK V, ^{9}1910 (= 1970), 184 beobachtet hier »das Entstehen eines allgemeinen Kirchenrechtes«.

57 Vgl. auch Röm 2,25f.

58 G. Bornkamm, Paulus, UB 119, 1969, 223 meint, gegenüber 1 Kor sei das Wort an den genannten Gal-Stellen »bedeutsam abgewandelt: an Stelle des Gehorsams gegen Gottes Gebote ist hier von dem in der Liebe tätigen Glauben ... die Rede«. Aber wirklich bewertbar wäre diese Abwandlung nur, wenn sich die zeitliche Abfolge von 1 Kor und Gal sicher bestimmen ließe.

bar zweierlei zeigen: Eine nachträgliche Änderung des bei der Berufung bestehenden Status des Menschen ist nicht gefordert bzw. wäre sogar unzulässig[59]; doch darüber hinaus hat auch der Status als solcher keine besondere Bedeutung, d. h. auch das Festhalten an ihm kann keinesfalls zur Heilsbedingung gemacht werden[60]. Der Status des Berufenen, so sagt v. 19, ist schlechterdings bedeutungslos; worauf es ankommt, ist, daß er jetzt Gottes Willen tut. Der Sinn von v. 19c erschließt sich, wenn man die Parallelität der Gedankengänge in v. 18–20 einerseits und v. 21–24 andererseits beachtet: Innerhalb von v. 21–24 geben v. 22a und v. 22b die Begründung dafür, warum der soziale Status des Berufenen für seine Beziehung zu Christus bedeutungslos ist (wobei v. 22b über v. 21 insofern hinausgeht, als von der κλῆσις des Freien bis dahin gar nicht die Rede gewesen war); dieselbe Funktion haben v. 19a und v. 19b im Blick auf die ethnisch-religiöse Zugehörigkeit der Berufenen. In v. 23 faßt Paulus die Aussagen von v. 22a.b zusammen und fügt eine Forderung an: μὴ γίνεσθε ... v. 19c hat innerhalb des Gedankengangs von v. 18–20 offenbar dieselbe Funktion: So wie die durch Christus befreiten Menschen (Freie wie Sklaven) nicht δοῦλοι ἀνθρώπων werden sollen (v. 23), so sollen sie als die jenseits von Beschneidung und Vorhaut Stehenden sich allein auf das Halten der Gebote einlassen[61]. So wenig man wird sagen können, Paulus denke hier womöglich nur an seine in 1 Kor 7 gegebenen Weisungen, so wenig wird man umgekehrt behaupten dürfen, er denke umfassend an die Gültigkeit der einzelnen Torabestimmungen[62].

Am deutlichsten ist der Abstand des Paulus von den Toranormen in 7,25–40 wahrnehmbar; nirgends wird die aus paulinischer Sicht beste-

---

[59] Der an erster Stelle erörterte Fall der Beschneidung ist vermutlich eher theoretischer Natur; Paulus beschränkt sich deshalb jeweils auf ein knappes μή + 3. Pers. d. Impt. (v. 18). Vgl. dagegen Gal 5,2: Die (nachträgliche) Beschneidung trennt definitiv von Christus.

[60] Dies spricht m. E. übrigens dafür, das umstrittene μᾶλλον χρῆσαι in v. 21 nicht so auszulegen, als solle der Sklave auch für den Fall einer möglichen Freilassung »umso lieber« an seinem Sklavenstand festhalten. Das μᾶλλον kann kaum dazu dienen, das μενέτω (v. 20) noch zu unterstreichen; denn dann bestünde beinahe die Gefahr, daß nun das μένειν Heilscharakter bekommt. Anders freilich H. Greeven, Das Hauptproblem der Sozialethik in der neueren Stoa und im Urchristentum, NTF III/4, 1935, 50–52.

[61] Zu τήρησις ἐντολῶν vgl. Sir 32,23f. LXX: ἐν παντὶ ἔργῳ πίστευε τῇ ψυχῇ σου· καὶ γὰρ τοῦτό ἐστιν τήρησις ἐντολῶν. ὁ πιστεύων νόμῳ προσέχει ἐντολαῖς... Anders der hebräische Text (vgl. Sauer JSHRZ III/5, 585).

[62] Nach Bultmann, Theologie, 342 unterscheidet Paulus zwischen der »kultischen« Tora und den »sittlichen« Geboten; die Freiheit vom Gesetz aktualisiere sich »in der Freiheit, innerhalb des überlieferten Gesetzes zu unterscheiden zwischen dem seinem Inhalt nach Gültigen und Ungültigen«. Aber Paulus nennt keine Kriterien für diese von Bultmann vermutete Differenzierung; sie würde auch der üblichen Tora-Interpretation widersprechen, für die der von Paulus in Gal 5,3 formulierte Grundsatz gilt: Wer sich auf die Tora einläßt, muß sie ganz halten.

hende Problematik des Ehestandes so nachdrücklich reflektiert wie hier – während doch für das Judentum der Wert der Ehe als einer guten Ordnung des Schöpferwillens außer jeder Diskussion stand. Paulus hat zu diesem Thema keine ἐπιταγὴ κυρίου, sondern er formuliert eine γνώμη (v. 25) – und dies, obwohl ihm von der Toratradition her einschlägige ἐντολαί ohne weiteres zur Verfügung gestanden hätten!

1 Kor 7 zeigt, daß die die Ehe betreffenden Toraaussagen für Paulus faktisch bedeutungslos sind. Während das Judentum die Ehe für den von Gott in der Schöpfung gewollten Normalzustand hält, dabei zugleich aber die Möglichkeit der Ehescheidung ohne besondere Vorbehalte konzediert, betont Paulus umgekehrt immer wieder die Höherwertigkeit der Ehelosigkeit gegenüber der Ehe (v. 38.40), übernimmt aber – ausgenommen den in v. 15 genannten Sonderfall – die Weisung des κύριος über die Unauflöslichkeit der Ehe. In kaum einem Abschnitt seiner Briefe geht der Apostel so detailliert und in geradezu kasuistischer Weise auf (individual-) ethische Probleme ein wie hier in 1 Kor 7; umso wichtiger ist die Beobachtung, daß er sich dabei an keiner Stelle auf irgendeine Aussage der Tora zu diesem Themenbereich bezieht.

Der große Abschnitt 1 Kor 8,1–11,1 steht insgesamt unter der Überschrift περὶ τῶν εἰδωλοθύτων; das ist das zweite der von den Korinthern brieflich angeschnittenen Themen. Die Gedankenführung in diesen drei Kapiteln bereitet gewisse Schwierigkeiten, so daß man immer wieder gemeint hat, literarkritische Operationen vornehmen zu sollen[63]. Aber das Vorgehen eines Redaktors bzw. Kompilators der zugrundeliegenden Brieffragmente kann ja kaum einsichtig gemacht werden, wenn man annehmen muß, die von ihm geschaffene Gedankenführung sei in sich so widersprüchlich, daß man sie jedenfalls Paulus nicht zutrauen darf[64]. Die Gedankenführung wird durchsichtig, wenn man erkennt, daß der ganze Abschnitt aufbaut auf einer in 8,1–6 angelegten doppelten Dialektik. Die erste dialektische Aussage lautet (v. 1): πάντες γνῶσιν ἔχομεν – aber der Gemeinde förderlich (Stichwort οἰκοδομεῖν) ist allein die ἀγάπη. Die

[63] Weiß, 1 Kor, 210–213 sieht in 10,1–22 (zusammen mit 6,12–20) den ältesten Teil, in dem Paulus einen rigorosen Standpunkt vertreten habe; später (Kap. 8 und 10,23ff.) habe er dann seine Haltung modifiziert. Ähnlich urteilen andere Autoren, die Teilungshypothesen zum 1 Kor vertreten.

[64] H. v. Soden, Sakrament und Ethik bei Paulus. Zur Frage der literarischen und theologischen Einheitlichkeit von 1. Kor. 8–10, in: Das Paulusbild in der neueren deutschen Forschung (hg. von K. H. Rengstorf), WdF 24, 1964, 359: »Wollte der Kompilator auch hier, wie es seinesgleichen ja öfter zugetraut wird, den Kritikern seine Entdeckung erleichtern, indem er sein Werk nur unvollkommen tat?« V. Sodens eigene Erklärung des Befundes ist freilich auch nicht recht befriedigend; vgl. jetzt H. Merklein, Die Einheitlichkeit des ersten Korintherbriefes, ZNW 75, 1984, 153–183 und insbesondere den Beitrag von D. Lührmann in diesem Band, vor allem Abschnitt II zu 1 Kor 8,1–11,1 (S. 308ff.).

zweite dialektische Aussage findet sich in v. 4.5: Wir wissen, daß οὐδὲν εἴδωλον ἐν κόσμῳ; und doch gilt, daß εἰσὶν θεοὶ πολλοί. Dies wird nun in 8,7–11,1 in mehreren Durchgängen von verschiedenen Aspekten her beleuchtet und entfaltet[65]. Die komplizierte Gedankenführung, die ja schon in 8,1–6 angelegt ist, entspricht der besonderen Komplexität des zur Debatte stehenden Themas. Aber warum ist die hier behandelte Materie eigentlich so komplex? Nach den Bestimmungen der Tora kann es ja überhaupt keinen Zweifel geben, daß sowohl das Essen von unreinem Fleisch wie auch die – sei es auch nur gastweise – Teilnahme an heidnischen Opfermahlen verboten ist[66]. Selbst wenn man nicht erwarten will, daß Paulus die korinthischen Christen unmittelbar auf diese Torabestimmungen verpflichtet[67], so müßte man doch damit rechnen, daß der Apostel sie zumindest als ein Argument unter anderen erwähnt; Paulus rechnet ja, wie 7,11f. zeigt, durchaus damit, daß die korinthischen Christen auch mit der besonderen Problematik von Juden innerhalb der Gemeinde vertraut sind. Und doch nimmt er auf diese Situation überhaupt nicht Bezug.

Ein etwas anderes Bild scheint der Abschnitt 9,1–18 zu bieten, denn hier spielt der Schriftbeweis für die Argumentation des Paulus doch eine wesentliche Rolle. Es geht dabei aber nicht um die Begründung sittlicher oder allgemein ethischer Weisungen; vielmehr gibt Paulus u. a. auch eine biblische Begründung dafür, weshalb die Apostel prinzipiell beanspruchen können, durch die Gemeinden finanziell unterhalten zu werden. In v. 7 führt er als erstes drei Beispiele aus dem Bereich der Alltagserfahrung an: Es gibt Menschen, die beanspruchen können, vom Ertrag ihrer Arbeit

---

[65] Ich kann dies hier lediglich andeuten:
8,7–13: Zwar ist Speise religiös neutral (»Wir alle haben γνῶσις ...«), aber man muß auf den Bruder Rücksicht nehmen (ἀγάπη...).
9,1–18: Paulus verfährt den Korinthern gegenüber ebenso: Er ist Apostel, verzichtet aber auf die Praktizierung der damit verbundenen ἐξουσία.
9,19–23: Paulus hat sich bei der Verkündigung des Evangeliums seinem Gegenüber jeweils angepaßt (vgl. v. 22: »den Schwachen ein Schwacher« – ein Pendant dazu fehlt).
9,24–27: So zu handeln ist ein erstrebenswertes Ziel; wer es verfehlt, der
10,1–13: vergeht sich gegen Christus – wie ja auch οἱ πατέρες, »uns« zur Warnung, gescheitert sind.
10,14–22: Folglich kommt Götzendienst keinesfalls in Frage; wer hier seine vermeintliche ἐξουσία demonstriert, der kommt mit Christus selbst in Konflikt (10,19f. liegt ganz auf der Linie von 8,4f.: Im Vollzug des Opfers wird das an sich nichtige εἴδωλον real.).
10,23–11,1 nennen das Fazit: Im Prinzip ist alles erlaubt; aber da nicht die Materialität der Speise zur Debatte steht, sondern die Relationalität, gilt als Kriterium für das Verhalten die Liebe zum Bruder und die Reinheit des Bekenntnisses.

[66] Bill III 377f. (zum Götzenopferfleisch) und III 420ff. (zur gemeinsamen Mahlzeit mit Heiden).

[67] Immerhin ist zu beachten, daß das »Aposteldekret« Apg 15,29 sehr wohl auf diesen Zusammenhang verweist; das Thema lag also auch der überwiegend heidenchristlichen Kirche nicht fern.

zu leben[68]. Dann folgt (v. 8) die rhetorische Frage, ob dies etwa nur κατὰ ἄνθρωπον gelte und ob nicht vielmehr auch der νόμος dies sage. Das – offenbar nach dem Gedächtnis angeführte – Zitat aus Dtn 25,4 wird auffallenderweise als ein Schriftwort ἐν τῷ Μωϋσέως νόμῳ eingeführt[69] und dann als Offenbarung des Willens Gottes gedeutet. Danach folgt der Hinweis auf das hermeneutische Prinzip der Typologie (δι' ἡμᾶς πάντως λέγει, v. 10a)[70]. Denselben Sinn hat das anschließende, so nicht belegbare Zitat in v. 10b[71]. Als weiteres Argument folgt in v. 13 der sehr allgemein gehaltene Hinweis auf den Altardienst der Priester; ein Bezug speziell zum jüdischen Kult und gar zu den entsprechenden Torabestimmungen ist nicht erkennbar[72] – die erwähnte Regel »gehört zum Grundbestand der Kultordnung überhaupt«[73]. Als abschließendes Argument folgt der Hinweis auf die διαταγή des κύριος[74]. Paulus betont dann aber, er mache – trotz all dieser Argumente – den Korinthern gegenüber von der erwähnten Bestimmung auch in Zukunft keinen Gebrauch (v. 15). Das Unterhaltsrecht der Apostel wird also von Paulus – in Bezug auf seine eigene Person freilich nur theoretisch[75] – auf vielfältige Weise begründet. Dabei spielen auch Aussagen der Tora eine Rolle; doch es wird ihnen kein herausragender Wert beigemessen, und schon gar nicht gelten sie als für die Entscheidung ausschlaggebend.

In 1 Kor 9,20f. expliziert Paulus seinen Satz, daß er »Allen alles geworden« sei, am Beispiel seiner Begegnungen mit den Menschen ὑπὸ νόμον bzw. mit den ἄνομοι. Dabei kann er zwar ohne weiteres sagen, er stehe nicht ὑπὸ νόμον (v. 20b)[76]; doch dem folgt in v. 21 nicht die korrespondierende Aussage, er sei nicht ἄνομος. Vielmehr differenziert Paulus

---

[68] Erwägen kann man, ob der Zusammenhang der Bilder vom Wehrdienst und vom Weinberg durch Dtn 20,6 beeinflußt ist.

[69] Vgl. 2 Kor 3,15: »Wenn Mose gelesen wird ...«

[70] Paulus deutet das Schriftwort nicht nur allegorisch, sondern zugleich typologisch, wie das δι' ἡμᾶς zeigt. Fragen kann man, ob das Subjekt von λέγει Gott ist (so könnte es sich von v. 9b her nahelegen) oder aber Mose bzw. die Schrift; für Letzteres spricht die Fortsetzung v. 10b.

[71] Es handelt sich wohl um ein schon vorpaulinisch gebildetes Mischzitat, dessen »apokrypher« Charakter dem Apostel offenbar nicht bewußt ist, wie die Einleitungsformel zeigt.

[72] Jedenfalls klingt keine der einschlägigen Textstellen (Num 18,8.31; Dtn 18,1–3) auch nur an.

[73] Conzelmann, 1 Kor, 193.

[74] Die nächste Parallele ist die sprichwortartige Sentenz in Lk 10,7.

[75] Anlaß ist sicher eine in Korinth lautgewordene Kritik an Paulus: Er verzichte unfreiwillig auf das den Aposteln zustehende Recht und zeige damit, daß er gar kein »richtiger« Apostel ist.

[76] Viele (überwiegend jüngere) Handschriften haben diese Aussage gestrichen. – Zwischen ὡς Ἰουδαῖος und ὡς ὑπὸ νόμον besteht sachlich kein Unterschied; Paulus hätte aber gewiß nicht formulieren können, er sei kein Jude.

hier: Er ist zwar gewiß nicht ἄνομος in Bezug auf Gott; aber er ist doch ἔννομος Χριστοῦ, er ist »im Gesetz Christi«[77]. Dies kann dem Zusammenhang nach nichts anderes bedeuten, als daß er nicht der Macht der Tora untersteht; denn dem »Gesetz Christi« korrespondiert ja die Absicht, gerade die ἄνομοι zu gewinnen. Der Ausdruck ἔννομος Χριστοῦ kann also keinesfalls bedeuten, daß Paulus von Christus her die Tora womöglich neu in Geltung gesetzt sieht.

In 10,1–13 erhalten biblische Texte bzw. biblische Erzählungen ein sachlich größeres Gewicht. Der Hinweis auf die Exodusüberlieferung (v. 1ff.) erfolgt, damit die damaligen Ereignisse als warnende Beispiele (v. 6) erkannt werden. Hier wird im Rahmen des Gesamtthemas von 8,1 erstmals klar gesagt, daß εἰδωλολατρία zu meiden sei. Geht dies darauf zurück, daß die Tora es immer schon so geboten hat? Paulus bezieht sich jedenfalls nicht auf Toraworte, die vor dem Götzendienst warnen[78]. Er zitiert aber (v. 7) einen Satz aus der Erzählung vom »Goldenen Kalb« (Ex 32,6 LXX wörtlich), der sich nach traditioneller jüdischer Auslegung auf den Götzendienst des Volkes bezieht[79]. Im Kontext der Argumentation des Paulus hat dieses Zitat nicht die Funktion, die Unzulässigkeit der εἰδωλολατρία zu begründen, sondern es setzt sie im Gegenteil voraus[80]. Dasselbe gilt für die in v. 8–10 erzählten bzw. erwähnten Beispiele: Daß πορνεύειν, πειράζειν τὸν Χριστόν und γογγύζειν unzulässig sind, wird als selbstverständlich vorausgesetzt, und Paulus braucht lediglich an die Strafen zu erinnern, die nach der biblischen Überlieferung die Übeltäter trafen; in v. 11 folgt, wie in v. 6, der Hinweis, dies sei τυπικῶς geschehen. Die wirklich entscheidende Begründung für die Warnung vor der Teilhabe an der εἰδωλολατρία ist, ähnlich wie im Fall von 6,12ff., die Feststellung der Unvereinbarkeit von ποτήριον κυρίου und ποτήριον δαιμονίων (v. 21).

In 10,25ff. geht es schließlich um zwei Sonderfälle: Darf man auf dem Markt angebotenes Fleisch ohne weiteres essen? Darf man die von Nichtchristen ausgesprochene Einladung zum Essen annehmen? Die erste

---

[77] In der Wendung μὴ ὢν ἄνομος θεοῦ ἀλλ' ἔννομος Χριστοῦ werden nicht nur die Adjektive ἄνομος und ἔννομος, sondern auch die beiden Genitivattribute einander gegenübergestellt; das ἀλλά ist wohl nicht lediglich adversativ, sondern zugleich in gewisser Weise auch steigernd gemeint.

[78] Hier wären Hinweise u. a. auf Weish 14,11ff. möglich gewesen, nicht zuletzt aber auch solche auf den Dekalog (vgl. Ex 20,4 LXX: οὐ ποιήσεις σεαυτῷ εἴδωλον).

[79] Paulus nimmt (vermutlich zu Recht) an, daß seine Leser die Erzählung kennen; denn er erwähnt nicht die das Volk treffende Strafe. Die in v. 8–10 folgenden Beispiele nennen dagegen jeweils das strafende Handeln.

[80] Paulus verweist also beispielsweise nicht auf das erste oder auf das – für seine Aussage als Beleg noch besser geeignete – zweite Dekaloggebot (Ex 20,5a LXX: οὐ προσκυνήσεις αὐτοῖς οὐδὲ μὴ λατρεύσῃς αὐτοῖς).

Frage wird bejaht (v. 26), wobei als einzige Begründung nun tatsächlich ein biblischer Text zitiert wird (Ps 23,1 LXX). Hat Paulus in diesem Psalmwort ein Wort der Tora gesehen? Das wäre dann möglich, wenn er den Titel ὁ κύριος hier als Gottesprädikat versteht und im Zitat also Gottes Schöpfermacht, nicht aber Christi Herrschaft über die Erde ausgesprochen findet. In der Tat scheint der Apostel die Aussage auf Gott zu beziehen: Er ist der Herr der Schöpfung, und darum kann das Geschaffene dem Menschen zur Verfügung stehen[81]. Der Hinweis auf die Schöpfung hat damit nun aber gerade die Funktion, die Geltung der Torabestimmungen über Rein und Unrein – wenn auch unausgesprochen – aufzuheben[82]. Sollte jedoch die christologische Deutung des Psalmworts die richtige sein, so hätte Paulus es benutzt, um zu zeigen, daß das Christusgeschehen die Normen der Tora zumindest mit Blick auf die Reinheitsvorschriften überbietet. – Noch auffälliger ist die paulinische Position dann in v. 27–30. Das hier erörterte Problem, wie man sich bei einer solchen Einladung zum Essen zu verhalten habe[83], ist in der Tora ausdrücklich angesprochen und ganz unzweideutig gelöst: Nach Ex 34,15 sollten die Israeliten eine Einladung zum Mahl mit Kanaanäern ablehen, weil die Gefahr bestehe, daß sie dann von deren Götzenopfer essen (LXX: καλέσωσίν σε καὶ φάγῃς τῶν θυμάτων αὐτῶν). Daß Paulus Ex 34 gekannt hat, zeigt 2 Kor 3,4ff.; offensichtlich aber fühlte er sich an die in Ex 34,15 gegebene Weisung nicht gebunden bzw. sah keinen Anlaß, die dortige Aussage auf den in Korinth zur Diskussion stehenden Vorgang zu beziehen. Auch seine in 10,28 gegebene Anweisung für das Verhalten in einer besonderen Situation nimmt

---

[81] In v. 31 wird die δόξα θεοῦ zum entscheidenden Kriterium erklärt; hier besteht wohl ein Zusammenhang mit v. 26, so daß ὁ κύριος tatsächlich = ὁ θεός wäre. Anders D.-A. Koch, Die Schrift als Zeuge des Evangeliums. Untersuchungen zur Verwendung und zum Verständnis der Schrift bei Paulus, HabSchr Mainz, 1983, 279; dort Anm. 2: Das Zitat spreche nicht von der Schöpfung, sondern von der Unterordnung der Welt unter den κύριος; auch der Kontext (v. 21f.) meine Christus, wenn vom κύριος die Rede ist. Sollte Kochs Deutung zutreffen, so wäre die paulinische Position in der Tat noch »wesentlich geschlossener« (Koch ebenda).

[82] Das πᾶν ... πωλούμενον ἐσθίετε nimmt vielleicht die bei Bill III 420f. referierten Diskussionen auf; vor allem aber überbietet es die Torabestimmungen darüber; welche Fleischsorten nach Gottes Gebot zu essen erlaubt sei und welche nicht (Lev 11). Man könnte einwenden, daß Paulus diese Bestimmungen deshalb übergeht, weil er das Thema als für Heidenchristen ganz abseitig ansieht. Apg 15,29 (vgl. daneben vor allem auch Gal 2,11–14) zeigt aber, daß im Zusammenleben von Juden und Heiden die Speisevorschriften von großer Bedeutung waren.

[83] Zur Frage, ob es sich um eine Einladung in ein Privathaus oder in ein »Tempelrestaurant« handelt, vgl. Conzelmann, 1 Kor, 217. – Es wäre falsch, das εἰ ... θέλετε im Sinne von »... wenn ihr unbedingt wollt« zu interpretieren (so Weiß, 1 Kor, 264). Würde θέλετε fehlen, so hätte Paulus die Teilnahme ja geradezu befohlen. Vgl. in der Sache im übrigen Lk 10,8.

nicht etwa auf die Tora Bezug, sondern argumentiert mit der συνείδησις dessen, der das servierte Fleisch für ἱερόθυτον hält[84].

Eine wichtige Rolle spielt die Frage nach der Geltung der Tora für Paulus im Zusammenhang der Auslegung von 1 Kor 11,2–16. Hier sieht es ganz so aus, als entsprächen die vom Apostel gegebenen Weisungen der biblischen bzw. jüdischen Tradition. Tatsächlich kann kein Zweifel sein, daß sich die Aussagen von v. 3 und v. 8f. an Gen 2.3 orientieren und darauf anspielen. Man darf aber nicht übersehen, daß das Thema des Abschnitts nicht die Überordnung des Mannes über die Frau ist, sondern daß es speziell nur um eine bestimmte Kleidung geht, die die Frau während ihres öffentlichen Betens und Predigens in der gottesdienstlichen Versammlung tragen sollen (v. 5.13b). Oft wird nun erklärt, Paulus kämpfe hier für die Einführung bzw. für die Beibehaltung der im Judentum geltenden Ordnung, derzufolge die verheiratete Frau in der Öffentlichkeit unbedingt eine Kopfbedeckung zu tragen hatte[85]. T. Holtz erklärt, Paulus könne seine Forderung »nur schwer überhaupt begründen«, wobei er annimmt, daß »ihm – natürlich – diese Ordnung wie alle Ordnung des Judentums als der Tora entsprechend gegolten haben wird«[86]. Das aber ist aus mehreren Gründen ganz unwahrscheinlich: In 11,2–16 geht es gar nicht um eine jüdische Sitte; denn zur Diskussion steht nicht allgemein das Auftreten der Frau außerhalb des Hauses, sondern ihr Verhalten in einer Situation, die es so im antiken Judentum gar nicht geben konnte[87]. Hätte dem Apostel die Tora tatsächlich als unbedingte Autorität gegolten, so wäre es ihm – entgegen der Vermutung von Holtz – keineswegs schwergefallen, eben mit dem Hinweis auf die Tora seine Forderung zu begründen. An der entscheidenden Stelle argumentiert Paulus überhaupt nicht mit dem Hinweis auf biblische Tradition, sondern er verweist auf das, was πρέπον ist (v. 13), d. h. er benutzt ein für die Stoa typisches Argument[88]. Und schließlich: Paulus setzt voraus, daß das Verhalten der korinthischen Christinnen in der *heidnischen* Öffentlichkeit Anstoß bereitet, nicht bei den Juden; nur so gibt die rhetorische Frage von v. 13 einen Sinn[89]. Die christlichen

---

[84] Die Bezeichnung des Fleisches als ἱερόθυτον (statt des polemischen εἰδωλόθυτον) sagt nichts darüber, ob der μηνύσας Heide oder (ängstlicher) Christ ist. Der korrekte Terminus zeigt nur, daß der andere mit seinem Hinweis eine Relation zu den mit dem Essen verbundenen Götzen herstellt; nun gilt also der von Paulus in v. 19f. (vgl. 8,1.5) aufgestellte Maßstab.

[85] Bill III 427ff.

[86] Holtz a.a.O. (Anm. 5) 392.

[87] Es gibt Zeugnisse für eine Debatte darüber, ob Frauen in der Synagoge öffentlich sprechen durften, doch war dies offenbar eine rein theoretische Diskussion (vgl. Bill III 467f.).

[88] Vgl. Conzelmann, 1 Kor, 232.

[89] Offenbar hielten die korinthischen Christen das Verhalten der Frauen für nicht πρέπον – und praktizierten es gerade deshalb, um so ihre ἐξουσία gegenüber der traditionellen Sitte zu demonstrieren.

Korintherinnen haben also – aus Gründen, über die sich Paulus nicht näher äußert – einen von ihrer Umgebung als verwerflich angesehenen Schritt vollzogen. Der Gedankengang in v. 2.3 macht es dabei wahrscheinlich, daß das Problem der Kopfbedeckung der im Gottesdienst predigenden und betenden Männer und Frauen nicht zu den von Paulus den Korinthern überlieferten παραδόσεις gehört hat. Zwar ist v. 2 sicher in erster Linie captatio benevolentiae; doch das θέλω δὲ ὑμᾶς εἰδέναι ist einfacher verständlich, wenn man annimmt, daß Paulus den Korinthern tatsächlich etwas für sie Neues mitteilt. Im übrigen darf man nicht übersehen, daß der Apostel in 11,2–16 nicht ausschließlich Weisungen an die Frauen formuliert; seine erste Anordnung (v. 4) richtet sich an den Mann[90]. Es scheint ihm also in erster Linie darauf anzukommen, daß die als traditionell geltenden Unterschiede zwischen den Geschlechtern gewahrt bleiben, wie H. Greeven m. R. betont hat[91]. Dabei führt der paulinische Gedankengang sogar eher von den biblischen Aussagen weg als zu ihnen hin: Zunächst (v. 7–9) gilt die Frau als dem Manne untergeordnet gemäß der Schöpfung[92]; dann jedoch erfolgt eine Korrektur: ἐν κυρίῳ sind Mann und Frau aufeinander bezogen (v. 11), und außerdem zeigt ja die Erfahrung, daß Mann und Frau nur gemeinsam existieren können (v.12)[93]. Weder für die paulinische Kritik an der Lage in Korinth noch für die von ihm für richtig erachtete Problemlösung spielt also die Tora bzw. die jüdische Tradition eine wesentliche Rolle.

Auf den thematisch verwandten Abschnitt 1 Kor 14,33b–36 braucht hier nur am Rande eingegangen zu werden. Der Schweigebefehl an die Frauen wird zunächst ganz pauschal konstatiert (v. 33b.34a)[94], bevor dann ebenso pauschal die Übereinstimmung dieser Weisung mit dem νόμος behauptet wird. Offenbar soll nicht das σιγάτωσαν, sondern das ὑποτασσέσθωσαν als der Tora entsprechend erwiesen werden, wobei anscheinend an Gen

---

[90] Man kann fragen, ob sich die Wendung καταισχύνει τὴν κεφαλήν in v. 4.5 jeweils auf die in v. 3 erwähnte κεφαλή (beim Mann also Christus, bei der Frau der Mann) bezieht; v. 5b.6 deuten aber darauf hin, daß κεφαλή tatsächlich den Kopf meint.

[91] Greeven a.a.O. (Anm. 60) 132: »Hier braucht nicht mehr gesagt zu sein, als daß Paulus für die Praxis im Gemeindegottesdienst die Konsequenzen gezogen wissen will aus der geschöpflichen Unterschiedenheit von Mann und Weib.«

[92] Die Anspielung auf Gen 1,27; 2,21–23; 2,18 ist deutlich.

[93] Der Nachsatz τὰ δὲ πάντα ἐκ τοῦ θεοῦ zeigt: Dies entspricht dem Willen Gottes. Vgl. in v. 14 den Hinweis auf die φύσις.

[94] 14,33b.34a sind nicht als aktuelle Anweisung formuliert; vielmehr verweist der Text auf einen schon in Geltung stehenden Sachverhalt (οὐ γὰρ ἐπιτρέπεται ...; vgl. v. 35b). G. Dautzenberg, Urchristliche Prophetie. Ihre Erforschung, ihre Voraussetzungen im Judentum und ihre Struktur im ersten Korintherbrief, BWANT 104, 1975, 257–273 hält mit guten Gründen v. 34.35 für eine frühchristliche Gemeinderegel, die durch v. 33b.36 situationsbezogen gerahmt wurde. Der ganze Abschnitt einschließlich v. 37f. sei nachpaulinische Interpolation (a.a.O. 297f.).

3,16 gedacht ist (vgl. 1 Tim 2,12)[95]. Da der Schriftbeweis nicht normierenden, sondern lediglich bestätigenden Charakter hat, ist es möglich, daß νόμος hier im allgemeinen Sinn von »die Schrift« gemeint ist, nicht im Sinne von Tora[96]. Ohnehin liegt mit hoher Wahrscheinlichkeit eine sekundäre (zugleich wohl die im Ersten Korintherbrief einzige) Interpolation vor, so daß die Stelle für die Paulusexegese nichts austrägt[97].

Für das hier erörterte Problem ist im Ersten Korintherbrief schließlich noch 14,21 von besonderem Interesse. Um seine Kritik an der Glossolalie zu bekräftigen, verweist Paulus auf Jes 28,11f., wobei er das (von LXX stark abweichende) Zitat als ein Wort des νόμος einführt. Für Paulus hat aber das Schriftwort keinen Beweischarakter oder enthält gar eine Weisung; vielmehr leitet Paulus aus ihm die Folgerung ab (ὥστε, v. 22), daß das Zungenreden ein σημεῖον lediglich für die Ungläubigen sei – daß es aber unter den korinthischen Verhältnissen nicht einmal diese Funktion erfolgreich wahrnehmen könne (v. 23). Normierenden Charakter für den

---

[95] ὑποτάσσομαι begegnet in bezug auf die wechselseitigen Beziehungen von den Menschen bei Paulus nur in Röm 13,1 und in 1 Kor 16,16; typisch ist das Verb dagegen für die Haustafeln (Kol 3,18; Eph 5,21f.; 1 Petr 3,1.5; vgl. vor allem auch Tit 2,5.9; 3,17).

[96] Vgl. O. Hofius, Das Gesetz des Mose und das Gesetz Christi, ZThK 80, 1983, 278 Anm. 554, der ebenfalls mit einer Interpolation rechnet.

[97] Die Argumente für die Interpolations-Hypothese sind oft zusammengestellt worden (vgl. Conzelmann, 1 Kor, 299). Nach Chr. Wolff, Der erste Brief des Paulus an die Korinther. Zweiter Teil: Auslegung der Kapitel 8–16, ThHK VII/2, 1982, 140–144 besteht zwischen 11,2ff. und 14,33ff. keine Spannung (und also kein Anlaß für die Annahme einer Interpolation); es gehe in Kap. 14 nur um das eigenmächtige Reden bzw. um »ein ›Dazwischenfragen‹ oder ›Drauflosreden‹« von Frauen im Gottesdienst (gegen diese Auslegung schon m. R. Greeven a.a.O. 132f., der die Stelle freilich nicht für interpoliert hält, sondern einen Selbstwiderspruch des Paulus konstatiert). Nach Wolff zeigt die Stelle die »unter den Korintherinnen verbreitete Disputierfreudigkeit«, die in der gottesdienstlichen Versammlung »zu einem Durcheinander« geführt habe (143); mit seinem Hinweis auf den νόμος erinnere Paulus die Leser an den jüdischen Gottesdienst: »Vermutlich ist daran gedacht, daß die Frau nur hörend am Tempel- und Synagogengottesdienst teilnimmt und dies aus der Thora hergeleitet wird« (144). – Aber es ist nicht zu erkennen, daß nach Meinung des Paulus für die in 14,1–33a geschilderten Zustände allein Frauen verantwortlich gewesen wären; σιγάτωσαν verbietet überdies ja nicht nur das »Drauflosreden«, sondern jedes Sprechen. Die für Paulus ungewöhnliche Terminologie und die inhaltliche Tendenz von v. 33b–36 verweisen auf das Umfeld der Pastoralbriefe (1 Tim 2,11ff.) und insbesondere auch des 1 Clem (vgl. 1,3; 21,7); beides könnte, sofern die Pastoralbriefe in Rom verfaßt wurden, auf die frühe römische Gemeinde als den Entstehungsort dieser Interpolation verweisen, womit auch erklärt wäre, warum die vv. in keiner Handschrift fehlen (freilich schwankt die Stellung von v. 34f.). Fragen muß man dann natürlich, ob der Interpolator die Spannung zu 11,2–16 nicht gesehen und warum er jenen Abschnitt nicht gestrichen hat. Aber (1) ist die Erweiterung eines Textes für den Bearbeiter leichter möglich als die Streichung eines so umfangreichen Abschnittes; und (2) enthält ja 11,2–16 – zumal aus der Sicht von 14,33ff. gelesen – auch schon eine restriktive Norm.

innergemeindlichen Umgang mit der Glossolalie hat der Hinweis auf Jes 28,11f. nicht[98].

III.

Die konkreten Weisungen des Paulus im Ersten Korintherbrief zeigen, daß Paulus sich nicht an den Inhalten der Tora orientiert, wenn er ethische Normen aufstellt oder in Konfliktfällen Entscheidungen trifft. Nun kann man natürlich sagen, daß in der Situation dieses Briefes (trotz 15,56, s. o.) die Gesetzesthematik als ganze von offenbar untergeordneter Bedeutung zu sein scheint und daß Paulus aus diesem Grunde keinen Anlaß sah, seine Entscheidungen explizit im Horizont bestimmter Toraaussagen zu formulieren bzw. von dorther zu begründen. Deshalb soll im folgenden zumindest kurz geprüft werden, ob sich der Befund in den späteren Paulusbriefen möglicherweise noch in charakteristischer Weise verändert hat.

In den beiden die Jerusalem-Kollekte betreffenden Brieffragmenten 2 Kor 8 und 2 Kor 9[99] finden sich an jeweils wichtiger Stelle ausdrückliche Hinweise auf Aussagen der Schrift. In 8,14 erklärt Paulus, die Kollekte für die ἅγιοι solle nicht zu einer Umkehrung der Besitzverhältnisse führen, wohl aber zu einem Ausgleich (ἰσότης), wofür in 8,15 ein Zitat aus der Erzählung vom Manna-Wunder in der Wüste folgt (zitiert wird Ex 16,18, mit geringen Abweichungen von LXX). Hier soll also zweifellos das angestrebte Ziel der ἰσότης als mit der Schrift übereinstimmend erwiesen werden; nicht jedoch wird die Unterstützung der Jerusalemer Gemeinde als solche als Erfüllung eines Toragebots (etwa des Almosengebens, Dtn 15,11) verstanden. Ähnliches gilt für 2 Kor 9,7: Das (gegenüber LXX veränderte) Zitat aus Prov 22,8a gibt kein Motiv für die Weisung selbst[100]; sondern es begründet, weshalb der Geber τῇ καρδίᾳ, nicht

---

[98] Zu den Einzelheiten des Zitats und seiner Veränderung durch Paulus vgl. Koch a.a.O. 255f. Paulus stelle klar, »daß die Wirkungslosigkeit der Glossolalie nach außen nicht auf Verblendung oder Verstockung der ἄπιστοι zurückzuführen ist, sondern im Phänomen der Glossolalie selbst begründet ist.«

[99] Ich vermute (ohne dies hier näher darlegen zu können), daß die Kapitel 8 und 9 zeitlich am Schluß der in 2 Kor erhaltenen paulinischen Korrespondenz stehen; die Abfassung von Kap. 8 läge nur wenig vor der Abfassung von Kap. 9. Jedenfalls geht der in 2 Kor 10–13 erhaltene Brief, in dem die Gesetzesproblematik ja zumindest indirekt von wesentlicher Bedeutung ist, voraus.

[100] Hätte Paulus unmittelbar auf eine biblisch begründete Weisung Wert gelegt, so hätte er nur den folgenden v. zu zitieren brauchen (Prov 22,9 LXX: ὁ ἐλεῶν πτωχὸν αὐτὸς διατραφήσεται· τῶν γὰρ ἑαυτοῦ ἄρτων ἔδωκεν τῷ πτωχῷ.); dies scheint ihm aber nicht wichtig zu sein. – Es ist im übrigen offenbar kein Zufall, daß Paulus im Zitat von Prov 22,8a das Verb εὐλογεῖν durch ἀγαπᾶν ersetzt; die Kollekte ist für ihn gleichsam die Antwort des Menschen auf die ihm durch das Christusgeschehen zuteilgewordene Liebe Gottes.

aber widerwillig von seinem Besitz abgeben soll. Und das (vollständig nach LXX angeführte) Zitat aus Ps 111,9 in 2 Kor 9,9 enthält keine Weisung, sondern es begründet die von Paulus in v. 8 angesprochene Verheißung, daß Gott in überreichem Maße Gnade gewähren werde.

Der Befund im paränetischen Abschnitt des Römerbriefes ist offensichtlich kein grundsätzlich anderer. Aus der Aussage von Röm 13,8–10, daß die ἀγάπη die Erfüllung (πλήρωμα) der Tora sei, wird zwar oft gefolgert, daß Paulus zumindest in diesem letzten uns erhaltenen Brief die für Christen geltenden konkreten ethischen Weisungen als mit den Normen der Tora übereinstimmend ansehe. Nach U. Wilckens ist sogar »das Gesetz die Autorität, die dem Tun der Liebe absolute Verbindlichkeit zuspricht«[101]. Man muß freilich beachten, daß Röm 13,8–10 eine gleichsam »systematische« Grundsatzaussage enthält, deren Sinn sich am besten erschließt, wenn man sie im Lichte der auch im Römerbrief vorhandenen konkreten Entscheidungen des Apostels liest. Das in Röm 14 ausführlich erörterte ethische Problem der Freiheit im Essen wird von Paulus nicht anders als im Ersten Korintherbrief ohne Rückgriff auf die Tora diskutiert und dann entschieden (14,23; 15,1)[102]. Die dabei in 14,14 getroffene Feststellung, daß nichts δι' ἑαυτοῦ unrein sei, steht sogar in einem eklatanten (freilich unerwähnt bleibenden) Widerspruch zur Tora – und stimmt auffällig mit der Tendenz von Mk 7,15.19 überein. Nicht die Rein und Unrein betreffenden Toragebote setzen im konkreten Konfliktfall den für das Verhalten der Christen gültigen Maßstab; entscheidend ist vielmehr das Christusgeschehen (14,15b). Wenn Paulus in diesem Zusammenhang betont, daß das »Betrüben« des Mitchristen im Widerspruch stehe zum Wandel κατὰ ἀγάπην, so zeigt dieser Hinweis auf die ἀγάπη eine Norm auf, die gerade jenseits aller Toraweisungen liegt[103]. Von hier aus ist m. E. auch der Abschnitt 13,8–10 zu interpretieren: Einziger Maßstab für das konkrete Verhalten der Christen ist der Erweis des gegenseitigen Liebens[104]. V. 8b zufolge hat der Liebende die gesamte Tora erfüllt; die Liebe bzw. »das Lieben« dient also nicht etwa dazu, das Tun der Toragebote zu ermöglichen, sondern sie tritt an die Stelle dieser Gebote[105]. Das wird durch v. 9 bestätigt: Die Aufzählung einzelner Gebote

---

[101] U. Wilckens, Der Brief an die Römer. 3. Teilband Röm 12–16, EKK VI/3, 1982, 71.

[102] Auch in Röm 13,1–7 erörtert Paulus ein ethisches Thema; aber er verhandelt es nicht als ein mit möglichen Konflikten behaftetes Problem. Zwar stimmt die hier von ihm gegebene Weisung mit Aussagen der jüdischen Tradition überein, doch fehlt jeder Hinweis auf die Schrift (etwa auf Weish 6,3f., wo freilich ein etwas anderer Akzent gesetzt ist).

[103] Es hat eben nicht nur »die Speisenfolge ... durch Christus ihre Relevanz verloren« (so Wilckens, Röm III, 92); die paulinischen Aussagen übe Rein und Unrein bedeuten die völlige Aufhebung eines Grundprinzips der Tora.

[104] Paulus verwendet in v. 8 nicht das Substantiv ἀγάπη, sondern das Verb; es geht um ein konkretes Handeln, nicht um ein »Prinzip«.

[105] So m. R. H. Hübner, Das Gesetz bei Paulus. Ein Beitrag zum Werden der paulinischen

des Dekalogs (Dtn 5,17–19.21 LXX) wird abgeschlossen mit dem Hinweis, daß dies alles »summiert«[106] sei im Liebesgebot, das Paulus nach Lev 19,18 LXX zitiert. Dabei erläutert Paulus in v. 10a den Charakter der ἀγάπη mit der Feststellung, Liebe sei das auf den Nächsten gerichtete Handeln, das das Tun des Bösen (κακόν) vermeidet. Indem Paulus daran anschließend in v. 10b die ἀγάπη als das πλήρωμα νόμου bezeichnet, setzt er nicht etwa nachträglich die Geltung der einzelnen Toragebote wieder in Kraft, sondern er macht deutlich, daß seine in v. 10a formulierte »Definition« der Liebe auch gerade gegenüber den Toranormen gilt[107]. Dieser Maßstab ist es, auf den Paulus dann in dem in Kap. 14 beschriebenen Konfliktfall verweist[108].

IV.

Paulus beruft sich in seinen Briefen in vielfältiger Weise auf biblische Texte, um die Übereinstimmung des von ihm verkündigten Evangeliums mit der Verheißung Gottes zu erweisen[109]. Dabei versteht er aber das Al-

---

Theologie, FRLANT 119, 1978, 78: Röm 13,8ff. enthalten eine Reduktion der Tora, 14,14.20 deren faktische Abrogation. Vgl. Hofius a.a.O. (Anm. 96): Röm 13,8ff. zeigt, daß Leben unter der Herrschaft des Geistes für Paulus zwar nicht »im Widerspruch zu der guten, sich in der Tora gültig bekundenden Rechtsforderung Gottes« steht (281), doch kenne Paulus andererseits keinen »tertius usus legis«, keinen »neuen ethischen Gebrauch der Mose-Tora für die christliche Gemeinde«; denn in der Tora »ist und bleibt die Rechtsforderung Gottes immer gebunden an die verklagende und verurteilende Bezeugung seiner Rechtsbestimmung« (278).

[106] ἀνακεφαλαιοῦσθαι, »ein sehr beziehungsreiches und vieldeutiges Wort«, ist in Röm 13,9 in dem überwiegend belegten Sinn von »etwas auf ein κεφάλαιον bringen, summieren, summarisch zusammenfassen« gebraucht (H. Schlier, Art. κεφαλή κτλ., ThWNT III, 1938, 681 Z 9–12.19).

[107] οὖν in v. 10b zeigt an, daß hier eine Folgerung vorliegt, nicht etwa eine Begründung für die Aussage von v. 10a.

[108] Wäre v. 10b anders zu deuten, so müßte man annehmen, daß Paulus zwischen dem Ritualgesetz und der ethischen Tora explizit und bewußt unterschieden hätte. Nach Holtz a.a.O. (Anm. 5) 394 hat es Paulus, ebenso wie schon vor ihm die Jerusalemer Hellenisten und auch Jesus, als einen Akt der Tora-Auslegung angesehen, kultisch-rituelle Gebote in gewissem Umfang nicht mehr anzuwenden; auch in bestimmten jüdischen Schriften spiele etwa die Beschneidung überhaupt keine Rolle, während die ethische Tora stark betont werde. Doch die von ihm genannten Texte belegen dies so nicht: Bei JosAs ist »auf alle Fälle [zu beachten], daß Aseneth eine Frau ist« (Chr. Burchard, Joseph und Aseneth, JSHRZ II/4, 1983, 611); Ps-Phokylides will von einem griechischen (!) Weisen verfaßt sein (vgl. N. Walter, JSHRZ IV/3, 1983, 192f.); und die Test XII schärfen dem Leser mehrfach ein, daß das ganze Gesetz zu halten sei (TJud 26,1; TIs 5,1), wobei die Beschneidung weder positiv noch negativ erwähnt wird.

[109] Die Schrift ist für Paulus tatsächlich ein »Zeuge des *Evangeliums*« (vgl. den Titel der Studie von D.-A. Koch; s. o. Anm. 81).

te Testament, seine Bibel, gerade nicht mehr als Tora im eigentlichen Sinne; sie ist ihm nicht mehr die Quelle der Weisungen Gottes für das Verhalten der Menschen, soweit sie Christen sind. Die paulinische Paränese ist, wie F. Lang zutreffend festgestellt hat, »ihrem Wesen nach nicht Gebrauch des Gesetzes (usus legis), sondern Konsequenz des Evangeliums«[110]. Der Durchgang durch den Ersten Korintherbrief hat das bestätigt: Paulus entscheidet in konkreten ethischen Konflikten nicht selten gegen die Tora; und er beruft sich umgekehrt auf sie als verbindliche Autorität auch dort nicht, wo er inhaltlich mit ihrer Weisung übereinstimmt[111].

Dem entsprechen diejenigen Aussagen im Römer- und im Galaterbrief, die sich innerhalb der Paränese grundsätzlich auf den Willen Gottes beziehen. Nach Röm 12,2 sollen die Christen δοκιμάζειν ... τί τὸ θέλημα τοῦ θεοῦ; mit keinem Wort sagt Paulus, der Wille Gottes könne doch an der Tora – oder auch nur speziell an den »sittlichen« Geboten des Dekalogs – zweifelsfrei abgelesen werden. Gewiß ist das in Röm 13,9 von Paulus als Erfüllung des νόμος genannte Liebesgebot eine biblische Weisung, und der Apostel weist darauf auch ausdrücklich hin. Aber das Liebesgebot steht nicht deshalb in Geltung, weil es von der Tora bezeugt wird, sondern deshalb, weil es dem Christusgeschehen entspricht (Röm 8,39; vgl. 14,15). Auch im Galaterbrief wird das Liebesgebot zitiert (5,14). Aber Paulus betont, daß es der auf das Christusgeschehen bezogene Glaube ist, der in dieser Liebe seine Wirksamkeit entfaltet (5,6), nicht die Tora; diese trennt vielmehr von Christus und seiner Gnade (5,4). In Gal 5,16ff. beschreibt Paulus präzise die Charakteristika des christlichen περιπατεῖν, wobei er ausdrücklich einen Gegensatz zwischen der vom πνεῦμα bestimmten Existenz und dem Sein ὑπὸ νόμον behauptet (5,18). Erst im Anschluß an die Auflistung des καρπὸς τοῦ πνεύματος (5,22.23a) folgt die Feststellung, daß der νόμος, die biblische Tora, zu diesen »Tugenden« nicht im Widerspruch stehe. Die das menschliche Zusammenleben ordnenden Worte und Maßstäbe stehen also nicht deshalb in Geltung, weil sie den inhaltlichen Normen der Tora entsprechen[112]; sondern nach Paulus

---

[110] F. Lang, Gesetz und Bund bei Paulus, in: Rechtfertigung. FS E. Käsemann (hg. von J. Friedrich/W. Pöhlmann/P. Stuhlmacher), 1976, 318.

[111] Einige der in 1 Kor zur Diskussion stehenden Konfliktfälle beziehen sich auf gleichsam »rituelle« Normen (so vor allem das Problem des Götzenopferfleisches); aber Paulus behandelt sie gar nicht als solche, sondern er bezieht die Konflikte auf die Grundnormen der zwischenmenschlichen Beziehungen (die ἀγάπη, die Rücksichtnahme auf den Bruder, entscheidet darüber, ob man am Mahl teilnehmen darf oder nicht). Auch von daher bestätigt sich noch einmal, daß der Apostel nicht zwischen Ritualgesetz und ethischer Tora trennt.

[112] Vgl. F. Mußner, Der Galaterbrief, HThK IX, ^{3}1977, 389: Der Hinweis auf den νόμος »taucht nicht deshalb auf, weil das Gesetz solche Tugenden gebietet, sondern weil die genannten Tugenden überhaupt nichts mit der Todesmacht des Gesetzes zu tun haben,

verdanken sie ihre Geltung dem πνεῦμα – und erst von daher wird dann ihre (teilweise) Konvergenz mit dem νόμος konstatiert[113]. Ethik ist für Paulus also keinesfalls die Praktizierung der Tora; ethische Entscheidungen trifft der Apostel vielmehr vom Bekenntnis her. Christen führen ihr Leben »in Christus«, der am Kreuz für Gottlose gestorben ist und in dem Gott die Sünder gerechtspricht. Dies ist für Paulus der Ursprung der ἀγάπη, an der als höchstem Wert sich das Handeln auszurichten hat[114].

---

sondern ›Frucht des Pneuma‹ sind. Das Pneuma, nicht das Gesetz, ›treibt‹ den Christen zu diesen Tugenden.« »Das Pneuma, nicht das Gesetz, ist das einzige ›Moralprinzip‹.«

113 Man kann also durchaus mit G. Ebeling, Die Wahrheit des Evangeliums. Eine Lesehilfe zum Galaterbrief, 1981, 345 vermuten, daß sich Paulus hier inhaltlich mit den Judaisten in Galatien »doch wohl im Konsens« befindet; aber es darf nicht übersehen werden, daß die von beiden Seiten anerkannte Geltung der erwähnten Normen unterschiedlich, ja, gegensätzlich begründet wird. Durch 5,23b werden ja die paulinischen Aussagen von 3,10.21 keineswegs aufgehoben.

114 Vgl. O. Merk, Handeln aus Glauben. Die Motivierungen der paulinischen Ethik, MThSt 5, 1968, 247f.: »Alles Begründen ethischer Weisungen ist für den Apostel nichts anderes als die Entfaltung des rechtfertigenden und versöhnenden Handelns Gottes, ist die Bezeugung des Anspruches Gottes auf die ihm gehörende Welt und die Bekundung seiner Treue zu seiner Gemeinde, die von Ostern her lebt und auf ihren kommenden Herrn wartet.«

Das apostolische Vermächtnis

– Zum paulinischen Charakter der Pastoralbriefe –

von Eduard Lohse

(Haarstraße 6, 3000 Hannover 1)

In den Briefen, die im Namen des Apostels Paulus an seine Schüler und Mitarbeiter Timotheus und Titus gerichtet sind, liegen Ansätze zu frühchristlichen Kirchenordnungen vor, die verantwortlichen Leitern von Gemeinden Hilfe bei der Wahrnehmung der ihnen anvertrauten Aufgaben bieten sollen. Dabei soll die Berufung auf die apostolische Autorität den Anweisungen für das Leben der Gemeinden sowie der Abwehr falscher Lehre Nachdruck verleihen. Zuständigkeiten und Verantwortlichkeit werden klar geregelt; die Übertragung des leitenden Amtes wird durch Handauflegung vorgenommen, und die Pflichten eines ἐπίσκοπος werden katalogartig aufgeführt, damit außer Zweifel steht, wer mit der Wahrnehmung des apostolischen Vermächtnisses und mit der Zurückweisung drohender Gefährdungen der Kirche betraut ist.

Im Rückblick auf die eingehende Diskussion, die über die Frage der Abfassung der Pastoralbriefe geführt worden ist, hat Hans v. Campenhausen mit Recht erklärt, ein Beweis für die nachpaulinische Entstehung der Pastoralbriefe brauche nicht noch einmal geführt zu werden.[1] Denn in 150 Jahren lang währender Auseinandersetzung um die Verfasserfrage sei bereits mehr als zur Genüge gezeigt worden, daß diese Schreiben in Wirklichkeit nicht von Paulus verfaßt sein können. Daher sei es angemessen, für alle weiteren Erörterungen die erwiesene Unechtheit der Pastoralbriefe nicht zum Ziel, sondern zur Voraussetzung zu machen. Diese Beurteilung trifft in der Tat zu, obwohl auch heute gelegentlich Stimmen laut werden, die an der paulinischen Verfasserschaft festhalten wollen. Sie können jedoch gegen die Fülle zwingender Gegenargumente schwerlich Gesichtspunkte beibringen, die eine erneute eingehende Prüfung erforderlich machen würden.

Das Bild, das die Briefe von Lehre und Verfassung der Kirche bieten, wird vielfach als frühkatholisch oder – wenn man behutsamer urteilt – als eine Vorstufe zum werdenden Frühkatholizismus bezeichnet. Bei dieser Beurteilung wird dann – grundsätzlich durchaus zu Recht – immer wieder auf die Unterschiede verwiesen, die zwischen der Theologie der Pa-

---

[1] H. v. Campenhausen, Polykarp von Smyrna und die Pastoralbriefe, 1951, 7.

storalbriefe und der authentischen Paulusbriefe bestehen.[2] Unversehens aber werden diese Gesichtspunkte dann so stark betont, daß nur noch der Abstand von Paulus betrachtet, aber nicht mehr gefragt wird, in welchem Maße die Pastoralbriefe denn trotz ihrer nachpaulinischen Entstehung Elemente der paulinischen Theologie bewahrt haben. Es trifft durchaus zu, daß die Frage nach dem Verhältnis der Pastoralbriefe zu Paulus zwar alt ist, ihre Beantwortung jedoch noch immer recht unterschiedlich ausfällt.[3] Will man aber den Ausführungen der Pastoralbriefe wirklich gerecht werden, so müssen sie an dem Anspruch gemessen werden, den sie als im Namen des Apostels redende Zeugnisse selbst geltend machen. Das aber heißt: In voller Würdigung ihrer nachpaulinischen Entstehung ist zu fragen, wie paulinisch denn die Pastoralbriefe sind. Zur Beantwortung dieser Frage seien einige einschlägige Abschnitte des näheren betrachtet, um aus diesen Analysen Kriterien zur genaueren Bestimmung der Theologie der Pastoralbriefe und des darin beschriebenen apostolischen Vermächtnisses zu gewinnen.

I.

Παῦλος ἀπόστολος Ἰησοῦ Χριστοῦ – so setzen die beiden Timotheusbriefe ein; Παῦλος δοῦλος θεοῦ, ἀπόστολος δὲ Ἰησοῦ Χριστοῦ – so sagt der Eingang des Titusbriefes. Damit werden Titel und Anspruch formuliert, wie sie auch in den unbestritten paulinischen Briefen aufgeführt werden. Durch Gottes Berufung und Befehl ist Paulus mit seinem apostolischen Amt betraut, damit er das Evangelium predige und Zeuge des gekreuzigten und auferstandenen Herrn sei. Die Erläuterungen, die der vorangestellten Titulatur hinzugefügt sind, sprechen dieses apostolische Selbstbewußtsein aus, geben ihm aber mit anderen Wendungen als in den Protopaulinen Ausdruck. Von der ἐπιταγὴ θεοῦ σωτῆρος ἡμῶν καὶ Χριστοῦ Ἰησοῦ τῆς ἐλπίδος ἡμῶν ist 1 Tim 1,1 die Rede. Paulus jedoch hat weder Gott als Heiland noch Christus als den Gegenstand der Hoffnung in dieser formelhaften Weise bezeichnet. 2 Tim 1,1 wird wie auch zu Anfang des 1. Korintherbriefes auf Gottes berufenden Willen hingewie-

---

[2] Den »wesentlichen Unterschied zwischen Paulus und Past.« arbeitet z. B. die umsichtige Untersuchung von H. v. Lips, Glaube – Gemeinde – Amt. Zum Verständnis der Ordination in den Pastoralbriefen, 1979, deutlich heraus (72; vgl. auch 280–283). Angesichts dieses Unterschiedes stellt sich jedoch um so schärfer die Frage, in welchem Verhältnis denn die Theologie der Pastoralbriefe zu der der authentischen Paulinen steht.

[3] So P. Trummer in seiner Grazer Habilitationsschrift: Die Paulustradition der Pastoralbriefe, 1978, 13. Zur Aufgabe vgl. zuletzt J. Roloff, Pfeiler und Fundament der Wahrheit – Erwägungen zum Kirchenverständnis der Pastoralbriefe, in: Glaube und Eschatologie – Festschrift für W. G. Kümmel zum 80. Geburtstag, 1985, 229–247: Der Verfasser der Pastoralbriefe »will von der festen Basis des paulinischen Evangeliums her im Namen des Apostels Lösungen für neu entstandene Probleme anbieten« (230).

sen, dann aber darüber hinaus die ἐπαγγελία ζωῆς τῆς ἐν Χριστῷ Ἰησοῦ genannt. Und der Titusbrief bringt mit einer für die Pastoralbriefe kennzeichnenden Wendung das Apostelamt des Paulus mit der πίστις ἐκλεκτῶν θεοῦ und ἐπίγνωσις ἀληθείας τῆς κατ' εὐσέβειαν in Verbindung (Tit 1,1). Erkenntnis der Wahrheit und rechte Frömmigkeit, zu der alle Menschen gelangen mögen, werden auf Gottes verborgenen, nun aber offenbar gewordenen Ratschluß zurückgeführt, den Paulus nach dem Befehl Gottes, unseres Retters, zu verkündigen hat (Tit 1,1–3). Der Gruß selbst lautet wie in den anderen Paulusbriefen auch im Titusbrief χάρις καὶ εἰρήνη, in den beiden Timotheusbriefen hingegen χάρις, ἔλεος, εἰρήνη.

Die Grundstruktur des paulinischen Briefformulars ist somit durchaus gewahrt. Das apostolische Amt des Paulus wird stark herausgehoben, und den Empfängern der Briefe wird gleich am Anfang in lapidaren Worten die rettende Heilsbotschaft zugerufen. Deren Inhalt wird jedoch mit Begriffen ausgesagt, die für die Pastoralbriefe kennzeichnend sind wie ἐπίγνωσις ἀληθείας, εὐσέβεια oder dem Hinweis auf die nunmehrige Kundgabe der vor ewigen Zeiten ergangenen Verheißung. Liegt in diesen Formulierungen lehrhaft geprägte Ausdrucksweise vor, so wird doch geltend gemacht: Paulus ist der Apostel der Völker. Die anderen Apostel oder die Zwölf werden nicht einmal erwähnt, mit niemandem hat Paulus sein unvergleichliches Amt zu teilen. Er ist von Gott und dem erhöhten Christus selbst berufen, in aller Welt die gute Nachricht bekannt zu machen. Denn er wurde gewürdigt, diesen Auftrag zu übernehmen und ihn in seinem missionarischen Wirken auszurichten.

Auf diese Beauftragung des Apostels wird nicht nur zu Beginn aller drei Briefe ausdrücklich hingewiesen, sondern von ihr wird auch in einem längeren Abschnitt im ersten Kapitel des 1. Timotheusbriefes ausführlicher gehandelt. Darin sagt der Apostel, der durch den Mund des Verfassers spricht, dem Kyrios Christus Jesus dafür Dank, daß er ihn stark gemacht, mit seinem Vertrauen beschenkt und zum Dienst berufen hat (1 Tim 1,12). Einst war er ein Lästerer, Verfolger und Frevler gewesen, jetzt aber ist ihm Erbarmung widerfahren, so daß er als Beispiel für den göttlichen Gnadenerweis schlechthin gelten kann (v. 13f.).

In diesen Sätzen werden Aussagen aufgenommen, mit denen Paulus selbst die entscheidende Wende seines Lebens beschrieben hat. »Ihr habt ja von meinem früheren Wandel im Judentum gehört«, – so redet er die Galater an –, »wie ich die Gemeinde Gottes über die Maßen verfolgte und sie zu vernichten suchte und im Jude-Sein viele meiner Altersgenossen in meinem Volk übertraf und besonders heftig um die Überlieferungen meiner Väter eiferte« (Gal 1,13f.). Daß er die Gemeinde Gottes verfolgt habe und darum nun allein aus Gottes Gnade sei, was er ist, sagt der Apostel auch zu den Korinthern (1 Kor 15,10). Er ist sich also durchaus dessen bewußt, daß – wie es im Philipperbrief heißt – sein Eifer um die

Gerechtigkeit unter dem Gesetz seine Feindschaft gegen die Gemeinde angetrieben hat (Phil 3,6). Aber während in diesen Worten nur in äußerster Knappheit die vorchristliche Zeit des Paulus erwähnt und ihr dann die von Gott gewirkte Wende entgegengestellt wird, wird im 1. Timotheusbrief der Hinweis auf den Lebensweg des Apostels erbaulich erweitert. Er war nicht nur ein Verfolger, sondern auch – so wird mit geläufigen Vokabeln der Lasterkataloge gesagt – ein Lästerer und Frevler. Paulus selbst aber hätte keinen Anlaß gesehen, dergleichen von sich zu behaupten, wie er sich auch nicht damit entschuldigt hätte, aus Unwissenheit im Unglauben gehandelt zu haben. Die Erklärung, Unkenntnis habe zu falschem Tun veranlaßt, bietet dagegen auch die Apostelgeschichte an, um begreiflich zu machen, warum die Juden Jesus ans Kreuz gebracht haben (Act 3,17). Die Schilderung, die der 1. Timotheusbrief vom Lebensweg des Paulus gibt, greift also auf geläufige Begriffe und Erklärungsmuster zurück, geht damit aber über die Angaben, die der Apostel selbst gemacht hatte, erheblich hinaus. Denn das Bild, das von Paulus gezeichnet wird, ist – wie Dibelius–Conzelmann zutreffend bemerken – »für den Gebrauch als Missionsparadigma stilisiert«.[4]

Die alles verwandelnde Wende seines Lebens führt Paulus auf Gottes Gnadenratschluß zurück, ohne jemals eine erbauliche Andeutung über seine Bekehrung zu machen. Nur in einem Nebensatz nennt er das für seinen Weg entscheidende Ereignis: »Als es aber Gott, der mich von Mutterleib an ausgesondert und durch seine Gnade berufen hat, gefiel, mir seinen Sohn zu offenbaren, damit ich ihn unter den Völkern verkündigte, da beriet ich mich nicht mit Fleisch und Blut« (Gal 1,15f.). Gottes gnädige Erwählung, die wie beim Propheten von Anfang an feststand, ereignete sich in der Offenbarung seines Sohnes, den Paulus fortan als den Herrn in aller Welt zu predigen hat. Nichts anderes als Gottes χάρις hat er darum zu preisen, »denn« – wie er zu den Korinthern sagt – »aus Gottes χάρις bin ich, was ich bin« (1 Kor 15,10). Insofern befindet sich die Schilderung, wie sie im 1. Timotheusbrief gegeben wird, durchaus in Übereinstimmung mit Paulus selbst, wenn sie – nun freilich in einem gewichtigen Hauptsatz – ausführt: »Um so reicher aber war die Gnade unseres Herrn« (v. 14). Der Begriff der χάρις wird dann aber mit denen von πίστις und ἀγάπη verbunden – die Gnade »samt dem Glauben und der Liebe, die in Christus Jesus ist« – und damit eine kurze Beschreibung des Christenstandes überhaupt vorgenommen. Dadurch wird Paulus als Exempel für das überwältigende Geschehen herausgestellt, daß Christus verlorene Sünder rettet, »unter denen ich« – Paulus – »der erste bin« (v. 15). Denn eben darum – so wird hinzugefügt – »ist mir Barmherzigkeit widerfahren, damit Christus Jesus an mir als erstem seine ganze Langmut erweisen könnte

[4] M. Dibelius–H. Conzelmann, Die Pastoralbriefe, ⁴1966, z. St.

zum Vorbild denen, die an ihn glauben sollen, um das ewige Leben zu erlangen« (v. 16).

Was Paulus widerfahren ist, wird damit als Paradigma einer Bekehrung verstanden, wie sie auch denen zuteil werden soll, die gleich ihm zum Glauben berufen werden sollen. Wie in der Apostelgeschichte in dreifacher Wiederholung und zugleich jeweils neu gestalteter erbaulicher Ausmalung von der Bekehrung des Paulus erzählt wird (Act 9,1–19; 22,3–21; 26,9–20), so wird auch im 1. Timotheusbrief das Beispiel des Paulus als Urbild für die Wende vom Unglauben zum Glauben verstanden.[5] Diese gewisse Nähe im beiderseitigen Verständnis der Berufung des Paulus darf jedoch nicht zu hoch bewertet und schon gar nicht zum Anlaß genommen werden, möglicherweise den Verfasser der Apostelgeschichte auch als den Autor der Pastoralbriefe anzusehen.[6] Denn für die Apostelgeschichte stellt das Damaskusgeschehen ein Ereignis dar, das die Befreiung aus der Finsternis zum wunderbaren Licht veranschaulicht, von der Paulus dann als auserwähltes Rüstzeug und Zeuge seines Herrn in aller Welt Kunde gibt (Act 9,15; 26,18). Aber der Titel eines Apostels wird ihm nicht zuerkannt,[7] sondern bleibt den Zwölf vorbehalten. Daher kann die Bekehrung des Paulus in der Apostelgeschichte auch nicht als Beauftragung mit dem Apostelamt verstanden werden. Doch eben in diesem, dem Selbstverständnis des Paulus entsprechenden Sinne bewertet der 1. Timotheusbrief das Damaskusereignis. Dort wurde Paulus die διακονία übertragen, für die der Kyrios ihm sein Vertrauen schenkte. Folglich ist er zum κῆρυξ καὶ ἀπόστολος eingesetzt, und das bedeutet – so unterstreichen die Pastoralbriefe –, daß er in dieser seiner Funktion διδάσκαλος ἐθνῶν ist (1 Tim 2,7; vgl. auch 2 Tim 1,11).

---

[5] Vgl. hierzu C. Burchard, Der dreizehnte Zeuge – traditions- und kompositionsgeschichtliche Untersuchungen zu Lukas' Darstellung der Frühzeit des Paulus, 1970, 127.

[6] Zu dieser Vermutung vgl. bes. A. Strobel, Schreiben des Lukas? Zum sprachlichen Problem der Pastoralbriefe, NTS 15 (1968/69), 191–210. Strobel weist darauf hin, daß zwischen den Pastoralbriefen und der Apostelgeschichte eine Reihe auffallender sprachlicher Übereinstimmungen besteht. So haben sie nicht nur Begriffe wie ἀγαθοεργεῖν, ἀχάριστος oder δυνάστης gemeinsam, sondern auch grammatische Konstruktionen wie δεῖ, ἔδει, δέον ἐστιν oder den Latinismus δι' ἣν αἰτίαν. Hier wie dort wird hervorgehoben, Christus sei in die Welt gekommen, um Sünder zu retten (1 Tim 1,15; Lk 19,10), oder: ein Arbeiter sei seines Lohnes wert (1 Tim 5,18; Lk 10,7). Doch die sprachlichen Übereinstimmungen beweisen nicht mehr, als daß in diesen Schriften hier wie dort eingeschobenes Koine-Griechisch verwendet wird. Und die inhaltlichen Berührungen beziehen sich auf geprägte Wendungen urchristlicher Lehre, die aus der mündlichen Tradition aufgenommen wurden. Zur Auseinandersetzung mit Strobel vgl. weiter N. Brox, Lukas als Verfasser der Pastoralbriefe?, JAC 13 (1970), 62–77.

[7] Zur Ausnahme von Act 14,4.14 vgl. die Kommentare z. St. und Burchard, a. a. O., 135 Anm. 315.

Wenngleich in dieser Darstellung, wie sie im 1. Timotheusbrief entworfen wird, das Interesse nicht beim Historischen bzw. Individuellen, sondern bei der erbaulichen Anwendung liegt,[8] so ist es eben doch die Gestalt des Paulus, dessen Berufung zum Apostel als Beispiel einer Bekehrung verstanden wird, wie sie sich an allen denen vollzieht, die künftig Glauben gewinnen und ewiges Leben empfangen sollen. Seine Bekehrung gilt als ὑποτύπωσις τῶν μελλόντων πιστεύειν, die als Urbild darstellt, wie Gottes Erbarmen Menschen zum neuen Leben führt. Ihm gelten darum Ehre und Preis in alle Ewigkeit (1 Tim 1,17). Wenn auch in typisierter Darstellung, so wird doch festgehalten, daß Paulus und kein anderer der Apostel, Prediger und Lehrer der Kirche ist, an dessen Verkündigung die Gemeinden sich zu orientieren haben. Weil er der erste ist, an dem sich Gottes Gnadenerweis auf wunderbare Weise mächtig gezeigt hat, darum haben alle, die nach ihm kommen, auf sein Beispiel zu blicken und seiner Lehre, die ihnen als sein Vermächtnis überliefert ist, zu folgen.

II.

Der Inhalt der Verkündigung, mit deren Ausrichtung Paulus beauftragt wurde, wird in den Pastoralbriefen in bekenntnisartigen Wendungen ausgesagt. So heißt es im Abschnitt, der die Berufung des Paulus zum Apostel darstellt, dieser λόγος sei fest, wahr und glaubwürdig: »daß Christus Jesus in die Welt gekommen ist, um Sünder zu retten« (1 Tim 1,15). Dabei liegt der Ton der Aussage wie auch in anderen urchristlichen Sätzen (vgl. Lk 19,10) auf dem rettenden Handeln des Christus σωτήρ. Die σωτηρία ist durch ihn ins Werk gesetzt und wird in der Verkündigung der Kirche als Gottes erlösende Tat ausgerufen.

In besonders hervorgehobenen Abschnitten seiner Briefe bezieht sich auch Paulus verschiedentlich auf urchristliche Bekenntnisaussagen, um damit anzuzeigen, daß es um das eine Evangelium vom gekreuzigten und auferstandenen Christus geht, wie es allerorten von allen bekannt wird, die den Namen des Herrn anrufen. So führt er zu Beginn der Auseinandersetzung, die er mit den Leugnern der Auferstehung in Korinth vornehmen muß, das Evangelium an, wie er es bereits empfangen und der Gemeinde als Inhalt und Grund ihres Glaubens weitergegeben hat, »daß Christus gestorben ist für unsere Sünden nach den Schriften und daß er begraben ist; und daß er auferstanden ist am dritten Tage nach den Schriften und daß er Kephas erschienen ist, danach den Zwölfen« (1 Kor 15,3–5). Was dieses Evangelium bedeutet, legt der Apostel dann im langen Gedankengang des 15. Kapitels seines Briefes dar, in dem er zunächst die Reihe der Zeugen des Auferstandenen weiterführt, mit seiner apostolischen Berufung zum Abschluß bringt und dann wiederholt auf die For-

[8] Vgl. Dibelius–Conzelmann, a.a.O. z. St.

mulierungen des Kerygmas zurückgreift, um sie auf die in Korinth gegebene Situation anzuwenden. »Ist aber Christus nicht auferstanden, dann ist unsere Predigt vergeblich, vergeblich auch euer Glaube« (v. 14), bzw.: »Ist aber Christus nicht auferstanden, so ist euer Glaube nichtig, so seid ihr noch in euren Sünden« (v. 17); »nun aber ist Christus von den Toten auferstanden als Erstling derer, die entschlafen sind« (v. 20).

Ebensowenig wie im 1. Korintherbrief begnügt sich Paulus in den Schreiben, die er an andere Gemeinden richtet, damit, eine überkommene Aussage nur anzuführen, um sich auf sie berufen zu können. Vielmehr legt er jeweils das von allen Christen gesprochene Bekenntnis aus, um die aktuelle Bedeutung des Glaubens aufzuweisen. So stellt sich im Eingang des Römerbriefes der Apostel der ihm persönlich noch unbekannten Gemeinde vor als »Knecht Christi Jesu, berufener Apostel, ausgesondert für das Evangelium Gottes« (Röm 1,1). Den Inhalt dieser ihm aufgetragenen Verkündigung aber gibt er mit dem Zitat eines judenchristlichen Bekenntnisses an, dessen Kenntnis er auch in der römischen Gemeinde voraussetzen kann. Im Evangelium – so heißt es – ist die Rede von Christus, »der seiner irdischen Herkunft nach aus dem Geschlecht Davids stammt, der zum Sohn Gottes eingesetzt wurde durch die Kraft des heiligen Geistes in Macht aufgrund der Auferstehung von den Toten« (Röm 1,3f.).[9] Mit dieser judenchristlichen Formulierung, die dem irdischen Davidssohn den erhöhten Gottessohn gegenüberstellt, verbindet Paulus die Hoheitstitel der hellenistischen Gemeinde, indem er an den Anfang den Begriff des Gottessohnes setzt und mit der vollen Wendung abschließt »Jesus Christus, unser Herr«. Ist auf diese Weise juden- und heidenchristliches Bekenntnis kraftvoll zusammengefaßt, so schließt Paulus dann an die zitierten Worte die Auslegung an, wie er sie in seiner Predigt vollzieht: Das Evangelium »ist Kraft Gottes zur Rettung für jeden, der glaubt, Juden zuerst und auch Griechen. Denn darin wird Gottes Gerechtigkeit offenbar aus Glauben in Glauben, wie geschrieben steht: Der Gerechte wird aus Glauben leben« (Röm 1,17f.). Diese Thematik aber wird dann im gesamten Gedankengang des Römerbriefs erläutert und in ihrer Bedeutung für Glauben und Leben der Gemeinde entfaltet.

Wie Paulus beschreibt auch der Verfasser der Pastoralbriefe in verschiedenen Zusammenhängen den Inhalt des christlichen Glaubens mit überkommenen Bekenntnisformulierungen. So erinnert er an die christologische Aussage, die zum Gedenken an Jesus Christus aufruft, »der von den Toten auferstanden ist, der aus dem Geschlecht Davids stammt« (2 Tim 2,8). Dabei sind freilich die Zeilen in umgekehrter Folge angeordnet, so daß nun zuerst vom Auferstandenen, dann erst vom irdischen Christus

---

[9] Zu den Einzelheiten der Abgrenzung und Bestimmung der urchristlichen Bekenntnisaussage vgl. die Kommentare z. St. und E. Lohse, Die Entstehung des Neuen Testaments, [4]1983, 21.

die Rede ist.[10] In einem anderen Zitat, das 1 Tim 2,5f. angeführt wird, heißt es: »Es ist ein Gott und ein Mittler zwischen Gott und den Menschen, nämlich der Mensch Christus Jesus, der sich selbst gegeben hat zur Erlösung für alle.« Dabei wird – wie deutlich zu erkennen ist – das Wort vom Lösegeld, das der Menschensohn mit der Hingabe seines Lebens für viele entrichtet (Mk 10,45 Par.), aufgenommen und in hellenistische Terminologie übertragen, indem von der universalen, allen Menschen geltenden Bedeutung des Kreuzestodes Jesu Christi gesprochen wird.[11] Ein hymnisches Fragment dient 1 Tim 3,16 dazu, den Inhalt des μυστήριον τῆς εὐσεβείας und die Kundgabe des göttlichen Geheimnisses zu nennen: »geoffenbart im Fleisch – gerechtfertigt im Geist; erschienen den Engeln – verkündigt unter den Völkern; geglaubt in der Welt – aufgenommen in Herrlichkeit.«[12]

In einer lehrreichen Abhandlung über die Christologie der Pastoralbriefe hat einst Hans Windisch überzeugend ausgeführt, daß der Verfasser der an Timotheus und Titus gerichteten Schreiben Christuslehre in Form von Sprüchen, Formeln und Hymnen darbietet, »die aus verschiedenen Lehrkreisen und Lehrstufen stammen.«[13] Er bezieht sich auf Aussagen des urchristlichen Bekenntnisses, legt sie aber seinerseits weder aus noch verwendet er sie in seiner weiteren Argumentation. Darin unterscheidet er sich in charakteristischer Weise von Paulus, der stets mit dem Zitat einer vorgegebenen Formulierung die konkrete Anwendung des einen Evangeliums verband, neben dem es kein anderes geben kann (vgl. Gal 1,6–9). In den Pastoralbriefen hingegen wird die rechte Lehre inhaltlich nur durch Zitate formulierter Bekenntnisse angegeben. Ihre Worte sind unverfälscht und unverändert zu wahren, um den Gefährdungen, die von Irrlehrern oder Vertretern libertinistischer Ethik ausgehen, widerstehen zu können. Es genügt, auf das Bekenntnis zum einen Gott und einen Mittler Jesus Christus den bekräftigenden Hinweis folgen zu lassen: »Eben dazu bin ich als Prediger und Apostel eingesetzt – ich sage die Wahrheit und lüge nicht –, als Lehrer der Heiden im Glauben und in der Wahrheit«

---

[10] Eine literarische Abhängigkeit von Röm 1,3f. ist jedoch kaum anzunehmen. So Trummer, a.a.O. (s. Anm. 3), 202f. Es dürfte vielmehr mündlich überliefertes Formelgut vorliegen.

[11] Vgl. E. Lohse, Märtyrer und Gottesknecht, ^{2}1963, 119.

[12] Zum Nachweis, daß ein hymnisches Zitat vorliegt, vgl. die Kommentare z. St. sowie Lohse, a.a.O. (s. Anm. 9), 23 und W. Stenger, Der Christushymnus in 1 Tim 3,16, TThZ 78 (1969), 33–48; ders., Der Christushymnus 1 Tim 3,16. Eine strukturanalytische Untersuchung. Regensburger Studien zur Theologie 6, 1977.

[13] H. Windisch, Zur Christologie der Pastoralbriefe, ZNW 34 (1935), 213–238, bes. 238. Zur Christologie der Pastoralbriefe vgl. weiter V. Hassler, Epiphanie und Christologie in den Pastoralbriefen, ThZ 33 (1977), 193–209 und L. Oberlinner, Die »Ephiphaneia« des Heilswillens Gottes. Zur Grundstruktur der Christologie der Pastoralbriefe, ZNW 71 (1980), 192–213.

(1 Tim 2,7). Der apostolischen Lehre, wie sie damit knapp bezeichnet ist, gilt es die Treue zu halten und sich weder von ihr abdrängen zu lassen noch von ihr zu weichen.

In den authentischen Paulusbriefen ist an einigen Stellen mit besonderer Betonung von der σωτηρία die Rede, die das Evangelium eröffnet – nicht nur in der Themaangabe des Römerbriefes (Röm 1,16) und in der Charakterisierung der ὁμολογία die εἰς σωτηρίαν abgelegt wird (Röm 10,10), sondern auch im 1. Korintherbrief, wo zum Wort vom Kreuz gesagt wird, es sei für uns, die wir gerettet werden (τοῖς δὲ σῳζομένοις ἡμῖν) Kraft Gottes (1 Kor 1,18). In den Pastoralbriefen wird die Wortgruppe σῴζειν/σωτηρῖα häufiger gebraucht, aber vor allem in formelhaften Sätzen verwendet. So werden Gott (1 Tim 1,1; 2,3; 4,10; Tit 1,3; 2,10; 3,4) und Christus (2 Tim 1,10; Tit 2,13; 3,6) als rettender σωτήρ bezeichnet. Gottes rettende Gnade ist erschienen (Tit 2,11), so daß sein gesamtes Erlösungshandeln als Rettung beschrieben werden kann (1 Tim 1,15; 2 Tim 1,9). Will Gott doch, daß alle Menschen gerettet werden und zur Erkenntnis der Wahrheit kommen (Tit 2,4), d. h. daß sie der σωτηρία in Christus Jesus teilhaftig werden (2 Tim 2,10; vgl. auch 2 Tim 3,15). Denn Gott, unser Retter, hat seine Güte und Menschenliebe offenbar gemacht und uns gerettet, damit wir nicht verlorengehen (Tit 3,4f.). Indem die σωτηρία auf diese Weise als Ziel und Inhalt des Evangeliums genannt wird, sind die christologischen Aussagen fest auf die apostolische Verkündigung bezogen, wie sie Paulus bei seiner Berufung aufgetragen wurde.[14]

Die gesunde Lehre, wie sie mehrfach in den Pastoralbriefen genannt wird (1 Tim 1,10; 2 Tim 4,3; Tit 1,9; 2,1), ist daher als paulinisches Evangelium verstanden, wie es im ersten Kapitel des zweiten Timotheusbriefes dem Nachfolger des Apostels vor Augen gehalten wird. Wie jener sich des Evangeliums nicht geschämt hat (Röm 1,16), so soll auch Timotheus sich »nicht des Zeugnisses von unserem Herrn noch meiner, seines Gefangenen, schämen« (2 Tim 1,8). Denn es geht im Evangelium um die von Paulus ausgelegte und bis an sein Ende treu gewährte Botschaft von Gott, »der uns gerettet hat und berufen mit heiliger Berufung, nicht nach unseren Werken, sondern nach seinem Ratschluß und nach der Gnade, die uns in Christus Jesus gegeben wurde vor ewigen Zeiten, aber jetzt offenbar gemacht ist durch die Erscheinung unseres Heilandes Christus Jesus, der dem Tode die Macht genommen und unvergängliches Leben ans Licht gebracht hat durch das Evangelium« (2 Tim 1,9f.). Partizipialstil, gedrängte Redeweise und parallele Anordnung der Zeilen lassen deutlich erkennen, daß in diesen beiden Versen eine vorgegebene Formulierung zitiert wird[15], die mit der Gegenüberstellung von Einst und Jetzt auf ein ge-

---

[14] Zur Soteriologie in den Pastoralbriefen vgl. weiter Oberlinner, a.a.O. (s. Anm. 13), passim.

[15] Vgl. Dibelius–Conzelmann, a.a.O. z. St.

bräuchliches urchristliches Predigtschema zurückgreift.[16] Der verborgene, aber schon von Urzeit an gefaßte Gnadenratschluß Gottes wird jetzt offenbar in der Proklamation des Evangeliums. Denn Christus hat – wie es auch andere urchristliche Bekenntnisaussagen hervorheben – die Macht des Todes zerbrochen und das Leben zum Sieg geführt (vgl. z. B. Kol 1,18; Eph 1,17f.).

Diesen überlieferten Wendungen ist eine ausgesprochen paulinische Antithese vorangestellt, die betont, Rettung und Berufung seien οὐ κατὰ τὰ ἔργα ἡμῶν ἀλλὰ κατὰ ἰδίαν πρόθεσιν καὶ χάριν erfolgt (v. 9). Die Problematik, mit der Paulus es in seiner Auseinandersetzung mit jüdischem bzw. judenchristlichem Verständnis einer Gerechtigkeit aus dem Gesetz zu tun hatte, liegt bereits in der Vergangenheit, so daß nicht mehr von Werken die Rede ist, wie sie das Gesetz fordert und deren sich rühmen zu können meint, wer seine δικαιοσύνη vor dem Gesetz zu erweisen bestrebt ist. Vielmehr wird von unseren ἔργα ohne jeden Zusatz gesprochen und festgestellt, daß zu keiner Zeit und in keiner Situation unser Tun – und sei es das denkbar beste – Grund zur σωτηρία oder Anspruch auf göttliche Berufung abgeben können. Sondern allemal ist die Rettung ausschließlich durch die göttliche χάρις bewirkt, die in Christus als Gottes rettendem Gnadenerweis offenbart ist.

Daß in einer geprägten Formulierung, die durchaus paulinische Züge trägt, eine so deutliche Ablehnung jeder Form von Werkgerechtigkeit vorgenommen ist, ist für die Theologie der Pastoralbriefe von besonderer Bedeutung. Denn in anderen Zusammenhängen spricht ihr Verfasser ebenso unbefangen wie unbedenklich davon, daß die Christen gute Werke zu tun haben, ja daß sie reich sein sollen ἐν ἔργοις καλοῖς (1 Tim 5,10.25; Tit 2,7.14; 3,8.14). Man gewinnt daraus den Eindruck, anders als bei Paulus heiße die Alternative nicht Glaube oder Werke, sondern rechter oder falscher Glaube und daher scheine die Verbindung von Glauben und Werken unproblematisch zu sein.[17] Doch ganz so spannungslos kann das Verhältnis von Glauben und Werken in den Pastoralbriefen nicht genannt werden. Denn das paulinische Evangelium, auf dessen lehrhafte Überlieferung zurückverwiesen wird, stellt sich einer naiven Werkgerechtigkeit in den Weg und weist sie in ihre Schranken.[18]

Eine vergleichbare Aussage, die in ähnlicher Weise gegen ein theologisches Fehlurteil Front macht, findet sich in einem anderen Zitat vorgegebener Formulierungen, das im dritten Kapitel des Titusbriefes ausgeführt wird. Darin wird das Erscheinen der Güte und Menschenfreundlichkeit Gottes gepriesen, die offenbar geworden ist. Denn er rettete uns »nicht um der Werke der Gerechtigkeit willen, die wir getan hatten, son-

[16] Vgl. hierzu P. Tachau, »Einst« und »Jetzt« im Neuen Testament, 1972.
[17] Vgl. v. Lips, a.a.O. (s. Anm. 2), 281.
[18] Vgl. Dibelius–Conzelmann, a.a.O. z. St.

dern nach seiner Barmherzigkeit durch das Bad der Wiedergeburt und Erneuerung im heiligen Geist« (Tit 3,4f.). Hier liegt wiederum eine paulinische Formulierung vor, die in den Gemeinden bereits in geprägte Formelsprache Eingang gefunden hat. Die polemische Auseinandersetzung um die vom Gesetz geforderten Werke spielt auch in diesem Satz keine Rolle mehr, so daß nur unsere Werke, die eine vermeintliche Gerechtigkeit begründen könnten, und Gottes Gnade einander gegenübergestellt werden. Diese Gegenüberstellung ist jedoch scharf ausgeprägt, so daß in den Gemeinden, die solche Sätze lehrend und bekennend festhalten, »das sola gratia getreulich bewahrt« worden sein muß.[19] Zugleich aber läßt sich nicht übersehen, daß die paulinische Antithese, die von der Rechtfertigung aus Gnaden – δικαιωθέντες τῇ ἐκείνου χάριτι (v. 7) – handelt, in einen durchlaufend von hellenistischer Terminologie geprägten Zusammenhang eingefügt ist. Von φιλανθρωπία, παλιγγενεσία und ἀνακαίνωσις ist die Rede. Dreimal wird die Wortgruppe σῴζειν/σωτήρ verwendet, ohne daß dabei eine Spannung empfunden wird, wenn zunächst Gott, dann aber Jesus Christus σωτήρ genannt wird (v. 4.6). Während bei Paulus Rechtfertigung und Taufe niemals in unmittelbare Verbindung miteinander gebracht werden, sondern nur auf Grund sachlich paralleler Aussagen einem sie übergreifenden Gedankenzusammenhang zugeordnet werden können,[20] sind sie hier – in konsequenter Fortführung der paulinischen Gedanken – fest miteinander verknüpft. Rechtfertigung, Wiedergeburt und Erneuerung, wie sie der heilige Geist bewirkt, haben sich in der Taufe ereignet, in der dem einzelnen das rettende Handeln Gottes und Jesu Christi widerfahren ist, so daß er fortan ἐν Χριστῷ Ἰησοῦ[21] lebt.

Auf diese Botschaft von Gottes rettendem Gnadenhandeln ist Verlaß, so daß die Anwartschaft auf das ewige Leben fest verbürgt ist. Denn der bereits geschehenen Epiphanie entspricht die künftige Erscheinung des großen Gottes und unseres Heilandes Jesu Christi, »der sich selbst dahingegeben hat, um uns von aller Ungerechtigkeit zu erlösen und sich ein reines Volk als sein Eigentum zu schaffen, das sich guter Werke befleißigt« (Tit 2,14). Läuft dieser Satz, der in wenigen Worten von Christi Erlösungswerk spricht, am Ende auf die Aufforderung hinaus, καλὰ ἔργα zu erbringen, so steht wiederum einer naiven Lehre von den Werken die im kirchlichen Bekenntnis bewahrte Theologie der Rechtfertigung entgegen.

Daher kann das apostolische Vermächtnis paulinischer Theologie im Zusammenhang der Pastoralbriefe als kritisches Prinzip dienen, um vul-

---

[19] Vgl. E. Käsemann, Exegetische Versuche und Besinnungen, I [6]1970, 299.

[20] Vgl. E. Lohse, Taufe und Rechtfertigung bei Paulus, KuD 11 (1965), 308–324; Die Einheit des Neuen Testaments, Göttingen 1973, 228–244.

[21] Während in den Protopaulinen sowohl die Formel ἐν Χριστῷ wie auch die Wendung ἐν κυρίῳ gebraucht werden, findet sich in den Pastoralbriefen durchgehend nur der Ausdruck ἐν Χριστῷ Ἰησοῦ.

gärchristliche Meinungen, die nur allzu leicht in Werkgerechtigkeit zurückzufallen geneigt sind, vom paulinisch verstandenen Kerygma her zu korrigieren.

III.

Als beispielhaftes Vorbild wird der Apostel nicht nur im Blick auf den ihm zuteil gewordenen Auftrag und die ihm aufgegebene Verkündigung hingestellt, sondern nicht zuletzt auch auf Grund seines vorbildlichen Wandels und seines Leidens, das er um Christi willen auf sich genommen hat. Christus Jesus hat an ihm – wie es in der Betrachtung über die Berufung des Paulus im 1. Timotheusbrief heißt – seine ganze Langmut erwiesen »zum Vorbild denen, die an ihn glauben sollen, um das ewige Leben zu erlangen« (1 Tim 1,16). Liegt darin zunächst der Gedanke, daß das rettende Handeln Christi, der ungeachtet der Feindschaft, in der der Jude Paulus ihm und seiner Gemeinde entgegengetreten war, sich seiner erbarmte und ihn nicht aus seiner Gnade fallen ließ, so dient doch der Hinweis auf das Leben des Paulus zugleich als Veranschaulichung der Wirkungen, die Christi rettendes Handeln zu zeitigen imstande ist. Denn als Paulus berufen wurde, wurde er für πιστός erachtet und ihm das Vertrauen geschenkt, daß er Treue halten werde. Unter diesem Stichwort ist der dankbare Lobpreis, in dem Berufung und Beauftragung des Apostels dargestellt werden, eingeführt: ἐπιστεύθην ἐγώ (1 Tim 1,11) – πιστόν με ἡγήσατο (ebda. v. 12). Die Verläßlichkeit der erneuernden Gnade des erhöhten Herrn kann daher am Beispiel des Paulus abgelesen werden, so daß aus der Betrachtung seines Vorbildes Ermutigung und Verpflichtung erwachsen, ihm im eigenen Lebensvollzug nachzueifern. »Halte dich« – so wird im 2. Timotheusbrief der Begriff ὑποτύπωσις wieder aufgenommen – »an das Vorbild der gesunden Worte, die du von mir gehört hast, im Glauben und in der Liebe in Christus Jesus« (2 Tim 1,13).

Auch Paulus konnte gelegentlich seine Gemeinden auf das Beispiel verweisen, das er ihnen gab. »Werdet meine Nachfolger« – so rief er den Korinthern zu, um den Auseinandersetzungen in der Gemeinde ein Ende zu setzen –, »wie ich Christus nachfolge« (1 Kor 11,1). Und den Thessalonichern stellte er das gute Zeugnis aus, sie seien seine und des Kyrios Nachfolger geworden, indem sie das Wort in vieler Bedrängnis mit vom heiligen Geist gewirkter Freude annahmen (1 Thess 1,6). Nachfolge ist damit als Nachfolge Christi und Gehorsam gegen das Wort verstanden. Die Pastoralbriefe nehmen diese Gedanken auf und fassen sie in den Begriff der ὑποτύπωσις, den die Protopaulinen nicht kennen. Dabei erhält das apostolische Vorbild seine besondere Prägung durch das im Leiden bewährte Zeugnis, dessen unveränderliche Gültigkeit damit festgestellt ist.

Dieser Zug des Paulusbildes ist besonders im 2. Timotheusbrief ausgeprägt, der den Charakter eines Testaments trägt und damit zugleich den endgültigen Abschluß der paulinischen Theologie bezeichnen will, an der nun keine Erweiterungen oder Veränderungen mehr vorgenommen werden dürfen. Zur Eigenart eines Testaments gehört es, daß derjenige, der anderen sein Vermächtnis anvertraut, sein bevorstehendes Ende ankündigt. So bereitet auch nach dem Bericht der Apostelgeschichte Paulus in der Abschiedsrede, die er vor den Ältesten aus Milet hält, seine Hörer auf seinen baldigen Tod vor: »Und nun siehe, als Gefangener im heiligen Geist reise ich nach Jerusalem, und ich weiß nicht, was mir dort begegnen wird, nur daß der heilige Geist in allen Städten mir bezeugt, daß Gefangenschaft und Bedrängnisse auf mich warten. Aber nach meinem Leben frage ich nichts, wenn ich nur meinen Lauf vollende und den Dienst tue, den ich vom Herrn Jesus empfangen habe, nämlich das Evangelium von der Gnade Gottes zu bezeugen« (Act 20,22–24).[22] Mit ähnlichen Worten wird auch im 2. Timotheusbrief der Lauf beschrieben, an dessen nahendes Ziel der Apostel gelangt ist:[23] »Ich werde schon geopfert, und die Zeit meines Scheidens ist gekommen. Ich habe einen guten Kampf gekämpft, ich habe den Lauf vollendet, ich habe Treue gehalten. Nun wartet auf mich der Kranz der Gerechtigkeit, den mir der Herr, der gerechte Richter, an jenem Tage geben wird, aber nicht nur mir, sondern auch allen, die seine Wiederkunft lieb haben« (2 Tim 4,6–8).

Sind in einigen Wendungen dieser Sätze deutlich Anklänge an Worte zu erkennen, die Paulus an die Gemeinden in Philippi und Korinth gerichtet hatte – »ich werde geopfert« (Phil 2,17), »ich sehne mich danach, aus der Welt zu scheiden und bei Christus zu sein« (Phil 1,23), »jeder aber, der kämpft, legt sich jeden Verzicht auf: jene nun, damit sie einen vergänglichen Kranz empfangen, wir aber einen unvergänglichen« (1 Kor 9,25) –, so ist darüber im apostolischen Testament des 2. Timotheusbriefes die grundsätzliche Bedeutung des apostolischen Leidens herausgestellt. Der Tod des Apostels drückt nicht nur der von ihm ausgerichteten Verkündigung das Siegel auf, das es gegen etwaige Verfälschung schützt, sondern zeigt zugleich, wohin der Weg weist, den Christen zu gehen haben. Denn auf dieses Wort ist Verlaß: »Sterben wir, so werden wir auch mit leben; dulden wir, so werden wir auch mit herrschen; verleugnen wir ihn, so wird er auch uns verleugnen; sind wir untreu, so bleibt er doch treu, denn er kann sich selbst nicht verleugnen« (2 Tim 2,11–13). In die-

---

[22] Zur Sache vgl. O. Knoch, Die »Testamente« des Petrus und Paulus. Die Sicherung der apostolischen Überlieferung in der spätneutestamentlichen Zeit, 1973 sowie die weiteren, dort verzeichneten Arbeiten zu Act 20,18–35.

[23] Zu den leidenstheologischen Aussagen in der Apostelgeschichte und den Pastoralbriefen vgl. auch Burchard, a.a.O. (s. Anm. 5), 127: »Ebenso ist für die nachapostolische Zeit das Bild des leidenden Apostels charakteristisch.«

sen Sätzen, die von hymnischem Klang getragen sind, liegt – wie auch die einleitende Formel πιστὸς ὁ λόγος anzeigt – offensichtlich wieder das Zitat eines geprägten Zusammenhanges vor.[24] Unserem Sterben und Dulden wird künftige Teilhabe an Leben und Herrschaft entsprechen. Unserem Versagen aber müßte göttliche Vergeltung antworten, doch größer als gerechte Entsprechung ist Gottes sich durchhaltende Treue. Weil er treu ist, darum sind auch seine Diener treu erfunden und ist auf das Beispiel wie auch das Wort, das sie in Leben, Leiden und Sterben ausgerichtet haben, Verlaß.

Die Leiter der Gemeinden, die als Evangelisten und Lehrer wirken, werden deshalb dazu angehalten, sich zu diesem Vorbild, das der Apostel gegeben hat, zu bekennen und mitzuleiden für das Evangelium in der Kraft Gottes (2 Tim 1,8), den guten Kampf des Glaubens zu kämpfen, das ewige Leben zu ergreifen, zu dem sie ja berufen sind (1 Tim 6,12), und selbst ein Vorbild der Gläubigen zu werden in Wort und Wandel (1 Tim 4,12). Verfolgungen, wie sie der Apostel erlitten hat und aus denen der Herr ihn errettete, bleiben denen nicht erspart, »die ein frommes Leben in Christus Jesus führen wollen« (2 Tim 3,12). Aber die Berufung zum ewigen Leben, die am Lebensweg des Apostels und seiner Vollendung beispielhaft abzulesen ist, kann niemand ihnen streitig machen – wenn sie nur treu bleiben, wie der Apostel es ihnen durch sein Vorbild gezeigt hat.

In einer Zeit, in der die Gemeinden durch Ausbildung einer geordneten Kirchenverfassung und Formulierung von Glaubenssätzen sich gegen Gefährdungen abgrenzten, die von gnostischen Spekulationen und libertinistischer Lebensweise ausgingen, wird in den Pastoralbriefen der Christenheit das Vorbild des Paulus vor Augen gerückt, der ihr als Apostel, Prediger und Lehrer den Weg zeigt, den sie zu gehen hat. Sein Wort, das die Prediger und Lehrer als das apostolische Vermächtnis der Gemeinde darreichen, hält sie dazu an, rechten und falschen Glauben voneinander zu unterscheiden. Wenn der 2. Petrusbrief erwähnt, daß unwissende und ungefestigte Leute Worte des Paulus, in dessen Briefen in der Tat manches schwer zu verstehen ist, verdrehten (2 Petr 3,16), so deutet er damit an, daß offenbar gnostische Gruppen sich auf den Apostel beriefen und ihn für sich in Anspruch zu nehmen suchten, um von christlicher Freiheit nach dem ihnen geläufigen Verständnis zu reden. Gegen solche Tendenzen machen die Pastoralbriefe Front und setzen jeder mißbräuchlichen Verwendung der paulinischen Theologie ihren Widerspruch entgegen. Diesen Vorgang hat einst Walter Bauer als den Versuch der Kirche bezeichnet, »Paulus unmißverständlich in die antihäretische Front einzugliedern und den Mangel an Vertrauen zu ihm in kirchlichen Kreisen zu behe-

[24] Vgl. Dibelius–Conzelmann, a.a.O. z. St.

ben«.[25] Doch dieses Urteil trifft nicht recht den Charakter der Pastoralbriefe. Denn sie brauchen nicht ein in Vergessenheit geratenes Bild des Apostels hervorzuholen, um ihm wieder zu Ansehen zu verhelfen. Vielmehr können sie sich mit der Berufung auf Paulus auf eine unbestrittene Autorität beziehen, um aus seinem Vorbild die für die Gegenwart erforderliche Orientierung zu gewinnen und damit zugleich die notwendigen Abgrenzungen gegen mißbräuchliche Berufung auf Paulus vorzunehmen.[26] Otto Merk hat daher den Standort der Pastoralbriefe zutreffend beschrieben, wenn er sagt, in ihnen werde gezeigt, »daß in der gegenwärtigen Lage der Kirche das Wort des einen Apostels, des Paulus, Recht und Gültigkeit beanspruchen darf und darum in seinem Namen anstehende Probleme der Kirche autoritativ gelöst werden können«.[27]

Es darf freilich nicht übersehen werden, daß manche Konturen, wie sie sich in den authentischen Paulusbriefen zeigen, in den Pastoralbriefen abgeschliffen sind und auch die Sätze, die von der Rechtfertigung aus Gnaden handeln, formelhaften Charakter tragen.[28] Der Verfasser der Pastoralbriefe hatte jedoch den unabweisbar geforderten Versuch zu unternehmen, durch den Entwurf einer Kirchenordnung sowie einer an den Fragen des Alltags orientierten Ethik zu beschreiben, wie christlicher Glaube sich in der Weltlichkeit seines Lebens und Handelns zu bewähren hat.[29] Dieser Aufgabe suchte er zu genügen, indem er verschiedene Überlieferungen aufnahm, sie zusammenfügte und unter das autoritative Wort des Apostels Paulus stellte. Daß bei dem Versuch, Weltlichkeit des Glaubens zu beschreiben, der Glaube sich nicht an diese Welt verlieren darf und sich der Gefährdungen, denen er ausgesetzt ist und standzuhalten hat, bewußt bleiben muß, hat der Verfasser der Pastoralbriefe durchaus empfunden. Es bleibt jedoch eine Spannung bestehen zwischen dem paulinischen Satz, daß die Gnade Gottes uns ohne alles Verdienst unserer Werke widerfahren ist, und der Aufforderung, guten Werken nachzueifern und sich darin zu bewähren. Wenn auch der Verfasser der Pastoralbriefe diese Spannung selbst kaum in ihrer vollen Stärke erkannt hat, so hat er doch

[25] W. Bauer, Rechtgläubigkeit und Ketzerei im ältesten Christentum, 1934 (^{2}1964), 228. Vgl. auch v. Campenhausen, a.a.O. (s. Anm. 1), 12.

[26] Vgl. W. Schmithals, Pastoralbriefe, RGG ^{3}V, Sp. 147.

[27] O. Merk, Glaube und Tat in den Pastoralbriefen, ZNW 66 (1975), 96; vgl. auch N. Brox, Die Pastoralbriefe, 1969, 115.

[28] Trummer, a.a.O. (s. Anm. 3), 193 spricht mit Recht von einer »geschichtlich bedingten Änderung und Entschärfung des paulinischen Ansatzes« in den Pastoralbriefen, übertreibt dann jedoch, wenn er dem eben genannten Sachverhalt »auch deutliche Tendenzen zu einer Ausweitung und Radikalisierung der paulinischen Thesen« meint gegenüberstellen zu dürfen.

[29] Der heute mißverständliche Ausdruck einer Bürgerlichkeit des Christentums, mit dem einst Dibelius den Charkater der Pastoralbriefe zu kennzeichnen suchte, wird m. E. besser durch den Begriff der Weltlichkeit des Glaubens ersetzt.

mit der Berufung auf den Apostel Paulus, der nicht nur aus den lehrhaften Sätzen, wie sie angeführt werden, sondern vor allem aus seinen eigenen Briefen spricht, aufgewiesen, daß es auf nichts anderes als die Wahrheit des Evangeliums ankommt. Insofern haben die Pastoralbriefe mit der Aufnahme und Fortführung der paulinischen Theologie, um die sie sich bemüht haben, zugleich auch die kritische Norm angegeben, an der sie gemessen sein wollen. Denn so notwendig in der damaligen Situation eine Konsolidierung der Kirche gefunden werden mußte[30], so unerläßlich bleibt die Aufgabe bestehen, eine bestimmte geschichtliche Situation nicht absolut zu setzen, sondern vielmehr die Probleme, denen sich die Kirche jeweils zu stellen hat, der stets neu zu bedenkenden Frage nach der Wahrheit des Evangeliums zu unterwerfen und die Antwort von dieser allein gültigen Botschaft her aufs neue zu suchen.

---

[30] Vgl. v. Lips, a.a.O. (s. Anm. 2), 160.

Die Frage nach dem Guten

Zu Mt 19,16–30 und Par.

von Ulrich Luck

(Königsweg 78F, 2300 Kiel 1)

I.

Die Perikope »Von der Gefahr des Reichtums«[1] gehört zu den Überlieferungsstücken der synoptischen Tradition, die die Exegese immer wieder vor zentrale überlieferungsgeschichtliche, religionsgeschichtliche, redaktionsgeschichtliche und theologische Fragen stellen. Dabei liegt, wie schon die Überschrift zeigt, das Interesse vor allem auf dem Ausgang der Perikope mit den Worten Jesu über den Reichtum. Es ist der Reichtum, der den Menschen bindet und hindert, den Weg der Nachfolge Jesu zu gehen und so den Weg zum ewigen Leben zu finden. In einer sozial bewegten und engagierten Zeit erscheint dies verständlich. Doch dieses Achtergewicht macht sich schon in der Überlieferungs- und Redaktionsgeschichte darin bemerkbar, daß Mt 19,16–22 eine ganze Reihe von Logien nach sich gezogen hat[2].

Demgegenüber hat die Einleitung des Stückes, in der »einer« an Jesus herantritt, um ihm die Frage zu stellen, was er tun müsse, um das ewige Leben zu erben, noch nicht die gebührende Beachtung gefunden, die ihr für das Verständnis der ganzen Perikope zukommt[3].

Aufgefallen ist natürlich immer schon, daß sowohl in der Anrede als auch in der Frage an Jesus sich die synoptischen Evangelien nicht unerheblich voneinander unterscheiden. Bei Mk wird Jesus mit »guter Lehrer« angeredet. Die Frage an ihn lautet: »Was muß ich tun, damit ich das ewige

---

[1] So der Titel der Perikope in A. Huck–H. Greeven, Synopse der ersten Evangelien, 1. Auflage der völligen Neubearbeitung von H. Greeven, 1981, 179.

[2] Dazu: N. Walter, Zur Analyse von Mc 10,17–31, ZNW 53, 1962, 206–218. – W. Harnisch, Die Berufung des Reichen, Festschrift für E. Fuchs, 1973, 161–176. Aus Platzgründen kann hier auf diese Fragen nicht näher eingegangen werden.

[3] K. Berger, Die Gesetzesauslegung Jesu I: Markus und Parallelen, WMANT 40, 1972, 396–417, behandelt die Funktion von Mk 10,17–19 im Aufbau von Mk 10,13–31. – J. Gnilka, Das Evangelium nach Markus (Mk 8,27–16,20), EKK II/2, 1979, 85 erkennt richtig: »Die Anrede ist ... mehr als eine captatio benevolentiae, sie ist der Vorausgriff auf den sich anbahnenden Konflikt.«

Leben erben werde?« (Mk 10,17). Auch Lk läßt den Vorsteher in dieser Form Jesus anreden und ihn die Frage stellen: »Was getan habend werde ich das ewige Leben erben?« (Lk 18,18).

Anders aber sind Anrede und Frage bei Mt. Hier wird Jesus nur mit »Lehrer« angeredet. Das Gute ist nicht Bestandteil der Anrede, sondern Gegenstand der Frage nach dem ewigen Leben: »Was Gutes soll ich tun, damit ich haben werde ewiges Leben?« (Mt 19,16). Demgemäß unterscheiden sich auch die Antworten, die Jesus gibt: Bei Mk und Lk weist Jesus den ihn anredenden Mann zurück: »Was nennst du mich gut? Niemand ist gut, außer der eine Gott!« (Mk 10,18; Lk 18,19).

Bei Mt erklärt sich Jesus für unzuständig für diese Frage und verweist auf Gott: »Einer ist der Gute!« (Mt 19,17). Von da aus verbindet er die Einleitung der Perikope mit der Fortsetzung: »Wenn du aber in das Leben hineinkommen willst, bewahre die Gebote!«[4].

Mk und Lk kommen ohne weiteren Übergang auf das Thema der Gebote mit dem knappen Hinweis »Die Gebote kennst du: ...« (Mk 10,19; Lk 18,20). Sie zitieren dann in verschiedener Reihenfolge: Du sollst nicht töten! Du sollst nicht ehebrechen! Du sollst nicht stehlen! Du sollst nicht falsch bezeugen! Du sollst nicht berauben! Ehre deinen Vater und die Mutter! Diese Gebote werden genannt als Antwort auf die Frage nach dem ewigen Leben. Auch hier unterscheidet sich Mt von Mk und Lk, wenn er mit Lev 19,18 noch das Gebot der Nächstenliebe hinzufügt[5].

Der Unterschied zwischen Mk und Lk auf der einen und Mt auf der anderen Seite hat die Exegese immer wieder beschäftigt. Eine Zusammenfassung der älteren Arbeiten bietet W. Wagner in seinem Aufsatz aus dem Jahre 1907[6]. Das Fehlen des Prädikates ἀγαθός in der Anrede bei Mt und die dadurch bedingte Änderung im Einleitungsdialog zwischen dem Fragenden und Jesus werden primär auf die christologischen Schwierigkeiten zurückgeführt, die die Ablehnung des Prädikates »gut« durch Jesus zur Folge hat: Wie verträgt sich das mit der Sündlosigkeit und sittlichen Vollkommenheit Jesu? In der Mk-Exegese spielt diese Frage bis in unsere Gegenwart eine erhebliche Rolle[7]. Die in der Zurückweisung der Anrede »Guter Lehrer« liegende Differenzierung zwischen Gott und Jesus wird zu begründen versucht. Diesem Problem weiche Mt aus, indem er Anrede und Frage auf seine Weise ändere. Ganz knapp wird dies von E. Klostermann so kommentiert: »Beide Male muß wohl Änderung aus vor-

[4] Der Zusammenhang zwischen der Auseinandersetzung über das Prädikat »gut« mit dem Hinweis auf die Gebote wird richtig vermerkt von R. Pesch, Das Markusevangelium II, HThK 2, 1977, 139.

[5] Vgl. dazu: Mt 5,43ff.; 7,12; 9,13; 12,7; 22,39 in gleichlaufender Tendenz.

[6] W. Wagner, In welchem Sinne hat Jesus das Prädikat ἀγαθός von sich abgewiesen? ZNW 8, 1907, 143–161.

[7] Vgl. E. Schweizer, Das Evangelium nach Markus, NTD 1, ^{2}1968, 120.

gefaßter dogmatischer Meinung ... angenommen werden.«[8] Auch R. Bultmann sieht die Dinge kaum anders: »Bei Mt kann Jesus die Anrede des Reichen, διδάσκαλε ἀγαθέ, natürlich nicht wie bei Mk zurückweisen; Jesu Antwort wird 19,17 ungeschickt korrigiert.«[9] In welchem Sinne das geschieht, wird von G. Bornkamm so formuliert: damit wird »Jesus selbst das von ihm Mk 10,18 abgewehrte Prädikat wieder zugesprochen.«[10]

Das Problem der verschiedenen Einleitungen wird also vorwiegend auf der Ebene der Christologien der Evangelien gesehen, die hinter der Redaktion der Evangelien stehen. Daß eine solche Sicht der Dinge ihre Berechtigung hat, ist unbestritten. Sie scheint mir aber bei weitem nicht auszureichen, wenn man die Bedeutung dieser Einleitung für das Verständnis der ganzen Perikope richtig in Anschlag bringen will. Dies gilt gerade auch für die Hintergründe der verschiedenen Gestalt dieser Einleitung bei Mk/Lk und Mt.

Bereits W. Wagner hat in seinem Aufsatz aus dem Jahre 1907 darauf hingewiesen, daß die relativ breite Diskussion um die christologischen Schwierigkeiten, die aufgeworfen werden, wenn Jesus für sich das Prädikat »gut« zurückweist, nur dann entstehen, wenn man ἀγαθός als »sündlos, sittlich vollkommen« versteht. Dagegen spricht aber schon eine von den Kirchenvätern an zu belegende Tradition, die an Justin, Ambrosius und Luther belegt wird, ἀγαθός als »gütig, gnädig« zu übersetzen. Unter dieser Voraussetzung wäre dann die Abweisung des Prädikates durch Jesus durchaus verständlich. Allerdings wird dann die Frage drängender: Warum hat dann Mt die Anrede und die Frage so geändert? Hat er bereits ἀγαθός als »sündlos und sittlich vollkommen« verstanden und damit doch wohl mißverstanden? Darauf gibt Wagner keine Antwort[11].

Mir scheint aber, daß gerade über die Version des Mt ein Weg zum Verständnis der ganzen Bedeutung der Einleitung für die Perikope führt. Erst von da aus können dann auch die Verschiedenheiten unter den Evangelisten zureichend erklärt werden.

Einen guten Einstieg bieten die Kommentare zum Markus- und Matthäusevangelium von J. Schniewind. In seiner Auslegung von Mk 10,17 stellt Schniewind zur Ablehnung des Prädikates »gut« durch Jesus die übliche Frage, ob dies nicht im Konflikt stehe zur Sündlosigkeit Jesu. Die Antwort ist dann eher dogmatisch als exegetisch: »Es steht überall im N. T. hart nebeneinander, daß Jesus ganz von ›den Sündern‹ getrennt (Hebr. 7,26) ist, und daß er ganz zu ihnen gehört, ganz versucht und ganz ohne

[8] E. Klostermann, Das Matthäusevangelium, HNT 4, ^{3}1938, 157.

[9] R. Bultmann, Die Geschichte der synoptischen Tradition, FRLANT 29, ^{2}1931, 383.

[10] G. Bornkamm, Enderwartung und Kirche im Matthäusevangelium, G. Bornkamm, G. Barth, H. J. Held, Überlieferung und Auslegung im Matthäusevangelium, WMANT 1, 1960, 13–47,26.

[11] W. Wagner, a.a.O. s. Anm. 6, 157–161.

Sünde (Hebr. 4,15): zwei Gedankenreihen, deren logische Einung nie gelingen kann, deren tatsächliche Einheit doch in jedem Wort des N.T. vorausgesetzt wird.«[12]

Anders in der Erklärung zu Mt 19,16f. Hier stellt er nicht nur fest, daß Mt »den Anstoß an der Überlieferung empfunden« habe, »der noch den heutigen Leser des Mk beschäftigt ...«, er arbeitet auch heraus, daß die Frage nach dem Guten (Neutr.) in einer langen biblischen Tradition steht: »Der Gute« ist »eine sonst im N.T. nicht vorkommende Bezeichnung Gottes. ›Das Gute‹ hingegen ist seit dem Propheten Amos ... die ständige Bezeichnung für das, was Gott will (Amos 5,14f.).«[13] Der Verweis auf Amos 5,4.6.14f.; Micha 6,8 findet sich in den Kommentaren zum Matthäusevangelium häufig[14]. Allerdings trägt dieser Hinweis wenig aus, wenn alttestamentliche und frühjüdische Belege nur eklektisch herangezogen werden. Sie müssen auf eine Basis gestellt werden, von der aus sich ihr Sinn und ihre Bedeutung erschließt. Dies soll nun versucht werden.

II.

Einen festen Grund für das Verständnis von »gut« und »böse« erhalten wir in Dtn 30,15–20:

> Siehe, ich habe dir heute vorgelegt Leben und das Gute, den Tod und das Böse. Wenn du dem Befehl Jahwes, deines Gottes gehorchst, den ich dir heute befehle, indem du Jahwe deinen Gott liebst, auf seinen Wegen wandelst und seine Gebote, Satzungen und Rechte beobachtest, so wirst du am Leben bleiben und dich mehren, und Jahwe, dein Gott, wird dich segnen in dem Lande, in das du einziehst, um es in Besitz zu nehmen. Wenn aber dein Herz abtrünnig wird und du dich ungehorsam zeigst, ... so kündige ich euch hiermit heute an: Ihr werdet sicher zugrunde gehen; ihr werdet kein langes Leben haben in dem Lande, in das du über den Jordan hinüberziehst, um es in Besitz zu nehmen. Ich nehme heute den Himmel und die Erde zu Zeugen gegen euch, daß ich dir Leben und Tod, Segen und Fluch vor Augen gestellt habe; so wähle denn das Leben, ...

Dieser Abschnitt ist in mehrfacher Hinsicht aufschlußreich. Er sagt zunächst ganz klar, worum es beim Gegenüber von gut und böse geht: Es geht um Leben und Tod. Die Entscheidung zwischen dem Guten und dem Bösen entspricht der Entscheidung zwischen Leben und Tod. Damit ist aber zugleich gesagt: Der Mensch steht in einer Grundsituation, in der er sich zwischen gut und böse, zwischen Leben und Tod zu entscheiden hat. Schon von hier aus fällt Licht auf unsere Perikope Mt 19,16ff.: Die Frage nach dem Guten und die Frage nach dem Leben gehören zusammen. Ja, man kann noch allgemeiner sagen: Mit dem Stichwort »gut« ist zugleich

---

[12] J. Schniewind, Das Evangelium nach Markus, NTD 1, ^{7}1956, 137.

[13] J. Schniewind, Das Evangelium nach Matthäus, NTD 2, ^{4}1950, 206.

[14] E. Schweizer, Das Evangelium nach Matthäus, NTD 2, 1973, 252. – W. Grundmann, Das Evangelium nach Matthäus, ThHK I, ^{5}1981, 432.

das Thema »Leben« gegeben. Die Frage nach dem Guten und die Frage nach dem Leben sind de facto identisch. Der Mensch, der leben will, der sein Leben gewinnen will, der muß das Gute tun.

Der Dtn 30,15–20 gegebene Hintergrund belegt nicht nur den Zusammenhang von »Gutem« und »Leben«. Zum Leben, so wie es im Deuteronomium vorausgesetzt ist, gehört auch wie selbstverständlich dazu: »Segen«, »langes Leben«, »Sich – mehren«, Wohlstand und Besitz[15]!

Da das Dtn den Weg des Guten mit dem Weg des Gesetzes identifiziert (Dtn 30,15f.), so ergibt sich schließlich, daß mit dem Stichwort »gut« alle Themen des Gespräches gegeben sind: Leben, Gesetz, Besitz. Doch zum wirklichen Verstehen unserer Perikope müssen wir noch einen Schritt weiter zurückgreifen. Die hier gemachte Voraussetzung, daß der Weg des Gesetzes zum Guten führt, ist deuteronomisch. Wir finden in den atlichen Überlieferungen noch einen anderen Weg, der zum Guten führt: die Weisheit. »Auch die Weisheit will den Weg des Lebens lehren.«[16] (Spr. 2,19; 5,6; 6,23; 12,18; 15,24; 16,17). Hier ist der Weg der Weisheit zugleich der Weg des Guten (Spr. 2,9.20). Sie, die Weisheit, verheißt den Guten Gutes (Spr. 2,20; 12,2; 13,2; 14,14.19). Das Problem dieses Nebeneinanders von Weisheit und Thora wird zumeist so gelöst, daß hier zwei ursprünglich selbständige Wege vorlägen, die später dann, nicht ohne Schwierigkeiten, identifiziert worden seien[17]. Dabei scheint mir die entscheidende Frage zunächst die zu sein, worin wir den älteren Weg zu sehen hätten: Im Weg der Weisheit oder im Weg des Gesetzes? Es dürfte keine Frage sein, daß der Merismus gut – böse ursprünglich weisheitlich ist. In ihm kommt die Grundsituation in unüberbietbarer Weise zum Ausdruck, in der der Mensch immer schon steht[18].

Aber es genügt nun nicht festzustellen, daß es zu einer Identifikation von Weisheit und Gesetz gekommen ist, sondern es muß klar werden, warum das Gesetz die Aufgabe der Weisheit übernimmt, in der Entscheidungssituation zwischen gut und böse den Weg zum Guten zu weisen.

Der Merismus gut – böse bezeichnet deshalb die menschliche Grundsituation, weil hier darüber entschieden wird, »was dem Leben nützt und was ihm schädlich ist«[19]. Die Weisheit führt den Menschen auf

---

[15] Vgl. dazu H. H. Schmid, Schöpfung, Gerechtigkeit und Heil. »Schöpfungstheologie« als Gesamthorizont biblischer Theologie, ZThK 70, 1973, 1–19 = Altorientalische Welt in der alttestamentlichen Theologie, 1974, 9–30,19f.: »Was über dem Halten der Gebote als Segen steht, ist nichts anderes als die heile, schöpfungsgemäße Weltordnung«.

[16] H. J. Stoebe, Art. טוֹב ṭob gut, THAT I, 651–664, 660.

[17] Vgl. M. Hengel, Judentum und Hellenismus, WUNT 10, ^{2}1973, 307–318. – M. Küchler, Frühjüdische Weisheitstradition, OBO 26, 1979, 33–45.

[18] H. J. Stoebe, a.a.O. s. Anm. 16, 658f. – I. Höver-Johag, Art. טוֹב, ThWAT III, 315–339, 329–331 (mit Wortstatistik),

[19] H. J. Stoebe, a.a.O. s. Anm. 16, 659.

dem Weg zum Leben, sie führt ihn auf dem guten Weg (Spr 2,9.20), damit er nicht dem Bösen und somit dem Tode verfällt.

III.

Das Problem besteht nun aber darin, daß die Weisheit den Menschen nicht aus dem Zwiespalt zwischen gut und böse herausführen kann, indem sie ihn auf dem Wege des Guten hält. Sie hat selbst teil an der Zwiespältigkeit der Welt (Spr. 5,1–14 u. a. aber auch Jak 3,15). Es entsteht die Frage nach der wahren Weisheit, eben der Weisheit, die zum Leben führt gegenüber der falschen Weisheit, die den Menschen täuscht und ihn in den Tod verführt[20].

Das Gesetz soll jetzt eindeutig sagen, was gut ist, und was Jahwe vom Menschen fordert (vgl. Micha 6,8). Damit steht es im Zusammenhang mit der prophetischen Tradition. Das Gute, das dem Menschen verheißen ist, ist die Folge des Guten, das er tut. Er kann es tun, wenn er den Weg des Gesetzes geht. So ist das Gesetz die Antwort auf die Grundfrage nach dem, was zu tun ist, welches Gute der Mensch tun muß, wenn er Gutes, d. h. Leben im Vollsinn des Wortes erlangen will. Insofern bestätigt sich die These von R. Pesch: »Der Hinweis auf die Gebote ist nach der Erörterung des Prädikates »gut« konsequent; die Gebote weisen den Weg zum ewigen Leben.«[21]

Doch nicht nur der Hinweis auf die Gebote ist nach der Erörterung des Prädikates »gut« konsequent, auch die Weiterführung des Gespräches hängt damit ebenso folgerichtig zusammen: Die Aufforderung Jesu an den Fragenden, seine Habe zu verkaufen und den Erlös den Armen zu geben ebenso wie die dann angehängte Diskussion über den Reichtum und seine Gefahren (Mt 19,21f.; 23–29). Dazu ist wiederum ein Rückgriff auf Dtn 30,15–20 nötig. Diese Paränese ist mit einer Verheißung verbunden:

> Wenn du dem Befehl Jahwes, deines Gottes, gehorchst, ... auf seinen Wegen wandelst, und seine Gebote, Satzungen und Rechte beobachtest, so wirst du am Leben bleiben und dich mehren, und Jahwe, dein Gott, wird dich segnen in dem Lande, in das du einziehst, um es in Besitz zu nehmen (Dtn 30,16).

Die Verheißung, die mit dem Guten verbunden ist, bedeutet »Leben« im Vollsinne des Wortes. Dazu gehören »Fülle«, Kinder, Besitz, reiche Ernten, gesundes Vieh. So wird denn auch das verheißene Land Dtn

---

[20] Diesem Phänomen ist noch nicht die ihm zukommende Aufmerksamkeit gewidmet worden. Hinweise finden sich bei M. Hengel, a.a.O. s. Anm. 17, 281f. Hengel sieht hier nur äußere Einflüsse wirksam. – H. H. Schmid, Wesen und Geschichte der Weisheit, BZAW 101, 1966, sieht die Geschichte der Weisheit dadurch bestimmt, daß die weisheitlichen Texte »zweideutig« werden (173).

[21] R. Pesch, a.a.O. s. Anm. 4, 139.

1–11 als ein »gutes« Land (Dtn 1,35; 3,25; 4,21f.) bezeichnet, dessen Qualität Dtn 8,7–10 eindrücklich beschrieben wird.

Leben mit Reichtum und Besitz ist hier die Erfüllung der Verheißung, die zum Guten gehört, für das der Mensch sich entscheiden soll. Auch hier ist der Zusammenhang mit der Weisheit mit Händen zu greifen: Auch sie verheißt Reichtum und Ehre (Spr. 3,16; 8,18). So kann ganz direkt der Rat gegeben werden:

> Wer immer Lust zum Leben hat
> und einmal Gutes sehen möchte,
> bewahre deine Lippen vor trügerischen Reden.
> Weiche vom Bösen und tue Gutes.
> Suche Frieden und jage ihm nach (Ps 34,13–15).

Nun lautet jedoch die entscheidende Weisung Jesu an den nach dem Weg zum ewigen Leben Fragenden gerade: Gehe hin, verkaufe deine Habe und gib sie den Armen und du wirst einen Schatz im Himmel haben (Mt 19,21)!

IV.

Hier ist zunächst festzuhalten: Auch Jesus verheißt einen Schatz und damit Reichtum. Doch dieser Schatz ist nicht im irdischen Leben unter den Bedingungen dieser Welt zugänglich, sondern »in den Himmeln«[22]. Dabei ist Himmel nicht nur der Ort des transzendenten Gottes, sondern der Bereich, in dem Gottes Wille, d. h. die gerechte Ordnung, herrscht (vgl. Mt 6,10)[23]. Es zeigt sich an dieser Stelle Kontinuität und Widerspruch. Kontinuität, insofern sich die Verheißung von Leben und Reichtum durchhält. Widerspruch, da dieses Leben und dieser Schatz nicht in dieser Welt zu haben sind und gerade die Hingabe des irdischen Besitzes zur unabdingbaren Voraussetzung haben. Andererseits muß gesagt werden: Der »Schatz« bleibt Verheißungsgut, aber er muß in einem radikalen Widerspruch zum irdischen Besitz gesehen werden.

Dieses eigenartige Verhältnis von Kontinuität und Widerspruch in der Verheißung von Leben und Reichtum im Wort Jesu gegenüber dem Deuteronomium muß noch genauer bestimmt werden, weil nur von hier aus auch die Stellung Jesu zu Reichtum und Besitz verständlich wird.

Die erste Frage, die zu stellen ist, muß lauten: Wie ist es zu diesem eigenartigen Verhältnis von Kontinuität und Widerspruch gekommen?

---

[22] K. Koch, Der Schatz im Himmel, Leben angesichts des Todes (Festschrift für H. Thielicke), 1968, 48–60. Koch geht den religionsgeschichtlichen Hintergründen der Vorstellung nach und führt sie auf die Auffassung von der »Tat als Sphäre« zurück (60).

[23] Aufschlußreich sind die Reisen Henochs im äth Hen. Ihm wird in der himmlischen Welt Einblick in die gute und gerechte Ordnung der Welt gegeben. Vgl. U. Luck, Das Weltverständnis in der jüdischen Apokalyptik, ZThK 73, 283–305, 295f.

Bereits in den Weisheitsüberlieferungen ist die Wertung von Besitz und Reichtum durchaus nicht eindeutig. Den oben genannten Belegen für die Auffassung, daß Reichtum und Ehre der Lohn für den sind, der den guten Weg, den Weg der Weisheit geht (Spr. 3,16; 8,18; Ps 112,3), stehen ganz andere gegenüber. Sie warnen vor Reichtum und Besitz (Ps 49,7; 52,9; 62,11; Jer 9,22). Nicht dem Guten geht es gut, sondern dem Frevler (Ps 73,3.12). Diese Erfahrung macht dem Menschen schwer zu schaffen. In der Welt kann sich die gerechte Ordnung nicht durchsetzen, es herrscht nicht Gottes Wille. Das ist der Eindruck, den man immer wieder haben muß. Die Zusagen Gottes verkehren sich in ihr Gegenteil. Gott ist in der Zwiespältigkeit dieser Erfahrung verborgen. Praktisch bedeutet das für den Menschen: Tun und Ergehen lassen sich nicht mehr in ihrem Zusammenhang sehen. Man kann sich nur an die Verheißung halten und darauf trauen, daß sie sich durchsetzen wird[24].

Dies ist auch die Voraussetzung für die Psalmen, in denen Gott als »gut« praediziert wird. Sie machen keine Seinsaussagen über das Wesen Gottes, sondern in ihnen kommt die Erfahrung zum Ausdruck, daß sich die gerechte Ordnung doch wieder einmal durchgesetzt hat. Er hat dem Gerechten, der Gutes tut, wieder einmal geholfen, daher:

> Schmeckt und sehet wie gut Jahwe ist.
> Wohl dem Manne, der auf ihn traut (Ps 34,9).

Der lobpreisende Ausdruck dieser Erfahrung ist zugleich ein Bekenntnis zu dem, der seine lebensrettende und fördernde Ordnung, seine Gerechtigkeit, immer wieder durchsetzt. So ist auch der vor allem die Psalmen 106 und 136 bestimmende Kehrvers zu verstehen:

> Danket Jahwe, denn er ist gut (ṭōb)
> und seine Güte (ḥáesaed) währet für immer[25].

Alles, was Jahwe getan hat, von der Schöpfung bis zur Rettung Israels ebenso wie sein Eintreten für den Gerechten, gibt von diesem Gut – Sein Ausdruck. Es besteht also Grund dazu, trotz der negativen Welterfahrung, seiner Verheißung des Guten, d. h. dessen, was Leben fördert, zu vertrauen (Ps 34,9).

Diese Verheißung allein, die auf dem Gesetz ruht und auf jeden kommen soll, der den Weg des Gesetzes geht, trägt zunehmend die schon in der alten Weisheit gehegte und gepflegte Erwartung, daß sich die Gerechtigkeit und damit das Gute durchsetzen wird (vgl. Ps 34,16), trotz der Enttäuschungen, die dagegen zu sprechen scheinen. Je größer nun aller-

---

24 Diese Erfahrung trägt die positive Sicht der Armut in bestimmten Kreisen des Judentums und im frühen Christentum. Von einer allgemeinen »Armenfrömmigkeit« sollte man deshalb nicht sprechen.

25 Zur Verbindung von טוב mit חֶסֶד: H. J. Stoebe, Art. חֶסֶד ḥaésaed Güte, THAT I, 600–621, 606.

dings die Differenz zwischen der Erwartung und der Erfahrung ist, der Erfahrung einer Welt, in der es dem Frevler gut geht und der Erwartung, daß der Gerechte im Vollsinn des Wortes »leben« wird, um so stärker, radikaler muß der Umschwung sein, der eintreten muß, wenn sich die Verheißung durchsetzen wird. Auf diese Weise kommt es zur Unterscheidung zwischen diesem Äon, der durch Ungerechtigkeit beherrscht wird, in dem die Bösen Gutes ernten, und dem kommenden Äon, in dem Gerechtigkeit herrscht und der Gute das ihm zustehende Erbe empfangen wird.

Auf dem Weg in diese scharfe Unterscheidung zwischen dieser und der kommenden Welt können mehrere Stufen beobachtet werden. Ist es zunächst die unbestimmte Hoffnung auf eine Zukunft in der noch absehbaren Zeit, in der sich durchaus noch unter den Bedingungen der Welt das Recht des Guten durchsetzen wird, so kommt es in der Apokalyptik und der dualistischen Weisheit zu einer qualitativen Differenz zwischen der Welt der Ungerechtigkeit und der kommenden Welt der Gerechtigkeit und damit des »Lebens« im Vollsinne des Wortes. Das Weltverständnis, gerade auch das Weltverständnis der Apokalyptik, hat seinen tragenden Grund in der Welterfahrung, wie sie sich dem auf Gerechtigkeit, auf Erfüllung der Verheißung wartenden Menschen darstellt[26].

V.

In unserem Text spiegelt sich dies darin wider, daß nunmehr die Verheißung für das Reich der Himmel (Mt 19,21) nicht mehr einfach für das Leben, sondern für das »ewige Leben« gilt. Die Verheißung zielt damit auf den neuen Äon, der sich von diesem Äon qualitativ unterscheidet. Der Topos, an dem sich der qualitative Unterschied besonders deutlich zeigen läßt, ist der Besitz. In diesem Äon geht es dem Gerechten schlecht, Besitz ist nicht mehr die Erfüllung der Verheißung für den, der den Weg des Guten, des Gesetzes, der Gerechtigkeit geht. Es ist der Böse, dem Reichtum und Macht zufallen. Der Lebenserfolg besagt nichts über die Qualität eines Lebens. Deshalb greift denn auch die Verheißung über diese Welt hinaus auf das ewige Leben, dessen Reichtum nunmehr ein Schatz im Himmel ist[27].

Während Dtn 30,15–20 die Zusammengehörigkeit von Gerechtigkeit und Wohlstand voraussetzen, hat sich im apokalyptischen Horizont eine Umkehrung vollzogen. Zu dieser Umkehr ist auch jeder gerufen, der in die Himmelsherrschaft eingehen, der das ewige Leben erben will. Der Schatz im Himmel und die irdische Habe stehen im krassen Gegensatz. Von dieser veränderten Situation her wird jetzt auch einsichtig, warum die

[26] Vgl. U. Luck, a.a.O. s. Anm. 23, 286f.

[27] Die Hintergründe für die Entstehung des »eschatologischen Rahmens« werden von K. Koch, a.a.O. s. Anm. 22, 54, nicht behandelt.

erste Antwort Jesu auf die Frage nach dem ewigen Leben mit dem Hinweis auf die Gebote nicht ausreicht, auch nicht mit dem Zusatz von Lev 19,18 (Mt 19,19), der gut matthäisch das Gesetz auf die Nächstenliebe zusammenfaßt: Angesichts der Verhältnisse in der Welt kann der Weg des Gesetzes nicht mehr als Weg zum Leben erfahren werden. Aber Jesus weist auch nicht den Weg des Gesetzes zu einem Leben im Glück und im Wohlstand, wie es Dtn 30,15–20 für unsere Verhältnisse »naiv« geschieht!

Auf die Anrede und die Frage, die ihm gestellt wird, reagiert Jesus zunächst so, daß er das Prädikat »gut« auf Gott eingrenzt: Niemand ist gut, außer: der eine Gott! (Mk 10,18; Lk 18,19) oder: Einer ist der Gute! (Mt 19,17). Herauszuheben ist zunächst das »Einer«. Hier handelt es sich höchstwahrscheinlich um eine bewußte Anspielung auf Dtn 6,4, den Eingang des Sch^ema Israel. Das Sch^ema bedeutet für Israel die Übernahme des Jochs der Gottesherrschaft, d. h. der Thora. Wer dieses Joch übernimmt, ist verpflichtet, den Weg der Thora zu gehen[28]. Damit ist der Hinweis auf die Gebote ganz und gar nicht unvermittelt oder überraschend. Er ergibt sich konsequent aus der Aufnahme von Anrede und Frage durch Jesus. Die besonderen Schwierigkeiten liegen nun aber bei der Eingrenzung des Prädikates »gut« auf den einen Gott. Daß dies nicht aus dogmatischen Gründen geschieht, dürfte klar sein! Hier können wir an bereits Gesagtes anknüpfen. Der Weg in die Apokalyptik, wie wir ihn in den alttestamentlichen und in den frühjüdischen Schriften verfolgen können, hat, wie eben gezeigt wurde, seinen inneren Grund in der Erfahrung, daß die gerechte, lebenschenkende Ordnung der Welt verborgen ist. Die Erwartung geht dahin, daß dem Gerechten Gutes vergolten wird (Spr. 13,21) und damit der Gute sich selber Gutes tut (Spr. 11,17). Die Erfahrung wird aber Pred 9,2f. ausgedrückt:

> Alles trifft alle gleicherweise:
> Ein Geschick hat der Gerechte und der Frevler,
> Der Gute und der Böse, der Reine und der Unreine,
> und der Opfernde und der keine Opfer darbringt.
> Wie dem, der Gutes tut, geht's dem Sünder,
> Wie dem, der schwört, dem, der den Schwur scheut.
> Das ist das Schlimmste unter allem, was unter der Sonne
> geschieht, daß alle ein Geschick haben.

Deshalb läßt sich auch nicht mehr sagen, wer in Wahrheit unter den Menschen gut ist (Pred 7,20). Im Grunde gilt doch, daß das Herz der Menschen des Bösen voll ist und Tollheit in ihrem Herzen, so lange sie leben (Pred 9,3; Ps 14,1.3; 53,2.4). Die Frage nach dem Guten kann eindeutig nur mit dem Verweis auf Gott selbst beantwortet werden, so wie es im Lobpreis der Psalmen geschieht (Ps 106; 136 u. a.).

---

[28] Belege dazu: Bill. I. 173f.

Was das für den Menschen bedeutet, der sich an das Gesetz gewiesen sieht, wird Ps 119,68 ausgesprochen:

> Du bist gut und tust Gutes, lehre mich deine Satzungen.

Es ist das Vertrauen zum Gut – Sein Gottes, das den Menschen am Gesetzt hält, auch wenn nicht festzustellen ist, ob es dem Guten wirklich gut geht[29]. Dies gibt ihm den Halt, auch angesichts der Verborgenheit Gottes an der Thora festzuhalten. In den Psalmen kann dieses Gut – Sein Gottes noch in den Beispielen aus der Geschichte, von der Schöpfung angezeigt werden. Hier liegt auch der Sinn des Geschichtsbezuges der Bekenntnisse Israels und des Lobpreises der Psalmen.

Angesichts des Bruches, der in der dualistischen Weisheit und in der Apokalyptik zwischen dieser Welt der Ungerechtigkeit und der kommenden Welt der Gerechtigkeit eingetreten ist, geben die Beispiele aus der Geschichte nicht mehr genug her, um Menschen daran festzuhalten, Gutes zu tun. In der Apokalyptik bedarf es deshalb einer Horizonterweiterung, in der der Apokalyptiker einen Zugang zu dieser Welt der Gerechtigkeit erschließt, um von hier aus seine Paränese zu begründen[30]. Am Ende seiner Reisen wird Henoch aufgefordert, die himmlischen Tafeln zu betrachten, auf denen die Taten der Menschen aufgezeichnet sind. Jetzt kann er Gott loben und die Gerechten selig preisen:

> Selig der Mann, der gerecht und gut stirbt, über den kein Buch der Ungerechtigkeit geschrieben und gegen den kein Tag des Gerichtes gefunden ist (äth Hen 81,4).

Zurückgekehrt in die irdische Welt soll Henoch seinen Kindern das kundtun, was ihm in der himmlischen Welt offenbart worden ist:

> Dein Herz sei stark, denn die Guten werden den Guten Gerechtigkeit kundtun, der Gerechte wird sich mit den Gerechten freuen, und sie werden einander beglückwünschen. Aber der Sünder wird mit dem Sünder sterben, und der Abtrünnige mit dem Abtrünnigen versinken (äth Hen 81,7f.).

Dieser Weg einer Verifikation der Gerechtigkeit und des Gut – Seins Gottes hält daran fest, daß zu diesem Leben Wohlstand, Erfolg, kurz »Fülle« gehören. Dies wird im Rückgriff auf die Geschichte oder im Vorgriff auf das Eschaton gezeigt.

VI.

Jesus hat in seiner Verkündigung Gottes Gut – Sein weder durch Beispiele aus der Geschichte, noch im Vorgriff auf das Eschaton zu begründen oder zu belegen versucht. Im Gegenteil: Gott läßt seine Sonne

---

[29] Im Grunde hat hier die Thora die gesamte Wirklichkeitserfahrung des Menschen zu tragen. Deshalb muß er sich Tag und Nacht allein darauf konzentrieren (Ps 1; Sir 6,37 u. a.).

[30] Vgl. U. Luck, a.a.O. s. Anm. 23, 303.

aufgehen über Böse und Gute und regnen läßt er über Gerechte und Ungerechte (Mt 5,45). Weder aus dem Blutbad unter den Galiläern, noch vom Einsturz des Turmes von Siloah darf man ableiten, daß die Opfer als Sünder ein verdientes Strafgericht erlitten hätten (Lk 13,1–5). Doch diese Verborgenheit Gottes im Weltgeschehen stellt seine unbedingte Gerechtigkeit nicht in Frage. Es gilt, sich auf die unbedingte Rechtsforderung einzulassen, ja, zu verlassen. Da nur Gott selbst gerecht und gut ist, bedeutet die unbedingte Rechtsforderung Gottes den Verzicht auf jede Orientierung an den Verhältnissen der Welt, die durch den Tat – Folge – Zusammenhang bestimmt sind.

So wird der Mensch an Gott selbst orientiert, an seinem Vollkommen – Sein, das ja gerade darin besteht, daß Gott die irdische Unterscheidung von Bösen und Guten nicht macht, sondern in seiner Schöpfungsordnung allen Leben ermöglicht. Die Feindesliebe erscheint in diesem Zusammenhang als nichts anderes als die Aufhebung der Grundunterscheidung von Guten und Bösen in der Beurteilung der Menschen untereinander (Mt 5,43–48)[31].

Auch die lukanische Version, die den Menschen auf das Barmherzig – Sein Gottes bezieht, meint jenes Handeln, das sich nicht an der Entsprechung von Tat und Folge orientiert, sondern an dem, was der andere zum Leben braucht, ganz gleich wer oder was er ist. Die lukanische Version des Gebotes der Feindesliebe, die bekanntlich nicht antithetisch gefaßt ist, bestätigt unsere Auslegung:

> Liebet eure Feinde, tut gut denen, die euch hassen, ... (Lk 6,27).

Das Verhalten, das Gutes – Tun wird hier unmittelbar am anderen orientiert. Gutes – Tun ist ganz und gar auf den Menschen und nicht mehr auf das Gesetz bezogen. So kommt auf diese Weise erst heraus, worum es primär auch im Gesetz geht: um das, was dem Leben nützt. Allerdings Leben in einer Welt, in der die Gerechtigkeit verborgen ist, in der der Mensch deshalb nicht über den anderen urteilen kann, sondern unter allen Umständen das Gute zu tun aufgerufen ist, weil Gott es will.

Diese Ausrichtung des Menschen und seines Tuns an einem Gott, der nicht unterscheidet zwischen Guten und Bösen, sondern gerade auf diese Weise das tut, was dem Leben seiner Geschöpfe nützt, hat bereits im Alten Testament viele Belege. Gott ist gut und gerecht, darum weist er den Irrenden den Weg (Ps 25,8). Er ist gut, weil er vergibt (Ps 86,5). Das nicht selten sich findende Nebeneinander von gut und gerecht zeigt, daß seine Gerechtigkeit lebenschenkendes Wirken ist[32].

---

[31] Das hat auch Folgen für das Verständnis der »besseren Gerechtigkeit« (Mt 5,20): Sie ist kein Urteil über gut und böse, sondern eine Tat, die zum Frieden, d. h. zum Heil des Ganzen und damit zur »schöpfungsgemäßen Weltordnung« führt (Schmid, s. Anm. 15).

[32] Zum Zusammenhang von טוֹב und צֶדֶק: I. Höver–Johag, a.a.O. s. Anm. 18, 327.

Konkret heißt das: Gott vergilt nicht jede Schuld des Menschen sofort und entsprechend. Er ist gut in seiner rettenden und so lebenschenkenden Zuwendung (Ps 100,5; 106,1; 107,1; 118,29; 136,1).

Dieses Verständnis ist auch in den Zeugnissen des hellenistischen Judentums zu registrieren. Gott ist der allein Gute (Philo Mut nom 7; Somn I, 149). Er ist gut, weil er die Gebote gegeben hat. An diesen Geboten ist nach Philo auffällig, daß sie ohne Strafbestimmungen gegeben sind. Gott ist der Urheber nur des Guten, nicht des Bösen. Das Böse ist hier das Strafgericht, das den Menschen trifft, der nicht das Gute gewählt hat. Die Gesetze sind aber gegeben, damit die Menschen aus freier, vernünftiger Entscheidung das Gute, das Leben wählen. Das Gericht über den, der nicht das Gute gewählt hat, ergeht durch die Gerechtigkeit, von der Philo sagt, daß sie bei Gott wohne. Sie ist von Gott zur Aufsicht über die menschlichen Handlungen gesetzt und steht in einer eigentümlichen Distanz zu ihm (Decal 176–178). Hier ist das Verständnis von gut in Bezug auf Gott mit seinem Wirken für den Menschen gleichgesetzt. Er wirkt im Menschen, indem der einzig Gute in die Seelen der Menschen einzieht (Somn I, 149)[33].

Einen solchen Einzug des Guten in die Seele kennt allerdings Jesus nicht, und ihn kennen auch die synoptischen Evangelien nicht. Gutes tun wird nicht durch Wirksamkeit des Guten in der Seele der Menschen möglich, sondern durch eine absolute Kehrtwendung. Dies zeigt sich einmal im Verhältnis zum Besitz. Entscheidend ist aber nun, daß der Mensch diese Ausrichtung zum Guten nicht an, in oder bei sich selbst findet, sondern in der Nachfolge Jesu. Das Gute kommt nicht in den Menschen hinein, sondern er muß Abschied nehmen von sich selbst und sein Leben eben in der Nachfolge Jesu suchen und finden[34]. Es ist unschwer zu erkennen, daß Mt 19,21 seine Entsprechung in Mt 16,25 hat, das dort in einer Reihe von

---

[33] Vgl. K. Berger, a.a.O. s. Anm. 3, 399f.

[34] An dieser Stelle ist ein Hinweis auf Paulus naheliegend, weil er zeigt, daß auch für ihn der Zusammenhang von Gesetz – Gutes – Leben selbstverständlich war. Seine Argumentation Röm 7,7–25 ist nur auf diesem Hintergrund verständlich: Das Gesetz ist das Gute, das zum Leben gegeben ist. Aber, so Paulus, das Gesetz führt nicht zum Leben! Vielmehr lebt durch das Gesetz die Sünde auf, der Mensch aber stirbt. Fazit: Das Gesetz gereicht dem Menschen statt zum Leben zum Tode (Röm 7,10). Gesetz und Gebot sind zwar »gerecht und gut« (Röm 7,12). Aber die Sünde bewirkt gerade durch das Gute, d. h. durch das Gesetz, den Tod. Wenn Paulus sagt, daß in ihm Gutes nicht wohne (Röm 7,18), so wird dies im Vergleich mit Philo Somn I, 149 verständlich. Dort wird die ψυχή zum Hause Gottes, weil das Gute in den Menschen einzieht. Für Paulus wohnt im Menschen die Sünde (Röm 7,19f.). Das hat zur Folge, daß der Mensch zwar das Gute, also das, was zum Leben führt, will. Aber es ist das Böse, das, was zum Tode führt, was bei seinem Tun herauskommt. Aus dieser hoffnungslosen Lage kann der Mensch sich nicht selbst befreien. Er kann das Gute, was zum Leben führt, nicht tun. Er muß durch Jesus Christus gerettet werden (Röm 7,25).

Nachfolgesprüchen steht, die eine Christologie erkennen lassen, die ihrerseits nun Licht auf unsere Perikope wirft. Nachfolge ist »Selbstverleugnung«. Selbstverleugnung heißt aber: Leben nicht bei sich selbst zu suchen, sondern es hinzugeben. So wird das Leben, ewiges Leben gewonnen. Jesus ist, wie die Nachfolgesprüche zeigen, ganz und gar Hingabe. Er ist nichts aus sich selbst. Um es einmal im Blick auf Philo zu sagen: Auch auf ihn geht das Gute nicht über, es zieht nicht in seine Seele ein, sondern er ist alles, was er ist, in der Hingabe[35].

Nachdem wir schon einleitend herausgearbeitet haben, daß mit dem Stichwort »gut« bereits die Hauptpunkte der ganzen Perikope angeschnitten sind: Leben, Gesetz, Besitz, so fällt nun vom Nachfolgewort her Licht auf die Einleitung: Als der, der in seine Nachfolge ruft, kann auch Jesus nicht »gut« sein! Er ist alles, was er ist, eben in der Hingabe. Nur Gott ist der Gute!

VII.

Es ist nun aber an der Zeit, noch einmal auf die Frage zurückzukommen, die uns am Anfang beschäftigte. Zwischen Mk/Lk auf der einen Seite und Mt auf der anderen Seite besteht darin ein nicht unbedeutender Unterschied, daß bei Mk/Lk Jesus als »guter Lehrer« angeredet wird und das Prädikat »gut« von sich wegweist auf Gott allein, während bei Mt Jesus nur als »Lehrer« bezeichnet wird und das Gute Gegenstand der Frage ist. Demgemäß braucht Jesus hier das Prädikat »gut« nicht von sich abzuwehren. Allen drei Evangelien gemeinsam ist dies, daß das Prädikat »gut« nur Gott zukommt. In unseren Überlegungen ließen wir uns leiten von der Gestalt der Perikope bei Mt. Der Grund dafür dürfte deutlich geworden sein: Bei Mt läßt sich die Herkunft des Prädikates »gut« und seine Bedeutung klarer erfassen als bei Mk/Lk. Mt hat dies in seiner Form herausgearbeitet: Die Frage nach dem Guten ist in der alttestamentlich-jüdischen Tradition identisch mit der Frage nach dem Gesetz. Ihr geht voraus die fundamentale Frage nach dem Leben im ursprünglichen Sinne und zwar einem glücklichen Leben mit allem, was dazu gehört. So steht denn bei Mt diese Perikope ganz im Kontext seiner theologischen Gesamtsicht: Wie wird das Gesetz erfüllt? Das heißt: Wie geschieht Gottes Gerechtigkeit? Es wird erfüllt in der Vollkommenheit (Mt 19,21, vgl. 5,48), die in der Nachfolge Jesu gelebt wird. Nachfolge ist Erfüllung des Gesetzes.

Bei Mk und auch bei Lk steht nicht das Gesetz im Vordergrund, sondern Jesus als Lehrer, der den Weg zum ewigen Leben weisen soll. Die

---

[35] Die Rede vom »Jesus Nachfolgen« ist in den synoptischen Evangelien schon christologisch und anthropologisch reflektiert. Das gilt von Mk 8,34–9,1/Mt 16,24–28 ebenso wie von unserer Stelle. Die knappen Ausführungen von G. Kittel, Art. ἀκολουθέω κτλ., ThWNT I, 210–216, bes. 213–215 (NT), sind hier immer noch voll gültig. Vgl. auch M. Hengel, Nachfolge und Charisma, BZNW 34, 1968, S. 68–70. 80–82.

Gebote, die der Fragende seit seiner Jugend beobachtet hat, haben nicht zum Ziel geführt. Jetzt weist ihm Jesus den Weg. Daß Jesus hier mit Autorität auftritt, wird durch den ansonsten schwer verständlichen Satz unterstrichen: Jesus aber blickte ihn an, liebte ihn und sprach ... (Mk 10,21). K. Berger vergleicht die Geste Jesu mit der Belehrung der Patriarchen in den Test XII. Sie küssen ihre zu belehrenden Kinder zum Beginn und am Ende ihrer Lehre (Test Rub 1,5; Test Dan 7,1)[36]. Noch weiter dürfte aber ein anderer Vergleich führen: Auch die Weisheit »liebt« die, die sich ihr zuwenden (Spr 8,17), das Verhältnis zwischen der Weisheit und dem Menschen wird als ein Liebesverhältnis dargestellt. Sie ist es, die den Menschen zum Leben führt.

Bei Mk führt Jesus den nach dem ewigen Leben Fragenden den entscheidenden Schritt weiter: »Eins mangelt dir« (Mk 10,21) heißt es bei Mk anders als bei Mt. Dieser entscheidende, zum ewigen Leben führende Schritt ist die Nachfolge Jesu und damit verbunden die Hingabe des Besitzes. Besitz und ewiges Leben erscheinen für Mk eher als Alternativen, wie schon die Nachfolgeworte zeigen (Mk 8,34–9,1). Das hat bei Mk jedoch nicht seinen Grund in einem Gefälle dieses Evangeliums zu einer Art Armenfrömmigkeit. Mk geht es um die Schwere der Entscheidung, die hier zu fällen ist. Sie steht in einem scharfen Gegensatz zu den leitenden Tendenzen im hellenistischen Judentum. Hier ist eigentlich keine Entscheidung nötig. Wer die Weisheit, d. h. die Thora, wirklich sucht, dem kommt sie freundlich entgegen, eine kurze Mühe wird reichlich belohnt. Das Weisheitslied Sir 51,13–20 schildert den Weg zur Weisheit-Thora, wie er von einem jungen Mann gegangen werden soll, der in der Welt umherirrt (Sir 51,13). Er soll ihr von Jugend an folgen und sie suchen. Er braucht sein Ohr nur ein wenig der Lehre zuzuwenden, dann wird er große Fortschritte machen (Sir 51,16f.). Er soll sich darum bemühen, Gutes zu tun, dann wird er nicht zuschanden werden. Schließlich erwirbt er sie als einen guten Besitz (Sir 51,21)[37].

Die Entscheidung Jesus nachzufolgen, ist demgegenüber unbedingt und klar: Sie fordert den Menschen mit allem, was er hat. Dennoch ist auch für Mk die Hingabe des Besitzes nicht nur eine Probe aufs Exempel! Er stellt auch die Frage: Was wird aus dem, der alles hingibt? Die Antwort wird Mk 10,30 gegeben: Er wird Hundertfältiges empfangen, jetzt in diesem Äon: Häuser und Brüder und Kinder und Äcker, unter Verfolgungen, und in dem kommenden Äon ewiges Leben. Besitz und ewiges Leben

---

[36] K. Berger, a.a.O. s. Anm. 3, 397f. Berger zieht in diesem Zusammenhang auch 2. Sam 15,4–6 heran.

[37] Zum Weisheitslied Sir 51,13–20: M. Hengel, a.a.O. s. Anm. 17, 242 betont, daß »gerade die dichterischen Stücke ... die theologischen Anschauungen des Verfassers zum Ausdruck« bringen. – Zur Bedeutung von Sir 51 im Matthäusevangelium vgl. U. Luck, Weisheit und Christologie in Mt 11,25–30, WuD/NF 13, 1975, 35–51, 41–46.

werden hier eschatologisch geschieden. Ewiges Leben ist Leben im kommenden Äon, der Besitz gehört in diesen Äon.

Anders bei Mt: Hier lautet gerade die eschatologische Verheißung:

> Und jeder, der ließ Häuser oder Brüder oder Schwestern oder Vater oder Mutter oder Kinder oder Äcker um meines Namens willen, Hundertfältiges wird er empfangen und ewiges Leben wird er erben. (Mt 19,29).

Der Schatz im Himmel ist für Mt nicht auf das »ewige Leben« beschränkt! Die alte Verheißung eines Lebens in »Fülle« wird durchgehalten.

Damit wird aber ein grundlegender Unterschied zwischen Mk und Mt erkennbar. Bei Mk ist es der Gehorsam gegenüber dem Wort des »Lehrers« Jesus und dem Evangelium (Mk 10,29), der den entscheidenden Schritt zum ewigen Leben führt.

Bei Mt führt der Gehorsam gegenüber Jesus und seinem Wort zur Vollkommenheit, damit zur Erfüllung des Gesetzes und so zum Erbe dessen, was mit dem Gesetz verheißen ist: »Leben« im Vollsinn des Wortes. Der Unterschied zwischen Mk/Lk und Mt hält sich von der Einleitung bis zum Schluß durch, er reicht in die Tiefe ihres theologischen Denkens.

Freundschaftsbrief trotz Spannungen

Zu Gattung und Aufbau des Ersten Korintherbriefs

von Dieter Lührmann

(Im Hainbach 9, 3550 Marburg-Cyriaxweimar)

Auch wer Teilungshypothesen zum 1 Kor nicht folgt, wird durch deren Verfechter auf Phänomene innerhalb des Textes hingewiesen, die einer Erklärung bedürfen, und ist genötigt, sich Gedanken zu machen über den Aufbau des uns vorliegenden 1 Kor und die diesen Aufbau bedingenden Faktoren. Zwar scheint jeder Teilungsversuch *a priori* diskreditiert durch die ja nicht unerheblichen Differenzen zwischen den einzelnen Hypothesen. Wenn aber etwas richtig ist an der Behauptung, sie alle seien im Grunde nur Variationen der These von J. Weiß[1], dann bedeutet dessen Argumentation die eigentliche Herausforderung, zumal J. Weiß sich einen Erfolg nicht schon für seine Zeit, sondern erst für die Zukunft erhoffte[2].

Eher »schüchtern« vorgetragen und die eigentliche Durchführung auf einen Kommentar zum 2 Kor verschiebend (XL), läuft seine Begründung darauf hinaus, daß »Inhalt und Disposition« nicht »ganz einwandfrei« sind (XLI), ja er spricht dann weiter von »den ungeheueren Schwierigkeiten . . ., die sowohl aus der Form wie aus dem Inhalt der Briefe entstehen« (XLI), aus 1 Kor wie aus 2 Kor, und deshalb sei es »eine methodische Pflicht, von der Annahme der Einheit zunächst einmal abzusehen« (XLI).

Das Ergebnis seiner Teilung: ein Brief A enthielt 10,1–22(23); 6,12–20; 9,24–27; 11,2–34; 16,7b–9.15–20, ein Brief B den ganzen Rest (»wenn auch nicht ohne Bedenken«), unter Abzug noch von »mancherlei katholisierenden Bemerkungen« des Redaktors, der für die heutige Gestalt verantwortlich ist (Interpolationen in 1,2; 4,17; 7,17; 11,16; 14,33; vielleicht auch 14,34f.; 10,29.30; 11,11f.), Den Gewinn dieser Hypothese sieht er in einem besseren Bild der Entwicklungsgeschichte der Gemeinde. Die Situation zur Zeit von Brief A liege »noch vor der Entstehung oder wenigstens vor der Verschärfung des Parteiwesens« (XLII); die Probleme gingen hier zurück »auf ein noch nicht völlig gebrochenes Heidentum« (XLII). In Brief B »tritt er (sc. Paulus) nun prinzipiell ganz ent-

[1] P. Vielhauer, Geschichte der urchristlichen Literatur, 1975, 141.

[2] J. Weiß, Der Erste Korintherbrief, Neudruck der 9. Aufl. von 1910, 1970, bes. XL–XLIII.

schieden auf den Standpunkt der Freien, fordert aber die Rücksicht der Liebe auf die schwachen Brüder« (XLII). Brief B präzisiert demnach den Standpunkt des Paulus, wo der in Brief A noch unklar gewesen sei: Kap. 7 gegenüber 6,12–20, Kap. 15 gegenüber 6,14, Kap. 12 und 14 gegenüber Kap. 11. Und Kap. 8 und 15, in denen Paulus nicht Bezug nimmt auf die Parteien, seien am besten als einer Zwischenphase zugehörig zu erklären, geschrieben noch bevor Paulus Nachricht erhalten habe über die Parteien in Korinth.

J. Weiß gesteht dann zu, daß auch in bezug auf den uns vorliegenden 1 Kor »über dem Ganzen eine geschickt disponierende Hand gewaltet hat« (XLIII), aber das kann ja auch die Hand des Redaktors gewesen sein. Die Begründung der Aufteilung liegt also einmal in Unterschieden der Situation in Korinth, zum anderen in unterschiedlichen Stellungnahmen des Paulus zu ein und derselben Frage. Das eigentliche Ziel aber war für J. Weiß wohl, das herauszuarbeiten, was Paulus abschließend und endgültig vertreten hat, nämlich den Standpunkt der Freien bei Rücksicht auf die Schwachen, deutlich ein Idealbild protestantischen Christentums des beginnenden Jahrhunderts.

Die sich an J. Weiß anschließenden Teilungshypothesen haben wie er immer wieder thematische Dopplungen und darin sich widersprechende Stellungnahmen des Paulus ebenso zum Ausgangspunkt genommen wie differierende Situationen in Korinth. Jüngst hat H. Merklein diese ganze Diskussion ausführlich dargestellt und selber für die Einheitlichkeit des 1 Kor plädiert unter dem Kriterium der »Kohärenz« sowohl der paulinischen Argumentation als auch der vorauszusetzenden Situation in Korinth[3]. Ich möchte seine Überlegungen ergänzen und, wie ich hoffe, seine These durch einige Beobachtungen zum Aufbau des 1 Kor stützen. In einem ersten, kürzeren Teil geht es um die Frage der Gattung des Briefes als ganzen und die daraus resultierende Bestimmung des Charakters von 1 Kor 1,10–16,18. Ein zweiter Teil beschäftigt sich mit dem Aufbau von 1 Kor 5,1–11,1, den Kapiteln also, die für die Teilungshypothesen entscheidend sind. Ich meine, daß sich hier ein Geflecht von thematischen Vor- und Rückverweisen aufzeigen läßt, das nicht erst von einem Redaktor geschaffen ist. Kann man 5,1–11,1 als von Paulus so intendierte Einheit verstehen, werden Teilungshypothesen zumindest fraglicher. Ein zusammenfassender dritter Teil ist wohl ebenfalls von einem Idealbild geleitet, doch überschritte eine aneignende Darstellung des paulinischen Freiheitsverständnisses den hier gesteckten Rahmen.

---

[3] H. Merklein, Die Einheitlichkeit des ersten Korintherbriefes, ZNW 75, 1984, 153–183; hier 154–156 eine Übersicht über die verschiedenen Teilungshypothesen. Zu ergänzen wäre noch R. Jewett, The Redaction of I Corinthians and the Trajectory of the Pauline School, JAAR 54, 1978, 389–444.

I.

1 Kor beginnt mit dem Präskript (1,1–3) in der für die Paulusbriefe typischen Form: Absender im Nominativ, Empfänger im Dativ, in einem neuen Satz ein Segenswunsch, der mit χάρις beginnt und damit das im griechischen Briefformular übliche χαίρειν[4] aufnimmt und variiert. Am knappsten in 1 Thess 1,1 ist diese Grundstruktur auch in der am meisten erweiterten Fassung Röm 1,1–7 noch klar zu erkennen. Es folgt in 1,4–9 das Proömium, wie bei Paulus üblich mit εὐχαριστῶ (vgl. Röm 1,8 Phil 1,3 Phlm 4 bzw. εὐχαριστοῦμεν 1 Thess 1,2) τῷ θεῷ einsetzend. Eine Ausnahme bildet Gal; dort ist das Fehlen des Dankes begründet in der Situation in Galatien. In 2 Kor 1,3ff. hingegen ist der Dank an Gott umgesetzt in einen Lobpreis Gottes.

Sind Präskript und Dank an Gott als Proömium konstitutiv für alle Paulusbriefe, so differieren sie in der Fortsetzung[5]. In 1 Kor 1,10 wird diese mit παρακαλῶ δὲ ὑμᾶς eingeleitet, also durch die farblose Partikel δέ angeschlossen und mit dem Verbum παρακαλῶ mit folgendem ἵνα-Satz[6] die Aufforderung aussprechend, die Gemeinde möge einig sein, im Unterschied zu ihrem derzeitigen Verhalten, wie sich im Fortgang des Briefes zeigt.

Solche mit παρακαλῶ bzw. παρακαλοῦμεν eingeleiteten Sätze finden sich in fast allen Paulusbriefen[7], und zwar in einer relativ festen Form, die auch in 1 Kor 1,10 vorliegt: παρακαλῶ/οῦμεν / Partikel / Personalpronomen / διά ... / Aufforderung.

1. Παρακαλῶ (Röm 12,1; 15,30; 16,17; 1 Kor 1,10; 4,16; 16,15) bzw. παρακαλοῦμεν (1 Thess 4,10; 5,14) steht am Satzanfang mit Ausnahme von 2 Kor 2,8 (διό davor; s. u. unter 4.), 2 Kor 10,1 (αὐτὸς δὲ ἐγώ betont voraus ähnlich wie) Phlm 9f., Phil 4,2 (betont voraus die angesprochenen Personen Euodia und Syntyche); in 1 Thess 4,1 gehen die Überleitungsfloskel λοιπὸν οὖν, die Anrede ἀδελφοί sowie ἐρωτῶμεν ὑμᾶς voraus. Vergleichbar sind wegen dieser Parallelität von παρακαλοῦμεν und ἐρωτῶμεν auch 1 Thess 5,12 (ἐρωτῶμεν steht zudem parallel zu παρακαλοῦμεν 5,14) und Phil 4,3[8], In 2 Kor 10,2 wird der in 10,1 mit παρακαλῶ formulierte Satz mit δέομαι wieder aufgenommen; in 2 Kor 5,20 nimmt δεόμεθα ὡς τοῦ θεοῦ παρακαλοῦντος auf, und δεόμεθα seinerseits ent-

[4] Vgl. im NT Apg 15,23; 23,26; Jak 1,1.

[5] Vgl. J. T. Sanders, The Transition from Opening Epistolary Thanksgiving to Body in the Letters of the Pauline Corpus, JBL 81, 1962, 348–362; dazu T. Y. Mullins, Disclosure. A Literary Form in the New Testament, NT 7, 1964/65, 44–50.

[6] Vgl. dazu BDR § 388.2.

[7] Röm 12,1; 15,30; 16,17; 1 Kor 1,10; 4,16; 16,15; 2 Kor 2,8; 10,1; Phil 4,2; 1 Thess 4,1.10; 5,14; Phlm 9f.; vergleichbar sind sonst im NT: Eph 4,1; 1 Tim 2,1; Hebr 13,22; 1 Petr 2,11; 5,1.

[8] Vgl. 2 Thess 3,12.

spricht παρακαλοῦμεν in 6,1. – Der Bedeutungsgehalt von παρακαλεῖν ergibt sich einerseits aus der Abgrenzung gegenüber ἐπιτάσσειν (Phlm 8), andererseits aus der Parallelsetzung zu δεῖσθαι und ἐρωτᾶν, er liegt eher beim Bitten, Auffordern als bei der deutschen Standardübersetzung mit »ermahnen«, die zu sehr eine Vorstufe der Bestrafung assoziiert[9].

2. Verbindende Partikel ist zumeist δέ (Röm 15,30; 16,17; 1 Kor 1,10; 16,15; 2 Kor 10,1; 1 Thess 4,10; 5,14) in kopulativer, nicht adversativer Bedeutung[10], sonst den Gedankengang fortsetzend οὖν (Röm 12,1; 1 Kor 4,16; 1 Thess 4,1) oder διό am Satzanfang 2 Kor 2,8 (vgl. Phlm 8).

3. Das personale Objekt steht im Akkusativ, und zwar durchweg im Plural die Briefempfänger ὑμᾶς, Phlm 10 der Singular σε; in Phil 4,2 sind die Personen namentlich genannt.

4. Die mit διά eingeleitete Begründung durch Verweis auf Gott oder Christus ist das am wenigsten konstante Element (Röm 12,1; 15,30; 1 Kor 1,10; 2 Kor 10,1, vgl. Phlm 9: Begründung in der Liebe). Ihr entsprechen in gewisser Weise die Einleitung des ganzen Satzes mit διό (2 Kor 2,8 Phlm 8) und das ἐν κυρίῳ in 1 Thess 4,1; vergleichbar ist vielleicht auch der Verweis auf die Lehre in Röm 16,17.

5. Der Inhalt des παρακαλεῖν steht im Infinitiv mit imperativischer Bedeutung[11] (Röm 12,1; 15,30; 16,17; 2 Kor 2,8; 10,2; Phil 4,2; 1 Thess 4,10), im Imperativ (1 Kor 4,16; 1 Thess 5,14 Phlm 17, in Röm 12,1; 16,17 auf den Infinitiv folgend) oder als ἵνα-Satz (1 Kor 1,10; 16,16; 1 Thess 4,1).

Auf die Struktur dieser παρακαλῶ-Sätze hat C. J. Bjerkelund[12] aufmerksam gemacht, ausdrücklich anknüpfend an die Untersuchung von P. Schubert[13] zu den εὐχαριστῶ-Sätzen. Da seine Arbeit m. E. in der ntl. Forschung zu wenig Beachtung gefunden hat, habe ich mit geringen eigenen Akzenten seine Strukturanalyse der Sätze noch einmal dargestellt. Festzuhalten ist sein Ergebnis, daß die παρακαλῶ-Sätze zum griechischen Briefstil gehören und mit der εὐχαριστῶ-Einleitung nach dem Präskript das Formular des »Freundschaftsbriefes« ausmachen, der damit als Dank und Bitte strukturiert ist. Die große Zahl der von ihm beigebrachten Belege zeigt das nachdrücklich[14].

---

[9] Vgl. T. Y. Mullins, Petition as a Literary Form, NT 5, 1962, 46–54: "παρακαλεῖν, the most personal of the verbs of petition" (49); H. Schlier, Die Eigenart der christlichen Mahnung nach dem Apostel Paulus, in: ders., Besinnung auf das Neue Testament, [2]1967, 340–357, bes. 340f.

[10] Vgl. BDR § 447.

[11] Vgl. 1 Thess 4,10 mit 4,1.

[12] C. J. Bjerkelund, Parakalô. Form, Funktion und Sinn der parakalô-Sätze in den paulinischen Briefen, BTN 1, 1967.

[13] P. Schubert, Form and Function of the Pauline Thanksgivings, BZNW 20, 1939.

[14] A.a.O. 44–50; vgl. auch das Material bei Mullins in dem in Anm. 9 angegebenen Aufsatz.

Problematisch bleibt seine Arbeit in zweierlei Hinsicht. Einmal begnügt sich Bjerkelund nicht mit diesem Ergebnis, sondern läßt als genauere Parallele zu den Paulusbriefen nur Briefe von Königen an Städte gelten wegen der »Ähnlichkeit der Situation«: »Die Könige wenden sich an verbündete Städte, um den Kontakt zu pflegen, innere Streitfälle zu lösen und den Abfall zu verhindern. Aus denselben Gründen schreibt der Apostel an die Gemeinden.«[15] Eine solche – in sich fragliche – inhaltliche Parallelität besagt jedoch nichts über die Gattung des »Freundschaftsbriefes«, die die Könige gegenüber befreundeten Städten verwenden. Warum Paulus das ebenfalls gegenüber seinen Gemeinden tut, ist noch einmal eine andere Frage.

Wichtiger ist ein zweiter Gesichtspunkt. So richtig es ist, daß Bjerkelund die παρακαλῶ-Sätze dem Briefstil zuordnet und sie nicht auf Formen mündlicher Paränese (Homilie o. ä.) zurückführt, so fraglich ist es, daß er nun auch auf der literarischen Ebene des Briefes gar keine Beziehung zur Paränese zuläßt[16]. Denn die Sätze haben innerhalb der Briefe durchaus die Funktion, den Übergang zur Paränese zu markieren[17]. Am augenfälligsten ist das bei Röm 12,1 und 1 Thess 4,1. Wo demgegenüber ein solcher παρακαλῶ-Satz fehlt, im Gal, ist die Bestimmung des Beginns der Paränese ein Problem, das in der Forschung unterschiedlich gelöst worden ist[18]. Im Gal fehlt aber ebenso eine Einleitung des Proömiums mit εὐχαριστῶ; die einzigen Reminiszenzen an den Freundschaftsbrief finden sich in dem werbenden Abschnitt 4,12–20[19], – verlorene Freundschaft verändert die Briefstruktur.

Die παρακαλῶ-Sätze enthalten nun mit Ausnahme allein von 2 Kor 10,1 immer eine Aufforderung zu einem bestimmten Verhalten (s. o. unter 5), münden also in Paränese in einem sehr allgemeinen Sinn. Auch wenn Paulus im Phlm lange zögert, eine solche Aufforderung zu formulieren, so erwartet der Leser damals wie heute nach dem wiederholten παρακαλῶ (9f.) eine Anweisung, die dann in 17 folgt.

Im Phil, sei er nun eine sekundäre Komposition aus verschiedenen Paulusbriefen oder nicht, markiert 4,2f. mit den Aufforderungen an bestimmte Personen den Übergang zum paränetischen Teil des Briefes; es folgen, abgesehen von 4,10–20, ab da solche Imperative. In Röm 15,30 und 16,17 fordert Paulus gegen Ende des Briefes unter Aufnahme des

---

[15] A.a.O. 66; das hat K. Berger aufgenommen: Formgeschichte des Neuen Testaments, 1984, 162f., 216f.

[16] A.a.O. 22f.58.189.

[17] Es überwiegt aber in der Literatur das Interesse an der inhaltlichen Zweiteilung der Briefe in Lehre und Ethik bzw. Indikativ und Imperativ, die sich freilich kaum einmal so deutlich zeigt.

[18] Vgl. dazu O. Merk, Der Beginn der Paränese im Galaterbrief, ZNW 60, 1969, 83–104, der ihn mit Recht in 5,13 sieht.

[19] Vgl. H. D. Betz, Galatians, Hermeneia Commentary, 1979, 221.

παρακαλῶ von 12,1 noch einmal zu bestimmten Verhaltensweisen auf, ebenso am Ende des 1 Kor in 16,15.

Auch die Komposition des uns vorliegenden 2 Kor[20] folgt diesem Schema, wenn 10,1 mit einem παρακαλῶ-Satz einsetzt, der aber zu keinem Imperativ führt; und auch die Wiederaufnahme in 10,2 mit δέομαι formuliert keine Anweisung an die Gemeinde, sondern soll eine nach Meinung des Paulus verhängnisvolle Reaktion von seiner Seite verhindern. Die Variation des Schemas ist wieder durch eine spezielle Situation bedingt; das Schema als solches ist mit der Abfolge von Präskript (1,1 f.), Proömium als Dank in der Form der Eulogie (1,3 ff.) und mit παρακαλῶ eingeleiteter Teil (10,1 ff.) auch hier erkennbar. Obwohl dieser letzte Briefteil dem »Tränenbrief« (2 Kor 2,4) entnommen ist, hat derjenige, der den 2 Kor zusammenstellte, ihm insgesamt also die Form eines »Freundschaftsbriefes« gegeben[21].

Betrachtet man die Teile des 2 Kor für sich, so enthält auch der »Zwischenbrief« 2,14–7,4 mit dem Dank an Gott (2,14: τῷ δὲ θεῷ χάρις) und dem δεόμεθα/παρακαλοῦμεν (5,20; 6,1) diese Abfolge und ebenso der »Versöhnungsbrief« 1,1–2,13; 7,5–16, aus dem die Eulogie stammt, die die Struktur der Briefkomposition bestimmt (1,3 ff.), und der mit dieser Eulogie und dem παρακαλῶ-Satz in 2,8, sich für die Liebe[22] zu entscheiden, die Elemente des »Freundschaftsbriefes« in reiner Form bietet.

Wenn also in 1 Kor 1,10 direkt auf das mit εὐχαριστῶ eingeleitete Proömium der παρακαλῶ-Satz folgt, ist damit alles bis 16,18 Folgende als Paränese charakterisiert; diese Paränese ist jedoch nicht »Ermahnung«, sondern »Bitte, Aufforderung«. Ähnlich besteht der 1 Thess eigentlich nur aus diesen beiden Teilen, nur daß hier das mit εὐχαριστοῦμεν eingeleitete Proömium überlang erscheint. In 1,2 beginnend wird es in 2,13 mit erneutem εὐχαριστοῦμεν wieder aufgenommen und erst nach der Frage 3,9 f., welche εὐχαριστία Paulus Gott abstatten könne, mit einem Gebet zu Ende geführt (3,11–13). Daran schließt sich die mit λοιπὸν οὖν, ἀδελφοί, ἐρωτῶμεν ὑμᾶς καὶ παρακαλοῦμεν ἐν κυρίῳ Ἰησοῦ eröffnete Paränese an, in der diese Stichworte mehrfach wiederholt werden (4,10; 5,12.14). Auch im 1 Kor folgen auf das παρακαλῶ von 1,10 ja noch 4,16[23] und 16,15.

---

[20] Vgl. dazu G. Bornkamm, Die Vorgeschichte des sogenannten Zweiten Korintherbriefes (1961), in: ders., Geschichte und Glaube II, BEvTh 53, 1971, 162–194.

[21] Über Bornkamms Hinweis hinaus, daß am Ende einzelner Schriften häufig Warnungen vor Irrlehrern begegnen (a.a.O. 180), läßt sich also auch von der Briefgattung her argumentieren.

[22] Vgl. Phlm 9.

[23] 4,16 leitet den Abschluß des Teils 1,10–4,21 ein, ergibt aber als Wiederholung von 1,10 kein Argument für Teilungshypothesen, die sich darauf berufen, 4,14–21 enthielte Elemente des Briefschlusses (dazu Merklein, a.a.O. 159 f.).

Es ergibt sich also ein allen Paulusbriefen gemeinsames Aufbauprinzip, das das Formular des antiken »Freundschaftsbriefes« ist; die einzige Abweichung, Gal, erklärt sich aus der besonderen Situation des Verhältnisses zwischen Paulus und den Galatern, die ihm, wie er meint, die Freundschaft gekündigt haben (1,6).

	Röm	1 Kor	2 Kor[26]	Gal	Phil	1 Thess	Phlm
Präskript	1,1–7	1,1–3	1,1f.	1,1–5	1,1f.	1,1	1–3
εὐχαριστῶ	1,8	1,4	(1,3)[27]	–	1,3	1,2 2,13 (3,9)	4
παρακαλῶ	12,1 15,30 16,17[24]	1,10 4,16 16,15	10,1	–	4,2	4,1.10 5,12.14	8–10
Grüße	16,1–23	16,19–22	13,12	–[28]	4,21f.	5,26[29]	23f.
Segensformel	15,33[25]	16,23f.	13,13	6,18	4,23	5,28	25

Überraschend an diesem Ergebnis ist, daß es fast ausschließlich für die Briefe gilt, die in der heutigen Forschung unbestritten als echte Paulusbriefe angesehen werden. In den Deuteropaulinen ist das Schema nur im Eph erkennbar: Präskript (1,1f.), Dank an Gott als Eulogie (1,3ff.), Einsatz der Paränese mit einem παρακαλῶ-Satz (4,1), keine Grüße, aber die Segensformel (6,23f.). Die anderen Briefe dagegen markieren den Übergang zur Paränese nicht mit παρακαλῶ, wenn sie mit einem durch εὐχαριστῶ eingeleiteten Teil beginnen[30]; wo umgekehrt in 1 Tim 2,1 dieser Teil zwar mit παρακαλῶ eröffnet wird, beginnt das Proömium nicht gleich nach dem Präskript, sondern erst in 1,12 mit χάριν ἔχω.

II.

Daß 1 Kor ab 1,10 durch den Einsatz mit παρακαλῶ δὲ ὑμᾶς als Paränese zu charakterisieren ist[31], verwundert natürlich nicht, sieht man den Inhalt der folgenden Kapitel. Es bedeutet für die Frage des Aufbaus

---

24 Die verwickelten Probleme von Röm 16 könnten vielleicht in ein neues Licht kommen?

25 Vgl. den textkritisch sekundären Segen 16,24.

26 In den Teilbriefen: Dank 2,14, Bitte 5,20/6,1; Dank 1,3, Bitte 2,8.

27 Als in ein Gebet umgesetzter Dank.

28 Mit eigener Hand (6,11) hier nicht ein Gruß wie 1 Kor 16,21.

29 Bjerkelund, a.a.O. 16, rechnet auch den ἐνορκίζω-Satz 5,27 zu den den παρακαλῶ-Sätzen vergleichbaren.

30 Bes. auffällig im 2 Thess, der ja das überlange Proömium des 1 Thess imitiert.

31 Enttäuschend im Blick auf die folgenden Fragen ist M. Bünker, Briefformular und rhetorische Disposition im 1. Korintherbrief, GTA 28, 1983. Er vergleicht zwar die Paulusbriefe mit der Gattung »Freundschaftsbrief« (22–34), aber nur im Blick auf die Topoi unter starkem Bezug auf K. Thraede, Grundzüge griechisch-römischer Brieftopik, Zet 49, 1970, sieht jedoch die Gattungsmerkmale nicht. Er verzichtet auch von vornherein

jedoch, daß man eine strenge Gliederung nicht erwarten kann; die Paränese ist ja gerade dadurch gekennzeichnet, daß die einzelnen Themen nur locker miteinander verknüpft sind[32]. Im Unterschied zu den paränetischen Teilen anderer Briefe behandelt 1 Kor vor allem *konkrete* Probleme des Verhaltens in der korinthischen Gemeinde, und diese Probleme geben daher die Themen des Briefes vor. Dabei geht Paulus einerseits auf Vorgänge ein, die ihm durch die Leute der Chloe berichtet worden sind (1,11), andererseits auf solche, von denen er gehört hat (5,1; 11,18), wie und von wem auch immer, und schließlich auf Probleme, die ihm in einem Brief vorgetragen worden sind, wozu wohl über 7,1 hinaus alle Themen gehören, deren Behandlung er mit περὶ δέ einführt (7,25; 8,1; 12,1; 16,1.12).

Sind Paulus damit zwar Themen für seinen Brief vorgegeben, so doch nicht unmittelbar auch die Reihenfolge, in der er sie behandelt; und selbst wenn er, wie häufig angenommen, den Brief der Korinther Punkt für Punkt beantwortet, bilden die Abschnitte in den Kapiteln 7–16, die nicht auf diesen Brief zurückzuführen sind, damit noch kein Argument gegen die Einheitlichkeit des 1 Kor[33], denn Paulus selber kann ja, aus welchen Gründen auch immer, in die fortlaufende Behandlung des Briefes der Korinther andere Themen einfügen. Der Aufbau des 1 Kor ist also nicht vorgegeben, sondern muß einer von Paulus selber intendierten Ordnung folgen. Zu fragen ist also nach möglicherweise erkennbaren Hinweisen auf diese Intention; leider hat Paulus uns hier so wenig wie in anderen Briefen eine Disposition hinterlassen.

Der mit 1,10 beginnende erste größere Block reicht bis 4,21; seine Integrität wird auch von Vertretern der Teilungshypothesen nicht in Frage gestellt[34]. Das Thema sind Gruppenbildungen in der Gemeinde, damit für Paulus aber sachlich die Frage des Verhältnisses zwischen Anfangsverkündigung und theologischem Fortschritt oder die der Identität von »Wort vom Kreuz« und christlicher »Weisheit«. Erkennbar ist weiter, daß in 11,2–14,40 insgesamt Fragen des Gottesdienstes der Gemeinde behandelt werden, in 11,2–16 beginnend mit der Kopfbedeckung der Frauen im Gottesdienst, ihre Mitwirkung bei Gebet und Prophetie unangefochten vorausgesetzt. 11,17–34 behandelt die Gestaltung des Herrenmahls, 12,1–14,40[35] insgesamt das Auftreten der Pneumatiker im Gottesdienst.

---

auf eine Bestimmung des Aufbaus des Briefes als ganzen wegen dessen behaupteter Uneinheitlichkeit. Der Vergleich mit Senecas *epistulae morales* (34–37) bleibt überaus blaß.

[32] Grundsätzlich ist festzuhalten an den Bestimmungen der Paränese durch M. Dibelius, Der Brief des Jakobus, KEK 15,⁸1956 (hg. von H. Greeven), 7–9.

[33] Vgl. Merklein, a.a.O. 177f.

[34] Vgl. Merklein, a.a.O. 159.

[35] Hier ist 14,33b–36 als sekundäre Interpolation anzusehen.

Eine solche thematische Verbindung kann natürlich nicht nur auf Paulus selber zurückgehen, sondern auch auf einen späteren Redaktor, der unter diesem Gesichtspunkt Teile aus verschiedenen Briefen zusammengestellt hätte. Unter den Argumenten, die für Teilungshypothesen angeführt werden, spielt aus diesem Komplex eigentlich nur eine Rolle, daß Paulus in 11,18f. das Problem der Spaltungen in der Gemeinde anders angehe als in 1,10–4,21, woraus dann eine Zuordnung der beiden Komplexe zu unterschiedlichen Briefen gefolgert wird[36].

1 Kor 15 greift ein neues Thema auf, ohne daß Paulus zu erkennen gibt, wie er über das Problem, das er in 15,12 nennt, informiert worden ist. Der Rekurs auf die Anfangsverkündigung (15,1–11) weist zurück auf die Thematik von 1,10–4,21, und Paulus gibt in 15,20–57 ein Beispiel christlicher »Weisheit« als Kreuzestheologie. Bevor er mit 16,1 zu nicht strittigen Fragen übergeht, zeigt sich also ein Rückbezug zum Anfang des Briefes. Die Vertreter der Teilungshypothesen weisen zum einen hin auf eine Diskrepanz zwischen seiner Selbstbezeichnung als »geringster der Apostel« (15,9) und seiner Verteidigung seines Apostolats in Kap. 9[37]. Wenn aber Paulus glaubt, dort nachgewiesen zu haben, daß er Apostel sei, kann er durchaus in 15,9 sich selber so nennen, freilich nicht wissend, daß diese Frage damit nicht erledigt ist, sondern in der Situation, auf die sich die im 2 Kor vereinigten Briefteile beziehen, erneut aufbrechen wird. Zum anderen wird darauf verwiesen, daß Paulus in 6,14 mit der Auferstehung argumentieren könne, die doch in Kap. 15 gerade ein Problem sei[38]. Dabei ist übersehen, daß Paulus sehr wohl in 6,14 vorgreifend ein Argument verwenden kann, dessen Begründung erst später folgt, weil ihm selber dieses Argument selbstverständlich ist und eine Begründung an dieser Stelle den Rahmen sprengen würde.

Sind also die Komplexe 1,10–4,21; 11,2–14,40; 15 und 16,1–18, letzterer als Behandlung von noch übrig gebliebenen nicht strittigen Fragen, als aneinander gefügte thematische Einheiten verständlich, so ist ein solcher einheitlicher Gesichtspunkt für 5,1–11,1 nicht ohne weiteres auszumachen, und erst in diesem Bereich finden die Vertreter der Teilungshypothesen ihre wesentlichen Argumente. Die bisher genannten Phänomene allein würden wohl kaum einem Exegeten die Annahme zwingend machen, der uns vorliegende 1 Kor sei in dieser Reihenfolge nicht von Paulus selber so konzipiert worden. Paulus beginnt in 5,1 unvermittelt mit der Erörterung eines konkreten Falles, von dem er gehört hat und den er unter πορνεία subsumiert. Es geht um ein männliches Gemeindemitglied, das mit der »Frau seines Vaters«, also seiner Stiefmutter, sexuelle Beziehungen hat, was nach jüdischem wie hellenistischem Recht unter das In-

[36] Vgl. dazu Merklein, a.a.O. 174f.
[37] Vgl. Merklein, a.a.O. 178.
[38] Vgl. Weiß, a.a.O. XLII.

zesttabu fiel[39]. Seine Stellungnahme ist eindeutig: Ausschluß aus der Gemeinde, ja Auslieferung an den Satan in einem formellen Rechtsakt der Gemeinde, der den Tod bewirken soll. Paulus votiert also gegen den, dessen Verhalten Anstoß erregt hat.

In 6,1–11 geht es ebenfalls um einen konkreten Fall, juristische Auseinandersetzungen zwischen Gemeindemitgliedern, vielleicht um die von der Antike bis in die Neuzeit stets delikate Frage deponierten Geldes[40]. Paulus ist auch hier eindeutig, indem er Prozessieren vor heidnischen Richtern ausschließt. Sein Vorschlag zur Regelung besteht zunächst darin, innerhalb der Gemeinde eine eigene Schiedsinstanz zu bilden; lieber wäre ihm jedoch ein grundsätzlicher Verzicht auf rechtliche Auseinandersetzungen. Er ergreift also Partei für den Beklagten.

6,12 dagegen benennt nicht wie 5,1 und 6,1 einen konkreten Vorfall, sondern formuliert parolenartig in zwei parallelen Sätzen: πάντα μοι ἔξεστιν mit jeweils durch ἀλλ᾽ οὐ(κ) eingeleiteter Einschränkung. Dies wird in 10,23 leicht variiert wiederholt; ἐξουσία ist aber nicht nur auch das Thema von Kap. 9, sondern die Wortgruppe begegnet in den Kapiteln 6–10 in auffälliger Häufung gegenüber nur vereinzelten Belegen in anderen Paulusbriefen[41]. Das läßt darauf schließen, daß es sich um ein Paulus aus Korinth vorgegebenes Stichwort handelt, das er jedoch nicht verwirft, sondern präzisiert. Gegenüber der bei Paulus sonst üblichen Wortgruppe ἐλευθερ-[42] enthält ἐξουσία mehr den Ton des Rechts, der Berechtigung.

Es folgt in 6,13a zunächst ein Satz, der am Beispiel der βρώματα positiv die Richtigkeit des πάντα μοι ἔξεστιν erweist; die Speisen haben nur mit dem Bauch zu tun, eins wie das andere aber nichts mit der den Tod überdauernden Gottesbeziehung. Nicht so ist es jedoch mit dem σῶμα und der πορνεία (6,13b), sondern der Körper gehört dem Herrn; deshalb ist die πορνεία nicht etwas, was einfach erlaubt ist. Der ganze Abschnitt 6,12–20 ist eine Paränese zum Thema πορνεία mit dem Aufruf: φεύγετε τὴν πορνείαν (6,18a), doch ohne daß Paulus hier wie in 5,1–13 und 6,1–11 direkt konkrete Vorgänge in der korinthischen Gemeinde benennt[43]. 6,12–20 sollte also wegen dieses anderen Charakters nicht mit den beiden vorangehenden Abschnitten unter welcher Überschrift auch immer verbunden, sondern als Neueinsatz verstanden werden[44].

---

[39] Vgl. dazu die Kommentare, z. B. H. Conzelmann, Der erste Brief an die Korinther, KEK 5, [12]1981, 123.

[40] Vgl. den kurzen Hinweis von R. Staats, Deposita fidei. Die Alte Kirche und ihr Geld, ZThK 76, 1979, 1–29, hier 16 Anm. 46, zu ἀποστερεῖν (6,7f.).

[41] Ἔξεστιν 6,12; 10,23; ἐξουσία 7,37; 8,9; 9,4.5.6.12(bis).18; ἐξουσιάζω 6,12; 7,4(bis)

[42] In 1 Kor 5,1–11,1: ἐλευθερία 10,29; ἐλεύθερος 7,21.22.39 9,1.19.

[43] 6,16 ist ein Beispiel innerhalb der Paränese, das keine Rückschlüsse auf konkrete Vorgänge zuläßt.

[44] Üblicherweise wird 5,1–6,20 ja unter »sittliche Mißstände« o. ä. zusammengefaßt.

Er dient nämlich der Vorbereitung von 7,1–40 und gehört mit diesem Abschnitt zusammen. Das Thema der ihm im Brief vorgelegten Anfrage ist das Verhältnis zwischen Männern und Frauen: »Ist Geschlechtsverkehr (überhaupt) erlaubt?«[45] Diese Frage ergibt sich im Kontext des Paulusbriefes aber auch aus 6,12–20[46]. Selbst ehelos lebend (7,7), seinen Körper nicht der Verfügungsgewalt einer Frau überlassend (6,12d, vgl. 7,4b), gibt Paulus deutlich der sexuellen Askese den Vorrang, nimmt aber dem ehelichen Geschlechtsverkehr den Ruch der πορνεία, auch dem mit einem ungläubigen Partner. Er behandelt das Thema nach einer ersten grundsätzlichen Aussage über Unverheiratete und Witwen (7,8f.) für Verheiratete (7,10–16), jungfräulich Lebende (7,25–38) und Witwen (7,39f.). War 6,12–20 eine allgemeine Paränese zur πορνεία, so konkretisiert Paulus diese in 7,1–40; beide Abschnitte gehören also eng zusammen, während 6,12–7,40 mit 5,1–13 nur das Stichwort πορνεία gemeinsam hat, dort auch nur ein Einzelfall behandelt wird, nicht wie in 7,1–40 eine die Gemeinde durchgehend betreffende Frage[47].

In 8,1 geht Paulus zu einem neuen Thema über, dem des Essens von Opferfleisch, wie die Einleitung περὶ δέ anzeigt ebenfalls vorgegeben durch den Brief der Korinther. Basis seiner Argumentation ist das monotheistische Bekenntnis, demzufolge es gar keine Götter gibt außer dem einen. Nun hatte Paulus bereits in 6,13a die βρώματα als Beispiel für das πάντα μοι ἔξεστιν genannt. Das nimmt er hier zunächst grundsätzlich auf, ohne es zu relativieren (8,1–6); allein die Rücksicht auf das Gewissen eines schwachen Bruders bringt ihn zu der schwurartigen Erklärung des Verzichts auf solches Fleisch. Gegenüber 6,13a ist er also nicht zu einer neuen Erkenntnis gekommen[48]; er übernimmt ja nicht das Urteil des schwachen Bruders, sondern hält die grundsätzliche γνῶσις (8,1) und die zu ihr gehörende ebenso grundsätzliche ἐξουσία fest.

Für den Aufbau des Briefes ergibt sich demnach eine innere Verbindung des ganzen Abschnitts 6,12–8,13: 6,12 nennt das Thema der ἐξουσία, 6,13a dafür als erstes Beispiel die βρώματα, 6,13b als zweites die πορνεία, die bis 6,20 grundsätzlich, ab 7,1 am konkreten Problem von Ehe und sexueller Askese behandelt wird; in 8,1–13 greift Paulus dann das in 6,13a bereits angezeigte Thema der βρώματα auf und behandelt es als konkretes Problem des Essens von Opferfleisch.

---

[45] Conzelmann, a.a.O. 146.

[46] Zumal, wenn sich Paulus im 1 Kor »nicht nur gegen überzogene Freiheitsparolen, sondern auch gegen asketische Ideale, die die weltlich-irdischen Relationen als sarkisch disqualifizieren«, wendet; W. Schrage, Zur Ethik der neutestamentlichen Haustafeln, NTS 21, 1974/75, 1–22, 4.

[47] Gegen die Behauptung, 6,12–20 müsse auf 5,1–13 folgen; dazu Merklein, a.a.O. 180.

[48] Auch in Röm 14,1–15,13 argumentiert er nicht grundsätzlich anders.

In 9,1 beginnt ein neuer Abschnitt mit vier rhetorisch gemeinten Fragen, deren erste die nach seiner Freiheit ist; erst die folgenden Fragen nach seinem Apostolat[49], der dann das Thema des ganzen Kapitels ist, und zwar unter dem Stichwort ἐξουσία. Seine Apologie (9,3) setzt erneut mit rhetorisch gemeinten Fragen ein, von denen erst die dritte (9,6), die nach seinem Recht, seinen Lebensunterhalt von der Gemeinde zu erhalten und ihn nicht selber erarbeiten zu müssen, dann ausgeführt wird. Paulus weist nach, daß er diese ἐξουσία durchaus habe, daß er von ihr aber keinen Gebrauch mache gerade wegen seiner Freiheit.

Die beiden 9,6 vorausgehenden Fragen werden in der Forschung offenbar einhellig von der dritten her interpretiert; man muß dann jeweils ergänzen »auf Kosten der Gemeinde«[50]. Vom Zusammenhang her legt sich aber durchaus auch eine andere Deutung nahe: Was ist mit der Freiheit des Paulus, wenn er sie in bezug auf das Essen gar nicht praktiziert? Diese Frage (9,4) und ihre Antwort ergeben sich aus 8,1–13. Und was ist mit der Freiheit des Paulus, wenn er selber in sexueller Hinsicht asketisch lebt? Diese Frage (9,5) und wieder auch ihre Antwort ergeben sich aus 7,1ff.. 9,4f. verklammern also die Apologie sehr eng mit den beiden vorangehenden Abschnitten, in denen Paulus bereits seine ἐξουσία reflektiert hatte. Dieses Stichwort selber weist zurück auf 6,12, wo Paulus das πάντα ἔξεστιν persönlich formuliert hatte als πάντα μοι ἔξεστιν. Die drei verschiedenen Probleme Sexualität, Essen, Lebensunterhalt des Apostels sind demnach für Paulus verbunden unter dem Thema der ἐξουσία, und nicht erst in Kap. 9, sondern schon in den vorangehenden Abschnitten hat er ja auch von sich selber gesprochen.

Die Apologie nun richtet sich gegen den Einwand, weil er sich seinen Lebensunterhalt selber verdiene, könne er kein Apostel sein. Paulus wendet sich mit den rhetorischen Mitteln der antiken ἀπολογία[51] an die Korinther als seine Richter und plädiert, Gegenargumente verwerfend, für sein Recht. Er erweitert diese Frage zu der grundsätzlicheren seiner eigenen Freiheit, die sich aus dem scheinbaren Widerspruch zwischen der von ihm proklamierten Freiheit und seiner eigenen Lebenspraxis nicht nur in bezug auf den Lebensunterhalt ergibt, und stellt diese seine Praxis als dem

---

[49] Vgl. die handschriftliche Überlieferung von 9,1, in der die Koiné die Fragen vertauscht hat. Bestimmt dies doch noch die Auslegung, wenn so durchgehend die zweite Frage als Leitfrage des Kapitels angesehen wird?

[50] Vgl. H. Lietzmann, An die Korinther I/II, HNT 9, ^{5}1969 (hg. von W. G. Kümmel), 40, der ab der 2. Aufl. dieses Verständnis vertreten hat, und viele andere; vgl. aber die Einschränkung für 9,5 bei H. J. Klauck, Herrenmahl und hellenistischer Kult, NTA NF 15, 1982, 249 Anm. 50.

[51] 9,3 ist Überschrift zum Folgenden, nicht zurückzubeziehen auf 9,1f. Wenn Paulus hier selber den Begriff einer rhetorischen Gattung verwendet, würde sich eine rhetorische Analyse eher anbieten als bei den Textpartien, die Bünker untersucht. Ihr Ergebnis spräche im übrigen für die Einheitlichkeit von 9,1–27.

Inhalt des Evangeliums entsprechend dar (9,16–23). Das theologische Thema des Verhältnisses zwischen Anfangsverkündigung und theologischem Fortschritt erscheint hier in sehr existentieller Weise wieder.

10,1–13 setzt erneut neu ein mit einer Paränese, die in einer Auslegung der Exodusgeschichte aufzeigt, daß auch diejenigen, die Taufe und Herrenmahl haben, nicht gefeit sind gegen die Versuchung. In 10,1–5 referiert Paulus die Geschichte; in 10,6–11 zieht er in parallel formulierten Aufforderungen paränetische Konsequenzen. Anders als die Israeliten damals sollen sie nicht ἐπιθυμηταὶ κακῶν sein (v. 6), nicht Götzendienst treiben (v. 7), nicht Hurerei (v.8), nicht den Herrn versuchen (v. 9) und nicht murren (v. 10).

Es entsteht also eine Art Lasterkatalog mit v. 6 als zusammenfassender Überschrift, Götzendienst (v. 7) und Hurerei (v. 8) voraus, die beiden traditionell als Hauptverfehlungen geltenden Verhaltensweisen, die auch in den Katalogen 5,10f.[52] und 6,9f. erscheinen. Während Paulus in den übrigen Aufforderungen die zugrunde liegenden Geschichten nur pauschal referiert, bringt er zum Thema des Götzendienstes in v. 7 ausdrücklich ein Zitat, Ex 32,6: ἐκάθισεν ὁ λαὸς φαγεῖν καὶ πεῖν, καὶ ἀνέστησαν παίζειν. Der Vers stammt aus der Geschichte vom Goldenen Kalb, deren Kenntnis wie die der ganzen Exodustradition Paulus bei seinen Lesern offenbar voraussetzt. Er zitiert aber einen Vers, der weniger als andere geeignet scheint, Götzendienst zu belegen, wenn nicht gesagt wird, wem der Tanz gilt. Das in Ex 32 nebensächliche Motiv des Essens und Trinkens tritt stark in den Vordergrund; dies aber weist zurück auf 10,3f. und auf 8,1–13, die Frage des Essens von Götzenopferfleisch, und auch auf 9,4 (φαγεῖν καὶ πεῖν).

Für die πορνεία verweist Paulus in v. 8 auf den Komplex Num 25[53], für das Versuchen auf Num 21 und für das Murren auf Num 14 und 16. Der Abschluß (10,12f.) zielt auf den paränetischen Topos des πειρασμός. »Versuchen« und »murren« sind über die Probleme des Briefes hinausweisende Motive. Daß Paulus aber die εἰδωλολατρία ausdrücklich mit Essen und Trinken verbindet, ist neu gegenüber 8,1–13, wo er, wenn nicht die Existenz , so doch zumindest die Macht von εἴδωλα bestritten hatte[54]. Wie die πορνεία, und dieses Stichwort hatte Paulus ja schon in 6,12–7,40 mehrfach gebraucht, gehört aber die εἰδωλολατρία in die Listen falscher Verhaltensweisen, die Paulus den Korinthern spätestens in seinem vorangegangenen Brief (5,9f.) vermittelt hatte, wahrscheinlich schon als Teil seiner Anfangsverkündigung[55].

---

52 In 5,10f. folgt auf die πορνεία die πλεονεξία – ein Vorblick auf 6,1–11?

53 Mit der bekannten Verwechslung der Zahlen, die in der handschriftlichen Überlieferung teilweise korrigiert wird.

54 Auch wenn er in 8,10 Kultmahle durchaus schon im Blick hatte; vgl. Klauck, a.a.O. 272.

55 Auch die Paränese, nicht nur das Kerygma gehört zur Anfangsverkündigung; vgl. die Rückverweise in 1 Thess 4,1ff.

Paulus nimmt nun dieses Thema der εἰδωλολατρία auf in dem anschließenden Imperativ: φεύγετε ἀπὸ τῆς εἰδωλολατρίας (10,14). Der entspricht dem Imperativ in 6,18: φεύγετε τὴν πορνείαν. Damit ist, wie in 6,14–7,40 die Frage der Sexualität auf den paränetischen Topos πορνεία gebracht wurde, nun die Frage des Essens in eine Beziehung gesetzt zur εἰδωλολατρία, die in 8,1–13 trotz der Diffamierung des Opferfleisches als εἰδωλόθυτον nicht hergestellt war. Das sich daraus ergebende Sachproblem liegt in der Frage, ob ein εἰδωλόθυτον bzw. ein εἴδωλον denn überhaupt eine Bedeutung haben kann; wenn die Verkündigung die Existenz der εἴδωλα bestreitet, warum warnt sie dann gleichzeitig vor der εἰδωλολατρία?

Diese Frage stellt Paulus sich selbst in 10,19–22 und beantwortet sie mit einer komplizierten Interpretation atl. Texte[56]. Sie zwingt aber Paulus auch zu einer erneuten Behandlung des Themas »Götzenopferfleisch« in 10,23–11,1. Er zitiert in 10,23 noch einmal den Grundsatz von 6,12, nun ohne μοι[57], aber mit dem auf 8,10 zurück- und auf 11,2–14,40 vorausweisenden Stichwort οἰκοδομεῖ, und er kommt nun zu einer endgültigen Stellungnahme zu dem in 8,1–13 bereits behandelten Problem: Trotz des Verbots der εἰδωλολατρία braucht man keine Nachforschungen anzustellen über die Herkunft des Fleisches, das man ißt, zu Hause oder als geladener Gast. Wird man jedoch hingewiesen auf den Charakter des Fleisches, soll man verzichten um des Gewissens desjenigen willen, der darauf hingewiesen hat (10,28.29a)[58]. Paulus bleibt also bei seiner Meinung von 8,1–13, präzisiert sie, modifiziert oder gar widerruft sie aber nicht. Wie sich aus der allgemeinen Paränese zum Thema πορνεία in 6,14–20 die konkrete Paränese in 7,1–40 ergab, so hier aus der Paränese zum Thema εἰδωλολατρία die zum konkreten Umgang mit Opferfleisch.

Grundsätzlich ist damit auch noch einmal die Frage der Freiheit angeschnitten (10,29b). Paulus aber streift sie nur und verweist insgesamt auf die Umwelt, in der die Korinther leben (Juden und Griechen), auf den Kontext der (von ihm gegründeten) Gemeinde(n) und auf sein eigenes Vorbild, also seinen freiwilligen Verzicht auf Realisierung der von ihm proklamierten Freiheit (11,1).

---

[56] Kompliziert nicht zuletzt durch die Unsicherheit der Textüberlieferung in 10,19b und 10,20, wo weithin dieselben Handschriften (p^{46} ℵ A C Ψ 33) in 19b ἢ ὅτι εἴδωλόν τί ἐστιν auslassen und in 20a τὰ ἔθνη einfügen. Letzteres ist nicht nur sinnvoller, sondern auch weitaus besser bezeugt (gegen B D F G).

[57] Es geht hier nicht um *seine* ἐξουσία.

[58] 10,28 bezieht sich nicht nur auf v. 27, sondern auch auf v. 25; dann ist der τίς nicht unter den Teilnehmern des Gastmahls von v. 27 zu suchen, sondern ein Mitglied der Gemeinde, Juden- oder Heidenchrist, das Anstoß nimmt.

III.

Es ergibt sich also für 5,1–11,1 ein Zusammenhang, der in sich verständlich ist als von Paulus selber fortlaufend so intendiert. 5,1–13 und 6,1–11 behandeln vorweg die zwei konkreten Probleme, die nur einzelne Personen betreffen, auch wenn sie die Gemeinde als ganze belasten. Warum Paulus sie hier placiert, ist müßig zu fragen; vielleicht stammen die Nachrichten darüber ebenfalls von den Leuten der Chloe (1,11) wie die für 1,10–4,21?

In 6,12–11,1 geht es dann vor allem um Fragen der Sexualität und des Essens von Opferfleisch, Fragen also des ethischen Verhaltens der Christen allgemein, nicht nur einzelner wie in 5,1–6,11, andererseits aber auch nicht Fragen der Gestaltung des Gottesdienstes wie in 11,2–14,40. Beide Themen gehen auf den Brief der Korinther zurück (7,1; 8,1). Hinzu kommen die Frage nach seinem Apostolat (9,1) und das Stichwort ἐξουσία, das als πάντα μοι ἔξεστιν zu einer wohl in Korinth formulierten griffigen Parole geworden ist, in der die aus der Begegnung mit dem Evangelium resultierende Freiheit zusammengefaßt ist[59].

Paulus macht dieses Stichwort zum übergreifenden Thema des ganzen Abschnitts, und πάντα (μοι) ἔξεστιν markiert dessen Beginn (6,12) wie Abschluß (10,23). Er verknüpft die einzelnen Teile aber auch untereinander durch voraus- und zurückweisende Beziehungen. 6,13 verbindet bereits das Thema der Speisen mit dem der πορνεία. Die Fragen 9,4f. greifen auf 6,12–7,40 und auf 8,1–13 zurück und leiten zu 9,6–27 über. 10,1–13 verbindet erneut 6,12–7,40 und 8,1–13, nun unter den Stichworten εἰδωλολατρία und πορνεία; der Imperativ 10,14 steht parallel zu dem in 6,18.

Läßt sich so der Zusammenhang 6,12–11,1 als in sich nicht nur sinnvoll erklären, sondern auch als einer durchgehenden Intention folgend, sind Teilungshypothesen nicht mehr erforderlich. Die Themen dieses Teils sind Paulus vorgegeben durch die Verhältnisse in Korinth; er verbindet sie miteinander unter dem Oberthema ἐξουσία. Das gelingt ihm, weil er nicht nur in der Apologie, sondern auch bei den Fragen der Sexualität und des Essens sich selbst einbezieht in die Reflexion, die Frage der ἐξουσία nicht nur als ein Problem der Korinther, sondern immer auch als sein eigenes sieht. Anders wäre Kap. 9 ein Fremdkörper in diesem Briefteil.

Neben der Situation in Korinth und dem Gestaltungswillen des Paulus hat noch ein dritter Faktor eingewirkt, die paränetische Tradition der Lasterkataloge. Die Imperative 6,18 und 10,14 unterstellen 6,12–11,1 ja

---

[59] Vgl. auch ἐξουσία in 11,10, wobei das griechische Wort ja nicht eine lexikalische Bedeutung im Sinne einer Kopfbedeckung hat; Paulus will das Tragen einer solchen als Zeichen von ἐξουσία verstanden wissen, oder zitiert er eine ironische Wendung korinthischer Frauen?

insgesamt dem Topos πορνεία καὶ εἰδωλολατρία[60]. Daß dieser Topos nicht von Anfang an das Paulus leitende Strukturprinzip für 6,12–11,1 war, zeigt sich darin, daß er erst in 10,7 und nicht schon in 8,1–13 auf das Stichwort εἰδωλολατρία kommt und dadurch in der »allmählichen Verfertigung der Gedanken beim Reden« gezwungen ist, die Frage des Essens von Opferfleisch noch einmal aufzunehmen.

Das aber deutet auf die prägende Kraft der paränetischen Tradition, aus der Paulus bereits in 5,10f. und 6,9f. zitiert hatte. Waren 6,12–20 wie 10,1–13 als Stücke allgemeiner Paränese zu bestimmen, 6,12–20 zum Thema πορνεία, 10,1–13 als paränetische Auslegung der Exodusgeschichte, so sind 7,1–40 und 8,1–13; 10,23–11,1 Beispiele für angewandte Paränese, in denen die großen Wörter πορνεία und εἰδωλολατρία reflektiert werden im Blick auf konkrete Probleme alltäglichen Verhaltens.

Die allgemeine Paränese in Tugend- und Lasterkatalogen wie in einzelnen Mahnungen läßt sich auf die Begegnung atl. und griechischer Traditionen im hellenistischen Judentum zurückführen. Paulus nimmt sie auf, entbindet sie aber von der Beziehung zur Tora, die ihr dort die konkrete Füllung gab; bei keinem der in 1 Kor 5,1–11,1 behandelten Probleme greift er auf dort ja durchaus vorhandene Regelungen als Kriterien zurück. Sowohl für Fragen der Sexualität als auch des Umgangs mit Fleisch wären in der Tora ausgeführte Verhaltensnormen zu finden gewesen; sie scheidet jedoch für Paulus nicht nur als »Heilsweg«, sondern auch als primäre Lebensorientierung aus[61]. Die Reduktion des Gesetzes auf das Liebesgebot (Gal 5,14; Röm 13,8–10) setzt konkrete Füllungen dieses Gebotes *der Tora* erst frei. Was πορνεία ist und was εἰδωλολατρία, entscheidet sich nicht in den autoritativen Bestimmungen des Gesetzes; dem Evangelium entsprechende Normen müssen erst gefunden werden[62].

Kriterium der ethischen Entscheidung ist für Paulus aber auch nicht ein einfacher Rückgriff auf eine als autoritativ verstandene Jesusüberlieferung. Auf sie verweist er in diesem Zusammenhang zwar zweimal (7,10f.; 9,14), beide Male übrigens nicht in Form eines direkten Zitats, sondern in indirekter Rede. In 7,10f. setzt er in der Parenthese jedoch entgegen dem Gebot Jesu (vgl. Mk 10,11f. parr.) voraus, daß es Geschie-

---

[60] Ich wiederhole damit nicht die These von Lietzmann, a.a.O. 25, der das Aposteldekret (Apg 15,23–29) als in Korinth bekannt erschließen wollte (dagegen Kümmel im Anhang 175); vgl. zur Verbindung von Opferfleisch und Hurerei auch Apk 2,14.20, zum Problem aber auch die in 1 Tim 4,3 abgewiesenen »Irrlehrer«.

[61] Vgl. den doch wohl spielerischen Umgang mit dem »Gesetz des Mose« in 9,9.

[62] Nachträglich sehe ich, daß in diesem Punkt Fragestellung und These sich eng berühren mit dem Aufsatz von A. Lindemann in diesem selben Band: Die biblischen Toragebote und die paulinische Ethik. Den Jubilar wird so etwas nicht verwundern, hat er doch selbst erleben können, wie frühere Zusammenarbeit in Bethel weiterwirkt.

dene gibt; Ehescheidung führt also nicht zum Ausschluß aus der Gemeinde. In 9,14 setzt er sich selber über das Gebot Jesu, daß die Jünger vom Evangelium leben sollen (vgl. Mt 10,8.10/Lk 10,7), hinweg. Ob er ein Jesuswort wie Mk 7,15 kannte, wissen wir nicht; jedenfalls zitiert er keines im Zusammenhang der Frage des Essens von Opferfleisch. Die Autorisierung der Paränese in 1,10 διὰ τοῦ ὀνόματος τοῦ κυρίου ἡμῶν Ἰησοῦ χριστοῦ bedeutet für Paulus also nicht, daß Jesusüberlieferung normative Regelungen für konkrete Probleme böte.

Die Verkündigung des Paulus zielte auf Bildung von Gemeinschaften, die in sich nicht homogen waren. Das Zusammentreffen unterschiedlicher Traditionen, bedingt durch Herkunft und soziale Stellung, führte erst zu den Problemen, die Paulus behandeln muß. Die Erfahrungen von Freiheit, auch gegenüber den gewohnten Orientierungen des alltäglichen Lebens, schufen Probleme im ethischen Bereich. Paulus, selber aus einem festen System ethischer Normen kommend, vollzieht diese Probleme als seine eigenen nach, bietet sich selbst an, macht aber seinen eigenen Lebensstil nicht zur autoritativen Norm (7,7a; 11,1). Die Behandlung des Falles in 5,1–13 zeigt zwar, daß es bestimmte Grenzen gibt; innerhalb dieser Grenzen aber ist ein großer Spielraum ethischer Freiheit möglich. Das »Wort vom Kreuz« als Anfangsverkündigung wie als christliche »Weisheit« bedeutet nicht die Schaffung eines neuen festen Systems ethischer Normen, sondern eine Krise der Weisheit einschließlich ihrer paränetischen Traditionen, die Paulus aufnimmt.

Der Streit um die Bergpredigt – ein exegetisches Problem?

Anmerkungen zum Umgang mit der Sprache

von Willi Marxsen

(von-Stauffenberg-Str. 40, 4400 Münster)

Die Auslegungs- und Wirkungsgeschichte der Bergpredigt zeigt, daß offenbar keine Generation mit ihr wirklich zurechtgekommen ist. Es ist daher kaum verwunderlich, wenn es uns heute nicht anders ergeht. Statt nun aber immer neue Versuche zu unternehmen, die bisher ausprobierten Möglichkeiten zu modifizieren oder um weitere zu vermehren (die mit hoher Wahrscheinlichkeit ebenfalls auf Widersprüche stoßen und dann schnell das Schicksal der früheren erleiden), sollten wir einmal innehalten und fragen, ob es für den Dissensus eine tieferliegende Ursache gibt. Es könnte doch etwas Grundsätzliches übersehen worden sein; und dann wären die Meinungsverschiedenheiten fast unvermeidbare Folgen daraus.

Nach meiner Überzeugung ist genau das der Fall. Ich möchte zu zeigen versuchen: Die Schuld am Streit um die Bergpredigt und um ihre Verwendbarkeit für christliche Ethik trägt kaum (oder höchstens zu einem sehr geringen Teil) eine immer noch unzureichende und darum verbesserungsbedürftige Exegese, sondern viel eher und sogar in erster Linie ein allzu sorgloser Umgang mit der Sprache. Vielfach werden für ganz unterschiedliche Gegenstände und Arbeitsschritte dieselben Vokabeln benutzt. Das hat zur Folge, daß man beim Gebrauch dieser Vokabeln unversehens von einer Bedeutung in eine andere hinübergleitet und dadurch permanent Mißverständnisse produziert. Dringend nötig sind daher Definitionen, über die man sich zwar zunächst einmal einigen, sie dann aber auch durchhalten muß. Ein möglichst präziser Sprachgebrauch zwingt zu methodisch kontrolliertem Arbeiten und macht zugleich das eigene Arbeiten für andere durchsichtig und so erst wirklich überprüfbar. Mancher Streit könnte sich dann als gegenstandslos erweisen. Das gilt zwar nicht nur für den Streit um die Bergpredigt. Diese soll aber (wegen der Aktualität) als Paradigma genommen werden.

I.

Wenn heute die Vokabel *Bergpredigt* benutzt wird, versteht man darunter sehr oft nicht etwa die Bergpredigt, sondern so etwas wie eine »Summe« für christliche Ethik oder das zentrale Dokument, an dem christliche Ethik sich auszurichten hat. Daß das nur durch eine schwerwiegende Bedeutungsverschiebung des ursprünglichen Sinnes von Bergpredigt möglich ist, macht man sich kaum klar.

Denn Bergpredigt ist eine eindeutige Größe: Mt 5–7. Doch reicht ein bloßer Hinweis auf diesen *Text* nicht aus, weil dieser »Text« in Wahrheit eine *Perikope* ist, also etwas »rundherum Abgeschnittenes«, und darum nicht eigentlich ein Text, sondern ein Abschnitt aus einem Text. Schon hier könnte ein präziserer Sprachgebrauch hilfreich sein. Das Neue Testament enthält 27 Texte, nicht mehr! Perikopen sind Abschnitte aus einem Text, manchmal in sich geschlossene Abschnitte, nicht selten aber auch Trümmerstücke.

Daß es sich bei der Bergpredigt um einen in sich geschlossenen Abschnitt handelt, berechtigt noch keineswegs, diesen isoliert zu betrachten. Man würde dann übersehen, daß es sich lediglich um einen der fünf Redenkomplexe des Matthäus-Evangeliums handelt, die der Evangelist selbst zusammengestellt und in sein Werk eingebaut hat. Er gibt sogar an, wie sie verstanden und benutzt werden sollen: Die Elf sollen taufen und zu halten lehren, was Jesus befohlen hat (28,20).

Wie Matthäus bei der Redaktion seines Werkes vorgegangen ist, ist nicht nur bekannt, sondern darüber besteht auch ein Konsensus: Er hat, im allgemeinen dem Faden des Markus-Evangeliums folgend, ältere Traditionen verschiedener Herkunft nicht nur gesammelt, sondern zugleich durch Eingriffe in seine Vorlagen kommentierend akzentuiert und zusammen mit einigen Neubildungen nach seinem eigenen Plan geordnet. Mögen Einzelheiten strittig sein (und strittig bleiben), tangiert das nicht das Gesamturteil: Wir haben es bei der Bergpredigt nicht mit einer Rede Jesu zu tun, sondern mit einer Schöpfung des Matthäus aus (etwa) den 80er Jahren des ersten Jahrhunderts. Der »Bergprediger« ist daher auch nicht Jesus, sondern das ist der Jesus, wie Matthäus ihn in seiner Zeit verstanden hat.

Die Vokabel Bergpredigt ist damit eindeutig definiert: die drei von Matthäus in seiner Zeit, aber auch für seine Zeit gestalteten Kapitel. Im Sinne des Evangelisten bilden sie eine Einheit.

Wer Perikopen aus der Bergpredigt herausschneidet und die von ihm (nach eigenem Bedarf) ausgewählten zitiert, darf dafür nicht das Wort Bergpredigt benutzen. Ein Trümmerstück ist nicht identisch mit dem Ganzen. Eine Perikope kann eben immer nur im Zusammenhang des Ganzen verstanden und darf darum auch nur so benutzt werden: eine Perikope aus Mt 5–7 nur im Zusammenhang der Bergpredigt und diese nur im Zusammenhang des ganzen Evangeliums.

Nun gibt es zwar noch die Möglichkeit, durch Literarkritik (also nicht einfach mit Hilfe der Schere!) Traditionen zu rekonstruieren, die dem Matthäus vorgelegen haben. Deren Wortlaut stimmt jedoch nur selten mit dem des Evangelisten überein. Selbst wenn das der Fall ist, muß unterschieden werden zwischen dem ursprünglichen Verständnis und dem matthäischen, das immer nur aus dem Zusammenhang erhoben werden kann. Bei diesen vormatthäischen Traditionen darf man auch nicht von »Bergpredigt« reden. Denn die Bergpredigt gibt es erst seit Matthäus.

Wer Bergpredigt sagt, muß daher die Bergpredigt *des Matthäus* meinen, sonst mißbraucht er das Wort. Wenn er dann der Auffassung ist, daß die Bergpredigt des Matthäus eine »Summe« der christlichen Ethik und als solche heute benutzbar ist, muß er das begründen: warum gerade die Ethik des Matthäus, warum nicht die irgendeines anderen Verfassers einer neutestamentlichen Schrift? Ohne solche Begründung mißbraucht er das Wort Bergpredigt. Die Frage ist nun aber nicht zuerst, ob eine solche Begründung möglich ist, sondern wie sie geschehen könnte.

II.

Ausgangspunkt kann nur die *Exegese* sein. Doch tauchen bei dieser Vokabel alsbald wieder Schwierigkeiten auf, da durchaus unklar ist, was mit ihr gemeint ist. Es führt zu nichts, wenn man, von der Vokabel ausgehend, die vielen Möglichkeiten ihres Verständnisses nebeneinander legt, sie erwägt und von dort aus eine Definition versucht. Auf diesem Wege wird kaum ein Konsensus erreicht werden. Wohl aber besteht eine Chance, wenn man die bisherigen Überlegungen einbezieht.

Da nicht zu bestreiten ist, daß die Bergpredigt ein durch Redaktionsarbeit entstandener Abschnitt aus dem Werk des Matthäus ist, mit dem der Evangelist in seiner Zeit den Christen seiner Zeit Anweisungen geben wollte, die sie zu befolgen haben, muß es zunächst darauf ankommen, zu verstehen, was *er ihnen* sagen wollte. Dieses Bemühen um Verstehen nenne ich Exegese. Allgemein könnte man definieren: Exegese ist das Nachsprechen dessen, was ein Verfasser in seiner Situation und unter seinen Bedingungen seinen Lesern in ihrer Situation und unter ihren Bedingungen sagen wollte – in meiner Sprache.

Was immer ich mit der Bergpredigt später anfangen will (und kann), man wird nicht bestreiten können, daß ich sie zunächst einmal verstehen muß. Dieses Bemühen um Verstehen ist also ein eigenständiger Arbeitsschritt. Wenn ich diesen Arbeitsschritt benenne und dafür gerade die Vokabel Exegese benutze, ist das natürlich Willkür. Ich könnte auch einen anderen Namen wählen. Spreche ich hier aber von Exegese, dann ist diese Vokabel »verbraucht«. Sie darf für weitere Arbeitsschritte nicht mehr benutzt werden. Umgekehrt gilt aber auch: Wer einen anderen (späteren) Arbeitsschritt oder mehrere Arbeitsschritte zusammen als Exegese bezeichnet, muß nun für den ersten Arbeitsschritt eine andere Vokabel benutzen, weil er sonst einem Sprachwirrwarr Vorschub leistet. Welche Vokabel er jetzt wählt, ist ihm unbenommen, *nennen* muß er sie aber. Ich spreche hier von Exegese.

Nun ist genau darauf zu achten, was die Exegese leisten kann und was nicht. Da es um den Versuch geht, das zu verstehen, was Matthäus damals seinen Lesern sagen wollte, ist Exegese immer historische Exegese. Der Exeget hat sich bei seiner Arbeit jeder Kritik zu enthalten. Er darf sich nicht davon beeinflussen lassen, ob er das, was Matthäus damals gesagt hat, für sinnvoll hält oder nicht, ob es ihm einleuchtet oder nicht, und auf gar keinen Fall, ob das (nach irgendwelchen Maßstäben) richtig ist oder falsch. Jede Kritik stellt sich dem Verstehen in den Weg; darum ist »historisch-kritische Exegese« keine Exegese mehr. Es geht bei der Exegese nur und um nichts anderes als um das verstehbare Nachsprechen einer alten Aussage.

Nun liegt es auf der Hand, daß verschiedene Exegeten zu verschiedenen Ergebnissen kommen. Das ist zwar bedauerlich, aber wahrscheinlich unvermeidbar. Doch was folgt daraus?

In jüngster Zeit kann man gelegentlich die Äußerung hören, daß neuere Exegese zu neuen Einsichten geführt habe und man daraus nun die entsprechenden Konsequenzen ziehen müsse – etwa im Blick auf die Stellung der Kirche zu Israel oder auf dem Gebiet ethischer Entscheidungen. Wenn man die Lehre von der Inspiration der Schrift in irgendeiner Weise (die man dann aber nennen sollte) voraussetzt, könnte das vielleicht zutreffen. Sonst aber ist das einfach ein Kurzschluß. Es kann ja in der Tat sein, daß eine neue Exegese der Bergpredigt durch Anwendung geeigneter Methoden (man denke an die Redaktionsgeschichte) oder durch ein deutlicheres Erkennen des zeitgenössischen Hintergrundes zu besseren Ergebnissen als den bisherigen kommt. Das heißt doch aber immer nur: Wir verstehen jetzt besser, was Matthäus damals seinen damaligen Lesern sagen wollte, als man es früher zu verstehen meinte. Das heißt doch aber nicht, daß wir deswegen heute die christliche Ethik umschreiben müßten. Der Ethiker darf sich doch nicht von den stets wechselnden und zudem oft umstrittenen Ergebnissen der Exegeten abhängig machen.

Andererseits darf der Exeget das nun auch nicht vom Ethiker verlangen. Er sollte sich klarmachen: Wenn er als Exeget mehr sein will als Exeget, setzt er sehr schnell seine Freiheit aufs Spiel. Bei der Exegese wird nicht darüber entschieden, was in einer christlichen Dogmatik oder Ethik zu gelten hat. Denn der Exeget ist als Exeget nichts anderes als Kirchen- und Dogmengeschichtler der Zeit bis etwa 130. Wenn er dann die Bergpredigt exegesiert, kommt als Ergebnis nichts anderes heraus als das, was Matthäus in seiner Zeit und für seine Zeit an ethischen Weisungen formuliert hat. Darüber und über nichts anderes streiten sich Exegeten und suchen im Gespräch miteinander einen Konsensus.

Daß Matthäus der Meinung war, die von ihm für seine Zeit formulierte Ethik sei christliche Ethik, darf man voraussetzen. Gleichwohl muß man bedenken, daß es sich um eine matthäische Behauptung handelt. Der Exeget wird das feststellen. Er hat aber als Exeget weder die Aufgabe noch die Möglichkeit, die Richtigkeit der Behauptung zu überprüfen. Und darum kann er als Exeget schon gar nicht verlangen, daß sein Ergebnis unmittelbar vom Dogmatiker oder Ethiker übernommen wird. Exegese ist nun einmal nur eine theologische Hilfswissenschaft. Sie ist zwar unverzichtbar, weil es ohne sie nicht zum Verstehen der 27 Texte des Neuen Testaments kommt und jede weitere Arbeit mit diesen Texten nur möglich ist, wenn diese zunächst einmal verstanden worden sind. Sie ist dennoch nur eine theologische Hilfswissenschaft. Diese Bescheidung ist der Grund für die Freiheit des Exegeten. Er sollte sie nicht leichtfertig dadurch aufs Spiel setzen, daß er seine Grenzen überschreitet. Er tut das, wenn er später notwendige Arbeitsschritte in seine Exegese hineinnimmt. Diese Gefahr ist deswegen so groß, weil er im allgemeinen ja selbst an den weiteren Arbeitsschritten interessiert ist und sie wohl auch tut. Nur tut er sie dann nicht mehr als Exeget. So ist es nicht nur eine Frage der Sprachdisziplin, sondern dient auch der methodischen Kontrolle der eigenen Arbeit, wenn jeder einzelne Schritt mit einem eigenen Namen bezeichnet wird.

Wenn wir nun einmal (selbstverständlich hypothetisch) unterstellen, daß eine solche Exegese der Bergpredigt gelungen ist, die die Aussage des Matthäus so adäquat wie nur möglich nachspricht (und das muß das Ziel des Exegeten bleiben), würde das also für heutige Ethik unmittelbar überhaupt nichts eintragen. Denn zunächst müßte jetzt doch die Frage beantwortet werden: Warum ist gerade die relativ späte Ethik des Matthäus die christliche Ethik par excellence? Warum nicht die Ethik *des Verfassers* (so sollte man immer präzise formulieren) einer anderen Schrift aus dem Neuen Testament: die des Verfassers des Jakobus-Briefes etwa, des Verfassers des Hebräerbriefes oder des Verfassers des 2. Thessalonicherbriefes? Der Ethik des Matthäus eine Sonderstellung einzuräumen, ist doch bare Willkür!

III.

Es kann hilfreich sein, sich zur Beantwortung dieser Frage zunächst einmal auf Luther zu besinnen. In seiner Vorrede zum Jakobus-Brief treibt er (selbstverständlich ohne schon die Vokabel zu benutzen) historische Exegese, und zwar als einen Arbeitsschritt für sich. Er stellt dar, was der (unbekannte) damalige Verfasser seinen damaligen Lesern sagen wollte: Der »gut frum Man« wollte Menschen, die sich auf einen Glauben ohne Werke verließen, zum Tun von Werken treiben, um dadurch Rechtfertigung vor Gott zu erreichen.

Nun kann man durchaus darüber streiten, ob Luther richtig exegesiert hat. Jede historische Exegese kann und muß *überprüft* werden. Man kann die Aussage des Verfassers ja aus Voreingenommenheit (seine Schrift steht im Neuen Testament) oder aus anderen Gründen mißverstanden haben. Luther war der Meinung, ihn richtig verstanden zu haben – und schrieb das Ergebnis seiner Exegese nieder.

Er dachte aber nicht daran, aus der (seiner Ansicht nach) richtigen historischen Exegese unmittelbar dogmatische Konsequenzen zu ziehen. Er fordert vielmehr (und fordert das für »alle Bücher«), daß nach der durchgeführten Exegese das Ergebnis der Exegese in einem zweiten Arbeitsschritt zunächst einmal *kontrolliert* werden muß. Hier (und nicht schon bei der Exegese!) kommt nun Kritik ins Spiel. Luther spricht in diesem Zusammenhang von einem »Prüfestein«, den er inhaltlich mit unterschiedlichen Wendungen umschreibt. Er spricht von »euangelisch art«, davon, »was Christum treibet«, und er versteht darunter Rechtfertigung allein aus Glauben.

Hier kann man nun wieder darüber streiten, ob Luther (1) den »Prüfestein« auf dem richtigen Wege gefunden und ob er ihn (2) inhaltlich richtig bestimmt hat. Beides muß man unterscheiden.

Daß Luther sich beim Finden des »Prüfesteins« an Paulus orientiert, hängt ganz offenkundig mit seiner eigenen Vergangenheit zusammen, mit seiner »Entdeckung« des Evangeliums durch sein neues Verständnis von Röm 1,17. Insofern liegt eine subjektive Entscheidung vor, die problematisch ist. Andere könnten mit demselben Recht ihre eigene (andere) subjektive Entscheidung dagegen setzen. Zu fordern ist daher, daß das Finden des »Prüfesteins« methodisch kontrolliert geschieht, weil er nur so einsichtig begründet werden kann. Darauf habe ich in einer anderen Festschrift (der für Präses Dr. Heinrich Reiß, Kirchlicher Dienst und theologische Ausbildung, Bielefeld 1985) hingewiesen. In unserem Zusammenhang brauche ich darauf nicht näher einzugehen, weil das eigentliche Problem dadurch nicht unmittelbar tangiert wird. Nicht in erster Linie um das Finden des »Prüfesteins« geht es, sondern um die Einsicht, daß es überhaupt eines »Prüfesteins« bedarf – wenn man nicht auf Inspirationslehre oder Lehramt ausweichen will.

Im Gefolge Luthers sind wir es gewohnt, von einem »Kanon in Kanon« zu reden. Das wird jedoch häufig mißverstanden. Man formuliert dann, daß die Schriften des Kanons von einem Kanon (= »Prüfestein«) aus »auszulegen« sind. Genau das aber ist falsch, wie Luthers Vorrede zum Jakobus-Brief zeigt. Jetzt werden nämlich zwei zu unterscheidende Arbeitsschritte (historische Exegese und Kontrolle ihres Ergebnisses) unversehens zu einem Arbeitsschritt zusammengelegt. Tatsächlich hat der »Kanon« bei der Exegese überhaupt nichts zu suchen. Er muß gesondert definiert und inhaltlich bestimmt werden.

Man kann nun durchaus darüber diskutieren, ob man den »Prüfestein«, wie Luther es tut, *im* Schriftenkanon *findet* (nachdem er das Evangelium »entdeckt« hatte), oder ob man ihn, wie ich es für sachgemäß halte, *vor* dem Schriftenkanon *sucht,* also vor dem Jahre 50, der Abfassung der ältesten erhaltenen Schrift (1. Thess). Die grundsätzliche Einsicht

Luthers bleibt jedoch unaufgebbar: Das Ergebnis der historischen Exegese bedarf (in einem zweiten Arbeitsschritt!) der Sachkontrolle. Dazu ist ein »Prüfestein« nötig.

Wird nun aber nicht genau diese Einsicht bei der Benutzung der Bergpredigt (allerdings keineswegs nur dort) unentwegt ignoriert? Sieht man überhaupt noch, daß es sich um zwei streng voneinander zu unterscheidende Arbeitsschritte handelt? Wirft man statt dessen nicht fast immer (um es mit Luther auszudrücken) methodisch ganz »vnördig eins ins ander«? Und dabei müßte doch (ganz unabhängig von Luthers methodischer Einsicht) wenigstens an diesem Punkt ein Konsensus zu erreichen sein: Man sollte Schriften (und natürlich auch Abschnitte oder gar Perikopen aus Schriften) erst dann (wozu auch immer) benutzen, wenn man sie (vorher!) verstanden hat. Doch genau dazu (und das heißt: nur zur Exegese) läßt man sich meist keine Zeit, weil man möglichst schnell »praktikable« Ergebnisse erreichen möchte. Verschleiert wird das dadurch, daß man die der Exegese folgenden Schritte auch mit der Vokabel Exegese benennt.

Ich meine, es müßte einzusehen sein: Beides, ob Matthäus damals mit seiner Bergpredigt eine Ethik vorgetragen hat, die als christlich bezeichnet werden kann, und, ob diese Ethik heute in eine christliche Ethik hineingeführt werden darf, das entscheidet sich nicht an der noch so adäquat ausgelegten Bergpredigt, sondern das entscheidet sich bei der Kontrolle des Ergebnisses der Exegese mit Hilfe des »Prüfesteins«.

IV.

Da mit einem »Prüfestein« (zumindest sachgemäß) so gut wie nie gearbeitet wird, besteht weder ein Konsensus darüber, wie er zu finden, noch darüber, wie er inhaltlich zu bestimmen ist. Hier liegt also eine Aufgabe vor, die noch auf ihre Lösung wartet.

Ich möchte dazu wenigstens einiges zu erwägen geben.

Unausrottbar scheint immer noch der Gedanke zu sein, den »historischen Jesus« als Maßstab zu nehmen. Dieser Maßstab wird jedoch nicht als »Kanon« an das Ergebnis der Exegese (etwa der Bergpredigt) gelegt, sondern man sucht (bzw. rekonstruiert) »authentische« Jesus-Worte und nimmt dann Jesu Ethik zum Kriterium für christliche Ethik. Das wirft indes eine Reihe von Fragen auf.

(1) Einzusehen muß zunächst sein, daß der, der diesen Weg geht, sich nicht mehr auf die Bergpredigt berufen darf, wenn er christliche Ethik begründen will. Wenn er das dennoch tut, darf er sich nicht mit sprachlicher Nachlässigkeit entschuldigen, denn er handelt gegen besseres Wissen. Das ist unredlich. – (2) Sodann muß er bedenken, daß er das christologische Problem verschleiert. Zwar erweckt er (bewußt oder unbewußt) den Ein-

druck, daß er ohne Christologie auskomme, da er sich »nur« und streng an Jesus orientiert. Tatsächlich aber setzt er eine massive Christologie bereits voraus. Denn wieso sollte die Ethik eines Rabbi aus Nazareth mehr bieten als (vielleicht) interessante und (vielleicht auch) erwägenswerte Denkmöglichkeiten? Erst die Christologie entscheidet doch darüber, daß und welche Verbindlichkeit Jesu Ethik haben könnte. War er etwa ein neuer Gesetzgeber, oder als wer ist er verstanden worden? Das muß ausdrücklich genannt werden, darf aber nicht in der Schwebe bleiben, wenn man sich heute auf Jesu Ethik berufen will. – (3) Nun besteht ja keineswegs ein Konsensus darüber, welche Jesus-Worte »authentisch« sind, welche nicht. Wird jetzt nicht von den (wechselnden!) Urteilen der Historiker abhängig gemacht, wie christliche Ethik auszusehen hat? – (4) Vor allem aber scheint mir übersehen zu sein, daß sich die (von Reimarus inaugurierte) Frage nach dem historischen Jesus inzwischen als eine falsche Fragestellung erwiesen hat. Fragen wir statt dessen (was allein möglich ist) historisch nach Jesus, kommen wir nie weiter als bis zu den Menschen, die Gehörtes oder Erlebtes dargestellt haben. Nun stellen diese Menschen aber einerseits immer nur eine Auswahl aus dem Gehörten oder Erlebten dar (nur das, was *sie* für wichtig hielten); und es gibt schlechterdings keine Methode, mit deren Hilfe man feststellen kann, ob der »historische Jesus« ebenso ausgewählt hätte. Andererseits (und das ist für unseren Zusammenhang wichtiger) stellen diese Menschen das Gehörte oder Erlebte immer so dar, wie *sie* es *verstanden* haben. Wieder gibt es keine Methode, mit deren Hilfe man feststellen kann, ob der »historische Jesus« es ebenso verstanden hat. Da sich auch nicht das Gegenteil beweisen läßt, folgt daraus: Wir können bei der historischen Frage nach Jesus die Menschen, denen wir das Traditionsgut verdanken, nie überspringen. Um das auch sprachlich deutlich zum Ausdruck zu bringen, sollte man nicht mehr von »Jesu Ethik«, sondern statt dessen präziser von »an Jesus orientierter Ethik« sprechen.

Hier kommt dann sofort Christologie in den Blick. Unsere Traditionen verdanken wir Menschen, die Jesus als einen erfahren haben, der ihnen in seinem Wirken (im Reden und im Verhalten) seinen Gott zugelebt hat. Indem er ihnen aber seinen Gott zugelebt hat, hat er ihnen zugemutet, sich auf ihn selbst und eben damit auf seinen Gott einzulassen.

Das müßte nun sehr viel genauer ausgeführt und inhaltlich gefüllt werden. (Ich hoffe, das in absehbarer Zeit nachholen zu können.) Vielleicht macht aber diese knappe Skizze schon deutlich: Hier kommen (wenn auch mit ganz anderen Vokabeln) Momente zum Zuge, die in der sogenannten Rechtfertigungslehre des Paulus begegnen, dem auf evangelischer Seite weithin anerkannten, wenn auch kaum je praktizierten »Prüfestein«. – Was könnte das für den Umgang mit der Bergpredigt bedeuten?

V.

Eine der meistdiskutierten Fragen war immer wieder (und ist es bis heute), ob die Forderungen der Bergpredigt erfüllbar sind. Da man bei der Suche nach der Antwort durchweg nicht streng die einzelnen Arbeitsschritte unterscheidet, rennt man sich im allgemeinen schnell fest. Behauptung steht gegen Behauptung.

Wir beschränken uns zunächst nur auf die Exegese. Die Frage lautet dann: War Matthäus der Meinung, seine Leser (und er) seien in der Lage, nach den Regeln der Bergpredigt zu leben? Da der Evangelist nicht erkennen läßt, daß er diese Frage überhaupt reflektiert, ist eine Antwort, zumindest unmittelbar, nicht möglich. Die Frage muß daher in einen größeren exegetischen Zusammenhang gestellt werden. Dabei muß man die Menschen in den Blick nehmen, für die Matthäus die Bergpredigt konzipiert hat, und man muß fragen, warum sie angehalten werden, sich in ihrem Tun an der Bergpredigt zu orientieren.

Hans Windisch war der Meinung, die Bergpredigt enthielte »die Einlaßbedingungen für den Eingang in das Reich«. Wenn wir unterstellen, daß diese Exegese richtig ist, ergibt sich daraus: Matthäus redet Menschen an, die durch dieses Leben hindurch unterwegs sind. Sie haben das Ziel, dermaleinst ins Reich zu gelangen. Schaffen werden sie das nur, wenn sie die Bedingungen erfüllen. Da man nun unterstellen darf, daß Matthäus dieses Ziel für erreichbar hielt, muß er auch der Meinung gewesen sein, daß die Forderungen erfüllbar waren.

Kontrolliert man jetzt das Ergebnis dieser Exegese mit Hilfe des »Prüfesteins«, stellt sich die Frage, ob Matthäus nicht in großer Nähe zum Verfasser des Jakobus-Briefes zu sehen ist, von dem Luther geurteilt hat, daß er »der sachen zu schwach« gewesen sei. Denn erwartet Matthäus von seinen Lesern nun nicht auch ein Tun von Werken, um das Ziel zu erreichen? Er formuliert Imperative, denen aber (zumindest ausdrücklich) kein Indikativ vorangeht. Es dürfte doch wohl mehr als nur problematisch sein, eine so exegesierte Bergpredigt in heutige Ethik zu überführen, wenn sie christliche Ethik sein soll. Eine andere Frage muß dann auch noch bedacht und darf keinesfalls übersehen werden: Ist eine heutige Ethik so an der Zukunft orientiert wie die des Matthäus? Zwar sollen die Einlaßbedingungen in der Gegenwart erfüllt werden, und das wird natürlich auch die Gegenwart selbst verändern. Nur liegt darauf beim Evangelisten gerade nicht der Akzent, sondern der liegt bei der Ermahnung an die Leser, heute die Voraussetzungen dafür zu schaffen, daß sie später in das Reich eingelassen werden. Diese deutliche Akzentverschiebung bedarf gründlicher Reflexion.

Nun kann die Exegese von Hans Windisch ja falsch sein. Häufig versucht man, bei Matthäus einen Indikativ zu entdecken. Dabei weist man auf die Christologie des Evangelisten hin. Möglich ist, daß das exegetisch zunächst gelingt, wenn auch kaum in der (matthäischen) Bergpredigt selbst, dann doch in der Gesamtkonzeption des Evangelisten. Das ist wieder ein Hinweis, daß man die Bergpredigt nicht isolieren darf.

Nun reicht es allerdings nicht aus, eine Christologie des Matthäus zu erheben und diese dann *neben* die Ethik zu stellen. Entscheidend ist doch, ob und wie Christologie und Ethik einen sachlichen Zusammenhang bilden. Anders formuliert: Ist der soteriologische Aspekt der matthäischen Christologie erkennbar, und zwar für die Menschen, die der Bergpredigt konfrontiert werden? Macht Matthäus deutlich, daß es nicht einfach »Menschen« sind, die nach der Bergpredigt leben sollen, sondern »veränderte Menschen«, die nach der Bergpredigt leben können? Das ist nur dann der Fall, wenn Matthäus seine Christologie nicht einfach als »Lehre« entfaltet, sondern als anredende Verkündigung, durch die Menschen, wenn sie sich darauf einlassen, verändert werden. Wenn sich das exegetisch am Werk des Evangelisten zeigen läßt (nicht aber nur an einzelnen Traditionen, die er, ganz gelegentlich sogar unverändert, übernimmt), dann wird das Ergebnis dieser Exegese einer Kontrolle am »Prüfestein« standhalten. Dann verdient die Ethik der Bergpredigt das Adjektiv christlich: Veränderte (= neu gewordene) Menschen *können* jetzt (und zwar immer, wenn sie sich verändern lassen) leben, wie die Bergpredigt es zeichnet. Ihr Tun ist dann »Frucht«, aber kein »Werk«.

Ich muß gestehen: Mir gelingt das nicht. Das kann an meiner unzureichenden Exegese des Evangeliums liegen. Sie muß überprüft werden, wie jede andere Exegese überprüft werden muß. So kann (und wird wohl auch) der Streit um die richtige Exegese weitergehen.

Nur tangiert dieser Streit nicht die Frage, wie christliche Ethik heute auszusehen hat. Der entscheidet sich eben nicht an der Exegese, sondern an der Christologie, dem eigentlichen »Prüfestein« für jede Exegese. Die Alternative lautet dann, wenn man sie auf eine kurze Formel bringt: Wird Jesus als einer verstanden, der Forderungen stellt, die erfüllt werden müssen, um ein Ziel zu erreichen? Oder wird Jesus als einer verstanden, der Menschen so verändert, daß sie dadurch (wirklich: *erst* dadurch) in der Lage sind, immer wieder Außerordentliches zu tun – für das sich dann auch in der Bergpredigt Beispiele finden?

New Evidence for the Question of the Original Language of the Diatessaron

by William L. Petersen

(Ridderschapstraat 18, 3512 CP Utrecht (Holland))

The question of the original language of Diatessaron has long vexed scholarship. It is a puzzle which has attracted the most formidable minds in New Testament textual studies: Zahn and Baumstark, Plooij and Burkitt. As one of our earliest witnesses to the NT text—it antedates the oldest uncials by a century and a half—the Diatessaron is of preëminent importance for recovering second-century gospel readings. "Pour retrouver les plus anciennes leçons évangéliques, la connaissance de l'œuvre de Tatien est d'une importance primordiale."[1]

Given this fact, it is disturbing to discover that Diatessaronic readings have been deleted from the apparatus of the latest (twenty-sixth) edition of Nestle-Aland. It is to be admitted that not all the editions and/or translations upon which these *lectiones variae* were based are reliable.[2] Hence, some of the "variants" in earlier editions of Nestle-Aland, as well as other NT editions (*e.g.*, Merk), are inaccurate and misleading.[3] (It follows, however, that the remainder of the readings were accurate ...) The result of this new exlusion is that we will soon be awash with a generation of NT scholars who do not even *think* of the Diatessaron when considering the NT text: out of sight, out of mind. The Diatessaron must now struggle to be readmitted to the apparatus of this most widely-used edition of the NT.

To its credit, the recently published first volume of *The New Testament in Greek*[4] includes Diatessaronic readings in its apparatus. The *opus magnum* of Prof. Heinrich Greeven, a complete renewal of Huck's *Synopsis,*[5] also includes Diatessaronic variants in its splendid apparatus.

---

1 L. Leloir, "Le Diatessaron de Tatien", *Orient Syrien* 1 (1956), p. 209.

2 *E. g.*, the criticism of Tj. Baarda, "In Search of the Diatessaron Text", in his *Early Transmission of Words of Jesus* (Amsterdam, 1983), pp. 67f.

3 The obvious solution is, of course, not to eliminate the *source* from the apparatus, but to engage the requisite experts to either retranslate the MS or check the variants against the MS, and eliminate those readings found to be inaccurate.

4 *The New Testament In Greek: The Gospel According to St. Luke (Pt. I, Chaps. 1–12)* (Oxford, 1984).

5 A. Huck, *Synopse der drei ersten Evangelien, fundamentally revised by H. Greeven* (Tübingen, 1981[13]).

The "Continuing Seminar On the Diatessaron", which meets under the auspices of Studiorum Novi Testamenti Societas, counts Prof. Greeven as one of its founders. It was there that I first met him. The interest he took in the work of a young *aspirant* was heartening; his personal kindness and generosity are matched by his intellectual integrity, acuity and depth. These are the rarest of qualities, in singular combination, and they bespeak a great man.

I am delighted to offer this essay to a man who honours me with his friendship; it is appropriate to present it to a scholar who is a member of what Quispel calls "an order within an order"—connoisseurs of the Diatessaron.

The Diatessaron is a harmony of the four canonical gospels and, perhaps, other early gospels. It was compiled by Tatian, "the Assyrian", as he calls himself. Justin Martyr was his teacher in Rome; after Justin's death about 165 AD, Tatian left Rome and returned to the East and obscurity.[6]

Today the Diatessaron is no longer extant. Instead, we possess various documents termed *witnesses* to the Diatessaron. Below are listed the most important, those pertinent to our study. On the basis of language and provenance, they are divided into Eastern and Western.[7]

Eastern Diatessaronic Witnesses:
- Ephrem's *Commentary* (Syriac & Armenian recensions, IV cent.)
- Aphrahat's gospel citations (Syriac, IV cent.)
- Arabic Harmony (Arabic, XII—XIII cent.)
- Persian Harmony (Persian, 1547 AD, copy of XIII cent. MS)
- Syriac NT Versions: $Syr^{s.c.p.pal}$ (Syriac, IV cent. & later)
- Ishoʿdad of Merv's *Commentary* (Syriac, IX cent.)

Western Diatessaronic Witnesses:
- Codex Fuldensis (Latin, VI cent.)
- Liège Harmony (Middle Dutch, XIII cent.)
  - Stuttgart, Cambridge, Haaren and Haagse Harmonies (all in Middle Dutch, XIV—XV cent., and textually related to the Liège Harmony)
  - Theodiscum Harmony (Middle German, XIV cent., also related to Liège)

---

6 A propos Tatian, see M. Whittaker's "Introduction" in her edition of Tatian's *Oratio ad Graecos And Fragments* (Oxford Early Christian Texts) (Oxford, 1982), pp. ix—xvii. On the Diatessaron, see my *The Diatessaron and Ephrem Syrus As Sources of Romanos the Melodist,* CSCO 475 (Louvain, 1985), pp. 20—51. The classic reference is C. Peters, *Das Diatessaron Tatians,* Orientalia Christiana Analecta 123 (Roma, 1939). Often overlooked is L. Leloir's excellent "Introduction" to his French translation of Ephrem's *Commentary: Éphrem de Nisibe: Commentaire de l'évangile concordant ou Diatessaron,* SC 121 (Paris, 1966).

7 Further descriptions of the individual witnesses are to be found in my *The Diatessaron (op. cit.),* or the handbooks of Peters, Vööbus or Metzger.

Tuscan Harmony (Middle Italian, XIII–XIV cent.)
Venetian Harmony (Middle Italian, XIII–XIV cent.)
Pepysian Harmony (Middle English, c. 1400 AD)

Each of these documents has its own textual history and, to a greater or lesser degree, each has been "Vulgatized". This is a process in which unique Diatessaronic readings are stripped from the Diatessaronic witnesses, and replaced with the standard canonical reading.[8] The concept of Vulgatization will be important in our study; we will see examples of it shortly.

Vulgatization, along with the linguistic and temporal diversity of the witnesses, presents Diatessaronic studies with its greatest problem: deciding what is a genuine Diatessaronic reading, and what is merely a chance agreement among Diatessaronic witnesses, or a "local" (speaking geographically) variant.

Some years ago, I developped three criteria which can aid in making these judgements.[9] Rather than being hard and fast rules, they offer an objective benchmark against which to measure readings. The criteria have met with approval, and are the standard by which we will measure readings in this study. They are:

(1) To be Diatessaronic, a reading should appear in both Eastern *and* Western Diatessaronic witnesses (thus guaranteeing a minimum of two sources, with linguistic and geographic diversity–a guard against local variants and chance agreements).
(2) The reading should not appear in any *non*-Diatessaronic sources, which might have contaminated our Diatessaronic witnesses (thus insuring the "purity" of the tradition, by limiting it to the Diatessaronic circle of texts).
(3) The genre of the sources with the reading should all be identical. All should represent harmonized Lives of Jesus or (as in the case of the Syriac Versions) sources which have a distinct possibility of having been influenced by the Diatessaronic tradition. (Should a "Diatessaronic" reading appear in a non-harmonized tradition, this criterion can help to determine if the outlier is related to or totally independent from the Diatessaronic texts).

What this means in practice is best illustrated by an example, given below. As can be seen in the lemma, Mt. 8.4 and parallels, Jesus tells the healed leper to "offer the gift which Moses commanded". But note the variant in the Eastern Diatessaronic witnesses: in both recensions of Ephrem's *Commentary*, Jesus tells the leper to *"fulfill the Law"*. Similarly Ishoʿdad: "offer a gift as *the Law* commanded".

Mt 8.4 (par.): ὕπαγε σεαυτὸν δεῖξον τῷ ἱερεῖ καὶ *προσένεγκον τὸ δῶρον ὃ προσέταξεν Μωϋσῆς*.

---

[8] The term "Vulgatization" is used regardless of what canonical version is used; it need not be the Latin Vulgate of Jerome. A Syriac source, for example, would have been brought into line with the Harklean or, perhaps, the Peshitta.

[9] Originally expressed in my "Romanos and the Diatessaron: Readings and Method", *NTS* 29 (1983), p. 490; see also my *The Diatessaron, op. cit.*, pp. 55–7.

Eastern Diatessaronic Witnesses:

Ephrem, *Comm.*, XII.23 (Syriac): dzl hw' npsk lkhn': *wml' nmws'* hw dbsyt 'lwhy.[10]
Vade, ostende teipsum sacerdotibus, et *imple legem* quam spernis.[11]

Ephrem, *Comm.*, XII.23 (Armenian): Vade tu, ostende teipsum sacerdotibus, et *perfice legem* quam spernis.[12]

Isho'dad, *Comm.*, (*ad loc.*): dn'zl lwt khn'. wnqrb qwrbn' 'yk dpqd *nmws'*.[13]
Go to the priests and offer a gift as *the Law* commanded.[14]

Western Diatessaronic Witnesses:

Liège Harmony, LVIII: ganc ten papen van der wet˙ eñ vertoegh di hen˙ eñ offer hen alselke offerande alse moyses gheboet *in der wet.*[15]

Venetian Harmony, XLII: va et mostrate a li prevedi e fa l'oferta che comanda *la leçe.*[16]

It is attractive to view this as a Syrian variant, perhaps originating with Ephrem. But note the readings of the Western Diatessaronic witnesses. In Middle Dutch (Liège): "offer them (*i. e.*, the priests) such an offering as Moses commanded *in the Law*"; in the Venetian Harmony, "make the offering which *the Law* commands". The Liège Harmony, by conflating the canonical "Moses" with the Diatessaronic "Law", makes it clear that we are dealing with something other than a simple substitution. Applying our criteria: (1) the reading has bilateral (Eastern and Western) support. (2) It is restricted to Diatessaronic witnesses; it occurs in *no* Greek or Latin MSS; it occurs in *no* Patristic or apocryphal sources. (3) *All* of the sources with the reading are either gospel harmonies or commenting on a gospel harmony.

Since there is no other source from which our witnesses might have taken the reading, and since the Diatessaron is the only known common denominator among them, one is compelled to accept the conclusion that the reading of the Diatessaron was "fulfill the Law". Given that, we now have before us a reading which antedates Codex Sinaiticus (א) by 150 years. We stand in the second century.

This is the textual importance of the Diatessaron. The gospel quotations of Justin, Marcion, Clement and Irenaeus provide incontrovertible

---

[10] L. Leloir, *Saint Éphrem, Commentaire de l'Évangile concordant texte syriaque,* Chester Beatty Monographs 8 (Dublin, 1963), p. 98; hereafter citd as: Leloir, *Beatty.*

[11] Ibid., p. 99.

[12] L. Leloir, *Saint Éphrem, Commentaire de l'Évangile concordant, version Armenienne,* CSCO 145 (Louvain, 1954), p. 126; hereafter cited as: Leloir, *CSCO.*

[13] M. D. Gibson, ed., *The Commentaire of Isho'dad of Merv,* Vol. II, Horae Semitica VI (Cambridge, 1911), p. 70.

[14] Ibid., Vol. I, HSem V, p. 42.

[15] D. Plooij, D. Phillips and A. Bakker, eds., *The Liège Diatessaron, Parts I–VII,* Verhand. nederlandse ak. van wetensch., Afd. letterkunde 19, 21 (Amsterdam, 1929–70), p. 104; hereafter cited as: Plooij, *Liège.*

[16] V. Todesco, *Il Diatessaron Veneto,* Pt. 1 of *Il Diatessaron in Volgare Italiano,* Studi e Testi 81 (Città del Vaticano, 1938), p. 50, hereafter cited as: Todesco, *Veneto.*

proof that the four gospels which we now call canonical were still in a state of textual flux in the second century. Since the Diatessaron was composed about the year 170—precisely in the midst of this period of textual diversity—its text would reflect the state of the gospels *as they stood then*. The text of the Diatessaron offers the researcher a "snapshot", as it were, of the gospels circa the year 170.

Often Diatessaronic readings are nothing more than an expansion or alteration of the standard Greek text which became canonical. In these cases, the Diatessaron's text is clearly secondary to the Greek text. But occasionally, and this example may be one such case, the Diatessaron offers a variant which appears to antedate the canonical text.[17] Whether the reader agrees or disagrees with that assertion is, however, not the issue. The point has been made to demonstrate what should be clear on purely chronological grounds: the Diatessaron holds the possibility of reaching behind the present canonical text.

Given that this is the case, it is all the more surprising that the original language of the Diatessaron is unknown. Now that we have a method for isolating Diatessaronic readings, let us address the main problem.

Modern research on the Diatessaron began with Zahn in 1881. With only the Curetonian Syriac and the Armenian recension of Ephrem's *Commentary* in hand—the other witnesses were either undiscovered or unpublished—Zahn concluded that "das Diatessaron existierte von Haus aus nur in syrischer Sprache".[18] He based his conclusion on agreements between the *Commentary*'s text and the text of the Vetus Syra, as found in the Curetonian MS. This method of citing versional agreements to determine the original language of the Diatessaron has been widely used since. As we will presently see, however, it is nonsense.

A. von Harnack and Vogels almost immediately assumed the opposite position, and cited agreements between the Armenian recension of the *Commentary* and the Greek and Latin (canonical) manuscript tradition. Greek, they said, was the original language.[19] The publication of von Soden's edition of the New Testament buttressed this position. As everyone knows, von Soden (incorrectly, of course) ascribed almost all cross-

[17] For other examples of readings which appear to antedate their canonical parallels, see my *The Diatessaron, op. cit.*, pp. 165–167; or my "Romanos and the Diatessaron", *op. cit.*, pp. 493–502.

[18] Th. Zahn, *Forschungen zur Geschichte des neutestamentlichen Kanons und der altkirchlichen Literatur,* Theil I: *Tatian's Diatessaron* (Erlangen, 1881), p. 238.

[19] A. von Harnack, "Tatian's Diatessaron und Marcion's Commentar zum Evangelium bei Ephraem Syrus", *Zeitschrift für Kirchengeschichte* 4 (1880), p. 475; H. J. Vogels, *Die altsyrischen Evangelien in ihrem Verhältnis zu Tatians Diatessaron,* Biblische Studien 15,5 (Freiburg im Breisgau, 1911), p. 144.

gospel harmonizations to Diatessaronic influence.[20] It took a Greek Diatessaron to influence Greek gospels, reasoned von Soden.

Burkitt took a variant position. Citing agreements between various Diatessaronic witnesses and the Vetus Latina, he suggested that Latin had been the original language.[21]

Note that in each case, the conclusion is based on versional agreements.

The emerging concensus behind a Greek original was challenged by Plooij in 1923. In that year he published a study of the Liège Harmony and pointed not only to agreements with the Vetus Syra, but also to Syriasms in its text.[22] These were explicable only if one presumed a Syriac original.

The matter was further complicated in 1935 when Kraeling announced discovery of the Dura Fragment. Only 14 lines long, this fragment of a Greek Diatessaron was found in Syria, in Dura. Since Dura was sacked by the Perisans in the winter of 256–57 AD, the fragment has a very early date. Citing agreements with the Greek NT MSS, and against the Syriac versions, Kraeling concluded that the language in which the Dura Fragment was written—Greek—had been the original language of the Diatessaron.[23] Burkitt also examined the Fragment, and felt that it demonstrated Syriac had *not* been the original language; but he still preferred Latin to Greek as the original language of the Diatessaron.[24]

Plooij was quick in responding. He adduced several places where the Dura Fragment agreed with the Syriac versions against the Greek,[25] thus countering Kraeling. Baumstark joined the defense of a Syriac original by conjecturing that several strange misspellings in the Dura Fragment's

---

[20] H. von Soden, *Die Schriften des Neuen Testaments* (Göttingen, 1911), Vol. I, Heft 2, p. 1634. Scholarship has since concluded that cross-gospel harmonizations are a common scribal tendency, either from unconscious memory lapse, or from a desire to bring accounts into agreement. They are a phenomenon not related (in most cases) to the Diatessaron.

[21] F. C. Burkitt, "Tatian's Diatessaron and the Dutch Harmonies", *JThS* 25 (1924), pp. 113–30.

[22] D. Plooij, *A Primitive Text of the Diatessaron* (Leyden, 1923). An example was Plooij's discovery of the reading "sat" in the Liège Harmony (Chap. 39, p. 253 (ed. Plooij): "so *sat* Jhesus altehant in en scheep": "Jesus presently *sat* in a boat") at Mk. 8.10. Yet the canonical Greek reads ἐμβάς, and the Latin gives *ascendens*. There is no precedent anywhere for *sat*—except in the Vetus Syra (Syr$^{s.c}$), which use the idiomatic Syriac excpression *ytb* (to *sit* in a boat: J. Payne Smith, *A Compendious Syriac Dictionary* (Oxford, 1903), p. 198).

[23] C. H. Kraeling, *A Greek Fragment of Tatian's Diatessaron From Dura*, Studies and Documents 3 (London, 1935).

[24] F. C. Burkitt, "The Dura Fragment of Tatian", *JThS* 36 (1935), pp. 257, 258f.

[25] D. Plooij, "A Fragment of Tatian's Diatessaron In Greek", *Expository Times* 46 (1935), pp. 471–6.

Greek could be explained if one presumed a Syriac original. For example, in place of the canonical ʿΑριμαθαία (Mt. 27.57 par.), the Dura Fragment reads ΕΡΙΝΜΑΘΑΙΑ. Baumstark suggested that the Dura Fragment's non-standard spelling arose from a mistake by a Syriac copyist. The lector slightly lengthened his pronunciation of the initial ʾālaph (in Syriac), and mistook the first *yūdh* for a *nūn* (an easy mistake in Syriac, where the sole difference is the height of the stroke). The scribe, hearing this misreading, would have written Syriac letters which, when transliterated into Greek, would give ΕΡΙΝΜΑΘΑΙΑ.[26] This and other examples, said Baumstark, demonstrated that the Dura Fragment had been translated from a Syriac *Vorlage*.

There the matter rests. Among experts, an informal consensus exists, favouring Syriac. But scant evidence has been produced in support of this, and what has been, is largely more of the same: citing versional agreements.

Before turning to some new evidence, derived with new methods, let us examine this method of citing versional agreements, and discover why it is so unsatisfactory, and has led to such an impasse.

First, Syriac. It is acknowledged that the Diatessaron preceeded and gave readings to the Vetus Syra.[27] Therefore, one would expect agreements to exist between the Diatessaron and the Vetus Syra. To reverse this order, and say that *because* a reading exists in the Syriac versions, then the Diatessaron must have been written in Syriac, is a manifestly circular argument. For example, when Plooij cited the reading ἦν δὲ ἡ ἡμέρα in the Dura Fragment at Mk. 15.24,[28] and pointed out that it agreed with Syr^s (as well as Codex Bezae), he may have found a Diatessaronic reading, but it says nothing about the original language of the Diatessaron, for I know of no reason why a *Greek* Diatessaron could not have read ἦν δὲ ἡ ἡμέρα,

---

26 A. Baumstartk, "Das griechische ›Diatessaron‹-Fragment von Dura-Europos", *Oriens Christianus* (ser. 3) 10 (1935), pp. 249f. Although Baumstark's conjecture has been repeated by numerous scholar (*e. g.*, B. M. Metzger, *Early Versions of the New Testament* (Oxford, 1977), p. 32), it is entierly unconvincing. As we will see *infra*, Exhibit II, the reading in all the Syriac editions for ʿΡαμά is *rmta*. The word begins with a *rēš*, and contains neither a *yūdh* nor a *nūn*! In short, Baumstark's hypothesized Syriac original form, from which the corruption supposedly arose, simply does not appear to have existed. I have cited before, and cite once again, the complaint of M. Goulder: "How can we trust ... conjectures that do not even fit the text as it is?" (*Midrash and Lection In Matthew*, p. 400, n. 53).

27 The issue is treated in scrupulous detail by M. Black, "The Syriac Versional Tradition", in K. Aland's *Die alten Übersetzungen des neuen Testaments, die Kirchenväterzitate und Lektionare*, Arbeiten zur neutestamentlichen Textforschung 5 (Berlin/New York, 1972), pp. 124–8.

28 D. Plooij, "A Fragment of Tatian's Diatessaron In Greek", *Expository Times* 46 (1935), p. 475.

and given that reading to the Syriac versions. In short, unless there is something distinctly Syriac in syntax, grammar or expression of the reading, the fact that it agrees with the Syriac versions says nothing about the original language of the Diatessaron.[29]

On the matter of the agreements with the Greek NT tradition as an argument for a Greek original, the flaw in the reasoning is even more obvious. We have commented on the phenomenon of Vulgatization before: everywhere, and at all times, the tendency has been to bring the Diatessaronic text into line with the canonical gospels. In our first example, only five of some dozen Diatessaronic witnesses read "fulfill the *Law*". The rest give the standard canonical reading. Yet it is clear that these Diatessaronic witnesses, which do *not* read "Law", have been Vulgatized, for only by assuming that the reading once stood in the Diatessaron can we account for its presence *only* in Dutch, Syriac and Italian sources connected with the tradition of harmonized Lives of Jesus.

Is it not patently nonsense, then, to cite agreements with the Greek tradition as evidence for a Greek original? Large portions of the original Diatessaron agreed word for word with the Greek gospels, as do all versions of the New Testament. What, then, can agreements with the Greek MS tradition prove, especially when the tendency has always been to bring divergent texts into conformity with the Greek gospels?

One fact emerges from these criticisms of past research. It is that any inquiry into the original language of the Diatessaron must being by presuming that it was Greek, and *then* searching for evidence to *disprove* this hypothesis. If it were written in Greek, then no evidence should emerge to falsify the hypothesis. If, however, some other tongue were the original language, then data would emerge which would falsify the Greek hypothesis—in addition to running counter to the usual pattern of Vulgatization and the natural tendency of any version of the gospels to agree with the Greek gospels. The "against the stream" character of evidence derived in this manner would render it a sound foundation upon which to base conclusions. For example, should certain undeniably Semitic features turn up in a reading which our criteria dictate to be Diatessaronic, and the reading cannot be found in the Graeco-Latin MS tradition, then we can be quite certain that the reading is of Semitic origin, and was transmitted only there, in a Semitic language. Note that we are not speaking of versional agreements here, but of "undeniably Semitic features". What might these be?

Three separate investigations were carried out. Each sought a particular hallmark of a Semitic language original, which would be absent from a Greek language original.

[29] This observation remains valid, even if one chooses to postulate the Vetus Syra as being older than the Diatessaron.

The first investigation (Exhibits I–III) sought to examine the OT quotations of the Diatessaron. First, all OT quotations in the gospels were isolated. Next, using our three criteria, the Diatessaronic reading was determined. This was then compared with the NT citation in the gospels. If the Diatessaron and the Greek gospels agreed in their quotation of the OT, it told us nothing, for the Diatessaron's text (1) might have been identical with the Greek gospels at this point, or (2) it might have been Vulgatized.

If, however, the Diatessaronic reading *diverged* from the canonical Greek NT citation of the OT, then further investigations were carried out. First, the Diatessaronic reading was checked against the Greek OT translations (LXX, Aquila, Symmachus, Theodotion), and against the Hebrew and Syriac OTs. If the Diatessaronic variant agreed with one of the Greek OT translations, then the Greek language hypothesis remained viable. If, however, the Diatessaronic reading agreed with a reading unique to a version of the OT which was Semitic in origin, then the finding was significant. Three readings emerged from this first line of investigation. They are presented below.

Exhibit I:[30]

Lk. 2.23: πᾶν ἄρσεν διανοῖγον μήτραν ἅγιον τῷ κυρίῳ κληθήσεται.

Ex. 13.2 (LXX): Ἁγίασόν μοι πᾶν *πρωτότοκον πρωτογενὲς διανοῖγον πᾶσαν μήτραν* ...

(Hebrew): קַדֶּשׁ־לִי כָל־בְּכוֹר פֶּטֶר כָּל־רֶחֶם בִּבְנֵי יִשְׂרָאֵל

(Syriac): Consecrate to me all *the firstborn* (*bwkra*) of the sons of Israel who open the wombs ...[31]

Eastern Diatessaronic Witnesses:

Syr^s (Lk. 2.33): Every *first-born* (*bwkra*) opening the matrix, the Holy one of the Lord shall be called ...[32]

Ephrem, *Comm.*, I.28 (Armenian; Syr. *hiat*): Omne *primogenitum,* quod aperit uterem, sanctum Domino vocabitur.[33]

Persian Harmony, I.6: Ogni maschio, *che primo* esce dal seno della madre, sarà chiamato santo di Dio.[34]

---

[30] It is distressing to find this important Diatessaronic reading omitted from the "collation" of Diatessaronic sources published by A. J. B. Higgins, "Luke 1–2 in Tatian's Diatessaron", *JBL* 103 (1984), pp. 193–222.

[31] A. M. Ceriani, *Syra Pescitto Veteris Testamenti ex Codice Ambrosiano* (Mediolani, 1876), p. 37; S. Lee, *Vetus Testamentum Syriace* (London, 1823), p. 52.

[32] F. C. Burkitt, *Euangelion da-Mepharreshe* (Cambridge, 1904), Vol. I, pp. 254f.; hereafter cited as: Burkitt, *Euangelion.*

[33] Leloir, *CSCO,* p. 21.

[34] G. Messina, *Diatessaron Persiano,* Biblica et Orientalia 14 (Rome, 1951), p. 21; hereafter cited as: Messina, *Persiano.*

Western Diatessaronic Witnesses:

Liège Harmony, XIII: dat die kneple kine die der moeder *irste vrocht* waten gode gof-fert mosten syn.[35]

Idem: Stuttgart (13), Haaren (13), Haagse (13), Cambridge (13), and Theodiscum (13).

Tuscan Harmony, 8: la quale dicea che ogni *primo* figliuolo maschio si dovesse presentare a Dio.[36]

The reading "first" or "firstborn" occurs in both Eastern and Western Diatessaronic witnesses (satisfying our first criterion); further, the reading is found in no NT sources other than the Diatessaronic witnesses listed above (satisfying our second criterion). The third criterion is met in that all sources with the reading are related to the harmonized Lives of Jesus tradition. The interpolation of "first" or "firstborn" must therefore be regarded as having stood in the Diatessaron. The next question is whence did the reading come?

It could not have come from the NT gospels, for it is lacking there (including all the NT MSS and versions–save the Vetus Syra). Only when we examine the OT versions does an answer appear. The reading occurs in the LXX, the Hebrew and Syriac OTs. Clearly, the Diatessaron is dependent upon one of these for the reading. Since, however, the reading appears in the LXX as well as the Semitic language versions, we cannot judge from which language the Diatessaron took the reading. It might have been from the LXX.

Although we must press on for more evidence, this reading has shown one important fact, namely, that the Diatessaron did not slavishly reproduce the Greek NT text. Rather, the Diatessaron either checked its OT citations against one or another OT version, or it followed a NT text other than what is the present Greek text.

Exhibit II:

Mt. 2.18: φωνὴ *ἐν ῾Ραμὰ* ἠκούσθη, κλαυθμὸς καὶ ὀδυρμός...

Jer. 38.15 (MSS א* & B of LXX): Φωνὴ *ἐν τῇ ὑψηλῇ* ἠκούσθη ...

(Hebrew): ... קול ברמה נשמע נהי

(Syriac): A voice is heard *brmt*ʾ (discussed below)[37]

Eastern Diatessaronic Witnesses:

Syr[s.c] (Mt. 2.18): A voice was heard *brmt*ʾ (discussed below)[38]

Western Diatessaronic Witnesses:

Codex Sangallensis, X.3: Stemma *in hóhi* gihorit uuard ...[39]

---

[35] Plooij, *Liège,* p. 27.

[36] M. Vattasso and P. A. Vaccari, *Il Diatessaron Toscano,* Pt. 2 of *Il Diatessaron in Volgare Italiano,* Studi e Testi 81 (Città del Vaticano, 1938), p. 211; hereafter cited as: Vattasso & Vaccari, *Toscano.*

[37] Ceriani, *op. cit.,* p. 341; Lee, *op. cit.,* p. 620.

[38] Burkitt, *Euangelion,* Vol. I, p. 10.

[39] E. Sievers, *Tatian, lateinisch und altdeutsch,* Bibliothek der ältesten deutschen Literatur-Denkmäler 5 (Paderborn, 1892^2), p. 29.

Cambridge Harmony, 16: die stimme ... wart ghehort *in der hogheded* ...[40]
Theodiscum Harmony, 16: die stimme wart erhoert *in der hoeche* ...[41]
Tuscan Harmony, 10: la voce è udita *da alti* ...[42]
Venetian Harmony, 5: Voce *in alto* audiva ...[43]

Other source with the reading:
Jerome/Ps-Bede/Hrabanus Maurus | Peter Comestor | Aquila

Establishing the reading as Diatessaronic is our first task. The reading "in/on the height" is prominent in the Western Diatessaronic witnesses, and is striking there, for it occurs in no Greek or Latin NT MSS. In the East, both MSS of the Vetus Syra, which were influenced by the Diatessaron and are Eastern witnesses, give the Syriac word *brmt*ʾ. The Syriac *b(ə)* is equivalent to the similar Hebrew preposition meaning "in". *Rmt*ʾ, however, has two meanings. In one, it is the name of a town, that indicated in Greek by Ῥαμά. However, the second meaning of *rmt*ʾ is "hill/height". The Vetus Syra, then, can be read either as "in Rama" *or* "in/on the hill/height". In his translation of the Vetus Syra, Burkitt gives "in Ramtha" at this point.[44] However, he translates the same word as "heights' at Lk. 3.3. We may conclude, then, that at least some of the readers of the Vetus Syra understood *brmt*ʾ as "in/or the height". This presumption is vindicated by the fact that the Palestinian Syriac Lectionary (Syr^{pal}) does not offer the ambiguous *rmt*ʾ of the Vetus Syra, but has changed the reading to *rʾm*ʾ—an exact transliteration of the Hebrew (or Greek, itself a transliteration of the Hebrew).[45] The reason for the change in the later Syr^{pal} is obvious: to remove the possibility of misreading the earlier, ambiguous *rmt*ʾ of $Syr^{s.c}$. Thus, the reading has eastern and western support.

The "Other" texts with the reading must be dealt with to satisfy our second and third criteria. Jerome, Pseudo-Bede and Hrabanus Maurus give the reading in virtually identical words, all in their respective *Commentaries* on Matthew.[46] Clearly, the latter two are dependent on Jerome who, in turn, may have known the ambiguous Syriac reading, the reading

---

40 C. C. de Bruin, *Diatessaron Cantabrigiense,* Corpus sacrae scripturae neerlandicae medii aevi, ser. minor, tome I, Vol. III (Leiden, 1970), p. 7.

41 C. Gerhardt, *Das Leben Jhesu,* Corpus sacrae scripturae neerlandicae medii aevi, ser. minor, tome I, Vol. 5 (Leiden, 1970), p. 12; hereafter cited as: Gerhardt, *Jhesu.*

42 Vattasso & Vaccari, *Toscano,* p. 213.

43 Todesco, *Veneto,* p. 30.

44 See *supra,* n. 38.

45 M. Gibson and A. S. Lewis, *The Palestinian Syriac Lectionary* (London, 1899), Chapter 173, p. 257.

46 Jerome, *Comm. in Mt.,* I (*CChr. SL* 77, p. 15); Ps.-Bede, *Exposito in Mt.,* I.2 (*PL* 92, 14c); Hrabanus Maurus, *Comm. in Mt.,* I.2 (*PL* 107, 763a). Peter Comestor, *Hist. Schol.-In Evang.,* 12 (*PL* 198, 1544c), uses similar phrases, and may also be dependent upon Jerome; in any event, it is clear that he could not be the origin of the reading in the Western witnesses. This reading has been noted by G. Quispel, *Tatian and the Gospel of Thomas* (Leiden, 1975), p. 113, but he draws no conclusions from it.

of Greek LXX codices א* or B, or the Greek translation of Aquila, which also read "in the height".

What is clear from these sources is that none could be responsible for the readings in the individual Diatessaronic witnesses. It is impossible to imagine that each of five Western Diatessaronic witnesses in five language or dialects abandoned the NT text at exactly the same point and, again acting independently, adopted the same reading from one of three Greek OT sources with the reading (and א's reading had already been removed by a corrector).

Our third criterion indicates that it is unlikely that the harmonized sources all, independently, should have appropriated the reading from Jerome or his imitators, for the genre of these sources is a commentary, not a harmonized Life of Jesus.

There is no need to reach outside the harmonized, Diatessaronic tradition to explain the reading, for, as we have seen, it already existed within the Eastern Diatessaronic family. From there it appears to have spread to the Western witnesses, marking them, of course, but no other Greek or Latin MSS. (The critic of this position must explain why *only* Diatessaronic witnesses abandon the NT text at this point, and chose to adopt the reading from the three (or two, if one excludes corrected א) Greek sources with the reading, or from Jerome. This appears to be an insurmountable obstacle.) We are confronted, then, with the reading of the Diatessaron: "in/on the heights".

Considering the implications of this reading for our research into the original language of the Diatessaron, we may conclude that the origin of the reading is clearly Syrian, for only in that language could the confusion have arisen. Hebrew and Greek are both unambiguous. Even in the Greek OT MSS with the reading, it would seem that Syriac must underlie the confusion.

But whence did the Diatessaron acquire the reading, and in what language? It could have been from the OT translation of Aquila, the OT of א* or B. If so, it would have been in Greek. Far more likely, however, is that the Diatessaron took the reading from the Syriac OT. It seems both unnecessary and awkward to presume that the Diatessaron re-imported a Syriac reading (via Aquila, א* or B) when the origin of the reading itself appears to have been Syriac.

Exhibit III:[47]

Lk. 1.31: ἰδοὺ συλλήμψῃ *ἐν γαστρὶ* καὶ τέξῃ υἱόν ...
Is. 7.14 (LXX): ἰδοὺ ἡ παρθένος *ἐν γαστρὶ* ἕξει καὶ τέξεται υἱόν ...
(Hebrew): הנה העלמה הרה וילדת בן
(Syriac): hʾ btwltʾ bṭnʾ wyldʾ brʾ ...[48]

---

[47] Like Exhibit I, this Exhibit is also lacking in A. J. B. Higgin's collation of Luke 1–2, see *supra*, n. 30.

[48] Ceriani, *op. cit.*, p. 300; Lee, *op. cit.*, p. 518.

Eastern Diatessaronic Witnesses:

Ephrem, *Comm.*, I.25 (Syriac): dh' bbtwlwtky tqblyn bṭn' wt'ldyn br' ...[49]

Ecce in virginitate tua concipies foetum, et paries filium ...[50]

Persian Harmony, I.3: ecco concepirai e portorirai un figlio ...[51]

Arabic Harmony, I.32: Tu concevras et tu enfanteras un fils ...[52]

Aphrahat, *Dem.* XVII.9: dh' btwlt' tbṭn wt'ld ...

Ecco Virgo concipiet et pariet ...[53]

Western Diatessaronic Witnesses:

Venetian Harmony, II: onde tu te gravidarai et se parturirai figliolo ...[54]

Pepysian Harmony, 2: And *þ*he angel ... seide ... *þ*at sche scholde conc[e]yun and beren a son ...[55]

Other sources:

[Aquila, Symmachus, Theodotion][56]

Protevangelium Iacobi, XI.2[57]

Ignatius, *ad Eph.,* XVIII.2[58]

Origen, *Hom. in Lc. VI* (MSS B and N only)[59]

Pseudo-Augustine, *Sermo CXCIII.2*[60]

Nestorius, *Homélie sur la seconde tentation*[61]

Versions: arm sah boh armen

This reading concerns the omission of the words ἐν γαστρί from the Diatessaronic witnesses. It may be argued that the Greek ἐν γαστρί is necessitated by the LXX verb ἕξει, and that it is included in the Hebrew verb הרה.[62] While this may be correct philologically, one cannot help but notice the prominence of the reading in Diatessaronic sources. It occurs in *no* Greek or Latin NT MSS. Also note that the most literal translations of the OT into Greek (those of Aquila, Symmachus and Theodotion) all appear

---

49 Leloir, *Beatty,* p. 23.

50 Ibid., p. 24.

51 Messina, *Persiano,* p. 11.

52 A.-S. Marmadji, *Diatessaron de Tatien,* (Beyrouth, 1935), p. 7; hereafter cited as: Marmadji, *Diatessaron.*

53 J. Parisot, *Aphraatis Sapientis Persae Demonstrationes,* PS 1 (Paris, 1894), cols. 805f.

54 Todesco, *Veneto,* p. 24.

55 M. Goates, *The Pepysian Harmony,* Early English Text Society o. s. 157 (London, 1922), p. 3.

56 J. Ziegler, *Septuaginta,* Vol. XIV (Göttingen, 1967^2), p. 147.

57 E. de Strycker, *La forme la plus ancienne du Protévangile de Jacques* (Bruxelles, 1961), p. 114.

58 F. X. Funk, ed., *Patres Apostolici,* Vol. I (Tübingen, 1901), pp. 226ff.

59 M. Rauer, ed., *Origenes Werke,* Vol. IX, *GCS* 49 (Berlin, 1959), p. 38.

60 Migne, *PL* 39, col. 2104.

61 F. Nau, ed., *Le livre d'Héraclide de Damas* (Paris, 1910), p. 344.

62 *E. g.,* at Gen. 16.4; Judges 13.3; etc. See under equivalent 45a in E. Hatch and H. Redpath, *Concordance to the Septuagint,* Vol. I (Oxford, 1897), pp. 586ff.

to omit ἐν γαστρί as well (Ziegler places the reading in brackets, indicating uncertainty).

To call the reading Diatessaronic, we must be sure that the Diatessaronic witnesses have not taken the reading from any of the "Other" sources with the reading. With such strong testimony from within the Diatessaronic family, this seems unlikely. If one rejects the Diatessaron as the purveyor of the reading to the Diatessaronic witnesses, then one must assume that each witness independently chose to omit ἐν γαστρί. This seems unlikely.

The *Protevangelium* is roughly contemporaneous with the Diatessaron, and could be another carrier of this early tradition. Origen would have known the reading from his *Hexapla,* of course. Nestorius would have known it from his Syrian homeland, where it was a well-known reading. The versions with the reading all show traces of Syriac influence; they are the recipients of the tradition, not the originators of it. And if the sermon of Pseudo-Augustine should prove genuine, then it might be a reading harkening back to Augustine's youth among the Manichees—who used the Diatessaron.[63] In short, the reading seems to have circulated outside the Diatessaron (Origen, the *Protevangelium*), but it also appears to have stood in the Diatessaron.

What can this reading tell us of the original language of the Diatessaron? Like Exhibit II, it is the standard reading of the Hebrew/Syriac OT. It survives in no NT MSS, nor is it found in the LXX. Nevertheless, there is a Greek route through which it could have come into the Diatessaron—namely, the translations of Aquila, Symmachus and Theodotion, if it actually stood in them. But, as in Exhibit II, Syriac would appear the more likely route, for the reading is omitted in the Syriac OT. Thus, this omission would seem to suggest that the Diatessaron was composed in Syriac—but one must always be cautious arguing from a passive omission, for it is an argument *e silentio.*

Summarizing this first avenue of inquiry, we note that when a Diatessaronic reading (as determined by our criteria) foresakes the NT text in OT citations, it invariably agrees with the Hebrew/Syriac OT. It must be acknowledged that there are often Greek interlopers (when I began the investigation, I had not reckoned with the literalness of the non-LXX Greek OT translations). But the *only* common denominator is the Hebrew/Syriac OT. While it can be argued that these Greek interlopers are responsible for the Diatessaronic readings, it seems unlikely. The reason is that one must then assume that the LXX is the source of Exhibit I, while

---

[63] Cp. G. Quispel, *Tatian and the Gospel of Thomas, op. cit.,* pp. 58–68; see also his "St. Augustin et Thomas", in *Mélanges d'histoire des religions offerts à Henri Charles Puech* (Paris, 1974), pp. 379–92.

Codex B of the LXX is the source of Exhibit II, and that Aquila is the source of Exhibit III. Such source-hopping on the part of the Diatessaron seems improbable, especially when one can point to a single source with all the readings: the Hebrew/Syriac OT.[64]

Since the results of this first series of investigations, although indicative of a direction, still left room for doubt, a second spoor was followed. At various points in the Greek NT, Hebrew words or names are used. Often these are translated into Greek for the benefit of the Greek readers of the NT, who would not have otherwise understood the significance of the foreign word. For example, "Rabbouni" is translated as "teacher" in Jn. 20.16.

Now, remembering that logic dictates that we can only search for clues which might *invalidate* the thesis of a Greek original for the Diatessaron, if we should find places where such translations were provided in the Greek NT, but omitted in the Diatessaron, then it would be a piece of evidence suggesting that the Diatessaron was not composed in Greek. Rather, it would suggest a Semitic language original, where such translations would have been superfluous, for the postulated Semitic-language reader would have understood the word: it would have been in his own or a sister language.

This investigation, which checked all places in the gospels where such translations are given, yielded one example. It alone met our criteria, and is given next.

Exhibit IV:

Jn. 9.7: ὕπαγε νίψαι εἰς τὴν κολυμβήθραν τοῦ *Σιλωάμ (ὃ ἑρμηνεύεται ἀπεσταλμένος).*

Eastern Diatessaronic Witnesses:

Syr[s] (Jn. 9.7): Go, wash thy face with a baptism of *Shiloah;* and I went ...[65]

Persian harmony, II.35: Va e lavati nella fontana di *Siloe.* Andò e si lavò ...[66]

---

[64] It would be desirable if one could find an indicator, a reading, which would allow us to decide if the Diatessaron's quotations came from the Hebrew OT or the Syriac OT. I have noted only one reading which might offer the possibility. At Mt. 4.6, the Greek NT, the LXX and the Hebrew OT all read "on their *hands*". However, the Syriac OT reads "on their *arms* (*dr'yhwn*). This singular reading is carried over into Syr[s.c] (Burkitt, *Euangelion,* p. 15), the Arabic Harmony (IV.48; Marmardji, *Diatessaron,* p. 39), the Persian Harmony (I.19; Messina, *Persiano,* p. 41), and the Armenian (Syriac *hiat*) recension of Ephrem's *Commentary* (IV.7; Leloir, *CSCO,* p. 36). I have not listed it as a Diatessaronic reading, however, for it lacks Western support; it is possible that these sources simply took it from the Syriac OT. But one cannot rule out the possibility that it stood in the Diatessaron, and thence spread to the Eastern Tatianic witnesses. If the latter were the case, then the reading would establish the Syriac OT (and *not* the Hebrew OT) as the source of the other readings in the Diatessaron which agree with both the Hebrew and the Syriac OTs.

[65] Burkitt, *Euangelion,* p. 479.

[66] Messina, *Persiano,* p. 145.

Western Diatessaronic Witnesses:

Liège Harmony, CLXXIX: ghanc eñ dauch ... in die ... borne die heet *syloa* eñ de ghene dede also eñ douch ...[67]

Venetian Harmony, 134: Vatene e lavate en la pisina di *Soloe*. E andossene quello e lavosse e vedè.[68]

Diatessaronic status is easy to establish, for the reading meets our criteria perfectly. It is found in both Eastern and Western Diatessaronic sources, but in *no* other documents. It is a uniquely Diatessaronic reading.

שלח, the root of the Hebrew word represented in the Greek NT by Σιλωάμ (note how all the Diatessaronic witnesses end on an open syllable, omitting the final μ of the Greek), is similar in both sound and meaning to the Syriac *šlḥ*. Just as a Dutch speaker can understand many German words, so a Syriac speaker would have understood the Hebrew. No translation would have been necessary for him. And that is exactly what we find: no translation in the Diatessaronic witnesses, although the Liège and the Venetian Harmony should have one, not only on the basis of linguistic necessity, but also if they have *any* connexion with the Graeco-Latin MS tradition, the whole of which gives the translation.

This evidence, like our first three Exhibits, indicates a Semitic language original for the Diatessaron. Once again, however, we must point out that this is an argument from an omission, and therefore must be viewed with some caution.[69]

While all of the foregoing evidence has pointed in the same direction, and is inexplicable if one presumes a Greek original for the Diatessaron, one final investigation was undertaken. In this, unambiguous evidence was sought. It is known, for example, that Greek is a hypotactic language, where a sentence usually has one finite verb, and a string of participles subordinated to that single verb. Moreover, good Greek style is spare, eschewing frequent conjunctions (participial subordination is preferred), and avoiding unnecessary use of the pronoun.

This is quite different from the Semitic languages, which link many finite verbs together, joining them with conjunctions (in Hebrew, the ubiquitous *waw-consecutivum*). Similarly, since both Hebrew and Syriac have suffix pronouns, which allow adding the pronoun by appending only a letter or two to either a noun or a verb, pronouns abound. Thus, our points for comparison were set. If, after fulfilling our criteria for being ge-

---

[67] Plooij, *Liège,* p. 514.

[68] Todesco, *Veneto,* p. 113.

[69] This reading and its importance for the matter of the Diatessaron's original language were noted by D. Plooij in his *A Primitive Text of the Diatessaron* (Leyden, 1923), p. 58: "... it seems to me a very strong (argument) in favour of the direct dependence of the Latin (*Vorlage* of Liège) on a Syriac original."

nuinely Diatessaronic, readings appeared in a passage which betrayed these hallmarks of the Semitic languages (paratactic construction with finite verbs, joined by conjunctions; frequent pronouns not found in the Greek parallel), then one would have further evidence to invalidate the thesis of a Greek language original Diatessaron, and in favour of a Semitic language original.

Luke was selected for this test, for his Greek is the most elegant among the Gospels—thus affording more points of comparison. In order to eliminate the confusing cross-currents of inter-gospel harmonizations, a pericope found only in Luke was selected. The results are displayed in Exhibit V.

Exhibit V:

Lk. 10.33–4: Σαμαρίτης δὲ τις ὁδεύων (*ἐν τῇ ὁδῷ ἐκείνῃ* 477*) ἦλθεν κατ' αὐτὸν καὶ ἰδὼν [αὐτὸν] ἐσπλαγχνίσθη,

Eastern Diatessaronic Witnesses:

Syr$^{s.c}$: šmry' dyn ḥd kd rd' *hw' bh b'wrḥ'* wmṭy lwth. ḥzyhy w'trḥm 'lwh*y*.
But a certain Samaritan, when he was journeying *that same way* and arrived by him saw him and had compassion *on him*.

Arabic Harm., 34: Et l'un des samaritains, pendant qu'il marchait, arriva à l'endroit ou il était et le vit et eut pitié *de lui*.

Persian Harm., III.25: Un samaritano passava nella strada, vide in quel luogo l'uomo e ne ebbe pietà.

Western Diatessaronic Witnesses:

Liège Harm., CLXXIII: Doe gheschide dat en samaritaen quam gaende *al din seluen wech*· eñ alse hi denghenen sach so ontfarments *hem*·

Theodiscum Harm., 165: Do geschach das ein Samaritani kam gande *den selben weg*. vnd do gein gesach do wart er mit barmherzekeit bewegt

Venetian Harmony, 65: Un Samaritano, coè a dire un homo mondano, andava per quel lugo e vecuto questo enfermo mossessi a misericordia

Lk: καὶ *προσελθὼν* κατέδησεν τὰ τραύματα αὐτοῦ *ἐπιχέων* ἔλαιον καὶ οἶνον,

Eastern:

Syr$^{s.c}$: w'tqrb *w'*ḳb mḥwth *wn*ḳl *'lyhyn* ḥmr' wmšḥ'.
and he drew neigh *and* bound up his wounds *and* poured *upon them* wine and oil

Arabic Harm.: Et il approcha *et* banda ses blessures *et y* versa du vin et de l'huile.

Persian Harm.: Si avvicino a lui e puli le sue ferite e pose vino e olio sulle sue ferite,

Western:

Liège: eñ hi ghinc ten ghenen daer hi lach *eñ* bant hem sine wonden *eñ* ghoet*er* in olie eñ wyn·

Theodiscum: vnd gieng zv ime da er lag *vnd* bant ime sine wunden *vnd* gos *dar* in oele vnd win

Venetian: et vene ad ello *e* lavò i *le plage* de vino *e* de olio e legali le plage e poselo

Lk: ἐπιβιβάσας δὲ αὐτὸν ἐπὶ τὸ ἴδιον κτῆνος [*et r*^{2}] ἤγαγεν [*δὲ* 1047] αὐτόν εἰς πανδοχεῖον καὶ ἐπεμελήθη αὐτοῦ.

Eastern:

Syr$^{s.c}$: w'rkbh ʿl ḥmrh. *w*'ytyh lpwtq' wtrsyh.

and made him ride on his ass *and* brought him to an inn and nourished him.[70]

Arabic Harm.: Et il le laissa fit monter sur l'âne *et* l'amena a l'hôtellerie et prit soin de lui.[71]

Persian Harm.: e legò e (lo) sedere sul suo asino *e* lo portò nella locanda, e quel giorno si fermò per lui.[72]

Western:

Liège: eñ dar na so sette hine op syn part *eñ* vurdene in ene herberge eñ plach syns.[73]

Theodiscum: vnd dar nach saste er in vf sine viche *vnd* furte in eine herberge vnd pflag sin.[74]

Venetian: en su lo caval suo *e* dusselo ad uno albergo et avene cura.[75]

Similarly: Stuttgart, Haaren, Haagse Harmonies and Syr^{p}.

Each of the features discussed below satisfies our criteria for being Diatessaronic. Let us being with the verbs. In the Greek of canonical Luke, προσελθών, ἐπιχέων and ἐπιβιβάσας are participles. They are underlined for emphasis. When we turn to the Diatessaronic witnesses, we find that in *every* witness cited, *each* of these participles has been turned into a finite verb—just as we predicted would be the case, if Greek were *not* the original language of the Diatessaron. The other features, conjunctions and pronouns, all added in the Diatessaronic witnesses, but absent from the Greek Luke, are listed tabularly below, commencing at the beginning of the verse.

Luke (Greek):	(ἐν τῇ ὁδῷ ἐκείνῃ 477*)	/ –	/ –	/ –	/ –	/ (δὲ 1047
Syr$^{s.c}$:	that same way	/ on him	/ and	/ and	/ upon them	/ and
Arabic Harmony:	–	/ de lui	/ et	/ et	/ y	/ et
Persian Harmony:	–	/ ne	/ e	/ e	/ sue ferite	/ e
Liège Harmony:	al din seluen weg	/ hem	/ en	/ en	/ (ghoet)er	/ en
Theodiscum:	–	/ –	/ vnd	/ vnd	/ dar	/ vnd
Venetian Harmony:	–	/ –	/ e	/ e	/ le plage	/ e

This table, together with the evidence of the verbs changing from participles to finite verbs, graphically demonstrates the imprint of the Semitic idiom on the text of the Diatessaron. Note especially how, although *totally* absent from the Graeco-Latin MS tradition, each of these features has af-

[70] Burkitt, *Euangelion,* p. 315.

[71] Marmardji, *Diatessaron,* p. 329.

[72] Messina, *Persiano,* p. 225.

[73] Plooij, *Liège,* p. 483.

[74] Gerhardt, *Jhesu,* p. 107.

[75] Todesco, *Veneto,* p. 67.

fected the *Western* harmonies—precisely those which should, were the original Diatessaron in Greek, show *no* trace of Semitic influence. Yet even these Western harmonies fall in step with their Eastern brothers, including the Vetus Syra. It would be hard to imagine a more compelling proof that the Diatessaron's text was *not* originally Greek, but a Semitic language.[76]

We began our study by pointing out how, from a point of method, one must begin by accepting the thesis of a Greek original, and then try to invalidate that hypothesis. All of our evidence, derived in three separate investigations, has pointed in the same direction. All of it speaks against a Greek language original. Indeed, as this last Exhibit has shown,[77] the Dutch, German or Italian Diatessaronic witnesses can be retranslated back into perfect Syriac, replete with suffix pronouns, conjunctions in the proper places, and the proper verb forms. But they *cannot* be retranslated back into Greek agreeing with any known form of the Graeco-Latin NT MS tradition.

This evidence, along with the tendency of the Diatessaron to follow the Hebrew/Syriac OT (Exhibits I–III), and the omission of the translation of a Hebrew word (Exihibit IV), compels one to conclude that Tatian's pen, when it composed the Diatessaron, wrote in Syriac.

Abbreviations

CSCO	Corpus Scriptorum Christianorum Orientalium
GCS	Die griechischen christlichen Schriftsteller
JBL	Journal of Bibilical Literature
JThS	Journal of Theological Studies
NTS	New Testament Studies
PL	Patrologia Latina (Migne)
PS	Patrologia Syriaca (Graffin)
SC	Sources chrétiennes

---

76 Among the Western witnesses, it might be argued that one or another of the languages had, idiomatically, similar syntax to Syriac, and therefore displays, solely by chance, readings similar to the Eastern Diatessaronic witnesses. This is correct. But the case can hardly be made that *three* Western languages each contained *all* of the syntactic features (*i. e.*, finite verbs, pleonastic pronouns, conjunctions) of the Semitic languages. The sheer number of Western witnesses, in three languages, each reproducing item after syntactic item of Semitic idiom must indicate a relationship with the East.

77 This is not the only passage where such striking agreements occur. To mention only one other case: Lk. 23.11.

Die Bitte um das Kommen des Geistes im lukanischen Vaterunser (Lk 11,2 v. 1.)

von Gerhard Schneider

(Hustadtring 65, 4630 Bochum-Querenburg)

Die Diskussion um die Ursprünglichkeit jener Textvariante, die im lukanischen Vaterunser um das Kommen des Heiligen Geistes bitten läßt, setzte vor rund hundert Jahren ein. Im Jahre 1882 wurde die Minuskelhandschrift der Evangelien für das Britische Museum gekauft, die heute mit dem Sigel 700 bezeichnet wird. Sie stammt aus dem 11. Jahrhundert. Der Textforscher H. C. Hoskier hat sie kollationiert und das Ergebnis seiner Arbeit 1890 vorgelegt[1]. Die zweite Bitte des Herrengebets lautet in 700: ἐλθέτω τὸ πνεῦμά σου τὸ ἅγιον ἐφ' ἡμᾶς, καὶ καθαρισάτω ἡμᾶς[2]. Diese Bitte steht hier an Stelle derjenigen um das Kommen des Reiches Gottes. Es gibt wahrscheinlich nur eine weitere Evangelienhandschrift, die eine entsprechende Lesart bezeugt, den Codex der Vatikanischen Bibliothek, der das Sigel 162 führt (geschrieben 1153)[3]. Die Minuskel 162 stellt in der Geist-Bitte σου vor τὸ πνεῦμα und läßt ἐφ' ἡμᾶς weg[4].

Durch das Bekanntwerden der Minuskel 700[5] kam bald die Erörterung in Gang, welchen textkritischen Stellenwert die betreffende Lesart in Lk 11,2 beanspruchen könne. Vor allem A. v. Harnack regte mit seiner Akademie-Abhandlung von 1904 den Streit um das Für und Wider an. Denn er veranschlagte den textgeschichtlichen Rang der Geist-Bitte so hoch, daß er deren Ursprünglichkeit im Lk-Evangelium annahm. Er hielt es für wahrscheinlich, daß Lukas »dem Herrngebet durch Voranstellung

---

1 Hoskier, Full Account, bes. 1–43. – N.B. Ein Verzeichnis der wichtigsten Literatur steht am Ende dieses Beitrages.

2 Eine Abbildung von folio 184 verso (mit dem Text des Vaterunsers nach Lk) findet sich bei Hoskier (a.a.O.) zwischen *Introduction* und *Collation*.

3 Harnack wurde durch Hans Frhr. v. Soden auf diese Minuskel aufmerksam gemacht; siehe Harnack, Über einige Worte 196.

4 So liest auch Maximus Confessor: PG 90, 884 B.

5 Sie hat bei Hoskier das Sigel 604 und wird im Britischen Museum unter der Nr. 2610 Egerton geführt. Die Lesart des Codex 700 mit der Geist-Bitte des Vaterunsers wurde schon früh beachtet; siehe Chase, Lord's Prayer (1891) 25; Scrivener, Introduction (1894) I 261. Auch in Deutschland fand sie (nicht erst durch Harnack) Beachtung: Resch, Paralleltexte (1895) 233f.; Blass, Evangelium sec. Lucam (1897) XLIII. 51.

der Bitte um den heiligen Geist den confessionellen Charakter gegenüber den Johannesjüngern[6] gegeben hat«[7].

H. Greeven hat in seiner wissenschaftlichen Erstlingsarbeit (1931) die Argumente Harnacks aufgegriffen und sich für die Ursprünglichkeit der Geist-Bitte im dritten Evangelium ausgesprochen[8]. Fünfzig Jahre später (1981) jedoch verweist Greeven in der von ihm erarbeiteten Synopse die Geist-Bitte Lk 11,2 in den kritischen Apparat und entscheidet sich für die Ursprünglichkeit der Reichs-Bitte im Lk-Text[9]. In der Synopse bot sich allerdings keine Gelegenheit, diese kritische Entscheidung zu begründen. Man fragt unwillkürlich, ob sich die Beurteilungsmaßstäbe der Textkritik in den dazwischenliegenden fünfzig Jahren geändert haben. Oder was führte dazu, daß heute die Ursprünglichkeit der Geist-Bitte im Lk-Evangelium nur noch selten behauptet wird?

Der vorliegende Beitrag stellt sich die Aufgabe, die nahezu hundertjährige Diskussion um die Geist-Bitte des Vaterunsers zu rekapitulieren. Dabei ist es nicht wichtig, die Vertreter des Pro und des Contra einfach zu registrieren. Es gilt vielmehr, deren Argumente zu würdigen. Zwar geht der Trend seit den dreißiger Jahren eher in Richtung einer Bestreitung der Ursprünglichkeit der Geist-Bitte im Urtext des dritten Evangeliums. Doch wird auch neuerdings noch deren lukanische Ursprünglichkeit verteidigt[10]. Die Zielsetzung der folgenden Berichterstattung liegt darin, die sich im Laufe der Diskussion herausbildenden methodischen Neuansätze aufzuweisen. Dann soll der Versuch gewagt werden, die schwierige Frage neu anzugehen und eine textkritische Entscheidung zu treffen.

1. Die Diskussion um die Geist-Bitte von Harnack (1904) bis Greeven (1931)

Noch vor der Publikation Hoskiers mit der Kollation des Codex 700 hatte A. Resch in der ersten Auflage seiner »Agrapha« (1889) die Geist-Bitte im lukanischen Vaterunser dem Evangelisten zugeschrieben und dazu auf Lk 11,13 (diff. Mt) verwiesen, um den »redaktionellen« Charakter der betreffenden Lesart zu unterstreichen[11]. Demgegenüber hielt F. H. Chase (1891), obwohl er die Kollation Hoskiers kannte[12], die Geist-Bitte für eine aus dem

---

[6] Vgl. Lk 11,1f.; Act 19,2–6.

[7] Harnack, Über einige Worte 206.

[8] Greeven, Gebet und Eschatologie 72–75.

[9] Greeven, Synopse 152.

[10] So z. B. von Gräßer, Problem (1956); Leaney, Lucan Text (1956) und Luke (1958); Ott, Gebet und Heil (1965); Freudenberger, Zum Text (1969).

[11] Resch, Agrapha (1889) 398f. Er beansprucht als Textzeugen neben Gregor von Nyssa und Maximus Confessor auch Marcion (nach Tertullian, Adv. Marc. IV 26). Resch, Paralleltexte 233f., wiederholt (nach Kenntnisnahme von Codex 700) die Auffassung, daß die Geist-Bitte vom Evangelisten stamme, bezeichnet dieses Urteil jedoch nur noch als »wahrscheinlich«. Nach Zahn, Vaterunser (1891), hat Marcion das Vaterunser des Lk-Evangeliums verfälscht, indem er die Geist-Bitte an die Stelle der Namens-Bitte stellte, die ihm unerträglich erschien (410f.).

[12] Chase, Lord's Prayer 25.

kirchlichen Gebrauch stammende Zutat zum dritten Evangelium[13]. Der einzige Forscher, der die Geist-Bitte von Lk 11,2 formell in den Lk-Text für aufnahm, war F. Blass[14].

A. v. Harnack konnte in seiner Akademie-Abhandlung am 21. 1. 1904 von der Kenntnis zweier Evangelien-Handschriften ausgehen, die die Geist-Bitte im dritten Evangelium bezeugen[15]. Er hält die Geist-Bitte im Lk-Text für ursprünglich[16] und führt dafür folgende Gründe an. Weil der Vaterunser-Text des Mt-Evangeliums im Lauf der Textgeschichte den des dritten Evangeliums nachweislich mehrfach beeinflußt hat, müsse man »auch den letzten Schritt thun« und die Reichs-Bitte Lk 11,2 als sekundär ansehen[17]. Ein Späterer habe doch wohl kaum den Mut aufbringen können, gegen einen gleichlautenden Mt-Lk-Text die Geist-Bitte einzusetzen, während umgekehrt leicht zu verstehen sei, daß man den Lk-Text auch hier mit Matthäus konformierte, »zumal, nachdem sich die von Matthäus gebotene Form in den Gottesdiensten durchgesetzt hatte«[18]. Weiterhin verweist Harnack auf den Kontext des lukanischen Vaterunsers, in dem der Evangelist die Folgerung »Um wieviel mehr wird euer himmlischer Vater denen, die ihn bitten, Gutes geben!« (so Mt 7,11b) abgeändert hat und liest: ». . . den heiligen Geist geben« (Lk 11,13b). Außerdem sei πνεῦμα ἅγιον ein Zentralbegriff in den Erzählungen der Apostelgeschichte, wo besonders Act 1,8; 11,15; 19,6 der Geist-Bitte des Herrengebets sehr nahe kämen[19].

Harnack kam zu seiner Einschätzung der Textüberlieferung, weil er den Befund nicht nur quantitativ bewertete, sondern bewußt wägte. Er vermutete, daß man bisher nur »ganz zufällig« auf zwei Zeugen gestoßen sei und man weitere Minuskel-Codices mit der betreffenden Lesart finden werde[20]. Doch hat sich diese Erwartung nicht erfüllt. Der Bestand an Textzeugen ist vielmehr bis heute jener geblieben, den schon Harnack kannte.

---

[13] Chase, a.a.O. 27f. Chase nimmt an, daß die Geist-Bitte in Handschriften vorhanden war, die sowohl Tertullian als auch Marcion vorlagen. Doch weist er (a.a.O. 28) darauf hin, daß die Geist-Bitte bei Marcion an die Stelle der Namens-Bitte des Vaterunsers tritt.

[14] Blass, Evangelium sec. Lucam 51.

[15] Harnack, Über einige Worte 196. Neben Codex 700 nimmt Harnack auch – auf Hinweis seines Schülers Hans Frhr. v. Soden – den Codex 162 zur Kenntnis.

[16] Harnack, a.a.O. 199: »Aus diesen Gründen darf man meines Erachtens nicht zweifeln, dass Lucas die Bitte um den heiligen Geist im Text des Vater-Unsers geboten hat.« Siehe auch a.a.O. 205f., ferner Harnack, Text (1923) 26–28; Marcion (^{2}1924) 207*f.

[17] Harnack, Über einige Worte 198.

[18] Harnack, a.a.O. 199.

[19] Ebd. Auch zu dem mit der Geist-Bitte verbundenen καθαρισάτω finde sich eine »schlagende Parallele« in den Acta, nämlich 15,8f.

[20] Harnack meinte: »es können zehn oder zwanzig oder noch mehr sein, welche diese Lesart bieten« (a.a.O. 199).

Es gibt vier Textzeugen, die an Stelle der Reichs-Bitte Lk 11,2 die Bitte um das Kommen des Geistes lesen. Dies sind zwei Minuskel-Handschriften und zwei Kirchenväter:

Codex 700 (11. Jh.) liest:

ἐλθέτω τὸ πνεῦμά σου τὸ ἅγιον ἐφ' ἡμᾶς,
καὶ καθαρισάτω ἡμᾶς.

Die *Handschrift 162* (geschrieben 1153) liest:

ἐλθέτω σου τὸ πνεῦμα τὸ ἅγιον,
καὶ καθαρισάτω ἡμᾶς.

Gregor von Nyssa († 394) liest[21]:

ἐλθέτω τὸ ἅγιον πνεῦμά σου ἐφ' ἡμᾶς,
καὶ καθαρισάτω ἡμᾶς.

Maximus Confessor († 662) liest[22]:

ἐλθέτω σου τὸ πνεῦμα τὸ ἅγιον,
καὶ καθαρισάτω ἡμᾶς.

Während Maximus[23] mit der Minuskel 162 übereinstimmt, indem er »auf uns« wegläßt, besteht andererseits eine Übereinstimmung zwischen Gregor und dem Codex 700, die beide ἐφ' ἡμᾶς lesen[24]. Neben diesen Zeugen ist noch der Vaterunsertext des *Marcion* heranzuziehen, den man im Anschluß an Tertullian, Adv. Marc. IV 26, rekonstruieren kann[25]. Bei Marcion lautete die Geist-Bitte vielleicht: ἐλθέτω τὸ ἅγιον πνεῦμά σου [ἐφ' ἡμᾶς], καὶ καθαρισάτω ἡμᾶς. Allerdings stand diese Bitte bei Marcion unmittelbar hinter der Vater-Anrede; auf sie folgte die Reichs-Bitte, während »Dein Wille geschehe!« fehlte[26].

Harnack stellte, indem er die Diskrepanz zwischen Marcion und den übrigen Zeugen der Geist-Bitte wahrnahm, die Frage: »Wo stand nach Lucas ursprünglich die Bitte um den heiligen Geist?«[27] Er kam zu der Antwort, bei Lukas habe weder die Bitte um Heiligung des göttlichen Namens noch die um das Kommen des Reiches gestanden; auch die »dritte« Bitte (nach Mt) habe gefehlt. Diesem lukanischen Text sei »aus Matthäus bald die eine, bald die andere Bitte (d. h. die 1. oder die 2.) hinzugefügt worden, und zwar schon in frühester Zeit«. Zuletzt, aber noch im 2. Jahr-

---

[21] Gregor von Nyssa, De oratione dominica III 5 (PG 44,1157 C). An anderen Stellen dieses Abschnitts begegnet diese Lesart ohne ἐφ' ἡμᾶς (44,1157 D) bzw. mit vorangestelltem ἐφ' ἡμᾶς vor τὸ πνεῦμα τὸ ἅγιον (ohne σου) (44,1160 D).

[22] Maximus Confessor, Expositio orationis dominicae 350 (PG 90,884 B).

[23] Irrtümlich wird als Zeuge dieser Lesart verschiedentlich Maximus *von Turin* genannt: Streeter, Four Gospels 277; Leaney, Lucan Text 103; Luke 59; Metzger, Textual Commentary 155; Marshall, Luke 458.

[24] Daß man ein ἐφ' ἡμᾶς gern mit den einleitenden Bitten des Vaterunsers verband, zeigt D in der Reichs-Bitte.

[25] Siehe Harnack, Über einige Worte 197.200. Dazu kritisch Freudenberger, Zum Text 420.

[26] Codex 700 enthält hingegen Lk 11,2 die »dritte« Bitte im Anschluß an die Geist-Bitte! Im Lk-Text haben folgende Zeugen die einfache Vater-Anrede mit zwei folgenden Du-Bitten (um Heiligung des Namens; um das Kommen des Reiches): P^{75} B 1. 118. 131. 209. vg sy^s Origenes (vgl. auch L).

[27] Harnack, a.a.O. 200.

hundert, sei »die Dreizahl der von Matthäus gebotenen Bitten *an die Stelle* der Bitte um den Geist gesetzt worden«[28].

Nicht nur die Auffassung Harnacks über die Entstehung der Vaterunsertexte, sondern speziell auch die über die Geist-Bitte ist bald auf Widerspruch gestoßen[29]. Harnack hat aber auch Zustimmung gefunden[30]. H. v. Soden bemerkt gegen Harnack kritisch, daß die beiden Minuskelhandschriften, die die Geist-Bitte bezeugen, auch sonst miteinander verwandt sind, »also wohl von einer und derselben Vorlage« stammen[31]. Außerdem vermutet er, »daß in jene beiden Kodices oder ihre gemeinsame Vorlage die Bitte aus der viel gelesenen Auslegung Gregors übertragen sei«; auch Maximus Confessor sei von Gregor abhängig[32]. Ob Marcion seinen Text mit der Geist-Bitte schon vorgefunden oder von sich aus hergestellt hat, läßt sich nach v. Soden nicht eindeutig entscheiden; möglich sei, daß er den ursprünglichen Lk-Text bewahrt hat[33]. H. v. Soden hält – gegen Harnack – die beiden mit dem Mt-Text übereinstimmenden ersten Bitten des lukanischen Vaterunsers für ursprünglich und die Geist-Bitte für eine sekundäre Einfügung[34]. Doch weiß er, daß man bei dieser Position erklären muß, wie Marcion und Gregor von Nyssa zu ihren Texten kamen[35].

H. v. Soden geht bei seiner Fragestellung nicht von den Textzeugen aus, sondern von inneren Gründen. Solche waren schon für Harnack ausschlaggebend. Die Nennung des Heiligen Geistes Lk 11,13 (diff. Mt) entspreche der hohen Wertung des πνεῦμα ἅγιον bei Lukas. Es sei jedoch nicht sicher, daß Lukas sich mit 11,13 auf das Vaterunser bezieht. Denn man muß sich fragen, warum hier »die Gegenstände der andern Bitten völlig ignoriert werden, die doch, auch nach Lukas, nicht in jener ersten

---

[28] Ebd.

[29] Siehe die Kritik v. Sodens, die schon am 3. 3. 1904 in der Zeitschrift »Die christliche Welt« unter dem Titel »Die ursprüngliche Gestalt des Vaterunsers« erschien.

[30] In bezug auf die Geist-Bitte im Lk-Text vgl. Spitta, Die älteste Form (1904) 337f.; Paslack, Bemerkungen (1905); Klein, Gestalt (1906) 35.40–50. Gegen Paslack wandte sich Schürer in seiner Rezension: ThLZ 30 (1905) 258f. Wellhausen, Evangelium Lucae (1904) 56, schreibt irrtümlich, daß bei Marcion die Geist-Bitte als *zweite* Bitte stehe. Die Frage, ob man sie als Korrektur dem Evangelisten Lukas zutrauen dürfe, lasse sich schwer beantworten. Die Geist-Bitte Lk 11,2 könne u. U. im Anschluß an 11,13 (als Korrektur) entstanden sein. Ähnlich unentschieden bleibt Wellhausen auch noch 1911: Einleitung 63f.

[31] v. Soden, Gestalt 219. Er vermerkt: »Obgleich jüngst alle, auch die spätesten Handschriften, welche Abweichungen von dem im Mittelalter herrschenden Text aufweisen, durchgesehen worden sind, ist die Bitte sonst nirgends aufgestoßen.«

[32] v. Soden, Gestalt 219.

[33] v. Soden, a.a.O. 220.

[34] v. Soden, a.a.O. 220f.

[35] v. Soden, a.a.O. 221.

Bitte aufgehen«. Zu Act 19 sei festzustellen, daß die Johannesjünger schon Christen seien (v. 2: sie sind »gläubig geworden«). Ihnen fehlte »nur die Taufe auf den Namen Jesu und die Handauflegung eines Apostels« und das damit vermittelte Kommen des Heiligen Geistes. In der Bitte der Jünger Lk 11,1, Jesus möge sie beten lehren wie Johannes seine Jünger lehrte, dürfe man keine »gegensätzliche Spitze« vermuten[36]. καθὼς καί beziehe sich »auf des Johannes bewährte Schulmethode«[37]. Somit sind nach v. Soden die von Harnack aufgezeigten Beziehungen der Geist-Bitte zu anderen Stellen des lukanischen Werkes unsicher. Zudem passe diese Bitte schlecht zur Anschauung des Lukas, insbesondere als tägliche Bitte[38]. Die Bitte um das Kommen des Geistes passe hingegen gut in ein Gebet der Johannesjünger[39]. Die Christen hätten diese Bitte »als Taufgebet« aus der Täuferschule übernommen und späterhin auch wohl in Verbindung mit dem Vaterunser gesprochen. »Marcion paßte diese Randnotiz vorzüglich; er sah sie als eine andere und glücklichere Fassung der ersten Bitte an . . . und verbesserte seinen Lukastext darnach mit dem Mut, der ihm bei seinen Textänderungen nie versagte.«[40] Im Evangelienexemplar Gregors von Nyssa sei die gleiche Randglosse dann an die Stelle der zweiten Bitte gerückt worden[41].

G. Klein knüpfte an v. Sodens Hypothese an, daß die Geist-Bitte aus dem Kreis um Johannes den Täufer stammt[42]. Christliche Kreise könnten sich das Taufgebet des Johannes angeeignet und ins Vaterunser eingebracht haben[43]. Später habe man – aus dogmatischen Gründen (vgl. Joh 20,21–23; Act 2) – die Geist-Bitte wieder getilgt. Sie habe sich im Lk-Text Marcions am längsten erhalten[44].

Th. Zahn behandelte in seinem Lk-Kommentar noch einmal das Vaterunser Marcions[45], diesmal unter Einbeziehung des Textes, den die Minuskel 700 bietet[46]. Zahn erkennt drei Möglichkeiten, den Befund der Textzeugen zu erklären: Entweder hat Marcion 1) den ursprünglichen Lk-Text bewahrt oder 2) seinen Text von sich aus geschaffen (er wäre von dort in kirchliche Handschriften übergegangen). Oder Marcion hat 3) seinen Text in einer kirchlichen Handschrift vorgefunden (vielleicht nur als Randglosse) und ihn dem vor-

---

36 Ebd.

37 v. Soden, a.a.O. 221f.

38 v. Soden, a.a.O. 222.

39 v. Soden, a.a.O. 223. Neben die Wendung »wie Johannes seine Jünger beten lehrte« (Lk 11,1), habe jemand die Geist-Bitte an den Rand notiert, der diesen Zusammenhang noch kannte!

40 Ebd. Auch Hönnicke, Forschungen 114, vermutete, daß die Geist-Bitte als Randglosse entstanden sei. Der Glossator habe die Reichs-Bitte erläutern wollen.

41 v. Soden, a.a.O. 223.

42 Klein, Gestalt 44.

43 Klein, a.a.O. 46f.

44 Klein, a.a.O. 47.

45 Zahn, Lucas 767–772. Vgl. Zahn, Vaterunser (1891).

46 Zahn, Lucas 768.

herrschenden Lk-Text vorgezogen[47]. Nach Diskussion der Möglichkeiten[48] entscheidet sich Zahn für die dritte Annahme: »Mn muß die Bitte um den hl. Geist in einem kirchlichen Lctext vorgefunden haben.«[49] Das Schwanken zweifelhafter Textbestandteile in bezug auf ihre Stellung (hier: als 1. oder 2. Bitte) ist »ein sehr häufiges Schicksal von Glossen, die zuerst am Rand geschrieben standen, dann aber . . . in den Text eingefügt wurden. So wird es also auch hier geschehen sein.«[50]

Die schon 1909 abgeschlossene Straßburger Dissertation über das Vaterunser von J. Hensler nahm ausführlich zu den Gründen Stellung, die Harnack für seine These über die Geist-Bitte im Gebet des Herrn genannt hatte[51]. Hensler selbst hält die Geist-Bitte des Lk-Textes für handschriftlich mangelhaft bezeugt[52]. Er macht auf die Störung der Struktur in den Du-Bitten des Gebets aufmerksam[53] und vermutet – entsprechend der Argumentation v. Sodens –, daß die Geist-Bitte, ein Taufgebet der Johannes-Jünger, als Randglosse zu Lk 11,1 notiert war. Danach habe Marcion seinen Evangelientext geändert[54]. Im Evangelienexemplar Gregors von Nyssa sei diese Glosse schon in den Text selbst geraten, und zwar als zweite Bitte[55].

J. Weiß[56] neigte dazu, die Geist-Bitte im Lk-Text für ursprünglich zu halten. Er weist zwar auf die Diskrepanz zwischen Marcion und den späteren Zeugen hinsichtlich der Stellung dieser Bitte gegenüber den anderen Bitten hin, hält es aber trotzdem für »nicht unwahrscheinlich«, daß schon Lukas die Geist-Bitte gelesen hat. Deutlich hebt er von der Frage der *lukanischen* Ursprünglichkeit die der *jesuanischen* Authentizität ab. Letztere hält er offensichtlich für unwahrscheinlich (weil der Heilige Geist im Rahmen der Verkündigung Jesu eine geringe Rolle gespielt habe). Die Geist-Bitte im Vaterunser entstamme also eher der christlichen Gemeinde.

In den zwanziger Jahren haben sich vier weitere Autoren für die Ursprünglichkeit der Geist-Bitte im dritten Evangelium ausgesprochen: H. Leisegang, A. Loisy, B. H. Streeter und E. Klostermann[57]. Gegen die Verankerung dieser Bitte schon im Lk-Text argumentier-

---

[47] Zahn, a.a.O. 769.

[48] Nach Zahn (a.a.O. 769) spricht gegen 1), daß die Geist-Bitte, falls sie ursprünglich ist, doch nicht fast überall verdrängt worden wäre, zumal sie für niemand religiös anstößig sein konnte. »Auch die Neigung, die beiden ev Berichte über das VU einander gleichzumachen, . . . würde nicht dazu taugen, die allgemeine Einführung der1. Bitte des Mt anstatt der angeblich von Mt bewahrten ursprünglichen 1. Bitte des Lc zu erklären; denn die ältesten und besten Zeugen für die wesentliche Identität der 1. Bitte bei beiden Evv: Orig., ℵ B L, Ss, Vulg haben den Text des Lc vom ersten bis zum letzten Wort von allen oder so gut wie allen Beimischungen aus Mt reingehalten.« Gegen 2): Die kirchlichen Zeugen für die Geist-Bitte bezeugen diese (gegen Marcion!) als Ersatz für die Reichs-Bitte.

[49] Zahn, a.a.O. 770. [50] Ebd.

[51] Hensler, Vaterunser (1914) 33–37.

[52] Hensler, a.a.O. 33f.37.

[53] Hensler, a.a.O. 37–42. Besonders die Zweiteiligkeit der Geist-Bitte spreche gegen ihre Ursprünglichkeit (39).

[54] Hensler, a.a.O. 43.

[55] Hensler, a.a.O. 45; vgl. v. Soden, Gestalt 223.

[56] Weiß, Schriften des NT I 450.

[57] Leisegang, Pneuma Hagion 109 (Lukas vermißte »in einem Kernstück christlicher Lehre, im Vaterunser«, den Heiligen Geist); Loisy, Luc 315f. (übernimmt die Geist-Bitte –

ten A. Plummer, H. v. Baer, P. Fiebig und M.-J. Lagrange[58], ferner J. M. Creed (1930) und F. Hauck (1934)[59].

H. Greeven behandelt die Geist-Bitte in einem »Exkurs über die ursprüngliche Form des Vaterunsers«. Er hält sie bei Lukas für ursprünglich: Dies werde schon dadurch sehr wahrscheinlich gemacht, »daß die Matthäus-Form des Vaterunsers alsbald die im Kult gebräuchliche wurde und schwerlich eine so stark abweichende Variante hätte neben sich aufkommen lassen, wenn diese ihren Anspruch nicht auf zuverlässige Überlieferung gründen konnte«[60]. Zweitens beruft sich Greeven auf den – wie wir heute sagen würden – lukanisch-redaktionellen Zusammenhang zwischen dem Bildwort Lk 11,11–13 (diff. Mt) und der Geist-Bitte 11,2. Das Wort erscheine 11,13 nicht mehr »allgemein gemünzt auf beharrliches Bitten«, sondern »auf beharrliches Bitten um den Heiligen Geist«[61]. Schließlich spreche auch 11,1 für die Echtheit der Geist-Bitte, »wenn man sie mit Act. 19,2f. vergleicht«[62]: Nach Lk 11,1 solle das folgende Gebet (11,2–4) »ein Spezifikum der Jesus-Jünger sein, wie es entsprechend auch die Johannes-Jünger hatten«[63].

Die Übereinstimmung Greevens mit Harnack erstreckt sich allerdings nur auf die Beurteilung der Geist-Bitte selbst, nicht aber auf die Rekonstruktion des Herrengebets im ältesten Lk-Text. Nach Harnacks Auffassung folgte hier auf die Vateranrede direkt die Geist-Bitte, dann sogleich die Brot-Bitte. Greeven sucht zu beweisen, daß die Bitte um das Kommen des Reiches bei Lukas auf die Geist-Bitte folgte[64]. Marcion habe m. a. W. den Urtext des dritten Evangeliums bewahrt. Indessen hält

---

wie Marcion – in den Lk-Text, d. h. vor der Reichs-Bitte); Streeter, Four Gospels 277; Klostermann, Lk 124 (»wohl authentischer Text des Lc«. Es frage sich nur, »ob Text der 2. Bitte allein, oder vielleicht für die 1. *und* 2. Bitte«).

[58] Plummer, Luke 295 Anm. 1 (Die Geist-Bitte sei vielleicht geschaffen worden für den Gebrauch des Vaterunsers bei der Handauflegung; so könne sie in einige Lk-Texte geraten sein.); v. Baer, Der Heilige Geist 152 (argumentiert gegen Leisegang); Fiebig, Vaterunser 21f. (Geist-Bitte stammt von Marcion; er hat sie geschaffen, weil ihm die Bitte um Heiligung des göttlichen Namens »zu ausgesprochen jüdisch« erschien); Lagrange, Luc 322f.(323: »Ce changement vient probablement de Marcion, qui aurait remplacé l'idée biblique du règne par celle de l'Esprit.« Doch bemerkt Lagrange selbst, daß Marcion, laut Tertullian, die Reichs-Bitte beibehielt!).

[59] Creed, Luke 156, betont, "the textual evidence is less homogeneous than Streeter [Four Gospels 277] states". Vielleicht stamme die Geist-Bitte aus dem liturgischen Gebrauch der Marcioniten. Hauck, Lk 149, hält die Geist-Bitte für eine Taufbitte, die irrig (vielleicht durch Marcion) Aufnahme ins Vaterunser fand.

[60] Greeven, Gebet und Eschatologie (1931) 73.

[61] Ebd.

[62] Greeven, a.a.O. 73f.

[63] Greeven, a.a.O. 74.

[64] Greeven, a.a.O. 74.76.

Greeven bei seiner Rückfrage nach dem Vaterunser *Jesu* im Gegensatz zu Harnack die Reichs-Bitte für echt. Bei den übrigen Bitten im ersten Teil des Herrengebets (um die Heiligung des Namens, um das Kommen des Geistes, um den Vollzug des Willens Gottes) »werden wir es allerdings mit Erweiterungen zu tun haben, die die Bitte um das Kommen des Reiches jeweils ausdeuten«[65].

2. Die Argumentation seit Lohmeyer (1946)

Bis in die dreißiger Jahre hinein war die Diskussion um die Geist-Bitte im Lk-Text des Vaterunsers weitgehend durch A. v. Harnack bestimmt[66]. Erst nach dem Zweiten Weltkrieg ist mit E. Lohmeyers Monographie über das Vaterunser[67] die Auseinandersetzung weitergeführt worden. Lohmeyer hält es für fraglich, ob die Geist-Bitte schon im ursprünglichen Lk-Text stand, meint aber doch, »daß schon die älteste Christenheit sie gekannt und verwandt hat«[68]. Marcion, der sie an den Anfang des Vaterunsers rückte, handelte dabei »willkürlich und künstlich«; »denn nun beginnen die beiden ersten Bitten auf fast unmögliche Weise mit einem ›es komme‹«[69]. Daß die Geist-Bitte selbst nicht von Marcion geformt ist, gehe daraus hervor, daß ihr Wortlaut aus alttestamentlichen Begriffen gebildet ist, z. B. »dein heiliger Geist« (Ps 51,13; 143,10; Weish 9,17); die Redeweise vom »Kommen« des Gottesgeistes (Ez 2,2; 3,24); »Reinigung« und heiliger Geist (Ez 36,25–27)[70].

Von den alttestamentlichen Zusammenhängen aus möchte Lohmeyer denn auch den Sinn der Geist-Bitte deuten. »Sie richtet sich auf eine eschatologische Gabe: Mit dem Kommen des heiligen Geistes soll der Tag der Vollendung ›für uns‹ anheben und sich damit erfüllen, was Gott seinem Volke einst verheißen hat.«[71] Wie aber konnte eine Gemeinde diese Bitte sprechen, die überzeugt war, den verheißenen Gottesgeist zu besitzen? Die Bitte stellt nach Lohmeyer kein »Initiationsgebet« dar; denn sie

---

[65] Greeven, a.a.O. 76.

[66] In der Zeit zwischen 1931 (Greeven) und 1946 (Lohmeyer) hat sich m. W. nur Hauck, Lk (1934) 149, zur Geist-Bitte geäußert; vgl. oben Anm. 59.

[67] Lohmeyer, Vater-unser (^{1}1946; ^{2}1947). Das Buch enthält ein eigenes Kapitel (XI.) über »Die lukanischen Formen (!) des Vater-unsers« (^{5}1962: 174–192). Lohmeyer ist der Ansicht, daß das Vaterunser von Anfang an in zwei verschiedenen Formen überliefert wurde und daß kein literarischer Zusammenhang zwischen beiden Fassungen besteht. Die Mt-Fassung gehöre nach Galiläa, die lukanische nach Jerusalem. Zur Kritik an Lohmeyer, die aber nicht auf seine Ausführungen zur Geist-Bitte eingeht, siehe vor allem Vielhauer, Vaterunser-Probleme.

[68] Lohmeyer, Vater-unser (^{5}1962) 186.

[69] Ebd.

[70] Lohmeyer, a.a.O. 186f.

[71] Lohmeyer, a.a.O. 188.

spreche nicht von der Begründung des Christenstandes, sondern vom Anbruch der Heilszeit »für uns«[72]. Sie sei »nicht das Gebet des Einzelnen vor seiner Taufe, sondern das einer Gemeinschaft, das sie täglich betet«[73]. Der Boden, auf dem die Geist-Bitte »möglich und begründet ist«, sei »ein Urchristentum, das eng an alttestamentliche Hoffnungen gebunden ist und in Johannes und Jesus die Wegbereiter des Herrn oder seines eschatologischen Werkes erblickt«[74].

In den fünfziger Jahren traten wiederum einige Forscher für die Ursprünglichkeit der Geist-Bitte ein. Während J. Schmid, H. J. Vogels und W. L. Knox die Verankerung der Bitte im lukanischen Vaterunser bestritten[75], haben neben G. W. H. Lampe[76] vor allem Gräßer und Leaney für ihre Ursprünglichkeit plädiert.

E. Gräßer meint beobachten zu können, daß Lukas das überlieferte Vaterunser »im Sinne der ausgebliebenen Parusie modifiziert hat«[77], und glaubt, diese an der Abweichung des Lk-Textes von der matthäischen 4. Bitte (Brot-Bitte) gewonnene »Beobachtung«[78] durch die Geist-Bitte stützen zu können[79]. »Daß die Geistbitte sekundäre Variation der Reichsbitte ist, scheint sicher.«[80] »Im Zuge der *Parusieverzögerung* tritt die Bitte um das Reich zurück hinter die um den Geist, der das Unterpfand dafür ist, daß Gott – wenn auch mit Verzug – doch zu seiner Verheißung steht!«[81] Lk 11,13 (diff. Mt 7,11) spreche dafür, daß *Lukas* diese Korrek-

[72] Lohmeyer, a.a.O. 188f.

[73] Lohmeyer, a.a.O. 189. Dieses Urteil gilt indessen nur, wenn die Geist-Bitte in das Vaterunser integriert ist!

[74] Lohmeyer, a.a.O. 191.

[75] Schmid, Lk 197 (Die Geist-Bitte »muß schon auf Grund der Textbezeugung als späterer Einschub gelten«. Wahrscheinlich war sie ursprünglich eine Taufbitte, »die dann aus dem Gebrauch des Vaterunsers bei der Taufe in den Text eingedrungen ist«.); Vogels, Handbuch 68 (Marcion hat den Text des Vaterunsers »gefälscht«)» Knox, Sources 26 Anm. 1 (Hinweis auf Creed, Luke; ferner: καθαρίζειν werde im NT nie in rein ethischem Sinn verwendet).

[76] Lampe, Holy Spirit 170, stellt die Geist-Bitte in den weiteren Rahmen der lukanischen Auffassung vom Heiligen Geist: Der Heilige Geist ist nach Lukas die vornehmliche Antwort auf das Gebet (Lk 11,13). Die Geist-Bitte gehört wahrscheinlich zum Vaterunser des Lukas. Für die lukanische Verwendung von καθαρίζειν verweist Lampe auf Act 15,9. Er vermutet für Lukas einen engen sachlichen Zusammenhang zwischen πνεῦμα und βασιλεία τοῦ θεοῦ (»identification of the Kingdom of God with the operation of the Spirit«, a.a.O. 184). Auf letzteren Zusammenhang gehen auch ein: Samain, L'Esprit (mir nicht erreichbar); Dunn, Spirit and Kingdom; Smalley, Spirit, bes. 69: »Spirit and kingdom are interchangeably associated in the context of petitionary prayer.« Siehe ferner George, L'Esprit Saint, der aber nicht auf Lk 11,2 v. l. eingeht.

[77] Gräßer, Problem (1956; ^{3}1977) 109.

[78] Gräßer, a.a.O. 107f.

[79] Gräßer, a.a.O. 109–111.

[80] Gräßer, a.a.O. 109.

[81] Gräßer, a.a.O. 110.

tur des Vaterunsers vornahm. Act 1,6–8 zeige, »daß sich Lukas des Geistphänomens zur Bewältigung des Parusieproblemes bedient, und zwar im Sinne des *Ersatzes*«[82].

A. R. C. Leaney verweist gleichfalls auf Lk 11,13, ferner (für καθαρίζω in einem geistig-metaphorischen Sinn) auf Act 10,15; 11,8; 15,9[83]. Besonders die letztgenannte Stelle, die von einer Reinigung der Herzen bei den Empfängern des heiligen Geistes spricht (15,8f.), wird als »ein Echo auf die lukanische Fassung des Vaterunsers« angesehen[84]. Ohne Harnack zu erwähnen, nimmt Leaney dann auch jene Tendenz der Textgeschichte für seine These in Anspruch, die vom Mt-Text her das lukanische Vaterunser beeinflußte[85]. Der Text Gregors von Nyssa könne infolgedessen der ursprüngliche des dritten Evangeliums sein. Allerdings sieht Leaney im Kommen des Geistes nicht den »Ersatz« des Lukas für das ausgebliebene Kommen der Basileia. Eher sei der Heilige Geist jene Kraft, durch die die Apostel das volle »Kommen« des Reiches herbeiführen[86]. Doch die Geist-Bitte habe Lukas schon vorgefunden; sie habe ihrerseits möglicherweise seine Konzeption vom Heiligen Geist geprägt[87]. Lukas habe die Geist-Bitte wohl im Vaterunser der Liturgie seiner Zeit gelesen, und diese Form des Gebets könne sogar »vom Herrn selbst« stammen[88].

Eine Kritik der auf die Geist-Bitte bezogenen Ursprünglichkeitsthese – besonders in der Form Harnacks – legt J. de Fraine vor[89]. Harnack folgt nach de Fraine dem Grundsatz, daß die lectio difficilior vorzuziehen sei. Aber im Fall der Geist-Bitte verliere die schwierigere Lesart hier ihren Wert, weil sie zu schwach bezeugt ist. Der erste sichere Zeuge sei Gregor von Nyssa[90]. Wenn Harnack behauptet, die Geist-Bitte könne nicht sekundär eingeschaltet worden sein, so müsse man dagegen auf Marcion hinweisen. Wenn nämlich diese Bitte auf ihn zurückgehe, brauche man sich nicht zu wundern; denn dieser »Häresiarch« habe sich nachweislich erkühnt, das Lk-Evangelium zu »korrigieren«[91]. Auch der Hinweis auf Lk 11,13 schlage nicht durch, weil hier »*ein* guter Geist« erwähnt werde[92].

---

[82] Gräßer, a.a.O. 111, mit Hinweis auf H. Conzelmann (Die Mitte der Zeit, Tübingen 1954, 100 Anm. 2 [siehe ^{4}1962, 127 mit Anm. 2]).

[83] Leaney, Lucan Text 104.

[84] Ebd. Vgl. ders., Luke 60f.

[85] Leaney, Lucan Text 105.

[86] Ebd. Conzelmann (vgl. oben Anm. 82) wird von Leaney nicht erwähnt. Siehe auch Leaney, Luke 61f.

[87] Leaney, Lucan Text 105.

[88] Leaney, a.a.O. 111; ders., Luke 68.

[89] de Fraine, Oraison Dominicale 789f.

[90] de Fraine, a.a.O. 789.

[91] de Fraine, a.a.O. 790, mit Hinweis auf Tertullian, Adv. Marc. IV 1–2; Cyrill von Jerusalem, Catech. VI 16 (PG 33,565).

[92] de Fraine, a.a.O. 790. Er bezieht sich wohl auf die Textvarianten zu Lk 11,13, die πνεῦμα ἀγαθόν lesen (P^{45} L vg).

Eine spätere Einfügung der Geist-Bitte in den Lk-Text erkläre sich leicht: Die Anspielung auf den Täufer (Lk 11,1) konnte an dessen Verheißung (laut Mt 3,11) erinnern: »Der nach mir kommt ... wird euch mit heiligem Geist und Feuer taufen.« Andererseits scheine es sicher, daß man das Kommen des Heiligen Geistes als den Inhalt des Gottesreichs ansah[93].

Im Lauf der sechziger Jahre sprachen sich die Lk-Kommentare W. Grundmanns und K. H. Rengstorfs[94] sowie der Lexikon-Artikel J. Gnilkas und die Untersuchung J. Carmignacs[95] gegen die Ursprünglichkeit der Geist-Bitte aus. Auf der anderen Seite traten Ott und Freudenberger – wenn auch nicht mit völlig neuen Argumenten – für diese Bitte ein.

Die Würzburger Dissertation von W. Ott behandelt die Gebetsparänese bei Lukas und ihre Bedeutung für die lukanische Theologie. Dem auf das Bittgebet bezogenen Abschnitt Lk 11,11–13 sowie der lukanischen Form des Vaterunsers (11,2–4) ist jeweils ein eigener Paragraph gewidmet[96]. Ott glaubt (nach Registrierung der Textzeugen für die Geist-Bitte) feststellen zu können: »Seit einiger Zeit mehren sich die Stimmen, die hier die ursprüngliche lukanische Lesart erhalten sehen oder dies für wahrscheinlich halten – trotz der schwachen Textbezeugung.«[97] Zunächst referiert Ott über Harnacks Argumente und über die Gegenargumente v. Sodens[98]. Seine eigene Auffassung begründet er vor allem mit dem Hin-

---

[93] Ebd., mit Hinweis auf Gregor von Nyssa (PG 44,1157 C): τὸ δὲ πνεῦμα τὸ ἅγιον βασιλεία ἐστίν. Doch dies ist bei Gregor nicht am Kontext des lukanischen Werkes abgelesen (vgl. dazu oben Anm. 76), sondern an der Geist-Bitte, die er an der Stelle der Reichs-Bitte fand.

[94] Grundmann, Lk (1963) 232, fügt zu Lohmeyers Beobachtungen über atl. Paralleltexte noch den Hinweis auf 1 QH III 21 hinzu. Doch spricht dieser Text nicht von der Reinigung durch den Geist Gottes, sondern von einer Reinigung des verkehrten Geistes! Dagegen spricht 1 QS IV 21 von der Reinigung durch heiligen Geist. – Rengstorf, Lk (^{10}1965) 145f. (»Ergebnis der Verknüpfung von Vaterunser und Taufe im Blick auf den mit dieser verbundenen Empfang des Geistes«; mögliche Wurzeln in Lk 11,13).

[95] Siehe Gnilka, Vaterunser 625. Carmignac, Recherches 89–91, denkt daran, daß die Geist-Bitte eine liturgische Formel darstellt, die Marcion seinem Vaterunsertext einfügte (90). Sie paßt formal nicht zur Bitte um Heiligung des Namens Gottes und zu der um das Kommen seines Reiches (91).

[96] Ott, Gebet und Heil 102–112. 112–123 (§§ 16.17).

[97] Ott, a.a.O. 113. Er beginnt mit Harnack, Über einige Worte (1904), und endet mit Gräßer, Problem (1956), und Leaney, Lucan Text (1956). In der Aufzählung der Anwälte für die lukanische Echtheit der Geist-Bitte fehlen: Paslack, Bemerkungen; Streeter, Four Gospels; Klostermann, Lk, und Lampe, Holy Spirit. Wellhausen (Evangelium Lucae; Einleitung) kann – gegen Ott, a.a.O. 113 – nicht als Zeuge benannt werden; siehe oben Anm. 30. – Bei den Gegenstimmen, die Ott, a.a.O. 111 Anm. 44, aufführt, vermißt man folgende Autoren: Schürer, Rezension Paslack; Hönnicke, Forschungen; Plummer, Luke; Creed, Luke; Hauck, Lk; Lohmeyer, Vater-unser; Vogels, Handbuch; Knox, Sources; Rengstorf, Lk.

[98] Ott, a.a.O. 113–115.

weis auf Gräßers Auffassung über den Heiligen Geist als »Ersatz« für die ausgebliebene Parusie[99]. Als Problem empfindet Ott eigentlich nur die Frage: »Wenn Lukas aber die Reichsbitte durch die Geistbitte ersetzt hat, wie erklärt sich dann die Tatsache, daß Marcion die Geistbitte und die Reichsbitte nebeneinander hat?«[100] Die Antwort lautet: Die Abweichung geht auf Marcion selbst zurück, der alles Jüdische aus dem Neuen Testament entfernen wollte. Er verschob daher die Geist-Bitte nach vorn, an die Stelle der Bitte um Heiligung des göttlichen Namens[101]. Marcion bezeugt somit nicht eine eigene Überlieferung, »sondern diese Stellung der Geistbitte an erster Stelle bei Marcion geht auf seine antijüdischen Tendenzen ... zurück«[102].

Wenn der ursprüngliche Lk-Text die Reichs-Bitte und nicht die Geist-Bitte geboten hätte, wäre nach Ott das spätere Aufkommen einer Geist-Bitte an Stelle der Reichs-Bitte »völlig unerklärlich«[103]. Lukas habe »die Naherwartung aufgegeben und überwunden«; daher habe er an die Stelle der »Bitte um die Ankunft des Reiches die Bitte um das πνεῦμα ἅγιον als um das Gut der Zwischenzeit eingefügt«[104]. Ott hält – im Gegensatz zu dem maßgeblichen Konsens der heutigen Vaterunser-Forschung[105] – das lukanische Vaterunser »mit großer Sicherheit« für »eine Überarbeitung und Verkürzung des Vaterunsers in der matthäischen Form«[106].

R. Freudenberger wendet sich gegen Autoren, die die Geist-Bitte als »unjüdisch, ja als typisch christlich« empfanden und infolgedessen den Häretiker Marcion als ihren Verfasser ansehen konnten[107]. Skeptisch äußert sich Freudenberger auch gegenüber der Vermutung, die Geist-Bitte sei durch die Verwendung des Herrengebets anläßlich der Taufe entstanden[108]. Auch die Ansicht, daß Lk 11,13 oder Act 1,6–8 hinter der Geist-Bitte stehe und diese somit von Lukas selbst stamme, läßt er nicht gelten; Lukas habe keinen Grund gehabt, die Reichs-Bitte zu streichen[109]. Viel-

---

[99] Ott, a.a.O. 115f.; vgl. Gräßer, Problem 111; dazu oben Anm. 82.

[100] Ott, a.a.O. 116.

[101] Ebd.

[102] Ott, a.a.O. 117. Ott, a.a.O. 116 Anm. 50, beruft sich dafür auf folgende Vorgänger: v. Soden, Hensler, Fiebig. Er erwähnt ferner v. Baer und Harnack.

[103] Ott, a.a.O. 118.

[104] Ott, a.a.O. 119, unter Berufung auf Gräßer, Problem 110.

[105] Dieser wird z. B. repräsentiert von Jeremias, Vater-Unser 157–160; Vögtle, Der »eschatologische« Bezug 344–347, und Schürmann, Gebet des Herrn 17–20.

[106] Ott, Gebet und Heil 122.

[107] Freudenberger, Zum Text 427. Er nennt hierzu neben v. Baer, Der Heilige Geist 149–152, auch G. Dalman, Die Worte Jesu (^{2}1930), Darmstadt 1965, 319f.

[108] Freudenberger, a.a.O. 427.

[109] Freudenberger, a.a.O. 429f.

mehr müsse der Evangelist »die Bitte um das Kommen des Geistes und die Reinigung« bereits in seiner Quelle gefunden haben[110]. Wenn auch die Geist-Bitte schon »in der Logienquelle« (!) stand, sei sie doch nicht ursprünglich. Zuvor habe das Vaterunser – entsprechend der Harnackschen Hypothese – nur aus der Anrede, der Brot-Bitte und den beiden folgenden Bitten (Vergebung, Bewahrung vor Versuchung) bestanden[111].

Die siebziger Jahre brachten – abgesehen von dem Textual Commentary Metzgers – nur kurze Stellungnahmen zum Problem der Geist-Bitte in einigen neuen Lk-Kommentaren. Sie sprachen sich ohne Unterschied gegen die lukanische Echtheit der Geist-Bitte aus. F. W. Danker[112] zeigt einerseits, daß die Reichs-Bitte sich gut vereinbart mit des Lukas »two-stage view of the Kingdom«: Das Reich ist gegenwärtig in der Person Jesu und in der Verkündigung der Botschaft; aber der Jünger muß dennoch beten um dessen Verwirklichung in seiner eigenen Existenz und um dessen Vollendung am Ende der Endzeit. Auf der anderen Seite paßt auch die Geist-Bitte zu der Auffassung des Lukas über die Bedeutung der Geist-Gabe (Lk 11,13). Doch die Geist-Bitte ist eher eine postlukanische Verdeutlichung, die später liturgischen Rang erhielt und die Reichs-Bitte verdrängte. – J. Ernst[113] hält die Geist-Bitte im Lk-Text für unecht. Ihre Einfügung sei allerdings ein interessantes Zeugnis für die liturgische Verwendung des Herrengebets (wahrscheinlich als Initiationsgebet bei der Taufe). – I. H. Marshall[114] meint, die Formulierung der Geist-Bitte sei gut lukanisch; er nennt dazu Lk 11,13; Act 4,31; 10,15; 11,8; 15,9. Die Bitte habe aber auch einen alttestamentlichen und jüdischen Hintergrund. Doch könnten alle Argumente zugunsten der Geist-Bitte nicht gegen das einmütige Zeugnis der griechischen Handschriften aufkommen, in denen die Geist-Bitte fehlt. Sie erkläre sich aus liturgischem Gebrauch, der den Lk-Text kontaminierte. – W. Schmithals[115] sieht in der Bitte um den Geist eine spätere Änderung des Lk-Textes, die »den für Lukas wichtigen Unterschied der gegenwärtigen Zeit des Geistes von der kommenden Gottesherrschaft« verwische.

Der Kommentar, den B. M. Metzger zum Greek New Testament schrieb, hält – wie die neueren Lk-Kommentare – die Geist-Bitte Lk 11,2 für eine nach-lukanische Änderung[116]. Er zeigt, daß das ἐφ' ἡμᾶς des Codex Bezae (in v. 2 vor der Reichs-Bitte) nicht als Argument zugunsten einer früher vorhandenen Geist-Bitte gewertet werden darf[117]. Die Bitte um den Geist sei aus dem liturgischen Gebrauch (bei Taufe oder Handauflegung) in das Vaterunser eingedrungen. Hätte die Bitte um Reinigung durch den Geist Gottes ursprünglich im Vaterunser gestanden, dann habe man keinen Grund gehabt, sie in den meisten Textzeugen zu beseitigen[118].

---

[110] Freudenberger, a.a.O. 430.

[111] Freudenberger, a.a.O. 431. Vgl. Harnack, Über einige Worte 208; siehe dagegen Greeven, Gebet und Eschatologie 75–77.

[112] Danker, Luke 135.

[113] Ernst, Lk 362.

[114] Marshall, Luke 458.

[115] Schmithals, Lk 132f.

[116] Metzger, Textual Commentary 154–156.

[117] Metzger, a.a.O. 155.

[118] Metzger, a.a.O. 156.

3. Zusammenfassung und methodische Überlegungen

Die unterschiedlichen Argumente, die seit hundert Jahren für und gegen die lukanische Ursprünglichkeit der Geist-Bitte vorgebracht wurden, haben zwar inzwischen dazu geführt, daß die Ursprünglichkeitsthese kaum noch vertreten wird. Die Argumente sind aber doch nicht dergestalt ins Spiel gekommen, daß man von der einen oder anderen Position gänzlich überzeugt worden wäre.

Zunächst sei in einer Übersicht zusammengestellt, wer sich *für* die Verankerung der Geist-Bitte im dritten Evangelium aussprach (linke Spalte) und wer sich *gegen* die Zugehörigkeit zum Lk-Text wandte (rechte Spalte):

Resch	1889	
	1891	Chase, Zahn
Resch	1895	
Blass	1897	
Harnack, Spitta	1904	v. Soden
Paslack	1905	Schürer
G. Klein	1906	Hönnicke
	1913	Zahn
	1914	Hensler
J. Weiß	1917	
Leisegang	1922	Plummer
Loisy, Streeter	1924	
	1926	v. Baer
	1927	Fiebig, Lagrange
Klostermann	1929	
	1930	Creed
Greeven	1931	
	1934	Hauck
	1946	Lohmeyer
Lampe	1955	Schmid, Vogels
Gräßer, Leaney	1956	
	1957	W. L. Knox
	1960	de Fraine
	1963	Grundmann
Ott	1965	Gnilka, Rengstorf
Freudenberger	1969	Carmignac
	1971	Metzger
	1972	Danker
	1977	Ernst
	1978	Marshall
	1980	Schmithals
	1981	Greeven

In methodischer Hinsicht ist zunächst einmal festzuhalten, daß die »äußeren« Kriterien für die Echtheit der Geist-Bitte im Lk-Text schwach sind. Zwar können für eine Geist-Bitte außerhalb des Herrengebets verschiedene Zeugnisse angeführt werden[119]. Doch gibt es für die Verankerung dieser Bitte im Vaterunser nur vier Textzeugen, von denen wiederum nur zwei Evangelienhandschriften sind. Die vier Zeugen (Gregor von Nyssa, Maximus Confessor sowie die Codices 700 und 162) sind außerdem vermutlich von einander nicht unabhängig[120]. Der rekonstruierbare Vaterunsertext Marcions zeigt zwar, daß man die Geist-Bitte schon früh mit dem Gebet des Herrn verband. Jedoch lag ihre Stellung im Gesamtgefüge der Einzelbitten offensichtlich noch nicht fest. Die Hypothese einer ursprünglich am Rande notierten Glosse, die schließlich als Textkorrektur (und nicht als Kommentierung) verstanden und in den Text selbst aufgenommen wurde[121], kann den Befund der Textzeugen erklären. Gegen die Möglichkeit, daß Gregor von Nyssa und die späteren Zeugen der Geist-Bitte von Marcion abhängig sein könnten, spricht zunächst die Vermutung, daß man kirchlicherseits kaum dem Erzhäretiker gefolgt sein würde.

Geht man einmal von der Hypothese einer ursprünglichen Randglosse aus, so fragt es sich, wie die Geist-Bitte – für sich genommen – entstand, wo sie selbständig existierte und wann sie möglicherweise als Glosse neben den Vaterunsertext geriet (4). Dennoch bleibt zu erörtern, ob sie nicht doch im Rahmen der lukanischen Geist-Theologie (auf »lukanisch-redaktionellem Wege«) entstanden sein kann (5). Die letztere Fragestellung ist zwar nicht neu, sie kann aber mit neuen redaktionskritischen Argumenten erörtert werden.

4. Zur Entstehung der Geist-Bitte

Schon Harnack erwähnte als Parallelen zur Geist-Bitte im lukanischen Vaterunser neben Acta Thomae 27 (ed. Bonnet) auch die Liturgie von Konstantinopel[122]. Die Thomasakten enthalten die Geist-Bitte in ei-

---

[119] Bisher wurden dafür vor allem folgende Zeugnisse angeführt: Acta Thomae 27 (ed. Bonnet); Liturgie von Konstantinopel (nach einem Ms. des 6. Jh.s; bei Chase, Lord's Prayer 29). Einen Hinweis gibt auch Tertullian, De bapt. 8: *Dehinc manus imponitur per benedictionem advocans et invitans spiritum sanctum.*

[120] Vgl. v. Soden, Gestalt 219. – Carmignac, Recherches 89, zählt zu den Zeugen für die Geist-Bitte auch »Anspielungen« bei Euagrios Pontikos († 399) und Severus von Antiochia († 538). Dazu verweist er auf koptische Übersetzungen bei A. Mallon, Grammaire copte ... Chrestomathie, Beirut ²1907, 80 bzw. 77. Euagrios hat das Ideengut des Origenes und des Gregor von Nyssa »eigenständig für eine Theorie der Vollkommenheit verarbeitet«; für Maximus Confessor war er der eigentliche Meister (K. Baus in: LThK² III 1140).

[121] Siehe v. Soden, a.a.O. 223.

[122] Harnack, Über einige Worte 197. Er spricht von »indirekten Zeugen«.

nem Initiationsgebet, und zwar als an den Heiligen Geist gerichteten Imperativ:

ἐλθὲ τὸ ἅγιον πνεῦμα
καὶ καθάρισον τοὺς νεφροὺς αὐτῶν καὶ τὴν καρδίαν,
καὶ ἐπισφράγισον αὐτοὺς
εἰς ὄνομα πατρὸς καὶ υἱοῦ καὶ ἁγίου πνεύματος.

In der Chrysostomus-Liturgie[123] wird bei der Eucharistie um das Kommen des Geistes gerufen:

Βασιλεῦ οὐράνιε, παράκλητε, τὸ πνεῦμα τῆς ἀληθείας ...
ἐλθὲ καὶ σκήνωσον ἐν ἡμῖν,
καὶ καθάρισον ἡμᾶς ἀπὸ πάσης κηλῖδος,
καὶ σῶσον, ἀγαθέ, τὰς ψυχὰς ἡμῶν.

In beiden Fällen wird der Heilige Geist direkt angerufen, um sein »Kommen« sowie um »Reinigung« gebeten. Diese drei Punkte sind beachtenswert.

1. Gegenüber der Geist-Bitte des Vaterunsers ist die direkt an das Pneuma gerichtete Bitte wahrscheinlich späteren Datums[124]. In den Thomasakten zeigt der trinitarische Schluß[125] und in der Liturgie von Konstantinopel die Paraklet-Bezeichnung[126], daß der Heilige Geist eindeutig »personal« verstanden ist und daher vom Beter »eingeladen« werden kann[127].

---

[123] Zitiert bei Chase, Lord's Prayer 29 (im Anschluß an C. A. Swainson, The Greek Liturgies, Cambridge 1884, 109).

[124] Vgl. dazu auch den mittelalterlichen Pfingsthymnus »*Veni Creator Spiritus*« (Hrabanus Maurus zugeschrieben, der 856 starb) sowie die Pfingstsequenz des Stephan Langton († 1228) *Veni Sancte Spiritus,* die erst 1570 (Pius V.) in das römische Missale Eingang fand. Zu vergleichen ist auch das wohl ältere *Veni, Sancte Spiritus, reple tuorum corda fidelium, et tui amoris in eis ignem accende,* das sich in folgenden Meßbüchern findet: Troyes (12. Jh.); Langres (13. Jh.); Agde (14. Jh.), siehe J. O. Bragança, L'Esprit Saint dans l'euchologie médiévale, in: Le Saint-Esprit dans la liturgie. XVIe Semaine d'études liturgiques (1969) (BEL. S 8), Rom 1977, 39–53, 41 Anm. 8. Siehe ferner das gleiche Gebet in der Liturgie der Priesterweihe und der Altarweihe im Pontificale des Durandus: M. Andrieu, Le Pontifical Romain au moyen-age III. Le Pontifical de G. Durand (StT 88), Rom 1940, 369,2; 492,1f.; 502,17 [Freundlicher Hinweis meines Bochumer Kollegen Dr. A. Gerhards].

[125] Vgl. dazu den »Taufbefehl« Mt 28,19b. In den Thomasakten (50) findet sich ein weiteres Gebet, in dem wenigstens der syrische Text die Zeile »Komm, heiliger Geist« liest.

[126] Siehe dazu Joh 15,26 und 16,13, wo nicht nur vom Parakleten, sondern auch von seinem künftigen »Kommen« (ἔρχομαι) die Rede ist. An beiden Stellen wird er τὸ πνεῦμα τῆς ἀληθείας genannt.

[127] Vgl. Tertullian, De bapt. 8; siehe oben Anm. 119. Zu beachten ist auch die gegen die Pneumatomachen geführte Argumentation zugunsten der Gottheit des Heiligen Geistes, bei der die ihm gebührende »Anbetung« und »Verehrung« hervorgehoben wird: Atha-

2. Vom ἔρχεσθαι des Gottesgeistes reden – außer Joh 15,26; 16,7.13[128] – im Neuen Testament nur noch Mt 3,16[129] und Act 19,6[130]. Jedoch sind auch noch jene Stellen einzubeziehen, die in diesem Zusammenhang ἐπέρχομαι verwenden: Lk 1,35; Act 1,8[131]. Die Redeweise vom Kommen des Geistes über/auf einen Menschen begegnet im Alten Testament z. B. Ez 2,2; 3,24[132]. An keiner dieser Stellen wird jedoch um das »Kommen« des Geistes *gebetet*[133].

3. Die Bitte um »Reinigung« (von »Herz und Nieren« bzw. »von jeglichem Schandfleck«) geht wahrscheinlich letztlich auf Ez 36,25–27 zurück, wo nach der Zusage καθαρισθήσεσθε (v. 25) die Gaben eines neuen Herzens und eines neuen Geistes (v. 26) sowie des Geistes Gottes (v. 27: τὸ πνεῦμά μου δώσω ἐν ὑμῖν) verheißen werden[134]. Die Geist-Bitte des Vaterunsers mit der Bitte um »Reinigung« wird verschiedentlich mit Act 15,8f. in Verbindung gebracht[135]. An dieser Stelle spricht Petrus aus, daß Gott für die Heiden Partei ergriffen hat, indem er ihnen den Heiligen Geist schenkte (v. 9; vgl. 11,17). Im Zusammenhang damit stellt er fest,

---

nasius, Vier Briefe an Serapion von Thmuis (358/62; SCh 15); Gregor von Nazianz, Fünf theologische Reden (380 in Konstantinopel; PG 36,9–172), z. B. V 28 (PG 36,165); Symbolum »Constantinopolitanum« (DS 150; vgl. Epiphanius von Salamis, DS 42). – Ein Beispiel für die m. E. »ältere« Bitte *an Gott* um den Heiligen Geist findet sich in den Homilien, die Makarios dem Ägypter († um 390) zugeschrieben wurden, deren Autor vielleicht jedoch Symeon von Mesopotamien, ein Schüler der Kappadokier, ist (H. C. Graef in: LThK² VI 1309f.): Macarius Aeg., Hom. XVIII 2. 11 (PG 34, 636 B. 641 B).

128 Vgl. oben Anm. 126.

129 Die Stelle spricht (diff. Mk 1,10) vom »Kommen« des Geistes Gottes auf Jesus (ἐπ' αὐτόν) bei der Taufe.

130 Durch die Handauflegung des Paulus »kam der heilige Geist« auf die Johannesjünger (ἐπ' αὐτούς).

131 Die beiden Stellen, die Maria und den Aposteln das Kommen des Heiligen Geistes ankündigen, sind nach Lukas wohl aufeinander bezogen (vgl. die Stellung am Anfang von Lk bzw. Act).

132 Das hat schon Lohmeyer, Vater-unser 186, beobachtet. Siehe auch Herm, m XI 43,17.21, wo jedoch vom ἔρχεσθαι im Hinblick auf den Ausgangspunkt (ἀπὸ τοῦ θεοῦ, ἄνωθεν) die Rede ist.

133 Siehe indessen den indirekten Zusammenhang Act 1,8 (mit 1,14); 19,6 (mit 8,15–17); ferner Lk 3,21f. (mit καταβαίνω).

134 Zu vergleichen ist auch Ps 50 LXX mit der Bitte καθάρισόν με (v. 4), dem zuversichtlichen καθαρισθήσομαι (v. 9), der Bitte um »ein reines Herz« und »einen bereitwilligen Geist« (v. 12), schließlich der Bitte: »deinen heiligen Geist nimm nicht von mir!« (v. 13).

135 Harnack, Über einige Worte 199, sah in Act 15,8f. »eine schlagende Parallele« zur Geist-Bitte. Dagegen schon v. Soden, Gestalt 222: Act 15,8f. »erscheint die Reinigung in der Nähe des heiligen Geistes, aber doch nicht als durch ihn, sondern als durch den Glauben bewirkt. Daß der heilige Geist reinige, ist nirgends im Neuen Testament gesagt, so viel von seinen Wirkungen geredet wird.«

daß Gott τῇ πίστει »ihre [der Heiden] Herzen gereinigt hat (καθαρίσας)« (v. 10). Da nun das Neue Testament davon überzeugt ist, daß die Getauften den Heiligen Geist *empfangen haben* und durch den Glauben *gereinigt sind,* ist es schwer vorstellbar, daß ein Christ im Zusammenhang mit dem täglich gesprochenen Gebet des Herrn[136] um das Kommen des Geistes und die Reinigung gebetet haben soll. Der Beter, der so spricht, hat eine nach-neutestamentliche Auffassung über das Kommen des Geistes, das sich je neu bei ihm ereignen kann[137]. Nimmt man aber die Bitte um den Geist für sich und nicht als das Gebet eines Christen, so kommen Beter in Betracht, die – wie die Johannesjünger[138] – das endzeitliche Kommen des Heiligen Geistes erflehen, oder solche, die anderen die Taufe spenden (Acta Thomae 27) oder selbst vor dem Empfang der Taufe stehen.

H. v. Soden wollte den Ursprung der Geist-Bitte in der Taufbewegung des Johannes finden. Der Heilige Geist sei »Gegenstand der Sehnsucht und der Verheißung des Täufers«, seine Taufe »nur ein Sinnbild der Buße«[139]. Erst der Messias, »der mit dem heiligen Geist und mit Feuer tauft« (Lk 3,16), bringe »Reinigung«[140]. Somit passe die Geist-Bitte trefflich »für die durch die Taufe sich für die messianische Zeit Rüstenden«[141]. Demgegenüber wird man die »messianische« Verkündigung des Täufers nicht einfach für sein Selbstverständnis und seine Taufauffassung beanspruchen dürfen. Die von ihm gespendete einmalige Bußtaufe zur Sündenvergebung bot in seinem Verständnis vielmehr die »allerletzte, einzige und einmalige Möglichkeit, ... eventuell vor dem Feuer bewahrt zu bleiben«[142] . Nur durch seine Taufe, verbunden mit der Umkehr, ist überhaupt noch Sündenvergebung möglich[143]. Ein Gebet um das Kommen des Gottesgeistes (in messianischer Zeit) zur »Reinigung« hat in einem solchen Horizont der Naherwartung des Gerichts kaum einen Platz.

Wenn man auch Johannes dem Täufer die Ankündigung einer Taufe »mit heiligem Geist« (Mk 1,8 par. Mt 3,11/Lk 3,16), die durch den »Kommenden« vollzogen werden soll, wird absprechen müssen, so ist doch klar, daß man in der christlichen Jesusüberlieferung den Unterschied zwischen Johannes und Jesus in jenem Logion von der künftigen Geist-Taufe charakterisiert sah. Es ist daher nicht auszuschließen, daß man im Anschluß an ein solches Wort dem Täuferkreis eine Bitte um das Kommen des Gottesgeistes zur Reinigung zuschrieb und diese dann als »Kommentar« neben Lk 11,1 notierte[144]. Doch scheint es eher so zu sein, daß die gleiche christliche Sicht über das Charakteristikum der christlichen Taufe (als einer

---

[136] Vgl. die Brotbitte Lk 11,3 par. Mt 6,11; ferner Did 8,3.

[137] Siehe z. B. die oben Anm. 124 erwähnten Gebete um das Kommen des Heiligen Geistes.

[138] Vgl. v. Soden, Gestalt 222f.; Klein, Gestalt 44. Letzterer vermutet, daß man in christlichen Kreisen »bezugnehmend auf Ez 36,25 das Taufgebet des Johannes sich aneignete« (46).

[139] v. Soden, Gestalt 222.

[140] Ebd., mit Hinweis auf Mt 3,12 par. Lk 3,17 »er wird seine Tenne reinigen«. Zu Mk 1,8 (par. Mt 3,11/Lk 3,16) siehe R. Pesch, Das Markusevangelium I (HThK II 1), Freiburg 1976, 83–85.

[141] v. Soden, a.a.O. 222.

[142] J. Becker, Johannes der Täufer und Jesus von Nazareth (BSt 63), Neukirchen 1972, 40.

[143] Ebd.

[144] Vgl. v. Soden, a.a.O. 223.

Geist-Taufe) sowohl dem Johannes zugeschriebenen Logion (Mk 1,8 par.) als auch einer christlichen Bitte anläßlich der Taufspendung zugrunde liegt.

Es gibt Hinweise darauf, daß man auf christlicher Seite dem bei der Taufe kommenden Heiligen Geist gerade die »Reinigung« von den Sünden zuschrieb. Zwei Beispiele dafür bieten die »Konstitutionen der ägyptischen Kirche« (um 500), die u. a. das nach der Taufe auf Befragung abzulegende Glaubensbekenntnis formulieren. In der koptischen und der äthiopischen Rezension der Konstitutionen wird dabei vom Heiligen Geist gesagt: *qui omnia purificat* bzw. *et qui purificat*[145].

Leider wissen wir nicht genau, seit wann anläßlich der Taufe das Vaterunser gebetet oder dem Täufling »übergeben« wurde. In liturgischem Zusammenhang scheint jedoch das Gebet des Herrn zuerst bei der Taufspendung verwendet worden zu sein[146]. Im Abendland bezeugt Augustinus den Brauch der Übergabe des Herrengebets kurz vor der Taufe[147]. Diese *traditio orationis dominicae* wurde etwa im 7. Jahrhundert zu einem feierlichen Ritus[148].

Nach dem Gesagten darf man wohl einen Ursprung der Geist-Bitte im Zusammenhang mit der Taufspendung als Möglichkeit in Rechnung stellen. Da wir nicht wissen, wann erstmals bei der Taufe das Vaterunser Verwendung fand, bleibt es zunächst noch offen, wann eine Geist-Bitte in das Herrengebet Eingang fand. Abgesehen davon, daß man die Bitte um das Kommen des Geistes kaum Jesus selbst zuschreiben kann[149], ist es auch unwahrscheinlich, daß man sie schon zur Zeit des Lukas mit dem Vaterunser verband. Trotzdem dürfen wir eine solche Möglichkeit nicht von vornherein ausschließen; ebensowenig darf es als unmöglich gelten, daß Lukas selbst die Geist-Bitte gebildet habe[150]. Hier ist indessen – von der möglichen Voraussetzung aus, daß diese Bitte separat existierte – zu fragen, wie sie in das lukanische Vaterunser eindrang, vor allem auch, wie es zu ihrer unterschiedlichen Einordnung in den Zusammenhang des Vaterunsers kommen konnte.

Bei der Frage, wann und aus welchen Gründen eine Bitte um das Kommen des Heiligen Geistes in das Vaterunser eingefügt worden sein

---

145 Siehe DS 62f. Vgl. Augustinus, Sermo 215 in redditione symboli (PL 38, 1072–1076).

146 Vgl. Const. apost. VII 45 (ed. F. X. Funk).

147 Siehe z. B. Augustinus, Sermones 56–59 (PL 38, 377–402); dazu F. van der Meer, Augustinus der Seelsorger, Köln 1951, 423; G. Kretschmar, Die Geschichte des Taufgottesdienstes in der alten Kirche, in: Leiturgia V, Kassel 1970, 1–348, näherhin 157f.

148 J. A. Jungmann, Vaterunser II, in: LThK² X 627–629.

149 Siehe E. Schweizer, Heiliger Geist, Stuttgart/Berlin 1978, 69: »Jesus hat kaum je vom Geist gesprochen.« Vgl. ders. in: ThWNT VI 400: »Matthäus und Markus enthalten erstaunlich wenige Geistaussagen. Nur eine einzige (Mk 13,11 Par) ist mit einiger Gewißheit in ihrer Substanz auf Jesus zurückzuführen.«

150 Diese Frage soll unten unter 5. behandelt werden.

könnte, ist von der ältesten erreichbaren Fassung dieses Gebets auszugehen, wie sie aus den Formen der Evangelien nach Matthäus und nach Lukas gewonnen werden kann. Diese Fassung hatte drei Abschnitte: die Anrede, zwei Du-Bitten und drei Wir-Bitten. Nach der Rekonstruktion von A. Vögtle ist etwa mit folgendem Wortlaut zu rechnen[151]:

I Vater!
II 1. Geheiligt werde dein Name,
2. es komme dein Reich!
III 1. Unser Brot ... gib uns heute
2. und vergib uns unsere Schulden
(wie auch wir vergeben unseren Schuldigern)
3. und laß uns nicht in Versuchung geraten!

Dieser Aufbau entspricht der bestbezeugten Lk-Fassung. Im Mt-Evangelium begegnet demgegenüber eine erweiterte Form. Daß es sich um wirkliche Erweiterungen handelt, geht aus zwei Beobachtungen hervor: Die Lk-Fassung ist in der des Mt-Evangeliums voll enthalten; die »Erweiterungen« stehen jeweils am Ende der Abschnitte: I. »unser, der in den Himmeln«; II. »es geschehe dein Wille (wie im Himmel so auch auf Erden)»; III. »sondern errette uns vor dem Bösen«. Dieses Verfahren, ein Gebet durch Zusätze oder Einschaltungen aufzufüllen, entspricht *liturgischem Gebrauch,* wie z. B. auch die in manchen Textzeugen angehängte Doxologie zeigt[152]. Ein anderes Verfahren wenden hingegen jene Textzeugen an, die im Vaterunser die Geist-Bitte bieten. Denn sie »ersetzen« jeweils eine der Du-Bitten. Ein derartiges Verfahren scheint eher auf das *individuelle Bemühen* eines Redaktors zurückzugehen.

Hinsichtlich der Frage, ob Marcion die Geist-Bitte in das Gebet des Herrn eingefügt haben könne – sei es, daß er sie als Einzelbitte schon vorfand, oder, daß er sie von sich aus schuf –, gehen die Auffassungen auseinander. Th. Zahn vertrat die Ansicht, daß Marcion die Bitte um Heiligung des göttlichen Namens »unerträglich« fand, weil Marcions Gott die Welt nicht geschaffen habe und nicht regiere. Seine Heiligkeit sei daher »auch durch das, was in der Welt des Demiurgen geschieht, gar nicht in

[151] Vögtle, Der »eschatologische« Bezug 347 (»als von Jesus selbst gesprochene Gebetsanweisung«). Siehe auch Jeremias, Vater-Unser 155, und Schürmann, Gebet des Herrn 17–20.

[152] Mt 6,13c nach L W Θ 0233 usw. (Didache 8,2). Vielleicht ist auch das »wie im Himmel ...« nach der dritten Du-Bitte als frühe sekundäre Erweiterung zu verstehen. Weil man die Erweiterungen in Mt 6,9–13 als solche des liturgischen Gebrauchs ansehen muß, entstammen sie wohl kaum der »Redaktion« des Evangelisten. – Zur Erweiterung von Gebeten im Judentum siehe z. B. Bill. IV 208–220 (18-Bitten-Gebet); I. Elbogen, Der jüdische Gottesdienst in seiner geschichtlichen Entwicklung, Hildesheim 1962 (= [3]1931), 92–98 (Kaddisch).

Frage gestellt«[153]. Zahn erkennt an, daß bei dieser Überlegung Marcion konsequenterweise auch die Reichs-Bitte hätte tilgen müssen[154]. Bei der Brot-Bitte hat Marcion nachweislich in den Text eingegriffen, indem er ἡμῶν durch σοῦ ersetzte. Geist-Bitte und Brot-Bitte geben der Reichs-Bitte (und dem Vaterunser insgesamt) eine geistliche, auf das himmlische Reich bezogene Note[155]. Dennoch kann man nicht sagen, daß die Geist-Bitte als solche und ihrem Inhalt nach spezifisch marcionitisch sei[156].

Geht man von der Voraussetzung aus, daß die Geist-Bitte schon (als Täufergebet?) am Rande des Lk-Textes stand, den Marcion »korrigierte«, so wird man nur bei Annahme eines Irrtums vermuten können, Marcion habe diese Bitte an die erste Stelle des Herrengebets gestellt. Geht man aber davon aus, daß es die Geist-Bitte (als christliche Taufbitte) schon gab, und daß Marcion sie von sich aus in das Vaterunser einfügte, so muß man ein Motiv dafür suchen, warum sie an die erste Stelle der Bitten rückte. Die gleiche Frage nach dem Motiv ist zu stellen, falls bei Marcion mit der Geist-Bitte nicht die Wendungen ἐφ' ἡμᾶς sowie καὶ καθαρισάτω ἡμᾶς verbunden waren[157]. Dieses Motiv konnte für Marcion Lk 11,13 bieten. Wenn es dort heißt, der himmlische Vater werde denen, die ihn bitten, »den heiligen Geist geben«, so wird Marcion daraus gefolgert haben, daß man als erste Bitte die um den Heiligen Geist aussprechen müsse. Bei diesem Verfahren wäre es möglich gewesen, die Geist-Bitte einfach vor die beiden vorhandenen Du-Bitten zu stellen. Doch wollte Marcion wohl das doppelte ἐλθέτω, das uns heute von der Form her stören mag, als Signal verstanden wissen: Das Kommen des Geistes ist mit dem des Reiches *identisch* oder geht diesem unmittelbar voraus. *Für uns* bedeutet das Kommen der Basileia, daß uns der Geist geschenkt wird. Eine derartige Hypothese kann sich darauf stützen, daß Marcion bei Paulus die Stichworte für seine Änderungen vorfinden konnte: »Das Reich Gottes ist

---

153 Zahn, Vaterunser 410. Nach v. Soden, Gestalt 223, erinnerte die erste Bitte Marcion »zu sehr an den Jehova der Juden«.

154 Zahn, a.a.O. 410f. So auch Harnack, Über einige Worte 200.

155 Vgl. Zahn, a.a.O. 411: »daß die Bitte um das Kommen des Reiches Gottes nun nicht mehr von irgend welcher Umwälzung der irdischen Welt, sondern nur noch von dem geistlichen und himmlischen Reiche verstanden werde, dessen einzige Güter [laut Röm 14,17!] ›Gerechtigkeit und Friede und Freude im heiligen Geist‹ sind«.

156 Spitta, Die älteste Form 336, meinte: »Die Theologie des Marcion gibt keinen Erklärungsgrund für eine Ersetzung der rezipierten Form der ersten Bitte durch dieses Gebet um den heiligen Geist.« Zu beachten ist auch, daß Tertullian gegen die Vaterunser-Fassung Marcions nicht polemisiert (Adv. Marc. IV 26). Doch will Tertullian nachweisen, daß sich sogar das verstümmelte Evangelium Marcions gegen die Unterscheidung des guten Gottes vom Schöpfergott sträubt; siehe Freudenberger, Zum Text 420.

157 Zur Rekonstruktion siehe außer Harnack, Marcion (^{2}1924) 207*, auch Freudenberger, a.a.O. 420.

nicht Essen und Trinken, sondern Gerechtigkeit, Friede und Freude *im heiligen Geist*« (Röm 14,17).

Bei Gregor von Nyssa, der die Geist-Bitte in seinem Lk-Text des Vaterunsers las, stand diese Bitte an der Stelle der Reichs-Bitte. Sie folgte als zweite Du-Bitte auf die Bitte um Heiligung des Namens[158]. Falls man der Hypothese von einer Geist-Bitte als Randglosse zu Lk 11,1 oder 11,2 folgt, kann man vermuten, daß diese Glosse schon in der Lk-Handschrift Gregors in den Text selbst geraten war und dort die Reichs-Bitte ersetzte. Doch müßte man in diesem Fall eher annehmen, daß die Geist-Bitte zu den übrigen Bitten *hinzugetreten* wäre. Falls sie hingegen die Reichs-Bitte verdrängte, kann hinter einem solchen Vorgehen nur Absicht gestanden haben. Wenn Marcion für seine »Korrektur« möglicherweise Lk 11,13 (und Röm 14,17) beanspruchen konnte, so konnte ein vor Gregor lebender Abschreiber des Lk-Evangeliums außer Lk 11,13 auch Act 1,6–8 mit in Betracht ziehen[159] und sich von dieser Stelle aus für berechtigt halten, die Reichs-Bitte durch die Geist-Bitte zu ersetzen[160].

Gregor kommt in seiner dritten Rede über das Gebet des Herrn[161] auf die Geist-Bitte des Lk-Textes zu sprechen. Die Geist-Bitte kommt ihm in seinem Kampf gegen die Pneumatomachen zustatten. Was Lukas Heiligen Geist nennt, heiße bei Matthäus das Reich. Wie können es da die Gegner verantworten, den Heiligen Geist zu einer Kreatur zu degradieren »und ihn statt mit der herrschenden mit der beherrschten Natur« auf gleiche Linie zu stellen? Aus dem Vergleich des ersten und des dritten Evangeliums ergebe sich die Gleichbedeutung von Heiligem Geist und Reich Gottes. Ist aber »Geist« gleich »Basileia«, »so folgt notwendig, daß er herrscht und nicht beherrscht wird«. Dem Heiligen Geist als besonderer Kraft und Wirksamkeit sei die Fähigkeit eigen, zu läutern (καθαίρειν) und die Sünden nachzulassen. Gregor, der im übrigen das matthäische Vaterunser erklärt, greift auf den Lk-Text zurück, weil er dort die Bitte um das Kommen des Geistes findet. Was er aus der Ersetzung der Reichs-Bitte durch die Geist-Bitte folgert, kann auch schon zuvor ein biblisch versierter Abschreiber des dritten Evangeliums – im Anschluß an Act 1,6–8 – durch eine »Korrektur« im Lk-Text verankert haben. Woher er seine Geist-Bitte bezog – aus der Überlieferung einer Taufbitte oder aus

[158] Sieh oben Anm. 21.

[159] Vgl. dazu die Argumentation bei Gräßer, Problem 111 (zugunsten eines *lukanischen* Ursprungs der Geist-Bitte).

[160] Act 1,6 läßt die Jünger nach dem Zeitpunkt der Errichtung der βασιλεία fragen. V. 8 antwortet Jesus positiv (mit einem ἀλλά eingeführt), daß die Jünger »den heiligen Geist empfangen« werden, »der auf sie kommt« (ἐπελθόντος ... ἐφ' ὑμᾶς). Zur Verwendung von ἔρχομαι und ἐφ' ἡμᾶς in der Geist-Bitte, die Gregor von Nyssa vorfand (siehe oben Anm. 21), siehe auch Act 19,6: ἦλθε τὸ πνεῦμα τὸ ἅγιον ἐπ' αὐτούς.

[161] Gregor von Nyssa, De oratione dominica III 5 (PG 44, 1157–1162).

dem Text Marcions –, wissen wir nicht. Sollte er von Marcion abhängig sein, so hätte er diesem gegenüber die erste Bitte wieder an ihren Platz gerückt. Diesem Abschreiber, dessen Text in der Minuskel 700 erhalten blieb[162], müßte man freilich eine hervorragende Kenntnis des lukanischen Doppelwerks zutrauen. Liegt es da nicht näher, in diesem »Kenner« des lukanischen Werkes dessen Verfasser selbst zu sehen und somit die Geist-Bitte doch für die ursprüngliche Lesart des Lukas zu halten?

5. Geht die Geist-Bitte auf lukanische »Redaktion« zurück?

Die unter 4. vorgeschlagene Hypothese, daß die Geist-Bitte des Vaterunsers auf bewußte »Redaktion« des Marcion oder eines späteren Abschreibers des Lk-Textes zurückgehe, wurde hauptsächlich auf zwei Beobachtungen gestützt. Zum ersten sprach für einen absichtlich »korrigierenden« Redaktor, daß sowohl Marcion als auch die späteren Zeugen Gregor von Nyssa und Codex 700 mit der Geist-Bitte eine andere Bitte verdrängen. Hinzu kam, daß die Fassung des Marcion vom dritten Evangelium her (Lk 11,13) inspiriert sein kann, die späteren Zeugen der Geist-Bitte jedoch wahrscheinlich das lukanische Gesamtwerk (vor allem auch Act 1,6–8) berücksichtigen, was einerseits dem Kanon Marcions, andererseits dem seit etwa 200 n. Chr. üblichen Kanon entspricht[163].

Obgleich die so begründete Hypothese angesichts der relativ schwachen »äußeren« Bezeugung der Geist-Bitte in Lk 11,2 an sich plausibel ist – zumal man für die Entstehung der Bitte um das Kommen des Geistes die Situation des Taufempfangs veranschlagen kann –, bleibt doch zu prüfen, ob nicht schon Lukas selbst diese Bitte in das Vaterunser einfügte. Bei dieser Prüfung sind zwei Möglichkeiten in Betracht zu ziehen: a) Die Geist-Bitte ersetzt die *erste* Vaterunserbitte (so Marcion); b) sie steht an Stelle der *Reichs*-Bitte (so die späteren Textzeugen).

a) Wo die Geist-Bitte als erste Vaterunser-Bitte erscheint, kann man vermuten, dies hänge mit dem lukanisch-redaktionellen Versteil 11,13b zusammen, wo Lukas das Textstück über die Gebetserhörung (aus Q) 11,9–13 (par. Mt 7,7–11) mit der Folgerung beschließt: Gott wird als Vater vom Himmel her »denen den heiligen Geist geben, die ihn bitten«[164]. Sieht man genauer hin, spricht Lukas hier nicht davon, daß man

[162] Siehe dazu oben Anm. 2. Der Vaterunser-Text von 700 enthält indessen bei Lk auch die »dritte« Bitte nach Mt; vgl. oben Anm. 26.

[163] Vgl. dazu Wikenhauser/Schmid, Einleitung in das Neue Testament, Freiburg ^{6}1973, 36–39 (zu Marcion); 39–44 (Abendland um 200 n. Chr.); 44–53 (kirchlicher Osten).

[164] Zum lukanischen Redaktionsverfahren, das ἀγαθά durch πνεῦμα ἅγιον ersetzt, siehe z. B. S. Schulz, Q. Die Spruchquelle der Evangelisten, Zürich 1972, 162; R. A. Piper, Matthew 7,7–11 par. Luke 11,9–13. Evidence of Design and Argument in the Collection of

um den Geist bitten solle, sondern er ersetzt die ἀγαθά des Q-Textes durch die größte Gabe, die Gott zu verschenken hat: den Heiligen Geist (vgl. Röm 5,5). Gott wird den Bittenden nicht nur das schenken, was sie erbitten, sondern *das* Geschenk Gottes *schlechthin.* Im lukanischen Werk wird denn auch nirgends eine Bitte um den Heiligen Geist formuliert (vgl. Lk 3,21f.; Act 1,14 mit 2,4; 4,24–30 mit 4,31). Die einzige Analogie zur Geist-Bitte kann in Act 8,15 gesehen werden: Die beiden Apostel »beteten für sie (προσηύξαντο περὶ αὐτῶν), daß (ὅπως) sie den heiligen Geist empfangen möchten«. Doch beten hier nicht die getauften Samariter, sondern die Apostel Petrus und Johannes »für sie«[165]. Die Geistverleihung erfolgt näherhin durch Handauflegung (8,17.18.19; vgl. 19,6). Gegen die Auffassung, Lukas habe wegen Lk 11,13b die erste Bitte des Herrengebets durch eine Bitte um den Geist ersetzt, spricht auch der zweite Teil der Geist-Bitte, d. h. die Bitte um »Reinigung«. Falls Marcion diesen Teil der Geist-Bitte las[166], wird er ihn kaum dem ursprünglichen Lk-Text verdanken. Denn Lukas verbindet den Gedanken der Reinigung nicht mit dem Geistempfang[167].

Es fragt sich weiterhin, ob die Zusammenstellung von Geist-Bitte und folgender Reichs-Bitte ihren Grund im Makrokontext des Lk-Evangeliums haben kann. Diese Frage ist zu bejahen. Lk 11,13b sieht im Heiligen Geist das Geschenk Gottes schlechthin an die Bittenden; 12,31 betont abschließend: »Vielmehr suchet sein Reich, und dieses wird euch dazugegeben werden!« Vielleicht bildete diese Aufforderung (par. Mt 6,33) ursprünglich den Abschluß einer Reihe von Texten, die in der Logienquelle zur Gebetsparänese zusammengefaßt waren[168]. Im Mt-Text steht die genannte Aufforderung noch näher beim Vaterunser als im heutigen Lk-Text. Dazu paßt, daß Mt 6,33 πρῶτον liest (mit Q[169]): Matthäus (Q) sieht in der Reichs-Bitte des Herrengebets die vorrangige Bitte[170]. Im dritten

---

Jesus' Sayings, in: Logia, hrsg. von J. Delobel (BEThL 59), Löwen 1982, 411–418, näherhin 414f.; D. R. Catchpole, Q and "The Friend at Midnight" (Luke XI. 5–8/9): JThS 34 (1983) 407–424, näherhin 414–416.

165 Zum Gebrauch von προσεύχομαι siehe H. Greeven, προσεύχομαι, προσευχή, in: ThWNT II 806–808; H. Balz, προσεύχομαι κτλ., in: EWNT III 396–409. – Greeven (a.a.O. 806) bemerkt mit Recht, daß προσεύχομαι »immer da bevorzugt ist, wo der Tatbestand des Betens ohne nähere Inhaltsangabe dargestellt werden soll«. Bei Lukas wird nach προσεύχομαι ein konkreter *Inhalt* des Gebets mit einem zusätzlichen verbum dicendi (Lk 11,2; 22,41; Act 1,24), durch ταῦτα (Lk 18,11) oder durch einen Infinitiv (Lk 22,40) eingeführt. Der Gedanke der Fürbitte wird durch περί mit Genitiv plur. (Lk 6,28; Act 8,15) ausgedrückt. Von einem αἰτεῖν/αἰτεῖσθαι gegenüber *Gott* spricht Lukas nur dann, wenn er von Quellen abhängig ist: Lk 11,9–13; Act 7,46; 13,21.

166 Zur Problematik siehe oben mit Anm. 157.

167 Zu Act 15,8f. siehe oben mit Anm. 84.135.

168 Siehe dazu Catchpole, a. Anm. 164 a. O. 423f.

169 So Schulz, a. Anm. 164 a. O. 152.

170 Die Bitte um Heiligung des göttlichen Namens kann als »Eröffnungswunsch« und die Reichs-Bitte als »der eine große Gebetswunsch« verstanden werden; siehe Schürmann, Gebet des Herrn 32.47f.

Evangelium steht der aus Q stammende Abschnitt über das Sorgen (Lk 11,22–31 par. Mt 6,25–33) nicht wie bei Matthäus im unmittelbaren Kontext des Vaterunsers, sondern in einem Kontext, der von der Einstellung zum Besitz handelt (Lk 12,13–15.16–21. 22–32.33f.)[171]. Es ist also nicht sehr wahrscheinlich, daß Lukas das von ihm 11,13 erwähnte Gottesgeschenk des Heiligen Geistes mit der Aufforderung zum Suchen der Basileia in Verbindung brachte und beides zum Vaterunser in Beziehung setzte. Eine solche Kombination kann man aber einem nach-lukanischen Redaktor des Lk-Textes zutrauen, wie es Marcion nachweislich war. Er hätte dann die vom dritten Evangelium hervorgehobenen »höchsten Güter«, den Gottesgeist und das Gottesreich (Lk 11,13; 12,31[172]), auch im Vaterunser verankern wollen.

Die für Marcion anzunehmende Fassung der Geist-Bitte (eher ohne als mit Zusatz: »und reinige uns«) kann also eher der korrigierenden Hand des nach-lukanischen Redaktors als dem dritten Evangelisten selbst zugeschrieben werden.

b) Ist eine entsprechende Erklärung auch im Falle der späteren Zeugen für die Geist-Bitte zu vertreten? Oder geht deren Geist-Bitte (mit der Bitte um »Reinigung«) als *zweite* Vaterunser-Bitte eher auf den Evangelisten zurück? Hier ist vor allem die Beweiskraft von Act 1,6–8 zu prüfen. Nach E. Gräßer, der H. Conzelmann folgt, ist beim dritten Evangelisten der Heilige Geist »Ersatz« für das eschatologische Wissen um die Parusie bzw. das Kommen des Reiches[173]. Dieser Konzeption könnte dann die Verdrängung der Reichs-Bitte des Vaterunsers durch die Bitte um den Geist entsprechen[174]. Gräßer geht davon aus, daß die Geist-Bitte »sekundäre Variation der Reichsbitte ist«[175].

Act 1,6–8 ist ein von Lukas mit Hilfe von Mk 13,10.32 gebildetes Apophthegma[176], in dem Jesus die Frage der Jünger nach dem *Termin* der

---

171 Siehe dazu H.-J. Degenhardt, Lukas, Evangelist der Armen, Stuttgart 1965, 68–97, der Lk 12,13–34 unter der Überschrift »Die rechte Einstellung zum Besitz« zusammenfaßt.

172 Lk 12,31 liest Marcion (mit anderen Textzeugen) statt τὴν βασιλείαν αὐτοῦ den Ausdruck »das Reich *Gottes*«.

173 Siehe H. Conzelmann, Die Mitte der Zeit. Studien zur Theologie des Lukas (BHTh 17), Tübingen (1954) ^{4}1962, 127; Gräßer, Problem 111.206.

174 Gräßer, a.a.O. 110f.: »Im Zuge der *Parusieverzögerung* tritt die Bitte um das Reich zurück hinter die um den Geist ... Die Frage, ob *Lukas* diese Korrektur zugetraut werden darf, läßt sich nicht mit letzter Sicherheit entscheiden; es spricht aber doch einiges dafür.« Als Argumente führt Gräßer dann Lk 11,13 (diff. Mt) und Act 1,6ff. an (111); zur Acta-Stelle siehe auch 205–207.

175 Gräßer, a.a.O. 109: »Erstens wegen des Übergewichtes der alten Zeugen, die alle die Bitte um das Reich lesen. Zweitens, weil die ältesten Christen sich des Geistes als eines dauernden Besitzes rühmten ...«. – Vielleicht darf man für die Ursprünglichkeit der beiden ersten Bitten (Name – Reich) auch das Kaddisch-Gebet anführen, in dem die gleiche Abfolge bezeugt ist; siehe J. Jeremias, Neutestamentliche Theologie I, Gütersloh 1971, 192f. Auch im Kaddisch stehen die beiden Bitten asyndetisch nebeneinander.

176 Siehe dazu G. Schneider, Die Apostelgeschichte I (HThK V 1), Freiburg 1980,

Basileia-Aufrichtung zurückweist und die Fragesteller (positiv) auf die durch den Geistempfang ermöglichte Zeugenaufgabe – von Jerusalem bis ans Ende der Erde – verweist. Damit ist indessen nicht die Erwartung des Reiches als solche zurückgewiesen. Vielmehr wird der missionarischen Zeugenaufgabe die aktuelle Vordringlichkeit zugesprochen. Man kann freilich sehr wohl davon sprechen, daß Lukas damit die Naherwartung der Basileia dämpfte. Da das Kommen des Geistes in Vers 8 durch ἐπέρχομαι ἐπί angekündigt wird, kann man sich an Lk 1,35[177] sowie an Act 19,6 und die Geist-Bitte (ἔρχομαι ἐπί) erinnert fühlen[178]. Doch wird man weder annehmen dürfen, daß Lukas Act 1,8a aufgrund einer schon vorhandenen Vaterunserbitte um den Geist entwarf, noch, daß er die Geist-Bitte Lk 11,2 im Hinblick auf Act 1,8 formulierte. Denn die Geist-Verheißung ist mit den »Pfingstwundern« der Juden (Act 2,1–4), der Samariter (8,14–17) und der Heiden (10,44–48) im wesentlichen bereits erfüllt. Im übrigen ist zu beachten, daß Lk 1,35 sowie Act 1,8 und 19,6 das Kommen des Heiligen Geistes auf bestimmte Menschen stets mit einer *besonderen* Wirkung – jedenfalls nicht mit einer »Reinigung« – verbunden wird: Maria wird als Jungfrau den Sohn Gottes gebären; die Apostel werden weltweit Auferstehungszeugen sein; die Johannesjünger reden »in Zungen« und weissagen.

Da Act 1,6–8 an exponierter Stelle steht und der Kontext außerdem die Geistverheißung des Auferstandenen mit der Wassertaufe des Johannes konfrontiert (1,4f.)[179], konnte es für einen nach-lukanischen Abschreiber-Redaktor naheliegen, die Geist-Bitte an die Stelle der Reichs-Bitte Lk 11,2 zu stellen. Möglicherweise knüpfte er dabei an den Marcion-Text an und »korrigierte« ihn in seinem Sinn, den er für besser »lukanisch« hielt. *Er* hätte dann den Heiligen Geist gewissermaßen als »Ersatz« für die ausgebliebene Basileia interpretiert. Es ist aber auch denkbar, daß er die Basileia als schon verwirklicht ansah[180]. Die »Reini-

---

201–204; ders., Jesu überraschende Antworten. Beobachtungen zu den Apophthegmen des dritten Evangeliums: NTS 29 (1983) 321–336, 331.

177 Beide Aussagen über das Kommen des Geistes (über Maria, über den Jüngerkreis) stehen am Anfang des betreffenden Buches, also an exponierter Stelle. Siehe auch oben Anm. 131.

178 Vgl. indessen auch Mt 3,16.

179 Vgl. dazu Lk 11,1 als Einleitung zum Vaterunser.

180 Vgl. Lk 10,9.11; 11,20; 12,32; 17,21. Siehe indessen neben 11,2 auch das Jesuswort 22,18 (»... bis das Reich Gottes kommt«). – Zu beachten ist auf jeden Fall, daß im Kontext des lukanischen Vaterunsers mehrere Aussagen stehen, die (wenigstens indirekt) von der *Gegenwart* des Gottesreiches sprechen: Lk 10,18.23f.; 11,20.21f.31f. Vgl. dazu H. Merklein, Die Gottesherrschaft als Handlungsprinzip (FzB 34), Würzburg 1978, 158–165. Siehe außerdem O. Merk, Das Reich Gottes in den lukanischen Schriften, in: Jesus und Paulus (FS W. G. Kümmel), Göttingen 1975, 201–220, näherhin 210–212.

gung«, die der Geist Gottes bei den Betern dieser Bitte bewirken soll, entspricht nicht der theologischen Konzeption des Lukas, sondern dürfte aus Ez 36,22–32 LXX herausgelesen sein. Da Ez 36,23 von der *Heiligung des Namens* Gottes spricht, lag es nahe, auch die Ankündigung der *Reinigung* (v. 25) und des *Geistempfangs* (v. 27) zu einer Gebetsbitte zu gestalten. Da Codex 700 nach der Geist-Bitte auch die »matthäische« Bitte um den Vollzug des Willens Gottes liest – möglicherweise las auch Gregor von Nyssa diese Bitte in seinem Lk-Text –, kann man damit rechnen, daß der Schöpfer dieser Abfolge von Vaterunser-Bitten bei der angenommenen Anlehnung an Ez 36 die Erfüllung der Anordnungen (d. h. des *Willens*) Gottes durch die Menschen mit Ez 36,27 als Folge der Geistmitteilung ansah. Ez 36 spricht nicht von der *Basileia*; somit konnte auch von daher dem angenommenen Redaktor eine Streichung der Reichs-Bitte als vertretbar erscheinen.

Als Ergebnis der Untersuchung kann festgehalten werden, daß die Vaterunser-Bitte um das Kommen des Heiligen Geistes im Lk-Text eher nach-lukanischen Abschreibern oder »Redaktoren« zugeschrieben werden darf als dem Verfasser des dritten Evangeliums.

Abgekürzt angeführte Literatur

v. Baer, H., Der Heilige Geist in den Lukasschriften (BWANT 39), Stuttgart 1926.

Blass, F., Evangelium secundum Lucam sive Lucae ad Theophilum liber prior secundum formam quae videtur Romanam, Leipzig 1897.

Carmignac, J., Recherches sur le «Notre Père», Paris 1969.

Chase, F. H., The Lord's Prayer in the Early Church (TaS I 3), Cambridge 1891.

Creed, J. M., The Gospel according to St. Luke, London 1930 (Neudruck 1965).

Danker, F. W., Jesus and the New Age. According to St. Luke. A Commentary on the Third Gospel, St. Louis (Missouri) (1972) ^{2}1974.

Dunn, J. D. G., Spirit and Kingdom: ET 82(1970/71) 36–40.

Ernst, J., Das Evangelium nach Lukas (RNT), Regensburg 1977.

Fiebig, P., Das Vaterunser (BFChTh.M 30,3), Gütersloh 1927.

de Fraine, J., Oraison Dominicale: DBS VI (1960) 788–800.

Freudenberger, R., Zum Text der zweiten Vaterunserbitte: NTS 15(1968/69) 419–432.

George, A. (†), L'Esprit Saint dans l'œuvre de Luc: RB 85 (1978) 500–542.

Gnilka, J., Vaterunser I. Biblisch: LThK^{2} X (1965) 624–627.

Gräßer, E., Das Problem der Parusieverzögerung in den synoptischen Evangelien und in der Apostelgeschichte (BZNW 22), Berlin (1956) ^{3}1977.

Greeven, H., Gebet und Eschatologie im Neuen Testament (NTF III 1), Gütersloh 1931.

–, Synopse der drei ersten Evangelien mit Beigabe der johanneischen Parallelstellen [13. Aufl. der Synopse von A. Huck], Tübingen 1981.

Grundmann, W., Das Evangelium nach Lukas (ThHK 3), Berlin 1963.

(v.) Harnack, A., Über einige Worte Jesu, die nicht in den kanonischen Evangelien stehen, nebst einem Anhang über die ursprüngliche Gestalt des Vaterunsers: SPAW 1904 (Berlin 1904) I 170–208.

–, Der ursprüngliche Text des Vater-Unsers und seine älteste Gestalt, in: ders., Erforschtes und Erlebtes. Reden und Aufsätze, NF IV, Gießen 1923, 24–35.
–, Marcion. Das Evangelium vom fremden Gott, Leipzig ²1924 (Neudruck Darmstadt 1960).
Hauck, F., Das Evangelium des Lukas (ThHK 3), Leipzig 1934.
Hensler, J., Das Vaterunser. Text- und literarkritische Untersuchungen (NTA IV 5), Münster 1914.
Hönnicke, G., Neuere Forschungen zum Vaterunser bei Matthäus und Lukas: NKZ 17 (1906) 57–67. 106–120. 169–180.
Hoskier, H. C., A Full Account and Collation of the Greek Cursive Codex Evangelium 604, London 1890.
Jeremias, J., Das Vater-Unser im Lichte der neueren Forschung (1962), in: ders., Abba. Studien zur neutestamentlichen Theologie und Zeitgeschichte, Göttingen 1966, 152–171.
Klein, G., Die ursprüngliche Gestalt des Vaterunsers: ZNW 7 (1906) 34–50.
Klostermann, E., Das Lukasevangelium (HNT 5), Tübingen ²1929.
Knox, W. L. (†), The Sources of the Synoptic Gospels II, Cambridge 1957.
Lagrange, M.-J., Évangile selon Saint Luc (EtB), Paris ³1927 (Neudruck 1948).
Lampe, G. W. H., The Holy Spirit in the Writings of St. Luke, in: Studies in the Gospels. Essays in Memory of R. H. Lightfoot, Oxford 1955, 159–200.
Leaney, A. R. C., The Lucan Text of the Lord's Prayer (Lk XI 2–4): NT 1 (1956) 103–111.
–, A Commentary on the Gospel according to St. Luke (BNTC), London 1958.
Leisegang, H., Pneuma Hagion. Der Ursprung des Geistbegriffs der synoptischen Evangelien aus der griechischen Mystik, Leipzig 1922.
Lohmeyer, E., Das Vater-unser, Göttingen (1946) ⁵1962.
Loisy, A., L'évangile selon Luc, Paris 1924.
Marshall, I. H., The Gospel of Luke, Exeter 1978.
Metzger, B. M., A Textual Commentary on the Greek New Testament, London/New York 1971.
Ott, W., Gebet und Heil. Die Bedeutung der Gebetsparänese in der lukanischen Theologie (StANT 12), München 1965.
Paslack, H. E., Exegetische Bemerkungen zu Matth. 6,9–13 und Luk. 11,2–4, Straßburg 1905.
Plummer, A., A Critical and Exegetical Commentary on the Gospel according to S. Luke (ICC), Edinburgh ⁵1922 (Neudruck 1960).
Rengstorf, K. H., Das Evangelium nach Lukas (NTD 3), Göttingen ¹⁰1965.
Schmid, J., Das Evangelium nach Lukas (RNT 3), Regensburg ³1955.
Schmithals, W., Das Evangelium nach Lukas (ZB 3,1), Zürich 1980.
Schürer, E., Rezension: H. E. Paslack, Exegetische Bemerkungen (1905): ThLZ 30 (1905) 258f.
Schürmann, H., Das Gebet des Herrn als Schlüssel zum Verstehen Jesu, Freiburg ⁴1981.
Scrivener, F. H. A., A Plain Introduction to the Criticism of the New Testament, 2 Bde., London ⁴1894.
Smalley, St. S., Spirit, Kingdom and Prayer in Luke-Acts: NT 15 (1973) 59–71.
v. Soden, H., Die ursprüngliche Gestalt des Vaterunsers: ChW 18 (1904) 218–224.
Spitta, F., Die älteste Form des Vaterunsers: MGKK 9 (1904) 333–345.
Streeter, B. H., The Four Gospels. A Study in Origins, London 1924 (Neudruck 1964).

Vielhauer, Ph., Vaterunser-Probleme [zu E. Lohmeyer, Das Vater-unser]: VF (München 1949/50) 219–224.
Vögtle, A., Der »eschatologische« Bezug der Wir-Bitten des Vaterunser, in: Jesus und Paulus (FS W. G. Kümmel), Göttingen 1975, 344–362.
Vogels, H. J., Handbuch der Textkritik des Neuen Testaments, Bonn [2]1955.
Weiß, J., Die Schriften des Neuen Testaments I, Göttingen [3]1917.
Wellhausen, J., Das Evangelium Lucae, Berlin 1904.
–, Einleitung in die drei ersten Evangelien, Berlin [2]1911.
Zahn, Th., Das Vaterunser eines Kritikers: NKZ 2 (1891) 408–416.
–, Das Evangelium des Lucas (KNT 3) ([1.2]1913), Leipzig/Erlangen [3.4]1920.

Ethische Tendenzen in der Textüberlieferung des Neuen Testaments

von Wolfgang Schrage

(Evang.-Theol. Seminare der Universität, Abtlg. f. Neues Testament, Am Hof 1, 5300 Bonn 1)

Ausgangspunkt dieser kleinen Studie, die die beiden Forschungsschwerpunkte des Jubilars zu verbinden sucht, ist die Frage, welche ethischen Tendenzen sich in der handschriftlichen Überlieferung des ntl. Textes niedergeschlagen haben. Eine Durchmusterung der verschiedenen textkritischen Apparate[1] ergibt allerdings sehr bald, daß ganze Passagen und Kapitel keinerlei sachliche Abweichung aufweisen. Selbst härteste und anstößigste Forderungen werden meist ohne jede sachlich abweichende Variante überliefert, und selbst an so situationsbedingten und radikalen Forderungen wie denen über die kärgliche Ausrüstung der Missionare (Mk 6,7f. par) ist kaum etwas verändert worden. Als nicht überraschendes Hauptergebnis ist jedenfalls zunächst die große Treue gegenüber dem Text des NT festzuhalten. Den vielfältigen Versuchungen zur Akkommodation an den jeweiligen Zeitgeist, zur Entschärfung und Ermäßigung, ist in einem Maß widerstanden worden, das alle Lügen straft, die da sagen, Kirche und Theologie hätten seit je von Anpassungen und Abschwächungen gelebt. Wie groß und vielfältig die hier lauernden Gefahren waren, zeigen gerade die vereinzelten Stellen, an denen dem Anpassungsdruck nachgegeben worden ist. Im großen und ganzen aber hat sich die Kirche ihre maßgebliche Instanz so bewahrt, daß diese ihr immer wieder kritisch ins Gewissen zu reden vermochte. Außerdem sind bei den meisten Veränderungen nur Tendenzen verstärkt worden, die sich mindestens ansatzweise schon im NT selbst abzeichnen.

Nun kann man freilich auch eine theologische Gegenrechnung aufmachen und auf die Zahl der Varianten verweisen, die eben doch auch Indiz dafür sind, wie wenig buchstabengläubig die Kirche gewesen ist. Je-

---

[1] Es wurden die Textausgaben von C. Tischendorf, Novum Testamentum Graece I. II Leipzig 1869/1872 (Neudruck Graz 1965) und von H. v. Soden, Die Schriften des NT. Text und Apparat, Göttingen 1913 benutzt, daneben auch der textkritische Apparat in den Editionen der Synopse von A. Huck/H. Greeven, Tübingen [13]1981 und die der alten Versionen.
Um des Umfangs und der Einheitlichkeit willen habe ich mich, zumal bei den Varianten, die auch in der 26. Auflage des Novum Testamentum Graece (1979) von E. Nestle/K. Aland bezeugt werden, im Regelfall an deren Sigla und Zeugenauswahl gehalten.

denfalls kann man heute nicht mehr das vielzitierte Dictum von F. J. A. Hort wiederholen: "Even among the numerous unquestionable spurious readings of the New Testament there are no signs of deliberate falsifications of the text for dogmatic purposes"[2]. So wenig man die vielen anderen Faktoren und Fehlerquellen unterschätzen wird – das ist die Gefahr bei E. Fascher[3] –, und so wenig man jeden Abschreiber zu einem reflektierenden Theologen machen und jede Variante auf theologische Motive hin abklopfen darf, so unbestreitbar ist, daß die Vorlagen nicht nur mechanisch abgeschrieben wurden und die Auslegung des ntl. Textes schon hier beginnt. Gewiß hat es immer wieder auch Stimmen gegeben, die – oft mehr aus apologetischen Gründen – eine Beziehung zwischen Textüberlieferung und christlicher Lehre und Praxis bestritten, jedenfalls aber betont haben, daß keine der textkritischen Varianten eine Revision der christlichen Lehre nahelegt[4]. Andererseits ist doch auch mehrfach durch Beispiele erhärtet worden, wie stark theologische Interessen und das eigene Verständnis von Glaube und Lehre die Textüberlieferung mitbestimmt haben[5]. Daß die Kirchenväter speziell den Irrlehrern vorgeworfen haben, häretische Lesarten einzuführen[6], ändert nichts daran, daß auch im Raum der Kirche die biblischen Texte nicht unberührt geblieben sind, und es steht von vornherein zu erwarten, daß das, was an dogmatischen Tendenzen herausgefunden wurde, auch seine ethisch-paränetischen Entsprechungen hat. Trotz mancher Fehlentwicklungen sind diese Textmodifikationen auch keineswegs nur negativ zu bewerten. Es gibt sehr tiefsinnige Änderungen, auch in einzelnen Handschriften. Nach pa^{c} zu Mt 12,36 z. B. müssen die Menschen am Tag des Gerichts Rechenschaft ablegen über jedes gute Wort, das sie nicht gesprochen haben statt – so der Urtext – über jedes schlechte, das sie gesprochen haben.

Zunächst einige Vorbemerkungen zu Ziel und Methode dieser Untersuchung: Der Aufweis bestimmter Tendenzen ist nicht von der Absicht

---

[2] Zitiert bei E. J. Epp, The Theological Tendency of Codex Bezae Cantabrigiensis in Acts, MSSNTS 3, Cambridge 1966, 1; weitere Belege ib. Anm. 3.

[3] E. J. Epp, a.a.O., 20; daß man so unbekümmert Paulustexte verändert habe wie Paulus atl. Texte (so E. Fascher, Textgeschichte als hermeneutisches Problem, Halle 1953, 13), dürfte jedenfalls übertrieben sein.

[4] Vgl. L. Vaganay, An Introduction to the Textual Criticism of the New Testament, St. Louis 1937, 12; F. Kenyon, Our Bible and the Ancient Manuscripts, New York 1940, 23; zitiert bei K. W. Clark, Textual Criticism and Doctrine, in: Studia Paulina. In Honorem J. de Zwaan, Haarlem 1952, 52–65.

[5] Vgl. K. W. Clark, a.a.O. (Anm. 4); E. W. Saunders, Studies in Doctrinal Influences on the Byzantine Text of the Gospels, JBL 71, 1952, 85–92; J. W. Burgon/E. Miller, The Causes of the Corruption of the Traditional Text of the Holy Gospels, London 1896, 211–231; weitere Literatur bei E. J. Epp, a.a.O. (Anm. 2), 2 Anm. 1.

[6] K. W. Clark, a.a.O. (Anm. 4), 55 z. B. verweist auf Ambrosius De Spiritu Sancti 2,6 und Didymus De Trinitate 2,11.

geleitet, eine Hilfestellung für die Rekonstruktion des Urtextes zu leisten. Gewiß ergibt sich indirekt eine gewisse Relevanz für die Beurteilung von Lesarten, aber das Hauptinteresse gilt hier der Frage, welcherart ethische Tendenzen in der Textüberlieferung erkennbar werden. Deshalb werden gerade auch eindeutig sekundäre und schwach bezeugte Lesarten in die Analyse einbezogen, auch wenn diese einen weniger starken Druck verraten als diejenigen Varianten, bei denen der Urtext umstritten ist. Es ist auch kein Beitrag zur Geschichte des Textes beabsichtigt, so daß hier auf Herkunft, Alter und Gruppenzugehörigkeit der einzelnen Handschriften kein Wert gelegt wird, auch wenn sich durchaus bestimmte Schlußfolgerungen nahelegen (vgl. z. B. die Häufigkeit der Belege aus dem sog. Westlichen Text).

Bei der Abgrenzung dessen, was speziell ethische Tendenzen sind, kann man natürlich im Einzelfall verschiedener Meinung sein, zumal oft Zusammenhänge mit anderen Theologumena bestehen. Bei der immer stärkeren Betonung der Jungfrauengeburt z. B. dürften sich dogmatische mit ethisch-asketischen Tendenzen vermischen, wenn etwa Mt 1,16 Josef nicht mehr der Mann der Maria genannt, sondern der Text in vielfacher Weise verändert wird, so daß aus dem Ehepaar Verlobte werden[7]. Auch die breit bezeugten antijudaistischen Tendenzen haben z. T. ethische Auswirkungen, so wenn Paulus nach D(gig w sy^{hmg} mae) zu Act 15,2 betont, daß heidenchristliche Konvertiten »so bleiben sollen, wie sie zum Glauben gekommen sind«[8].

Es versteht sich von selbst, daß die bekannten Hauptfehlerquellen[9] auch bei der Überlieferung ethischer Texte eine entscheidende Rolle spielen. Entsprechend kann man im einzelnen immer wieder schwanken, ob man die als tendenziös bezeichneten Lesarten tatsächlich zu den beabsichtigten oder unbeabsichtigten Fehlern zu zählen hat. So würde ich – um nur ein Beispiel zu nennen – die Auslassung von Mt 5,47 durch k sy^{s} eher als Homoioteleuton verstehen, während H. Vogels[10] meint, der Vers sei Tatian unerträglich gewesen. Daß auch ein lapsus calami bezeichnend sein kann, ist auch ohne allzu intensive psychologische Motivforschung leicht zu begreifen. Gleichwohl gibt es auch in ethischen Texten ganz eindeutige Fälle für die typischen Versehen wie Homoioteleuton (vgl. die Auslassung von 1 Kor 10,26f. durch 177 337, die von παρ' ὃ δεῖ φρονεῖν in Röm 12,3 durch F G oder die jeweiligen Auslassungen von ἀδιάκριτος durch 915 bzw. ἀνυπόκριτος durch 614 in Jak 3,17). Überhaupt muß man sich hüten, in die meisten Varianten allzuviel Tiefsinn hineinzugeheimnissen, zu-

7 Vgl. E. Fascher, a.a.O. (Anm. 3), 48ff.

8 Vgl. E. J. Epp, a.a.O. (Anm. 2), 101f.

9 Vgl. H. Vogels, Handbuch der Textkritik des NT, Bonn ²1955, 162ff.; B. M. Metzger, Der Text des NT, Stuttgart–Berlin–Köln–Mainz 1966, 188ff.

10 H. Vogels, a.a.O. (Anm. 9), 179.

mal viele Varianten durchaus ambivalent bleiben oder sich in der jeweiligen Tendenz aufheben. Daß man gegenüber *allen* Menschen auf Gutes bedacht sein soll, schien 𝔓^{46} A^{1} D* F G 436 pc it in Röm 12,17 vielleicht zu weit zu gehen, weshalb sie πάντων ausgelassen bzw. durch den Artikel ersetzt haben. Andererseits aber wird, offenbar unter Einfluß von Röm 12,17, πάντων in 2 Kor 8,21 von 255 256 1319 2127 eingefügt. Beide Beobachtungen zusammen warnen vor voreiligen Schlußfolgerungen. Nach 2 Thess 2,17 soll Jesus Christus die Adressaten stärken in jedem guten Werk und Wort. F G K al vertauschen die Reihenfolge von Werk und Wort (vgl. Röm 15,18; 2 Kor 10,11; Kol 3,17), 33 pc bezeugen nur das gute Werk, 642 nur das gute Wort. Man könnte daraus zwar allgemein auf die Priorität des guten Werks schließen (vgl. die Beispiele unten), sei es, daß es an die erste Stelle gerückt, sei es, daß es allein genannt wird, aber die Lesart in 642 läßt auch für 33 pc ein mögliches Versehen zu. Und was könnte man nicht alles – um ein weiteres Beispiel anzuführen – aus der Auslassung von ἔπαινον δὲ ἀγαθοποιῶν durch 049* 1241 1505 pc in 1 Petr 2,14 herauslesen! Sollen Statthalter nur strafen? Widerspricht die Erfahrung der Abschreiber solcher Aussage zu stark? Viel ungezwungener ist die Annahme eines Homoioteleuton (vgl. das vorangehende κακοποιῶν). Gerade in langen Tugendkatalogen ist das Auslassen einzelner Begriffe wie etwa εὐσέβεια durch ℵ* sa oder von ἀγάπη durch 1912 in 1 Tim 6,11 kaum etwas anderes als ein Schreibfehler. Bisweilen zeigt sich, daß die Abschreiber selbst nicht genau wußten, wie sie den Text zu verstehen hatten. In Apk 2,20 wird »Ich habe wider dich« sowohl durch πολύ bzw. πολλά (ℵ 2050 𝔐^{A} gig (it) sy^{ph}) als auch durch ὀλίγα (pc vg^{cl}) ergänzt (dasselbe in Apk 2,4 durch g), wobei ὀλίγα wahrscheinlich durch Einfluß von 2,14 zustandegekommen ist.

Selbstverständlich hängt die Bewertung an einzelnen Stellen von der Exegese des Urtextes ab. 1 Kor 10,29 wird das »andere Gewissen«, das eincm nicht seine Freiheit nehmen kann, von F G a b d vg^{mss} Cyp als das des ἄπιστος charakterisiert. Ob das eine sinnvolle Ergänzung ist, wird von J. Weiß[11] verneint, von Ch. Wolff[12] bejaht. In Mk 10,24 bieten A C D Θ f$^{1.13}$ 28 565 (1241) 𝔐 lat sy bo^{pt} Cl den Text, daß die, die auf Besitztümer vertrauen, schwer ins Reich Gottes kommen. Wer diese Wendung gegenüber der allgemeinen Aussage, daß es überhaupt schwer ist, in das Reich Gottes zu kommen, für weniger radikal hält, wird urteilen, daß "the rigor of Jesus' saying was softened"[13] und τοὺς πεποιθότας ἐπὶ χρήμασιν eher für einen Zusatz halten. Desgleichen wer in der Textüberlieferung eine asketische Radikalisierung in der Stellungnahme zu Besitz und Besitzver-

[11] J. Weiß, Der erste Korintherbrief, KEK 5, Göttingen ^{9}1910, 266.

[12] Ch. Wolff, Der erste Brief des Paulus an die Korinther, ThHK VII 2, Berlin 1982, 61.

[13] B. M. Metzger u. a., A Textual Commentary on the Greek New Testament, London–New York ^{2}1975, 106.

zicht ausmacht. Mit gleichem Recht aber kann derjenige, der nicht die Verallgemeinerung, sondern die konkrete Zuspitzung als härter beurteilt, für die Ursprünglichkeit der Lesart plädieren, zumal wenn ihre Auslassung einer auch sonst zu beobachtenden Erweichungstendenz entspräche (vgl. Punkt 3). Ein weiteres Beispiel ist etwa die Umstellung von D E G F sy^{p} in 1 Thess 4,4.

1. Unspezifische Varianten

Zunächst sei kurz belegt, daß neben den erwähnten unbeabsichtigten Varianten auch in ethischen Texten die üblichen Glättungen, Klarstellungen und Ergänzungen begegnen, die u. U. durchaus sinnvoll sind und der Absicht der ntl. Autoren gerecht werden. So wenn z. B. in 1 Kor 4,16 104 614 (629) pc a vg^{cl} (in Analogie zu 1 Kor 11,1) καθὼς κἀγὼ Χριστοῦ anfügen. In Röm 14,6 wird von Ψ 𝔐 sy der Vollständigkeit halber wie beim Essen so auch bei der Tagewählerei die entsprechende Umkehrung eingefügt: »der, der den Tag nicht beachtet, beachtet ihn nicht für den Herrn« (vgl. die entsprechende auf Essen und Trinken sowie Nicht-Essen und Nicht-Trinken bezogene Erweiterung durch Epiph in Röm 14,3). Nach C^{3} D^{2} Ψ 𝔐 vg^{ms} sy zu zu 1 Kor 6,20 soll Gott nicht nur am Leib gepriesen werden, weshalb hinzugefügt wird καὶ ἐν τῷ πνεύματι ὑμῶν, ἅτινά ἐστιν τοῦ θεοῦ (Vigil liest freilich *glorificate deum cordibus vestris*). Außerdem fügen c f g t und lateinische Väter *et portate deum in corpore vestro* ein. Verdeutlichungen tendieren oft zu Übertreibungen: Nach f^{13} 1093 1241 1604 zu Lk 8,15 geht es um das Fruchtbringen in »viel« Geduld, nach $ℵ^{2}$ Ψ F G^{c} 104 365 pc zu 1 Thess 4,3 um das Vermeiden »aller« Unzucht, nach A zu Röm 6,17 um den Gehorsam aus »reinem« Herzen, nach 255 zu 1 Petr 3,1 um einen »guten« Wandel der Frauen, nach 1 Petr 1,22 um Liebe aus »reinem« ($𝔓^{72}$ ℵ* C P Ψ 𝔐 t vg^{mss} sy^{h} co) bzw. »wahrem« Herzen ($ℵ^{2}$ vg^{ms})[14] usw.

Ein Punkt bedarf noch besonderer Beachtung, der der Parallel- und Kontexteinflüsse. Jeder Kundige weiß, welches Gewicht diesem Faktor gerade in den Evangelien zukommt. Gerade wenn im Regelfall nicht einfach stumpfsinnige Abschreiber am Werk waren, genügt es aber nicht, hier einfach auf den bekannten Einfluß des Matthäus auf die anderen Synoptiker zu verweisen, denn erstens ist darauf zu achten, an welchen Stellen sich dieser Einfluß bemerkbar macht, und zum anderen gibt es einen wenn auch weniger wirksamen Einfluß auch auf Matthäus. Es ist z. B. charakteristisch, wenn in Mt 9,15 bei der Frage, ob Hochzeitsleute trauern können, πένθειν von D W 1424 pc it $sy^{p.hmg}$ sa mae bo^{mss} unter synoptischem Paralleleinfluß durch νηστεύειν verdrängt wird, während der parallele

---

14 Vgl. die bei C. Tischendorf II 278 genannten Lesarten verschiedener Versionen: *ex corde puro et perfecto* und *in corde sancto*.

Markus- und Lukastext unbestritten sind (vgl. auch die Einfügung von »diese Art fährt nicht aus außer durch Gebet und Fasten« durch ℵ^{2} C D L W f$^{1.13}$ 𝔐 lat (sy$^{p.h}$) (mae) bo^{pt} Or in Mt 17,21 unter Einfluß von Mk 9,29, wobei alle νηστεία bieten, das schon bei Markus die meisten Handschriften bezeugen; vgl. unten). Gerade in Fällen, wo der Matthäus-Text nur aufgefüllt zu werden braucht, haben auch die anderen Synoptiker Einfluß genommen, wenn z. B. in Mt 5,44 von D L W Θ f^{13} 𝔐 lat sy$^{(p).h}$ Cl Eus »segnet die euch fluchen, tut wohl denen, die euch hassen, bittet für die, die euch beleidigen« im Anschluß an Lk 6,27 f. eingefügt wird. Meist steht es freilich so wie Mk 12,31, wo die matthäische Gleichstellung der beiden Hauptgebote von A (D) W (Θ) f$^{1.13}$ 𝔐 lat (sy) auch für den Markustext bezeugt wird (Hinzufügung von ὁμοία), Mt 22,39 aber unbestritten bleibt. Natürlich findet man auch in ethischen Partien das, was man sonst immer wieder findet, nämlich Kombinationen: Wenn Mk 12,28 nach dem »ersten« Gebot von allen gefragt wird und Mt 22,36 nach dem »größten« Gebot im Gesetz, so bietet sy^{c} vg^{ms} in Mt 22,36 μεγάλη καὶ πρώτη (ähnlich aber Matthäus selbst in v. 38) Als Beispiele für Kontexteinfluß seien erwähnt die Hinzufügung in Mt 18,10, wo D pc it vg ^{mss} sy^{c} sa^{mss} unter Einfluß von v. 6 die verbotene Verachtung »keines dieser Kleinen« ergänzt wird durch »die an mich glauben«, außerhalb der Evangelien die Ergänzung von »die nicht nach dem Fleisch wandeln« durch A D^{1} Ψ 81 365 629 pc vg (sy^{p}) Spec, wozu ℵ^{2} D^{2} 𝔐 a sy^{h} noch hinzufügen »sondern nach dem Geist« in Röm 8,1 (unter dem Einfluß von Röm 8,4).

Beeinflussungen finden sich natürlich auch außerhalb der Evangelien, etwa beim Einschieben von Formeln wie »im Herrn« (vgl. F G in 1 Thess 5,16 und D* in Phlm 19) oder »in Christus Jesus« (vgl. F G in Phil 3,15) oder von Wendungen wie »Mann und Frau« (vgl. D* F G 629 it vg^{mss} Hil Ambr in Kol 3,11 nach Gal 3,28). Vor allem ist zu beobachten, daß geformte paränetische Stücke wie Haustafeln, Tugend- und Lasterkataloge, Bischofsspiegel, Sendschreiben u. ä. stark aufeinander eingewirkt haben, wobei freilich auch hier die Details von Belang sind. So werden in Lasterkatalogen aus anderen Katalogen bekannte Begriffe nachgetragen: φόνοι in Gal 5,21 von A C D F G Ψ 0122 𝔐 lat sy$^{(p)}$ bo (Cyp) (vgl. Mk 7,21 par; Röm 1,29), ἀσέλγεια von 440 in Kol 3,5 (vgl. Mk 7,22; Röm 13,13; Gal 5,19). Unter dem Eindruck des Tugendkatalogs von Gal 5,22 wird bei 𝔓^{46} D^{2} Ψ 𝔐 sy^{h} aus der »Frucht des Lichtes« (Eph 5,9) die »Frucht des Geistes«. Freilich kann solche Komplettierung auch ohne alle Analogien erfolgen, z. B. Phil 4,8 durch ἐπιστήμη bei D* F G a vg^{cl} Ambst. Sehr starke Beeinflussung weist speziell die Haustafel des Kolosserbriefes von seiten des Epheserbriefes auf, wozu hier nur beispielhaft erwähnt seien: statt ἐρεθίζετε bieten A C D* F G L 0198 33 81 104 365 1175 1241^{s} 1739^{mg} 2495 al vg^{mss} Ambst in Kol 3,21 wie Eph 6,4 παροργίζετε (kein einziges Beispiel für eine Beeinflussung in umgekehrter Richtung!), in Kol 3,23 haben 203 506 1912 wie Eph 6,7 μετ' εὐνοίας und A pc δουλεύοντες (keine Beispiele für Auslassung im Eph), und endlich findet sich die Auslassung von κατὰ πάντα in 𝔓^{46} 81 1241^{s} pc vg^{ms} sa in Kol 3,22 (vgl. Eph 6,5; dort wiederum ohne diesbezügliche Ergänzung). Gerade bei dieser letzten Auslassung in der Mahnung an die Sklaven stellt sich die Frage, ob nicht zugleich eine verständliche Entschärfung beabsichtigt war. In den Sendschreiben der Offenbarung wird in 2,9 von ℵ 𝔐 sy^{h} und in 2,13 vom 𝔐 sy^{h} τὰ ἔργα (σου) eingetragen (in Analogie zu Apk 2,2.19; 3,1.8.15). Im Bischofsspiegel von 1 Tim 3,3 wird μὴ αἰσχροκερδῆ von 326 365 614 630 2495 pm in Analogie zu Tit 1,7 hinzugefügt.

Paralleleinfluß gibt es freilich auch außerhalb geformter Paränese. »Was sollen wir tun?« (Lk 3,10) wird von Act 16,30 her von D sy^{c}? sa^{mss} ergänzt durch ἵνα σωθῶμεν (in Lk 3,12.14 wird diese Ergänzung nur noch von D geboten). Da die übliche Reihenfolge bei Paulus Glaube – Liebe ist, wird sie in Phlm 5 von 𝔓^{61vid} D 323 365 629 945 1739 1881 pc a b vg^{mss} sy^{p} Ambst wieder hergestellt (vgl. das Gegenbeispiel zu Punkt 7) usw.

Endlich ist der Einfluß atl. Zitate zu beachten, zumal beim Dekalog. So fügen ℵ (P) 048 81 104 365 1241 1506 (2495) pm a b vg^{cl} (sy^{h}) bo in Röm 13,9 im Anschluß an Ex 20,16 »Du sollst nicht falsch Zeugnis reden« ein. In Jak 2,11 rücken C Ψ 614 630 945 1241 1505 1739 1852 2464 2495 al das Verbot des Mordens vor das des Ehebruchs, womit sie gegen die LXX der masoretischen Reihenfolge entsprechen[15] (ähnlich Lk 18,20). Umgekehrt steht es wahrscheinlich Mk 10,19/Mt 19,18, wo das Mord- vor dem Ehebruchverbot steht, aber unter Einfluß von Röm 13,9; Jak 2,11; Lk 18,20 und LXX die Reihenfolge bei Mk 10,19 von A W Θ f^{13} 𝔐 lat sy^{h} Cl umgedreht wird. Wahrscheinlich unter Einfluß von Matthäus/Lukas, aber wohl auch von Ex 20,16/Dt 5,20, wird in Mk 10,19 das μὴ ἀποστηρήσῃς von B* K W Δ Ψ f$^{1.13}$ 28 700 1010 al sy^{s} Ir Cl ausgelassen.

2. Größere Allgemeingültigkeit

Während die bisherigen Beispiele kaum etwas für die Ethik Typisches aufweisen, wird das in den folgenden Beispielen nun anders. Deutlich greifbar wird durch verschiedene Indizien die Absicht, die ntl. Ethik als dauernd gültig zu erweisen. Das beginnt schon bei der Umwandlung von Imperativen des Aorist in solche des Präsens (vgl. als Beispiel 𝔓^{71vid} B D 565 in Mt 19,17 oder 33 81 467 in 1 Petr 1,22), auch wenn es vereinzelt Gegenbeispiele gibt. Bei der Bewertung der Verwandlung der 2. Person in die 1. Person bin ich mir allerdings nicht sicher, zumal hier viele Gegenbeispiele genannt werden können und zweifellos auch der Kontext eine

[15] Vgl. M. Dibelius/H. Greeven, Der Brief des Jakobus, KEK 15, Göttingen ^{11}1964, 182 Anm. 3.

große Rolle spielt (vgl. den Ersatz der 2. durch die 1. Person in 1 Kor 10,10 durch ℵ D F G 33 pc bo in Angleichung an v. 8f.). Genannt sei als Beispiel nur Röm 13,11, wo es nach 𝔓^{46vid} ℵ^{c}D F G Ψ 𝔐 latt sy^{p} sa Zeit ist, daß *wir* vom Schlaf aufstehen (weitere Beispiele in 1 Kor 6,15; 7,15 u. ö.).

Eindeutiger ist die Auslassung oder Erweiterung der ursprünglichen Adressaten. Die Auslassung von »seiner Jungfrau« in 1 Kor 7,38 bei Ψ 𝔐 gibt den paulinischen Aussagen eine größere Allgemeingültigkeit[16]. In dieselbe Richtung weist wahrscheinlich auch die Auslassung des σοί in Röm 13,4 durch F G bo^{ms}, des σέ in 1 Kor 8,10 durch 𝔓^{46} B F G latt, des zweimaligen μου in 1 Kor 8,13 durch (D*) F G a (b) (Cl) Cyp Ambst und des μοί durch C in 1 Kor 6,12 (vgl. aber als Gegenbeispiel die Hinzufügung von μοί unter Einfluß von 1 Kor 6,12 in 1 Kor 10,23 bei ℵ^{2} C^{3} H (P) Ψ 𝔐 t vg^{cl} sy). Symptomatisch sind auch Hinzufügungen von Pronomen wie ἕκαστος in 1 Kor 10,24 bei D^{2} Ψ 𝔐 sy und in Gal 6,1 bei G F it Vict, oder πάντες in Mt 7,23 bei L Θ f^{13} 1424 al b vg^{s} (zwar unter Paralleleinfluß von Ps 6,9 und Lk 13,27, doch wird es in Lukas von niemandem ausgelassen), von Adverbien wie πανταχοῦ in 1 Kor 11,2 bei F G b d, oder von πάντοτε (anstelle von πάντα bei P 2004). Typisch ist auch die Hinzufügung von πᾶς: Christen sollen sich nach ℵ^{2} Ψ (F G^{c}) 104 365 pc zu 1 Thess 4,3 ἀπὸ πάσης (τῆς) πορνείας enthalten; ebenso naheliegend ist das Einschieben von πάντα in 1 Kor 10,11 durch ℵ C D F G Ψ 81 𝔐 lat sy bo Ir^{lat}: alles ist dem atl. Gottesvolk widerfahren und dient zur νουθεσία der Christen. Auch hier konnte aber an ntl. Gebrauch angeknüpft werden. Wenn man schon »alle Zeit« Arme hat, kann und soll man auch »alle Zeit« Gutes tun: Mk 14,7 fügen deshalb ℵ^{2} B L 892 (1241) pc ein zusätzliches πάντοτε ein[17] (vgl. auch den Ersatz von ποιῆσαι durch ποιεῖν im selben Vers durch Ψ Δ D* 179 1588).

3. Formale Verstärkung und inhaltliche Abschwächung

Aus der Kanonisierung des Textes ergab sich von selbst, daß die Mahnungen des NT an Gewicht gewannen und ihre Autorität verstärkt wurde. Es braucht hier nicht auf die Fälle verwiesen zu werden, wo außerhalb ethischer Partien auf den autoritativen Charakter verwiesen wird, wenn z. B. 2 Petr 2,10 Verachtung der Engelmächte und der hinzugefügten θεῖαι δυνάμεις von 2138 pc auf eine Stufe mit der der ἐκκλησιαστικαὶ ἀρχαί gestellt wird, oder wenn in 1 Tim 5,19 b Cyp Ambst Pel die Einschränkung, daß man keine Klage gegen einen Presbyter annehmen soll,

---

16 Vgl. G. Zuntz, The Text of the Epistles, London 1953, 165 Anm. 1.

17 Joh 12,8 ist möglicherweise auch erst unter Einfluß von Mk 14,7/Mt 26,11 von der Mehrheit der Zeugen (außer D sy^{s}) eingefügt worden, doch ist das umstritten.

es sei denn auf Aussage von 2 oder 3 Zeugen hin, wohl schon zu weit ging, so daß sie das Zitat von Dt 19,15 ausließen. Doch greift auch hier eins ins andere.

Das Mysterium hat Gott nach G F zu Kol 1,26 nicht seinen Heiligen, sondern seinen Aposteln anvertraut (Eph 3,5 ist hier von Einfluß). Weil D F G Ψ 𝔐 a b sy^h Ambst Pel die Frage nach dem Apostelsein des Paulus für entscheidender halten als die nach seiner Freiheit, haben sie die Reihenfolge der beiden ersten Fragen in 1 Kor 9,1 vertauscht. Die Hochschätzung der apostolischen Autorität gilt dabei vor allem den Zwölfen, wie die Auslassung der Negation in Gal 2,5 bei D* b Ir^{lat} Tert MVict Ambst zeigt, nach denen Paulus in Jerusalem nachgegeben haben soll, auch wenn das z. B. damit begründet wird, *ut scandalum imminens vitaretur*[18]. Während nach Act 15,2 die antiochenische Gemeinde Paulus und Barnabas nach Jerusalem abordnet (ἔταξαν), macht D (gig w sy^{hmg} mae) die Jerusalemer Autoritäten zum Subjekt des Anordnens und bezeugt damit die sich ausbildende Praxis, »kirchliche Streitigkeiten vom übergeordneten Amt entscheiden zu lassen«[19]. Das hat Konsequenzen auch für die ntl. Ethik. Petrus und die übrigen Apostel werden nach D E it sy^{hmg} in Act 2,37 nicht nur gefragt »Was sollen wir tun?«, sondern es wird hinzugefügt ὑποδείξατε ἡμῖν. Die Verbindlichkeit der ntl. Weisungen wird dadurch gesteigert, daß »neutrale« Verben wie λέγω durch παραγγέλλω (so 255 in 1 Kor 7,12) oder Überlieferungen durch *praecepta* ersetzt werden (so f vg Pelag in 1 Kor 11,2). Möglicherweise ist auch ἐντολή $\mathfrak{P}^{46}$ $\aleph^2$ B 048 0243 33 1241^s 1739 1881 pc vg^{ms} bzw. ἐντολαί (D^2 Ψ 𝔐 lat sy sa) in 1 Kor 14,37 nachträglich hinzugefügt worden, falls D* F G (pc) b Ambst mit κυρίου ἐστίν den Urtext bilden, was aber nicht sicher ist[20]. Auffallend ist auch, daß die apostolischen Weisungen als πανταχοῦ geltend eingeführt werden (zu 1 Kor 11,2; vgl. oben).

Bei der zunehmenden Bedeutung der apostolischen Autorität und der Vorbildfunktion der Apostel steht beinahe von selbst zu erwarten, daß die schon bei den Synoptikern beginnende Retuschierung des Jüngerbildes sich in den Handschriften fortsetzt. Daß *alle* geflohen sein sollen (Mk 14,50), war z. B. schwer zu verkraften, weshalb bekanntlich schon Lukas die ganze Notiz ausgelassen hat. Darin ist ihm zwar keiner der Abschreiber des Markus- und Matthäus-Tertes gefolgt, wohl aber haben einige das πάντες ausgelassen, in Mk 14,50 N 485 565 sy^p, in Mt 26,56 1424 r^2. Ähnlich ging 206 die Aussage von 2 Tim 1,15, daß *alle* sich von Paulus abgewandt haben sollten, wohl zu weit, weshalb πάντες ausgelassen wurde.

[18] C. Tischendorf, a.a.O. (Anm. 1), II, 633.

[19] E. Haenchen, Die Apostelgeschichte, KEK 3, Göttingen [13]1961, 383 Anm. 7; vgl. auch E. Fascher, a.a.O. (Anm. 3), 32f.

[20] Vgl. G. Zuntz, a.a.O. (Anm. 16), 139f.; W. Schrage, Die konkreten Einzelgebote in der paulinischen Paränese, Gütersloh 1961, 114 Anm. 179.

Gerade wenn die Verbindlichkeit gesteigert, jedenfalls ernst genommen wird, mußten die Forderungen andererseits oft als zu steil und schwer erfüllbar gelten. So fügt die große Mehrzahl der Zeugen (außer 𝔓^{67} ℵ* B pc vg Iu Or^{pt}) in Mt 5,22 ein εἰκῇ ein, läßt also nicht mehr den Zorn, sondern nur den grundlosen Zorn von Jesus verboten sein, weil das generelle Zornverbot als zu radikal galt. Wahrscheinlich ist trotz der Möglichkeit eines Itazismus auch der Ersatz der Hyperbel vom Kamel und Nadelöhr durch Seil und Nadelöhr in allen 3 Evangelien (in Mk 10,25 bei 13 28 pc; in Mt 19,24 bei pc; in Lk 18,25 bei S f^{13} 1010 1424 al) als Abschwächung zu bewerten, die die Unmöglichkeit für Reiche, in das Reich Gottes zu kommen, ermäßigt. In Lk 9,23 wird von ℵ^{1} C D 𝔐 it sy$^{s.hmg}$ sa^{ms} καθ' ἡμέραν ausgelassen, gewiß unter Paralleleinfluß, aber auffallend ist doch, daß keine einzige Handschrift die Wendung in Mt 16,24/Mk 8,34 einträgt (in Lk 17,4 hat dagegen kein einziger Zeuge trotz Mt 18,21 das τῆς ἡμέρας ausgelassen). Ob das Verlassen der Frau in Mt 19,29 ausgelassen wird oder aber ἢ γυναῖκα hinzugefügt wurde, ist nicht sicher (vgl. zu Punkt 4). Möglicherweise ist auch der Ersatz von μηδέν durch μηδένα in Lk 6,35 von solcher Abschwächungstendenz mitbestimmt, auch wenn Dittographie nicht auszuschließen ist. Jedenfalls wird nach ℵ W Ξ pc sy$^{s.p}$ nun nicht mehr erwartet, daß man beim Leihen »nichts« zurückerhofft, sondern an »niemandem« verzweifelt[21]. Das Auslassen des bekannten Wortes in Apk 3,15 »O daß du kalt oder heiß wärest« durch A 1006 pc könnte ebenfalls auf das Erschrecken vor diesem radikalen Widerspruch gegen alles Halbe und Unentschiedene zurückgehen, doch liegt Homoioteleuton als Erklärung vielleicht doch näher. 1 Petr 3,9 wird zwar festgehalten, daß man Böses nicht mit Bösem und Schmähung nicht mit Schmähung vergelten soll, aber statt des absoluten Gebotes zum Segnen beschränkt 1898 das auf die Segnenden (τοὺς εὐλογοῦντας εὐλογοῦντες). Daß die Adressaten nie mehr einen Fehltritt tun werden, schien A Ψ pc h Ambr wohl durch οὐ μή + Konjunktiv stark genug ausgedrückt, weshalb sie das ποτε in 2 Petr 1,10 ausließen. Nach dem m. E. wahrscheinlichen, aber umstrittenen Urtext von 𝔓$^{45.75}$ C* W Θ pc (A Ψ f^{13}𝔐) lat sy$^{c.p.h}$ sa bo^{ms} in Lk 10,42 ist nur »eines nötig«, nach 38 Or sy^{pal} arm georg »weniges«, nach (ℵ L al) 𝔓^{3} B C^{2} f^{1} 33 pc »eines oder weniges«. "The absoluteness of ἑνός was softened by replacing it with ὀλίγων"[22]. Die dritte Lesart ist wohl eine Kombination. Daß die Abschreiber eine ursprüngliche Äußerung, daß Jesus auch mit einfacher Bewirtung zufrieden sei, spiritualisiert haben sollten[23],

---

[21] Vgl. H. Schürmann, Das Lukasevangelium, HThK III 1, Freiburg 1969, 355 Anm. 90; Rudolf Bultmann, ThWNT II 531.

[22] B. M. Metzger u. a., a.a.O. (Anm. 13), 154.

[23] I. H. Marshall, The Gospel of Luke, The New International Greek Testament Commentary, Exeter 1978, 453; F. Hauck, Das Evangelium des Lukas, ThHk III, Leipzig 1934, 148.

leuchtet dagegen weniger ein[24], auch wenn eine Spiritualisierung generell nicht zu leugnen ist (vgl. die Brotbitte von Mt 6,11 in der Vulgata: *panem supersubstantialem*).

In den Zusammenhang der Abschwächung von Jesu Radikalität gehört schon die Auslegung der Didache. Nach Did 1,4 soll man tun, was man kann; wer aber auch beim Schlag auf die rechte Wange die andere darbietet (Mt 5,39), dem wird gesagt καὶ ἔσῃ τέλειος. Hinzu tritt hier eine pragmatische Begründung mit Nützlichkeitserwägungen, z. B. des Gebotes der Feindesliebe (καὶ οὐχ ἕξετε ἐχθρόν Did 1,3) oder des Gebotes, daß man dann, wenn einem jemand das Seine nimmt, es nicht zurückfordern soll (οὐδὲ γὰρ δύνασαι Did 1,4)[25].

4. Askese

In einer gewissen Spannung zu der zuletzt erwähnten Abschwächungstendenz steht eine asketische Verschärfung. Allerdings betrifft sie weit überwiegend das Gebiet der Sexualität, wobei hier die Parallelität zu den gnostischen Schriften besonders auffällt[26]. Das Wort ἄσκησις selbst ist allerdings offenbar nur in Röm 14,17 von der Minuskel 4 eingeführt worden[27], so daß danach das Reich Gottes in Gerechtigkeit und Askese, Friede und Freude im Heiligen Geist besteht. Vor den zahlreichen Fällen sexualethischer Askese zunächst einige Beispiele aus anderen Bereichen: Häufig wird z. B. das Fasten zusätzlich eingefügt, meist neben Beten: In Mk 9,29 wird es von 𝔓^{45vid} ℵ^{2} A C D L W Θ Ψ f$^{1.13}$ 𝔐 lat sy^{h} co eingefügt, zudem von sy$^{s.p}$ bo^{ms}auch noch dem Beten vorangestellt (vgl. auch die Beispiele oben); in Act 10,30 sehen 𝔓^{50} A^{c} D$^{(*)}$ E Ψ 𝔐 it sy sa mae das Gebet des Cornelius eben vom Fasten begleitet, und in 1 Kor 7,5 ist Fasten bei ℵ^{2} 𝔐 sy ein weiterer Grund für eheliche Enthaltsamkeit. Röm 14,5 wird κρίνειν zweimal von 1827 in νηστεύειν verändert (vgl. auch oben zu Mt 9,15 und 17,21). Die Altlateiner e und l wollen die Hochzeit zu Kana offenbar deutlicher von einer Weinorgie abheben und erklären das Ausgehen des Weines in Joh 2,3 mit der großen Zahl der Hochzeitsgäste: *et factum est per multam turbam vocitorum vinum consummari.*

Speziell in sexualibus werden asketische Züge an folgenden Stellen erkennbar: Nach sy^{s} Ephr hat die Prophetin Hanna nach ihrer Jungfrau-

[24] M. Dibelius, Die Formgeschichte des Evangeliums, Tübingen ^{4}1961, 115.

[25] L. E. Wright, Alterations of the Words of Jesus as Quoted in the Literature of the Second Century, Harvard Historical Monographs XXV, Cambridge Mass., 1952, 15 spricht von "prudential motivation"; vgl. S. 16 zu Did 1,4; "a prompting to realistic appreciation of inalterable fact".

[26] Vgl. bloß das Ägypter-Evangelium bei Clem Strom III 9,13: »Ich bin gekommen, die Werke des Weiblichen zu zerstören ...«; vgl. L. E. Wright, a.a.O. (Anm. 25), 93f.

[27] B. M. Metzger, a.a.O. (Anm. 9), 205.

enschaft nicht sieben Jahre (so alle anderen Zeugen in Lk 2,36), sondern nur sieben Tage mit ihrem Mann zusammengelebt. Nach dem Mehrheitstext fordert Paulus in 1 Kor 7,3 von den christlichen Ehepartnern nicht die sexuelle Gemeinschaft als Pflicht, sondern nur geschuldete εὔνοια. Aufschlußreich ist auch der Ersatz des adversativen δέ durch begründendes γάρ in 1 Kor 7,7 durch $\aleph^{2}$ B D^{2} Ψ 𝔐 vg^{cl} sy Cyp. Zeigt es doch, daß die paulinische Konzession nicht mehr auf den zeitweiligen Verzicht auf Ehe- und Geschlechtsgemeinschaft bezogen wird, sondern auf diese Gemeinschaft selbst, was dann v. 7 mit dem Hinweis auf die paulinische Ehelosigkeit begründet. 1611 fügt hinter das »wie ich« noch zusätzlich ἐν ἐγκράτεια hinzu. 1 Petr 3,7 bietet ℵ* συνομιλοῦντες[28] statt συνοικοῦντες (vgl. auch *concordes et caste viventes* bei Aug), spricht also nicht mehr von voller Lebensgemeinschaft inklusive der Geschlechtsgemeinschaft (vgl. Sir 25,8 u. ö.). In 1 Kor 9,5 wird vom apostolischen Recht gesprochen, Frauen (so F G a b Tert Ambst Pel) oder (so die anderen) eine Schwester als Frau auf den Missionsreisen mitzuführen, während mehrere Kirchenväter[29] den Aposteln nur eine Frau als Schwester konzedieren. Daß die Ehe »von allen« in Ehren gehalten werden soll (Hebr 13,4), scheint 38* 460 623 1836 1912* und einigen Kirchenvätern unangemessen gewesen zu sein, weshalb sie ἐν πᾶσιν ausgelassen haben. Vermutlich wird man auch die Einfügung von ἢ γυναῖκα, falls es sich um eine solche handelt, in Mt 19,29 durch alle Handschriften bis auf B (D) pc a n (sy^{s}) und Mk 10,29 bei A C Ψ f^{13} 𝔐 f q $sy^{p.h}$ bo^{ms} nicht einfach auf Einfluß von Lk 18,29 abschieben dürfen (dort nur von 1241 vg^{ms} $sy^{h\ ms}$ ausgelassen), sondern als nachdrückliche Erinnerung daran, daß natürlich auch die Ehefrau hinter die Nachfolge zurückzutreten hat[30]. Junge Männer sollen nicht nur zur Besonnenheit, sondern nach C 88 256 263 330^{c} 436 642 915 1845 c^{1} sy^{h} arm auch zur Keuschheit ermahnt werden (Tit 2,7); dasselbe Wort wird im Tugendkatalog von Gal 5,23 von D* F G it vg^{cl} Ir^{lat} Cyp Ambst eingeschoben, und eine Vulgatahandschrift gibt die θεοσέβεια der Frauen in 1 Tim 2,10 mit *pudicitia* wieder.

Vor allem die ntl. Warnung vor πορνεία wird immer mehr hervorgehoben, z. B. zusätzlich in den Urtext eingeschoben. So wird in Mk 10,19 selbst in den Dekalog von D (Γ pc) k Ir das μὴ πορνεύσῃς eingeschoben und in Lasterkatalogen, wo das nicht ohnehin schon der Fall war, πορνεία an die erste Stelle gerückt: in Mt 15,19 von L 1604 q (wohl unter Paralleleinfluß von Mk 7,21, wo unter Matthäus-Einfluß freilich auch eine star-

[28] Nach L. Goppelt, Der 1. Petrusbrief, KEK XII/1, Göttingen ^{8}1978, 221 Anm. 3 »eine rein geistige Gemeinschaft«.

[29] Nach C. Tischendorf, a.a.O. (Anm. 1), II 505; vgl. aber G. Zuntz, a.a.O. (Amn. 16), 138. Vgl. Clem Strom III 6,23 οὐχ ὡς γαμετάς, ἀλλ᾽ ὡς ἀδελφὰς περιῆγον τὰς γυναῖκας.

[30] Die Ursprünglichkeit in Mt 19,29 ist freilich umstritten; vgl. J. W. Burgon/E. Miller, a.a.O. (Anm. 5), 209; B. M. Metzger u. a., a.a.O. (Anm. 13), 50.

ke Gegentendenz vorliegt, meist mit Voranstellung von μοιχεία). Röm 1,29 wird von Ψ 𝔐 πορνεία an erster Stelle nachgetragen. Die Mahnung vor πορνεία in 1 Thess 4,3 wird von Minuskel 5 mit den vielerlei Arten von Zügellosigkeit begründet (διὰ τὸ πολλὰ εἶναι τῆς ἀκολασίας τὰ εἴδη). Das »Brennen« von 1 Kor 7,9 ist in der lateinischen Handschrift g ein *uri in malo fornicationis*. Weniger oft erscheint zusätzlich μοιχεία, das etwa Gal 5,19 von ℵ^{2} D (F G) Ψ 0122 𝔐 (b) sy^{h} (Ir^{lat} Cyp) Ambst eingefügt wird. Erstaunlich ist, daß Joh 7,53 ff. Aufnahme gefunden hat, da doch die Bedenken auf der Hand lagen: *peccandi impunitatem dari mulieribus* (Augustin De Conj Adult 2,7) und die Schwierigkeiten der Abgrenzung gegenüber Leichtfertigkeit dadurch nur wachsen konnten.

Endlich gehört in diesen Zusammenhang wohl auch der oft sekundäre Zusatz von ἐπιθυμία(ι), von A pc sy^{h} in 2 Tim 3,6 noch durch ἡδοναί (vgl. Tit 3,3), sowie die Charakterisierung des Fleischesleibes als σῶμα τῶν ἁμαρτιῶν τῆς σαρκός in Kol 2,11 durch ℵ^{2} D^{1} Ψ 𝔐 (b) sy Epiph Aug^{pt}, wohl unter Einfluß von Röm 6,6, aber charakteristisch ist doch der Plural (vgl. auch die Charakterisierung der »Glieder« durch *et sunt vobis suavissima* in Jak 4,1 bei PsAug).

5. Antifeminismus

Es hängt wohl auch mit der Askese und ihren Motiven zusammen, daß die Textüberlieferung in ihrer Einstellung zur Frau, die schon in den Spätschriften des NT negativer wird, gewisse antifeministische Tendenzen zu erkennen gibt[31]. Daß 485 in Mt 12,50 ἀδελφή durch ἀδελφοί ersetzt, wird man wohl nicht überbewerten dürfen. In Mt 14,21 wohl auch nicht die Tatsache, daß D Θ f^{1} it die Kinder vor die Frauen rücken (vgl. immerhin 15,38, wo dasselbe bei ℵ d (Θ f^{1}) lat sy^{c} sa bo geschieht), erst recht nicht den Ersatz von γυναῖκες durch τινες in der Kreuzigungsszene von Mk 15,40 durch sa. Daß D lat in Act 17,4 aus vornehmen Frauen »Frauen der Vornehmen« macht, ist dagegen kaum Zufall, da D* auch in Act 17,12 in der Wendung »nicht wenige der angesehenen Frauen und Männer« die Hervorhebung der vornehmen Frauen ändert und daraus »von den Vornehmen viele Männer und Frauen« werden läßt. D fügt auch in Act 1,14 καὶ τέκνοις hinzu, weil dadurch die erwähnten Frauen zu Ehefrauen der Apostel werden und ihre unabhängige Aktivität in der Urgemeinde reduziert wird[32]. In Act 17,34 läßt D endlich eine Frau namens Damaris unter denen aus, die sich Paulus anschlossen.

Man darf das freilich nicht überziehen. Die ursprüngliche Reihenfolge von Aquila und Priscilla in Act 18,26 ist zwar umstritten, doch m. E. ist

---

[31] Zu Kodex D vgl. B. Witherington, The Anti-Feminist Tendencies of the "Western" Text in Acts, JBL 103, 1984, 82–84.

[32] Vgl. E. Haenchen, a. a. O. (Anm. 19), 121 Anm. 2.

die unbestrittene Reihenfolge Priscilla und Aquila in Act 18,18 ein Zeichen dafür, daß es keine prinzipielle Tendenz zur sekundären Voranstellung der Männernamen gibt. Das spricht aber dafür, in Act 18,26 (anders z. B. Nestle/Aland) die von D Ψ 0120 𝔐 gig sy sa^{mss} bezeugte Reihenfolge Aquila und Priscilla als ursprünglich anzunehmen, was dann von $𝔓^{74}$ ℵ A B E 33 pc vg bo an Act 18,18 angeglichen worden ist. Es geht hier also weniger um Antifeminismus als um Kontextangleichung. Auch in Röm 16,3 (vgl. auch 2 Tim 4,19) ist die Reihenfolge Priscilla und Aquila unbestritten (1 Kor 16,19 auch die umgekehrte Reihenfolge). Auch die Vertauschung der Reihenfolge von »Mutter oder Vater« in Mk 10,29 ist wohl auf den überstarken Druck von Mt 19,29 sowie Ex 20,12 und Dt 5,16 zurückzuführen, doch wird nach D k a ff^{2} vg^{ms} der Vater sogar ausgelassen, also nicht verlassen, und in Mt 15,6 wird das Ehren der Mutter wahrscheinlich von ℵ B D pc a e sy^{c} sa sekundär ausgelassen (Homoioteleuton), nicht umgekehrt nachträglich hinzugefügt. In Act 2,18 rückt ℵ τὰς δούλας sogar vor τοὺς δούλους.

Schwerer könnte wiegen, daß in Mt 5,32b D pc a b k Or? den Schlußsatz »und wer eine Geschiedene heiratet, bricht die Ehe« auslassen. B. Witherington will darin die Tendenz erkennen, "to highlight and protect male privilege, while also relegating women to a place in the background"[33]. Aber der ebenfalls an den Mann gerichtete und sachlich unbestrittene v. 32a mit seinem Verbot der Scheidung ist im Grunde ein größerer Schutz der Frau als das Verbot der Heirat einer Geschiedenen in v. 32b, das doch eher frauenfeindlich als -freundlich wirkt. So könnte man erwägen, daß pedantische Abschreiber v. 32b für überflüssig hielten[34]. Immerhin ist es richtig, daß nur v. 32b im Rahmen der Scheidung vom Ehebruch des Mannes spricht. Hält man H. Greevens textkritische Entscheidung zu Mt 19,9 für richtig und betrachtet den zu 5,32b par v. 9b als ursprünglich[35], dann zeigte sich hier eine Tendenz zur Auslassung derselben Wendung, falls es nicht doch umgekehrt steht und hier von B C* W Θ 078 $f^{1.13}$ 𝔐 lat $sy^{p.h}$ bo sekundär aufgefüllt worden ist.

1 Kor 7,2 wird der zweite Versteil, daß auch jede Frau ihren Mann haben soll, von F G pc ausgelassen, und ob hier tatsächlich ein an sich gut mögliches Homoioteleuton vorliegt[36], kann man durchaus fragen. Vielleicht sollte das Recht der Frau auf die Ehe eingeschränkt werden. In 1 Kor 7,36 machen D* F G 2495 pc d vg^{st} sy^{p} den Mann allein zum Subjekt des Eheschlusses, indem sie γαμείτωσαν durch γαμείτω ersetzen. Das ursprünglich wohl eher auf die Gottesdienstordnung bezogene ὑποτάσσε-

---

[33] B. Witherington, a.a.O. (Anm. 31), 84.

[34] B. M. Metzger u. a., a.a.O. (Anm. 13), 14.

[35] Anders freilich E. Nestle/K. Aland, Novum Testamentum Graece, Stuttgart ^{26}1979 und B. M. Metzger u. a., a.a.O. (Anm. 13), 48.

[36] E. Nestle/K. Aland mit Fragezeichen.

υθαι der Frauen in 1 Kor 14,34 wird von A (in Analogie zu den Haustafeln) auf die Männer bezogen. Nach ℵ* sollen die Ehemänner ihre Frauen nicht wie ihre eigenen Leiber (Eph 5,28), sondern wie ihre eigenen Kinder lieben.

Zweifellos im Sinn einer Abwertung der Frau ist es zu werten, wenn Kol 4,15 von D (F G) Ψ 𝔐 sy$^{p.hmg}$ *seiner* statt *ihrer* Hausgemeinde sprechen und Νύμφαν als Männername (Νυμφᾶν) verstehen. Ähnliches gilt für die Fassung von 2 Tim 2,2 in der Minuskel 2. Danach soll Timotheus das von Paulus Gehörte nicht treuen Menschen, sondern treuen Männern anvertrauen. In der lateinischen Handschrift E und bei Ambst wird aus dem Gebot, den Eltern zu gehorchen (Kol 3,20) *obaudite patribus,* in q wird aus dem doppelten μία Mt 24,41 ein doppeltes *unus*. Die Trilingue 460 fügt in Tit 1,9 unter anderem neben der Mahnung, daß solche, die zweimal geheiratet haben, nicht gewählt und zu Diakonen gemacht werden sollen, auch noch an: »auch keine Frauen, die in einer zweiten Ehe leben; man soll sie nicht zum Altardienst zulassen«. Auffallend ist auch, daß den Frauen des alten Bundes von Ψ 460 919 arm in 1 Petr 3,5 das Heiligkeitsprädikat abgesprochen wird und 1898 die Frauen in 1 Petr 3,7 nicht das weibliche, sondern das fleischliche σκεῦος nennt (vgl. auch den Ersatz von τέκνα durch *filii* in 1 Petr 3,6 bei den Lateinern 65Δ^{L} 262* Epiph).

Eine gegensätzliche Tendenz wird kaum greifbar, wenn man nicht das eindeutig als Frauennamen zu verstehende Julia von 𝔓^{46} 6 a b vg bo in Röm 16,7 dazu rechnen muß[37], wobei freilich auch das von den anderen Zeugen gebotene Junian entgegen einer verbreiteten Auslegungstendenz Frauenname ist[38]. Daß in 1 Kor 11,11 die beiden Satzhälften von D^{2} K L al vg sy umgedreht werden und also zuerst gesagt wird, der Mann sei nicht ohne die Frau, ist wohl von der in v. 12 genannten Naturordnung her zu verstehen. Ein bloßes Versehen ist es möglicherweise, wenn Θ A in Lk 8,3 Jesus nicht von vielen anderen (ἕτεραι) Frauen, sondern vielen Freundinnen (ἑταῖραι) umgeben sein läßt[39].

6. Loyalität

Ein immer wieder erkennbar werdender Zug ist das Bemühen, das Verhältnis von Gemeinde und Staatsordnung in ein möglichst günstiges

---

[37] Vgl. 𝔓^{46} auch in 1 Kor 11,9, wonach die Frau nicht um des Mannes, sondern um des Menschen willen geschaffen wurde.

[38] Vgl. dazu E. Gerstenberger/W. Schrage, Frau und Mann, Biblische Konfrontationen (Kohlhammer Taschenbuch 1013), Stuttgart 1980, 133; B. Brooten »Junia ... hervorragend unter den Aposteln« (Röm 16,7), in: Frauenbefreiung. Biblische und theologische Argumente, hg. v. E. Moltmann/Wendel, 1978, 148–151.

[39] So H. Vogels, a.a.O. (Anm. 9), 163 zur ähnlichen Verschreibung von ἑτέροις in ἑταίροις im Gleichnis von Mt 11,16 bei G 700 1010 pm aur ff^{1} l vg sa Hipp Or.

Licht zu rücken, wobei auch hier Ansätze des NT verstärkt werden und beider Loyalität unterstrichen wird. Schmähung und Verfolgung dürfen nicht auf wirkliche Vergehen der Christen zurückgehen (vgl. schon 1 Petr 4,15), sondern nur auf lügnerische Verleumdung. Deshalb fügen im Makarismus von Mt 5,11 alle Handschriften außer D it sy^{s} georg Tert ψευδόμενοι ein[40] (vgl. auch den Zusatz von κακοποιοῦντες zu ἁμαρτάνοντες in 1 Petr 2,20 durch 69). In Act 16,37 legt D (sy^{p}) Wert darauf, daß Paulus und Silas unschuldig (ἀναιτίους) Stockhiebe und Gefängnis erduldet haben. Dem entspricht, daß nach D (614 pc sy^{h**}) zu Act 16,39 die römischen Beamten mit vielen Freunden im Gefängnis erscheinen und versichern, daß sie nur aus Unkenntnis die christlichen Missionare nicht für ἄνδρες δίκαιοι gehalten haben[41]. Nach der Minuskel 2147, die in Act 25,8 τῶν Ἰουδαίων als Qualifizierung des νόμος ausläßt, heißt es in der Verteidigungsrede des Paulus vor Festus nun, er habe weder gegen das Gesetz (wahrscheinlich nun als das römische verstanden) noch gegen den Tempel noch gegen den Kaiser etwas verbrochen. Apk 13,10b wird wahrscheinlich unter Einfluß von Mt 26,52 die ohnehin schwierige Konstruktion von ℵ al und in ähnlicher Weise von 𝔓^{47vid} C 051 al so verändert, daß der, der mit dem Schwert tötet, mit dem Schwert getötet wird bzw. getötet werden muß. Das wird zwar auch so beurteilt: "Persecutors will be requited in strict accord with the lex talionis"[42]. Aber die genannten Veränderungen dürften kaum allein auf die Verfolger zielen, sondern auch den Widerstand gegen Rom im Auge haben. Die Christen sollen sich nicht bewaffnet gegen die kaiserliche Macht zur Wehr setzen. W. Bousset, der die Variante für den Urtext hält, fragt freilich, ob das für Christen überhaupt realistisch war, doch hält er für möglich, daß solche »wahnwitzigen Gedanken« hier und da gehegt worden seien[43], was für die Zeit der Varianten allerdings noch schwerer vorstellbar ist. Immerhin wird auch von Jesus in 1 Petr 2,23 (wahrscheinlich unter Einfluß der Passionsgeschichte Mk 15,19 par und speziell von Lk 6,29) gesagt, daß er geschlagen wurde und nicht zurückschlug (so Ir^{lat} Ambr^{pt}).

Angesichts solcher Apologien ist es nicht verwunderlich, daß auch der römische Staat und seine Beamten vereinzelt noch positiver beurteilt werden als ohnehin schon bei Lukas. In Act 25,24 verweigert Festus die Übergabe des Paulus an die Juden nach sy^{hm}, denen er Paulus *sine defensione ad tormentum* übergeben soll, u. a. folgendermaßen: *Non potui autem tradere eum propter mandata quae habemus ab Augusto*[44]. Auch die Auslassung von ἀνθρωπίνῃ durch ℵ* in 1 Petr 2,13 könnte mehr sein als

40 B. M. Metzger u. a., a.a.O. (Anm. 13), 12f. erwägen eine sekundäre Auslassung unter Paralleleinfluß von Lukas.

41 Zum Kontext vgl. E. Fascher, a.a.O. (Anm. 3), 38.

42 B. M. Metzger u. a., a.a.O. (Anm. 13), 748.

43 W. Bousset, Die Offenbarung Johannis, KEK 16, Göttingen ^{5}1896, 423.

44 So H. v. Soden, a.a.O. (Anm. 1), 600.

ein Versehen, nämlich eine Aufwertung der Obrigkeit. Möglicherweise ist die Lesart ἐστάθην von 051 𝔐 vg^{mss} sy^{ph} co in Apk 12,18, die den vom ursprünglichen Text (»*er* trat«) angedeuteten Zusammenhang zwischen dem Drachen (= Satan) und dem Tier aus dem Abgrund (= römisches Imperium) durch die 1. Person beseitigt, mit in diesen Zusammenhang einzubeziehen, auch wenn eine Angleichung an das folgende εἶδον in 13,1[45] in Rechnung zu stellen bleibt.

Das ändert freilich nichts daran, daß letztendlich auch der Staat nichts gegen Gottes Sache vermag. So wird in die Rede des Gamaliel, daß der Hohe Rat alles das, was von Gott kommt, nicht zunichte machen kann (Act 5,39), von D h sy^{h**} mae eingefügt, daß das auch βασιλεῖς und τύραννοι nicht vermögen, so daß die Machtlosigkeit gegenüber Gottes Vorhaben und Werk auch für die politischen Mächte gilt. 460 hat außerdem zu Tit 1,9 den Zusatz, daß Herrscher, die ungerechte Richter, Räuber, Lügner und Unbarmherzige sind, vom Bischof als θεοῦ διάκονος zurechtgewiesen werden sollen. Interessant und bezeichnend ist auch die Konstruktion von Röm 13,1 in c f t: *quae autem sunt a deo, ordinatae sunt.* Wenn üblicherweise Matthäus auf Markus eingewirkt hat, muß man auch besonders beachten, daß in Mt 20,25 statt οἱ ἄρχοντες von 473 δοκοῦντες ἄρχειν gelesen wird, Matthäus aber keinen Einfluß auf Mk 10,42 ausgeübt hat.

Mit der Respektierung der staatlichen Ordnung war nach einzelnen Handschriften auch die der religiösen und familiären Ordnung gegeben. So wird in der Verhandlung vor Pilatus die politische Anklage der Aufwiegelung und Steuerverweigerung – und damit deren Entkräftung! – um die religiöse Dimension erweitert, wenn it Mcion in Lk 23,2 die Auflösung von Gesetz und Propheten erwähnen und Marcion selbst als weiteren Anklagepunkt die Entfremdung von Frauen und Kindern hinzufügt (vgl. auch (c) e in v. 5: *et filios nostros et uxores avertit a nobis, non enim baptizantur sicut et nos nec se mundant*[46]. Jesus wird also gegen den Vorwurf in Schutz genommen, die jüdische Lebens- und patriarchalische Familienordnung aufzulösen. Es ist gerade ein Zeichen der Auflösung aller sittlichen Ordnung in der Endzeit, wenn sich nicht nur Kinder gegen ihre Eltern, sondern nach 579 zu Mk 13,12 auch Eltern gegen ihre Kinder erheben. Jetzt aber gilt, daß Kinder, die ihre Eltern mißhandeln oder schlagen, gehindert, zurechtgewiesen und ermahnt werden sollen (460 zu Tit 1,11).

7. Ideale und Kriterien

Von vornherein zu erwarten ist, daß die ethische Vorbildlichkeit Jesu gesteigert wird. Nicht nur sollen die Jünger wie Jesus einander die Füße

---

[45] So B. M. Metzger u. a., a. a. O. (Anm. 13), 746.

[46] Bei F. Fascher, a. a. O. (Anm. 3), 54f. wird sogar Ursprünglichkeit erwogen.

waschen (Joh 13,14), sondern diese Verpflichtung besteht nach D Θ it (sy$^{s.p}$) bei ihnen πόσῳ μᾶλλον. 1 Joh 4,17 heißt es nach 2138 pc nicht »wie jener ist«, sondern »wie jener in der Welt untadelig und rein war«. Vielleicht darf man, gerade weil man Jesu Wort ernst nahm und sich an seinem Vorbild zu orientieren suchte, auch den Ersatz von ὀργισθείς durch σπλαγχνισθείς in Mk 1,41 durch alle Handschriften bis auf D a ff^{2} r^{1} von hier aus verstehen, denn m. E. ist ὀργισθείς Urtext[47]. Nur schwach dringt dagegen die imitatio dei ein: So wird 2 Tim 1,8 von 1319 κατὰ μίμησιν θεοῦ hinzugesetzt.

Verwunderlich ist, daß καλοκαγαθία nur ein einziges Mal erscheint, und zwar in Jak 5,10 bei ℵ anstelle von κακοπαθία, vielleicht aufgrund eines Versehens. Im übrigen aber sind bei den Tugendkatalogen weniger Varianten zu beobachten als bei den Lasterkatalogen.

Die schon im Neuen Testament selbst zurücktretende Radikalität im Gesetzesverständnis setzt sich fort. Charakteristisch ist Gal 3,19. Nach D* Cl ist der νόμος nicht um der Übertretungen willen gegeben, sondern um der Überlieferung willen. 𝔓^{46} F G al it sprechen vom νόμος τῶν πράξεων und konstruieren um. Daß das Gesetz die befristete Aufgabe habe, die Übertretungen zu mehren, war offenbar allen denen anstößig, die das Evangelium als neues Gesetz verstanden[48]. Möglicherweise ist auch die Auslassung von καὶ νόμου durch B in Hebr 7,12 von hierher begründet: Veränderung des Priestertums war notwendig, impliziert aber keine Änderung des Gesetzes (v. 18 bleibt unbestritten, doch ist dort von der Aufhebung nur eines Gebotes die Rede). Vielleicht konnte sich D^{2} (L) Ψ 𝔐 sy^{p} schon nicht mehr vorstellen, daß Paulus nicht mehr ὑπὸ νόμον sei (1 Kor 9,20), so daß sie das auslassen, doch bleibt auch Homoioteleuton möglich[49]. *Peccator et impius* ist nach Patricius offenbar eo ipso ein *transgressor legis,* wie sein Zusatz in 1 Petr 4,18 zeigt. Nach 33 pc zu Jak 1,25 wird dem vergeßlichen Hörer nicht einfach der handelnde ποιητὴς ἔργου gegenübergestellt, sondern der ἀκροατὴς νόμου καὶ ποιητὴς ἔργου. Wenn Jak 1,22 von C^{2} 88 621 1067 1852 al λόγος durch νόμος ersetzt wird, ist das zwar durch 1,25 und 4,11 zu erklären, aber auffällig bleibt doch, daß nicht λόγος den νόμος verdrängt und νόμος bis auf 1241 in Jak 2,8 unbestritten bleibt. Ähnlich steht es in Mt 15,6, wo τὸν λόγον τοῦ θεοῦ von ℵ^{*2} C 084 f^{13} 1010 pc Epiph durch τὸν νόμον τοῦ θεοῦ, in L W 0106 f^{1} 𝔐 lat sy^{h} Cyr durch τὴν ἐντολὴν τοῦ θεοῦ verdrängt wird (letzteres wahrscheinlich unter Einfluß von v. 3 und Mk 7,8). Auch in Mk 7,13 wird

---

47 Anders H. Greeven, a.a.O. (Anm. 1), E. Nestle/K. Aland, a.a.O. (Anm. 1); vgl. dagegen mit Recht G. Stählin, ThWNT V, 428 Anm. 326; J. Gnilka, Das Evangelium nach Markus, EKK II/1, Zürich/Neukirchen 1978, 92 Anm. 15 u. a. Entscheidend ist, daß σπλαγχνισθείς sonst nirgendwo ersetzt worden ist.

48 E. Fascher, a.a.O. (Anm. 3), 94.

49 So H. Vogels, a.a.O. (Anm. 9), 166.

λόγος τοῦ θεοῦ unter Einfluß von v. 8 durch τὴν ἐντολὴν τοῦ θεοῦ ersetzt (so f[1]) bzw. ergänzt (so W), ἐντολὴ τ.θ. in Mt 15,3/Mk 7,8 dagegen bleibt unbestritten. Apk 22,14 wird die Seligpreisung derjenigen, die ihre Kleider waschen (πλύνοντες τὰς στολὰς αὐτῶν) von 𝔐 gig sy[(h)] bo Tert ersetzt durch die Seligpreisung der ποιοῦντες τὰς ἐντολὰς αὐτοῦ. In 2 Kor 10,6 wird von 206 1758 πᾶσαν παρακοήν durch πᾶσαν παράβασιν ergänzt, in Kol 2,13 von 1836 »tot durch Verfehlungen« ebenfalls durch τῆς παραβάσεως.

Das ist freilich nicht allzu viel für die oft betonte Vergesetzlichung der Ethik. Immerhin ist die Sorge vor allzu großer Freiheit unübersehbar. Die berühmte Seligpreisung des Sabbatarbeiters in Lk 6,4 bei D ist bei aller »geistigen Echtheit« gegen libertinistische Gefahren gerichtet und will die treffen, die aus Freiheit Gesetzlosigkeit werden lassen[50]. Ähnlich wird man auch die Umformung des Gleichnisses von den anvertrauten Talenten Mt 25,14ff. im Nazarener-Evangelium 18[51] zu bewerten haben, wo die Drohung nicht dem dritten Knecht gilt, der sein Talent ängstlich vergräbt, sondern dem ersten, der das Vermögen mit Huren und Flötenspielerinnen durchbringt und darum von seinem Herrn ins Gefängnis geworfen wird, während der Nichtstuer nur getadelt wird. Eine gewisse Ängstlichkeit vor allzu großer Vergebungsbereitschaft ist auch die Beschränkung von Mt 18,21f. im Hebräer-Evangelium 15a[52], wo die zu vergebende Sünde auf Wortsünden beschränkt und von der Bedingung der Genugtuung abhängig gemacht wird: *Si peccaverit . . . in verbo et satis tibi fecerit.*

Deutlicher treten Rücksicht und Liebe in den Vordergrund. 1 Kor 13,13 wird die Liebe von 255 2298 nicht nur als größte τούτων (sc. der drei genannten Größen), sondern πάντων bezeichnet. Daß sie alle anderen Gebote »zusammenfaßt« (ἀνακεφαλαιοῦται) wird unter Einfluß von Röm 13,9 auch in Gal 5,14 von 365 pc eingetragen. In Jak 5,12 fügt aeth hinzu *at quod vero omnium primum est, amate vos invicem*[53]. Im Unterschied zur Angleichung von Phlm 5 (vgl. oben) haben in 2 Tim 2,22 F G die Liebe vor den Glauben gerückt, in Tit 2,10 lassen ℵ* 33 den Glauben aus, und statt ἀγαθήν liest 33 ἀγάπην. Der Westliche Text fügt ins Aposteldekret die Goldene Regel ein, in Act 15,20 D 323 945 1739 1891 pc sa Ir[lat], in Act 15,29 D 323 614 945 1739 1891 pc l p w sy[h**] sa Ir[lat] Cyp (die negative Fassung auch Did 1,2). Daß man sich der Neuheit durchaus bewußt ist, zeigt Justins Abwandlung von Mt 5,46 in Apologie I 15: »Wenn ihr die liebt, die euch lieben, was tut ihr Neues (καινόν)? Denn

---

[50] So W. Käser, Exegetische Erwägungen zur Seligpreisung des Sabbatarbeiters Lk 6,5 D, ZThK 65, 1968, 414–430, besonders 425.

[51] Euseb Theophanie, Griechischer Text bei H. Greeven, a.a.O. (Anm. 1), 229; vgl. L. E. Wright, a.a.O. (Anm. 25), 97.

[52] Hier Dial Adv Pelag III 2, Lateinischer Text bei H. Greeven, a.a.O. (Anm. 1), 147.

[53] So C. Tischendorf, a.a.O. (Anm. 1), II 270.

das tun auch die πόρνοι«[54]. Daß man nicht mit Wort und Zunge, sondern mit Tat und Wahrheit lieben soll, schränkt a f in 1 Joh 3,18 durch »nicht allein, sondern« ein und läßt damit erkennen, daß auch Wort und Zunge von der Liebe bestimmt sein sollen. In Lk 14,12 wird die Mahnung, nicht Freunde, Brüder, Verwandte oder reiche Nachbarn einzuladen, von D it vg^{s} dadurch verstärkt, daß die Reichen als selbständiges Glied genannt werden, und sy^{s} fügt in v. 13 zu den Armen, Krüppeln, Lahmen und Blinden noch »die Verachteten und viele andere« hinzu (vgl. auch die Hinzufügung in v. 21: »und die Verworfenen«). Nach D it Spec zu Act 2,45 erfolgt nicht das Verharren im Tempel (so Act 2,46), sondern das Verkaufen und Verteilen von Gütern und Habe καθ᾿ ἡμέραν. Der Verkauf der Habe beim reichen Jüngling wird vom Nazaräer-Evangelium sozial begründet: »Siehe, viele deiner Brüder, Söhne Abrahams, starren vor Schmutz und sterben vor Hunger, und dein Haus ist voll von vielen Gütern, und gar nichts kommt aus ihm heraus zu ihnen«[55]. Auch die Rücksicht auf das schwache Gewissen wird verstärkt: Röm 14,21 fügen 𝔓^{46vid} ℵ^{2} B D F G Ψ 0209 𝔐 lat sy^{h} sa ἢ σκανδαλίζεται ἢ ἀσθενεῖ hinzu. Andererseits ist die Auslassung von ἀσθενοῦσαν in 𝔓^{46} Cl in 1 Kor 8,12 vielleicht darum geschehen, um Rücksicht auf das Gewissen des Bruders nicht nur im Fall eines schwachen Gewissens nahezulegen[56]. Solche Rücksichtnahme wird freilich auch kirchlich verengt (vgl. die Hinzufügung von τῶν ἐν τῇ ἐκκλησίᾳ in Mt 18,10 durch Or Eus (Tischendorf I 106).

8. Moralisierung

Wer den gehäuften Numeruswechsel vom Singular zum Plural Moralisierung nennt, kommt auf seine Kosten. Früchte statt Frucht bezeugen in Phil 1,11 Ψ 𝔐 sy, in Lk 6,43 (par Mt 7,17) D it (vg) sy$^{s.p}$, Begierden statt Begierde in 2 Petr 2,10 C P 323 614 630 945 1241 1505 1739 2495 al (vg^{mss}) sy^{h} bo Hier Cass, τὰ θελήματα τοῦ θεοῦ anstelle des Singulars in Mk 3,35 B und in Mt 7,21 ℵ*. Der Plural soll dabei wohl die einzelnen Akte stärker erfassen. Vor allem auf gute Werke wird größter Wert gelegt, in Anknüpfung an andere Stellen des Neuen Testaments. Nach ℵ* f^{1} 28 1424 al it vg^{cl} sy$^{c.p.h}$ co zu Mt 16,27 wird der Menschensohn jedem nicht κατὰ τὴν πρᾶξιν αὐτοῦ vergelten, sondern κατὰ τὰ ἔργα αὐτοῦ (die Änderung entspricht freilich Ps 62,13; vgl. dasselbe Zitat Röm 2,6, wo es unverändert bleibt). Nach 1515 in Mt 12,37 wird man nicht durch Worte (so alle anderen Handschriften), sondern durch Werke gerechtfertigt oder verdammt (Θ kombiniert beides und fügt ἔργων hinzu). In Jak 1,22 läßt 431 μόνον aus, wodurch der Gegensatz Hören/Tun schärfer heraustritt.

---

54 Vgl. L. E. Wright, a.a.O. (Anm. 25), 61f.

55 Lateinischer Text bei H. Greeven, a.a.O. (Anm. 1), 179.

56 Vgl. B. M. Metzger u. a., a.a.O. (Anm. 13), 557.

In Jak 3,17 fügen C 322 323 945 1241 1243 1739 pc Did zu καρπῶν als Apposition noch ἔργων an. PsAug hat in 1 Pt 5,3 den Zusatz *in operibus bonis in omni conversatione quae secundum deum.* Nach F G pc vg^{cl} kommt es in Phlm 6 auf die Erkenntnis des guten Werkes an, nicht einfach auf die des Guten.

Es gibt aber auch Gegenbeispiele. Zum einen für den Numeruswechsel in den Singular (vgl. Lk 3,8 in D W pc e r^1 sy^h, unter Einfluß von Mt 3,8, wo freilich auch der Plural eingedrungen ist; in Röm 13,14 haben $\mathfrak{P}^{46*}$ A C pc in den Singular ἐπιθυμίαν verändert). Außerdem ist im Einzelfall Kontexteinfluß zu berücksichtigen, z. B. Röm 13,13 unter Angleichung an die vorangehenden Begriffspaare, die im Plural stehen, so daß B sy^h sa (Cyp) auch »Hader und Streit« in den Plural verändern (ähnlich Gal 5,20). Zum anderen ersetzt 1245 in 1 Tim 6,18 gute Werke durch gute Worte, vielleicht weil zwischen der Mahnung zum Gutestun und zur Freigebigkeit eine nochmalige Betonung der Werke als redundant erschien. Der Plural kann auch eine gewisse Individualisierung bedeuten, wenn z. B. nach ℵ A C F G Ψ 𝔐 sy^h zu 1 Thess 1,7 die Gemeinde nicht mehr als ganze τύπος genannt wird, sondern statt dessen der Plural erscheint. Nach dem von A B bo^{pt} gebotenen Plural ὡς κλέπτας in 1 Thess 5,4 soll der Tag die Gemeinde nicht ὡς κλέπτης überraschen, d. h. entweder (bildlich) nicht »wie Diebe« oder (stellvertretend für alle Laster und damit moralisierend) nicht »als Diebe«.

Man kann zur Moralisierungstendenz auch die bekannte Wendung vom Kult zur Moral rechnen. Man muß das freilich sogleich präzisieren. Denn zweifellos macht sich in der Textüberlieferung hier und da auch der christliche Kult bemerkbar, wenn etwa Jak 5,14 das Öl von 1838 als »heiliges« qualifiziert wird oder man nach D* F G t vg^{mss} Ambst zu Röm 12,13 nicht an den χρεῖαι, sondern an den μνεῖαι der Heiligen teilnehmen soll. Hier dürfte nicht nur »eine alte mechanisch entstandene Korruptel« vorliegen[57], sondern »die Sitte der Fürbitte für die Verstorbenen, wenn nicht gar beginnender Heiligenkult« zu vermuten sein[58]. Die Uminterpretation betrifft die jüdischen und judenchristlichen Kult- und Zeremonialgebote. Bekanntestes Beispiel einer solchen Uminterpretation ist die moralische Fassung des sog. Aposteldekrets, das in Entsprechung zu Lev 17f., wonach vier Vorschriften auch für die in Israel wohnenden Nichtjuden gelten sollen, Enthaltung von Götzendienst, von Unzucht (d. h. wohl von sexuellen Beziehungen in bestimmten Verwandtschaftsgraden) und von Ersticktem und Blut fordert[59]. Diese ursprünglich kultische Fassung wird in der

[57] So H. Lietzmann, An die Römer, HNT 8, Tübingen ^{4}1933, 111.

[58] So E. Käsemann, An die Römer, HNT 8a, Tübingen ^{4}1980, 331. H. Vogels, a.a.O. (Anm. 9), 163 rechnet unsere Stelle freilich zu den unbeabsichtigten Fehlern.

[59] Vgl. E. J. Epp, a.a.O. (Anm. 2), 107ff. (Literatur!); E. Fascher, a.a.O. (Anm. 3), 34. Vgl. im übrigen das kultkritische Jesuswort im Hebräer-Evangelium (Epiph Adv Haeres XXX 16. »Ich bin gekommen, die Opfer aufzulösen ...«).

Textüberlieferung moralisch gedeutet, d. h. die zeremoniellen Teile werden ausgelassen und εἰδωλόθυτα im Sinn des Götzendienstes und αἷμα im Sinne des Mordens uminterpretiert. Ein Versehen ist hier völlig ausgeschlossen, da die entscheidenden Veränderungen sowohl in Act 15,20 als auch in 15,29 und 21,25 erfolgen, jedenfalls bei D, der das Erstickte an allen drei Stellen ausläßt, in Act 15,20 unterstützt von gig und Ir^{lat}, in 15,29 von l Ir^{lat} Tert und in Act 21,25 von gig. Die ethische Interpretation bestätigt vor allem die hinzugefügte »Goldene Regel« (vgl. oben) in 15,20 und in 15,29[60]. Schwieriger ist die Beurteilung von Lk 11,40 wo $\mathfrak{P}^{45}$ C D Γ 700 pc a c e Inneres und Äußeres umstellen. Ursprünglich fragt Jesus hier wahrscheinlich[61], ob der (d. h. Gott), der das Äußere gemacht hat, nicht auch das Innere gemacht hat, was heißen soll, daß alles auf die innere Einstellung und nicht die rituellen Äußerlichkeiten ankommt. Daraus aber wird nun, daß »der, der das Innere getan (= in Ordnung gebracht) hat, das auch mit dem Äußeren getan hat«. Das legt das Urteil nahe: "This statement appears to give surprising support to ritual observance"[62]. Doch ist das mindestens für D schwierig, da hier v. 42b (ταῦτα δὲ ἔδει ποιῆσαι κἀκεῖνα μὴ παρεῖναι) ausgelassen wird. Wahrscheinlich ist Subjekt des Satzes nun der Mensch, der damit, daß er das Innere gereinigt hat, auch das Äußere erledigt hat.

Am ehesten wird man von Moralisierung dort sprechen, wo das Verhältnis von Indikativ und Imperativ außer Blick gerät. Auffälligstes Beispiel ist die mehrfache Auslassung des οὖν-paraeneticum, das Indikativ und Imperativ bei Paulus verknüpft, was offenbar nicht mehr verstanden wird. Zwar ist es Kol 3,5 unbestritten stehengeblieben und 3,12 nur von L ausgelassen, Röm 12,1 aber wird es von 81 durch δέ ersetzt und in 1 Thess 4,1 von B* 33 629 630 1175 1739* vg^{mss} sy^{p} bo, in Gal 5,1 von D* 69 1912 vg sy^{h} ausgelassen. Auch in 1 Kor 5,7 ist es m. E. nicht sekundär eingefügt[63], sondern von $\mathfrak{P}^{46}$ ℵ* A B D F G 614 629 2464 pc lat sy^{p} Tert Cl ausgelassen worden (immerhin gibt es auch eine Gegentendenz: in 1 Petr 2,13 von P 𝔐 vg^{ms} sy^{h}). Mt 6,33 ist von B die Reihenfolge von Reich und Gerechtigkeit umgekehrt worden, wobei Gerechtigkeit nun wohl als Bedingung des Reiches Gottes gilt. Nach A* zu 2 Tim 2,19 bleibt nicht »der feste Grund Gottes« bestehen, sondern der Grund Gottes für die Standhaften, wobei freilich eine Verschreibung (ὁ μέντοι στερεός → ὁ μὲν τοῖς στερεοῖς) am Anfang gestanden haben wird. Immerhin sollen sich auch nach ℵ A Ψ 81 614 (623) 630 1505 1852 (2464) 2495 al h vg sy

---

60 Vgl. H.-W. Bartsch, Traditionsgeschichtliches zur »Goldenen Regel« und zum Aposteldekret, ZNW 75, 1984, 128–132, bes. 129f.

61 J. Wellhausen, Das Evangelium Lucae, Berlin 1904, 61, z. B. hält diese Lesart aber für sekundär.

62 So L. H. Marshall, a.a.O. (Anm. 23), 498.

63 So E. Nestle/K. Aland.

co zu 2 Petr 1,10 die Adressaten befleißigen, διὰ τῶν καλῶν ἔργων ihre Berufung und Erwählung festzumachen. In Lk 2,14 gilt die Verheißung nach der Vulgata den Menschen *bonae voluntatis* (vgl. auch die Umstellung von Bösen und Guten in Mt 5,45 durch lat sy). Vielleicht darf man in diesen Zusammenhang auch den gut bezeugten Zusatz von Röm 11,6 einordnen. Hier wird über Paulus hinaus, nach dem Gottes Gnadenwahl nicht aus Werken geschieht, weil sonst Gnade nicht Gnade bliebe, der Satz von (ℵ^2 B Ψ (365 2127) 𝔐 vg^{ms} (sy) auch umgedreht: »Wenn aber aufgrund von Werken (die Gnadenwahl erfolgt), dann (handelt es sich) nicht um Gnade, weil anders das Werk nicht mehr Werk bliebe«. Das könnte zunächst den überzeugenden Gedanken zum Ausdruck bringen, daß nur durch die allein wirksame Gnade auch das notwendige Werk des Menschen als Werk rein erhalten bleibt (vgl. auch B: »weil dann das Werk nicht Gnade bliebe«). Man muß dann für ἔργον und ἔργον aber einen verschiedenen Sinn annehmen: verdienstliches Werk – gebotenes Werk. Näher liegt, mit B. Weiß[64], der diese Variante für ursprünglich hält, anzunehmen, daß das Werk darum nicht mehr Werk bliebe, »weil ein Werk, das nicht durch sich selbst erwirbt, was seine Folge ist, keine wirkliche Leistung mehr ist«. Das aber soll es eben bleiben, wenn auch nicht für die Gnadenwahl, so doch für den Jüngsten Tag, aber eben nach diesen sekundären Abschreibern.

Von Einfluß scheint auch die Synergismusproblematik. Gal 2,8 bietet 920 statt ἐνεργήσας das im NT sonst seltene συνεργήσας, das sich freilich hier auf Gott bezieht. Umgekehrt aber hatte man offenbar Schwierigkeiten mit dem συνεργὸν τοῦ θεοῦ als Qualifikation des Timotheus in 1 Thess 3,2. Entweder man ließ τοῦ θεοῦ aus (B pc vg^{mss}) oder man ersetzte συνεργόν durch διάκονον (ℵ A P Ψ 6 81 629* 1241 1739 1881 2464 pc lat co) oder man kombinierte wenigstens (𝔐 al). Die Varianten haben wohl tatsächlich die Absicht, "to remove the objectionable character which the bold designation συνεργὸς τοῦ θεοῦ appeared to have"[65] (vgl. auch die Hinzufügung von μου in Kol 4,11 zu συνεργοὶ εἰς τὴν βασιλείαν τοῦ θεοῦ durch D F G 505 it arm Or).

Zusammenfassend läßt sich feststellen, daß die Textüberlieferung vor allem Tendenzen verstärkt hat, die schon in den Spätschriften des NT selbst zum Vorschein kommen, daneben aber deutlich bestimmte Tendenzen greifbar werden, die in der Ethik der frühen und mittelalterlichen Kirche eine besondere Rolle gespielt haben.

---

64 B. Weiß, Der Brief an die Römer, KEK 4, Göttingen ^{8}1891, 471.

65 B. M. Metzger u. a., a.a.O. (Anm. 13), 631.

Haben Jesu Worte über Armut und Reichtum Folgen für das soziale Verhalten?[1]

von Hans-Hartmut Schroeder

(Albertsdorf 18, 2448 Landkirchen/Fehmarn)

Wenn wir die Worte Jesu über Armut und Reichtum auf ihre sozialethische Wirkung hin befragen, so tun wir dies möglicherweise mit einem Vorverständnis oder einer bestimmten Absicht. Denn wenn Jesus der Mensch schlechthin war, dann – so meinen wir – müßte er uns auch verbindlich sagen können, wie wir uns in ethischen Fragen zu entscheiden haben. Und mit dem Thema »Arm und Reich« ist ja in der Tat ein so umfangreiches Feld ethischen Verhaltens bezeichnet, daß unser Interesse an einer Weisung durch Jesus nicht unbegründet ist. Es geht ja nicht nur um unsern persönlichen Umgang mit Geld und Besitz; sondern es geht um die Eigentumsfrage als solche; es geht um Wirtschaftssysteme; es geht um die Frage der Unterdrückung und Abhängigkeit, um Hunger und Armut in der Dritten Welt. Kann Jesus uns dazu etwas sagen?

Angesichts dessen nun, daß Jesu Predigt Ansage der Nähe der Königsherrschaft Gottes war, geht es um die rechte Einschätzung ethisch relevanter Aussagen im Munde Jesu. Weder dürfen wir ihm Worte in den Mund legen, die er gesagt haben könnte, noch dürfen wir Worte, die er gesagt hat, ohne Berücksichtigung der kerygmatischen Absicht, der sie dienen, deuten oder in ihrer Tendenz bis in unsere Gegenwart ausziehen. Dabei bleibt aber die Frage, ob Jesus heute, wenn er z. B. durch Bolivien ziehen würde, ganz anders als damals reden und zum Thema ›Armut‹ anders Stellung beziehen würde.

Wir können aber auch umgekehrt fragen: Wenn ein Sozialarbeiter oder Arbeiterpriester, der gerade die sozialen Mißstände im Auge hat, damals so wie Jesus durch Galiläa gezogen wäre – wie hätte er wohl die sozialen Verhältnisse beurteilt? Worauf hätte er den Finger gelegt? Hätte er Anlaß gehabt, revolutionären Umsturz zu predigen? Hätte er Bodenreformvorschläge gemacht? Hätte er das Sklaventum abgeschafft? Hätte er – entsprechend dem vierten Gebot, das die Versorgung der alten Eltern sicherstellte – auch ein Gebot zur Sicherung der alleinstehenden Witwen und Waisen oder der unverhofft in Not geratenen Menschen gefordert?

---

[1] Diesem Aufsatz liegt ein Referat zugrunde, das Verf. 1977 im «seminario de profesores» der Facultad de Teología ISEDET in Buenos Aires gehalten hat, abgedruckt in : Los Pobres, Buenos Aires, Argentina 1978, S. 29–43.

Und wie sehen im Vergleich dazu die Worte Jesu aus, in denen von Armut bzw. Reichtum die Rede ist? Hat Jesus in wünschenswerter Klarheit Not und Armut in seinem Land gesehen? Hat er etwas unternommen, um die Armut zu beseitigen? Wer wäre dafür der richtige Adressat gewesen? Oder hat er das Volk hinter sich zu bringen versucht, gerade auch in dieser Frage?

Ferner: Was ist Armut? Ist uns aus dem Neuen Testament ersichtlich, ob es damals in Galiläa eine weitverbreitete Armut gab? Oder waren es einzelne Fälle? Und wenn es Armut gab, kennen wir dann auch die Ursachen dafür? Vielleicht neigen wir dazu, das Sklaventum für ungerecht und also für eine Ursache der Armut zu halten. Andererseits wissen wir, daß damals die Zuordnung von Herr und Sklave als genau so naturbedingt angesehen wurde wie das Verhältnis von Mann und Frau oder Eltern und Kinder. Gibt es Hinweise darauf, daß Jesus an dieser Zuordnung Anstoß genommen hat? Etwas anderes ist es, wenn innerhalb solcher vorgegebenen Strukturen Unrecht geschieht, was aber kein ausreichender Grund wäre, um die Institution als solche aufzulösen. Es wäre also unbegründet zu vermuten, Jesus habe mit gelegentlichen sozialkritischen Äußerungen auch tendenziell die ganze soziale Zuordnung oder Struktur angegriffen und aufheben wollen.

Wir müssen also prüfen: Wo sagt Jesus etwas zum Thema ›Armut‹ in genereller Weise? Wo sagt er etwas dazu in einer konkreten Einzelsituation? Weiter müssen wir fragen: Wenn er nicht eindeutig über Armut im konkreten und sozialen Sinne spricht, welche Bedeutung haben solche Worte dann für die soziale Wirklichkeit? Ist der von den Jüngern geforderte Besitzverzicht nur an die damalige konkrete Situation der Nachfolge gebunden? Oder wird er von allen verlangt? Hat Jesus dabei zugleich an eine gerechtere Umverteilung der Güter gedacht? So könnte ja Jesu Antwort an den reichen Jüngling verstanden werden: Gehe hin, verkaufe alles, was du hast, und gib es den Armen. Man könnte auch alternativ zugespitzt fragen: Predigt Jesus das Lob der Armut, oder will er, daß alle das gleiche Einkommen haben?

Wenn wir uns nun die Texte ansehen, so scheint es mir auf den ersten Blick so zu sein, daß wir einerseits wertneutrale Äußerungen Jesu haben, die die damaligen Zustände widerspiegeln. Daneben gibt es andererseits Worte, in denen er den Verzicht auf Reichtum fordert. Die Armen werden glückselig genannt. Ihnen wird das Evangelium gebracht. Hingegen ist Reichtum ein Hindernis auf dem Weg ins Reich Gottes. In Abgrenzung gegen diese Wortgruppe gibt es Äußerungen, die sich auf konkrete soziale Bedingungen beziehen und in denen Jesus sich kritisch zu ihnen äußert.

Es ist nun zu fragen, ob diese unterschiedlichen Wortgruppen dennoch in einem inneren Zusammenhang miteinander stehen; bzw. wie soll solche konkrete Kritik verstanden werden auf dem Hintergrund des generellen Besitzverzichts? Stünde die Kritik nicht im Widerspruch zur positiven Bewertung der Armut? Jedenfalls dann, wenn der Verzicht konkret gemeint ist. Ließe sich solch ein Widerspruch aus unterschiedlicher Motivation der Worte Jesu begreifen? So daß ein unterschiedliches Verhalten im Konkreten bedingt ist durch die unterschiedliche Absicht?

Sollten sich nun aber aus den unterschiedlichen Äußerungen Jesu nicht eindeutig Weisungen für das konkrete sozialethische Verhalten ergeben, so bliebe zu untersuchen, ob sich nicht schon aus dem Liebesgebot unmißverständlich auch das Gebot der Hilfe für die Armen ergibt. Ja, es wäre weiter zu fragen, ob diese soziale Hilfe füreinander nicht ohnehin ein Gebot der Vernunft ist, diese also möglicherweise gar keine spezifische Forderung des Neuen Testaments ist, entsprechend wie wir im NT deutliche Spuren dafür finden, daß gerade die praktische Morallehre aus der Umwelt übernommen wurde und lediglich in die Klammer des ἐν κυρίῳ gesetzt wurde.

So könnten wir zu dem Ergebnis kommen, daß das Spezifische an Jesu Worten über ›arm und reich‹ gerade das ›Lob‹ der Armut und das ›Wehe‹ über die Reichen bzw. die Aufforderung zum Besitzverzicht ist. Dies würde nicht im Widerspruch zum Liebesgebot stehen. Denn wer auf Besitz verzichten kann, kann auch in der Not anderer besser helfen als der, der sein Geld festhält.

Schließlich wäre noch zu fragen nach den Traditionen, von denen her Jesu Worte geprägt worden sind bzw. gegen die sie sich abheben.

Damit mögen einige Anhaltspunkte genannt sein, mit denen wir uns den Worten Jesu über arm und reich zuwenden. Ich unterscheide – wie schon oben angedeutet – zwischen drei Wortgruppen.

1. Die Worte, die unkritisch etwas aussagen über die Verhältnisse zur Zeit Jesu und in denen sich die herrschende Auffassung zu Sozialfragen spiegelt.

2. Die radikalen Worte Jesu, die zum Verzicht auf Besitz auffordern und in denen die Armut gelobt und der Reichtum getadelt wird; sowie die, in denen zwischen Gott und Mammon unterschieden und auf die Gefahren des Reichtums hingewiesen wird.

3. Die Worte, in denen die konkrete Praxis zu erkennen ist.

Zur ersten Gruppe gehört zum Beispiel Matthäus 20,15: Steht es mir nicht frei, mit dem Meinigen zu tun, was ich will? Ein Wort aus dem Gleichnis von den Arbeitern im Weinberg. Es steht nur bei Matthäus. Man könnte es so deuten, daß Jesus das Privateigentum anerkennt. Ferner: Matthäus 24,45ff. = Lukas 12,42ff.; das Gleichnis vom guten und bösen Knecht scheint den Großbesitz anzuerkennen. Matthäus 25,14–30 = Lukas 19,11–27 lehnt die Nutzung der Güter bzw. des Geldes ab. Das Geld soll Zinsen bringen. Darüber hinaus machen dieses und andere Gleichnisse deutlich, daß das Herr-Knecht-Verhältnis fraglos als die bestehende Zuordnung auch von Jesus vorausgesetzt wird. Daß es Arme gibt, kommt in vielen Anspielungen zum Ausdruck: Markus 12,41ff. =

Lukas 21,1ff. (Das Scherflein der armen Witwe); Matthäus 26,11 = Markus 14,7 (»Arme habt ihr alle Tage«).

Die zweite Wortgruppe könnte unter der Überschrift stehen: Du kannst nicht Gott dienen und dem Mammon (Matthäus 6,24 = Lukas 16,13). Gott und Geld werden als zwei sich ausschließende Alternativen gesehen. Geld erhält einen religiösen Rang im negativen Sinne. Entsprechend bekommt Armut eine positive religiöse Färbung. Den Armen wird das Heil verheißen und somit der gerechte Ausgleich geschaffen gegenüber den Reichen, die ihren Trost dahin haben (Lukas 6,24).

In Lukas 1,52f. kündigt es Lukas als Erscheinung der Heilszeit an, daß der Herr »die Mächtigen von den Thronen stoßen und die Niedrigen erhöhen wird. Die Hungernden hat er mit Gütern überhäuft und die Reichen leer fortgeschickt. «Ähnlich die Seligpreisung Matthäus 5,3, die bei Lukas ergänzt wird durch die Weherufe über die Reichen (Lukas 6,24). Hierher gehört das Gleichnis vom reichen Mann und armen Lazarus, in dem der Reiche die ewige Höllenpein empfängt, der Arme aber am seligen Mahle teilnehmen darf. (Lukas 16,19ff.).

Die Gründe für das Wehe über die Reichen und das Lob der Armut werden deutlich im Gleichnis vom törichten Reichen (Lukas 12,15ff.). Der Reiche sorgt für seinen Leib und vernachlässigt seine Seele. Die Gier nach Geld, die von den Pharisäern ausdrücklich berichtet wird (Lukas 16,14–15), ist Gott ein Greuel. Wenn Geld und Reichtum so generell verworfen werden, so liegt dem wohl eine ähnliche Auffassung zugrunde wie Aristoteles' Urteil über das Geld: Gelderwerb geschieht um seiner selbst willen. Das heißt die Gier nach Geld ist unendlich. Und entsprechend definiert Plutarch den Reichtum als das, was den Hunger nach Reichtum nicht stillen kann. Während jedes andere Bedürfnis des Menschen befriedigt werden kann – der Hunger durch Speise, der Durst durch Getränke –, ist der Reichtum unersättlich.[2]

Im Gegensatz hierzu definiert Seneca die Armut als das »genug haben«. So fragt er: Willst du viel haben oder genug? Und er fährt fort: Wer viel hat, will mehr, woraus man folgern kann, daß er nicht genug hat. Aber wer genug hat, hat die Bestimmung seines Lebens erreicht, was dem Reichen nie passieren wird.[3]

Auch Epiktet sagt, daß er glücklich sein kann in der Armut. Er will also sagen, daß für die Stoiker Glück und Reichtum einander entgegengesetzte Alternativen sind, weil, wie Seneca formuliert, die materiellen Güter auf den Geist drücken.[4] Deshalb hat vielen ihr Reichtum den Weg zur Philosophie verbaut.[5]

---

[2] Plutarch, Moralia, Leipzig 1942, S. 114.

[3] Seneca, Epistolae, ed. O. Hense, Leipzig 1914, 119,6.

[4] Seneca, Ad Helviam matrem de consolatione, 9,2; 11,6.

[5] Seneca, Epistolae, 17,3.

So hat die Alternative: Gott – Mammon in der Stoa die Parallele: Philosophie – Reichtum.

Dennoch scheint die Forderung Jesu, auf Besitz und Reichtum zu verzichten, sehr viel rigoroser und radikaler als die der Stoa zu sein, wenn wir allein in Rechnung stellen das Wort Mk 10,25 parr.: Es ist leichter für ein Kamel durch das Nadelöhr zu gehen, als daß ein Reicher in das Reich Gottes komme.

Bindung an Reichtum wurde so denn auch mit Bindung an die Welt gleichgesetzt. So entspricht der Alternative: Gott – Mammon die von Gott – Welt überhaupt bzw. die von altem und neuem Äon. Die Naherwartung gibt dieser Alternative zusätzlich einen aktuellen Akzent. Die Dringlichkeit der Entscheidung wird unterstrichen durch die konkrete Verzichtforderung. Der unmittelbar bevorstehende Anbruch der Königsherrschaft macht den tatsächlichen Verzicht auf Reichtum zwingend erforderlich. Von diesem Hintergrund her muß man Lk 12,32ff. verstehen: Es ist eures Vaters Wohlgefallen, euch das Reich zu geben. Verkauft, was ihr habt, und gebt Almosen. Macht euch Beutel, die nicht veralten, einen Schatz, der nimmer abnimmt, im Himmel, wo kein Dieb zukommt und den keine Motten fressen. (vgl. Mt 6,19–21)

Hier muß auch erwähnt werden, daß die Jünger, die auf Jesu Ruf in die Nachfolge hören, tatsächlich aufgeben, was sie besitzen: Mk 1,16–20; Mt 4,18–22; vgl. Lk 5,1–11; 5,27f.; s. auch Lk 14,33 (vgl. 14,26); Mk 8,34ff.; Mt 16,24ff., Lk 9,23ff.; Lk 9,59ff.; Mk 10,28–30 parr. Mt 19,27–29; Lk 18,28–30. Sie ziehen mit Jesus und teilen sein Schicksal als Wanderprediger, der von sich sagt, daß er nicht hat, wo er sein Haupt hinlegen soll (Lk 9,58 par.).

Daß er auf der Wanderschaft in Häusern von wohlhabenden Menschen einkehrt (Mk 2,15 = Mt 9,10; Lk 5,29; Lk 7,36; 11,371 14,1; 19,1–10), braucht nicht im Widerspruch hierzu zu stehen. Entscheidend ist ja, daß sie von aller Sorge um eigenen Reichtum und Besitz frei sind. So ist ja garantiert, daß sie nur das Notwendige zum Leben erhalten. Wer sich aber nur das Notwendige verschafft, der ist frei von der schädlichen Begierde. Hinzu kommt dies, daß es Brauch war, die Wanderprediger in ihrem Lebensunterhalt zu unterstützen. So braucht die Aufforderung an die Jünger, keinen Beutel mitzunehmen (Lk 10,4 par.), nicht als generelle Aufforderung an alle verstanden zu werden, nicht einmal für das Notwendigste des eigenen Lebensunterhalts zu sorgen. Entsprechend wie auch mit der Sorge in der Bergpredigt (Mt 6,25–34 = Lk 12,22–31) nur die falsche Sorge gemeint ist, die über das heute Notwendige hinaus geht.

Wenn Jesus also auf mancherlei Weise zum Besitzverzicht auffordert bzw. die Armut lobt, so hat er dabei offenbar die Begierde des einzelnen im Auge. Es bleibt aber zu fragen, ob er ebenso auch das Unrecht, das anderen dadurch zugefügt wird, anprangern will. Mit Anspielung auf die Begierde der Pharisäer tadelt er zwar, daß sie der Witwen Häuser fressen

(Mt 23,14). Und er prangert die Gelübdepraxis der Pharisäer an, die dazu führen kann, daß Eltern ihres Lebensunterhalts durch den eigenen Sohn beraubt werden (Mk 7,9–13 par.). Jedoch haben diese Worte, die eher der eingangs erwähnten dritten Gruppe angehören, nicht die radikale Konsequenz und Allgemeingültigkeit wie die zuvor genannten Worte Jesu. Geschweige denn, daß sich eine generelle Sozialethik von ihnen ableiten ließe.

Man könnte vielleicht so sagen: Da Jesus in der Begierde des Menschen die Wurzel des sozialen Unrechts sieht, richtet sich sein Appell in erster Linie an den einzelnen, statt einer revolutionären Neuordnung der sozialen Verhältnisse das Wort zu reden. So taucht auch in der Geschichte vom reichen Jüngling (Mk 10,17–31 = Mt 19,16–30 = Lk 18,18–30), dem Jesus sagt, er solle den Erlös aus dem Verkauf seines Besitzes den Armen geben, das soziale Problem wohl mit auf. Aber die soziale Fürsorge scheint hier nicht das Hauptanliegen Jesu zu sein. Vielmehr geht es um die Gefahren des Reichtums für den Reichen selber.

Im konkreten sozialen Bezug haben die Worte Jesu deshalb auch nicht die Schärfe und Radikalität wie im individual-ethischen Anspruch. Der Zöllner Zachäus (Lk 19,1–10) korrigiert das, was er an konkretem Unrecht getan hat, behält aber selber die Hälfte seines Vermögens. Diese »vernünftige« Halbierung dessen, was man besitzt, kommt auch in den Worten Johannes des Täufers zum Ausdruck: Wer zwei Röcke hat, gebe einen dem, der keinen hat (Lk 3,11). Jesus stimmt auch nicht dem Tadel der Jünger zu, die sich über das verschüttete Nardenöl entrüsten (Mt 26,6–13 = Mk 14,3–9). Seine Äußerung: Arme habt ihr alle Tage, hat beinahe etwas Abwertendes. Jedenfalls wird deutlich, daß Jesus in konkreten sozialen Fragen nicht rigoros ist. Puristen und Fanatiker überrascht er vielmehr – auch in wichtigen sozialen Fragen – durch unerwartete Antworten.

So hebt sich die Gruppe der radikalen Worte Jesu zu Armut und Reichtum in ihrem spezifischen Charakter umsomehr von den konkreten Forderungen ab. Erstere wollen gerade nicht als direkte soziale Handlungsanweisungen verstanden werden. Sie wollen aber – so könnte man vorläufig formulieren – eine Haltung im Menschen erzeugen, aus der heraus das Unrecht vermieden wird oder doch korrigiert werden kann. Dies schließt natürlich auch eine gerechte Vermögensverteilung und als Ziel die Beseitigung von Armut und Unterdrückung ein.

Entsprechend den Wortgruppen, die wir unterschieden haben, redet Jesus in unterschiedlicher Weise über Armut. Einmal fordert er den Verzicht auf Besitz überhaupt, lobt die Armut und tadelt die Reichen. Zum anderen scheint er im konkreten Umgang am Reichtum keinen Anstoß zu nehmen. Er kehrt gern ein bei vermögenden Männern; ebenso wie er sich auch nicht scheut, Umgang mit Deklassierten und Entrechteten zu haben.

Er spricht von der Hilfe, die einem seiner geringsten Brüder zuteil werden soll (Mt 25,40); aber er kann auch halb verächtlich von den Armen reden, wenn er sagt: Arme habt ihr alle Tage.

Während solche Worte verdeutlichen, daß Jesus soziale Forderungen nicht mit revolutionärer Gewalt durchsetzen möchte, enthalten seine Verzichtforderungen eine unbedingte und absolute Schärfe. Im Falle der Jüngernachfolge scheinen sie konkret und direkt gemeint zu sein. Als generelle Forderungen jedoch leuchten sie nicht ein, wenn Jesus in andern Situationen diese Unbedingtheit nicht zu fordern scheint.

Daraus können wir nun aber auch nicht folgern, daß Jesus in jeder gegebenen Situation anderes fordert; so daß auch die Forderung des Besitzverzichts nur eine unter anderen möglichen Forderungen ist. Vielmehr scheint diese in besonderer Weise die Meinung Jesu wiederzugeben, so wie sie in ihrer Schärfe auch kaum verglichen werden kann mit entsprechenden Forderungen philosophischer Art. Zugleich hat die Forderung nach Besitzverzicht aber auch einen so allgemeinen Charakter, daß sie über die konkrete Situation der Jüngerwerbung bzw. -unterweisung hinausgeht. Ihre Radikalität vermag sowohl inhaltlich als auch in ihrer Form einen jeden Menschen so unmittelbar zu treffen, daß es schwer fällt, sie als eine zufällige historisch bedingte Forderung abzutun. D. h. es gelingt einem nicht, diese Äußerung nur aus dem Zusammenhang der Naherwartung des Königsreichs Gottes heraus zu erklären; so daß man sagen könnte, sie habe in einer weitergehenden Geschichte keinen Platz mehr. Zu sehr ist mit dieser auf das Ende der Geschichte verweisenden Forderung zugleich auch der Mensch schlechthin vor sein Ende gerückt. D. h. wenn damals auch das tatsächlich als bevorstehend gedachte Ende die Art der Forderung Jesu mitgeprägt hat, so ist doch auch noch für den heutigen Hörer die Unbedingtheit des göttlichen Anspruchs in diesen Worten deutlich vernehmbar. Nun aber nicht in der Weise, daß er sich herausgefordert sieht, genau das Gleiche zu tun, was damals von den Jüngern gefordert war. Denn das Hinter-Jesus-hergehen mit dem entsagungsvollen Leben eines Wanderpredigers war ja gebunden an die kurze Zeitspanne der Predigttätigkeit Jesu und in gewandelter Form auch noch gefordert in der Zeit der Mission der frühen Gemeinden.

Wenn aber diese rigorosen Worte auch noch später überliefert wurden, so sicher nicht um des faktischen Anspruchs willen, sondern vielmehr um der in diesen Worten erkennbaren unbedingten Forderung Gottes willen, die jeweils in neuen geschichtlichen Situationen zu neuen konkreten Verhaltensweisen herausforderte. Diese Herausforderung Gottes darf nun allerdings nicht so allgemein gefaßt werden, daß von der in diesen Worten konkret gemeinten Sache nichts mehr übrig bleibt und der Verzicht auf Besitz lediglich noch als ein Bild erscheint für unbedingten Gehorsam gegen Gott im generellen Sinne oder auch als ein Bild, in dem die Weltentsagung ausgedrückt ist, die der Christ vollziehen müsse. Vielmehr darf die konkrete Sache des Besitzes nicht aus dem Auge verloren werden.

Mindestens ließe sich doch soviel sagen, daß auch heute noch vom Glaubenden gefordert wird, daß die Bindung an Besitz etwas Zweitrangiges ist gegenüber der Liebe zu Gott. Bzw. daß angesichts des Betroffenseins durch den Anspruch Gottes deutlich wird, daß man seine Existenz nicht aus dem Besitz von Gütern und Reichtum begründen kann. Wenn dem Reichtum aber diese Existenz-begründende und Existenz-sichernde Dignität genommen ist, dann könnte man allerdings davon reden, daß der Mensch eine neue Freiheit dem Mammon gegenüber gewonnen hat, die es ihm ermöglicht, in den jeweils gegebenen Lebenssituationen Forderungen zu erfüllen, die einen materiellen Einsatz beinhalten. Insofern bezeichnen die Worte Jesu, damals angesichts des bevorstehenden Endes gesprochen, doch auch heute noch etwas Konkretes. Nur dürfen sie nicht direkt und wörtlich übertragen werden, wie es z. B. Graf Tolstoi tat. Dann wäre die Forderung rein gesetzlich mißverstanden. Vielmehr muß aus der jeweils gegebenen neuen Situation die angemessene Forderung entwickelt werden, die insofern den Geist Jesu widerspiegeln sollte, als an ihr deutlich wird, daß sich der Mensch heute – so wie die Jünger damals – ganz und gar als auf Gott angewiesen begreift.

Wenn aber der Mensch sein Leben nicht eigenmächtig aus sich selbst heraus zu begründen versucht, dann heißt dies zugleich auch, daß er den andern als Mitgeschöpf Gottes und als Bruder ansieht und ihm in eben demselben Maße zum Notwendigen des Lebens verhilft, wie es auch ihm zu Gebote steht.

Wie dies zu geschehen hat, hängt von den konkreten Bedingungen ab. Diese wiederum haben ihre Herkunft aus der Vergangenheit und sind ausgerichtet auf die Zukunft. In diesen Ablauf von Vergangenheit, Gegenwart und Zukunft gehört auch die mitlaufende Tradierung und Interpretation der Worte Jesu. So ist auch die gegenwärtige Interpretation dieser Worte eingebunden in einen geschichtlichen Prozeß, der letztlich auf Jesus selber rückverweist und insofern auch die ursprüngliche historische Bedeutung der Worte verständlich macht und mit ins Spiel bringt.

Insofern kann man auch von einem historisch vermittelten Anspruch Jesu reden. Und insofern wir geschichtliche Wesen sind und zu dieser einen Geschichte der Menschheit gehören, können die Worte Jesu auch heute noch in ihrem geschichtlich vermittelten Anspruch in ihrer selben Gestalt vernommen werden und uns auch noch unmittelbar etwas bedeuten für die konkrete geschichtliche Gestaltung unseres Lebens.

Hermeneutisch-ethische Folgerungen, die sich aus dem Spannungsverhältnis von radikalen Worten Jesu und »vernünftiger« Sozialkritik ergeben.

Um einen Anhalt zu haben, ob und in welcher Weise die Worte Jesu zu Armut und Reichtum für eine Sozialethik der Gegenwart relevant sein könnten, fügen wir einige Überlegungen an.

Wir neigen dazu, konkrete Handlungsanweisungen aus dem Neuen Testament zu gewinnen. Dabei befinden wir uns in dem Widerspruch, einerseits nach Regeln und Geboten Ausschau zu halten, entsprechend wie sie im Alten Testament vorgegeben sind und wie sie in ihrer Praxisbezogenheit, wenn auch in etwas abgewandelter Form, auch heute noch angewendet werden könnten. Und andererseits sehen wir uns den radikalen Worten Jesu gegenüber, die den Praxisbezug zu sprengen scheinen und über die konkrete Situation hinaus auf eine andere Wirklichkeit zu verweisen scheinen.

Das Dilemma besteht nun gerade darin, daß wir in den letzteren die spezifischen Aussagen des Neuen Testaments sehen. Denn gerade sie gehen über das hinaus, was im Alten Testament gesagt ist. Aber gerade diese spezifischen Aussagen erschweren auch die Anwendung auf die Praxis.

Dies nun wiederum hat zur Folge, daß sie einerseits als Soll-Forderung verstanden werden, die im Sinne einer Ethik des summum bonum den Menschen zur ethischen Höchstleistung anspornen sollen; und andererseits werden sie im Sinne des usus legis elenchticus zum Signal dafür, daß der Mensch diesen Forderungen doch nicht entsprechen könne. Daraus folgt dann Resignation, bzw. man verweist die Forderungen ins Reich der Utopie, damit wir darauf hoffen, dereinst sie mal erfüllen zu können. Fürs Hier und Jetzt bleibt nur das Vertrauen auf die Gnade Gottes. Dieser Verweis auf die Gnade, weil man dem eigentlich Geforderten doch nicht entsprechen könne, mindert aber die Entschlußkraft, wenigstens das Notwendige und Machbare zu tun.

In beiden Fällen schießt man über das konkret Gegebene und konkret Erforderliche hinaus. Im ersten Fall wird ein Eifer entwickelt, der in Ausrichtung auf das ferne Ideal in der Regel an dem konkret Notwendigen vorbeischießt. Bezeichnend für diese Haltung ist die Unterscheidung zwischen bürgerlicher und christlicher Ethik. Wobei sich die christliche Moral gerade als das »mehr« versteht, als die Zugabe, als das donum superadditum. Dabei fällt gar nicht auf, daß solches Übermaß an Gutem oft den anderen, dem Gutes zugefügt wird, gerade zum Objekt des eigenen Handelns erniedrigt. Er wird zum Opfer meiner Wohltätigkeit; und ich sammle mir einen Schatz im Himmel durch den Mißbrauch des andern, den ich so ja gerade nicht als freien und selbständigen Menschen anerkenne und den ich so gerade nicht zur Entfaltung seiner eigenen

Kräfte anspome. Im anderen Fall, dem der Resignation, verfehle ich das konkret Gebotene, da ich dahinter zurückbleibe. Ja, es kann aus dieser Haltung heraus sogar zur Rechtfertigung von Verbrechen kommen, da der Mensch ja zugegebenermaßen nicht gut sein kann, also mit Notwendigkeit das Böse tun muß. Häufig gibt es dabei aber auch die Variante, daß das tatsächlich Böse für gut erklärt wird – als Ergebnis der Tatsache, daß man sich soweit von der Wirklichkeit entfernt hat, daß man das konkret Gute nicht mehr erkennen kann. Es kann dabei zu einer Kombination von beiden Haltungen kommmen. Einerseits wird eine Forderung für absolut im Sinne des idealen Zieles erklärt, andererseits verfolgt man dieses Ziel ohne Rücksicht auf die konkreten Folgen bzw. nimmt in Kauf, daß man in Schuld gerät, die einem ja durch die Gnade Gottes vergeben wird.

Beide möglichen Interpretationen ethischer Forderungen des Neuen Testamentes versuchen eine direkte Übertragung derselben in die Gegenwart. Dabei werden aber weder die historischen Bedingungen voll in Rechnung gestellt, unter denen die Worte Jesu entstanden sind; noch wird eine genaue Standortbestimmung der Gegenwart vorgenommen. Bei dem besonderen Charakter des Neuen Testaments genügt es aber auch nicht, nur eine historische Bestimmung vorzunehmen. Es gilt vielmehr, nach der besonderen Sache zu fragen, die zu derart radikalen Forderungen geführt haben könnten.

Wenn sich dabei herausstellt, daß sowohl die apokalyptische Erwartung des Endes der Geschichte als auch die eschatologische Hoffnung auf den Anbruch des Reiches Gottes bestimmend gewesen ist für die Radikalität der Forderungen, dann ist insofern eine unvergleichliche Situation bezeichnet, als dieselbe Konstellation nicht für irgend einen anderen Zeitpunkt der weitergehenden Geschichte angenommen werden kann; d. h., daß eine schlechthinnige Verallgemeinerung der radikalen Forderungen Jesu ausgeschlossen ist. Vielmehr entsteht hier die Frage, welches denn die angemessene Form ist, in der zu einem anderen geschichtlichen Zeitpunkt dieselbe Intention Jesu, die damals so ihren Ausdruck gefunden hat, heute ihren Ausdruck finden könnte. Dies ist aber keine Sache, die wir aus beobachtender Distanz zu beurteilen haben; sondern wir sind jeweils mitten darin im Entscheidungsprozeß der vorgegebenen historischen Situation. Nun meine ich aber, daß auch die Intention Jesu, so wie sie damals in Jesu Worten unter gegebenen Bedingungen zum Ausdruck kam, im geschichtlichen Fortgang ihren Niederschlag gefunden hat und insofern bis in die gegenwärtige Situation hineinreicht. Und da wir auch ein Stück der Gegenwart sind und von der Geschichte geprägt sind, reicht die Intention Jesu auch bis in unsere Existenz hinein, sofern wir uns der Geschichte Jesu bewußt sind und seine Wirksamkeit als eine auch-geschichtliche verstehen. Wenn wir uns aber so verstehen, kann es nicht anders sein, als daß wir auch geschichts- und d. h. gegenwarts- und zukunftsbezogene Entscheidungen fällen, die von ethischer Relevanz sind und die, im Glauben vollzogen, die gleiche Ausrichtung haben wie Jesu eigene Intention.

Wenn ich Jesu Intention, wie sie im Geschichtsprozeß wirksam geworden ist, umschreiben soll, so würde ich schematisierend dies sagen: die radikalen Forderungen Jesu sind auf dem eschatologisch-apokalyptischen Hintergrund zu verstehen. Sie heben angesichts der Naherwartung und angesichts des völlig anderen Charakters und Wesens der Königsherrschaft Gottes alle irdischen und sozialen Bedingungen auf. In Konfrontation mit Gott werden sie total infrage gestellt. Auch die Gebote, die auf soziales Verhalten ausgerichtet sind, sowie die Gebote der Pietät und Frömmigkeit gelten nicht mehr. Sie sind nicht mehr Ziel oder auch nur Mittel zum Zweck, mit denen man am Reich Gottes Anteil gewinnen könnte. Jetzt gilt nur noch das eine, sich auf die Herrschaft Gottes vorzubereiten und an der Verkündigung der Botschaft vom nahen Reich teilzunehmen. Familie und Ehepartner gelten genau so wenig wie Reichtum und Besitz. Der nichts hat, ist Gott gerade recht; der Arme; d. h. der nicht nach Besitz strebt, also auch keine entsprechende Mentalität hat, also der ›arm im Geiste‹ ist.

Diese Aussagen, gesprochen in einer eschatologisch-apokalyptischen Situation, haben in der weitergehenden Geschichte eine bleibende Wirkung gehabt. Sie sind verstanden worden als Forderungen, die in ihrer Radikalität den Menschen stets neu unmittelbar vor Gott rücken und ihn das Ende seiner Existenz erkennen lassen. In dieser Weise verstanden, haben sie Gültigkeit bis in die Gegenwart hinein. D. h. angesichts dieser Worte Jesu vollzieht sich auch heute noch so etwas wie Aufhebung der eigenen Existenz, Herauslösung aus den sozialen Bindungen und Verpflichtungen angesichts der Wahrheit Gottes.

Und es kann auch heute noch geschehen, daß ein Mensch in solcher Konfrontation sich ganz zum Dienst für Gott gerufen weiß, ähnlich wie es den Jüngern damals ergangen ist; nur mit dem Unterschied, daß er heute nicht mehr konkret Jesus auf seiner Wanderschaft durch Galiläa begleitet, sondern daß er heute anders dem Ruf Jesu folgt, sei es als Diakonisse oder Priester oder Mönch. Es gibt aber auch in solchem Anspruch den entschiedenen Ruf in eine weltliche Existenz, in einen Beruf. Es ist darüber hinaus aber auch denkbar, daß geschichtliche Situationen eines Volkes oder der Menschheit insgesamt eintreten, wo es gilt, eine besondere Wende in der Geschichte herbeizuführen, die nur durch radikalen Einsatz oder Opferbereitschaft zu erreichen ist.

Das ist die eine Seite der Wirkungsgeschichte Jesu. Die andere wäre erkennbar an den Aussagen Jesu zu konkreten sozialen Problemen seiner Zeit. Hier scheint Jesus keine sachlich neuen Aussagen zu machen. Er korrigiert lediglich. Verweist auf die bekannten Gebote, wendet Klugheitsregeln an, scheint also lediglich seine Vernunft zu gebrauchen, verbunden mit einem gesunden Selbstbewußtsein und Vertrauen in die Situation, wie sie nun einmal vorgegeben ist. Hier im konkreten Bezugsfeld fallen keine großen Worte, wie man alles besser machen oder revolutionieren könnte, keine Vorschläge zur Bodenreform, keine Abhandlungen über die Abschaffung der Sklaverei, kein neues Steuergesetz (sondern: Gebt dem Kaiser, was des Kaisers ist). Was wir heute von ihm erwarten: Stellungnahme zu wichtigen politischen und sozialen Fragen – dessen enthält er sich damals ganz und gar. Wenn wir auch vermuten können, daß Jesus lediglich angesichts der nahen Königsherrschaft daran kein Interesse gehabt hat, so hat diese Ausrichtung seines Denkens doch auch ihre Fortsetzung in der weitergehenden Geschichte gehabt. Zunächst bei Paulus und den frühen Gemeinden, die soziale und politische Fragen doch nicht eigentlich als solche traktieren, sondern nur sofern sie im Rahmen ihrer Gemeinden vorkommen: Der dem Herrn entlaufene Sklave; die Verwaltung des Eigentums innerhalb der Gemeinde; Armenpflege.

Auch die ethischen Normen werden selbstverständlich aus der Umwelt übernommen. Es ist geradezu bezeichnend, daß die radikalen Forderungen Jesu auch dort, wo sie im Widerspruch zu den überkommenen Geboten stehen, solche Spannung nicht einmal als Problem erkennen lassen. Die Forderung Jesu, um seinetwillen Vater und Mutter zu verlassen, wird nicht als Widerspruch zum 4. Gebot gesehen, das weiterhin gilt. Ein Zeichen dafür, daß man das eschatologisch Geforderte wohl zu unterscheiden wußte von dem konkret-sozial Geforderten. Diese konkret-vernünftige Linie im Denken Jesu und der frühen Gemeinde hat sich dann auch auf ihre Weise durchgehalten in der Geschichte.

Die Frage ist nun: Wie können wir beide Linien in konkreten Entscheidungssituationen zusammenbringen – die eschatologische und die ethisch-praktische?

Ich will es so versuchen:

1. Die idealistische Ausrichtung auf ein nicht erreichbares summum bonum halte ich für ein Mißverständnis, das sich aus der generalisierenden Anwendung eschatologisch bedingter radikaler Forderungen auf die konkrete soziale Praxis ergeben hat.

2. Die Einsicht in das totale Unvermögen des Menschen angesichts dieses Mißverständnisses der eschatologischen Forderung als einer absoluten, mit der Folge der Resignation und der Rechtfertigung auch des Bösen, halte ich für eine Abirrung des Denkens.

3. Ich kann die radikalen Forderungen nur so verstehen, daß sie auch in der weitergehenden Geschichte den Menschen direkt mit Gott konfrontieren und ihn so den jeweiligen konkreten Willen Gottes in einer gegebenen Situation besser erkennen lassen. Oder anders gesagt: Wenn der Mensch im Angesicht Gottes seine eigene Existenz infrage gestellt sieht bzw. sich selber hinter sich gelassen und überwunden hat, ist er in neuer Weise frei, die konkreten Forderungen Gottes zu vernehmen.

4. Diese konkreten Forderungen Gottes liegen dann aber mehr in der Richtung, in der sich Jesus konkret zu sozialen Fragen geäußert hat. Es sind praktikable Aufforderungen und Gebote, die der Mensch nun hört. Man könnte auch so sagen, daß es Gebote sind, die gleichsam auf der Mitte liegen, mehr Forderungen der Vernunft, des Maßes, der Besonnenheit und der praktischen Durchsetzbarkeit als solche utopischen Charakters.

5. D. h. in bezug auf das, was konkret an den Armen zu tun ist, daß man aus der gegebenen Handlungssituation heraus die Vernunft und das Gefühl sprechen läßt und daß man bedenkt, welche Handlungsmodelle aus der Vergangenheit auf uns überkommen sind. Wenn wir dabei die Geschichte der Armenpflege und sozialer Reformen sowie der Liebestätigkeit der Kirche in unsere Überlegungen mit einbeziehen, wird uns jedoch bewußt, daß wir in der Gegenwart sozialen Problemen von einem solchen Ausmaß gegenüberstehen, daß alle bisherige Praxis neu überdacht werden muß. Weltwirtschaftliche Fragen der Dependenz müssen ebenso bedacht werden wie die Frage nach der Wechselbeziehung zwischen Unterdrückungsstrukturen und der Sünde des einzelnen.

Bedeutet die Ansage der Königsherrschaft dann nicht nur Vergebung und Befreiung von der individuellen Sünde, sondern auch den Anfang der Aufhebung der strukturellen Sünde, wie sie sich in der Armut von Millionen darstellt? So daß, parallel zur Befreiung des einzelnen von der Habgier, durch das Evangelium auch die wirksame Befreiung von Armut und Not auf der Ebene des Staates und der internationalen wirtschaftlichen Beziehungen in Gang gesetzt werden müßte?

Diese schwierige Frage – auch gerade unter Berücksichtigung des zuvor Gesagten – zu beantworten, bedarf einer weitergehenden Erörterung, die in diesem Rahmen nicht mehr geschehen kann.

Reform der theologischen Ausbildung

*Eine Bilanz der Arbeit der »Gemischten Kommission für die Reform des Theologiestudiums« seit Verabschiedung des Ausbildungsgesamtplans.**

von Georg Strecker

(Nikolausberger Weg 5b, 3400 Göttingen)

Man kann fragen, ob das, was seit 1965, dem Gründungsjahr, in der Gemischten Kommission – dem durch Vertreter der Ausbildungsreferentenkonferenz und des Fakultätentages[1] besetzten, unter der Obhut der Evangelischen Kirche in Deutschland stehenden Gremium – betrieben wurde, den Namen »Reform« verdient. Wer mit diesem Begriff die Vorstellung einer tiefgreifenden Wandlung verbindet, mag – wenn er die Ergebnisse der Reform der Theologenausbildung Revue passieren läßt – zu dem Urteil gelangen, daß »die Geschichte der Reform der Theologischen Ausbildung in starkem Maß eine Geschichte des Scheiterns von Reformbemühungen und -hoffnungen« ist[2]. Dieses Urteil setzt freilich weitgespannte Erwartungen voraus, die keineswegs zu Anfang der Gemischten Kommission allgemein geteilt wurden und angesichts der besonderen Lage des Theologiestudiums im Spannungsfeld von staatlicher universitärer Ausbildung und kirchlicher Praxis auch nicht realistisch gewesen wären[3]. Zudem war die staatliche Hochschulpolitik, die sich Ende der 60er und Anfang der 70er Jahre um den Ausgleich verschiedenartiger Reformvor-

---

* Heinrich Greeven hat als erster Rektor der Universität Bochum nicht nur wesentlich zum Aufbau der dortigen evangelisch-theologischen Fakultät beigetragen, sondern auch als Präsident des Fakultätentages seit 1965 seine Arbeitskraft der Gestaltung und Entwicklung des Theologiestudiums gewidmet. Im folgenden soll dargelegt werden, wie im letzten Jahrzehnt in der »Gemischten Kommission für die Reform des Theologiestudiums« Überlegungen zur Struktur des Theologiestudiums angestellt wurden und welche Aufgaben sich daraus für die Planung der theologischen Ausbildung in der näheren Zukunft ergeben.

1 Die im Text abgekürzt gebrauchten Bezeichnungen lauten vollständig: »Gemischte Kommission für die Reform des Theologiestudiums« (GK), »Konferenz der Ausbildungsreferenten der Evangelischen Kirche in Deutschland« (ARK) und »Fakultätentag der evangelisch-theologischen Fakultäten in Deutschland« (FT).

2 Wolf-Dieter Hauschild, Reform der theologischen Ausbildung. Eine problematische Unternehmung zwischen Veränderung und Beharrung, in: Kirchlicher Dienst und theologische Ausbildung. Festschrift für Präses Dr. Heinrich Reiß, Bielefeld 1985, 125–138 (Zitat aus S. 138).

3 Vgl. Reform der theologischen Ausbildung (RthA) IX, 1972, 53–61.

stellungen bemühte, primär auf eine Änderung der überkommenen Personal- und Institutsstrukturen und in einem weit geringeren Ausmaß auch auf das inhaltliche Lehrangebot ausgerichtet. Daher war es folgerichtig, daß der »Ausbildungsgesamtplan«[4] nur behutsam Veränderungen anzubahnen suchte. Wenn auch die Gemischte Kommission wie auch der Fakultätentag von den Veränderungen der Personalstruktur der Universität nicht unberührt blieben[5], so war ihre Arbeit doch im wesentlichen von den Vorstellungen bestimmt, wie sie von Fakultäten[6] und den Landeskirchen gemeinsam verantwortet werden konnten, um dem Wandel der geistigen Situation und den neuen Anforderungen des Pfarramtes entsprechend die theologische Ausbildung zu planen. Von hier aus kam es zu einschneidenden Vorschlägen hinsichtlich der Methode und Inhalte der theologischen Ausbildung. Zwar wurden die bisher geltenden Sprachanforderungen gegenüber Volltheologen und Religionsphilologen im wesentlichen beibehalten, jedoch didaktischen Änderungen der Weg geebnet. Die Interdisziplinarität und Praxisbezogenheit des Studiums wurde ebenso reflektiert, wie im Bereich der zweiten Ausbildungsphase die sog. Handlungswissenschaften zu einem Bestandteil der theologischen Ausbildung wurden. Es hatte zunächst den Anschein, als ob nach der Verabschiedung des Ausbildungsgesamtplans durch den Rat der EKD am 8. 7. 1977 die Reformarbeit der Gemischten Kommission zu ihrem Ende gekommen war. In Wahrheit ergab sich jedoch durch die veränderte hochschulpolitische Situation ein neues Aufgabengebiet, das durch das im Dezember 1975 von den Bundesbehörden verabschiedete Hochschulrahmengesetz umrissen, durch die anschließende Hochschulgesetzgebung der Länder aufgenommen und sodann in die universitäre Praxis übergeleitet wurde[7]. Im Hochschulrahmengesetz wurde die Bildung von Studienreformkommissionen vorgesehen, welche »zur Förderung der Reform von Studium und Prüfungen und zur Abstimmung und Unterstützung der an den einzelnen Hochschulen geleisteten Reformarbeit« dienen sollten. Hierbei sollten neben Vertretern aus dem Bereich der Hochschulen auch staatliche Stellen sowie Fachvertreter aus der Berufspraxis beteiligt werden (§ 9). Zur Koordinierung der Kommissionsarbeit sollten auf Bundesebene

---

[4] »Theologiestudium – Vikariat – Fortbildung. Gesamtplan der Ausbildung für den Pfarrerberuf. Empfehlungen des Rates der Evangelischen Kirche in Deutschland, herausgegeben von der Kirchenkanzlei der Evangelischen Kirche in Deutschland, Stuttgart–Berlin 1978 (RthA XII)«. Im folgenden = »Ausbildungsgesamtplan«.

[5] Ein Vertreter der Studenten war von Anfang an Mitglied der GK. Zu den Sitzungen der Gemischten Kommission wie auch des Fakultätentages wurden seit 1970 je 2 Vertreter der Mitarbeiter und der Studenten als stimmberechtigte Mitglieder, die von ihren übergeordneten Gremien zu entsenden waren, hinzugezogen.

[6] Der im folgenden benutzte Ausdruck »Fakultäten« schließt auch die theologischen Fachbereiche und kirchlichen Hochschulen ein.

[7] Das Niedersächsische Hochschulgesetz trat z. B. am 1. 10. 1978 in Kraft.

Bundesstudienreformkommissionen entstehen. Jedoch wurde in der Folgezeit eine Bundeskommission für die Reform des Theologiestudiums nicht einberufen, dies mit ausdrücklichem Verweis auf den Ausbildungsgesamtplan, der die Arbeit einer solchen Kommission faktisch vorweggenommen habe[8]. Von besonderer Bedeutung für die theologische Ausbildung ist auch § 18 des Hochschulrahmengesetzes, wonach durch die Hochschulprüfung ein berufsqualifizierender Abschluß erworben wird, der zur Führung des Diplomgrades mit Angabe der Fachrichtung berechtigt. Die Hochschule kann den Diplomgrad auch aufgrund einer staatlichen oder kirchlichen Prüfung, mit der ein Hochschulstudium abgeschlossen wird, verleihen. Dies ermöglichte in der Folgezeit einer größeren Anzahl von Absolventen der kirchlichen Prüfungen in der Konföderation der niedersächsischen evangelischen Kirchen, den von der Universität Göttingen verliehenen Grad »Dipl. theol.« zu erwerben.

Die Aufgabe der Gemischten Kommission nach Verabschiedung des Ausbildungsgesamtplanes war es im wesentlichen, diese und andere Entwicklungen in der allgemeinen Hochschulpolitik wie auch in der theologischen Ausbildung an den Fakultäten zu beobachten. Sie nahm damit faktisch die Aufgabe der nichtkonstituierten Bundesstudienreformkommission für (evangelische) Theologie wahr[9].

---

[8] Protokoll der Gemischten Kommission, XIII. (Sitzung, TOP) 3a (im folgenden abgekürzt zitiert).

[9] Die X.–XX. Sitzung der Gemischten Kommission fand an den folgenden Tagen und Orten statt: X. 27.–28. 10. 1977 Berlin; XI. 6. 3. 1978 Hannover; XII. 24. 10. 1978 Göttingen; XIII. 11.–12. 5. 1979 Berlin; XIV. 11. 1. 1980 Hannover; XV. 12. 2. 1982 Göttingen; XVI. 10.–11. 9. 1982 Frankfurt; XVII. 27.–28. 5. 1983 Frankfurt; XVIII. 3.–4. 2. 1984 Stuttgart; XIX. 2.–3. 11. 1984 Berlin; XX. 10. 5. 1985 Stapelage. – Die X.–XIV. Sitzung stand unter dem Vorsitz von Hans-Joachim Birkner und Hans-Martin Müller (letzterer bis 1979), die XV.–XX. Sitzung unter dem Vorsitz von Georg Strecker und Klaus Dirschauer. – In dieser Zeit wirkten als Vertreter des Fakultätentages mit: Hans-Joachim Birkner (1974–1981), Peter C. Bloth (seit 1974), Eilert Herms (seit 1980), Horst-Dietrich Preuß (seit 1976), Georg Strecker (seit 1974). Vertreter der Ausbildungsreferentenkonferenz: Hans-Martin Müller (1974–1979), Klaus Baschang (seit 1977), Klaus Dirschauer (seit 1976), Helmut Frik (seit 1979), Ernst Kampermann (seit 1982), Hartmut Löwe (1977–1980); als Ständige Gäste waren beteiligt: der Vorsitzende des Fakultätentages: Hartmut Stegemann (1977–1981), Hans-Joachim Birkner (1981–1983), Friedemann Merkel (seit 1983), der stellvertretende Vorsitzende des Fakultätentages (jeweils der Amtsvorgänger des Vorsitzenden des Fakultätentages), Vertreter der Kirchenkanzlei bzw. (seit 1983) des Kirchenamtes der Evangelischen Kirche in Deutschland: Birger Maiwald (1978–1980), Eckhard von Nordheim (1982), Friedrich G. Lang (seit 1982); der Vertreter der Kommission für die zweite Phase der Theologischen Ausbildung: Hermann Rück (seit 1975); der Vertreter der Fachbereiche Evangelische Theologie an kirchlichen Fachhochschulen: Karl Foitzik (seit 1978); der Vorsitzende der Gemischten Kommission II: Hartmut Aschermann (seit 1977); ferner die Sekretäre der Kommission: Günter Goldbach, Jürgen-K. Schulze, Eilert Herms, Karin Hirschgän-

1. Trotz des Schlagwortes von der »humanistischen Illusion«, welcher die Exegeten angeblich anhängen, hat der Ausbildungsgesamtplan nicht mit dem Prinzip gebrochen, daß ein volltheologisches Studium nur unter der Voraussetzung der *alten Sprachen,* d. h. nach vorhergehender Ablegung der Sprachprüfungen in Latein, Griechisch und Hebräisch, einen wissenschaftlichen Charakter besitzt. So sind die Empfehlungen zum Unterricht der alten Sprachen und zu den entsprechenden Prüfungsanforderungen ein wesentlicher Bestandteil des Ausbildungsgesamtplanes[10], und es hat nicht an Bemühungen gefehlt, durch Ausarbeitung von Fernstudiengängen[11] oder von Übungsbüchern, die auf die spezifisch theologischen Sprachanforderungen zugeschnitten sind[12], den Theologiestudenten das Erlernen der alten Sprachen zu erleichtern. Dabei wurde der Grundsatz aufrechterhalten, daß es die Aufgabe der Schulen, die beanspruchen, zur Universitätsreife zu führen, ist, die notwendigen Voraussetzungen auch für das Theologiestudium bereitzustellen. Daher werden die Sprachexamina im allgemeinen als Ergänzungsprüfungen dem Abitur zugeordnet. Von hier aus versteht sich der wiederholte Aufruf der Gemischten Kommission wie auch des Fakultätentages, daß sich die zuständigen Kultusbehörden für eine Erweiterung des Lehrangebotes von altsprachlichem Unterricht an den Gymnasien einsetzen möchten, als Anmahnung einer staatlichen Bringschuld, die nicht in Vergessenheit geraten sollte[13].

Die Sprachanforderungen sind den unterschiedlichen Studiengängen entsprechend verschieden gewichtet. Während Lehramtskandidaten für Grund- und Hauptschulen im allgemeinen keine, dagegen angehende Realschul- oder Gewerbeschullehrer allenfalls Sprachkenntnisse im Griechischen, gelegentlich auch im Lateinischen nachweisen müssen, wird als Zulassungsvoraussetzung für die Prüfung des Lehramtes der Sekundarstufe II in der Mehrzahl der Fakultäten das neutestamentliche Graecum sowie ein Latinum gefordert. Nur die Volltheologen haben einen dreifachen

---

ger, Hans-Georg Babke; außerdem je zwei Vertreter der Mitarbeiter- und Studentenschaft (siehe oben Anmerkung 5).

10 RthA XII, 1978, 37–49.

11 Zur Vorbereitung auf das Hebraicum wird ein Fernstudiengang vom EKD-Kirchenamt angeboten: W. Schneider u. a., Hebräisch – ein Fernstudium in 24 Lektionen, hg. vom Kirchenamt der EKD, 2. revidierte Auflage, Hannover 1983. Für das Erlernen der griechischen Sprache ist ein solcher in Vorbereitung.

12 Vgl. Eklogai. Einführung in das neutestamentliche Griechisch, hg. von L. Lenz u. a., Neukirchen ^{6}1983; F. Stolz, Hebräisch in 53 Tagen, Göttingen ^{3}1982; Latinitas-Christianitas. Lateinisches Textbuch für das Theologiestudium, hg. von W.-D. Hauschild in Zusammenarbeit mit O. Utermöhlen, Stuttgart 1975 u. a.

13 Vgl. XVII 4; auch G. Strecker, Der Stand der neutestamentlichen Wissenschaft in Deutschland, in: O. Merk (Hrsg.), Schriftauslegung als theologische Aufklärung. Aspekte gegenwärtiger Fragestellungen in der neutestamentlichen Wissenschaft, Gütersloh 1984, 11f.

Sprachnachweis zu erbringen: Latinum, Graecum und Hebraicum. Eine neue Diskussion wurde eingeleitet, als die Kultusministerkonferenz (KMK) mit Wirkung vom 26. 10. 1979 eine Änderung der bestehenden Richtlinien beschloß und für Kandidaten des Lehramtes der Sekundarstufe II allgemein ein qualifiziertes Latinum mit dem Schwierigkeitsgrad von Cicero-Texten forderte[14]. Dies bedeutete eine Verschärfung der bis dahin bestehenden Situation, da in vielen Ausbildungsstätten bisher das Kleine Latinum als ausreichende Grundlage des Lehramtstudiengangs für Sekundarstufe II akzeptiert worden war[15]. Dies berührt auch die volltheologische Ausbildung, da sich nunmehr die Frage stellt, ob bei einem Wechsel des Studiengangs die Sprachprüfungen des theologischen Studiums anerkannt werden, da an zahlreichen theologischen Fakultäten allein das Kleine Latinum gefordert wird. Die Gespräche, die auf verschiedenen Ebenen stattfanden, zeigten, daß die zuständigen Gremien unterschiedliche Positionen einnahmen[16], und erbrachten das Ergebnis, daß eine Änderung der KMK-Vereinbarung zur Zeit nicht erreichbar sei, daß aber die Bundesländer unterschiedliche Auslegungen akzeptieren und damit auch in Zukunft verschiedene Regelungen praktizieren werden. Als Resümee läßt sich feststellen, daß die KMK-Vereinbarung für das Theologiestudium de facto weniger zur Einheitlichkeit geführt als einer größeren Pluralität in den Sprachanforderungen den Weg geebnet hat.

2. Für die Prüfung im *Magisterstudiengang,* der an theologischen Fakultäten mit besonderer Rücksicht auf ausländische Studierende angeboten wird, liegt eine Rahmenordnung vom 2. 10. 1964 vor, die von der Westdeutschen Rektorenkonferenz und der Kultusministerkonferenz – übrigens als einzige theologische Prüfungsordnung – verabschiedet wurde. Durch das Hochschulrahmengesetz kam es in den Fakultäten zu einer neuen Gremienstruktur und wurde insbesondere das Verhältnis zwischen der Prüfung des Magisterstudienganges und der Diplomtheologenprüfung bzw. dem kirchlichen ersten theologischen Examen fraglich. Der Fakultätentag beschloß daher am 16. 4. 1977 eine Novellierung der Magisterprüfungsordnung und beauftragte die Gemischte Kommission, diese Novellierung vorzubereiten. Eine Unterkommission (Peter C. Bloth, Hans-

---

[14] »Vereinbarung über Kenntnisse in Latein und Griechisch – Beschluß der Ständigen Konferenz der Kultusminister der Länder in der Bundesrepublik Deutschland vom 26. 10. 1979« (2.1); entsprechend für die Ablegung des Graecums: Schwierigkeitsgrad von Platon-Texten (a.a.O. 2.2).

[15] Vgl. die Umfrage der Gemischten Kommission, die der XVII. Sitzung vorlag; auch die Umfrage des Kirchenamtes der EKD vom 4. 8 1983 zu »Sprachanforderungen für Religionsphilologen (Gymn/Sek II)«.

[16] Während die Ausbildungsreferentenkonferenz eine Gleichstellung der Religionsphilologen mit den Volltheologen anstrebte, sprach sich die Schulreferentenkonferenz der EKD dafür aus, daß die Religionsphilologen keinen anderen Bedingungen unterliegen sollten als die übrigen Philologen (XVII 4).

Martin Müller, Georg Strecker) legte auf der 11. Sitzung der Gemischten Kommission ihre Arbeitsergebnisse in der Form eines Empfehlungskatalogs zur Rahmenordnung der Magisterprüfung vor. Eine Neufassung der Rahmenordnung von 1964 wird danach nicht als notwendig angesehen. Doch sollten bei der Neufassung einzelner Ordnungen die folgenden Grundsätze beachtet werden: Die Magisterprüfung dient dem Nachweis besonderer wissenschaftlicher Urteilsfähigkeit. Für die Zulassung sollen die gleichen Voraussetzungen gelten wie beim ersten theologischen Examen und bei der äquivalenten akademischen Abschlußprüfung. Soweit die genannten Prüfungen abgelegt worden sind, können die Prüfungsleistungen entsprechend gemindert werden. Für ausländische Kandidaten können darüber hinaus Ausnahmeregelungen vorgesehen werden. Was die Anrechnung von Leistungen der Magisterprüfung auf das erste theologische Examen angeht, so wird auf den Beschluß des Fakultätentages vom 4. 4. 1975 verwiesen: Allgemeine Regelungen sollen nicht getroffen werden, doch sind Dispensregelungen im Einzelfall ausdrücklich zugelassen worden[17].

Billigte der Fakultätentag am 13. 4. 1978 diese Empfehlungen ohne Gegenstimme[18], so wurde das Problem der Magisterprüfung in der Folgezeit noch mehrfach verhandelt: In Mainz fiel der Magister- dem Diplomstudiengang zum Opfer, was der Fakultätentag insbesondere im Blick auf die ausländischen Studierenden, die diesen Abschluß anstreben, bedauerte[19]; in Göttingen wurde aufgrund eines Beschlusses des Fachbereichsrats vom Dezember 1983 der Magisterstudiengang zugunsten eines Magisteraufbaustudiums ebenfalls abgeschafft. Dies veranlaßte die Gemischte Kommission zu einem energischen Einspruch, der durch den Vorsitzenden in einem Brief an den Niedersächsischen Minister für Wissenschaft und Kunst am 1. 3. 1984 übersandt wurde. Hier wurde darauf hingewiesen: »Grundsätzlich soll an der ›Rahmenordnung für die Magisterprüfung der evangelisch-theologischen Fakultäten‹ festgehalten werden, die im Jahre 1964 von der Westdeutschen Rektorenkonferenz und der Ständigen Konferenz der Kultusminister der Länder beschlossen wurde«; auch könne der Magisterstudiengang wegen seiner großen Bedeutung für ausländische Studenten aus der Ökumene nicht preisgegeben werden[20].

Ein besonderes Problem wurde durch eine Anfrage aus der evangelisch-theologischen Fakultät der Universität Münster aufgeworfen, welche

---

17 X 3 (auch die Anlage: »Rahmenordnung für die Magisterprüfung«).

18 Vgl. XII 3: Beschluß des Fakultätentages vom 13. 4. 1978.

19 Vgl. XVII 2a (Beschluß des Fakultätentages vom 15. 10. 1982): »Die theologische Magisterprüfung soll dort, wo sie eingeführt ist oder eingeführt werden soll, neben dem Fakultätsexamen bzw. neben der Diplom-Prüfung erhalten bleiben, insbesondere wegen ihrer Bedeutung für Theologiestudenten aus dem Ausland«.

20 XVIII 10 (Anlage).

die Anregung enthielt, speziell Religionsphilologen die Möglichkeit, den theologischen Magistergrad zu erwerben, zu eröffnen[21]. Eine Unterkommission der Gemischten Kommission (Hartmut Aschermann, Hans-Joachim Birkner, Peter C. Bloth) befaßte sich mit dieser Frage und legte der 18. Sitzung eine Beschlußvorlage vor. Die Gemischte Kommission entschied daraufhin, daß eine eigenständige Magisterprüfung für Religionsphilologen nicht sinnvoll sei, vielmehr für die theologische Magisterordnung die Rahmenordnung von 1964 weiterhin verbindlich bleiben solle. Allerdings sind die darin vorgesehenen Ausnahmeregelungen auch auf die Gruppe der Religionsphilologen anzuwenden. Dies gilt insbesondere für die Einbeziehung eines nichttheologischen Faches in die Magisterprüfung. Darüber hinaus wurde darauf hingewiesen, daß das Fach Theologie auch im Rahmen der philosophischen Magisterprüfung zur Geltung gebracht werden kann[22].

3. Die Anordnung des § 18 des Hochschulrahmengesetzes, an den Universitäten den Diplomgrad mit Angabe der Fachrichtung allgemein einzuführen, hat zunächst in den katholisch-theologischen Fakultäten, sodann auch an evangelisch-theologischen Fakultäten Überlegungen hervorgebracht, ob und in welcher Weise sich ein *Diplomstudiengang* einrichten lasse. Eine solche Anfrage aus der Marburger Fakultät wurde der Gemischten Kommission und dem Kontaktausschuß zur Bearbeitung zugewiesen und – auch ohne daß ein schriftlicher Antrag vorlag – mit der Antwort beschieden, daß eine theologische Diplomprüfung neben dem ersten theologischen Examen keine Alternative darstelle[23]. Dieser Beschluß wurde – nachdem entsprechende Initiativen aus der Göttinger Fakultät bekanntgeworden waren – in der 14. Sitzung der Gemischten Kommission bekräftigt: Ein zusätzlicher Studiengang mit dem Abschluß der Diplomprüfung sei keineswegs anzuraten. Die Anforderungen der angepaßten Prüfungsordnung eines Diplomstudiengangs sollten denen der herkömmlichen theologischen Abschlußprüfung entsprechen. Eine solche Anpassung sei in Tübingen und Kiel erfolgt, ohne daß der Charakter der Abschlußprüfung und des Kolloquiums hierdurch eine substantielle Änderung erfahren habe[24]. – In Göttingen beschloß der Fachbereichsrat die Umwandlung des Fakultätsexamens in eine Diplomprüfung, die als Abschluß des Theologiestudiums den Grad »Dipl. theol.« verleiht. Am 18. 8. 1982 wurde hier die theologische Diplomprüfungsordnung in Kraft gesetzt. Die Empfehlungen zur Neuordnung des Studiengangs Evangelische Theologie mit dem Abschluß Diplom/Kirchliche Prüfung, die von der Studienreformkommission des Landes Niedersachsen im Mai 1983 vorge-

---

[21] XVII 3 (Brief vom 15. 4. 1984).

[22] XVIII 10.

[23] XIII 3 (3e) + 7.

[24] XIV 6.

legt wurden, orientieren sich weitgehend an der Göttinger Diplomprüfungsordnung. Die Diskussion dieser Empfehlungen in der Gemischten Kommission konzentrierte sich einmal auf die Regelstudienzeit, die hier auf 10 Semester festgesetzt wurde[25]; dies mit Rücksicht auf die KMK-Vereinbarung, wonach Lateinkenntnisse mit dem Schwierigkeitsgrad von Cicero-Texten zu fordern seien[26]; vor allem aber auf die Diplomvorprüfung, die an die Stelle des im Ausbildungsgesamtplan vorgesehenen Kolloquiums bzw. der Zwischenprüfung getreten war.

Hatte der Ausbildungsgesamtplan ein *Kolloquium,* auch *Zwischenprüfung* genannt, vorgesehen, das den Übergang des Grundstudiums zum Hauptstudium darstellen sollte[27], so wurde dies in der Praxis unterschiedlich gehandhabt, indem einerseits der Prüfungs-, andererseits der studienberatende Charakter stärker hervorgehoben wurde. Sonderregelungen wurden in Tübingen, Heidelberg und Erlangen getroffen, wo das Kolloquium/Zwischenprüfung deutlich als Prüfung konzipiert wurde und teilweise die Ablegung eines Biblicums einschloß[28]. Auch die Diplomvorprüfung, wie sie in Göttingen mit dem Diplomstudiengang geplant wurde, stieß auf das Bedenken, daß hierdurch Schwierigkeiten beim Wechsel des Studienortes hervorgerufen werden könnten. Dies war der Anlaß, daß die Gemischte Kommission am 4. 5. 1982 in einem Rundschreiben die im Fakultätentag zusammengeschlossenen Fakultäten um eine Äußerung zu der neuen Entwicklung ersuchte. Die eingegangenen Antworten erbrachten das Ergebnis, daß sich die Mehrzahl der Fakultäten mit den neuen Ordnungen zwar einverstanden erklären konnte, jedoch den Charakter des Kolloquiums als einer Studienberatung beibehalten wollte[29]. Auf dieser Grundlage bemühte sich die Gemischte Kommission um einen mittleren Weg zwischen den Rahmenempfehlungen des Ausbildungsgesamtplans, die ihrerseits die »Allgemeinen Bestimmungen für Diplomprüfungsordnungen, Beschluß der Westdeutschen Rektorenkonferenz vom 10. 2. 1970 in der Fassung vom 12. 11. 1974; Beschluß der Kultusministerkonferenz vom 12. 3. 1970 in der Fassung vom 21. 3. 1975« voraussetzen[30], und einer Diplomprüfungsordnung nach Göttinger Vorbild. Sie stellte fest, daß das Kolloquium, wie es im Ausbildungsgesamtplan empfohlen wird, selbst schon einen Prüfungscharakter besitze, und richtete an die Fakultäten die Bitte sicherzustellen, daß durch gegenseitige Anerkennung

25 Sonst neun Semester; anders Ausbildungsgesamtplan S. 15f.: vier Jahre (einschl. Hebraicum), zuzüglich je ein Jahr für das Erlernen der lateinischen und griechischen Sprache (dazu unten Anmerkung 33 und 39).

26 XVII 5b.

27 RthA XII, 1978, 57–60.

28 XV 2.

29 XVI 3.

30 RthA XII, 1978, 62.

von Kolloquium/Zwischenprüfung der Wechsel des Studienortes weiterhin möglich sei. Eine gegenseitige Anerkennung werde erleichtert, wenn in Zukunft bei der Abfassung von Kolloquiums-/Zwischenprüfungsordnungen erschwerende Bestimmungen vermieden werden und an der durch die Rahmenempfehlungen des Ausbildungsgesamtplans genannten Vierzahl von Leistungsnachweisen festgehalten werde. Dabei solle das »Biblicum« oder »Philosophicum«, soweit dieses im Rahmen der Zwischenprüfung eingeführt worden sei, als Äquivalent für einen der vier Leistungsnachweise gelten. Schließlich sprach sich die Gemischte Kommission dafür aus, daß die Studienberatung ein verbindlicher Bestandteil des Grundstudiums bleiben und im Rahmen der Zwischenprüfung angeboten werden solle[31]. Dieses Votum wurde dem Fakultätentag zugeleitet und von diesem zur Grundlage eines Beschlusses gemacht[32]. Auch die Konföderation der Niedersächsischen Kirchen machte sich das Votum der Gemischten Kommission zu eigen und gab eine entsprechende Erklärung gegenüber dem Niedersächsischen Minister für Wissenschaft und Kunst ab. Darin wird die Notwendigkeit hervorgehoben, daß das theologische Studium durch Freizügigkeit, insbesondere bei der Wahl des Studienortes und in der Möglichkeit zum Studienortwechsel, gekennzeichnet sein müsse[33].

4. Wenn auch der Ausbildungsgesamtplan sich wesentlich auf Rahmenempfehlungen für Examensordnungen beschränkte, so griff die darin vorausgesetzte Unterscheidung zwischen Grund-, Überblicks- und Schwerpunktwissen[34] doch weitgehend in das Gefüge der *Studienordnung* ein. Es war nur folgerichtig, daß in der hier zur Besprechung anstehenden Arbeitsphase der Gemischten Kommission das Problem der Studienordnungen zweimal ausdrücklich behandelt wurde. In der 12. Sitzung wurde festgestellt, daß die Gemischte Kommission keine Studienverlaufsordnung, sondern allenfalls »Richtlinien für die Erstellung von Studienord-

---

[31] XVI 3. Es verdient hervorgehoben zu werden, daß im universitären Bereich allein die theologische Ausbildung mit einer obligatorischen Studienberatung verbunden ist.

[32] XVII 2c; Fakultätentag vom 14. 10. 1982: »1. Es ist sicherzustellen, daß durch gegenseitige Anerkennung der Kolloquien (Zwischenprüfungen) der Wechsel des Studienortes weiterhin möglich ist . . ., 2. . . . die Studienberatung verbindlicher Bestandteil des Grundstudiums bleibt und im Rahmen der Zwischenprüfung angeboten wird.«

[33] Vgl. XVIII 5. – Die Konföderation der Niedersächsischen Kirchen sprach sich in diesem Zusammenhang auch für eine Regelstudienzeit von zehn Semestern (ohne Sprachen) aus. Die Bafög-Regelung bezog sich demgegenüber auf zwölf Semester (unter Einschluß der Sprachen); ähnlich der Fakultätentag; vgl. Gemischte Kommission XIII 3: Regelstudienzeit von acht Semestern, dazu je ein Semester für Griechisch und Hebräisch, ein freies Semester und ein Examenssemester. – In der folgenden Diskussion ist das Problem der Regelstudienzeit zurückgetreten, da die ursprünglich damit verbundene staatliche Absicht, die Höchstdauer des Studiums rechtswirksam zu begrenzen, aufgegeben wurde.

[34] RthA XII, 1978, 66f.

nungen« erarbeiten könne und die hierbei anzuwendenden Kriterien sich aus dem Ausbildungsgesamtplan ergeben müßten[35]. Die für die 13. Sitzung aufgrund einer Umfrage an den Fakultäten angefertigte Vorlage ergab das Vorhandensein von fünf Studienordnungen. Diese weisen untereinander in den Rahmenbedingungen Übereinstimmungen auf, sind jedoch andererseits durch örtliche Eigentümlichkeiten bestimmt, insbesondere durch verschiedene qualitative und quantitative Festschreibungen. Zur Komplexität trägt bei, daß offenbar unterschiedliche Adressaten (Studenten, Hochschullehrer, kirchliche oder staatliche Instanzen) vorausgesetzt sind und daß die Studienordnungen einmal als studentische Orientierungshilfen, ein anderes Mal als Rechtstexte konzipiert worden sind. Die Kommission einigte sich auf das Vorgehen, lediglich »Gesichtspunkte« zu formulieren, »die bei Abfassung von Studienordnungen zu berücksichtigen sind«. So wurde es durch eine Unterkommission[36] vorbereitet und auf der 14. Sitzung verabschiedet[37].

Das Problem der Studienordnungen wurde aufgrund einer Anfrage der Evangelischen Kirche in Deutschland bei den Ländervertretungen in Bonn auf der 18. und 19. Sitzung der Gemischten Kommission noch einmal aufgegriffen. Hiernach existieren mit Ausnahme von Bremen, Baden-Württemberg und Berlin in allen Bundesländern landeseigene Rahmenempfehlungen, die über die »Grundsätze für Studium und Prüfungen« der Ständigen Kommission für die Studienreform vom 4. 6. 1982 hinausgehen. Allerdings handelt es sich dabei um formale Empfehlungen zur Erstellung von Studienordnungen, welche Aussagen über den Geltungsbereich, die Studien- und Prüfungsdauer, die Studienvoraussetzungen, die Ziele, Inhalte und den Aufbau des Studiums, die Leistungsnachweise, die Veranstaltungsarten und die Studienberatung enthalten sollen. Die fachspezifischen Studienordnungen der theologischen Fakultäten konkretisieren diese Empfehlungen, stimmen etwa in der Unterscheidung von Grund- und Hauptstudium mit dem Ausbildungsgesamtplan überein, unterscheiden sich jedoch u. a. in der Festsetzung der Regelstudienzeiten[38]. So zeigt es die Synopse von fünf Studienordnungen, die der Sekretär der Gemischten Kommission, Hans-Georg Babke, auf der 19. Sitzung vorlegte[39]. Die Gemischte Kommission hatte schon auf der 18. Sitzung den Be-

---

35 XII 5a.

36 Mitglieder: Hartmut Löwe (ARK), Enno Konukiewitz (wissenschaftlicher Mitarbeiter) und Detlev Rosenboom (studentischer Vertreter).

37 Die beschlossenen »Gesichtspunkte« wurden der Ausbildungsreferentenkonferenz und am 20. 3. 1980 dem Fakultätentag zugeleitet; dieser hat die Vorlage am 3. 10. 1980 einstimmig angenommen.

38 XVIII 9.

39 XIX 9; besonders auffallend waren in den Mitgliedsinstitutionen Bochum, Bonn, Erlangen, Göttingen und Oberursel die Differenzen bei den Sprachanforderungen, in der Studienberatung, Studiendauer und in der Gestaltung von Kolloquium/Zwischenprüfung.

schluß gefaßt, den Fakultätentag zu bitten, darauf hinzuwirken, daß die Fakultäten ihre Studienordnungen künftig bereits im Entwurfstadium der Kommission zuleiten, damit noch vor der Verabschiedung Änderungen eingetragen werden können. Es besteht kein Zweifel, daß hier eine noch unabgeschlossene Aufgabe vorliegt, die unter Berücksichtigung der neueren Studiensituation Gegenstand der künftigen Arbeit der Gemischten Kommission sein sollte.

Zu unterscheiden von Studienordnungen, die primär die formale Struktur des Studiums betreffen, sind *Stoffpläne,* die den Inhalt der im Studium zu erwerbenden Kenntnisse beschreiben. Hatten die Verfasser des Ausbildungsgesamtplans auf Rahmenempfehlungen zu Stoffplänen bewußt verzichtet, so war doch nicht ausgeschlossen worden, daß solche Anforderungskataloge zur Orientierung der Studenten und Hochschullehrer hilfreich sein könnten[40]. In den Landeskirchen ist es weitgehend geübte Praxis, derartige Stoffkataloge den Studenten zuzuleiten und die darin angegebenen Lerninhalte im ersten theologischen Examen abzurufen[41]. Es ist eine noch unbeantwortete Frage, ob bzw. in welchem Ausmaß die Gemischte Kommission sich künftig mit Rahmenempfehlungen zur Erstellung von Stoffplänen zu befassen haben wird. Auch wenn man die Gefahr von übermäßig vereinzelnden Anforderungskatalogen für die Studierfreiheit als nicht gering einschätzt, bleibt es im Interesse der Einheitlichkeit des Theologiestudiums eine wichtige Aufgabe, sich dafür einzusetzen, daß die vorhandenen Stoffpläne nicht zu sehr divergieren und bei der Auswahl und Gewichtung der theologischen Lehrinhalte den Studenten durch Beispielkataloge Hilfen an die Hand gegeben werden.

Nicht eine Reglementierung des Studiums, sondern eine Hilfe zur Examensvorbereitung soll auch der *Studienbericht* sein, der im Ausbildungsgesamtplan empfohlen wurde[42] und an einigen Fakultäten in Ge-

---

Was die Studienzeit angeht (vgl. oben A 25), so empfiehlt Bochum: 8 + 1 Semester (ohne Hebräisch), pro Sprache 1 weiteres Semester, mindestens 6 sprachfreie Semester; Bonn: 8 + 1 (einschl. Hebräisch), pro Sprache 1 Jahr zusätzlich; Erlangen: 9 (einschl. Hebräisch und Examen), pro Sprache ein weiteres Semester; Göttingen: 10 (einschl. Examen), zusätzlich 1 Semester für jede Sprache; Oberursel: 8 sprachfreie Semester.

40 RthA XII, 1978, 61ff.67. – Empfehlungen zu »Anforderungskatalogen« wurden schon RthA IV veröffentlicht; sie waren auch Gegenstand einer Umfrage des Vorsitzenden der Gemischten Kommission am 30. 11. 1977 (XI 4).

41 XVI 5b.

42 RthA XII, 1978, 75: »Damit die Prüfungszulassung begründet ausgesprochen werden kann, muß die Prüfungsordnung den in diesen Rahmenempfehlungen geforderten *Studienbericht* verlangen. Der Prüfling soll darin den Aufbau seines Studiums, seine Studienschwerpunkte sowie seine wissenschaftlichen und berufspraktischen Interessen darstellen (z. B. durch Benennung der Lehrveranstaltungen, der Themenkomplexe und der Literatur, die ihn besonders beschäftigt haben, sowie der angefertigten Studienarbeiten). Die Prüfungsinstanz soll ihm dafür ein *Merkblatt* zur Verfügung stellen.«

brauch ist[43]. Die Gemischte Kommission hat sich in mehreren Sitzungen mit der Frage beschäftigt, wie ein »Merkblatt zur Erstellung des Studienberichtes« gestaltet sein könnte. Das Ergebnis, auf der 12., Sitzung noch kontrovers diskutiert, wurde auf der 13. Sitzung verabschiedet und zur Stellungnahme den beteiligten Gremien zugeleitet[44]. Besonders die Vertreter der Ausbildungsreferentenkonferenz kritisierten nicht so sehr die Tatsache eines Studienberichtes, der vor der Zulassung zum Examen von den Studierenden eingereicht werden könnte, als vielmehr die Einzelheiten der Merkblattempfehlung. Vor allem wurde festgestellt, daß die geistige Entwicklung im Verlauf des Studiums und die theologische Sozialisation und Persönlichkeitsentwicklung, die außerhalb von Lehrveranstaltungen gewonnen werden, mit zu berücksichtigen seien. Daher wurde das Merkblatt an die Prüfungsämter mit der zusätzlichen Bemerkung verabschiedet, die Empfehlungen nach eigenem Ermessen anzuwenden[45].

Auf ein positives Echo stieß die Ausarbeitung eines *Muster-Seminarscheins.* Aufgrund der Erfahrung, daß die Zulassung zum ersten theologischen Examen von Leistungsnachweisen abhängig gemacht wird, die in den Instanzen, welche über die Zulassung zu entscheiden haben, unterschiedlich bewertet werden, beschloß die Gemischte Kommission eine einheitliche Gestaltung von Seminarscheinen zu empfehlen. In Zukunft sollten die Seminarscheine eindeutig Auskunft geben über den Leiter der Lehrveranstaltung, die Disziplin, Art und Thema der Veranstaltung und der individuellen Leistung sowie eine Bewertung mit Notenschlüssel[46]. Ein Muster wurde von Horst Dietrich Preuß auf der 19. Sitzung vorgelegt[47]; es wurde dem Fakultätentag zu einer vorläufigen Stellungnahme zugeleitet und in der 20. Sitzung der Gemischten Kommission verabschiedet[48].

5. Über die Ausbildung der *Religionslehrer* wurde seit 1974 in einer eigenen Kommission zunächst unter dem Vorsitz von Klaus Koch, seit 1977 unter dem Vorsitz von Hartmut Aschermann, gearbeitet. Sie hat »Empfehlungen zur Erarbeitung von Studienordnungen für künftige Religionslehrer« ausgearbeitet; diese wurden im Dezember 1979 von dem Rat und der Kirchenkonferenz der EKD verabschiedet[49]. Seit dieser Zeit war die »Gemischte Kommission II« (GK II) nicht mehr zusammengetreten. Wohl aber hatte Hartmut Aschermann als Ständiger Gast an den Sitzungen der Gemischten Kommission (GK I) teilgenommen. Da die GK II

---

[43] Formblätter für die Erstellung eines Studienberichtes lagen vor in Tübingen, Göttingen sowie in der hannoverschen und badischen Landeskirche (XII 4).

[44] XII 4; XIII 5. [45] XIV 4 (Anlage).

[46] XVIII 3a; Beschluß des Fakultätentages vom 12. 10. 1983.

[47] XIX 3.

[48] XX 7; Beschluß des Fakultätentages vom 12. 10. 1984 und vom 11. 10. 1985.

[49] Veröffentlicht als RthA XIII, 1980.

nicht reaktiviert wurde, legte es sich nahe, das Problem der Magisterprüfungsordnung für Religionsphilologen in der Gemischten Kommission zu verhandeln[50]. Darüber hinaus wurde auf der 17. Sitzung über die Ergebnisse der Studienreformkommission in Niedersachsen hinsichtlich der Teilstudiengänge Evangelische Religion für die Lehrämter an Grund-, Haupt- und Realschulen, Gymnasien und Berufsbildenden Schulen beraten. Hierbei machte sich die Gemischte Kommission die Stellungnahme von Hartmut Aschermann zu eigen, wonach insbesondere die zu knappe Stundenzahl für Religion als drittes Lehrfach (12 Semester-Wochenstunden) die Frage stellt, ob hierdurch »ein didaktisches Ganzes« zu erreichen ist[51]. Kontrovers ist auch das Problem, welche Sprachanforderungen für angehende Realschul- und Gymnasiallehrer obligatorisch sein sollen. Gegenüber dem Sondervotum, das im Zusammenhang der Beratungen der Studienreformkommission in Niedersachsen abgegeben wurde und für Realschul- und Gymnasiallehramtskandidaten Sprachkenntnisse gemäß der KMK-Vereinbarung forderte, wurde festgestellt, daß sinnvoller als die Anhebung der Sprachanforderungen die Präzisierung der Studieninhalte sei. Bei der ohnehin geringen Stundenzahl der Realschullehrerausbildung bedeute der Spracherwerb auf höherem Niveau eine zusätzliche Belastung und einen Einschnitt in andere Inhalte[52].

Die sprachlichen Anforderungen für Lehramtskandidaten waren noch einmal Gegenstand der Beratungen auf der 18. Sitzung der Gemischten Kommission[53]. Hier wurde festgestellt, daß speziell für das Lehramt der Sekundarstufe I in den Bundesländern eine große Variabilität der Sprachanforderungen besteht: vom Maximum der KMK-Vereinbarung über die Forderung von Kenntnissen im neutestamentlichen Griechisch bis hin zum Verzicht auf altsprachliche Kenntnisse. Da als vorrangiges Ziel anzuerkennen ist, daß die Durchlässigkeit der verschiedenen Studiengänge sicherzustellen ist, konnte sich die Gemischte Kommission nicht dazu entschließen, Sprachanforderungen für Lehramtskandidaten im Sekundarstufenbereich I festzuschreiben; denn durch das Fehlen einer solchen Festschreibung ist ein Studiengangwechsel eher zu gewährleisten als durch eine Vermehrung von Sprachkursen auf unterschiedlichem Niveau. Im Blick auf die Sekundarstufe II zeigt eine Synopse der geltenden Sprachanforderungen eine erhebliche Uneinheitlichkeit in den einzelnen Bundesländern auf, die das anstehende Problem zunächst an die vorrangig betroffenen Fakultäten zurückgehen läßt und einer globalen Regelung widerrät[54].

---

[50] Dies geschah auf der XVII. und XVIII. Sitzung (s. o. S. 416).

[51] XVII 5a.

[52] Ebd.

[53] XVIII 11 (Bezugnahme auf den Brief von Hartmut Aschermann an den Fakultätentag vom 7. 9. 1983).

[54] Vgl. die von Friedrich G. Lang angefertigte Synopse vom 12. 8. 1983.

6. Die Neukonstituierung der Gemischten Kommission im Februar 1982 wurde wesentlich durch den Auftrag des Fakultätentages vom Oktober 1981 veranlaßt, eine Broschüre zu erarbeiten, die über die Studienmöglichkeiten unterrichten sollte, welche von den evangelisch-theologischen Fakultäten über den klassischen Fünf-Fächer-Katalog hinausgehend angeboten werden. Dabei sollte vor allem eine übergreifende Standortbestimmung ins Auge gefaßt werden[55]. Vorbereitet wurde eine solche Übersicht über das *Angebot der Randfächer* an den evangelisch-theologischen Fakultäten auch durch eine Zusammenstellung von speziellen Lehrangeboten, die durch die Ausbildungsreferentenkonferenz vorgelegt wurde. Hier war eine Umfrage zu den Bereichen Mission und Ökumene durchgeführt worden. In der württembergischen Landeskirche stand darüber hinaus ein Papier für die Ausbildung in der ersten Phase im Fach Diakonie zur Verfügung. Nach Vorarbeiten durch Klaus Dirschauer und Hermann Rück zur grundsätzlichen Problematik, die auf der 16. Sitzung diskutiert wurden[56], entschloß sich die Gemischte Kommission, zunächst die besonderen Lehrangebote, die an den im Fakultätentag zusammengeschlossenen evangelisch-theologischen Fakultäten vorhanden sind, aus den Vorlesungsverzeichnissen zu erheben. Darüber hinaus wurde eine Umfrage auf der Grundlage von detaillierten Fragebogen durchgeführt, die mit Ausnahme von zwei Fakultäten auch vollständig beantwortet wurden. Die auf dieser Basis zusammengestellte Sammlung enthielt eine nach Hochschulorten gegliederte Darstellung der Randfächer, ein alphabetisches Schlagwortregister und ein Merkblatt über Kurse in den alten Sprachen. Allerdings zeigte eine eingehendere Analyse die Ergänzungs- und Korrekturbedürftigkeit auf, auch, daß das zusammengestellte Material außerordentlich zeitgebunden war, so daß fortdauernde Korrekturgänge zu planen gewesen wären[57]. Da sich der Fakultätentag am 12. 10. 1983 für eine knappe Darstellung aussprach, dagegen die Ausbildungsreferentenkonferenz einer Weiterentwicklung zu einem Studienführer den Vorzug gab[58], stand die Gemischte Kommission vor der Frage, ob sie sich zu einer großen, kleinen oder mittleren Lösung entschließen sollte. Eine Unterkommission wurde beauftragt, die verschiedenen Modelle zu überprüfen und eine Entscheidung der Gemischten Kommission vorzubereiten[59]. Diese legte in der 19. Sitzung das Ergebnis ihrer Arbeit vor: Drei unter-

---

[55] XV 1; vorausgegangen war das Votum der ARK vom 9.–11. 12. 1981 sowie das noch weiter zurückliegende Memorandum der Arnoldshainer Konferenz, das sich für eine Integration des Kirchenrechts in die theologische Ausbildung aussprach (XIII 8).

[56] XVI 4.

[57] XVII 6.

[58] XVIII 3a.b.

[59] XVIII 4; Mitglieder: Hans-Georg Babke, Klaus Dirschauer, Eilert Herms, Ernst Kampermann, Friedrich G. Lang, Georg Strecker.

schiedliche Modelle waren geprüft worden, die sämtlich nicht den Anforderungen genügen konnten, da sie entweder den Funktionszusammenhang der Spezialgebiete mit den Hauptfächern nicht deutlich gemacht oder zu viele variable Daten enthalten hätten. Daher habe man sich darauf verständigt, auf der Grundlage des vorhandenen Materials Übersichtstabellen zu erstellen, die auf der einen Seite kurze Angaben über die Hauptfächer und ihre Ausstattung, auf der anderen Angaben über die institutionalisierten Spezialgebiete auflisten sollten. Diese Übersichten sollten mit einer ausführlichen Einleitung (Arbeitsauftrag: Friedrich G. Lang) und einem abschließenden Register verbunden werden. Der Titel dieser Broschüre soll lauten: »Gesamtverzeichnis der Studienmöglichkeiten Evangelische Theologie in der Bundesrepublik Deutschland«[60]. Die Ausführung dieses Planes wurde in der 20. Sitzung vorgestellt und ein nochmaliger Rücklauf bei den Fakultäten vereinbart[61]. Das Gesamtverzeichnis wurde im Herbst 1985 dem Fakultätentag, der Ausbildungsreferentenkonferenz und dem Kirchenamt der EKD zugeleitet.

7. Nach Verabschiedung des *Ausbildungsgesamtplans* am 17. 9. 1977 stellte sich erstmals im Jahr 1983 die Frage, wie nach den Erfahrungen mit der Studienreformkommission in Niedersachsen und angesichts der steigenden Zahlen von Theologiestudenten mit dem Ausbildungsgesamtplan in Zukunft umzugehen sei[62]. Die Ausbildungsreferentenkonferenz ergriff die Initiative und veranstaltete auf der Grundlage eines von Klaus Baschang ausgearbeiteten Fragebogens eine Umfrage bei den Kirchenleitungen über das Verhältnis der landeskirchlichen Prüfungsordnungen zum Ausbildungsgesamtplan. Hierbei wurde festgestellt, daß sich die kirchlichen Prüfungsordnungen weitgehend an den Rahmenempfehlungen ausrichten[63]. Dies wurde zum Anlaß genommen, die Vertretungen der Bundesländer in Bonn darauf hinzuweisen, welchen Stellenwert der Ausbildungsgesamtplan für die Gestaltung der theologischen Ausbildung in der Bundesrepublik hat, dies auch im Blick auf die künftige Arbeit der Studienreformkommissionen auf Länderebene[64].

Aufgrund des Interesses, das der Fakultätentag auf seiner Sitzung vom 12. 10. 1983 bekundet hatte, wurde beschlossen, daß nunmehr auch eine Umfrage unter den Fakultäten durchgeführt werden sollte, um festzustellen, welche Funktion und welcher Stellenwert der Ausbildungsgesamtplan für den didaktischen Aufbau des Lehrangebots und für die Prüfungsordnungen hat[65]. Das Ergebnis dieser Umfrage wurde synoptisch

---

[60] XIX 4.

[61] XX 1.

[62] XVII 7 (1).

[63] XVII 2a.

[64] XVIII 3b.

[65] XVIII 6. – Das Problem einer Neuauflage des Ausbildungsgesamtplans stellte sich noch nicht. Vorsorglich wurde überlegt, ob der Ausbildungsgesamtplan in einer zweiten Aufla-

ausgewertet und in der 19. Sitzung diskutiert: Alle angeschriebenen Fakultäten hatten die Fragebogen ausgefüllt zurückgeschickt. Generell wurde dabei die Bitte ausgesprochen, die Gemischte Kommission möge weiterhin für die Vergleichbarkeit und Einheitlichkeit des Theologiestudiums sorgen. Darüber hinaus ergab sich, daß – trotz unterschiedlicher Gestaltung des Studiums im einzelnen und divergierender Prüfungsordnungen – Aufbau und Struktur des Theologiestudiums und auch die Prüfungsanforderungen einander ähnlich sind und mit den Empfehlungen des Ausbildungsgesamtplans in Einklang stehen. Freilich sind einige Unterschiede nicht ohne Bedeutung; so das Fehlen einer obligatorischen Studienberatung in Göttingen und Tübingen; auch wird nur in etwa 50% der Prüfungsordnungen die Einreichung eines Studienberichtes verlangt. Besonders zu bemängeln ist, daß die Empfehlung des Ausbildungsgesamtplans in Hinsicht auf integrierte Sprachkurse und studienbegleitende Lernkontrollen nur wenig Beachtung gefunden hat. Eine Unterkommission wurde beauftragt, dieses Ergebnis zusammenzufassen und nach Abstimmung mit der Gemischten Kommission dem Fakultätentag zuzuleiten[66].

Die Gemischte Kommission hatte unmittelbar nach der Verabschiedung des Ausbildungsgesamtplans festgestellt, daß hiermit ihre Arbeit nicht beendet sei, vielmehr auch in Zukunft bestimmte Auftragsarbeiten zu erledigen seien und – auch im Austausch mit dem Fakultätentag und der Ausbildungsreferentenkonferenz– sie sich Rechenschaft über den weiteren Verlauf der Studienreform zu geben habe. So ist es – wie die voranstehenden Ausführungen zeigen – im einzelnen durchgeführt worden und dies hat zweifellos auch zu einem besseren Verständnis zwischen Fakultäten und Landeskirchen beigetragen. Am Ende der Wahlperiode im Jahr 1984, die dann um ein weiteres Jahr verlängert wurde[67], stellte sich die Frage nach den künftigen Arbeitsgebieten[68]. Auch wenn in den entsendenden Gremien unterschiedliche Auffassungen zur Funktion der Gemischten Kommission artikuliert wurden, so ergab sich doch unter den Mitgliedern der Gemischten Kommission Übereinstimmung in der Ansicht, daß auf eine kontinuierliche und langfristige Zusammenarbeit zwischen Fakultäten und Landeskirchen nicht verzichtet werden dürfe. Die Aufgabe der Gemischten Kommission sollte es auch in Zukunft nicht nur sein, die Entwicklungen in der theologischen Ausbildung reaktiv zu begleiten, sondern sie sollte darüber hinaus Herausforderungen neu benennen.

---

ge unverändert abgedruckt werden könne, wobei die neueren Beschlüsse der Gemischten Kommission als Fortschreibung des Ausbildungsgesamtplans angefügt und in einer Einleitung die Entwicklungen seit 1977 skizziert werden sollten (XVIII 8).

[66] XIX 5; XX 4 (Anlage); Mitglieder der Unterkommission: Ernst Kampermann, Friedrich G. Lang, Georg Strecker.

[67] Beschluß des Fakultätentages vom 12. 10. 1984; XVIII 12b.

[68] XVIII 12b.

Wegen der künftig geringer werdenden finanziellen Mittel, auch um die Arbeitskraft der Kommission wirksamer zu nutzen, erarbeitete die Gemischte Kommission einen Vorschlag zur künftigen Zusammensetzung. Danach sollen in Zukunft nur drei Professoren (bisher vier) und ein wissenschaftlicher Mitarbeiter (bisher zwei) vom Fakultätentag entsandt werden. Die Ausbildungsreferentenkonferenz benennt vier Vertreter, zu denen auch der Fachreferent des Kirchenamtes der EKD gezählt wird, der bisher als Ständiger Gast teilnahm. Von der Vereinigung evangelischer Theologiestudenten/Konferenz theologischer Fachschaften (VeTh/KthF) soll ein Student als stimmberechtigtes Mitglied, ein weiterer als Ständiger Gast nominiert werden. Der Vorsitzende des Fakultätentages wird wie bisher als Ständiger Gast geladen werden. Im übrigen können zu einzelnen Beratungsgegenständen insbesondere hinzugezogen werden: der zweite Vorsitzende des Fakultätentages, der Vorsitzende der Gemischten Kommission für die Religionslehrerausbildung, ein Vertreter der Predigerseminare und ein Vertreter der Fachbereiche Evangelische Theologie an kirchlichen Fachhochschulen[69].

Sind diese Vorschläge auch durch die einzelnen Gremien noch zu bestätigen, so dürfte doch schon jetzt klar sein, daß auch in der neuen Amtsperiode viele Aufgaben für die Gemischte Kommission bereitstehen, um so mehr, als sich seit dem Erlaß des Hochschulrahmengesetzes und der Verabschiedung des Ausbildungsgesamtplanes die Studiensituation tiefgreifend geändert hat: Das soziale Umfeld wie auch die schulischen Voraussetzungen der Studienanfänger haben sich gewandelt; die Berufsperspektive, die gerade in der Zeit der zurückliegenden Studienreform die theoretische Ausbildung prägte, ist eine andere geworden. Stand noch vor wenigen Jahren jedem Theologiestudenten der Weg ins Pfarramt offen, so wird es nunmehr für die Mehrzahl der Studenten zu einem Problem werden, ob und wie sie die im Studium erworbenen Kenntnisse in der Praxis anwenden können. Die Bevölkerungsstatistik zeigt an, daß sich in absehbarer Zeit das Bild der verfaßten Kirchen erheblich wandeln wird. Auch die veränderten Kommunikationssysteme in unserer Gesellschaft werden neue Anforderungen an die Kirche und ihre Verkündigung stellen. Die Folgerungen, die für die theologische Ausbildung gezogen werden müssen, sind noch nicht wirklich in den Blick gekommen. Sie systematisch zu durchdenken, müßte eines der künftigen Arbeitsthemen sein.

Darüber hinaus zeigt die Erfahrung der Prüfer in den theologischen Prüfungen, daß die Studierenden mehr und mehr begründete wie auch unbegründete Examensängste zu überwinden haben. Da die zweite Ausbildungsphase entsprechend dem Ausbildungsgesamtplan voraussetzt, daß die Studenten während ihres Studiums eine ausreichende theologische Kompetenz erworben haben, ist zu fragen, ob die allgemein übliche Anla-

[69] XIX 6; XX 6

ge des Studiums noch in der Lage ist, eine solche Kompetenz zu vermitteln. Zweifellos ist in diesem Zusammenhang auch erforderlich, die Struktur der zweiten Ausbildungsphase kritisch zu bedenken. Viele Erwartungen, die man an die Einbeziehung der »Handlungswissenschaften« in die zweite Phase des theologischen Studiums knüpfte, sind nicht in Erfüllung gegangen; eher wurde ein Dilettantismus gefördert, der dem Erwerb eines soliden theologischen Wissens und Urteilsvermögens entgegensteht. Es gilt, die theoretische Perspektive der theologischen Ausbildung neu zu erfragen, nicht zuletzt im Verhältnis der beiden Ausbildungsphasen zueinander.

Selbstverständlich kann das Theologiestudium, insbesondere wenn es für das Pfarramt vorbereitet, auf den Zusammenhang mit der kirchlichen Wirklichkeit nicht verzichten. Solcher Kontext mag auch in kirchlicher Begleitung der Studierenden zum Ausdruck kommen. Freilich sollte an dem Grundsatz festgehalten werden, daß das Studium der evangelischen Theologie zu eigenständiger, selbstverantworteter Urteilsbildung führen soll – dies schließt auch nur den Versuch aus, klerikale oder professorale Machtansprüche im Studium zu etablieren.

Die Geschichte der Gemischten Kommission hat gezeigt, daß sich das Verhältnis von Fakultäten und Landeskirchen durch eine solche Arbeitsgemeinschaft positiv fördern läßt. Bestehende Vorurteile konnten überwunden und ein besseres gegenseitiges Verstehen erreicht werden. Die aufgrund gemeinsamer Verantwortung gebotene Zusammenarbeit verwirklichte sich in einer Atmosphäre des Vertrauens. Auch das Verhältnis der Fakultäten zueinander konnte durch die Arbeit der Gemischten Kommission enger gestaltet werde. Es ist zu wünschen, daß diese Arbeit in der eingeschlagenen Richtung weiter vorangehen und hierdurch die theologische Ausbildung an den Fakultäten auch in Zukunft vergleichbar und im Interesse der künftigen Theologen und Pfarrer weitgehend einheitlich gestaltet werden wird.

»... einander durch Demut für vorzüglicher halten ...« Zum Begriff »Demut« bei Paulus und in paulinischer Tradition[1]

von Klaus Wengst

(Claus-Groth-Straße 2a, 4630 Bochum 1)

Bei Paulus und in der paulinischen Tradition hat »Demut« ihren Ort im Raum der Gemeinde. Die an sie gerichtete Forderung, sich »demütig« zu verhalten, ergeht nicht innerhalb einer hierarchischen Struktur – eine Einschränkung ist in dieser Hinsicht jedoch beim ersten Petrusbrief zu machen –, sondern sie erfolgt im Horizont von Gleichheit und Gegenseitigkeit. Das gibt ihr hier ihr besonderes Gepräge[2].

1. Nach dem Verständnis des Begriffs »Demut« in den Briefen des Paulus zu fragen, ist darüber hinaus in dreifacher Hinsicht interessant. Einmal wird in der Beurteilung seines Auftretens durch andere und durch ihn selbst das Einwirken verschiedener – griechischer und jüdischer – Traditionen sichtbar. Diese Traditionen zeigen sich in charakteristischer Weise auch in der eigenen Bewertung der sozialen Situation des Apostels, die differenziert zu beschreiben ist. Schließlich wird in der christologischen Begründung der Demutsforderung an seine Gemeinden deutlich, woran sein Reden von »Demut« letztlich ausgerichtet ist und was ihm eigenes Profil verleiht.

---

[1] Der folgende Beitrag war ursprünglich wesentlich breiter angelegt. Er sollte die verschiedenen Verwendungen des Begriffs »Demut« in urchristlichen Schriften im Rahmen der entsprechenden griechischen und alttestamentlich-jüdischen Traditionen untersuchen. Der bekannten Beobachtung, daß »Demut« in der griechischen Tradition negativ und in der alttestamentlich-jüdischen positiv gewertet wird, sollte unter der Fragestellung nachgegangen werden, wer diesen Begriff wem in welcher sozialen und politischen Situation zuschreibt. Davon nämlich hängt es weitgehend ab, was unter »Demut« verstanden und wie sie bewertet wird. Auch die festzustellenden Verschiebungen im Verständnis von »Demut« innerhalb der einzelnen Traditionsbereiche sind – zumindest teilweise – sozial und politisch bedingt. – Die Ausarbeitung nahm dann aber Ausmaße an, die als Festschriftbeitrag unzumutbar sind. Daher beabsichtige ich zu einem späteren Zeitpunkt eine selbständige Veröffentlichung und lege hier vorab einen Ausschnitt vor.

[2] Die nächste Analogie hierzu findet sich in den Qumrantexten, wo »Demut« erstmals nicht ein Verhalten zwischen Niedriggestellten und Höhergestellten beschreibt, sei es als Unterwürfigkeit auf der einen und Bescheidenheit und Milde auf der anderen Seite, sondern wo sie das Verhalten zwischen Gleichgestellten bestimmen soll: 1QS 5,1–7.24f. Den Rahmen bildet hier die klosterähnliche Sektengemeinschaft.

a) In 2 Kor 10,1 spricht Paulus von sich selbst als einem, »der ich zwar bei meiner persönlichen Anwesenheit unter euch ταπεινός, abwesend aber mutig gegen euch bin«. Daß er hier einen gegen ihn erhobenen Vorwurf aufnimmt, ergibt sich deutlich aus v. 10, wo er als über ihn in Umlauf gebrachte Aussage zitiert, »daß die Briefe zwar gewichtig und stark seien, die persönliche Anwesenheit jedoch schwächlich und die Rede verächtlich«. In solchem Zusammenhang gibt sich ταπεινός in v. 1 als von griechischer Tradition geprägt zu erkennen. Es kennzeichnet das Auftreten des Paulus als niedrig, kriecherisch, sklavisch, schwächlich[3]. Der konkrete Anlaß für diese Beurteilung dürfte darin liegen, daß es Paulus nicht vermocht hatte, bei dem sog. Zwischenbesuch in Korinth die in Gruppen zerfallene und sich zu einem beträchtlichen Teil gegen ihn wendende Gemeinde wieder in den von ihm gewünschten Zustand zu bringen, sondern daß er erfolglos nach Ephesus hatte zurückreisen müssen[4]. Bei dem Besuch war es zu einem Paulus besonders demütigenden Zwischenfall gekommen; er spricht davon, daß ihm Unrecht angetan und daß er betrübt worden sei[5].

Paulus setzt nun dem Vorwurf, sein persönliches Auftreten sei ταπεινός, nicht einfach die Behauptung entgegen, er treffe gar nicht zu. Daß er nicht stark sein will, sondern bewußt seine Schwäche annimmt, führt er in 2 Kor 12,7–11 aus; darauf sei hier nicht weiter eingegangen. Er nimmt auch die erlittene Demütigung an, nicht als Urteil der Menschen, sondern von Gott her. Doch setzt er hier die Akzente bezeichnend anders. In 2 Kor 12,20f. schreibt er: »Ich fürchte nämlich, daß ich vielleicht, wenn ich komme, euch nicht so antreffe, wie ich will, und ich bei euch so angetroffen werde, wie ihr nicht wollt; daß vielleicht Streit, Eifersucht, Zornausbrüche, Streitereien, Verleumdungen, Ohrenbläsereien, Aufgeblasenheiten und unordentliche Zustände da sind. Damit mein Gott mich nicht wiederum, wenn ich komme, vor euch erniedrigt/demütigt (ταπεινώσῃ) und ich nicht viele von denen beklage, die vorher gesündigt und nicht Umkehr geübt haben über ihrer Unreinheit, Unzucht und Zügellosigkeit, die sie

---

3 Vgl. Walter Grundmann, Art. ταπεινός κτλ., in: ThWNT VIII 1969 (1–27), 20,12: »servil, unterwürfig, machtlos, niedrig«; Stefan Rehrl, Das Problem der Demut in der profangriechischen Literatur im Verhältnis zu Septuaginta und Neuem Testament, AeC 4, 1961, 175: »mutlos, feige, kleinlaut«.

4 Der Vorwurf »gründet sich zum mindesten darauf, daß Paulus beim letzten Aufenthalt der Gemeinde nicht hatte Herr werden können, sondern sogar die c. 2 und 7 erwähnte Kränkung hatte über sich ergehen lassen müssen und abgereist war, ohne, wie zuerst in Aussicht genommen, wiederzukommen« (Hans Lietzmann, An die Korinther I. II, HNT 9, ⁴1949, 140). – Zur Literarkritik des 2 Kor und zum Ablauf der Ereignisse verweise ich hier nur auf Philipp Vielhauer, Geschichte der urchristlichen Literatur. Einleitung in das Neue Testament, die Apokryphen und die Apostolischen Väter, 1975, 143–155, ohne mit den dort aufgestellten Hypothesen in allen Einzelheiten übereinzustimmen.

5 2 Kor 2,5; 7,12.

begangen haben.« Was Paulus bei seinem Zwischenbesuch in Korinth, auf den er hier zurückblickt, erleben mußte, hat er als Erniedrigung und Demütigung erfahren. Als Subjekt dessen nennt er an dieser Stelle aber Gott. Von ihm her akzeptiert er für sich die erlittene Demütigung, ohne jedoch dieses Geschehen damit zu legitimieren. Die Aussage von seiner Schwäche gilt prinzipiell, aber nicht die von der Demütigung. Solche Erfahrung will er nicht noch einmal machen. Das Urteil, Paulus sei im persönlichen Auftreten ταπεινός, beruhte ja vor allem auch darauf, daß er Korinth hatte erfolglos verlassen müssen. Akzeptanz der ihm zugefügten Demütigung kann für ihn auf keinen Fall heißen, die Gemeinde verlorenzugeben. Er kämpft weiter um sie; und als er hört, daß sie durch Titus wieder zurechtgebracht ist, erfährt er das als Erhöhung des Gedemütigten durch Gott. Er interpretiert also diese Erfahrung mit Hilfe alttestamentlicher Tradition, wenn er 2 Kor 7,6 schreibt: »Gott, der die Gedemütigten tröstet, hat uns getröstet durch die Ankunft des Titus«, der ihm von der wiedergewonnenen korinthischen Gemeinde berichtete[6]. Nicht zuletzt dürfte es aber dieses Wissen von Gott sein, daß er die Gedemütigten tröstet, das Paulus Demütigungen annehmen läßt, um dann gerade nicht zu resignieren, sondern zu kämpfen.

b) So wenig es Paulus nach aktuellen Demütigungen verlangt, ist doch die Entscheidung, ein Leben in niedrigen Verhältnissen zu führen, die Existenzweise eines ταπεινός zu haben, für ihn von prinzipieller Bedeutung. Das ist angedeutet in dem Abschnitt Phil 4,10–20, in dem er sich für eine Unterstützung durch die Gemeinde in Philippi bedankt. Er gibt zwar betont seiner Freude darüber Ausdruck, stellt aber zugleich heraus, daß er so nicht »aus Bedürftigkeit« rede. Daß er bedürftig ist, leidet keinen Zweifel, aber er legt es nicht darauf an und ist auch nicht darauf angewiesen, aus dieser Bedürftigkeit herauszukommen, da er es gelernt habe, sich in seiner Lage genügen zu lassen (v. 11). Er fährt dann fort: »Ich verstehe mich sowohl darauf, in armseligen Verhältnissen zu leben (ταπεινοῦσθαι), als auch verstehe ich mich darauf, im Überfluß zu leben. In alles und jedes bin ich eingeweiht, sowohl satt zu sein als auch zu hungern, sowohl im Überfluß zu leben als auch Mangel zu leiden« (v. 12). ταπεινοῦσθαι steht parallel zu πεινᾶν und ὑστερεῖσθαι und in Opposition zu περισσεύειν und χορτάζεσθαι, ist somit eindeutig durch die materielle Lage bestimmt. Daher bezeichnet es hier nicht den freiwilligen Verzicht auf Sättigung, hat also nicht die technische Bedeutung »fasten«[7], sondern beschreibt die Mangelsituation des Armen, der nicht genug zu essen hat[8].

---

[6] Bei allen, die literarkritische Operationen am 2 Kor für nötig halten, ist es unumstritten, daß der »Versöhnungsbrief«, zu dem diese Stelle gehört, zeitlich nach dem »Tränenbrief« (Kap. 10–13) anzusetzen ist.

[7] Gegen Albrecht Dihle, Art. Demut, in: RAC, III 1957 (735–778), 750.

[8] Vgl. Heinz Giesen, Art. ταπεινός κτλ., in: EWNT, III 1983 (798–804), 803: »in Entbehrungen leben«

Wenn Paulus sich für die ihm in solcher Situation widerfahrene Hilfe zwar freudig bedankt, aber doch zum Ausdruck bringt, daß diese Hilfe für ihn nicht von unbedingter Notwendigkeit sei – und das schließt die Konsequenz ein, daß sie von ihm aus betrachtet auch unterbleiben könne –, weist er damit auf eine grundsätzliche Bedeutung seiner Lebensweise als ταπεινός hin. Wer formuliert, daß er sowohl das eine als auch das andere vermag, im Mangel zu leben und auch im Überfluß[9], ist kaum von Haus aus ein Armer. Die Lebensweise als ταπεινός ist daher für Paulus offenbar nicht ihm von vornherein vorgegebener Zwang, sondern bewußte Wahl. Das macht die andere hier zu besprechende Stelle noch deutlicher.

In 2 Kor 11,7 fragt Paulus: »Oder habe ich eine Sünde begangen, als ich mich selbst erniedrigte (ἐμαυτὸν ταπεινῶν), damit ihr erhöht würdet, da ich euch unentgeltlich das Evangelium Gottes verkündigt habe?« Er hat hier im Blick, daß er zur Schaffung der materiellen Voraussetzung seiner Missionstätigkeit Handarbeit verrichtete. Das bezeichnet er als Erniedrigung seiner selbst. Damit findet sich hier dieselbe negative Wertung der Handarbeit wie in der uns überlieferten griechischen Literatur[10]. Das dürfte auch bei Paulus dieselbe soziale Basis zur Voraussetzung haben, also einen gehobenen Sozialstatus: Von Haus aus ist er offenbar kein Handarbeiter[11]. Der entscheidende Punkt ist jedoch, daß Paulus zwar an der negativen Wertung der Handarbeit durch die bessergestellten Kreise der griechisch-römischen Welt partizipiert[12], daß er aber doch diese als negativ eingeschätzte Arbeit durch eigenen Entschluß auf sich nimmt und dieses Tun ganz gewiß nicht negativ wertet. In dieser Selbsterniedrigung ist er höchst »ungriechisch« und »unrömisch«. Er macht sich denen, die Gott erwählt hat, den Geringen und Verachteten (1 Kor 1,27f.), solidarisch, fällt ihnen nicht zur Last (2 Kor 11,9), damit sie Erhöhung erfahren. Er, der von Haus aus die Perspektive eines »Hohen« hat, macht sich die Perspektive der Geringen durch seine Lebenspraxis zu eigen. Darin erweist sich seine »Demut«.

---

[9] Im Blick auf den Überfluß ist allerdings mit Wolfgang Schrage, Ethik des Neuen Testaments, NTD Ergänzungsreihe 4, 1982, 213, festzustellen, daß »Paulus vor allem ein entbehrungsreiches Leben geführt hat«.

[10] Ich nenne als Belege hier nur Aristot. pol. VIII 2,1 (1337b) und Lukian. somnium 9.13.

[11] Vgl. auch die sachlich parallele Stelle 1 Kor 9,19, wo Paulus im Blick auf seine Handarbeit von Versklavung seiner selbst spricht. Beide Stellen hat Ronald F. Hock für die Frage nach der sozialen Position des Paulus ausgewertet: Paul's Tentmaking and the Problem of His Social Class, JBL 97, 1978, 555–564. Vgl. auch den Exkurs in Teil III 2a bei Klaus Wengst, PAX ROMANA. Anspruch und Wirklichkeit. Erfahrungen und Wahrnehmungen des Friedens bei Jesus und im Urchristentum, 1986.

[12] Insoweit ist Hock, a.a.O. (Anm. 11), 562, zuzustimmen, wenn er schreibt, die Sprache des Paulus an diesen Stellen spiegele »die snobistische und verächtliche Haltung« zur Handarbeit wider, »die für Griechen und Römer der Oberschicht so typisch ist« (vgl. 560). Doch damit ist allenfalls erst die Hälfte gesagt.

c) Paulus fordert die bessergestellten Christen in seinen Gemeinden nicht dazu auf, seine Lebensweise zu imitieren. Sie ist Teil seiner besonderen apostolischen Existenz[13]. Aber die in ihr sich zeigende Haltung und Praxis der Solidarität mit den Geringen, diese »Demut«, ist doch auch Gegenstand und Ziel seiner Paränese. So schreibt er in Röm 12,16 innerhalb einer Reihe von Mahnungen: »Trachtet nicht nach Hohem, sondern laßt euch zu den Niedrigen (τοῖς ταπεινοῖς)[14] herabziehen!« Unmittelbar anschließend bittet er, nicht klug für sich selbst zu sein. Das wäre eine Klugheit, die abgesondert von den anderen gewonnen wird und das eigene Interesse im Auge hat, die sich »oben« orientiert. Sie entspricht dem Trachten nach Hohem, dem Aufstiegsstreben. Solche Klugheit und solches Trachten entsolidarisieren und führen in die Konkurrenz[15]. Paulus aber zielt auf die »Einmütigkeit untereinander«, zu der er am Beginn von v. 16 mahnt. Sie kann es in der Gemeinde nur geben, wenn sie sich an den Möglichkeiten sowie an den Bedürfnissen und der Not ihrer schwächsten Glieder orientiert – sich zu ihnen »herabziehen« läßt, ihnen solidarisch wird[16]. Hiermit gehört die Mahnung von v. 13a sachlich zusammen: »Nehmt Anteil an den Bedürfnissen/der Not der Heiligen!«[17]

---

[13] Vgl. 1 Kor 9.

[14] τοῖς ταπεινοῖς kann natürlich auch neutrisch verstanden werden; dann stünde es in genauer Parallele zu τὰ ὑψηλά. Dafür tritt Heinrich Schlier, Der Römerbrief, HThK VI, 1977, 380f., ein, der den Vers als Mahnung zum Verzicht auf hohe Stellung und Vorrang interpretiert. Beide Möglichkeiten offen lassen Ulrich Wilckens, Der Brief an die Römer 3. Röm 12–16, EKK VI 3, 1982, 23 Anm. 113; Grundmann, a.a.O. (Anm. 3) 20. Letzterer erklärt die neutrische in dieser Weise: »so denkt Paulus an die kleinen und geringen Dienste, in denen einer dem anderen beisteht« (20,25f.). Da diese »Dienste« jedoch vor allem die Schwachen nötig haben, ist auch hier im Grunde an die ταπεινοί gedacht. Vom unmittelbaren Kontext her – Einmütigkeit, nicht für sich selbst klug sein – ist wohl der Gegensatz zwischen Aufstiegsstreben und Solidarität mit den Schlechtergestellten intendiert. Für ein maskulines Verständnis von τοῖς ταπεινοῖς vgl. auch Giesen, a.a.O. (Anm. 8) 799; Ernst Käsemann, An die Römer, HNT 8a, 1973, 332, nach dem es hier darum geht, daß »die Gemeinschaft mit den Niedrigen und Unterdrückten festgehalten werden (muß)«.

[15] Vgl. Wilckens, a.a.O. (Anm. 14) 23: »Als Christ kann man vernünftig nur sein, wenn man es für andere ist.«

[16] Käsemann, a.a.O. (Anm. 14) 332, folgert aus dieser Stelle: »Was man heute Mitmenschlichkeit nennt, ist unabdingbar daran gebunden, daß die Gemeinde Jesu auf der Seite der Niedrigen zu stehen und auch sozial das Ghetto der Klassen zu durchbrechen vermag.« Karl Barth, Der Römerbrief, ^{7}1933 (= ^{2}1922), sprach in der Auslegung dieser Stelle in folgender Weise vom Christentum: »Es hört das heimliche Krachen im Gebälk. Und es kann nicht *über*sehen und *über*hören, was es sieht und hört. Es liebt darum die Armen, die Leidtragenden, die Hungernden und Dürstenden, die Unrechtleidenden« (447). »Es hat – und *darum* haben die Sozialdemokraten auf weite Strecken seinen Beifall! – eine gewisse parteiische Vorliebe für die Bedrückten, zu kurz Kommenden, Unfertigen, Grämlichen und in Auflehnung Begriffenen« (448). Vgl. aber auch die bis S. 450 folgen-

Von daher erscheint es nicht als zufällig, daß das Miteinander in der Gemeinde im Blick ist, wo Paulus ausdrücklich zur »Demut« mahnt. Das ist in Phil 2,3 der Fall. Dieser Vers steht innerhalb des Abschnitts 2,1–11, dessen Aufbau zunächst in den Blick zu nehmen ist, wenn die Forderung der »Demut« angemessen verstanden werden soll. In v. 1 nennt Paulus in vier Bedingungssätzen zunächst die Voraussetzung, von der ausgehend er die in v. 2–4 folgenden Imperative formuliert. Den zweiten Imperativ bringt er in der Form eines ἵνα-Satzes und entfaltet ihn anschließend in Partizipien. Die entfalteten Imperative faßt er dann in v. 5a in einem einzigen knapp zusammen und gibt in v. 5b deren Norm an, die er ihrerseits wieder in v. 6–11 durch Zitierung des bekannten Christusliedes[18] entfaltet. Die folgende kolometrisch angeordnete Übersetzung von v. 1–5 versucht, die Struktur des Textes sichtbar zu machen:

Wenn es so etwas wie Zuspruch und Anspruch[19] in Christus gibt,
wenn etwas wie von der Liebe gewährten Trost,
wenn etwas wie vom Geist geschenkte Gemeinschaft,
wenn etwas wie Herz und Barmherzigkeit,
  dann bringt meine Freude zur Vollendung:
    Seid doch einträchtig,
      indem ihr dieselbe Liebe habt,
      einmütig nach dem einen trachtet,
      in keiner Weise selbstsüchtig noch ruhmsüchtig,
      sondern indem ihr einander durch Demut für vorzüglicher haltet als euch selbst,
      indem ihr ein jeder nicht auf das Eigene den Blick lenkt,
      sondern alle auf das der anderen!
    Danach trachtet unter euch,
wonach auch in Jesus Christus (zu trachten angemessen ist)!

---

de dialektische – jedoch gerade nicht ausgewogene, sondern klar gewichtende – Relativierung »in der *Anwendung* auf *konkrete* ›Höhen‹ und ›Niederungen‹ unseres Daseins« (448). In der 1. Auflage (vgl. jetzt: Der Römerbrief [Erste Fassung] 1919, hg. v. Hermann Schmidt, 1985) hatte Barth zu Röm 12,16 von »einseitiger und entschiedener Parteinahme« gesprochen. »Ihr gehört nicht zu den Herren. Ihr könnt auch nicht neutral sein und es allen Leuten recht machen. Ihr gehört unter allen Umständen zum gemeinen Volk ... Denn Gott ist wohl ein Gott der Juden *und* der Heiden, aber nicht ein Gott der Hohen *und* der Niedrigen, sondern einseitig ein Gott der Niedrigen, nicht ein Gott der Großen *und* der Kleinen, sondern rücksichtslos ein Gott der Kleinen« (489f.).

17 Wilckens, a.a.O. (Anm. 14) 17, übersetzt treffend: »Wo die Heiligen in Not sind, teilt mit ihnen.«

18 Zum Christuslied in Phil 2,6–11 sei hier nur auf Joachim Gnilka, Der Philipperbrief, HThK X 3, ^{2}1976, 131–147, hingewiesen.

19 παράκλησις läßt sich hier mit nur einem Wort kaum angemessen übersetzen. Zu παρακαλεῖν/παράκλησις bei Paulus vgl. ausführlich Heinrich Schlier, Die Eigenart der christlichen Mahnung nach dem Apostel Paulus, in: Ders., Besinnung auf das Neue Testament. Exegetische Aufsätze und Vorträge, II ^{2}1967, 340–357.

Die Mahnung erfolgt »in (Jesus) Christus« (v. 1.5); der Indikativ schließt den Imperativ ein[20]. So macht schon der Aufbau klar, daß das Christusgeschehen Grund und Norm des Handelns der Gemeinde ist. Als Objekt des Heilshandelns Gottes wird die Gemeinde von Paulus als ethisches Subjekt angesprochen. Er spricht sie in v. 1 auf ihre christliche Erfahrung hin an und will, daß sie sich als christliche Gemeinde bewährt. Dabei ist hier nicht die Bewährung nach außen im Blick – darauf war er in 1,27–30 eingegangen –, sondern es geht um die innergemeindliche Praxis. Dafür nennt er als Richtungsanzeige in mehreren Formulierungen die Einmütigkeit. Wie sie zu erstreben ist, legt er in v. 3f. negativ und positiv dar. Ausgeschlossen werden Selbst- und Ruhmsucht, der Drang, vor den anderen herauszuragen. Aufsteigermentalität verhindert das einträchtige Ausgerichtetsein der Gemeinde. Als positives Gegenbild führt Paulus an, den jeweils anderen für höher als sich selbst einzuschätzen. Eben das bewirkt die »Demut« (ταπεινοφροσύνη), die die eigene Person gegenüber den anderen »unten« orientiert und damit das genaue Gegenteil von Aufsteigermentalität ist. Demut läßt nicht den eigenen Vorteil suchen, sondern den der anderen. Dabei ist noch einmal zu betonen, daß diese Mahnungen nicht isolierten Individuen gegeben werden, sondern den einzelnen als Gliedern der Gemeinde[21].

Die Mahnung zur Demut erfolgt im Horizont der Gemeinde. Das ist im Zusammenhang dessen weiter zu bedenken, daß die von Paulus an dieser Stelle gegebenen Forderungen dem gesellschaftlichen Trend entgegenstanden. Die Gesellschaft der römischen Kaiserzeit hatte eine »Stände-Schichten-Struktur«, in der die Scheidelinie zwischen Oberschicht und Unterschicht besonders ausgeprägt war; die Herkunft, vor allem sozial, aber auch geographisch, spielte die entscheidende Rolle[22]. Doch waren die Grenzen innerhalb der hierarchischen Gesellschaftsstruktur keineswegs hermetisch gegeneinander abgeschottet. In bestimmten Bereichen war sozialer Aufstieg nahezu die Norm: Der städtische »Sklave hatte in der Regel die Aussicht, freigelassen zu werden, und erhielt die Freiheit,

[20] Vgl. hierzu Ernst Käsemann, Kritische Analyse von Phil. 2,5–11, in: Ders., Exegetische Versuche und Besinnungen, I 1960 (51–95), 90f.

[21] Das ist durchaus »eine Forderung nach kollektiver Demut«, die nicht als »absurd« abgetan werden kann, wie es Aleksander Radler, Art. Demut VIII. Ethisch, in: TRE, VIII 1981 (483–488), 486, in seiner Betonung der Demut als einer »individualethischen Größe« tut. Die Gemeinde als ethisches Subjekt kommt bei ihm nicht in den Blick. – Eine individualisierende Auslegung von Phil 2,3, die den Horizont der Gemeinde nicht wahrnimmt, bietet Dihle, a.a.O. (Anm. 7) 749: »Die ταπείνωσις oder ταπεινοφροσύνη gegenüber dem Nächsten ist das einzig angemessene Verhalten für den, dem Gott im Nächsten begegnet, vor dem alle Menschen rechtlose, ihm verfallene und begnadigte Sünder sind, die keine Ansprüche zu stellen haben.«

[22] Vgl. Géza Alföldy, Römische Sozialgeschichte, ^{2}1979, 83–138; besonders 93–102.130–138.

falls er dieses Alter erlebte, spätestens zumeist um sein 30. Lebensjahr«[23]. Das nach der Freilassung geborene Kind des Freigelassenen galt bereits als freigeboren[24]. Neben sozialem Abstieg[25] gab es auch schon vor der Kaiserzeit immer wieder auch Fälle größeren sozialen Aufstiegs, in der Kaiserzeit jedoch in verstärkter Anzahl[26]. Werden die innergesellschaftlichen Abgrenzungen von vielen nicht mehr als selbstverständlich akzeptiert[27], bedarf es allerdings auch der Möglichkeit sozialen Aufstiegs und ihrer gelegentlichen Verwirklichung zur Legitimation und damit auch Erhaltung der bestehenden Gesellschaftsstruktur[28]. Es kann dann suggeriert werden, daß jeder durch entsprechende Leistung seine Position verbessern könne[29]. Aufstiegsbewußtsein wird dann ein verbreitetes Phänomen.

---

23 Ebd. 121.

24 Ebd.

25 Nach ebd. 135 war sozialer Abstieg »unter den konsolidierten Verhältnissen der frühen Kaiserzeit ein seltener Vorgang ... Massenweise betroffen waren davon höchstens die Einwohner der Provinzen in den ersten Generationen nach ihrer Unterwerfung, in der Kaiserzeit also immer engere Kreise. Verarmte und verschuldete Familien, vor allem auf dem Lande, die z. B. ihre Kinder als Sklaven verkaufen mußten, gab es zwar immer, aber breite Bevölkerungsschichten erlebten selten gleichzeitig einen derartigen Abstieg.« Diese Beschreibung ist etwas schönfärberisch: Wenn in der frühen Kaiserzeit die Latifundienwirtschaft expandierte, mußte das zwangsläufig auf Kosten kleinerer Landbesitzer gehen.

26 Zur sozialen Mobilität in der frühen Kaiserzeit vgl. Gerd Theißen, Christologie und soziale Erfahrung. Wissenssoziologische Aspekte paulinischer Christologie, in: Ders., Studien zur Soziologie des Urchristentums, WUNT 19, ^{2}1983 (318–330), 321–324, sowie die dort Anm. 6–8.10 genannte Literatur. Theißen stellt zusammenfassend fest: »Es gab also begrenzte Aufstiegschancen. Wie oft sie realisiert wurden, ist weniger wichtig. Entscheidend ist, daß die Erwartungen der Menschen davon geprägt werden konnten, daß jeder in seinem Leben einen Schritt ›nach oben‹ tun konnte« (321).

27 Vgl. das Beispiel Lukians, der als Kind kleiner Leute seinem Milieu entflieht und sich mit Hilfe der Bildung den ihm möglichen »Weg nach oben« sucht (somnium).

28 Vgl. Alföldy, a.a.O. (Anm. 22) 135: »Immerhin wies das römische Gesellschaftssystem vielfache soziale Aufstiegschancen auf, die man zumindest anstreben konnte; diese Elastizität trug zu seiner Stärke und Stabilität wesentlich bei.«

29 Das gilt besonders für den militärischen Bereich. So rühmt Aelius Aristides die Kaiser, daß sie angeworbenen Fremden die Hoffnung gaben, »daß sie es nicht bereuen würden, wenn sie sich als tüchtige Männer erwiesen; denn nicht Leute aus altem Adel würden die sein, die stets den ersten Platz einnehmen, und Leute aus der zweiten Klasse den zweiten Platz, und auch bei den übrigen Rängen werde es nicht so sein, sondern jeder werde den Rang einnehmen, den er verdiene, da die Tüchtigen hier nicht nach Worten, sondern nach Taten beurteilt würden« (Aristeid. Romrede 85). – Die oben gemachte Aussage, daß die Möglichkeit sozialen Aufstiegs nur gelegentlich verwirklicht wurde – und nur gelegentlich zu verwirklichen war –, bezieht sich auf die Gesamtzahl der in der Unterschicht Lebenden. – Bei aller Unterschiedlichkeit, vor allem verursacht durch die große Bedeutung der Herkunft (vgl. Alföldy, a.a.O. [Anm. 22] 98.101), bildet doch die amerikanische Legende »vom Tellerwäscher zum Millionär« eine moderne Analogie. Auch wenn es solche

In der Konkurrenz gegeneinander gilt es konsequent den eigenen Vorteil zu suchen, um »hochzukommen«. Wenn Paulus auf solchem Hintergrund nicht den isolierten einzelnen, sondern die Glieder der Gemeinde zu einem Verhalten auffordert, das dem für die Gesellschaft charakteristischen entgegengesetzt ist, dann wird dieser Raum »in Christus« zu einer anderen Gesellschaft, zur Gegengesellschaft als solidarischer Gemeinschaft. Dann aber ist »Demut« nicht individueller Verzicht[30], sondern Grundbedingung einer neuen Gesellschaft, die wirklich alle einschließt.

So gewiß der Raum »in Christus« durch solches Verhalten seiner Bewohner konkret auszugestalten ist, bildet doch dieser vorgegebene Raum selbst schon den Grund und die Norm dafür. Inwiefern das der Fall ist, führt Paulus durch die Zitierung des Liedes in v. 6–11 aus, das von Christus als dem spricht, der seine Gottgleichheit nicht wie »ein gefundenes Fressen« festhielt[31], sondern sich entäußerte und erniedrigte (ἐταπείνωσεν), die Daseinsweise eines Sklaven annahm und am Kreuz getötet wurde, den Gott daraufhin zur höchsten Höhe erhob und zum Herrn aller machte. »In Christus« ist daher der Raum, in dem die Herrschaft des

---

Karrieren tatsächlich gegeben hat – wie ja auch das kaiserzeitliche Rom erstaunliche Karrieren aufzuweisen hatte –, sind sie in einem bestimmten Sinn des Wortes »legendär«: Man erzählt von ihnen als einem einmal wahr gewordenen Traum, der im System festhält und faktisch für die allermeisten eine unerreichbare Möglichkeit bleibt – und bleiben muß: wie sollte sonst das System Bestand haben? Da es aber die Möglichkeit, wenn auch noch so eingeschränkt, nun doch gibt, kann die allgemeine Meinung jedem, der den Aufstieg nicht schafft, das als persönliches Versagen anrechnen und damit versklavende Strukturen verschleiern. – Theißen, a. a. O. (Anm. 26), nennt neben der Tüchtigkeit »die Loyalität gegenüber einem Herrn« als wichtigen Aufstiegsfaktor (321) und belegt das an Beispielen (322–324); beide Faktoren gehören zusammen (325). Auf dem Hintergrund der den gesellschaftlichen Aufstieg fördernden Loyalität versucht Theißen, den »Glauben an den erhöhten Herrn« als »ein Angebot von Aufstiegsloyalität für jeden« zu verstehen (324; ähnlich in der Zusammenfassung 326). Mir scheint jedoch, daß die paulinische Intention der gesellschaftlichen Wirklichkeit viel weniger entspricht, als ihr vielmehr zuwiderläuft. Zumindest kann nicht undifferenziert von »Aufstiegsloyalität für alle« und »jeden« die Rede sein. Nach 1 Kor 1,27f. macht die Erwählung der Törichten, Schwachen und Unedlen durch Gott die Weisen und das Starke zuschanden und das, was etwas gilt, zunichte. Nach 1 Kor 7,22 ist zwar der im Herrn erwählte Sklave ein Freigelassener Christi, aber der erwählte Freie Sklave Christi. Jeder macht die Erfahrung des jeweils anderen; wenn man so will: der eine die des Aufstiegs, der andere die des Abstiegs. Selbstverständlich ist »Sklave Christi« für Paulus eine »höhere« Bezeichnung als »Freier«, aber wenn er die sozialen Termini so differenziert gebraucht, scheint es mir nicht angemessen zu sein, von »Aufstiegsloyalität für alle« zu sprechen.

[30] Die Kategorie des Verzichts bestimmt sehr stark die Interpretation von Stefan Rehrl, Art. Demut III. Neues Testament, in: TRE, VIII 1981 (463–465), 464f.

[31] Zu ἁρπαγμόν τι ἡγεῖσθαι in v. 6 und verwandten Wendungen vgl. Werner Foerster, Art. ἁρπάζω, ἁρπαγμός, in: ThWNT, I 1933 (471–474), 472f.; zur Diskussion um das Verständnis von v. 6 Gnilka, a.a.O. (Anm. 18) 115–117.

durch diese »Karriere« bestimmten Herrn ausgeübt wird und jetzt schon zum Zuge kommt. Es ist nicht die Herrschaft eines Menschen, der zum Gott gemacht wird, wie das beim römischen Kaiser der Fall ist[32], also die Herrschaft eines »Aufsteigers«, die deshalb auch nur »von oben« erfolgen kann und Unter-Ordnungen setzt. Es ist vielmehr die Herrschaft eines »Absteigers«, die Herrschaft dessen, der seinem Sein nach ganz und gar der Sphäre Gottes zugehört, der aber den Menschen zutiefst solidarisch wurde[33]. Wenn das Lied davon spricht, daß er die Daseinsweise eines Sklaven annahm, dann tut es das wohl nicht nur dazu, um menschliche Existenz generell als sklavisch zu kennzeichnen[34], sondern doch auch deshalb, weil der Sklave die unterste soziale Stufe einnimmt[35]. Diese Linie zieht Paulus weiter aus, wenn er als Tiefpunkt nicht wie das Lied den jeden Menschen treffenden Tod angibt, sondern mit einem Zusatz den schmählichen Verbrechertod am Kreuz (v. 8). Wenn dann im zweiten Teil des Liedes (v. 9–11) von der Erhöhung und Herrschaft dessen gesprochen wird, der mit dieser absoluten Anti-Karriere ausgezeichnet ist, dann bestreitet das nicht nur faktisch ausgeübte andere Herrschaft, sondern ist seine Herrschaft selbst auch anderer Art. Die Herrschaft des Gottgleichen, der sich aller Macht begeben und sich auf dem Weg nach ganz unten den Geringsten solidarisch gemacht hat, vollzieht sich in einer solidarischen Praxis der von ihm Beherrschten. Solcher Praxis gibt seine »Demut« Raum.

2. Auf das Miteinander in der Gemeinde bezogen findet sich der Demutsbegriff auch in deuteropaulinischen Texten. So wird in Kol 3,12 gemahnt: »Zieht nun als Auserwählte Gottes, als Heilige und Geliebte, an: herzliches Mitgefühl, Güte, Demut (ταπεινοφροσύνη), Sanftmut (πραΰτης), Langmut!« »Demut« steht hier innerhalb einer Reihe von Tugenden, die das Zusammenleben in der Gemeinde fördern. Daß eine geschwisterliche Gemeinschaft der Gleichen im Blick ist, zeigt der vorangehende v. 11, der für den neuen Menschen im Bereich der Gemeinde ethnische, religiöse, soziale und kulturell-zivilisatorische Trennungen negiert

---

32 Als »Herr und Gott« ließ sich zwar erst Domitian anreden, aber gottgleiche Verehrung wurde schon Augustus – verbunden mit der Göttin Roma – im Osten des Reiches zuteil. Indem er sich *divi filius* nannte, umgab er sich auch selbst mit einem göttlichen Nimbus. Zur religiösen Überhöhung des Kaisers vgl. die Abschnitte II 7b.c bei Wengst, a.a.O. (Anm. 11).

33 Vgl. Roger Mehl, Art. Demut IV. Systematisch, in: RGG^3, II 1958 (80–82), 81: »Es handelt sich für Gott darum, sein Geschöpf aufzusuchen, ihm in Jesus Christus der Nächste zu werden. Hier liegt der Prüfstein aller wahren Demut, der Punkt, an welchem sie sich radikal scheidet von aller Herablassung, zu der sich der Hochmut bequemen kann.«

34 Die Erläuterung von δοῦλος durch ἄνθρωπος (v. 7) »kann nur bedeuten, daß das Menschsein als δουλεία verstanden ist« (Gnilka, a.a.O. [Anm. 18] 120).

35 Theißen, a.a.O. (Anm. 26) 325, spricht im Blick auf das Sklavesein des Gottgleichen von der »größtmöglichen Statusdissonanz«.

und Christus als alles durchdringende und Einheit stiftende Macht betont[36]. Alle aufgezählten Tugenden stehen somit im Zusammenhang der Gegenseitigkeit; es kommt nicht etwa den einen Demut als Niedrigkeit, den anderen Sanftmut als sich herablassende Huld zu. Den Aspekt der Gegenseitigkeit hebt auch der folgende v. 13 hervor, wenn er in großer Nüchternheit dazu mahnt, einander zu ertragen und zu vergeben und dafür »auf das Handeln des Herrn« verweist, »das für die Glaubenden Grund und Richtung ihres Tuns bestimmt«[37]. Schließlich werden alle Tugenden der Liebe als »Band der Vollkommenheit« unterstellt (v. 14). Von daher ist es deutlich, daß πραΰτης in v. 12 nicht von der griechisch-römischen Tradition der Herrschertugend her verstanden werden kann, sondern aus alttestamentlich-jüdischer Tradition kommt und gleichsinnig neben ταπεινοφροσύνη steht. Wie in Phil 2,1–4 meint »Demut« damit an dieser Stelle negativ den Verzicht auf das Herausstellen der eigenen Person in der Gemeinschaft der Gemeinde, den Verzicht auf Wettbewerb und Konkurrenz, und positiv das förderliche Sich-Einbringen ins Miteinander[38].

Die Aufnahme von Kol 3,12 in Eph 4,1–3 gewinnt ihr besonderes Profil durch die Mahnung zu ökumenischer Einheit. Der Verfasser des Epheserbriefes stellt heraus, daß der Kirche die Einheit in doppelter Weise vorgegeben ist[39]. Sie ist bereits von Gott her in Christus ein für allemal gesetzt und wird im Bekenntnis festgehalten[40]; sie liegt aber immer auch vor der Kirche und ist in einem ökumenischen Lernprozeß je konkret zu erstreben[41]. In diesem Kontext bedeuten dann die in 4,2 genannten Tugenden der Demut, Sanftmut und Langmut, die anderen Christen, Gemeinden und Kirchen in ihrer Andersartigkeit wahrzunehmen und wahr sein zu lassen, sie auszuhalten und gemeinsam mit ihnen nach Einheit zu

---

[36] Vgl. auch Kol 3,15.

[37] Eduard Lohse, Die Briefe an die Kolosser und an Philemon, KEK IX 2, 1968, 213.

[38] Ein ganz anderer Gebrauch von »Demut« begegnet in Kol 2,18.23, wo der Verfasser sich auf Aussagen der von ihm bekämpften Häresie bezieht. Dort findet sich Demut einmal neben »Engeldienst« und zum anderen neben »freiwilligem Dienst« und »Strenge gegen den Leib«. Sie steht im Zusammenhang der Mächteverehrung der kolossischen Philosophie, die sich in kultischen Vollzügen (2,17), in der Beobachtung von Tabuvorschriften (2,21) und in Askese (2,23) äußert. »Demut« ist hier Unterwerfung unter sich aufdrängende Macht, um auf diese Weise an ihr partizipieren zu können; vgl. Klaus Wengst, Versöhnung und Befreiung. Ein Aspekt des Themas »Schuld und Vergebung« im Lichte des Kolosserbriefes, EvTh 36, 1976 (14–26), 15f.

[39] Vgl. Rudolf Schnackenburg, Der Brief an die Epheser, EKK X, 1982, 165: Dem Verfasser geht es »um die Einheit, die zwar von Gott her der Kirche vorgegeben ist, aber für alle Christen zur ständigen Aufgabe wird«.

[40] Eph 4,4–6; besonders v. 5.

[41] Eph 4,13–16.

suchen. »Demut« ist damit das Gegenteil von jeder Art Absolutsetzung seiner selbst[42], sie ist eine ausgesprochen ökumenische Tugend.

3. Der in paulinischer Tradition stehende erste Petrusbrief nimmt ebenfalls die Demutsforderung gemeindebezogen und unter Hervorhebung der Gegenseitigkeit auf, wenn es in 5,5b.6 heißt: »Alle aber umkleidet euch im Verkehr miteinander mit Demut; denn Gott widersteht den Hochmütigen, den Demütigen aber gibt er Gnade. Demütigt euch also unter die starke Hand Gottes, damit er euch erhöhe zur rechten Zeit!«[43] Allerdings folgt diese Mahnung hier auf eine klare Anweisung zu innergemeindlicher Über- und Unterordnung. Auf der einen Seite stehen die Presbyter, die »die Herde Gottes« zu weiden haben. Selbstverständlich sollen sie nicht profitsüchtig sein und nicht gewalttätig herrschen (5,1–4). Auf der anderen Seite werden die jüngeren Leute aufgefordert, sich den Presbytern unterzuordnen (5,5a). Der Verfasser versucht hier also, die Tradition wechselseitiger Demut in eine hierarchische Struktur einzubringen. Kann das aber wirklich gelingen? Kann die Forderung zur Demut für die »Oberen« dann etwas anderes bedeuten als die Mahnung zur Herablassung im Sinn der griechisch-römischen Herrschertugend, der πραΰτης/*clementia*? Und wird dann für die »Unteren« nicht auch der griechische Sinn von ταπεινοφροσύνη bestimmend werden – nur jetzt eben in einer Umkehrung der Werte positiv verstanden[44]?

[42] Vgl. Heinrich Schlier, Der Brief an die Epheser, ^{4}1963, 181: »Die ταπεινοφροσύνη ist die Gesinnung und das Verhalten desjenigen, der von dem anderen mehr hält als von sich selbst, und das nicht wiederum, um sich dadurch über ihn zu erhöhen, sondern aus echter Bescheidenheit, die das dem anderen und ihm selbst von Gott Beschiedene als solches erkennt und anerkennt.« Wenn Schlier allerdings die Ausführungen des ersten Clemensbriefes für einen »Kommentar zu unserer Stelle« hält, ist das ein Fehlurteil. Für die Begründung dieser Aussage muß ich auf den Abschnitt zum ersten Clemensbrief in der Anm. 1 angekündigten Arbeit verweisen.

[43] Vgl. auch 1 Petr 3,8f.

[44] Nach Norbert Brox, Der erste Petrusbrief, EKK XXI, 1979, 235, bewegt sich diese Ethik »auf dem schmalen Grat zwischen dem wirklichen Gelingen der Gegenseitigkeit ... und der Dekadenz zur trivialen Ordnungs-Moral«.

Ethics and the Gnostics

by R. McL. Wilson

(St. Mary's College, St. Andrews, Fife Ky 16 9JU (Schottland))

Several years ago, when the study of the Nag Hammadi texts was still in its infancy, it was asserted that these new documents showed the gnostics to have been 'even blacker' than they were painted by the early Fathers. At the time, at least one reader wondered how the author knew. The texts were not then readily accessible – in fact they were locked away in the Coptic Museum in Cairo, pending settlement of questions of ownership. Only one codex had been smuggled out of Egypt, and the process of editing and translating its contents extended over a period of some twenty years[1]. The first direct access to the texts, as distinct from the various reports and inventories published by J. Doresse, H. C. Puech and others, came with the appearance of the *editio princeps* of the Gospel of Truth and Pahor Labib's photographic edition containing a number of pages belonging to the Codex Jung and the greater part of five treatises from Codex II[2]. There was nothing here to support the assertion. In contrast, Jean

[1] The Gospel of Truth from the Codex Jung was published in 1956, the final part of the Tractatus Tripartitus in 1975. The delay was occasioned at least in part by the problems of co-ordinating translations of the Coptic into three different modern languages, which entailed circulation and discussion of the material by correspondence among a group of eventually seven scholars in several different countries. In the event, complete co-ordination proved to be impossible, and the translations accordingly differ, sometimes quite appreciably. James M. Robinson is not altogether fair in speaking of a monopoly (*Religious Studies Review* 3, 1977, 17–29), since the group was expanded at least twice, first by the inclusion of Wilson and Zandee and then by the addition of Kasser and Vycichl. Prior to their publication, the texts in this codex were admittedly not available to other scholars, but that was to prevent premature release – and the editors were themselves bound by contract not to publish articles of their own on a given text for a period of some months after its publication. In retrospect it might have been better to have adopted a simpler and more basic form of publication, as suggested at the time by W. C. Till, but that is another matter. Incidentally, the draft English translation circulated by the Claremont Coptic Gnostic Library project in preparation for *The Nag Hammadi Library in English* carried on every page a notice restricting its use to authorised persons.

For bibliography relating to the Nag Hammadi library, see D. M. Scholer, *Nag Hammadi Bibliography 1948–1969* (NHS 1, Leiden 1971), supplemented annually, apart from 1976, in *Novum Testamentum*.

[2] *Coptic Gnostic Papyri in the Coptic Museum at Old Cairo*, Cairo 1956. Plates 1–46 contain pages belonging to the Codex Jung, and plates 47–158 the first four treatises of Cod-

Doresse, in the first full-scale survey of the library[3], says bluntly: 'Nothing in these documents leads us to suppose that the Gnostics in question were addicted to licentious rites: one finds oneself almost disappointed in this, so freely had the heresiologists given us to understand that mysteries of that description were common practice in the principal sects!'

Scholars had long been accustomed to noting the curious phenomenon that asceticism and lubricity could both spring from the self-same root, the gnostic denigration of this present world and its Creator, and explanations lay readily to hand. On the one side, the gnostic did not belong to this world and should have nothing to do with it. His mind was set on higher things, and the daily concerns of the ordinary citizen in this life had no relevance for him; they were to be avoided so far as possible. On the other side, it was alleged, the gnostic was 'saved by nature'. Nothing that he did could affect that fact, and he was therefore at liberty to do whatsoever he chose. Indeed, hostility to the Demiurge could be construed to mean that the gnostic had a positive duty to disobey his commands, and hence to transgress against the laws imposed by the God of the Old Testament. On the one side the road led straight to asceticism, on the other to practices of a libertinarian character.

More recent studies have placed the whole matter in a different perspective, particularly in the light of the Nag Hammadi texts. As K. Rudolph notes[4], 'Gnosis is not a "theology of salvation by nature," as the heresiologists caricature it; it is rather thoroughly conscious of the provisional situation of the redeemed up to the realisation of redemption after death. Otherwise the extant literature which relates to existential and ethical behaviour is inexplicable. Naturally the fact remains that the pneumatic element cannot perish and its entry into the Pleroma is preordained, but the why and the how are not independent of the right conduct of its bearer'. In point of fact, the gnostics were wrestling with problems which have perplexed adherents of more orthodox traditions, in particular the reconciliation of divine grace and human freedom. The Westminster Confession of Faith for example affirms effectual calling, by which the elect are regenerated and renewed, and determined to that which is good (ch. X); but the last sentence of the preceding chapter declares 'The will of man is made perfectly and immutably free to do good alone in the state of glory only'. A later chapter (XX: Of Christian Liberty) is quite specific: 'They who, upon pretence of Christian liberty, do practise any sin, or cherish any lust, do thereby destroy the end of Christian liberty; which is, that,

---

ex II with some twelve pages of the anonymous treatise which was given the title On the origin of the World. This was just under half the text of the latter work.

[3] *The Secret Books of the Egyptian Gnostics,* London 1960, 251 (ET of *Les livres secrets des gnostiques d'Egypte,* Paris 1958).

[4] *Gnosis,* Edinburgh 1983, 117 (ET of *Gnosis,* Leipzig 1977, 135).

being delivered out of the hands of our enemies, we might serve the Lord without fear, in holiness and righteousness before him, all the days of our life'. In Pauline terms, it is by grace that we are saved, and not of works; yet conduct and good works are not irrelevant to Christian living.

At a later point[5], Rudolph echoes Doresse's comment: 'It is at any rate striking that thus far no libertine writings have appeared even among the plentiful Nag Hammadi texts. The witnesses for the libertine tendency are restricted to the Church Fathers and even here the evidence is uneven and in particular not easy to put into chronological sequence. At times it looks as if libertinism appeared rather late ... and as if individual sects (for example, the Simonians, the Basilidians and the Valentinians) first arrived at these conclusions in the course of their further development'.

Here a number of points call for attention. In the first place, the Fathers were engaged in polemic, concerned to refute and denounce what they regarded as a dangerous heresy; and it is not uncommon for polemic to degenerate into vilification. 'Une fois l'aversion contre une classe d'hommes créée et enracinée par un motif quelconque, dans l'objet haï tout devient haïssable: l'opinion préconçue donne naissance ou crédit à des fables, à des calomnies, qui contribuent, à leur tour, à la généraliser et à la fortifier, quelquefois même survivent à ses véritables causes'[6]. These words were written with reference to the slanders against the Jews which appear in Greek and Roman authors, but this 'loi fatale' is capable of wider application. We may recall the slanders directed against early Christians, the accusations of atheism, Thyestian banquets, promiscuity. In the light of this, the patristic statements must be viewed with some reserve. It is possible that some groups, or some individual gnostics, were guilty of the practices alleged, but we have no ground for assuming that all were guilty or that these practices were characteristic.

A second point is that the allegations vary from one Father to another: it may be not that libertinism appeared rather late, as Rudolph suggests, but that later Fathers were more inclined to bring such charges, with or without foundation. Certainly the most extreme cases are recorded by Epiphanius, and Epiphanius is notoriously not the most reliable of witnesses. Irenaeus is severe in his condemnation of Carpocrates (I 25. 1–6) and the Cainites (I 31. 1–2), but these are groups for whom we have no direct evidence, and may have been quite exceptional. Moreover we can see in the case of Jews and Christians how some of the allegations might have arisen through misunderstanding or misrepresentation, and the same may hold for the gnostics. One need only consider what a rite called 'the bridal chamber' might suggest to an outsider who had no knowledge of its real nature, the more especially if he knew of the sacred prostitution asso-

[5] Op. cit. 254 (German ed., 260).

[6] T. Reinach, *Textes d'auteurs grecs et romains relatifs au judaïsme*, Paris 1895, xvi.

ciated with some other cults. In the Gospel of Philip however it is the highest of the sacraments, symbolised by the Holy of Holies in the Temple at Jerusalem, and as 'the marriage undefiled' is expressly contrasted with earthly marriage. As Rudolph notes[7], Irenaeus provides us with the necessary background: at the consummation, according to the Valentinians, the gnostic is to be re-united with his celestial counterpart in the Pleroma (the bridal chamber). Since the human predicament originates in a disruption of the primal unity, symbolised by the separation of Adam and Eve (cf. Gospel of Philip 68.22–26; 70.10–22), 'the return of the soul to the arms of her partner or ideal prototype, prefigured in that of Sophia herself, is the decisive event at the end of time'. It is of course possible that some groups sought to symbolise this consummation by some form of ritual intercourse, but we have no proof that they did. The emphasis on continence even within the bonds of marriage in such works as the Acts of Thomas suggests otherwise.

Irenaeus at one point (I 6.3f.) speaks of some who 'secretly seduce women', or even openly parade their shameless conduct, and others who 'initially made an impressive pretence of living with (women) as sisters' but 'were convicted in course of time when the "sister" became pregnant by the "brother"'[8]. This passage, in his report on the Valentinians, is det-

---

[7] Op. cit. 245 (German ed., 251); see his discussion, 245–247. Following H. G. Gaffron, he regards it as 'probably even a kind of sacrament for the dying'. Irenaeus says nothing of any sexual act in this connection; 'it would be contrary to the "spiritual" interpretation of this"marriage"'.

[8] The passage recalls one interpretation of the 'famous crux' (Chadwick, NTS 1, 1954–5, 267) of I Cor. 7: 36–38, which some scholars have understood to refer to "the elementary, early relationship which soon afterwards developed into the *virgines subintroductae* of the later Church" (Moffatt, *First Corinthians,* London 1938 (repr. 1947), 99. So too NEB: "partner in celibacy"; but the footnotes suggest another interpretation: "virgin daughter"). As the NEB margin indicates, reference to a "spiritual" marriage is only one of several possible interpretations of the Corinthians passage (cf. Barrett, *First Corinthians,* London 1968, 182–185; Conzelmann, *Der erste Brief an die Korinther,* Göttingen 1969, 160–161. Like Chadwick and Prof. Greeven (NTS 15, 1968–69, 375), they understand it of an engaged couple; cf. RSV "betrothed"). That there were "libertine" trends in Corinth is evidenced by 1 Cor. 5:1ff., 6:12ff., but it should be noted a) that the first of these passages refers to a single case, and b) in the second instance the preceding verses (9–11) are a reminder that "some" of the Corinthians had formerly not led irreproachable lives – but they were washed, sanctified, justified, and are therefore under an obligation to glorify God in their bodies (6:20). In neither case is there ground for thinking that Paul's censure applies to all the Corinthian Christians, or even to a large number. Their fault was that they tolerated the offender of 5:1ff., and were in danger of being misled by the claims of the (possibly quite small) group in view at 6:12ff. It may be added that it is by no means certain that Paul's opponents in Corinth were fully "gnostic" in the second-century sense of that term, and that there were also tendencies in the direction of asceticism.

ached from its context in Werner Foerster's anthology and adduced separately, on the ground that it does not correspond with the rest of the account of Valentinian gnosis. 'Nor can any libertinism be recognised in the letter of Ptolemaeus to Flora, in the central section of the *Excerpta ex Theodoto,* or in the fragments of Heracleon's Commentary on John'[9]. Foerster deduces that Irenaeus is not referring to the common doctrines of ordinary Valentinians, but to 'a mere group'. Frederik Wisse, in a cogent presentation of the case for the 'ascetic' view[10], observes 'Dies muß im Licht des valentinianischen Mysteriums vom Brautgemach gesehen werden, dem offenbar in bestimmten Fällen ein enthaltsames Zusammenleben eines Bruders und einer Schwester folgte. Es ist kein Wunder, daß die Gegner für diese Praxis nur Zynismus und Spott übrig hatten. Doch war dieses asketische Ideal auch bei den Orthodoxen weitverbreitet, und daß dahinter ernster religiöser Eifer stand, läßt sich nicht bezweifeln, auch wenn es nicht immer erfolgreich verwirklicht wurde'. Comparing the similar situation in the Acts of Thomas, he suggests that wives converted to the gnostic faith might have abandoned their husbands to devote themselves to a life of *encrateia.* The husbands evidently complained to Irenaeus that the gnostics had stolen away their wives; and finally, when the wives returned in penitence they would portray their gnostic teachers in the darkest colours, in order to present themselves as the innocent victims of wicked deceivers. This certainly has the ring of truth about it, and would provide another indication of the way in which these aspersions grew and developed.

In this context, reference should be made to some characteristics of polemic. In the first place, in Reinach's words, 'dans l'objet haï, tout devient haïssable'. Therefore even what might otherwise be accounted good must be taken *in malam partem.* Thus Irenaeus writes of Saturnilus (I 24.2) that 'many of his followers abstain also from animal food, and through this feigned continence they lead many astray'. Similarly Epiphanus writes (XL 2.4) that some Archontics 'pretend to an affected abstinence and deceive the simpler sort of men by making a show of withdrawal from the world in imitation of the monks'. Gnostic abstinence, in the eyes of the Fathers, is thus not genuine but a sham and a pretence, intended to deceive the unwary into thinking them other than they really are. On the other hand Irenaeus in the same context notes that for Saturnilus marriage and procreation 'are of Satan', and even Epiphanius writes of the followers of Severus that they 'abstain completely from wine', because of the evils which it produces, and say that those who consort in

[9] *Gnosis* i, Oxford 1972, 313 (ET of Die *Gnosis* i, Zürich and Stuttgart 1969, 400).

[10] 'Die Sextus-Sprüche und das Problem der gnostischen Ethik', in Böhlig-Wisse, *Zum Hellenismus in den Schriften von Nag Hammadi,* Göttinger Orientforschungen VI. Reihe, Bd. 2, Wiesbaden 1975, 70

marriage 'fulfil the work of Satan' (XLV 1.8; 2.1). In neither case in there any suggestion of hypocrisy or deceit.

A second feature of polemic is a tendency to generalise from particular cases: a practice known or alleged to be indulged in by some is simply assumed to be characteristic of all. It is possible, as already noted, that some groups, or some individual gnostics, were guilty of such practices, but that is no justification for the assumption that all were tarred with the selfsame brush. We have to look for the general trend, the dominant tendency, and from all that we know of the period that seems more likely to have been ascetic in character rather than libertine. As Wisse writes (p. 72): 'Zum mindesten ist klar, daß solche Exzesse bei den Gnostikern Ausnahmen waren: sie sind kein Kriterium, nach dem man die ganze Bewegung beurteilen kann. Die jetzt zahlreich bekannt gewordenen gnostischen Originalwerke zeigen, daß das ethische Interesse der Gnostiker entschieden asketisch war'.

Wisse takes as his starting-point the presence in the Nag Hammadi library of a Coptic version of the Sentences of Sextus, which he describes as a typical example of hellenistic religious ethics. The popularity of this work is shown by its translation into Latin and Syriac, and in part into Armenian and Georgian. Introducing his translation in *The Nag Hammadi Library in English*[11], Wisse calls it a collection of maximes with a strongly ethical and ascetic tone, and adds 'Although the tractate itself cannot really be considered a Gnostic treatise, its esoteric, moral asceticism seems to make it quite compatible with the other tractates from the Nag Hammadi collection . . . the evidence indicates that the library was the property of a group which placed a strong emphasis upon sexual asceticism'. The presence of non-gnostic works in a largely gnostic collection was initially the cause of some perplexity, but is probably to be explained on the assumption that these works were congenial to the owners, if they were gnostics, or at least were thought to be of the same general character as more strictly gnostic works. Several years ago, Wisse noted that if there is a unity in the library, it is to be found not in doctrine but in the ethical stance of the tractates[12], and in a recent study G. Sfameni Gasparro writes: 'La conclusione più prudente è quella di riconoscere come, nella complessità e varietà delle tendenze dottrinali espresse nei trattati copti di Nag Hammadi, l'elemento unificante sia costituito – nello sfondo sostanzialmente gnostico – da un interesse peculiare per tematiche di astensionismo, sessuale sopratutto ma talora anche alimentare che, a titolo diverso, emerge dalla maggior parte di essi'.[13]

---

[11] *The Nag Hammadi Library in English* (General Editor: James M. Robinson), New York, London, Leiden 1977, 454 (abbreviated NHLE).

[12] 'The Nag Hammadi Library and the Heresiologists', *Vigiliae Christianae* 25, 1971, 220.

[13] *Enkrateia e Antropologia:* Le motivazioni protologiche della continenza e della verginità

The Coptic version of Sextus is unfortunately extant only in part, and the missing 'sentences' include most of those which Wisse (p. 75) adduces as evidence for the ascetic tendency. However, there are two blocks more or less complete (157–180, 307–397), and in Wisse's view 'es ist so gut wie sicher, daß die dazwischenliegenden Maximen 181–306 ursprünglich nicht gefehlt haben, und dasselbe kann für die ersten 156 der Sammlung angenommen werden'. In that case practically all of the relevant 'sentences' would have been included, and moreover in a text showing a remarkable agreement with the Greek version edited by Chadwick (Wisse 74). Even the extant Coptic however contains pointers to an ascetic morality: 'It is better to die [than] to darken the soul because of [the] immoderation of the belly' (345); 'Say with [your] mind that the body [is] the garment of your soul; keep it, therefore, pure since it is innocent' (346); 'Unclean demons do lay claim to a polluted soul; ⟨the⟩ evil demons will not be able to lay hold of a soul which is faithful and good in the way of God' (348–9; perhaps one might compare 'saying' 61 in the Gospel of Philip (65.1–27). Here too there is an ascetic element: he who comes out of the world is above desire and fear, master over nature (lines 28–30)).

The second work adduced by Wisse is the Teachings of Silvanus, 'a rare example of an early Christian Wisdom text' (NHLE 346) showing Platonic and Stoic as well as Biblical influences. Here again we read: 'The soul which is a member of God's household is one which is kept pure, and the soul which has put on Christ is one which is pure' (109.4–8). The opening lines speak of 'the struggle against every folly of the passions of love and base wickedness, and love of praise, and fondness of contention, and tiresome jealousy and wrath, and anger and the desire of avarice' (84.20–26). The soul is bidden to bring in mind as its guide, and reason as its teacher (85.24–26). Later we find 'Turn toward the rational nature and cast from yourself the earth-begotten nature' (94.16–18), and towards the end 'My son, first purify yourself toward the outward life in order that you may be able to purify the inward' (117.25–28). The admonition 'Be sober and shake off your drunkenness, which is the work of ignorance' (94.20–22) recalls the New Testament use of this metaphor, but at the same time the reference to 'ignorance', like the mention of 'robbers' at 85.2; 113.33, may indicate how these works could be interpreted in ways congenial to gnostics. Silvanus also refers to the bridal chamber (94.28), in which according to Wisse the mind is illuminated (p. 78). That would provide a link with such works as the Gospel of Philip, but possibly some reserve is called for here: the preceding words refer to

nel cristianesimo dei primi secoli e nello gnosticismo, Rome 1984, 148. The chapter relating to Gnosticism extends over pages 115–166. Reference may also be made to the papers delivered at the colloquium on 'La tradizione dell' *enkrateia*: motivazioni ontologiche e protologiche' held in Milan in 1982 (ed. U. Bianchi). Rome: Edizioni dell' Alenes 1985.

natural birth, and slight modification of the translation could convey a different impression: 'When you entered into a bodily birth, you were begotten. You came into being inside the bridal chamber. You were illuminated in mind'. A gnostic, of course, would understand the phrase of the celestial bridal chamber, but if originally it went with the preceding sentence it would have referred to natural birth. This is just one case, and there are others, in which it may be that we have not yet completely resolved the problems of understanding and interpretation.

Wisse's third text, the Authoritative Teaching, is described as 'weniger deutlich christlich als Silvanus und gleichzeitig ausgeprägter gnostisch' (p. 78f.). The gnostic character of this text has however been disputed (cf. Gasparro 158), and Wisse himself elsewhere calls it 'not obviously heretical'[14]. In that respect it is like another tractate which shows some similarities in theme and content, the Exegesis on the Soul, which Ménard calls 'bel et bien un traité gnostique'[15], whereas Wisse considers it merely heterodox and questions whether the use of certain concepts in the text is really gnostic. More important for present purposes is an earlier comment: 'Only celibacy would be consistent with the teaching of the tractate (i. e. ExSoul). Repentance remains, of course, the dominant theme, but an ascetic way of life appears to be a part of it'[16]. If Krause's reconstruction is correct, incidentally, the Exegesis offers a clear statement of salvation by grace alone: 'So wird die Seele durch die Wiedergeburt gerettet werden. Das aber kommt nicht durch asketische Worte, auch nicht durch Künste, auch nicht durch geschriebene Lehren (= Lehrbriefe), sondern es ist die Gna[de Gott]es, vielmehr ist es das Geschenk Got[tes für den Men]schen'[17]. H. M. Schenke however offers a different restoration of the lacunae, while *The Nag Hammadi Library in English* makes no attempt to fill them[18]. Here again we are confronted by problems of translation and interpretation, in this case complicated by lacunae in the manuscript. Edi-

---

14 'On exegeting "The Exegesis on the Soul"', *Les Textes de Nag Hammadi* (ed. J. E. Ménard), Leiden 1975, 69.

15 'L'"évangile selon Philippe" et l'"exégèse de l'âme"', *Les Textes de Nag Hammadi* 67.

16 Art. cit. 78. For the questioning of the concepts mentioned, see p. 79.

17 *Die Gnosis* ii, Zürich and Stuttgart 1971, 133 (ET Oxford 1974, 108); cf. also Krause-Labib, *Gnostische und hermetische Schriften aus Codex II und Codex VI,* Glückstadt 1971, 81f. for the Coptic text (134.28–33).

18 'Sprachliche und exegetische Probleme in den beiden letzten Schriften des Codex II von Nag Hammadi', OLZ 70, 1975, 8 and 12; NHLE 185 reads: 'Thus it is by being born again that the soul will be saved. And this is due not to rote phrases or to professional skills or to book learning. Rather it is the grace of the [. . ., it is] the gift of the [. . .].' See also Wisse, art. cit. 76, who says 'the lacunae resist reconstruction in places', but adds 'The fact that salvation comes only through grace is used by the author as a further ground for the soul to repent and call upon God for mercy (135.4–15)'. The Greek word ἄσκησις of course does not necessarily carry the connotation of asceticism.

torial reconstruction, however well-meant and however plausible, may be misleading.

According to G. W. MacRae[19], the Authoritative Teaching contains no typical gnostic cosmogonic myth but appears to presuppose 'a generally gnostic, i. e. anticosmic dualist, understanding of the fate of the soul in the material world'. Reference to the Pleroma (22.19) and to 'her bridegroom' (22.23) naturally suggests the Valentinian concept of the bridal chamber; but at least one Christian hymn from a later age salutes Jesus as 'Shepherd, Husband, Friend', and a footnote in the edition runs: 'The imagery is common in the Bible, the Fathers, Gnosticism (especially Valentinian)'. A later reference to 'her true shepherd' (33.2) evokes the comment 'The precise expression is not Johannine but invites comparison with Jn 10:11 and the Johannine use of ἀληθινός in other contexts'.[20] Curiously, there is no reference to the Johannine passage at 32.10f., where it would seem to be equally apt: here the soul 'runs into her fold, while her shepherd stands at the door'. Rev. 3:20 is however cited. In the light of the references now available in the edition, the Christian influence may perhaps be considered slightly stronger than Wisse originally allowed.

Wisse's final example, the Testimony of Truth, is also now available in edited form, with an extensive introduction and notes by B. A. Pearson[21]. Right at the outset, the 'old leaven' of the scribes and Pharisees is identified with 'the errant desire of the angels and the demons and the stars' (29.15–18). The Pharisees and scribes are 'those who belong to the archons', and 'no one who is under the law will be able to look up to the truth, for they will not be able to serve two masters' (29.18–24). The law in fact is rejected – because it commands one to take a wife or husband, and to multiply like the sand of the sea (29.26–30.5). When John the Baptist saw the power which came down upon the Jordan river, he knew 'that the dominion of carnal procreation had come to an end' (30.25–30). A later section (38.27–41.4) urges the necessity for radical rejection of all that pertains to carnal generation. 'No one knows the God of truth except solely the man who will forsake all of the things of the world' (41.4–8).

It could be argued that some of this material is not particularly ascetic, but simply represents fairly conventional morality. The point is however that it is definitely not libertinarian in character. The gnostics were people of their time, and shared with other groups the attitude and outlook of the period. The evidence of the Nag Hammadi texts, like that of the extracts quoted by the Fathers from the Valentinians (see above), suggests a moral standard at least as high as that of other contemporary groups, and on occasion even stricter. The tendency was in the direction of asceticism

[19] *Nag Hammadi Codices V, 2–5 and VI,* Leiden 1979, 258.

[20] Op. cit. 282–3.

[21] *Nag Hammadi Codices IX and X,* Leiden 1981, 101–203.

and encratism, rather than towards libertinism. Gasparro, after reviewing the documents mentioned and some others, speaks of 'le decisive tendenze encratite che percorrono sia gli scritti di più evidente ispirazione diteista e di impostazione "mitica" sia quelli a carattere didattico-parenetico, poco o nulla interessati a speculazioni teo-cosmologiche'[22].

In a recent book G. A. G. Stroumsa writes 'At the root of the Gnostic rejection of the material world and its creator lies an obsessive preoccupation with the problem of evil'[23]. Whatever its form, the 'gnostic myth' is intended to provide an explanation for the human predicament, for the trials and tribulations of the human race in the world as we know it. Gnostic ethics is dominated by a concern for purity, for the restoration of a lost ideal, for the recovery of a primal innocence, and is therefore in the main of an ascetic or encratite character. Some groups, or some individuals, may have drawn conclusions leading to libertinism, but all the evidence suggests that they were exceptional. Two points deserve some mention in conclusion: in the first place, if the gnostics were predominantly encratite, this does not mean that all encratites were gnostic; nor does it justify attaching the label 'gnostic' to any document showing encratite features. We need to refine our categories and definitions, as indeed the discussion of some of the texts above has shown, for example by restricting the use of the label to those cases in which there is reasonably clear evidence of gnostic mythology in the text. The Nag Hammadi library has made it abundantly clear that if its owners were gnostics they were perfectly prepared to make use of hermetic or other literature which was congenial to their own ideas, or could be interpreted in conformity with them. If they were not gnostics, of course, it shows that the kind of confusion which has beset modern investigation was already prevalent in the ancient world: the people who brought these texts together presumably thought they belonged together. And secondly we need to reconsider some of the implications. In the past the view that asceticism and lubricity could both spring from the same root has led to the designation of both encratite and libertinarian texts as 'gnostic', which in turn has fostered the kind of *Pangnostizismus* that by ignoring important differences has found gnostics under every stone and behind every bush. A case in point is the ethical section in Galatians, which has sometimes been regarded as directed against antinomian 'gnostics'. To the contrary, the evidence of the Nag Hammadi texts would suggest that gnostics would have welcomed Paul's injunctions. They too could speak in terms of bondage to the flesh and freedom in the Spirit.

---

[22] *Enkrateia e Antropologia* 165.

[23] *Another Seed:* Studies in Gnostic Mythology, Leiden 1984, 17.

Bibliographie Heinrich Greeven

(*4. 10. 1906)

von Rudolf Linßen

1931

Gebet und Eschatologie im Neuen Testament. [= Greifswald, Theol. Diss. vom 6. 12. 1930] Gütersloh 1931. (Neutestamentliche Forschungen Reihe 3, Heft 1)

1935

Das Hauptproblem der Sozialethik in der neueren Stoa und im Urchristentum. [= Greifswald, Habil. Schr.] Gütersloh 1935. (Neutestamentliche Forschungen Reihe 3, Heft 4)
Fotomechanischer Abdruck der Ausgabe Gütersloh 1935, Münster 1983.[1]

Artikel: »δέομαι, δέησις, προσδέομαι«. In: Theologisches Wörterbuch zum Neuen Testament [= ThWbNT], hg. v. G. Kittel, Bd. 2, Stuttgart 1935, S. 39–42.

Artikel: »ἐρωτάω, ἐπερωτάω, ἐπερώτημα«. In: ThWbNT Bd. 2, Stuttgart 1935, S. 682–686.

Artikel: »εὐσχήμων«. In: ThWbNT Bd. 2, Stuttgart 1935, S. 768–770.

Artikel: »εὔχομαι, εὐχή, προσεύχομαι, προσευχή«. In: ThWbNT Bd. 2, Stuttgart 1935, S. 774–782. 799–808.

Artikel: »ζητέω, ζήτησις, ἐκζητέω, ἐπιζητέω«. In: ThWbNT Bd. 2, Stuttgart 1935, S. 894–898.

1938

Die Entstehung des Neuen Testamentes. Verlag des Evangelischen Bundes, Berlin 1938. (Heliand 49)

Artikel: »κατανύσσω, κατάνυξις«. In: ThWbNT Bd. 3, Stuttgart 1938, S. 628.

---

[1] Ohne Wissen des Autors.

1948

Krankheit und Heilung nach dem Neuen Testament. Stuttgart 1948 (Lebendige Wissenschaft 8).

1949

Rezension: Bruce M. Metzger, Lexical Aids for Students of New Testament Greek, Princeton 1946. In: Theologische Literaturzeitung 74 (1949) Sp. 291.

Rezension: Anton Gerardus Hamel, Mythe en historie in het oude Ierland, Amsterdam 1942. In: Theologische Literaturzeitung 74 (1949) Sp. 401–403.

Rezension: A. Trouw, Het Katastrofale, Assen 1946. In: Theologische Literaturzeitung 74 (1949) Sp. 492–493.

1951

Propheten in der Kirche. In: Die neue Furche 5 (1951) S. 143–151.

Martin Dibelius, Aufsätze zur Apostelgeschichte, hg. v. Heinrich Greeven, Berlin 1951 und Göttingen 1951 (Forschungen zur Religion und Literatur des Alten und Neuen Testaments 60, N.F. 42).
3. Aufl. Berlin 1956 und Göttingen 1957; 5. durchgesehene Aufl. Göttingen 1968.

Die Textgestalt der Evangelienlektionare. In: Theologische Literaturzeitung 76 (1951) Sp. 513–522 [= Rezension von Bruce M. Metzger, The Saturday and Sunday Lessons from Luke in the Greek Gospel Lectionary, Chicago 1944.].

1952

»Wer unter euch . . .?«. In: Wort und Dienst. Jahrbuch der Theologischen Schule Bethel (als Festschrift für H. Girgensohn, hg. v. J. Fichtner) N.F. 3 (1952) S. 86–101.
Wiederabgedruckt in: Gleichnisse Jesu. Positionen der Auslegung von Adolf Jülicher bis zur Formgeschichte. Hg. v. W. Harnisch, Darmstadt 1982, S. 238–255. (Wege der Forschung 366)

Propheten, Lehrer, Vorsteher bei Paulus. Zur Frage der »Ämter« im Urchristentum. In: Zeitschrift für die neutestamentliche Wissenschaft 44 (1952/53) S. 1–43.
Wiederabgedruckt in: Das kirchliche Amt im Neuen Testament, hg. v. K. Kertelge, Darmstadt 1977, S. 305–361. (Wege der Forschung 439)

1953

An die Kolosser, Epheser, an Philemon. Erklärt von Martin Dibelius, 3., neubearbeitete Auflage von Heinrich Greeven, Tübingen 1953. (Handbuch zum Neuen Testament 12)

1954

Artikel: »πάλη«. In: Theologisches Wörterbuch zum Neuen Testament. Begründet von G. Kittel, hg. v. G. Friedrich, Bd. 5, Stuttgart 1954, S. 717–718.

Die Weisungen der Bibel über das rechte Verhältnis von Mann und Frau. In: Ehe und Eherecht. Mit Beiträgen von Heinrich Greeven u.a., Stuttgart 1954, S. 5–17. (Kirche im Volk 12)

Die Frau im Beruf. Tatbestände, Erfahrungen und Vorschläge zu drängenden Fragen in der weiblichen Berufsarbeit und in der Lebensgestaltung der berufstätigen Frau. In Zusammenarbeit mit L. Präger, E. Schwarzhaupt, A. Rudolph und E. Metzke, hg. im Auftrag der Studiengemeinschaft der Evangelischen Akademien von Heinrich Greeven, Hamburg 1954. (Soziale Wirklichkeit 1)

Prüfung der Thesen von J. Knox zum Philemonbrief. In: Theologische Literaturzeitung 79 (1954) Sp. 373–378. [John Knox, Philemon among the letters of Paul. A new view of its place and importance, Diss., Chicago 1935.]

1955

Die Heilung des Gelähmten nach Matthäus. In: Wort und Dienst. Jahrbuch der Theologischen Schule Bethel (anläßlich ihres 50jährigen Bestehens, hg. v. H. Krämer) N.F. 4 (1955) S. 65–78.
Wiederabgedruckt in: Das Matthäus-Evangelium, hg. v. J. Lange, Darmstadt 1980, S. 205–222. (Wege der Forschung 525)

1956

Der Brief des Jakobus. Erklärt von Martin Dibelius. 8., durchgesehene Auflage mit einem Ergänzungsheft hg. v. Heinrich Greeven, Göttingen 1956. (Kritisch-exegetischer Kommentar über das neue Testament 15)
11. Auflage hg. und ergänzt von Heinrich Greeven, Göttingen 1964.

Die lästige Ehe. In: Deutscher Evangelischer Kirchentag Frankfurt 1956. Dokumente. Stuttgart 1956, S. 188–198.

Rezension: Wilfred L. Knox, The sources of the Synoptic Gospels. Vol. I., St. Mark. Ed. by H. Chadwick, London 1953. In: Theologische Literaturzeitung 81 (1956) Sp. 439–442.

Martin Dibelius, Studies in the Acts of the Apostles. Ed. by Heinrich Greeven, trans. by M. Ling and P. Schubert, London 1956. (SCM IX)

1957

Artikel: »Comma Johanneum«. In: Die Religion in Geschichte und Gegenwart. Handwörterbuch für Theologie und Religionswissenschaft. 3., völlig neu bearbeitete Auflage, hg. v. K. Galling [= RGG^3], Bd. 1, Tübingen 1957, Sp. 1854.

Zu den Aussagen des Neuen Testaments über die Ehe. In: Zeitschrift für evangelische Ethik 1 (1957) S. 109–125.

Rezension: Johannes Munck, Christus und Israel. Eine Auslegung von Röm 9–11. København 1956. (Acta Jutlandica. Aarsskrift for Aarhus Universitet XXVIII 3) In: Theologische Literaturzeitung 82 (1957) Sp. 693–694.

1958

Artikel: »Ehe im NT«. In: RGG^3 Bd. 2, Tübingen 1958, Sp. 318–320.

Artikel: »Frau im Urchristentum«. In: RGG^3 Bd. 2, Tübingen 1958, Sp. 1069–1070.

Artikel: »Griesbach«, Johann Jakob, In: RGG^3 Bd. 2, Tübingen 1958, Sp. 1876.

Artikel: »Gregory«, Casper René. In: RGG^3 Bd. 2, Tübingen 1958, Sp. 1850.

Jede Gabe ist gut, Jak 1,17. Rudolf Hermann zum 70. Geburtstag. In: Theologische Zeitschrift 14 (1958) S. 1–13.

Die missionierende Gemeinde nach den apostolischen Briefen. In: Sammlung und Sendung. Vom Auftrag der Kirche in der Welt. Festgabe für Heinrich Rendtorff zu seinem 70. Geburtstag am 9. April 1958, hg. v. J. Heubach und H.-H. Ulrich, Berlin 1958, S. 59–71.

Rezension: K. H. Rengstorf, Mann und Frau im Urchristentum. In: Arbeitsgemeinschaft für Forschung des Landes Nordrhein-Westfalen 12 (1954) S. 7–52. und H. Conrad, Grundprobleme einer Reform des Familienrechts. Zu den familienrechtlichen Gesetzesentwürfen der Bundesrepublik. In: ebd. S. 53–93. In: Zeitschrift für evangelisches Kirchenrecht 6 (1958) S. 196–200.

Rezension: Pierre Thévenaz, L'homme et sa raison. I.: Raison et consience. II.: Raison et histoire. Neuchâtel 1956 (Être et Penser. Cahiers de Philosophie 46,47) In: Evangelische Theologie 18 (1958) S. 576–578.

1959

Artikel: »Hort«, Fenton John Antony. In: RGG^3 Bd. 3, Tübingen 1959, Sp. 453.

Artikel: »περιστερά, τρυγών«. In: ThWbNT Bd. 6, Stuttgart 1959, S. 63–72.

Artikel: »πλησίον«. In: ThWbNT Bd. 6, Stuttgart 1959, S. 309–310. 314–316.

Artikel: »προσκυνέω, προσκυνητής«. In: ThWbNT Bd. 6, Stuttgart 1959, S. 759–767.

Artikel: »Protestantische Exegese«. In: Lexikon für Theologie und Kirche, Bd. 3, Freiburg 1959, Sp. 1290–1293.

Die Geistesgaben bei Paulus. In: Wort und Dienst. Jahrbuch der Theologischen Schule Bethel (als Festschrift für W. Brandt zum 65. Geburtstag, hg. v. Ch. Maurer) N.F. 6 (1959) S. 111–120.

Die Frau im Urchristentum. Vortrag im Rahmen der »Universitätstage« Kiel 1958 [Gesamtthema: Die Frau in Geschichte und Gegenwart.] In: Zentralblatt für Gynäkologie 81 (1959) S. 295–301.

1960

Artikel: »Nestle«, Eberhard. In: RGG^3 Bd. 4, Tübingen 1960, Sp. 1403–1404.

Erwägungen zur synoptischen Textkritik. In: New Testament Studies 6 (1959/60) S. 281–296.

Der Urtext des Neuen Testaments. Rektoratsrede am 16. 5. 1960. Kiel 1960. (Veröffentlichungen der Schleswig-Holsteinischen Universitätsgesellschaft N.F. 26)

Rezension: Wilfred L. Knox, The Sources of the Synoptic Gospels. Vol. II: St. Luke and St. Matthew. Ed. by H. Chadwick, London 1957. In: Theologische Literaturzeitung 85 (1960) Sp. 589–592.

1961

Rezension: Jean Duplacy, Où en est la critique textuelle du Nouveau Testament? Paris 1959. In: Gnomon 33 (1961) S. 91–92.

1962

Artikel: »Text und Textkritik der Bibel. Neues Testament«. In: RGG^3 Bd. 6, Tübingen 1962, Sp. 716–725.

Artikel: »Westcott«, Brooke Foss. In: RGG^{3} Bd. 6, Tübingen 1962, Sp. 1659.

Artikel: »White«, Henry Julian. In: RGG^{3} Bd. 6, Tübingen 1962, Sp. 1674.

Artikel: »Wordworth«, John. In: RGG^{3} Bd. 6, Tübingen 1962, Sp. 1807.

1963

Artikel: »Dekalog«. In: Evangelisches Soziallexikon, hg. v. Fr. Karrenberg, 4., vollständig neubearbeitete Aufl. Stuttgart 1963, Sp. 246–248.

Artikel: »Frau«. In: Evangelisches Soziallexikon, 1963, Sp. 407–415. [zusammen mit E. Schwarzhaupt].

Artikel: »Gleichberechtigung von Mann und Frau«. In: Evangelisches Soziallexikon, 1963, Sp. 524–528. [zusammen mit E. Schwarzhaupt und H. Ranke].

1964

Artikel: »συναναμείγνυμι«. In: ThWbNT Bd. 7, Stuttgart 1964, S. 850–853.

Kirche und Parusie Christi. In: Kerygma und Dogma 10 (1964) S. 113–135.

1965

Evangelium und Gesellschaft in urchristlicher Zeit. In: Festschrift zur Eröffnung der Universität Bochum. Hg. v. H. Wenke und J. H. Knoll, Bochum 1965, S. 105–121.

1966

Gottes Wort an Mann und Frau. In: Wege zum Menschen 18 (1966) S. 385–394. [Leicht verändert abgedruckt in: Ist die Ehe überholt? Hg. v. Ruthe, München 1966, 2. Aufl. 1971, S. 30–43.]

1967

Konzeption und Aufbau der Ruhr-Universität Bochum. In: Die Umschau in Wissenschaft und Technik. Halbmonatszeitschrift über die Fortschritte in Naturwissenschaft, Medizin und Technik, Frankfurt 67 (1967) S. 143–146.

Die Zukunft der Korporationen. Rede beim Bochumer Verbände-Kommers am 26. 11. 1966. In: Der Convent 18 (1967) S. 81–85. Abgedruckt in: Akademische Monatsblätter 80 (1967) S. 60–64 und in: Schwarzes Brett, Heft 19 (1968) S. 3–6.

1968

Ehe nach dem Neuen Testament. In: New Testament Studies 15 (1968/69) S. 365–388.[2]

1969

Ehe nach dem Neuen Testament. In: Theologie der Ehe. Veröffentlichung des Ökumenischen Arbeitskreises evangelischer und katholischer Theologen. Mit Beiträgen von Heinrich Greeven, J. Ratzinger, R. Schnackenburg, H. D. Wendland, mit einem Vorwort von L. Jaeger und W. Stählin, hg. v. G. Krems und R. Mumm, Regensburg/Göttingen 1969, S. 37–79. [2. Aufl. 1972][2]

1976

Martin Dibelius. A Commentary on the Epistle of James, rev. by Heinrich Greeven, trans. by M. A. Williams, ed. by H. Koester, Philadelphia 1976. (Hermeneia Commentary Series)

1977

Nochmals Mk IX.1 in Codex Bezae (D, 05). In: New Testament Studies 23 (1977) S. 305–308.

1978

The Gospel Synopsis from 1776 to the present day. In: J. J. Griesbach: Synoptic and textual-critical studies 1776–1976. Ed. by B. Orchard and Th. R. W. Longstaff. SNTS Monograph Series Vol. 34 (1978) S. 22–49.

1981

[Huck-Greeven] Synopse der drei ersten Evangelien mit Beigabe der johanneischen Parallelstellen / Synopsis of the First Three Gospels with the Addition of the Johannine Parallels. 13. Auflage, völlig neu bearbeitet von / 13th edition, fundamentally revised by Heinrich Greeven, Tübingen 1981.

---

[2] Der Aufsatz ist in beiden Publikationen gleichzeitig und wortgleich erschienen.

Judentum, Urchristentum, Kirche

Festschrift für Joachim Jeremias
2., vielfach berichtigte und ergänzte, um eine wissenschaftliche Würdigung und einer Bibliographie des Jubilars erweiterte Auflage

Herausgegeben von Walther Eltester

Groß-Oktav. XXX, 259 Seiten, 1 Bildnis. 1964. Kartoniert DM 71,– ISBN 3 11 005594 5
(Beiheft zur Zeitschrift für die neutestamentliche Wissenschaft, Band 26)

Apophoreta

Festschrift für Ernst Haenchen zu seinem 70. Geburtstag am 10. Dezember 1964

Groß-Oktav. VIII, 299 Seiten, 1 Bildnis. 1964. Ganzleinen DM 71,– ISBN 3 11 005596 1
(Beiheft zur Zeitschrift für die neutestamentliche Wissenschaft, Band 30)

Beiträge zur Theorie des neuzeitlichen Christentums

Wolfgang Trillhaas zum 65. Geburtstag

Herausgegeben von Hans-Joachim Birkner und Dietrich Rössler

Groß-Oktav. VIII, 142 Seiten. 1968. Ganzleinen DM 34,50
ISBN 3 11 006314 X

Geist und Geschichte der Reformation

Festgabe für Hans Rückert zum 65. Geburtstag, dargebracht von Freunden, Kollegen und Schülern

In Verbindung mit Kurt Aland und Walther Eltester herausgegeben von Heinz Liebing und Klaus Scholder

Groß-Oktav. VIII, 486 Seiten und Frontispiz. 1966. Ganzleinen DM 122,–
ISBN 3 11 001236 7 (Arbeiten zur Kirchengeschichte, Band 38)

Preisänderungen vorbehalten

Walter de Gruyter · Berlin · New York

Text – Wort – Glaube

Studien zur Überlieferung,
Interpretation und Autorisierung biblischer Texte
Kurt Aland gewidmet

Herausgegeben von Martin Brecht

Groß-Oktav. VIII, 397 Seiten, Frontispiz. 1980. Ganzleinen DM 128,–
ISBN 3 11 007318 8 (Arbeiten zur Kirchengeschichte, Band 50)

Vom Amt des Laien in Kirche und Theologie

Festschrift für Gerhard Krause zum 70. Geburtstag

Von Gustaf Wingren, Clemens Thoma, Antonius H. Gunneweg, Henning Schröer, Gerhard Müller. Grußwort von Gerhard Brandt,
herausgegeben von Henning Schröer und Gerhard Müller

Groß-Oktav. XII, 431 Seiten, Frontispiz. 1982. Ganzleinen DM 158,– ISBN 3 11 008590 9
(Theologische Bibliothek Töpelmann, Band 39)

Denkender Glaube

Festschrift für Carl Heinz Ratschow
zur Vollendung seines 65. Lebensjahres am 22. Juli 1976 gewidmet
von Kollegen, Schülern und Freunden

Herausgegeben von Otto Kaiser

Groß-Oktav. VIII, 364 Seiten, Frontispiz. 1976. Ganzleinen DM 116,–
ISBN 3 11 004155 3

Prophecy

Essays presented to Georg Fohrer on his sixty-fifth birthday
6. September 1980

Edited by J. A. Emerton

Large-octavo. VIII, 202 pages, frontispiece. 1980. Cloth DM 92,– ISBN 3 11 007761 2
(Beiheft zur Zeitschrift für die alttestamentliche Wissenschaft, volume 150)

Preisänderungen vorbehalten

Walter de Gruyter · Berlin · New York